Infant and Toddler Development and Responsive Program Planning

A Relationship-Based Approach

Second Edition

Donna S. Wittmer
University of Colorado Denver

Sandra H. Petersen
ZERO TO THREE: The National Center for Infants, Toddlers, and Families

PEARSON

Boston   Columbus   Indianapolis   New York   San Francisco   Upper Saddle River
Amsterdam   Cape Town   Dubai   London   Madrid   Milan   Munich   Paris   Montreal   Toronto
Delhi   Mexico City   Sao Paulo   Sydney   Hong Kong   Seoul   Singapore   Taipei   Tokyo

Vice President and Editor in Chief: Jeffery W. Johnston
Senior Acquisitions Editor: Julie Peters
Editorial Assistant: Tiffany Bitzel
Vice President, Director of Sales and Marketing: Quinn Perkson
Marketing Manager: Erica DeLuca
Marketing Coordinator: Brian Mounts
Senior Managing Editor: Pamela D. Bennett
Senior Project Manager: Linda Hillis Bayma
Senior Operations Supervisor: Matthew Ottenweller

Senior Art Director: Diane Lorenzo
Cover Designer: Ali Mohrman
Cover Art: SuperStock
Media Project Manager: Rebecca Norsic
Full-Service Project Management: Connie Strassburg and Kelly Keeler, GGS Higher Education Resources
Composition: GGS Higher Education Resources
Printer/Binder: Hamilton Printing
Cover Printer: Lehigh Phoenix
Text Font: Berkeley Book

Credits and acknowledgments borrowed from other sources and reproduced, with permission, in this textbook appear on appropriate page within text.

Every effort has been made to provide accurate and current Internet information in this book. However, the Internet and information posted on it are constantly changing, so it is inevitable that some of the Internet addresses listed in this textbook will change.

Photo Credits: Teri Stratford/PH College, p. 1; Donald and Lori Easton-Brooks, pp. 3, 4, 13 (both), 16, 138, 271, 289, 314 (top), 316; Carla Mestas, pp. 7, 189, 200, 266, 273, 278, 284, 314 (bottom), 318; Sandra Petersen, pp. 25, 26, 29, 35, 45, 57, 59 (both), 82 (all), 89, 94 (both), 95, 110, 113 (all), 127, 132, 162, 167 (all), 173, 179, 220, 223, 226, 228, 243, 244, 245, 246, 251, 356, 367 (all); Jamie West, p. 28; Donna Wittmer, pp. 69, 72 (both), 87 (both), 192, 265, 296, 300, 340, 373; Jen Sieminski, Boulder Journey School, pp. 135, 143, 145, 147, 148, 149, 198, 210, 311, 315, 339; Dan Naven and Yanira Rodriguez, p. 328; Cara Martinez, p. 346; Anthony Magnacca/Merrill, p. 375; Barbara Schwartz/Merrill, p. 390.

Library of Congress Cataloging-in-Publication Data

Wittmer, Donna Sasse.
    Infant and toddler development and responsive program planning: a
relationship-based approach / Donna S. Wittmer, Sandra H. Petersen. — 2nd ed.
        p. cm.
    Includes bibliographical references and index.
    ISBN-13: 978-0-13-715263-6
    ISBN-10: 0-13-715263-9
1. Child development—Study and teaching.   2. Infants—Development—Study and teaching.   3. Toddlers—Development—Study and teaching.   I. Petersen, Sandra H.   II. Title.
    RJ131.W56 2010
    618.9200076—dc22

                                                                                                2009005905

10 9 8 7 6 5 4 3 2 1

www.pearsonhighered.com

ISBN-13: 978-0-13-715263-6
ISBN-10:   0-13-715263-9

To my husband, Dennis; our daughters, Deanna and Dana;
my mother, Vera; son-in-law, John; and grandson, Kai.
My relationships with you are a constant source of
joy and inspiration.
—Donna Wittmer

To the four people who live the mutuality of relationship
with me every day: my husband, Neil Rose, and our daughters,
Emily Adams, Juliette Petersen, and Alyssa Rose.
—Sandy Petersen

Preface

This second edition of a comprehensive, applied text covers infant and toddler development from prebirth through age 36 months, curriculum and program planning, and guidance using a relationship-based model. In addition, it focuses on the importance of families' and teachers' relationships and responsiveness in interactions with children, the latest developmental research, an emphasis on child-centered planning, a particularly strong coverage of infants and toddlers with special needs, and an emphasis on the effects of culture, families, and quality programs on infant-toddler development and interactions. It is research based *and* written so that the information is accessible and highly motivating to a wide range of readers.

RELATIONSHIP-BASED APPROACH

Infants and toddlers have emotional and social needs to feel safe, valued, loved, appreciated for their individuality, and to be deeply connected with their family, culture, important adults, and peers. Relationships meet these needs and create the environment in which development proceeds.

Infant and Toddler Development and Responsive Program Planning uses a relationship-based model as a framework for understanding how infants and toddlers grow and learn with the support of their families and teachers. A relationship-based model respects the effects of an individual child's characteristics and the child's environment on the quality of the child's relationships. These relationships then become the filter and the catalyst for children's sense of well-being and development. As you use the relationship-based model to discover the importance of the infant and toddler years, we hope that you will gain a sense of enthusiasm and excitement about the influence that infant and toddler professionals can have on the quality of experiences and programs for young children and their families.

WHAT THIS BOOK PROVIDES FOR OUR READERS

Our text provides a foundation in how infants and toddlers develop, in typical and atypical ways, and in program planning.

Why and How of Developmental Practice

We present all aspects of development within the context of brain development and the foundational structure of emotional development and early relationships. We want students to understand *why,* according to the science of child development, certain practices support or hinder an infant's or toddler's optimal development—and *how* to provide responsive, high-quality care. This book integrates theory, research, and practice in usable language for teachers.

Program Planning

In addition to including developmental content, it also uniquely includes program planning, which highlights the following components:

1. developing the foundation of a program
2. the teacher's roles
3. the importance of relationships with families and how to provide culturally sensitive care
4. a responsive planning process
5. conducting sensitive transitions and routines
6. creating responsive and relationship-based environments
7. providing responsive experiences and opportunities for children
8. a relationship-based approach to guidance

AN EMPHASIS ON CULTURE AND CHILDREN WITH DISABILITIES

To fully respect the impact of culture on early development, information on this and on the importance of inclusion of children with disabilities in early education and development programs is included throughout the book. These topics are presented as they relate to the major content of each chapter, such as how disabilities may affect learning or how people from different cultures approach learning.

NEW TO THIS EDITION

myeducationlab

When you see a margin note like this, go to www.myeducationlab .com to watch a video, answer questions, and build teaching skills.

- *MyEducationLab* video resources integrated into book margins and assignable exercises pertaining to them are online
- A comprehensive review of the literature regarding the key elements of a relationship-based approach and the research that supports it (chapter 1)
- Chapter on observation, documentation, and assessment (chapter 4)
- Information on language and motor development theories (chapters 9, 10)
- The most recent research on infant and toddler development, individualized planning, and curriculum
- Discussion of issues such as the effect of multiple attachments and bilingual opportunities for infants and toddlers
- *Portraits of Development* tables (Appendix A and Appendix B [in Spanish]), a snapshot of development at each age group from birth to 36 months.
- *Developmental Trends and Responsive Interactions* tables in Spanish (Appendix C)
- Additional and updated references, resources, and Web sites

SPECIAL PEDAGOGICAL FEATURES

The special features of this book include:

- *Observation Invitations* in the development chapters (chapters 6 through 10) invite readers to enter the world of a child to reflect on what a photo or written observation reveals about the child's development and goals.

- At the end of each development chapter, a ***Strategies to Support*** box summarizes specific strategies for teachers and other adults that facilitate the child's development in that domain.

- Observation and planning forms for individuals and groups in Chapter 13 and Appendix D.

- Each development chapter presents a comprehensive chart, ***Developmental Trends and Responsive Interactions,*** which describes the capacities of the child as well as developmental milestones, includes examples of development to help students connect theory with practice, lists teacher or parent interaction strategies to support development and learning, and includes a list of toys, materials, and equipment and other environmental supports that enhance development. These tables also appear in Spanish in Appendix C.

- "Reflections and Resources for the Reader" at the end of each chapter provides follow-up questions and reinforcing material to correspond with the chapter's content. Relevant Web links are provided as well.

- *Vignettes* are woven throughout the chapters to illustrate how theories and concepts look in real settings where infants and toddlers are cared for and educated.

- *Glossary terms* are defined in the margin of the page where the term is used.

- *Quotes* from a variety of early childhood education and child development authors are highlighted throughout the book to illuminate specific points of interest.

- A complete *Summary* at the end of each chapter highlights the major points of that chapter.

ORGANIZATION

Chapters 1 through 3 set the stage by focusing on early experiences, family relationships, and theoretical perspectives. Chapter 1 describes the current status of the infant and toddler field. Powerful research informs us that the early years matter. Science is establishing that the child's attitudes, knowledge, and skills developed during the first 3 years provide a foundation for a lifetime of learning and loving. Families, as the primary influence on their child's development, build this foundation, and the factors that influence how families function are explored in chapter 2. Infant and toddler professionals also have a strong influence on whether babies thrive, and it is important that professionals build their practice on knowledge of theoretical perspectives. In chapter 3, the theories that guide teachers to become purposeful about their work, understand how infants and toddlers develop, know what they need, and appreciate how they learn are described. The observation and documentation strategies highlighted in a new chapter, chapter 4, provide methods for teachers to learn about children—how they develop and think and what they need to thrive.

The second section of this book describes the remarkable development of children in the prenatal period (chapter 5), and in the emotional (chapter 6), social (chapter 7), cognitive (chapter 8), language (chapter 9), and physical or motor (chapter 10) domains. Each domain of development is explored on several levels that relate to the relationship-based model presented in the first chapter. We describe the capacities that each child brings to that domain, and then explore individual attributes such as gender or temperament. Early disabling conditions and intervention strategies are included in "Children with Special Needs." The development of the child within his or her family, culture, and an infant and toddler program is emphasized, along with strategies for supporting that aspect of development. At the end of these chapters, we describe components of programs that support and enhance the development of infants, toddlers, and their families.

The third section of the book (chapters 11 through 16) takes you, the infant and toddler professional, into the world of responsive program planning that happens day to day, the relationship way. Equipped with the knowledge of the importance of the early years, theoretical perspectives, and the amazing development of infants and toddlers, you will learn how to plan a program that meets their needs and supports them as they learn. This process includes *respecting* the child's experience, *reflecting* on his or her intentions and your own reactions, and *relating* to the child through your response.

Nurturing and responsiveness are key elements of being an infant and toddler professional, and you will learn ways to promote the emotional development of young children within a program setting. With an emphasis on responsive interactions and relationships, you will discover how to set up an enriched environment full of learning opportunities (chapter 13). The guidance strategies recommended (chapter 14) respect the child's culture and individuality, require reflection on the part of the professional, and build infants' and toddlers' capacity to be in constructive relationships with others. Since programs include children with disabilities as well as children with diverse interests, needs, and abilities, chapter 15 discusses how to individualize for children with special needs and how to work with the early intervention system.

The quest for quality experiences for very young children leads us to focus on what it means to be a professional who works with infants, toddlers, and their families. Chapter 16 describes the professional's journey toward developing an identity as an infant and toddler professional; becoming reflective; creating and nurturing relationships for professional development; and advocating for teachers, children, families, programs, and the community to move the profession forward.

We hope this book inspires you to promote the well-being, competence, and quality of life for infants and toddlers and their families. We also hope that it is the beginning of a new or renewed journey to develop a community of caring that recognizes the importance of the infant and toddler years. Infants and toddlers are depending upon it.

SUPPLEMENTARY MATERIAL FOR THIS TEXT

MyEducationLab Videos and Assignable Questions and Exercises

Margin notes within each chapter enable students and instructors to access MyEducationLab, a carefully selected collection of video clips, artifacts, and assignable questions in "Activities and Applications," and more elaborate exercises in "Building Teaching Skills and Dispositions."

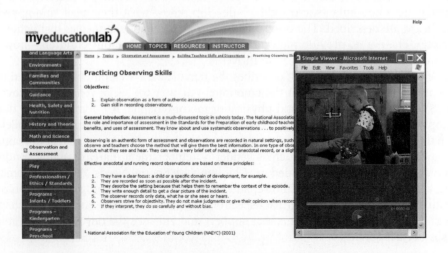

Instructor Resources

The following ancillaries can be downloaded from www.pearsonhighered.com by instructors who adopt this text. Click on "Educators," then "Download Instructor Resources."

Online Instructor's Manual. An extensive *Online Instructor's Manual* includes discussion points, a multitude of active learning strategies, and an annotated bibliography of resources such as videos, DVDs, manuals, articles, and books to accompany each chapter in the book.

Online Test Bank. The Test Bank contains multiple-choice and essay items for every chapter.

Online PowerPoint Slides. These slides cover the major points and strategies of each chapter.

Online Test Generator Software. Known as TestGen, this test-generator software permits instructors to create and customize exams. TestGen is available in a dual Macintosh and PC/Windows version.

Course Management. The assessment items in the Test Bank are available in WebCT and Blackboard formats.

ACKNOWLEDGMENTS

No book is written without affecting the lives of the friends and families of the authors. We especially want to thank our husbands, children, and sons-in-law for their never-ending support and encouragement. They, and our grandchildren, provide a secure and joyous base from which to explore this field. We thank Deanna, Donna's daughter, for an excellent first edit of the first edition of this book.

We have shared numerous professional and personal experiences, and we have been influenced by many of the same individuals and programs. Together, we gratefully acknowledge and thank Dr. Ron Lally and Peter Mangione for their mentorship, friendship, and untiring leadership in their efforts to improve the quality of early care and development programs for young children. Because they embrace their Fellows as family, we thank everyone at ZERO TO THREE who has led to the promotion of relationship-based practice. These people have deepened our understanding of the infant family field and have been a constant source of support for us.

To our friend, Jo Koehn, we offer deep respect, affection, and gratitude. Her wisdom and fortitude has provided us with endless opportunities to deepen and refine our understanding of infant and toddler care through the Colorado Department of Education's statewide infant and toddler training, Expanding Quality for Infants and Toddlers. We offer our heartfelt appreciation to the faculty, community teachers, and participants across the state who are endlessly supporting quality care.

Special thanks to Julie Peters, our editor at Pearson, who strives for quality in all she does. We definitely could not have completed this book without her positive regard and constant encouragement. We thank Connie Strassburg of GGS Higher Education Resources, who masterfully wove the writing into a book, and Carol Sykes of Pearson for her good humor in working with amateur photographers.

We would also like to thank Carla Mestas; Jen Sieminski; Don and Lori Easton-Brooks; Ellen Hall and the Boulder Journey School; Diane Trujillo at SPIN ECE Center (a program of Starpoint); Janelle, a wonderful family child care provider; Terri Liggins of Calvary Baptist Church Child Care Center; Denny McGihan of Creative Options Early Head Start and Child Care; Family Star Early Head Start; and all of the parents who provided the photographs of loving and skilled teachers and beautiful children throughout this book.

We would like to say a special thank you to Dr. Alice Honig, Professor Emeritus at Syracuse University, and a mentor and friend of Donna's since graduate school, for her continuous warm support and her infinite wisdom about infants and toddlers. For their influence on our visions of quality for infants, toddlers, and families, we also offer our gratitude and affection to Rose Bromwich, Jeree Pawl, Judith Pekarsky, Lillian Sugarman, Judie Jerrald, and Tammy Mann.

Finally, we would like to acknowledge the following second edition reviewers for their insight and comments: Susan Churchill, University of Nebraska, Lincoln; Irene Cook, California State University, Bakersfield; Michelle Koppelman, Owens Community College; Mary Beth Mann, Missouri State University; Rhonda D. Richardson, Sam Houston State University; Joanne Labish Taylor, Sussex County Community College; Rebecca L. Ward-Smith, Aims Community College; and Deborah Young, Naropa University.

Brief Contents

Chapter 1   A Relationship-Based Model and the Importance
of the Infant and Toddler Years   1

Chapter 2   Infants, Toddlers, and Their Families   25

Chapter 3   Understanding and Using Theories   45

Chapter 4   The Power of Observation: Learning About Infants and
Toddlers   69

Chapter 5   Brain and Prenatal Development, Birth, and the Newborn   89

Chapter 6   Attachment and Emotional Relationships   110

Chapter 7   Social Development and Learning with Peers   135

Chapter 8   Cognitive Development and Learning   162

Chapter 9   Language Development and Learning   189

Chapter 10   Motor Development and Learning   220

Chapter 11   Responsive Programs: Quality, Health, Safety, and
Nutrition   243

Chapter 12   Creating a Relationship-Based Curriculum   265

Chapter 13   Routines, Environments, and Opportunities: Day to Day
the Relationship Way   296

Chapter 14   Respect, Reflect, and Relate: The 3 R Approach to
Guidance   328

Chapter 15   Including Infants and Toddlers with Disabilities in Child
Development and Education Programs   356

Chapter 16   The Infant-Toddler Professional: Identity, Relationships, and
Resources   372

Contents

Chapter 1   **A Relationship-Based Model and the Importance
of the Infant and Toddler Years   1**

A Relationship-Based Model   2

How the Ecology Affects Relationships   3

How Children's Attributes and Capacities Affect Relationships   4

*Research on the Importance of Relationships for Children, Families,
and Infant-Toddler Professionals   5*

The Importance of the Infancy Period (Prenatal to 3 Years of Age)   6

*Recent Understanding of the Importance of the Infant and
Toddler Years   7*

Research on Brain Development   8

Sensitive Periods and Windows of Opportunity   9

Core Concepts of Prenatal, Infant, and Toddler Development   10

Both Nature and Nurture Affect Children's Development   11

*Culture Influences Development and Child-Rearing Beliefs
and Practices   11*

Self-Regulation Is an Important Indicator of Development   11

*Children Contribute to Their Own Development Through Active
Exploration   11*

*Human Relationships, and the Effects of Relationships on Relationships,
Are the Building Blocks of Healthy Development   12*

There Is a Broad Range of Individual Differences   12

The Development of Children Is Both Continuous and Discontinuous   12

Infants and Toddlers Are Both Vulnerable and Resilient   12

*The Timing of Early Experiences Can Matter and Children Are Open to
Change   15*

Early Intervention Can Make a Difference   15

Conclusion of the 10 Core Concepts   15

Changes in Demographics That Affect Infants and Toddlers
and Their Families   15

A Changing Population in the United States   15

Poverty   17

Early Development and Education Programs   18

Child Care   18

Early Intervention Programs for Children at Risk   20

Early Intervention for Children with Disabilities   21

Infants' and Toddlers' Irreducible Needs   21

Summary   22

Key Terms   23

Reflections and Resources for the Reader   23

Chapter 2   **Infants, Toddlers, and Their Families   25**

Biological and Cultural Effects on the Family   26
Our Biology Affects Our Parenting   26
Cultural Effects on Parenting   26

Variations in Parenting   29
Becoming a Mother   31
Becoming a Father   32
The Transition from Partners to Parenthood   33
The Imagined Baby and the Real Baby   34
Parenting Styles   34

Family Structure   35
Divorce   36
Single Parents   36
Same-Sex Parents   37
Grandparents   38
Adoptive Parents   38
Foster Parents   39

Care and Education Programs That Support
Families   40
Parent Education   40
Family Support Programs   41

Summary   42

Key Terms   43

Reflections and Resources for the Reader   43

Chapter 3   **Understanding and Using Theories   45**

What Are Theories?   45

Our Theoretical Framework   46
Relationship-Based Theory   47
Transactional Theory   49
Bioecological Systems Theory   51
Summary of the Major Theories   52

Theories of Emotional Development: A Sense of Self
and Relationships with Others   53
Theory of Psychosocial Development   53
The Hierarchy of Human Needs   54
Separation and Individuation   54
Attachment Theory   56
Interpersonal Development Theory   57
Summary of Theories of Emotional Development   58

Theories of Cognitive Development: Learning About the World   58
   Constructivist Theory of Learning   58
   Sociocultural Theory   61
   Social Learning/Cognitive Theory   62
   Core Knowledge Theory   62
   Summary of Theories of Cognitive Development   63

Theories of Language Development   63
   Kuhl's Perceptual Mapping Model   63
   Social Interaction Theory   64

A Theory of Motor Development: Learning to Move   64

Applying Theories in Programs   65
   Child Development Programs   66
   Relationship-Based Programs   66
   Summary of Applying Theories in Programs   66

Summary   67

Key Terms   67

Reflections and Resources for the Reader   68

Chapter 4   The Power of Observation: Learning About Infants and Toddlers   69

Observing—A Powerful Skill   70
   Why Observation Is Important   70
   Observation and Theory Have Changed How Children Are Understood   70

The Ethics of Observing   72

What to Observe   73

How to Observe and Record Observations   75
   Anecdotal Records and Running Records   75
   Event Sampling   78
   Charts   80
   Documentation   81
   Summary of Observation Methods   83

Observation as Part of Assessment   83
   Developmental Profiles   83
   Screening Tools   85

What Method to Use?   85

Bring Information Together: Portfolios of Observations/Documentations   86

What the Observer Brings to Observations   86
   Past Experiences, Beliefs, Values   87
   Culture   87
   Presence   87

Summary   88

Key Terms   88

Reflections and Resources for the Reader   88

Chapter 5   **Brain and Prenatal Development, Birth, and the Newborn   89**

Brain Development: An Overview   90
The Structure of the Brain   90
The Importance of Early Experiences for Brain Development   93
The Effects of Stress and Violence on Brain Development   94

Genetics and Prenatal Development   95

The Fetus   97
The First Trimester   97
The Second Trimester   98
The Third Trimester   98

The Womb as an Environment for Development   99
Nutrition   100
Toxins and Teratogens   101
Structural/Metabolic Birth Defects and Maternal Infections   102
Prenatal Testing   102

The Mother's Experience as an Environment   103
Maternal Stress, Anxiety, and Other Factors   103

The Newborn   104
Postnatal Brain Development   105
Developmental Milestones of the Newborn   106

Unique Beginnings   106

Summary   107

Key Terms   108

Reflections and Resources for the Reader   108

Chapter 6   **Attachment and Emotional Relationships   110**

The Uniqueness of Each Child   110
Capacities   111
Attributes   114

Development and Learning Through Relationships   116
Cultural Differences and Emotional Development   116
Emotional Expression and Understanding   117
The Attachment Relationship   119
Impact of Maternal Depression   123

Children with Special Needs   124

Programs That Enhance Emotional Development
and Learning   125
Infant Mental Health   125

Strategies to Support Emotional Development
and Learning   125
Child Care Experiences and Emotional Development   127

Summary   132

Key Terms   133

Reflections and Resources for the Reader   133

Chapter 7   **Social Development and Learning with Peers   135**

The Uniqueness of Each Child   136
Capacities   136
Attributes   137

Development and Learning Through Relationships   140
Culture and Peer Relationships   140
Social Development with Peers   141
Prosocial Development in Infants and Toddlers   144
Learning Through Relationships   152

Strategies to Support Social Development
and Learning   153

Children with Special Needs   154

Programs That Enhance Social Development
and Learning   155
Quality Child Development and Education Programs   155
Continuity of Peer Groups   155
Ratios, Number of Adults, and Group Size   155
Relationship with the Infant-Toddler Teacher   155
Socialization Strategies of the Teacher   160

Summary   160

Key Terms   161

Reflections and Resources for the Reader   161

Chapter 8   **Cognitive Development and Learning   162**

The Uniqueness of Each Child   162
Capacities   163
Sensory Perceptions   166
Attributes   171

Development and Learning Through Relationships   172
Culture and Relationships   172
Tools of Learning   173
Learning Through Relationships   176
Concepts Infants and Toddlers Learn   177

Children with Special Needs   180

Programs That Enhance Cognitive Development
and Learning   181
*Child Care: Rich Environments and Responsive
Relationships   181*

Strategies to Support Cognitive Development
and Learning   182
Programs for Infants and Toddlers at Risk   183
Early Intervention   183

Summary   186

Key Terms   187

Reflections and Resources for the Reader   187

Chapter 9   Language Development and Learning   189

The Uniqueness of Each Child   189
Overview of Language Capacities   190
Attributes   192

Development and Learning Through Relationships   193
Culture and Language   193
Bilingual and Bidialectical Children and Families   195
Language Development in Relationships   199
Strategies to Encourage Language Learning   206

Children with Special Needs   211
Hearing Impairment   211

Programs That Enhance Language Development
and Learning   212
Child Care: Relationships and Responsive Interactions   212
Early Intervention Programs   212

Strategies to Support Language Development
and Learning   213

Summary   218

Key Terms   218

Reflections and Resources for the Reader   218

Chapter 10   Motor Development and Learning   220

The Uniqueness of Each Child   220
Capacities   221
Attributes   223

Development and Learning Through Relationships   224
Culture and Motor Development   224
Motor Development Through Relationships   225
Movement   226
Using Tools   229
Perceptual-Motor Coordination   232

Strategies to Support Motor Development
and Learning   233

Children with Special Needs   233
Motor Concerns   234
Effects of Motor Disorders   234

Programs That Enhance Motor Development
and Learning   235
Child Development and Education Programs   235
Physical and Occupational Therapy   236
Movement Psychotherapy   237

Summary   240

Key Terms   241

Reflections and Resources for the Reader   241

Chapter 11   **Responsive Programs: Quality, Health, Safety, and Nutrition**   243

What Is Quality . . . and Why Does It Matter?   244
- *Structural Variables of Quality*   245
- *Process Variables of Quality*   248

An Emphasis on Health and Safety   249
- *Sanitizing and Preventing the Spread of Disease*   250
- *Promoting Safety and Preventing Injuries*   253
- *Adopting Policies That Promote and Protect Health*   254

The Importance of Good Nutrition   256
- *Nutritional Needs of Infants and Toddlers*   256
- *Child Development and Education Programs Supporting Safe and Healthy Nutrition*   258

Evaluating Quality in Child Care Programs   260
- *Infant-Toddler Environmental Rating Scale* (ITERS)   260
- *Observational Record of the Caregiving Environment* (ORCE)   261
- *Teacher Interaction Scale*   261
- *Program Review Instrument for Systems Monitoring* (PRISM)   261

Policies, Laws, and Systems That Support Quality Programs   261
- *Child Care Development Fund* (CCDF)   261
- *Licensing*   262
- *Quality Rating Systems and Tiered Reimbursement*   262
- *Accreditation*   263

Summary   263

Key Terms   263

Reflections and Resources for the Reader   264

Chapter 12   **Creating a Relationship-Based Curriculum**   265

Component 1: The Foundation—A Way of Thinking About Infants and Toddlers   267
- *What Are the Beliefs and Assumptions About the Nature of Infants and Toddlers?*   267
- *What Are the Needs of Infants and Toddlers?*   268
- *What Is Important for Infants and Toddlers to Learn?*   269
- *How Do Children Develop and Learn?*   271

Component 2: The Infant-Toddler Professional's Role—Creating a Relationship-Based Program   275
- *A Special Kind of Person*   275
- *Creating a Relationship-Based Community*   276
- *Adult-Child Interactions and Relationships in a Relationship-Based Program*   276

Component 3: Relationships with Families and Culturally Sensitive Care   283
- *Strategies for Developing Relationships with Families*   283
- *Strategies for Developing Relationships with Families from Diverse Cultures*   284

Component 4: Responsive, Relationship-Based
Planning   287

Summary   293

Key Terms   294

Reflections and Resources for the Reader   294

Chapter 13   **Routines, Environments, and Opportunities: Day to Day
the Relationship Way   296**

Component 5: Transitions and Routines—A Time for
Relationships   297

Transition of Entering a New Child Care Education Program   298
Transitions During the Day   298
Responsive Routines   299

Component 6: Creating Responsive, Relationship-Based
Environments   300

A Quality Environment for Centers and Child Care Homes   300
Cozy Spaces and Special Places   304

Component 7: Responsive Opportunities   307

Planning Opportunities   307
Quiet and Calm Opportunities   308
Nurturing Opportunities   309
Social Opportunities   310
Language Opportunities   310
Cognitive Opportunities   312
Delighting-the-Senses Experiences   312
Creative Opportunities   313
Writing and Drawing Opportunities   315
Opportunities with Blocks   315
Music, Song, and Creative Movement Opportunities   317
Literacy Opportunities   318
Math, Space, and Shape Opportunities   320
Opportunities for Active Play and Motor Development   322

Curriculum Approaches   323

The Program for Infant/Toddler Care (PITC)   325
High/Scope   325
The Creative Curriculum for Infants, Toddlers & Twos   325
Reggio Emilia   325

Summary   326

Reflections and Resources for the Reader   327

Chapter 14   **Respect, Reflect, and Relate: The 3 R Approach to Guidance   328**

The Difference Between Guidance and Discipline   329

Component 8: A Relationship-Based Approach to
Guidance   329

Respect   329
Reflect   331
Relate   332

Relationship Realignments   339
  Separation Anxiety   339
  Toddler Resistance   340
  Tantrums   341
  Children Who Bite   342
  Toilet Learning   346

Challenging Behavior and Mental Health Issues   347
  Anxious, Fearful, Vigilant   348
  Angry and Defiant   349
  Children Who Behave Aggressively   350
  Posttraumatic Stress Disorder   350
  What Philosophy Will You Use?   352

Summary   353

Key Terms   354

Reflections and Resources for the Reader   354

Chapter 15   Including Infants and Toddlers with Disabilities in Child Development and Education Programs   356

What Disabilities Do We See in Infants and Toddlers?   357
  Groups of Disabilities   357
  Chromosomal Abnormalities and Genetic Syndromes   358
  Sensory Impairments   359
  Metabolic Disorders   359
  Central Nervous System Disorders   360
  Congenital Infections   361
  Disorders Secondary to Exposure to Toxic Substances   361
  Chronic Illness   361
  Conditions of Risk for Poor Development   361

Early Intervention: Part C of IDEA   362
  Eligibility   363
  Individualized Family Service Plan (IFSP)   363
  Early Intervention Services   364
  Making Referrals   365
  Child Development and Education as a Natural Environment   366

Teacher Attitudes and Strategies in the Child Development and Education Program   366
  Maintain a Positive Attitude   366
  Ask for Information Sharing   367
  Document Children's Competence   368
  Adapt Materials and Activities   368
  Arrange the Environment   369
  Use Group Affection Activities   369
  Meet Therapeutic Goals   370

Summary   370

Key Terms   371

Reflections and Resources for the Reader   371

Chapter 16   **The Infant-Toddler Professional: Identity, Relationships, and Resources   372**

The Infant and Toddler Profession   372
Professional Identity   373
Professional Standards   374

The Professional's Experience   377
What's Different About Being an Infant and Toddler Professional?   377
Infant and Toddler Professionals Must Know Themselves Well   378

Professional Development: Visions, Values, and Philosophy   379
Your Vision   379
A Professional Philosophy Statement   380
Developing and Using a Code of Ethics   380

Organizational Structure, Programs, and Policies   380
The Organization of a Program: Are You Treated Like a Professional?   381
Shared Decision Making   381

Developing Relationships and Community Within the Program for Professional Development   383
Developing a Professional Relationship-Based Community   383
A Reflective Practice Model   386
Reflective Supervision   386
Mentoring and Being Mentored   387

Becoming an Advocate   388

Summary   389

Key Terms   390

Reflections and Resources for the Reader   390

Appendix A   Portraits of Development   392

Appendix B   Portraits of Development (Spanish)   410

Appendix C   Developmental Trends and Responsive Interactions (Spanish)   432

Appendix D   Planning Guides   456

References   461

Name Index   483

Subject Index   491

A Relationship-Based Model and the Importance of the Infant and Toddler Years

Infants and toddlers are remarkable, delightful, and engaging human beings who require sensitive and responsive families and teachers in order to develop into capable and caring adults. Connections with others—family, teachers, and peers—support infants and toddlers as they figure out who they are, sustain meaningful relationships, and gain knowledge about their world. As you walk through the incredible developmental journey that infants and toddlers take, you will appreciate how children influence their families and teachers—and in turn how families, cultural perspectives, and the larger world influence who these infants and toddlers become.

In this book, our goal is that you gain an appreciation for how vitally important the prenatal period and the first 3 years of life are. Our hope is that you will become knowledgeable about and gain a passion for promoting the (1) well-being, (2) competence, (3) good developmental outcomes, and (4) quality of life of infants and toddlers and their families. To better understand these goals for infants and toddlers, we will define each one.

Well-being, refers to "how a child feels and thinks about him- or herself and the joy and satisfaction that the child experiences in regard to his or her relationships and accomplishments" (Erickson & Kurz-Riemer, 1999, p. 26). *Competence* refers to how effectively the child adapts

to day-to-day changes; how adaptable and flexible a child is. This is the outward manifestation of "*good developmental outcomes*" (p. 26, italics added). *Quality of life* refers to the child's feelings about the value, worth, living conditions, and relationships that he or she experiences. We hope that your enthusiasm and excitement about these four goals will grow and guide you in your interactions with, beliefs about, and support for infants and toddlers.

The theoretical basis for this book is a relationship-based model that promotes infants' and toddlers' optimal *mental health* in the context of the children's family, culture, community, and world. When toddlers reach age 3, they will be mentally healthy if they (1) feel competent and confident, (2) enjoy intimate and caring relationships, (3) feel safe, (4) have basic trust in others, (5) regulate and express emotions in healthy ways, (6) communicate and are understood, (7) feel valued for their unique personalities, (8) have the energy and curiosity to learn, and (9) enjoy excellent health and nutrition. The term **mental health** describes infants' and toddlers' social and emotional well-being.

mental health
The emotional and social well-being of a person.

A RELATIONSHIP-BASED MODEL

This book will focus on a relationship-based model for understanding infant and toddler development and responsive program planning.

A **relationship-based model** (see Figure 1.1) recognizes that constructive, caring relationships are fundamental to the human experience. As adults we know that intimate rela-

relationship-based model
A model whereby constructive, caring relationships are fundamental to infant and toddler development.

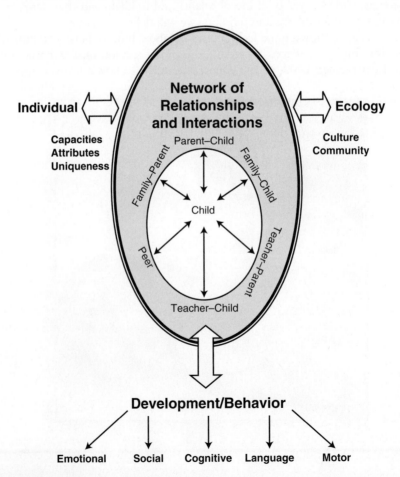

Figure 1.1   Relationship-based model for infant and toddler development and program planning.

tionships and worthwhile friendships are a source of joy. Relationship-building skills such as initiating interactions, maintaining congenial associations with others, and social problem solving are often the key to success at home, as well as in the workplace. Positive relationships are vital for infants and toddlers as well. To thrive, infants and toddlers need loving adults who protect, nurture, and help them learn. Adults who respond to children and treat them with respect promote their strengths. In fact, respectful responses from others are *essential* to infants' and toddlers' sense of security, self-worth, self-confidence, and motivation to learn. Infants' and toddlers' experience of healthy relationships is the foundation for their ability to love and learn.

Infants and toddlers exist within a network of relationships: mother–child, father–child, mother–father, mother–grandmother, father–neighbor, mother–employer, and many more that are influenced by and in turn influence infants' well-being (See Figure 1.1). A relationship-based model predicts that the quality of the relationship in one dyad (2 people who interact with each other)

Constructive, caring relationships are fundamental to the human experience.

affects the quality of relationships in another dyad (Hinde & Stevenson-Hinde, 1987). For example, a parent's positive relationship with the infant can affect the expectations that the infant or toddler has for a relationship with an infant or toddler teacher. Both of these relationships can then have an impact on the nature of the child's peer interactions. Aggression between a mother and father is related to infants withdrawing from social interaction (Crockenberg, Leerkes, & Lekka, 2007). The array and quality of children's relationships exist within and throughout a web of interconnected circles, with each relationship influencing the other.

Both the *ecology* (environment), including culture, and the child's individual characteristics influence the features of the relationships that a child experiences. We will discuss the theories supporting this in detail in chapter 3; however, here we will briefly discuss how first the ecology and then a child's individual attributes and capacities influence the child's relationships with parents, families, and teachers.

How the Ecology Affects Relationships

When infants and toddlers are physically, emotionally, and cognitively healthy and experiencing positive relationships, it is because of a support system that involves family, culture, the neighborhood, community, and a society that knows and cares deeply about the importance of the first 3 years of life. According to **bioecological systems theory** (Bronfenbrenner, 1979, 1986, 2004), the ecology—the personal and physical environment—influences the nature of the relationships that the child experiences. These relationships are most influenced by the immediate settings: namely, family and the early care and education program that the child is experiencing.

Families are also influenced by their **culture**—the values and beliefs about what is important in life, including traditions, celebrations, languages, and styles of interacting with others (Gonzalez-Mena, 2008). According to Haviland, culture comprises "the abstract values, beliefs, and perceptions of the world that lie behind people's behavior, and which are reflected in their behavior" (Barrera, 2003). For example, a family's culture may value a baby sleeping with the

bioecological systems theory
How the settings in which a developing child lives interact with the child's biological characteristics to influence development.

culture
The beliefs, way of life, abilities, and arts of a particular group of people that are held and/or passed along to future generations.

parents rather than alone in a separate room. Their belief is that babies need to be close to a parent to feel safe and a part of the family. These values and beliefs guide the decisions about where the baby will sleep. The importance of cultural perspectives, as a key part of the ecological model, is highlighted in this book.

National and international laws and policies are a part of the ecology that influences the quality of a child's relationships with parents, family, and teachers. For example, how a nation's citizens view families in poverty, welfare reform, or the importance of quality child care intensely affects life's possibilities for infants and toddlers. Also, in addition to being influenced by the environment, infants and toddlers play a role in a relationship-based model and influence the relationships that children have with their parents and families. Infants and toddlers are born with unique characteristics, attributes, and capacities that have an effect on how we, as adults, interact and relate to them.

How Children's Attributes and Capacities Affect Relationships

transactional theory
Emphasizes the effect of a child's behavior or characteristics on his or her environment and relationships.

Transactional theory highlights how the feelings and reactions of families and teachers are affected by their children's *attributes*—age, biological makeup, gender, temperament, appearance, and actions (Sameroff & Feise, 2000) (see Figure 1.1). These attributes influence how the infant or toddler is treated by the family or teacher. Not all babies within the same family or progam are treated the same. A baby who is fussy influences the adult–child dynamics. For example, a toddler who reminds the family of a favorite uncle has a different impact than a child who resembles a relative who isn't liked by the family.

How much a child's characteristics influence a family, however, may depend on the ecology of the particular family and how the ecology affects the relationships within the family. A family under stress that has outside support from relatives, friends, or a community program may do well with a fussy baby. A family that is isolated from relatives or friends may have a difficult time with the same type of baby, who cries often and requires sensitive adult responses. The stress of the family may contribute to insensitive caregiving, which then possibly leads to a neglected infant, who in turn becomes a challenging toddler. On the other hand, when families perceive that they have social support from a shared community, then the family and the children in that family are more likely to thrive (Child Welfare Information Gateway, 2008; Runyan et al., 1996).

A child's capacities blossom within loving relationships.

Infants and toddlers come into this world with many capacities. They have the ability to be social, express emotions, learn, communicate, and move. These capacities blossom throughout the infant and toddler years within loving relationships with family members and other caring adults and peers.

domains
The specific areas of development that include emotional, social, cognitive, language, and motor development.

In a relationship-based model of infant and toddler development, there is a constant interplay between children's attributes and capacities and the ecology, and all of these—together and separately—influence the quality of children's relationships. It is the quality of the relationships that then affects the experiences and development of the children—their development in the emotional, social, cognitive, language, and motor **domains** (see Figure 1.1).

Research on the Importance of Relationships for Children, Families, and Infant-Toddler Professionals

The research on the importance of infants' and toddlers' positive, caring relationships with family members, teachers in centers and child care homes, and early interventionists (who work with children with special needs) is clear. Research conducted in the United States found that young infants and toddlers who feel safe and secure with their mother, father, and other family members feel less stressed (Gunnar & Cheatham, 2003) and can express and control emotions in healthy ways (self-regulation) (Feldman, Greenbaum, & Yirmiya, 1999; Gunnar & Quevedo, 2007) compared to young children who experience fearful or anxious relationships. The quality of the parent–child relationship also influences the quality of peer relationships. Children with less positive parent–child relationships are more likely to be aggressive than children who experience more positive relationships (McElwain, Cox, Burchinal, & Macfie, 2003).

How do parents help young children feel secure? Children feel secure when parents are responsive and affectionate (de Wolff & van IJzendoom, 1997; Harel & Scher, 2003), and also when adults support the children's self-directed activities and autonomy (NICHD Early Child Care Research Network, 2004). Parents' sensitivity to their children's needs and distress is important. Parents' *sensitivity* to infant distress at 6 months relates to infants feeling secure (McElwain & Booth-LaForce, 2006). Ziv, Aviezer, Gini, Sagi, and Koren-Karie (2000), researchers in Israel, reported that among 687 Israeli mother–infant dyads, higher mother *emotional availability* scores predicted more secure attachment. Conversely, mothers' intrusiveness with their children in different cultural groups—European American, African American, and more or less acculturated Mexican American low-income families—when infants were 15 months old led to aggression when these children were 25 months old (Ispa et al., 2004).

Support for families to help them become responsive makes a difference. When mothers of adopted 6-month-old children were given video feedback to become more sensitively responsive, their children were more likely to be secure at 12 months than were children of mothers who did not receive the intervention (Jeffer, Bakermans-Kranenburg, & van IJzendoorn, 2005). With children who were deaf-blind, parents who completed a five-module curriculum communicated with their infants and toddlers more and the quality of communication interactions improved (Chen & Haney, 1999). Parents reported that they felt more effective in observing and responding to their young children's special needs.

Responsiveness is a key term that is used frequently in this book. Babies communicate through their facial expressions, body postures, gestures, and words. **Responsiveness** refers to both how well the adult understands what the infant or toddler is trying to communicate (their cues) and how the adult acts in response to the child. A responsive adult is "tuned in" to the child and is sensitive and caring in response to the child. The responsiveness may occur moment to moment in an interaction with the child, or over time as the adult plans future interactions, an environment, and experiences that meet the child's needs and interests. A family's responsiveness is important at home and a care teacher's responsiveness is important in a program.

Infants' and toddlers' secure relationships with care teachers in child care and education programs also are vital for the children's development. When children feel secure within caring relationships with teachers they are more socially competent (Howes, Phillips, & Whitebook, 1992), have better language development, can regulate their emotions, and participate more in problem-solving activities (Howes & Smith, 1995). What do care teachers do that help infants and toddlers feel secure?

Young children feel secure to love and learn when care teachers are highly involved with the children—hold them, hug them for comfort, and engage them in conversations (Howes & Hamilton, 1992). Teachers can also promote security by providing many opportunities for the infants and toddlers to make choices in an interesting environment (NICHD Early Child Care

myeducationlab

Go to the Activities and Applications section in Chapter 1 of MyEducationLab at www.myeducationlab. com. to watch the video *Infant Feeding*. Observe how the care teacher is sensitive and responsive.

responsiveness
Adult sensitivity and reaction to a child's facial expression, body postures, gestures, and words.

Research Network, 2004). The more sensitive (warm, attentive, and engaged) the teacher is with children as compared to harsh (critical, threatening, and punitive) or detached (low levels of interaction) the more secure the child feels with the teacher (Howes & Hamilton, 1992).

Continuity of care in child care and education programs is important for infants' and toddlers' feelings of security. Helen Raikes (1993) observed infants and toddlers in child care centers and found that 91% of the children who stayed with a teacher over 1 year felt secure, whereas only about 50% of those children who were with a teacher for a shorter period of time felt secure. A more recent study of more than 1,000 toddlers found that when at least one care teacher "moves up" with the group or all care teachers stay with the group as they age the following occurs:

- Children and teachers develop close trusting affectionate relationships.
- At child care, children are more positive with peers.
- At home, children are less negative and less aggressive.
- Children have increased cognitive and language skills. (NICHD, 2001b)

When care teachers do not move with the children and the children experience the loss the results are not as positive. The more caregiver losses infants and toddlers have experienced by the time they are preschoolers the more likely they are to be socially withdrawn and aggressive with peers (Howes & Hamilton, 1993). Infants and toddlers learn to trust adults and learn *how* to be in quality relationships with continuous care.

In this book, stories of children, families, and communities are shared to bring to life the attributes and capacities, the relationships, and the ecology of infants and toddlers in the first 3 years of life. Our hope is that we can share these stories, the results of research, information on development and responsive care, ideas about relationship-based programs, and how to help infants love, laugh, and learn in such a way that you, too, will become an advocate for the importance of the early years.

THE IMPORTANCE OF THE INFANCY PERIOD (PRENATAL TO 3 YEARS OF AGE)

While you have been reading this, a newborn baby has opened her eyes for the first time and sensed the closeness of her mother gazing lovingly into her eyes, and a toddler, seeking nurturing, has reached up for his father's hand. In this moment a mobile infant is learning to walk, falling down every 5 seconds but quickly getting up to master the task. Who are we talking about when we use terms like *infants, mobile infants,* and *toddlers?*

> The word infant *derives from Latin words meaning "not yet speaking." It emphasizes what the child cannot do and reflects the baby's total dependence on adults. The word* toddler, *however, demonstrates our change in perspective, for it focuses on the child's increasing mobility and burgeoning independence. (Kutner)*

infants
Birth to approximately 18 months of age.

toddlers
18 months to 36 months of age.

prenatal
The time period (usually 9 months) prior to birth or during pregnancy.

The general term *infants and toddlers* refers to children from birth to 36 months of age. An **infant** is a baby from birth to approximately 18 months of age. At 8 months, the baby is crawling and some babies are even beginning to walk; it is then that infants are often referred to as mobile infants. From age 18 to 36 months, infants become **toddlers**, walking and even running in a straight-legged manner that causes them to toddle—sometimes wobble, weave, and bobble—as their physical and mental abilities develop at lightning speed. The infancy period refers to development from birth to age 3. In this textbook, the terms *babies, infants and toddlers,* and *infancy* are used to refer to children from birth to age 3. **Prenatal** development occurs prior to birth. From the prenatal period to 3 years old, babies grow from helpless dependency to children with a rich collection of relationships, skills, attitudes, and behaviors.

Who are the professionals who work with infants, toddlers, and their families? We use the term **infant and toddler professional** to refer to the broad range of specialists who teach or administer child development and education programs, which include *center child care* and *family (home) child care* programs. *Infant and toddler professionals* also refers to professionals who support families in the care and education of their children through home visits, early intervention, and family support programs. (These types of programs will be defined and discussed later in the chapter and book.) The term **care teacher** refers to a professional who has received specialized training to work with young children individually and/or in groups, and/or is in a position of responsibility with infants and toddlers in a classroom or home setting. We have chosen to use the word care *teacher* rather than the more commonly used term *caregiver* because of the mistaken notion that caregivers give care but do not teach. The reality is that with infants and toddlers, *teaching* is (1) taking care of infants' and toddlers' physical needs, (2) interacting with them in ways that meet their emotional and social needs and facilitate their development, (3) setting up an environment that promotes learning in all domains, and (4) working closely with the families of the children to build trusting relationships with them. In this book when the term **caregiver** is used, it is in the context of any adult who takes care of and cares about young children. Caregivers include parents, teachers, and grandparents.

infant and toddler professional
The broad range of specialists who teach in or administer child development and education programs.

care teacher
A professional who has received specialized training to work with young children.

caregiver
Any adult who takes care of and cares about young children. Includes parents, teachers, and grandparents.

Recent Understanding of the Importance of the Infant and Toddler Years

It is easier to build a child than to rebuild an adult. (Author unknown)

No other stage of human development requires as much learning and results in as many changes as in the first 3 years of life. Some infants and toddlers are healthy, have enough to eat, feel safe and loved, are talked to in responsive ways, and feel like valued members of their families and cultures. Sadly, other infants and toddlers are hungry, fearful, surrounded by violence, or abused and neglected. Do these early experiences make a difference? Yes, without a doubt. What happens during this time period may largely determine the well-being of not only children and their families but also their communities and the world in which they live. Educators and parents now know, definitely, that what happens during the first 3 years of a child's life has a long-lasting effect on who that person is and will become. It is worth repeating that infants' and toddlers' early experiences will influence their ability to learn, feelings of self-worth, sense of competence, and capacity to love and care for others. The infancy years do matter—and you can make a difference in promoting the health, wellness, quality of life, and happiness

Children's emotional, social, and learning needs are met when caring teachers read to them.

of children and families in these important years of development. The work of parenting, caring for, and educating young children from birth to 3 years of age, during this time of rapid growth and development, is among the most important work that exists.

Scientific evidence is proving what parents and child development professionals have known for many years regarding the importance of the prenatal and infancy period. Families, educators, legislators, and community professionals are paying more attention to the birth-to-3 age period as critically important in the development of a capable and contributing person. Parents and professionals are learning more each day about how the kind of environment in which an infant or toddler lives has a strong and lasting influence on that baby's development.

> *Early childhood is both the most critical and the most vulnerable time in any child's development. (Brazelton & Greenspan)*

The kind of nutritional, physical, social, and emotional environment that adults provide for infants and toddlers can make an enormous difference in how infants and toddlers experience their present and future life. Sammy, age 2, opens his eyes after a nap and cries out for his mother. As she comes to the side of the crib, she says soothingly, "Hello, you're awake? How are you feeling?" He wiggles around and then turns over and gradually stands up to see her better. His face relaxes and he smiles as she asks, "Are you ready to get out of your crib?" He answers by reaching up with his hands, getting ready for her to reach in the crib and pick him up. In this short but important interaction, Sammy is learning that he is important enough to be responded to quickly, that he can make things happen in this world, and that adults can be trusted to meet his needs most of the time. He is learning about who he is, how to be a generous partner in a relationship, and important concepts about the world in which he was born. These are the most important things for him to be learning at this time in his life, and these lessons will serve him well in years to come. If Sammy consistently receives this kind of responsive care, he will continue to thrive.

The latest scientific discoveries concerning prenatal, infant, and toddler development have significantly influenced the renewed interest concerning how babies think and what they need not only to survive, but also to thrive. The landmark publication *From Neurons to Neighborhoods: The Science of Early Childhood Development* (Shonkoff & Phillips, 2000) highlights important research and practice that illustrate the significance of these early life experiences. This book focuses on the central role of positive and loving relationships in a child's life and the powerful capabilities of young children. On the other hand, the authors express concern about the features of modern life that contribute to the stress of families: The potential damage to developmental outcomes from **risk factors** such as poor quality of child care, poverty, stresses, trauma, and violence are emphasized. The authors, following rigorous scientific scrutiny of the research and writings of infant and toddler specialists, strongly and with certainty recommend that families, teachers, communities, advocates, policy makers, businesses, government officials, and scientists come together to ensure an environment that facilitates "a rewarding childhood and a promising future for all children" (p. 15). As we move into the 21st century, research results, particularly the astounding new knowledge of brain development, have changed the way parents and professionals view the importance of the early years.

risk factors
Personal, environmental, and relationship features that are threats or a danger to the optimal development of a child.

Research on Brain Development

Brain development will be covered in detail in chapter 5 of this book. Here we highlight how research on brain development has influenced parents' and professionals' beliefs about the importance of the early years.

A ray of sunlight dances across 6-month-old Tamara's line of vision. Her dad talks warmly to her about the bright light, her eyes, and what she is seeing. We can't see inside of Tamara's head as new signals race along neural pathways in her brain. If we look closely, though, we can see it in her eyes, as they show curiosity, wonder, and joy.

In another home, the stresses of life have caused Jo's parents to reach the end of their coping skills. As Jo, barely 1 year old, reaches for a forbidden cookie, her hands are slapped hard, as they are frequently. We can't see how hormones of fear surge in her brain, and how development is hindered by the constant fear and vigilance that Jo must maintain to protect herself, but if we look closely we can see it in her eyes, as they show sadness, panic, anger, and pain.

The discoveries about the brain development of Tamara, Jo, and other infants and toddlers have been remarkable. They are providing a bright, sharp lens to focus on the complex and multifaceted picture of the capabilities of these very young children. They also identify experiences that are crucial for optimal child development.

As a mom, dad, or teacher talks to a baby, a song is sung, or the baby is positioned on the parent's body where he can see the playing dog, the baby reacts to these events, taking in information, processing it, and storing it. The synapses and the pathways formed actively create a web of learning in the brain. This is why early responsive experiences are so crucial: Those synapses that have been activated many times by virtue of repeated early experience tend to become permanent to ensure optimal emotional, social, language, and thinking development. Scientists have also discovered that there are *sensitive periods* and *windows of opportunity* for development in the prenatal period and during the infant years. As stated in *From Neurons to Neighborhoods:*

> Our conclusion is unequivocal: What happens during the first months and years of life matters a lot, not because this period of development provides an indelible blueprint for adult well-being, but because it sets either a sturdy or fragile stage for what follows. (Shonkoff & Phillips, 2000)

Let's examine how the study of sensitive periods of development and windows of opportunity have made a remarkable difference in how we view the importance of the early years.

Sensitive Periods and Windows of Opportunity

There is always one moment in childhood when the door opens and lets the future in. (Graham Greene)

There are windows of opportunity for learning that nature seems to fling open. These **windows of opportunity** are periods in the development of the brain when specific types of learning take place. Later, like windows stuck with age, they are more difficult to open and use. For example, the learning window for language is from birth to 10 years. However, circuits in the auditory section of the brain are wired by age 1, and the more words used in meaningful ways that a child hears by age 2, the larger her vocabulary will grow. Early life windows of opportunity have been discovered for vision, hearing, math and logic, cognition, problem solving, and emotional development.

Sensitive periods also occur early in a child's life. **Sensitive periods**, also known as *prime times* (Shore, 1997; Thomas & Johnson, 2008), are periods of development when positive or negative experiences are more likely to have serious and sustained effects.

We must remember, however, that all is not lost if the infant, toddler, or preschooler has a less than optimal start. There are too many examples of competent adults who overcame difficult and challenging starts in life. The human brain has a remarkable capacity to change, but timing is essential. Often, time and effort are required to help older children or adults compensate for negative and damaging experiences in their lives. For example, a child whose world has been mostly silent during the first 2 years of life because of a hearing loss or lack of responsive language talk with an adult will likely be delayed in language development. This child will need intensive support to learn how to use language to communicate in a variety of ways. In the future, brain imaging techniques may help unravel the mysteries of when sensitive periods occur and how intervention can remediate losses (Spelke, 2002; Stanford University Medical Center, 2007).

windows of opportunity
Periods in the development of the brain when specific types of learning take place.

sensitive periods
Periods of development when positive or negative experiences are more likely to have serious and sustained effects.

"Readiness—or unreadiness—begins in the first three years of life" (ZERO TO THREE, 1992). As this quote indicates, the first years truly do have a lasting effect. The brain power developed during the first 3 years is a foundation for the child to build on for learning and loving, just as a house must have a strong foundation to continue standing. Will the foundation be strong and sturdy, upon which one can build solidly, or will the foundation crumble easily under the weight of future challenging times—the emotional windstorms, sleet, hail, and drought that may occur in a person's life? The exciting research on the early years, brain development, windows of opportunity, and sensitive periods has led to a better understanding of human development and the importance of the first 3 years of life. Ten core concepts of development during the infancy period summarize the findings of all of the latest and best research.

CORE CONCEPTS OF PRENATAL, INFANT, AND TODDLER DEVELOPMENT

After analyzing what is known about the brain, early experiences, and child development, the Committee on Integrating the Science of Early Childhood Development from the National Research Council Institute of Medicine (Shonkoff & Phillips, 2000) proposed that 10 core concepts frame our current understanding of early development. These core concepts of human development are based on clinical and research findings from 1925 to 2000 and "help to organize what is known about infants and families and to suggest what is yet to be discovered or understood" (p. 13). These concepts provide a framework for thinking about what is important for infants and toddlers to develop optimally, how and when infants and toddlers best learn, and how problems in development can be prevented. Parents and professionals can use these core concepts as guides for interacting with very young children; for developing quality programs that support infant development and families; and for creating systems, laws, and public policies that value the amazing early years. These concepts are briefly introduced here and they will be revisited numerous times throughout the text. We have rewritten the titles of the core concepts to capture the primary meaning expressed in the concept (see Figure 1.2).

1. Both nature and nurture affect children's development.
2. Culture influences development and child-rearing beliefs and practices.
3. Self-regulation is an important indicator of development.
4. Children contribute to their own development through active exploration.
5. Human relationships, and the effects of relationships on relationships, are the building blocks of healthy development.
6. There is a broad range of individual differences.
7. The development of children is both continuous and discontinuous.
8. Infants and toddlers are both vulnerable and resilient.
9. The timing of early experiences can matter and children are open to change.
10. Early intervention can make a difference.

Figure 1.2   10 core concepts of human development.
Source: Shonkoff and Phillips (2000), pp. 23–32.

1. Both Nature and Nurture Affect Children's Development

It has often been asked which has more effect on a child's development: **nature** (genetic influences on growth and development) or **nurture** (environment, experiences, and education influences on growth and development). This is no longer a controversy in the early childhood field. There is a complex interplay between these two in the development of an infant (Gottlieb, 1992). Both play their parts in shaping who the infant will become. The impact of the child's experiences is dramatic and specific; it actually affects how the brain is wired for future learning (nurture). The quality of early care has a decisive and long-lasting impact on how people develop, their ability to learn, and their capacity to regulate (control) their own emotions. On the other hand, scientists are making remarkable discoveries about the genes that govern the color of our eyes, the shape of our nose, and our susceptibility to certain diseases (nature). Those discoveries will further enhance our understanding of the interaction effects of environment and heredity (Collins, Maccoby, Steinberg, Hetherington, & Bornstein, 2000; Olson, Vernon, Harris, & Jang, 2001).

nature
Genetic influences on the growth and development of a child.

nurture
The influences of the environment, experiences, and education on the growth and development of the child.

2. Culture Influences Development and Child-Rearing Beliefs and Practices

All families and cultures have different backgrounds, experiences, dreams for their children, habits, and customs that guide their thinking about raising children (Coll & Magnuson, 2000; Gonzalez-Mena, 2008). Everyone sees the world through the lens of their own culture (Small, 1998), and these beliefs about development, child-rearing practices, and family and community customs and routines continually influence the child's and the family's thinking and feeling. A rich and valuable array of beliefs and practices define who children and families are, how they interact and care for others, their traditions, and their way of life.

3. Self-Regulation Is an Important Indicator of Development

When infants begin to recognize when they are hungry or sleepy, focus on what is important, and tune out extraneous noise they are regulating their reactions to the world. When toddlers begin to express sadness or happiness without falling apart, attend without often becoming distracted, wait a few minutes for lunch, touch a flower gently, and process information without becoming overwhelmed, they are demonstrating **self-regulation**. One can see how these behaviors provide the foundation for all further learning. The ability to self-regulate is the backdrop of capabilities that allow the child to concentrate on a task, focus on another person's feedback in a social situation, and control emotions in positive ways (Bronson, 2000a, 2000b; Kopp, 2000).

self-regulation
The process of adapting reactions to sensory experiences, feelings, the environment, and people.

4. Children Contribute to Their Own Development Through Active Exploration

Infants don't need lessons to learn to walk, or drill practice to learn to talk. Rather, babies desire to walk and talk; they practice on their own and with responsive peers and adults. They act on their environment: They put objects in containers to figure out where they go. They shake, bang, roll, and stack objects to see what will happen. They make all kinds of funny sounds to get a response from a laughing sibling. They have goals, such as getting a favorite adult to look at them or opening a door, and they experiment with different strategies to make these events happen. When all is going well, infants and toddlers are curious, energetic, and motivated to figure things out. They are communication partners who need to take a turn in a conversation, even if the communication turn is a sneeze or a soft cooing sound. When given the opportunity (and this is how they learn best), they pursue their interests with adults who keep them safe, talk to them, nurture them, and support their learning. They are *motivated* to learn about themselves, others, and the world in which they live.

5. Human Relationships, and the Effects of Relationships on Relationships, Are the Building Blocks of Healthy Development

Relationships have an effect on relationships (Hinde & Stevenson-Hinde, 1987). This concept means that what infants learn in their first relationships is how to *be* in relationships. If the initial relationships are satisfying and enjoyable, then young children learn to trust, communicate, negotiate, show empathy, and cooperate with parents, peers, and others they meet—the building blocks of satisfying relationships. How they are cared for in these first relationships influences their sense of self-worth and whether they view themselves as lovable. As will be emphasized a number of times in this book, how infants and toddlers experience their first relationships influences not only the quality of future relationships but also their ability to learn. When relationships are comfortable, stable, and constant rather than anxiety producing, confusing, or frightening, then babies have the emotional energy and feelings of safety to focus on exploring and investigating—important aspects of learning.

6. There Is a Broad Range of Individual Differences

One infant walks at 8 months of age and another at 14 months. One infant is babbling "Dada" when he turns 1 year old and another infant begins to say words on his first birthday. A toddler learns to use the toilet on her second birthday, while another waits until she is 3 years old. These are all normal variations in motor, language, and adaptive development. However, while some children who aren't saying clear words by 2 years of age may eventually start to talk, others may have a hearing impairment or auditory disorder that must be diagnosed early in the infant's life so that appropriate intervention can occur. Because of the broad range of individual differences, it is sometimes difficult to distinguish between an *individual difference* in development and what might be a *developmental delay* that requires intervention. When there are questions about a child's development, adults can review developmental sequences as found in this book at the end of chapters 6 through 10.

7. The Development of Children Is Both Continuous and Discontinuous

Terri, 4 months old, likes to learn about the shape and texture of a safe, soft rattle by sucking and chewing on it. By 9 months she is trying different ways to learn about the object. She shakes, bangs, switches hands, turns the rattle over to inspect the other side, tries to roll it and sit on it, and throws it many times, only to retrieve it by crawling very quickly across the floor. This trajectory or path of development is *continuous*, as Terri seems to progress forward in her acquisition of skills that help her learn about objects such as rattles. One skill seems to build on the previous skill. Discontinuity occurs at significant points of development when the child's behavior seems very different from the age before. For example, 7-month-olds (as opposed to 2-month-olds) have a cluster of skills that propel them to be social partners who "act as if they understand that their thoughts, feelings, and actions can be understood by another person" (Zeanah, Boris, & Larrieu, 1997, p. 166). Toddlers also seem worlds apart from infants because they have developed a whole constellation of skills that contribute to their emerging independence, a marked contrast to only a year before. These points of rapidly increasing skills in development are considered transition points, as they have an effect on both how the baby views the world and how the teachers and caregivers interact with the infant or toddler. For example, when a baby begins to walk, the infant views the world differently and the caregiver views the child as more capable.

8. Infants and Toddlers Are Both Vulnerable and Resilient

vulnerable
The state of being helpless, defenseless, or open to criticism or danger.

Shana, a 1-year-old, has experienced much anguish in her short life: excessive hunger, hours of crying for someone to come to her crib to take her out, and bouts of severe diarrhea. She feels **vulnerable** (helpless and defenseless) and open to further trauma. What are her sources of vulnerability? They may be parent alcoholism, mental illness, criminality, poverty that contributes

Chelsea learned many skills as she grew from an infant (left) to a toddler (right).

to overwhelming stress in the family, or maternal/paternal abuse. These are just a few of the risk factors that increase the likelihood that something negative will happen to Shana's well-being in the future—her own drug abuse, dropping out of school, or social problems. Yet, there are sources of *resilience* (ability to thrive despite risk factors) in Shana's and in many children's lives that contribute to **positive turnarounds** (Werner, 2000). The source of resilience may be within the child—an easygoing, engaging temperament, for example, or a curious mind. Resilience may come from the child's family—a loving grandfather or a mother who is at first neglectful of her child but then goes to school or gains support for new, positive ways of interacting with her baby. The source of competence for Shana could come later in life in the form of a caring circle of friends, counseling, or an adult mentor. Every person has sources of vulnerability and sources of resilience (Poulsen, 1993; Rouse, 1998; Werner, 1993, 2000).

positive turnarounds
Refer to the resilience of a person to recover from challenging life experiences.

Let's explore the topic further. "Risks to development can come both from direct threats and from the absence of normal, expectable opportunities" (Garbarino & Ganzel, 2000, p. 77). Risk conditions (see Figure 1.3) can influence current and later outcomes for children in learning, language, social, and emotional development. The most serious detrimental effects occur when multiple risk factors are present in a child's life (Garbarino & Ganzel, 2000; Sameroff, 1998; Sameroff & Chandler, 1975). There are, however, personal and environmental characteristics that contribute to resilience in children who are experiencing risk factors.

"Resilience is the ability to thrive, mature, and increase competence in the face of adverse circumstances" (Rouse, 1998, p. 47). Resilient children have aspects within themselves or their environment that help them withstand more stress and cope better than many other children. Breslin (2005) notes that it is not helpful to label a child "at risk," but rather to focus on the strengths and competencies in each child that can help them thrive—the resiliency factors. Resiliency factors (see Figure 1.4), or features that contribute to the resiliency in the child, can be divided into three groups: personal, environmental, and relationship based.

Just as many threads woven tightly together hold up well against outside forces, the more threads of resiliency there are for a child the more likely that they will create a durable tapestry that resonates strength and transformation despite risk and adversity. Werner (2000) demonstrated the

- Poor nutrition
- The child's own biological risks—such as injury, low birth weight, or health
- Living in poverty or near poverty
- Parents who are addicted to drugs or alcohol
- Negative and abusive parenting
- Parents' use of harsh physical punishment
- Lack of social support for the family
- Living in a community with a high rate of violence
- Unemployed parents
- Low-wage jobs for parents
- Lack of quality child care
- Lack of access to health and medical care
- Low parent-education levels
- Moving frequently (transience)
- Parent in jail or prison

Figure 1.3   Risk conditions.
Sources: Hodgkinson (2003); Werner (2000).

protective factors
Shield the child from harmful effects of the environment or relationships and support the child's development.

importance of **protective factors** (factors that shield and protect the child) in forming resiliency in a study of 698 multiethnic children born into high-risk environments in 1955. In a follow-up report when those children were 45 years old, Werner found that primarily positive caregiving during the first years of life is a protective factor that results in better adjusted adults. Also, the emotional support of close friends, spouses, adult mentors, and parent education classes contributed to the resiliency of the adults. Werner's work inspires us to think about the importance of

1. *Personal factors*—characteristics of the infant or toddler
   - Energetic
   - Tolerant of frustration
   - Cooperative
   - Internal locus of control
   - Strong social skills
2. *Environmental factors*—characteristics of the environment
   - Social support for the mother
   - Social support for the family
   - Caregiver with education
   - A safe community
3. *Relationship factors*—characteristics of the child's relationships with others
   - Strong caregiver–child bond
   - Nurturing adults in the child's life
   - Responsive caregiver
   - Parents and teachers who allow ample exploration time within a safe environment
   - Peers
   - Adults who give positive feedback about strengths

Figure 1.4   Resiliency factors.

personal, environmental, and relationship factors when planning policy and redesigning programs for infants, toddlers, and their families. When adults recognize risk and resiliency factors for young children and their families, then they can make important decisions in community and business practices that recognize the significance of loving, responsive adults for infants and toddlers.

9. The Timing of Early Experiences Can Matter and Children Are Open to Change

The importance of a responsive, caring environment during the first 3 years of life cannot be disputed. However, a wonderful infancy is not a magical immunization against later troubles in life. A 3-year-old may be bright, full of zip, caring, and engaging and yet face unbelievable trauma as a 4-year-old or as a teenager. Due to stress and trauma, there could be an erosion of the child's trust in others and her own sense of self-worth. The developing child remains vulnerable to risks at all ages. Conversely, a child is still open to protective factors after 3 years of age. For example, a child who has an emotionally difficult first 3 years and has challenging behaviors may respond beautifully to a loving adult who sincerely believes in the child's positive characteristics and supports the child through several years of learning new, more productive behaviors (Zeanah et al., 1997).

10. Early Intervention Can Make a Difference

Early intervention includes services and programs for children at risk and children with disabilities and their families. We will discuss these types of programs later in the chapter. Early intervention with children and support for families can reduce the risk factors, ameliorate vulnerabilities, and increase protection factors and resiliency (Shonkoff & Meisels, 2000).

Conclusion of the 10 Core Concepts

Clearly, the main ideas represented in these 10 core concepts are that positive, responsive, mutual, and protective adult–infant and adult–toddler relationships promote a child's development and have sustaining effects on the young child's ability to be in a relationship. Very young children need adults to help them become an important part of their community and culture, and support them in learning how to become healthy, caring, and constructive members of society.

CHANGES IN DEMOGRAPHICS THAT AFFECT INFANTS AND TODDLERS AND THEIR FAMILIES

Two demographic factors (characteristics of a population) that influence the vulnerabilities, protective factors, and character of relationships for infants and toddlers—a changing population, and the increase in families and children experiencing poverty—will be discussed next. Let's start, however, with information on how the population of the United States is becoming more diverse.

A Changing Population in the United States

As illustrated in Figure 1.5, there is great diversity in the United States. There are approximately 21 million children under the age of 5 in the United States (U.S. Census Bureau, American Fact Finder 2007). The U.S. census of 2000 confirms that there are approximately 12 million infants and toddlers (birth to age 3) living in the United States (The Annie E. Casey Foundation, 2008). Fifty-eight percent of children under 5 years of age are White, 19% are Hispanic, and 22% are other races (The Annie E. Casey Foundation, 2008). Approximately 20% of people in the United States 5 years or older speak a language other than English at home and approximately 5% speak English less than "very well" (The Annie Casey Foundation, 2008).

- 76 would have at least one parent in the labor force
- 68 would live with two parents
- 41 would live in a two-parent family where both parents are in the labor force
- 38 would be minorities
- 28 would live in a central city
- 23 would live only with their mother
- 22 would have at least one parent who graduated from college
- 20 would have no parent who graduated from high school
- 19 would live in a rural area
- 17 would be poor
- 11 would live with a parent who never married
- 10 would live with a parent who is divorced
- 4 would live only with their father
- 2 would live with a grandparent

Figure 1.5   If the United States were a village of 100 children . . .
Source: From *The State of America's Children,* Children's Defense Fund, 2001, p. xxviii. Copyright 2001 by the Children's Defense Fund. Reprinted with permission.

An increase in the numbers of children and families from diverse cultures has an impact on public policy, health systems, and education systems. Thoughtful consideration must be given to several questions posed by this change in demographics. One question involves the type of training that infant and toddler professionals should receive to help them become culturally competent, in order to respectfully create a menu of responsive services. A second question relates to how communities, child development and education centers, and family support programs can demonstrate how they appreciate and embrace people of many cultures and races (Barrera & Corso, 2003). The United States truly is a **kaleidoscope of cultures** with different values, customs, and languages (Lynch & Hanson, 1998, p. 492) that are interconnected, and when this diversity of cultures and races is respected by professionals, then children benefit. Both teachers and children must become **culturally competent** in our diverse world in order to thrive.

kaleidoscope of cultures
Refers to a society with a variety of values, customs, and languages.

culturally competent
Possessing skills that enable a person to interact effectively with people from a variety of different cultures.

The United States is a kaleidoscope of cultures.

Poverty

Another issue that affects the quality of children's relationships with their families and teachers is poverty, which affects everyone either through experience or through the effects that it has on a nation. Poverty in the United States is defined by income. According to the 2006 U.S. census figures (U.S. Census Bureau, American Fact Finder, 2006), 21% of children under the age of 5 live in poverty, defined by the United States Department of Health and Human Services (2008b) as an annual income of $21,200 or less for a family of four in the 48 contiguous states, $26,500 in Alaska, and $24,380 in Hawaii. Furthermore, according to KIDS COUNT Census Data Online (2006), almost 10% percent of U.S. children under the age of 5 live in extreme poverty, with household incomes less than 50% of the poverty line. For children under the age of 5, approximately 11% of White children, 33% of African American children, and 28% of Hispanic children live in poverty. Of children under age 5 in families with a single mother 49.5% live in poverty and in families with a single father 23.9% live in poverty (KIDS COUNT Census Data Online, 2006). Every 35 seconds a baby in the United States is born into poverty (Children's Defense Fund, 2006).

Poverty is a global concern (Penn, 2005). From a basic needs approach to defining poverty there are seven elements that children need: "drinking water, sanitation, nutrition, health, shelter, education, or information" (Delamonica & Minujin, 2007). When a child lacks one of the seven elements in his life, he is considered as living in poverty. Delamonica and Minujim report that in 46 developing countries one billion children—one half of the population—are deprived of at least one of these elements. An organization of the United Nations—the United Nations Children's Fund, or UNICEF (UNICEF, 2008)—reports in its publication *The State of the World's Children 2008* that while vast improvements have been made in the number of newborns who do not live to see their fifth birthday, there are still estimated to be almost 10 million children worldwide who do not due to the lack of one or more of the seven elements children need to survive.

Living in poverty, whether defined as low income or lack of basic rights, is difficult and challenging, to say the least, for families of infants and toddlers. Families that are in or near poverty face challenges that include the need for well-paying jobs, access to high-quality affordable child care and health care, adequate nutrition, decent housing, and basic services provided by the community (e.g., see the National Center for Children in Poverty Web site, http://www.nccp.org). These stresses for families in poverty can negatively affect children's academics, health, and social outcomes. The information in Figure 1.6 emphasizes how reducing child poverty is one of the smartest investments that nations can make in the future.

In summary, there are many parents and professionals, legislators, and policy makers who are working hard toward building a nation and world that can do something about racial and ethnic injustice, poverty, and eliminating risk factors, but we can do more. We each have a part to play to support infants, toddlers, and their families as they strive for a meaningful life. They deserve our best efforts.

Reducing child poverty is one of the smartest investments that Americans can make in their nation's future. Fewer children in poverty will mean:

- More children entering school ready to learn
- More successful schools and fewer school dropouts
- Better child health and less strain on hospitals and public health systems
- Less stress on the juvenile justice system
- Less child hunger and malnutrition, and other important advances

---

Figure 1.6   Reducing poverty.
Source: Child Poverty Fact Sheet (2001).

EARLY DEVELOPMENT AND EDUCATION PROGRAMS

early development and education programs
Programs for children from birth to age 5 that include, but are not limited to, child care, early intervention for children at risk, and early intervention for children with disabilities.

Early development and education programs are an important part of the lives of infants and toddlers and their families in the United States. Quality programs that support parents can reduce infants' and toddlers' exposure to risk factors and build resiliency and positive relationships (Wittmer & Petersen, 2009). Let's examine three different types of early development and education programs available to families of infants and toddlers and a few of the issues related to these programs: (1) child care, (2) early intervention for children at risk, and (3) early intervention for children with disabilities.

Child Care

Child care programs offer varying hours of care for infants and toddlers, usually during the day while parents are at work. The number of families utilizing child care has increased. Fifty-five percent of women with babies younger than 1 year of age were employed part-time or full-time in 2007 (Bureau of Labor Statistics, 2008) compared with 31% in 1976 (Children's Defense Fund, 2006). Sixty-five percent of mothers with children younger than 3 were in the workforce in 2000 (Oser & Cohen, 2003). In fact, this employment rate of young mothers means that families have a desperate need for child care that nurtures their young children's emotional and learning development. As the demand for child care increases, so does the urgent need for public and private resources to improve the quantity and quality of child care. Parents often use an assortment of child care services that may change and may blend with each other to create an array of types of experience for infants and toddlers. These choices include child care provided in private homes (family child care) or in child care centers. Family child care homes may be of the following types:

- Small, family child care (or fewer children in the home of the care provider)
- Large, family, or group child care homes (typically no more than 7 to 12 children in the home of the care provider, who has a full-time assistant)
- In-home care (by a nonrelative in the family home)
- Kith and kin care (provided by a relative or friend)

Center child care includes the following:

- Nonprofit (community or agency supported)
- Local for-profit (privately owned)
- National chain for-profit (centers found across a region, or nationally or internationally owned by one company)
- Church supported (sponsored by and usually located in a church)
- On-site business (child care operated by a company, on-site for its employees)

There are many ecological and relationship-based factors that contribute to parents' decisions about *how much* child care they will use and *the type* of child care they choose for their infants and toddlers (see Figure 1.7). These factors include their hours of employment and financial situation, workplace policies that govern how soon a new parent has to return to work after the birth of a baby, the number of relatives who live in the same community, and the availability of affordable child care. Cultural factors play a part in parents' decisions; some cultures firmly believe in parents exclusively taking care of their children during the early years, while other cultures believe in shared care. National policies also play a role.

National policies concerning the importance of parental care versus child care outside the home contribute significantly to parents' choices. For example, an employed mother in the United States usually must use her accumulated sick and personal days to stay home with her

1. Family Variables
   - Cost of care
   - Cost subsidies available
   - Family geography

2. Family Beliefs and Cultural Variables
   - Culture/faith preferences
   - Parental beliefs about the need for caregiver training

3. Child Factors
   - Age, sex, temperament, disability, and health of the child
   - Number of children needing care

4. Caregiver and Facility Factors
   - Size of facility, group size, ratios, time the facility operates
   - Caregiver characteristics
   - Curriculum issues
   - Parent-provider relationships

5. Political, Business, and Community Supports for Choice
   - Businesses and unions: Supports for family child-care choice
   - Accreditation and referral agencies

Figure 1.7　Reasons for family choice of child care.
Source: From "Playing it out: The aftermath of September 11th in early care and education" by A. Honig, 2002, *Zero to Three*, 22, p. 416. Copyright 2002 by A. Honig. Adapted with permission.

newborn baby for approximately 6 to 12 weeks. In 128 other countries, on the other hand, mothers are provided an average of 16 weeks *paid* and job-protected leave before and after the birth of their baby with benefits provided by a combination of sources—government, employers, and health insurance. For example, Sweden provides full parental leave at 80% of the previous salary for 18 months. Leaves in some countries may be extended if the father stays home with the child for a period of time, as in Austria, where 3 years of extended leave is provided, but only if the father takes 6 months of the leave. Several countries—for example, the United Kingdom—also provide parents choices as to how the leave is spread out over the first 18 months after the birth the child ("Mother's Day," 2002). Parents in the United States, because of work leave policies, may not have as many choices about how and when they use child care services.

Parents want a setting where their children will be safe and where teachers show they care about their children (Gable & Cole, 2000). The challenge is to find infant-toddler child care that has adequately trained teachers and the individualized, affectionate attention that children need to thrive. Unfortunately, parents have difficulty locating affordable and excellent care for their children.

There is a crisis concerning the availability of affordable and quality care. In a study of 400 child care centers located in four states, only 8% of infant classrooms were judged to be good or excellent quality. An astonishing 40% of the centers observed were rated poor on the Infant/Toddler Environment Rating Scale (ITERS), a widely used measure of the physical and emotional characteristics of a child care environment (Helburn, 1995).

The Early Child Care Research Network of the National Institute of Child Health and Human Development (NICHD, 1996) also conducted a longitudinal study of more than 1,000 children to determine the characteristics and quality of child care for infants, toddlers, and preschoolers. Researchers conducting the study report that among infants and toddlers who attend child care, the ones who attend higher quality facilities as compared to lower quality settings develop higher language, intellectual, and social skills (NICHD Early Child Care Research Network, 2000a, 2000b). We know that higher quality care that emphasizes the importance of an adult's gentle and considerate responsive interactions, well-organized learning toys and materials, language development, and friendly and reciprocal program–family relationships has a positive effect on the development of infants and toddlers.

Because the quality of early development and education settings is so important, we will devote five chapters (chapters 11 through 16) to the development of programs for infants and toddlers that are responsive to babies' and families' needs, promote learning, and are relationship based.

A Web site (http://www.childcare.gov) has been created to bring together in one place all of the federal agency resources concerning child care. Parents, professionals, and providers will benefit from information on this site on health, safety, family child care, staff training, regulations, and funding. Also, the results of research studies, news, and publications are included at the site.

Early Intervention Programs for Children at Risk

Early intervention programs for children at risk comprise a second type of resource for families and children. One such program is Early Head Start (EHS), which has been said to mark "a turning point in America's commitment to our youngest children and their families" ("Shalala Calls," 1995). An example of a nationally supported intervention program that provides support to families living in poverty, EHS reduces infants' and toddlers' risk factors, builds resiliency, and provides child and family development services. As Donna Shalala, secretary of the Department of Health and Human Services, described it, "Early Head Start is about giving our youngest and most disadvantaged children a chance to grow up healthy, to learn, and to prepare for school" (U.S. Department of Health and Human Services, 2001). The federally funded program provides services to families who are expecting a child or who have a child 3 years of age or younger and helps parents support their children's development. Services include child development classes, family involvement and parent education, health and nutrition, and prevention and early intervention. These services may take place as home visits, as child care services, or as center-based programs. The detailed and comprehensive Head Start Program Performance Standards (HSPPS), which EHS programs must meet, are used often as a base of comparison as individual states and others develop their own program standards.

In each of the 650 EHS programs that exist across the United States, there is an emphasis on collaborating with community agencies to provide services. Specific services that EHS provides, in collaboration with its community partners, include prenatal and postpartum education, counseling services, infant and toddler education programs, family parenting classes, medical and dental services, referrals and assistance to families to access comprehensive prenatal and postpartum care and, in some cases, child care services. These services are also provided through home visits planned collaboratively with the family, infant and toddler group socialization experiences, family support groups, and a multitude of other creative ways.

The results of a comprehensive national study (Early Head Start Research and Evaluation Project [EHSRE], 1996–Current) of the effectiveness of EHS that included approximately 3,000 infants and toddlers from 17 different sites demonstrate that EHS is making a difference for children and families. Half of the 3,000 children who participated in the study were enrolled in EHS (the experimental group) and half were not (the control group). EHS children scored higher than the control group on measures of cognitive (thinking) and language (vocabulary and complex sentences), had better attention with play objects, were more emotionally engaged with their parents, and scored lower in aggressive behavior at age 3 (Love et al., 2005). Only 50%, though, of the EHS children moved into formal programs at age 3 and those who did had higher reading-related skills at age 5. At age 5, the EHS children had significantly fewer behavior problems and scored higher on approaches to learning. This study highlights the benefits of EHS as well as the importance of the EHS children attending a formal preschool, but unfortunately, due to limited federal funding, only 3% (45,000) of the poorest infants and toddlers in the United States attend EHS.

The program is making a difference for families as well as children. When the EHS children were 3 years old the EHS families were observed to have more supportive attitudes toward learning than the control group families, were more likely to read to their children, were more emotionally supportive of their children, and scored higher on measures of the quality of home environment, parenting behavior, and knowledge of infant-toddler development. Parents who attended EHS reported that they spanked their children less and were more likely to resolve problems by using distraction, explanation, or mild responses rather than physical punishment. EHS families reported lower levels of parenting stress and family conflict and were more likely to attend school or a job training program (EHSRE, 1996–Current; Love et al., 2005). When the EHS children were 5 years old the parents of the EHS children read more to their children, provided a more enriched home environment, and were at lower risk for depression (EHSRE, 1996–Current, 2006). Web sites that provide additional information and resources for families and professionals include the Early Head Start National Resource Center @ ZERO TO THREE (http://www.ehsnrc. org/) and the Administration for Children and Families site (http://www.acf.hhs.gov/).

Early Intervention for Children with Disabilities

Early intervention services for children with disabilities and their families are the third type of early development and education program we will discuss. All infants and toddlers in the United States are entitled to a comprehensive assessment to determine whether or not they have a disability. A disability may include a developmental delay in how the child communicates and relates with others, moves, or thinks. This comprehensive assessment is provided by the school district in which the family lives. If a child has a disability, then the family and the professionals involved develop a plan for the child and family that builds on the family's strengths, priorities, concerns, and resources. The early intervention program may offer home visits and family support to "enhance the ability of families to work toward their own goals and deal effectively with their own concerns" about their child and family (Blasco, 2001, p. 159). Infants and toddlers may also receive special help from professionals while attending a child development and education center or family child care home.

The Individuals with Disabilities Education Act (IDEA) (http://www.idea.ed.gov/) provides federal funds, paired with a high proportion of state funds, for special education services for children with disabilities. Part C of IDEA provides funds and directives for providing early intervention services to infants and toddlers with disabilities. The act specifies which intervention services must be available for children but also sets policies that ensure that parents function as active members of the team and determine the goals for their own children. A high value is placed on the full inclusion of individuals with disabilities in their communities by specifying that early intervention services must be offered in natural settings—homes, parks, child care programs, and other places where very young children without disabilities would be spending time.

The number of children identified with disabilities and served under Part C of IDEA is increasing, from a total of 165,351 in 1994 (the first year that state-reported data are considered reliable) to 247,433 in 2001 (Oser & Cohen, 2003, p. 65). Children's disabilities will be discussed in many of the chapters and will receive special attention in chapter 15.

INFANTS' AND TODDLERS' IRREDUCIBLE NEEDS

Meeting young children's irreducible needs is the thread that ties these three types of early development and education programs together. **Irreducible needs** are the needs of children that are absolutely necessary for them to survive and thrive (see Figure 1.8). Brazelton and Greenspan (2000) emphasize that when these seven needs are met, a child will grow, learn, and flourish. We can think of these from the child's perspective and imagine what it must feel like

irreducible needs
The needs of children that are absolutely necessary for them to survive and thrive.

1. Ongoing nurturing relationships
2. Physical protection, safety, and regulation
3. Experiences tailored to individual differences
4. Developmentally appropriate experiences
5. Limit setting, structure, and expectations
6. Stable communities and cultural continuity
7. Adults to protect the future

Figure 1.8   Infants' and toddlers' irreducible needs.
Source: Brazelton and Greenspan (2000).

to the infant or toddler whose irreducible needs are met compared to the infant or toddler whose irreducible needs are not met. This book contains research and description of practice that will provide strategies to meet children's irreducible needs. It is our hope that all adults, including those who read this book, can work together to meet infants' and toddlers' needs so that they can thrive—feel secure, be able to relate (feel warm and close) to others, communicate, solve problems, express feelings in culturally appropriate ways, appreciate their own and others' individuality, and have a sense of self-worth.

SUMMARY

myeducationlab)

Go to MyEducationLab and complete the Building Teaching Skills and Dispositions exercise in Chapter 1.

The goal of this book is that you will become knowledgeable about and gain a passion for promoting the well-being, competence, and good developmental outcomes of infants and toddlers and their families.

- The prenatal period and the first 3 years of life are vitally important for children and the future adults they will become.
- A relationship-based model of infant and toddler development informs and influences the content and organization of this book.
- The ecology of the child and the individual attributes and capacities of the child influence the quality of the relationships that the child experiences.
- The quality of the child's relationships influences the experiences and the development of the child.
- Research on brain development has influenced the way parents and professionals view the significance of the first 3 years of life.
- The core understandings of infant and toddler development are highlighted by the book *From Neurons to Neighborhoods.*
- Two demographic trends that affect both infants and toddlers and those who care for them are a changing population and the number of children experiencing poverty.
- Early development and education programs are available for infants and toddlers.
- There is a strong need for quality early development and education programs—programs that have adequately trained teachers, responsive and affectionate adult interactions with children, and mutually beneficial relationships with families.

When we see the sparkle in an infant's eyes and the curiosity of a healthy toddler, then we know that the focus on healthy relationships and ecological factors that influence these relationships is a very worthwhile endeavor.

Key Terms

bioecological systems theory
caregiver
culturally competent
culture
domains
early development and education
    programs
infant and toddler professional
infants

irreducible needs
kaleidoscope of cultures
mental health
nature
nurture
positive turnarounds
prenatal
protective factors
relationship-based model

responsiveness
risk factors
self-regulation
sensitive periods
teacher
toddlers
transactional theory
vulnerable
windows of opportunity

REFLECTIONS AND RESOURCES FOR THE READER

Reflections

1. Why do infants and toddlers need responsive, continuous caring relationships with parents, families, and teachers?
2. Create a list of why the first 3 years of life are so important for the well-being of infants and toddlers.
3. How are children's irreducible needs met in your community?
4. How has the research on brain development influenced the way parents and teachers think about the importance of the first 3 years of life?

Observation and Application Opportunities

1. Choose one of the 10 core concepts and discuss how that concept plays out in your life.
2. Discuss how your individual attributes influence the relationships in your life.
3. Brianna lives in a family that is experiencing poverty. What are some of the risk and resiliency factors that may influence the quality of relationships that she is experiencing?
4. Choose one of the irreducible needs of children and discuss what would happen to a child, from the child's perspective, if this need is met or not met.

Supplementary Articles and Books to Read

Baker, A. C., Manfredi/Petitt, L. A. (2004). *Relationships, the heart of quality care: Creating community among adults in early care settings.* Washington, DC: NAEYC.

Brazelton, T. B., & Greenspan, S. I. (2000). *The irreducible needs of children: What every child must have to grow, learn, and flourish.* New York: Perseus Books.

McMullen, M. B., & Dixon, S. (2006). Research in review. Building on common ground: Unifying practice with infant/toddler specialists through a mindful, relationship-based approach. *Young Children, 61*(4), 46–52.

Interesting Links

http://www.childrensdefense.org/

Children's Defense Fund   The mission of the CDF is to Leave No Child Behind® and to ensure every child a healthy start, a head start, a fair start, a safe start, and a moral start in life and successful passage to adulthood with the help of caring families and communities.

http://www.childtrends.org/

Child Trends   Child Trends is an organization that seeks to impact policy decisions and programs that affect children through conducting and disseminating research, collecting and analyzing data, and sharing this information with those who set policy and provide services.

http://www.naccrra.org/

National Association of Child Care Resource & Referral Agencies   NACCRRA is a leading voice for child care. This organization works with resource and referral agencies nationwide to ensure that families have access to high-quality child care. It also leads projects that support professionals, conduct research, and advocate child care policies.

myeducationlab

These and other web links are included in this chapter on MyEducationLab.

http://www.nccp.org/

National Center for Children in Poverty   NCCP highlights 25 initiatives in the United States that improve the lives of infants and toddlers.

http://nccic.acf.hhs.gov/

National Child Care Information and Technical Assistance Center   NCCIC is a service of the Child Care Bureau that provides comprehensive child care information resources.

http://www.parentsaction.org/

Parent Action Network (formerly "I Am Your Child")   This Web site has several articles on emotional development and some video clips, a national public awareness and engagement campaign to make early childhood development a top priority for the country and show the importance of the first 3 years of life.

http://www.unicef.org/

UNICEF (the United Nations Children's Fund)   UNICEF was created by the United Nations after World War II. It works in 190 countries and focuses on children's rights to protection, education, health care, shelter, and good nutrition. Its work depends entirely on voluntary contributions of time and money. UNICEF is the author of *The State of the World's Children 2008* that can be accessed on its Web site.

http://www.zerotothree.org/

ZERO TO THREE   ZERO TO THREE is an organization that develops publications dedicated to advancing the healthy development of infants and toddlers. This Web site offers cutting-edge research, demonstrated best practices, parenting tips, publications, and conference information.

Infants, Toddlers, and Their Families

Looking around the room at the parent meeting, Sammie was impressed with the diversity of the group they served at the Metro Infant-Toddler Center. Some of the differences were racial. Some were cultural. Given their neighborhood, they tended to serve people of many backgrounds and religions. Nevertheless, there was more depth to the diversity. Susan was a single physician who had adopted a baby from Cambodia. Jewel was raising her grandbabies. Mare and Ernesto were adjusting from being a young married couple to becoming parents. Each family seemed to have a unique situation regarding parenting, unique needs for support and information, and unique—and very strongly held—beliefs about parenting!

As Sammie understands, families come in all shapes and sizes—and all kinds of families have happy, healthy, well-developing babies. All families are similar in some ways and each is unique in some ways. There are vast differences in size and composition, the roles of parents and children, the beliefs and values of their different cultures regarding infants and parents, even the rituals and processes surrounding birth itself. While we explore the basic similarities and differences, we also look beyond the immediate family to the support they receive from programs and agencies as they utilize health care, child care, and other services. These services, in turn, are affected by policies and regulations made by state and federal legislators. Although these policies

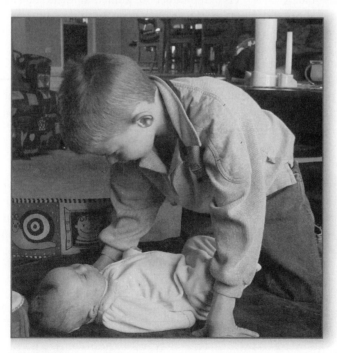

may seem far removed from any one family's daily life, they may have great effect on access to resources, services, and information, as reflected in the bioecological theory (see chapter 3).

BIOLOGICAL AND CULTURAL EFFECTS ON THE FAMILY

All humans share common beginnings. The very biology of conception, birth, and early development that will be described in chapter 5 is much the same for all human babies. However, even within this basic prototype of early development, each beginning is different. Some mothers welcome the birth of their child; some fear birth, or don't want the child. Some biological fathers are present and active participants in the pregnancy and birth; some are not. Like birth, parenting is always an intensely personal experience. Each family creates its own, unique identity while responding to or incorporating its culture, current societal norms, personal history and characteristics, resources, stresses, and family structure.

Our Biology Affects Our Parenting

Biology and evolution have determined some of our parenting patterns. Because babies are born so dependent, parents around the world have developed ways to closely care for and protect their infants. Humans are born with large but not fully developed brains. The baby cannot stay in the mother's womb long enough for the brain to fully develop, as both the mother's body and the placenta can support only the developing baby's needs until the baby reaches a certain size. The baby's size is also an important factor in the birth process; the woman's pelvic structure was better suited to childbirth before humans became upright and started walking on two feet. Birth is now a long and arduous process for many mothers and babies, and in most cultures the event is planned for and helpers attend the mother (Ellison, 2001).

Along with these biological aspects of reproduction, human mothers and fathers react to newborns similarly across the world. Upon seeing their newborn for the first time, mothers and fathers hold the baby so that they can gaze into each other's eyes. They touch the baby's fingers, the palms, the arms and legs, and then the trunk (Goodnow, Cashmore, Cotton, & Knight, 1984). Babies, in turn, are born ready to participate in human interactions (Gopnik, Meltzoff, & Kuhl, 1999).

The long gestation, difficult birth process, dependency of the infant, and predictable responses of the parents to the newborn are constant factors across humanity. Together they promote long-term, closely attentive, highly invested parenting. However, the exact nature of that parenting varies widely across cultures.

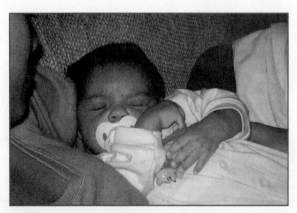
This very young baby sleeps in her mother's embrace.

Cultural Effects on Parenting

Our parenting decisions today may be based in part on human biology, but they are also based on cultural adaptations made by our ancestors. Particular parenting adaptations served certain people well as hunters and gatherers, as farmers, or as members of industrialized societies. The following definition of *culture* can help clarify this idea:

> Each member of a group lives by a set of social rules, operates within a particular spiritual belief system, and adheres to an ideology that helps the society run smoothly. Each group can be described relative to the subsistence pattern, the production of goods and their distribution, the interpersonal interactions and social rules, and the history of its society. (Small, 1998, p. 74)

So, for example, consider a spiritual belief system that "babies are godlike" versus one that believes "babies must be trained to be god-serving members of the community." These cultural beliefs would result in very different parenting practices. The first might cause parents to quickly and responsively meet every expressed need of their children; in the latter, parents might actively teach infants patience and generosity from the beginning. Economics also affects our view of children and parenting. If a society depends on its children to watch the livestock on the farm or to care for the infants while the mothers work, the expectations of the children (and the ways they are treated) will be very different from an industrialized country where we generally see the "work" life beginning in adulthood.

Differing Cultural Values

Values concerning the relationships among people differ by culture. **Individualist cultures**, such as much of the United States, emphasize the importance of each individual over the whole group. They tend to value independence, competition, production, and personal responsibility. **Collectivist cultures**, such as Latino and Asian cultures, value cooperation, process (rather than production), and interdependent relationships. The individual is primarily responsible to the harmony and well-being of the group, setting aside individual interests (Keller, 2002; Keller et al., 2006).

individualist cultures Emphasize the importance of the individual over the group.

collectivist cultures Emphasize cooperation and interdependent relationships over individuality.

These basic cultural belief systems about people are transmitted to babies through their earliest interactions with their caregivers as we help babies become members of our family and community (Borke, Larsen, Eickhorst, & Keller, 2007; Keller, 2002).

> *Andrea and Neil brought their newborn, Alyssa, into their bed at night. They all slept comfortably and Andrea was able to breast-feed easily during the night. Sleeping together even made them feel closer as a family. But their friends, their pediatrician, and their family all warned them to get her into her own bed quickly or she would be spoiled. They were very torn between what felt right and what their culture told them was right.*

The assumption as to whether the new baby sleeps alone or in the mother's bed is, in part, one that reflects cultural beliefs. It is a very early step toward teaching the child to be a member of his own culture.

Many cultures assume the primary importance of the mother–infant bond as a way of keeping the infant fed, safe, and drawing him into the family group: "In almost all cultures around the globe today, babies sleep with an adult and children sleep with parents or other siblings" (Small, 1998, p. 112). Mayan parents, for example, expressed pity for American babies who have to sleep alone. These parents slept with their babies as a part of their commitment to their children and because of a strong belief that co-sleeping fosters family closeness and attachment, a belief held in cultures that are based on group harmony and interdependence (Small, 1998). This value is demonstrated by patterns of mothers and infants co-sleeping for an extended period, by extending breast-feeding over several years, and by quickly comforting crying babies (Small, 1998). Current research finds that there is, indeed, a synchrony in the mother's and infant's heart rates, breathing, and shifts from active to deeper sleep when they sleep together. Mother and child both get longer periods of sleep and nursing is more frequent and of longer duration (McKenna, nda; Stein, Colaruso, McKenna, & Powers, 2001). Recent research suggests that *consistency* in sleep arrangements with infants leads to more positive mother-child interaction (Taylor, Donovan, & Leavitt, 2008).

The idea of co-sleeping is a difficult one for many Americans on both cultural and scientific levels. For many Americans, our values for independence and competition—which may be seen as a reflection of our economic system—promote the practice of leaving babies to sleep alone and to comfort themselves. This is not a rejection of the baby, but rather is a way of teaching the baby the cultural norms of society. In the United States, we often see the married couple (if that

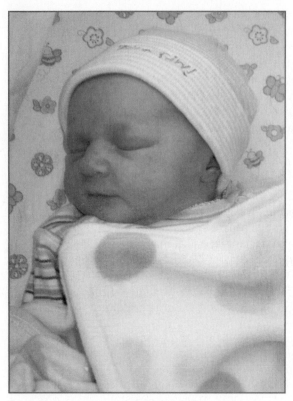

This newborn sleeps securely in her bassinet.

is the structure of the family) as having the primary relationship (rather than the mother and child) and the bed is seen as the site of their sexual relationship. We sometimes have discomfort with the idea of including the baby in the marital bed, but a newborn may be kept in the parent's bedroom, in a bassinet near the bed. Other reflections of the value of independence are apparent in that American babies are weaned earlier and comforted less often and less speedily than in many other cultures—again, not as rejection but to promote competence, independence, and self-sufficiency (Small, 1998).

The strongest argument against co-sleeping comes from the American Academy of Pediatrics (AAP) in a series of policy statements (AAP, 2000b, 2005a and b). In 1992, drawing conclusions from overwhelming evidence that sleeping position was a major risk factor for sudden infant death syndrome (SIDS), an event in which an apparently healthy young baby goes to sleep and then dies in his sleep, the AAP began a public awareness campaign called "Back to Sleep." In this campaign, the AAP makes a series of recommendations, primarily that infants always sleep on their backs, but including that parents not share beds with their babies. The success of the campaign has been clear, with a 56% drop in SIDS deaths between 1992 and 2001. However, the issue of co-sleeping continues to be controversial (National SIDS/Infant Death Resource Center, 2007; Stein et al., 2001). Further information on preventing SIDS through the "Back to Sleep" campaign and recommendations for safe co-sleeping are in chapter 10.

Cultural Questions in Infant and Toddler Child Care

Cultural differences create many questions for teachers and others who study child development. Teachers and parents may have different opinions on how they want an infant handled in feeding, sleeping, being helped, developing language, or many other issues. When this happens, it is important to consider if the differences are grounded in each person's own invisible, cultural beliefs about babies. If so, respectful negotiations may lead to everyone agreeing on how these issues will be handled in group care. For example, consider a teacher who was working with a mother who lived in a very cramped, dirty housing situation. The mother always carried her baby son because, within her culture, carrying your baby signifies your love and protection of the baby and because she felt that she could not clean the carpet enough to have her baby lie on it safely. Her concerns extended into the child care program. If the baby were allowed to play and crawl on the floor in child care, how would the mother be able to stop him from doing so at home? The teacher felt equally strongly that floor time was good for physical development and it was impossible for her to care for four babies when she was constantly carrying one. When the mother and teacher took time to discuss their positions, trying to respect and listen to each other, they were able to resolve their differences. The teacher supplied the mother with an extra mat to use on the floor at home, assuring her that sitting nearby and playing with her baby on the clean surface would maintain their closeness. The teacher also agreed to more holding and carrying of the baby than she would do naturally, as a way of providing the kind of care the baby had come to expect.

Nobody has ever before asked the nuclear family to live all by itself in a box the way we do. With no relatives, no support, we've put it in an impossible situation. (Margaret Mead)

Sometimes, even when differences may be seen as cultural, there are areas that cannot be negotiated. An example that often arises is a parent who insists: "I was spanked as a child and I'm fine. I want you to spank my child if she gets out of line." Spanking, or any form of corporal punishment, may go against your cultural beliefs or may be part of your cultural beliefs—but it is definitely not allowed under child care licensing regulations. No discussion of cultural differences is required with this one. A simple "Our licensing does not allow us to spank children" should end that discussion. Providing information as to why licensing would have such a rule would be a useful parent education effort.

This happy dad and mom describe parenting as adding joy to their life together as a couple.

Changing Times

It is also important for us to learn whether our current, industrialized, technological society is handling babies in ways that fit our own current evolution. Human beings evolve slowly, over thousands of years. The baby's brain and instincts may be much better suited to the close, one-on-one relationship of less industrialized societies than to the current American culture of busy schedules, meals on the run, and electronic toys that play music and flash lights at our babies.

VARIATIONS IN PARENTING

Teachers meeting very young infants in child care are often fascinated by the quick pace of change and development they are able to observe. Sometimes it seems as though a baby is changing before your very eyes. The huge changes the parents are experiencing in themselves are not always as obvious, but they are equally profound and teachers can be very helpful as people make the transition to parenthood.

Our common biological and evolutionary heritage and our cultural variations, although each a huge factor in parenting, barely begin to describe the many influences on how people act as parents. An ecological approach to parenting describes a number of factors that account for the variation we find across families and that have a significant influence on how the family forms and functions (Susman-Stillman, Appleyard, & Siebenbruner, 2003). These factors include attitudes, early experiences, and current circumstances, as follows:

- The family's attitudes toward family membership and marriage
- The impact of childhood family and attachment experience
- The impact of economic opportunity
- The impact of the parents' relationship
- The mother's influence on paternal involvement
- The influence of a single parent's other adult relationships
- Economics as a factor affecting parent–child interactions

The family's attitudes toward family membership and marriage. Studies show that women respect marriage and have a positive attitude toward it, but often delay it. When they have had unstable and abusive relationships with men, they choose to delay marriage until they are economically self-sufficient and have raised their own young children. They see this delay as providing them with more power and control in the marriage, balancing their desires for a partner who can make their lives better against their fears of domestic violence and unfaithful partners (Edin, 2000; Fitchen, 1995).

The impact of childhood family and attachment experience. The structure of one's own family growing up seems to have less impact on choosing marriage than perceptions of marital happiness and day-to-day family life (Golombok, 2000). While the translation of early attachment relationships into marital relationships has not been widely studied, it appears that when both adults had secure relationships as children, they report less ambivalence about their marriage and more competence in parenting (Volling, Notaro, & Larsen, 1998).

The impact of economic opportunity. The relative economic opportunities of the two adults affect their relationship and their willingness to marry. If a woman sees the man as having the potential to raise her economic state, she is more likely to marry. If her economic status seems more secure if she is single, she is more likely to want to live separately or cohabit, rather than marry (Edin, 2000).

The impact of the parents' relationship. The ability of the adults to negotiate conflict and maintain positive feelings between them increases their ability to attend to their young children and meet their needs (Gable, Belsky, & Crnic, 1992). Fathers in satisfying, stable marriages are more involved with their children and feel greater competence and satisfaction as fathers (Yeung, Sandberg, Davis-Kean, & Hofferth, 2001). Marital satisfaction often declines during the years with a young child in the home; it can be a strain even for loving couples who choose to have a family. Couples who had consistently unhappy marriages seem least able to provide nurturing parenting (Kerig, Cowan, & Cowan, 1993).

The mother's influence on paternal involvement. The mother's positive attitude toward the father and her support of the father's involvement are important factors in both married and unmarried families (Carlson & McLanahan, 2002). Mothers draw fathers into involvement with their children by having child-centered conversations, encouraging fathers to take on caregiving tasks, and having a harmonious mother–father relationship (Coley & Chase-Lansdale, 1999).

The influence of a single parent's other adult relationships. Single parents and their children benefit when the parents have other helpful adult relationships. Strong social networks of friends and/or family can increase the success of single parents in their ability to maintain strong, positive relationships with their children. Single parents are often able to meet their own needs through friendships or support groups (Olson & Haynes, 1993). However, extended families without resources, or with additional difficulties of their own, can intrude on the parent–infant relationship and be an impediment (Fitchen, 1995).

Economics as a factor affecting parent–child interactions. Economics may have more impact on children's socioemotional development than does family structure (Kesner & McKenry, 2001). Fathers with fewer economic resources tend to have less involvement with their children (Coley & Chase-Lansdale, 1999). Fathers who are employed in higher socioeconomic levels and with good jobs tend to be more involved with their children, but work schedules can interfere with consistent parenting opportunities (Yeung et al., 2001).

The foregoing description of personal history, attitudes and beliefs, social environment, and economic resources describes some of the impact these factors may have on parenting. Past relationships, current relationships, economic resources, and social resources may each affect whether adults choose to marry to raise a family, choose to live within extended families, or choose highly alternative family structures. What is clear, however, is that becoming a parent has a huge and completely unique impact on each person.

Becoming a Mother

Nan woke up each morning feeling she could barely face the day. She had always wanted children and thought this should be the happiest time of her life. Her husband, Roy, had been increasingly distant since she announced her pregnancy and now he was out playing basketball almost every evening. Her family called and sent flowers when the baby was born, but lived too far away to help. Friends from work seemed a lifetime away. She felt very much alone, and felt like a very bad mother for not just being grateful and happy that she had a baby. She was worried that she didn't know enough, or care enough, to ever be the kind of mother her baby deserved.

The personal, psychological work of becoming a mother takes longer than the 9 months of physical work. Yet, few of us could articulate exactly what changes as one goes from not being a parent to being a parent for the first time. In his book *The Motherhood Constellation,* Daniel Stern (1995) lists a set of beliefs that he sees as influencing parenthood in our current, postindustrial American society—beliefs we see as "truths" because they are so pervasive that it would never occur to us to question them. They are:

1. The society places a great value on babies—on their survival, well-being, and optimal development.
2. The baby is supposed to be desired.
3. The culture places a high value on the maternal role, and a mother is, in part, evaluated as a person by her participation and success in the maternal role.
4. The ultimate responsibility for care of the baby is placed with the mother, even if she delegates much of the task to others.
5. It is expected that the mother will love the baby.
6. It is expected that the father and others will provide a supporting context in which the mother can fulfill her maternal role, for an initial period.
7. However, it is more true to say the family, society, and culture do not provide the new mother with the experience, training, or adequate support for her to execute her maternal role alone easily or well. (Stern, 1995, p. 173)

If we see these cultural beliefs as *truths,* it is easy to imagine how difficult it may be for a new mother or father who does not meet these cultural norms. What additional pressures does a woman feel if she does not want her baby, or does not receive support from her husband or others?

While the mother is behaviorally organizing the baby's world—his cycles of sleep and hunger—the baby is helping her to reorganize her own representational world. He is turning her into a mother . . . (Daniel Stern)

Stern (1995) describes American women today as struggling with questions concerning three major themes. The first is the *Life-Growth* theme, in which the mother wonders if she can keep her baby alive and help the baby grow and thrive. The second theme, *Primary Relatedness,* involves the mother's internal questions as to whether she can love her baby, feel her baby's love, and read and respond sensitively to the baby's moods, cues, and needs. The third theme, the *Supporting Matrix,* questions whether the mother or couple will be able to build a "protecting, benign, support network, so that she can fully accomplish the first two tasks of keeping the baby alive and promoting his . . . development" (p. 177).

Implications for Teachers

Teachers can be helpful to new mothers who are struggling with questions about becoming a mother. Sometimes a woman will actually tell a teacher that she is feeling unsure of herself in this new role; sometimes the concern comes out as a little joke. Either way, a teacher who is aware of these developmental themes in new mothers can be reassuring about how all of these feelings are part of the work of becoming a loving, caring, competent mother.

Becoming a Father

Craig grew up thinking he wanted to have children someday, but he really believed that being a parent was something special between mothers and babies. Now he is the head-over-heels-in-love dad to 6-month-old Caitlin. When he picks up Caitlin from child care every day, her teacher always greets him saying, "Just look at how excited she is to see you. She just lights up when you enter the room!"

Teachers also have an important role in welcoming and valuing the child's father. Men struggle with the changes in their lives, dealing with the biological, cultural, and personal aspects of becoming fathers. For many men, the concept of paternity has enormous meaning, in both a biological and cultural context.

All human cultures recognize the importance of men in children's lives and have roles for men that keep them involved with infants and children in paternal ways, such as uncles or grandfathers being responsible for fatherless children (Beckerman & Valentine, 2002; Lamb, 2004; Yogman, 1982). Over the last century, fewer children have been left fatherless by the death of the father, but increasing numbers of children are fatherless due to divorce, desertion, and out-of-wedlock births (Popenoe, 1999).

Through years of increasing fatherlessness in America (only 50% of children born in the early 1980s still lived with both parents by age 17), there has been an increasing understanding and emphasis on the importance of fathers, not just as providers for the family but for their unique contributions to positive development in their children (Tamis-Lemonda & Cabrera, 2002). In fact, in 1997 UNICEF issued a report on the importance of involving men in the lives of children (Foumbi & Lovich, 1997) and in 2001, the Administration for Children and Families in the U.S. Department of Health and Human Services identified increasing male involvement and father-hood as a top priority for federally funded programs at the beginning of the 21st century.

> *The guys who fear becoming fathers don't understand that fathering is not something perfect men do, but something that perfects the man. The end product of child raising is not the child but the parent. (Frank Pittman)*

Ross Parke has studied fathers extensively (Parke, 1996, 2000, 2002, 2004). He stated in 1996 that ". . . many fathers are active partners in parenting and a direct influence on their children's development" (p. 2). Fathers make unique contributions to their children's development in many ways. Boys with more involved fathers have higher IQs (Yogman, Kindlon, & Earls, 1995) and are more sociable with their mothers, fathers, and strangers (Frascarolo, 2004). Fathers who are affectionate and who spend time with their young infants tend to have more securely attached 1-year-olds than do distant and negative fathers (Cox, Owen, Henderson, & Margand, 1992). Children with involved fathers have fewer behavior problems, more positive attitudes, and greater involvement with others and activities (Amato & Rivera, 1999).

> *Sherman made the terrible discovery that men make about their fathers sooner or later . . . that the man before him was not an aging father but a boy, a boy much like himself, a boy who grew up and had a child of his own and, as best he could, out of a sense of duty and, perhaps love, adopted a role called Being a Father so that his child would have something mythical and infinitely important: a Protector, who would keep a lid on all the chaotic and catastrophic possibilities of life. (Tom Wolfe)*

Fathers' perceptions of their role will differ based on culture and social group. Bronte-Tinkew, Carrano, and Guzman (2006), based on an Early Childhood Longitudinal Study, found that the more fathers *perceived that they had important roles to play* the more they were involved in caregiving activities, paternal warmth, nurturing activities, physical care, and cognitively stimulating activities. This has implications for teachers.

Implications for Teachers

Infant-toddler teachers should be aware of their own attitudes in making fathers feel welcome and appreciated for their relationship with the baby. Including posters of fathers with babies as part of the room decor, offering pamphlets and brochures specifically for fathers, and even including a few sports magazines in the foyer can help fathers feel welcome. It is also helpful for new fathers to hear from their child's teacher that they are doing a good job as a dad, that they have a wonderful baby, and that it is clear that the baby loves them very much. Parent education for first-time fathers can be effective in teaching interaction skills: if active learning strategies are used (Magill-Evans, Harrison, Benzies, Gierl, & Kimak, 2007).

The Transition from Partners to Parenthood

Becoming a parent is a unique, personal experience for each man and woman—and for each couple. The transition to parenthood has both personal meaning and consequences for the couple. One of the major studies in this area was done by a pair of researchers who were married themselves. Cowan and Cowan (1992) completed a 10-year study of 96 couples (72 expectant couples and 24 nonparent couples) from their pregnancies in 1979 or 1980 through their child's kindergarten year. They found that becoming a parent certainly changes everything—and they identified five "domains of family life" that undergo changes as couples make the transition to parents. These domains are:

- Changes in identity and inner life
- Shifts in the roles and relationships within the marriage
- New parenting roles and relationships
- Shifts in the three-generational roles and relationships
- Changing roles and relationships outside the family

These five domains illustrate how pervasive the changes can be in people's lives, as they become parents. Every relationship a person has (with yourself, with your spouse, with your own parents, and with others in your life) may be changed by the arrival of the baby.

Cowan and Cowan (1992) complement Stern's thinking, describing new mothers and fathers as going through *changes in identity and inner life*. Fathers may have questions of identity as they integrate new roles of caregiving and nurturing into their self-image. Mothers may feel overwhelmed at their new feelings of being completely responsible for another human being. The second domain of change, *shifts in the roles and relationships within the marriage,* describes how a couple needs to adjust to changes in the sharing of household chores and providing for the family. The new father may adopt the role of "protector" or "primary breadwinner" for the family. This can be a frightening prospect for a man whose partner has always brought in an income and functioned competently in the world. Becoming the sole wage earner, even for a limited amount of time, may be daunting. The new mother may also have concerns about becoming dependent on her husband and losing her sense of equality in the relationship. The third domain, *new parenting roles and relationships,* addresses how parents must deal with their differences on parenting issues such as how much the baby needs to be protected or stimulated during play, a common difference of opinion between men and women.

The remaining two domains, *shifts in the three-generational roles and relationships* and *changing roles and relationships outside the family,* describe how changes in their own identities may play out for the new parents in their relationships with their own parents and with friends and colleagues. The parents' parents may welcome becoming grandparents or they may find that new role very challenging. They may find it hard to support their own children's further steps into adulthood and independence.

Implications for Teachers

Although teachers are primarily responsible for the children in their care, providing opportunities for parents to meet other parents and explore both personal and practical issues of parenting can be very valuable. Merely understanding and appreciating the huge impact that becoming a parent has on the individuals and on the couple can make the baby's teacher a great source of support for the entire family.

The Imagined Baby and the Real Baby

Long before we become parents, long before we experience pregnancy, early in our own childhoods, we play at being parents. In our play, during teen years of babysitting, watching younger siblings or cousins growing up, we form ideas about what babies are like. During pregnancy, parents wonder about their baby and imagine what she will look like and how she will be. Mental health providers, who specialize in the relationships between babies and their parents, believe that expectant parents use the months of pregnancy to imagine the ideal child they hope to have (attractive, smart, athletic, happy) as well as deal with their fears of who the child might be (malformed, weak, ugly—or ultimately violent, alcoholic, or mean, like some disliked member of the family). Part of the process of becoming a parent to a real baby after the birth is getting to know and accept the real baby (Stern, 2000). This may involve letting go of some imagined attributes while having the time to learn who this new baby really is. Infant teachers need to be aware that new parents are very vulnerable to the thoughts and comments of others during the early parts of infancy, and their comments about each baby's character should be both true and positive.

Parenting Styles

Even with considerable appreciation for the importance that nurturing, involved mothers and fathers have in the lives of children, it is important to recognize that mere presence does not ensure positive contribution. The parent's emotional availability, mental health, and reasonableness all affect what it feels like for the child to be with the parent. Even the good effects of having an involved, nurturing father disappear if the father is a highly restrictive, authoritarian disciplinarian (Radin, 1982).

The term *parenting styles* describes the normal variation in patterns of how parents try to control their children (Baumrind, 1991). Parenting style includes both parent responsiveness and parent demands (Maccoby & Martin, 1983). Four parenting styles are commonly identified in the literature: *indulgent* (or *permissive*), *authoritarian, authoritative,* and *uninvolved.*

Indulgent (or permissive) parents are highly responsive but seldom demand mature behavior from their child, depending instead on the child's self-regulation.

Authoritarian parents are demanding, but not responsive. They demand obedience to extensive sets of rules.

Authoritative parents are demanding and responsive. They hold high standards for their children but are supportive in their discipline.

Uninvolved parents are neither responsive nor demanding, but not to the point of being neglectful. (Baumrind, 1991)

In Western cultures, parenting styles are related to child outcomes, especially in adolescence. Children of indulgent parents have higher self-esteem but are more likely to have problems in school and in their behavior. Children from highly authoritarian families do well in school but

indulgent (or premissive) parents Responsive but seldom demand mature behavior from their child, relying instead on the child's self-regulation.

authoritarian parents Unresponsive, but demand obedience from their child.

authoritative parents Responsive, but also demanding, holding high standards for the child while being supportive in their discipline.

uninvolved parents Neither responsive nor demanding, although not to the point of being neglectful.

tend toward poor self-esteem, depression, and poor social skills. Children whose parents are authoritative are rated more socially and intellectually competent than those of other parents. Children of uninvolved parents do most poorly in all areas (Darling, 1999). However, parenting style is also related to culture. In America, with a predominant emphasis on individualism and freedom, authoritarian parents seem restrictive and constraining. However, children of Chinese families with highly authoritarian styles develop very well, possibly reflecting the cultural attitude toward authority as serving the harmony of the group (Chao, 1994), and because strict and extensive rules are usually paired with great warmth and closeness (Marcus & Kitayama, 1991).

Implications for Teachers

Infant-toddler teachers may find it helpful to share this information on parenting styles with the families they serve. However, this may also be useful information for self-reflection: As an infant-toddler teacher, you have a relationship with the children that is very similar to that of a parent. Reflection on whether your style of relating to the children is permissive, authoritarian, authoritative, or uninvolved could be very enlightening.

FAMILY STRUCTURE

As we continue to wrestle with the complexity of understanding families, one large task would be simply defining the word *family*. A **family** may meet the traditional image of two married, biological parents and their children—or it may mean single parents, grandparents raising children, same-sex couples raising children, adoptive parents, or foster parents. Parents may be of the same or different religions and of the same or different races or cultures. The changing composition of the family does not change what is important to the child about being a member of a family, however. A recent report from the American Academy of Pediatrics states, "Children's optimal development seems to be influenced more by the nature of the relationships and interactions within the family unit than by the particular structural form it takes" (Perrin, 2002, p. 341).

family
Individuals related by birth, marriage, or choice.

In the recent past, we considered the two-biological-parent family as "normal" and regarded any other family structure as having deficits. The many changes in the structure of families have caused us to look at this differently. We currently view all families as having both risk factors and protective factors (Seifer, Sameroff, Baldwin, & Baldwin, 1992). As defined in chapter 1, *risk factors* are those life events or personal characteristics that threaten a child or family's well-being. *Protective factors* are the events and characteristics that act against risk factors (Donahoo, 2003). Any family structure may have risk factors and protective factors, given the particular characteristics of the family. For example, a calm, nurturing single-parent home would provide more protection than a two-biological-parent home affected by alcohol and violence.

This father finds that participation in Early Head Start increases his understanding and enjoyment of his daughter.

Children can grow up happily, healthy, and without serious problems in all kinds of families, but children in two-parent households are more likely to escape poverty, teenaged unmarried childbearing, and school and mental health issues (Child Trends, 2002; Weitoft, Hjern, Haglund, & Rosén, 2003). The majority of American children live in two-parent households; however, according to census reports, that percentage has been steadily decreasing since the 1960s. About 70% of children live with two parents (biological or stepparents), 23% live with only their mother, 3% live with only their father, and 4% live with neither parent (U.S. Census Bureau, 2004). In order to work effectively with extremely diverse families and their infants and toddlers, it is helpful to understand some of the issues that may be related to family structure. There are so many variations to the American family, and the issues surrounding them are so complex, that the following discussion should be considered a brief introduction to a topic worthy of deeper study.

Divorce

Each year nearly 1 million American children experience the divorce of their parents and, before they reach adulthood, over half of all children will live in a home with one parent only (Cathcart & Robles, 1996).

Parents of infants and toddlers have particular issues to consider when they divorce. Infants and toddlers may not be able to understand the difficulties their parents are experiencing, but they are very aware of the emotional tone of their environment. The sadness, tension, and anger of divorce can be stressful to even very young infants (Doescher, Hare, & Morrow, 1996). The baby's ability to develop a sense of trust in others depends on the adults' predictability and consistent emotional availability. Custody issues concerning parenting time are quite complex when it comes to infants and toddlers. Breast-feeding, for example, can be a significant factor in determining how much time the baby can spend with the father, away from the mother (Baldwin, Friedman, & Harvey, 1997). A recent study (George & Soloman, 2003) suggests that overnight visitation with fathers in divorced or separating families relates to a high occurrence of disorganized attachment in 12- to 18-month-olds. Two thirds more of these children demonstrated disorganized attachment, compared to infants who saw their fathers only during daytime visits. Disorganized attachment occurs when infants are unable to signal their distress to parents in order to elicit contact and comfort. These babies were unable to utilize their parents as a resource for handling stress. The degree of harmful effects of the overnight visits was related to the parents' ability to remain responsive to the baby's behavior, to communicate and cooperate about the baby's well-being, and to keep conflicts away from the baby.

Implications for Teachers

An infant-toddler teacher needs to be sure that she relates fairly to both divorced parents, supporting each parent's relationship with the child. She must remain neutral in a situation that can be fraught with difficult feelings. In supporting the child's relationship with each parent, the teacher must keep both parents well informed about the child and find ways, when necessary, to describe the effect that the parent's relationship, or the custody situation, is having on the child.

Single Parents

Some of the issues for infants and toddlers concerning divorce are also relevant for children raised by a single, never-married parent. The percentage of children born to women who have never married is increasing dramatically:

> In the early 1960s, less than 1 percent of children lived with a never-married parent. By 2000, nearly one in 10 children lived with a never-married parent. . . . Today nearly one-third of all births occur to unmarried women. (Child Trends, 2002)

In his book *Fatherneed,* Kyle Pruett recounts the importance of fathers in the lives of their children. He then provides this advice for the single mothers of infants and toddlers:

- Take care of yourself first, especially if you are alone. Surround yourself with all of the support you can find—emotional, physical, nutritional, and spiritual. Don't let loneliness, bitterness, and isolation take root.

- Invite close males, relatives and friends, to hold, walk, rock, play with, or babysit your child. Be sure these men have an important relationship with you, because your child can tell the difference even at this age.

- Have close male friends or relatives engage in physical play and rough-and-tumble exploration with your child.

- Have close male friends or relatives read to and comfort your child.

- Try to find child care arrangements or play groups in which men or older male siblings are involved as staff or regular volunteers. (Pruett, 2000, pp. 161–162)

Implications for Teachers

Teachers need to be particularly sensitive to infants and toddlers who are growing up with only one parent, as these children need and long for safe, nurturing contact with adults of both sexes. Because child care is predominantly female, it is easier to provide female experiences to children being raised by fathers than male experiences to children of single mothers.

Same-Sex Parents

Same-sex parents are estimated to be raising as many as 9 million of America's children, but accurate statistics are impossible to find. Gay and lesbian parents share the same concerns and worries of all parents but face additional issues unique to their situation. If the child was not originally conceived within an earlier heterosexual relationship, there are questions of adoption, artificial insemination, or surrogate mothers. There are legal issues wherein the biological or adoptive parent may have full parental rights, but the same-sex partner may not be allowed to adopt the child as an equal parent. Children of gay and lesbian parents also experience more teasing during their school years (Patterson, 1992).

The majority of children of same-sex couples have experienced the divorce of their biological parents' heterosexual marriage. Research studies describe them as looking much like other children of divorced parents with no significant differences in gender identity, social roles, or sexual orientation (Patterson, 1992). Children of lesbian mothers look very similar to children of heterosexual divorced mothers in terms of self-esteem, behavior, academic success, and peer relationships (Golombok, Tasker, & Murray, 1997). They were rated higher in terms of tolerating diversity, being protective of younger children, and seeing themselves as more lovable (Steckel, 1987). Patterson (2006) summarized the research in this way, "More than two decades of research has failed to reveal important differences in the adjustment or development of children or adolescents reared by same-sex couples compared to those reared by other-sex couples. Results of the research suggest that qualities of family relationships are more tightly linked with child outcomes than is parental sexual orientation" (p. 241).

Implications for Teachers

The teacher's primary responsibility is to support the relationship between the infant and the parents. When same-sex couples bring an infant or toddler to a program, they may share the questions anyone may bring to the experience of being a new parent. The teacher should, as always, be ready to share information on development and early parenting practices. However, same-sex parents may face more complicated questions about each person's new role. How does a baby have two mommies or two daddies? How does each person understand sharing this role? The teacher should listen to these questions with the same compassion and acceptance as she would with any other's parent's issues about adjusting to the role.

A bigger question for same-sex couples may be whether they and their child will be genuinely welcomed into the program or will staff or families have animosity toward the couple based on religious or personal objections. These are issues that may also arise when families of a different race or religion enter an otherwise homogeneous program. As in dealing with any feelings of discomfort based on differences, the teacher should begin by examining her own feelings; perhaps in supervision or with the mental health consultant. The teacher may also want to practice with that person how to politely, but firmly, put a stop to cruel remarks from other parents. For example, "I can see you have strong feelings about Jami having two mommies, but this is not the time or place to talk about it. Our director will be happy to have a conversation with you, but we keep this room calm for the babies."

While no one is free of bias toward others, each teacher is expected to behave in a professional manner and always work to support the relationship between the child and his family.

Grandparents

Grandparents raising grandchildren is an increasing phenomenon in America. Parents may or may not live in the same household, but grandparents are increasingly providing primary care for grandchildren. According to the U.S. Census Bureau, in 1997 3.9 million children were living in homes maintained by their grandparents, up 76% from 2.2 million in 1970. The steady increases are due to a variety of factors: substance abuse by parents, teen pregnancy, family violence, illness, and incarceration. Grandparents are sometimes able to offer a stable home to their grandchildren; however, they often care for their grandchildren without any legal rights. This leaves them in precarious conditions for accessing health care or other social supports for the children (Minkler, 2002).

Implications for Teachers

Both the grandparents and the infant and toddler will need sensitive understanding from educators. "While the home-school connection is critical for every young child, it is especially crucial in grandparent-headed households. Education professionals need unique insight and information about custodial grandparents' particular circumstances" (Smith, Dannison, & Vach-Hasse, 1998). The infants and toddlers may be grieving for the loss of a parent, and grandparents may be struggling with transforming their role of doting grandparent into one of parent with multiple responsibilities for their grandchildren.

Adoptive Parents

Adoption is another subgroup of parenting with so many variables that it is tempting to say it can only be understood on a family-by-family basis. Given that about 120,000 adoptions occur annually in the United States and about 1 million children live with adoptive parents, there are endless differences (CWIG, 2004). Infants may be adopted at birth from parents who relinquish their rights immediately, they may be adopted by family members, or they may be removed from their birth parents because of abuse or neglect and spend years in foster care without a permanent home. They may have been exposed to drugs or alcohol in utero. Obviously, the circumstances leading up to the adoption will have considerable effect on the child's outcomes.

For infants and toddlers, the work of developing relationships and establishing trust is highly dependent on consistent, responsive caregiving. Achieving a balance between a secure attachment to a caregiver and a healthy ability to move out into the world to explore can be challenging for any baby. Infants and toddlers who have experienced many disruptions in early relationships may have particular difficulties in establishing trust and in feeling safe enough to explore the world (CWIG, 2004).

Implications for Teachers

Teachers may also need to support adoptive parents as they struggle with particular issues. In an earlier section of this chapter, we described some of the issues men and women struggle with as they become parents. While the process of adoption is very time-consuming, many adoptive parents have only a few days between being notified that their child is available and actually receiving the child. In contrast to a 9-month pregnancy, this can leave very little time for emotional preparation. In order to protect themselves from disappointment, the adoptive parents may not dream and fantasize about parenting as much as the pregnant couple. They may be afraid at first to become too attached to the baby. They may worry whether they will love the baby or whether the baby can love them, given the lack of genetic connection. Adopting families may be acting in opposition to their own families' cultural beliefs and values concerning adoption (Frank & Rowe, 1990). They may also need help in determining whether issues that arise are typical behavioral issues for infants and toddlers or whether they are related to the adoption.

Foster Parents

When children are abused or neglected, they enter the child welfare system and often are placed in foster homes. More than 30% of all children in foster care are under 5 years of age. Infants comprise the largest cohort of the young child foster care population, accounting for one in five admissions, and they remain in care twice as long as older children (Dicker, Gordon, & Knitzer, 2001). These children are possibly the most vulnerable in our country. In order to be placed in foster care in the first months or years of life, they have already experienced deficient or dangerous parenting. They may not have received prenatal care, and they may have been poorly nourished and substance exposed in utero. Nearly 80% of these children are at risk for medical and developmental problems due to prenatal exposure. They may have witnessed or been victims of physical or sexual violence.

More than 40% of foster children are premature and/or of low birth weight. More than half have serious health problems and more than half have developmental delays—4 to 5 times the rate of children in the general population. With all of these problems, children in foster care are also unlikely to receive basic health care such as immunizations, and are highly unlikely to receive early intervention or mental health services due to fragmented systems and record keeping (Dicker et al., 2001).

Implications for Teachers

Participation in high-quality early childhood programs is included as one of five strategies to promote the healthy development of young children in foster care proposed by the National Council on Poverty. High-quality early childhood programs provide stimulating, engaging, and nurturing environments that can be inherently supportive of development. Early childhood teachers can also provide information, strategies, ideas, and emotional support to foster parents.

In recognition of the important role early childhood programs can play in the foster care system, Early Head Start (EHS) and the Children's Bureau launched a collaborative effort in 2002. Twenty-four EHS programs received grants to enhance and expand services for children and their families who are part of the child welfare system, as well as to provide more intensive services throughout communities. This initiative emphasizes both the important role that quality programs can play in children's development and the need for early childhood programs to develop the specific skills and knowledge necessary to serve these children effectively.

Another acknowledgment of the benefits of high-quality child care programs comes from the Illinois Department of Child and Family Services (IDCFS). IDCFS has implemented an extensive system of developmental screening and services for children in foster care. As one of its available services, the IDCFS has appropriated $2 million of child care funds to cover the costs of private early childhood programs for children in foster care.

CARE AND EDUCATION PROGRAMS THAT SUPPORT FAMILIES

Although the previous section was meant to describe how families might identify themselves as a unit, the many references to programs that serve families or laws that affect programs provide an idea of how dynamic the ecological relationship is between a family and its surrounding social environment.

Parent Education

parent education
The array of government and private programs that provide informational services to young children and their families.

In a broad sense, all programs that provide informational services to young children and their families might be called **parent education**. The specific purpose of the program may lie anywhere along what the National Parenting Information Network (NPIN) calls the "parenting education spectrum." This includes an increasing intensity of services and supports, such as resources and referrals, suggestions or strategies, informal community programs or groups, formal instruction through classes, and counseling and one-on-one support for parents (Robertson, 1998). Parent education may be delivered through an equally wide variety of strategies including brochures and pamphlets, magazine articles and newspaper columns, parent and tot groups, parenting groups and classes, and home visiting. The content of parent education ranges from general developmental information to topics of focused specific interest. Thomas and Footrakoon (1998) describe the methods used in presenting material as falling into one of three categories—transmitting, transacting, and transforming—each having a different perspective on the role of the teacher and the learner. The *transmitting* perspective assumes the presenter chooses the content, views the material as scientific facts to be learned, and sees the participants as absorbing the knowledge. The *transacting* perspective has teacher and participants determining together the content to be covered and includes scientific fact and personal experience and understandings as relevant content. The *transforming* perspective has the learner choosing the content in relationship to his or her own interests, seeing scientific knowledge as information to be acquired as related to one's own needs, and wanting that knowledge to be incorporated into new understandings and transformed into new actions.

A meta-analysis of parenting education program evaluations (Layzer, Goodson, Bernstein, & Price, 2001), suggests that certain aspects of programming are likely to contribute to particular outcomes. Programs such as Early Head Start and Parents as Teachers, which provide services directly to children as well as parents, are more likely to affect children's cognitive development. Programs that provide opportunities for parents to have peer support and professional staff have greater effects on children's cognitive and socioemotional development and are more effective in producing positive outcomes for parents. Of the programs reviewed, nearly two thirds had little or no effect on parents' understanding of child development or attitudes on childrearing or behavior with their children. More than half the programs had little or no effect on family functioning (Layzer et al., 2001). Those programs that are successful, according to Schorr (1997), share certain attributes. Successful programs:

- Are comprehensive, flexible, responsive, and persevering
- See children in the context of their families
- Deal with families as parts of neighborhoods and communities
- Have a long-term preventive orientation, a clear mission, and continue to evolve over time
- Are well managed by competent and committed individuals with clearly identifiable skills
- Operate in settings that encourage practitioners to build strong relationships based on mutual trust and respect
- Train and support staff to provide high-quality, responsive services (pp. 17–18)

Given almost limitless possible combinations of content specificity, delivery strategies, learning approaches, and intended outcomes, it is difficult to define parent education or to understand exactly which elements are most important to include in planning. Parents of infants and toddlers often need information on the predictable course of development. They need the professionals involved to be able to understand and accept cultural variations in parenting practices. They also benefit from opportunities to exchange ideas and information with other parents as they work out exactly what they really believe about parenting.

The infant-toddler teacher provides parent education on a daily basis through casual conversation or perhaps more formally through parent meetings or conferences. Programs such as Early Head Start promote parent education as a major element of their curriculum. Being a parent educator, without working directly with children, is also a possible vocation within the field of early childhood education.

Family Support Programs

All families need support at various stages of family life and at select times. **Family support programs** provide and coordinate a variety of services and supports for families—such as prenatal care for the mother, health services for children, quality child care and child care options, assessment and services for special needs, education, and social services. Different agencies in a city, county, or state may collaborate to provide the services and supports in a coordinated way that creates a strong infrastructure to support families and children prenatally to 5 years of age.

family support programs
Provide and coordinate a variety of services and supports for families, including prenatal care, assessment for special needs, and other medical, educational, and social services.

While family support programs are often organized by states, counties, and cities, family support can be provided by a single child care and education program where staff believe in the importance of strong and positive family–infant relationships and realize the potential for child care to be a source of educational and resource support. Specific ways to partner with parents in early care and education programs will be highlighted in chapters 12, 13, 14, and 15.

Family support programs are likely to ensure that the basic needs of children and families are met, attempt to prevent children's and families' problems from occurring, and provide more intense services to support children at risk and vulnerable families—for example, parents in poverty or who have a history of substance abuse or child abuse. These programs are essential in order for all families to ensure their children's healthy and happy start in life and the families' abilities to access resources that facilitate healthy family functioning.

Programs for Parents of Children with Special Needs

Perhaps there is no other group of parents for whom such a variety of education and support services are available as parents of children with disabilities. The parents themselves represent every race, culture, economic status, and family structure. Assisting them, are programs that provide information about legal, developmental, financial, and medical aspects of disabilities, as well as parent-to-parent connections and advocacy.

When infants or toddlers are identified with disabilities, parents may have any number of reactions, influenced by many factors including their personal history with disabilities, their religious or cultural beliefs about disability, the nature or severity of the particular disability, and their own capacity to be open to someone other than the wished-for perfect child.

Despite a prevailing societal assumption that the discovery of a disability in one's child is a tragedy for the parent, parents describe many kinds of reactions. One study reported parents as describing themselves in a constant state of tension between feelings such as "joy and sorrow," "hope and no hope," and "defiance and despair." Parents also identified their own optimism and resourcefulness in meeting the ongoing challenges of their child's disability (Kearney & Griffin, 2001). Other parents have less positive experiences and describe their reactions as including fear over the child's future ability to live a satisfying life or guilt over having possibly caused the disability through a physical or spiritual act. Some parents feel confusion over the new situation, often trying to understand complex medical information at a time when anxiety and lack of sleep make understanding anything difficult. Parents may feel powerless to control their own lives, may feel disappointed by the child they have produced, and even feel rejection of the child or the professionals who carry this image of the child (Smith, 2003). Many parents describe themselves as having all of these feelings at different times—sometimes even having contradictory feelings at the same time!

The only disability is having no relationships. (Judith Snow)

Each state has at least one parent training and information center (PTIC) with the purpose of providing parents with training and information about disabilities, parent and children's rights under the relevant laws, and resources in the community, state, and nation (Müller, 2007). These centers are funded through the Individuals with Disabilities Education Act (IDEA), which mandates special education services for children with disabilities. The parent center staff members are often parents of children with disabilities themselves. They provide information over the phone, through workshops, and through conferences, helping parents to understand their own child's needs and to learn what options might be available. They encourage parents to actively participate in making decisions about their child's services and in negotiating with providers and intervention systems to ensure their child's legal rights to services are fulfilled.

Parent-to-Parent support programs are also available all over the country and through national clearinghouses. Parent-to-Parent is a program that matches parents of children with similar needs to provide support and information to each other. A parent whose child is newly identified may contact a Parent-to-Parent program and be matched with an experienced parent trained to discuss the new parent's concerns. Parent-to-Parent may provide an understanding friend with whom the parent can share experiences of stress, confusion, or optimism. Strategies for utilizing resources, making decisions, and simply gaining confidence in trusting one's own feelings and understandings may be shared. Lifelong friendships sometimes begin in Parent-to-Parent matches (Santelli, 2003).

Teachers should be considered part of the early intervention team serving an infant or toddler with disabilities and should have a good knowledge of the resources and programs in the local community. However, the role of the child care provider as a partner to the parent may be even more important in day-to-day life. Teachers can contribute ongoing observations and information about a child's new interests and accomplishments. They can help parents sort out what new behaviors may be related to the disability and what is typical toddler behavior. Most importantly, teachers can provide a genuine welcome to and true affection for a child whose acceptance in other settings may be of great concern to parents.

myeducationlab

Go to MyEducationLab and complete the Building Teaching Skills and Dispositions exercise in Chapter 2.

SUMMARY

Many aspects of life affect how families form and function in their parenting:

- Human families all over the world share a common biology of reproduction that determines some aspects of their parenting—attending births, caring for vulnerable young infants, and valuing the bonds between parents and their children.

- Cultural beliefs about how people relate to each other and the role of children within the culture directly, if sometimes invisibly, determine the guidance parents offer their children.

- The transition to parenthood is a powerful and significant life change for the individual and for the couple, which can be supported or undermined by factors such as personal history, support from the partner, social support, and economic stability.

- Personality, culture, and the experiences of one's own childhood will influence the parenting styles each parent adopts—indulgent (or permissive), authoritarian, authoritative, or uninvolved.

- Families created through marriage, divorce, nonmarried individuals, same-sex couples, grandparents raising grandchildren, adoption, and foster care may each provide very different experiences for the family members. Nonetheless, the quality of caring, responsiveness, and relationship will have a greater impact on the child's mental health and overall developmental well-being than the configuration of the family.

- Finally, many early childhood programs provide information and support to help parents do the best jobs they can with their children. These programs include parent education, family support programs, and early intervention parenting programs.

Every early childhood program must respect the primacy of the family in the lives of infants and toddlers. Parents are our best partners, our best sources of information and guidance concerning their own children, and often our real reason for existence.

Key Terms

authoritarian parents	family	indulgent (or permissive) parents
authoritative parents	family support programs	parent education
collectivist cultures	individualist cultures	uninvolved parents

REFLECTIONS AND RESOURCES FOR THE READER

Reflections

1. In your own family, do you think your parents believed their job was basically to teach you to be independent and self-sufficient or to be interdependent? How did they communicate these messages to you?
2. Looking at Stern's list of current American beliefs about becoming a mother, do you know women who have struggled with their own disappointment because some of these beliefs are not true in their lives? Is there a difference between our ideals of becoming a mother and the supports available to young women becoming mothers?

Observation and Application Opportunities

1. As you observe parents with their young children at child care, in a store, or on a bus, what do you see parents do that suggests to you whether they might be authoritative, authoritarian, indulgent (permissive), or uninvolved?
2. Children are able to grow and develop well in all sorts of families. What unique strengths have you seen in families of different structures such as grandparents raising children, single parents, divorced parents sharing custody, or others?
3. Visit a parenting class in your community. Using Schorr's list of attributes that make a program successful, evaluate the program.

Supplementary Articles and Books to Read

Behrman, R. (Ed.). (2001). Reports from the field. *The Future of Children: Caring for Infants and Toddlers, 11*(1), 110–157.

Finn, C. D. (2003). Cultural models for early caregiving. *Zero to Three, 23*(5), 40–45.

Gottman, J. *The four parenting styles.* Available at the Parenting Counts Web site (http://www.parentingcounts.org/toddler_spot_4styles.htm).

Homeier, B. (2008). *How becoming parents affects your relationship*. Available at the KidsHealth for Parents Web site (http://www.kidshealth.org/parent/positive/family/becoming_parents.html).

Raikes, H. H., Summers, J. A., & Ruggman, L. A. (2005). Family involvement in Early Head Start programs. *Fathering*, 3(1), 29–58.

Saracho, O. N., & Spodek, B. (Eds.). (2005). *Contemporary perspectives on families, communities, and schools for young children*. Greenwich, CT: Information Age.

myeducationlab ⟩

These and other web links are included in this chapter on MyEducationLab.

Interesting Links

http://npen.org/

National Parenting Education Network   The National Parenting Education Network is a national organization that promotes parenting education. The Web site has many articles and resources on parenting education.

http://www.childwelfare.gov/pubs/

Child Welfare Information Gateway.   This government Web site provides research briefs, statistics, and issue papers.

http://www.taalliance.org/

Technical Assistance Alliance for Parent Centers   The Web site provides an array of data about parent training and information centers (PTICs) and community parent resource centers. PTICs are funded by the federal government to support parents of children with disabilities.

http://www.talaris.org/

Talaris Research Institute   This Web site offers a section called Research Spotlights, including both text and video clips describing current research findings in early development. An interactive timeline demonstrates the projection of typical development.

Understanding and Using Theories

It is not unusual for the new teacher or parent to discover contradictory information on child development. One book instructs adults to let babies cry themselves back to sleep if they awaken in the night, another tells them to respond with a comforting pat on the back. Still others advocate for a "family bed" where the children sleep with the parents. Women who are told by their mothers to keep babies on a strict feeding schedule—regardless of their cries of hunger, even during growth spurts—may be told by their pediatricians to feed their babies on demand. Parents and teachers are alternately seen as too strict or too lenient in guiding children's behavior. It is not surprising that people feel frustration in trying to sort out what, if anything, is really known about supporting development in children.

WHAT ARE THEORIES?

Child development is similar to any other body of knowledge. From early in history, people have had a desire to understand how the world works (a desire we see reflected in even the youngest infants). In trying to make sense of human development, just as in trying to understand

the changing seasons or the patterns of stars in the skies, people developed ideas about how things *might* work. Some of those ideas may have been scoffed at and lost to history. Others were recognized, acknowledged, and adopted by thinking people of their day. These ideas were developed into theories.

Theories are explanations of information, observations, and life experiences. They are attempts to provide continuity and meaning between past and present events and to provide a way of thinking about, or anticipating, future events. Theories are based on the thoughts and studies of one person or one group of people. Oftentimes, the theorist has been primarily interested in one area of development and proposes ideas about that area without trying to encompass every aspect of development. The limits of the theory depend on the conception of those who first proposed it, or those who follow—taking the idea, adding new information, examining it from new perspectives, and testing its application to reality. The benefit of a theory is that it helps us understand the possible relationship between separate events. The limitation of a theory is that reality is so complex that a single theory is unlikely to explain anything entirely.

OUR THEORETICAL FRAMEWORK

There are theories of child development throughout all of recorded history. This chapter will not provide a history of all theories or even an overview of recent theories. Instead, we will introduce the theories that inform the beliefs and values expressed throughout this book. These include general theories of development such as relationship-based theory, transactional theory, and bioecological theory. Theories addressing one or two related areas of development are also described including theories of emotional development, cognitive development, language development, and motor development. The theoretical framework of this book derives from many important developmental theorists. These popular theories are each described here, but a major common theme among them is that infants and toddlers achieve their development within relationships with responsive, caring adults. This book is based on these beliefs:

- Optimal growth and development for children, families, and communities occurs within nurturing relationships.
- Children influence the relationships within their families, and families influence the children's relationships.
- Experiences in the early years affect the course of development across the life span—the brain becomes wired to expect stress or to thrive within relationships.
- Children are able to learn when they feel safe enough to explore, when they feel they can have an effect on the people and things in their environment, and when they have an adult partner who listens to them and talks and reads to them.
- Early developing attachment relationships may be disturbed by parental histories or relationships such as unresolved losses and traumatic life events.
- The relationships that parents have with other adults affect their ability to build positive, secure relationships with their children.
- A child is part of a family, which is part of a culture, which is part of a community, which is part of a country, and each of these elements affects the others.
- Service delivery models, community programs, and public policy can and should build strong relationships and reduce the risk of relationship failure.

The clear emphasis on the importance of quality relationships for the well-being of infants and toddlers and their families reflects the *relationship-based theory* of child development

(Emde & Robinson, 2000; Hinde, 1992b). *Transactional theory* points out that the child and family affect each other (Sameroff & Chandler, 1975). *Bioecological systems theory* sees the child in the wider context of his family and society (Bronfenbrenner, 2004). Each of these theories acknowledges the power of the cultural lens through which people make decisions, as well as the family and individual differences that exist within that person's particular culture (Barrera & Corso, 2003). Each of these complements and, to some extent, includes the others. Among these theories, the relationship-based theory most clearly describes the individual child's experience while simultaneously holding the social network in which he lives, as described by Hinde (1992b):

> A relationships approach involves the recognition that children must be seen not as isolated entities, but as forming part of a network of social relationships; and requires a delicate balance between conceptions of the child as an individual and as a social being. (p. 1019)

Relationship-Based Theory

> *When Tara, the infant-toddler teacher, welcomes Jaime into her arms in the morning, her warmth, the meeting of their eyes, and the sound of pleasure in her voice all make Jaime feel that Tara remembers him and is happy to see him. As Tara is welcoming Jaime, however, her words also address her relationship with his mother: "Have a good day. I'll take good care of Jaime today, we'll be fine, and then he'll be very happy when you come and get him after work."*

Recall from chapter 1 that relationship-based theory offers an understanding of development that is consistent with our current knowledge about brain development, our experience with the effects of adverse relationships such as abuse and neglect, and—perhaps most importantly—with our own personal experiences. We understand the power of a loving relationship to support us through difficulties. We know, most of us, that we somehow feel more whole and safer when we are known by others—not known casually and pleasantly by strangers, but known and understood deeply, over long periods of time, known by someone who cares and shares experiences with us over a variety of life's situations.

Jeree Pawl (1995), an infant–parent psychotherapist, wrote a wonderful description of the power of the baby's relationship with his care teacher:

> A two-month-old held facing outward will drop his head back to look at the holder from time to time, if he's well nurtured. By the time you are a sitting baby, with good enough ordinary experiences, your very back feels safe, held. You know you are watched—that is, that you exist, are held, in someone's mind. You feel secure, and secured. . . .
>
> But this only develops if you truly are consistently in the mind of someone, so that you are noted, noticed, spoken to over distance, rescued, protected, appreciated, and tethered across space and out of mutual sight. It is the teacher that creates and confirms this, by her continual surveillance and by holding the child in continual existence in her mind. This becomes a crucial part of a child's internal sense and experience. (p. 5)

The infant-toddler care teacher's relationship with each baby, holding the baby in her mind, is very important. Her relationship with each parent and other family members is also important because all of the adults' relationships may affect their relationship with the baby. So much of each baby's ability to develop well depends on the availability of a meaningful relationship, on the capacities of the adult to hold the infant in her mind, on the surrounding social and physical environments to support the adult in the relationship, and on the condition of the society in which they live.

Care for your children as you wish them to care for your grandchildren. (Solnit & Provence)

What makes relationship-based theory stand out is its explicit detail in defining relationships. Within this construct, *relationship* is not a general word used to describe casual contacts or moments of interaction. Relationship-based theory says that relationships are effective as the organizing force of development, the element that gives an action or a feeling greater meaning and importance. According to this theory, relationships can differ depending on the following dimensions:

- Content of the interactions
- Diversity of the interactions
- Qualities of the interactions
- Qualities that emerge from the relative frequency and patterning of different types of interactions
- Complementarity versus reciprocity of the interactions
- Intimacy
- Interpersonal perception
- Commitment (Hinde, 1992b)

- *Content of the interactions.*   The content of infant–parent interactions may include established routines, play, affection, discipline, and sharing interests and experiences. The content may have a predominantly positive or negative affective tone, depending on whether the interactions are begun and completed pleasantly or with conflict.

- *Diversity of the interactions.*   Infant–parent interactions could be comprised only of routine caregiving, such as diapering and feeding. Other parents and babies may share a wide range of interactions as the parent includes the infant or toddler in conversation, singing, walks, and household activities. For one parent the routines may seem boring and repetitive; for another each diapering is a new opportunity to share a moment of closeness.

- *Qualities of the interactions.*   Relationships vary in how well the behavior of one partner coordinates with the other. In infant–parent relationships, the quality depends in large part on the sensitivity of the adult to the child's cues. Sensitivity includes perceiving the signal, correctly interpreting it, selecting an appropriate response, and delivering the response in a timely, continent fashion (Ainsworth, Bell, & Stayton, 1971).

- *Qualities that emerge from the relative frequency and patterning of different types of interactions.*   Behaviors are meaningful in a relationship not because they occur a certain number of times, but because the *pattern of frequency* of touching, smiling, and nuzzling amidst the more neutral behaviors comes to have meaning. If touching occurs relatively often but only when the parent feels like it, it may be less satisfying to the baby than if it occurs less frequently but always in response to his signal that he desires contact.

- *Complementarity versus reciprocity of the interactions.*   Complementary interactions are a negotiation of different behaviors in the two partners. Reciprocal interactions are characterized by both partners using similar behaviors. When parents cooperate with and facilitate the baby's behavior, they establish the foundation of a reciprocal relationship where the partners can adjust their actions for the benefit of a goal-corrected partnership (Bowlby, 1969).

- *Intimacy.*   A relationship with intimacy provides a warm emotional tone, a desire for closeness, a sense of security in the close presence of the other, and a willingness to act on behalf of the well-being of the other.

- *Interpersonal perception.*   Relationships are also characterized by how each partner feels the relationship affects himself or herself. This perception, or assessment of the effect of the relationship, may depend on the person's emotional availability and cognitive understanding of self and of the other person.

- *Commitment.*   The final dimension is the willingness to act on the other's behalf and work for the other's well-being, in a relationship that endures over time. It is this aspect of endurance, allowing for memories of past experiences and expectations of future experiences, that makes relationships so powerful even when the partners are not in each other's presence, as described by Hinde (1988):

> At the behavioural level, a relationship involves a series of interactions between two individuals, each interaction being relatively limited in duration but affected by past interactions between the same individuals and affecting future ones. But a relationship can persist in the absence of interactions, and involves also subjective aspects—including especially memories of past interactions and expectations of future ones, which have both cognitive and affective aspects. (p. 1)

The relationship-based theory of development is appealing because it is at once very simple in focusing on the quality of the moment-to-moment experiences of the infant, as well as focusing on the depth of intimacy and commitment between the baby and the adult. At the same time it can be all-encompassing, because it respects the effect of all possible surrounding ecological systems on the relationships that nurture the baby (Emde & Robinson, 2000).

Teachers utilizing the relationship-based theory of development commit to deep, meaningful relationships that endure over time with infants, toddlers, and families. They are capable of incorporating intimate relationships within their professional role.

Transactional Theory

A professional football player whose entire life is dedicated to rough physical contact becomes a father to a baby girl. This little girl is very sensitive about how she is handled and fusses unless treated gently. Her daddy does not want her to cry and he adjusts his handling of her so that she feels safe and comfortable in his arms. Over time, being close to her daddy becomes a high priority for this baby, and she learns to tolerate play that is more active because she feels his pleasure in it.

These silent, instantaneous transactions are negotiated in each moment between infants and toddlers and those around them. As discussed in chapter 1, *transactional theory*, as first proposed by Sameroff and Chandler (1975), emphasizes characteristics of both the child and the environment, and their dynamic interplay over time. For example, the child is seen as bringing certain biological and genetic characteristics such as gender, temperament, physical health, and genetic predispositions toward intellectual and other abilities—or in the previous story, a desire to be handled gently. The environmental influences include the psychological resources and behaviors of the most important people in the child's life: parents, siblings, extended family, peers, friends, schools, and neighborhood communities. In the previous example, one influence was the dad's ability to be responsive but another is the dad's pleasure in active, physical sports.

Transactional theory was first developed as a way of understanding why children with similar biological risk factors at birth could have very different courses of development. Sameroff and Chandler (1975) proposed that the child's biological status is only one contribution to development. The parent's understanding of the child and the appropriateness or helpfulness of the parent's response also have enormous impact. A case in point would be a premature baby who is very sensitive to touch and sounds, doesn't eat well, and is not an active partner in developing a relationship. A parent may respond to that baby with understanding of the physical stresses and be very sensitive in maintaining contact while being careful not to overload the baby's senses. Over time, the baby would grow stronger, and grow up with a feeling of being understood and respected. Gradually, she could become a devoted emotional partner. Another parent might feel rejected, irritated, and helpless around this baby. Due to these uncomfortable inner feelings, the parent might limit contact with the baby to absolutely necessary tasks, and approach those with anxiety and hostility. This baby would probably grow to feel unloved and uncomfortable with others. She might not even try to develop communicative skills.

Children affect their environment and environments affect children. Children are neither doomed nor protected by their characteristics or by the characteristics of their caregivers alone. (Sameroff & MacKenzie)

The transactional theory identifies the "bi-directional, reciprocal relationships between infants and their caregivers" as providing several points as the basis for intervention (Sameroff & MacKenzie, 2003, p. 19). Transaction is seen as a three-part sequence, offering three different points at which to intervene. First, the baby stimulates the parents, either through their appearance or through their behavior. The parents then attribute some meaning to the baby's message. Finally, the parents react with some form of caregiving. As seen in Figure 3.1, the dynamic between infant and parent (or teacher) could be changed at any of these three points, changing the child through remediation, the parent's meaning through redefinition, and the parent's caregiving reaction through reeducation or increasing skills and knowledge (Sameroff & Fiese, 2000).

Transactional theory makes explicit the process in which babies and parents are constantly affecting each other's experiences. Transactional theory is particularly helpful in looking at factors that may put a child's development at risk. In child care a healthy, sturdy child may be able to manage a separation from a parent for a while if he is used to a predictable environment, has strong emotional bonds to that parent and to extended family, and if he receives loving support during the separation. That same child may not do so well if the environment is less supportive. On the other hand, a more vulnerable child—a poor eater with irregular sleeping patterns, for instance, who is often fussy and unhappy—may make it very difficult for the well-intentioned caregiver to be consistently helpful during the separation.

Transactional theory is a way to focus on the effects the child and adult have on each other, as well as the effect their surrounding environment may have on them. Teachers utilizing transactional theory would seek additional information and education for themselves when they need to change the trend of a relationship that does not serve the child. For example, when the teacher's handling never comforts a young infant, she might consult with the parents, or even an occupational therapist, for suggestions about better techniques knowing that it could, in turn, improve the relationship.

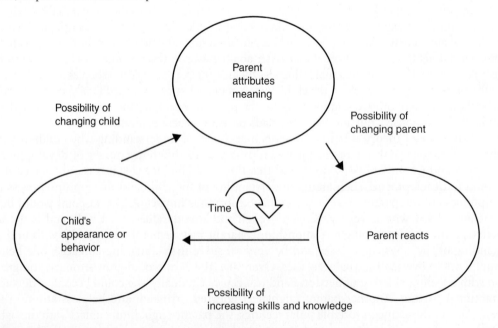

Figure 3.1   Transactional theory of development and points of intervention.
Source: Based on Sameroff and MacKenzie (2003).

Bioecological Systems Theory

Perry loved being a home family provider. She had close relationships with the children and their families. But her city council was putting new restrictions on home businesses and she was worried about meeting the new requirements. Other providers were also concerned and they were meeting with the state child care administrator, hoping for some help.

The many levels that affect Perry's child care program are addressed within bioecological systems theory (Bronfenbrenner, 2004). Bioecological systems theory projects beyond the interpersonal relationships into the effects of the community and society on the child. Beginning with Bronfenbrenner's belief that the primary relationship needs to be with someone who can provide a sense of caring for a lifetime, and that children need stable families who provide constant mutual interaction with their children, he then looks to the structure of society to determine whether society supports this level of relationship. A society where both parents work teachers in child care come and go is not supporting the child's need for consistent relationships.

The bioecological systems model is usually portrayed as a series of concentric circles emanating from the child, as seen in Figure 3.2.

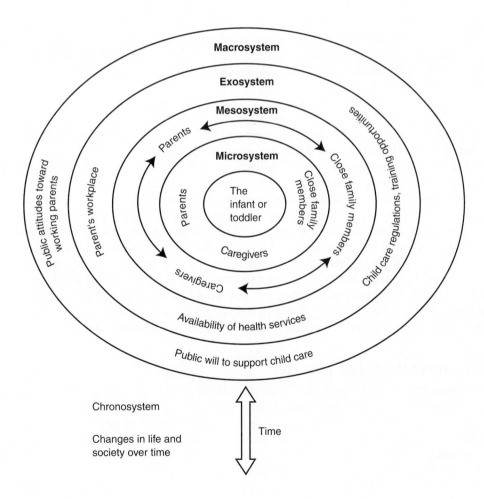

Figure 3.2   Bioecological systems theory of development, adapted to child care.

microsystem
The child's most immediate relationships.

The innermost circle is the **microsystem** that describes the child's direct relationships with his family, and which relates most closely to relationship-based theory. Perry, in the previous example, creates her own microsystem in the child's life as each child spends much of his or her waking time with her. In echoes of the transactional theory, the family members, friends, and teachers in the microsystem affect the child—but the child affects them as well. This sense that influences are bidirectional within the microsystem is repeated as influences are seen as bidirectional between the systems as well.

mesosystem
The child's relationships among the microsystems.

The next circle is the **mesosystem** this includes relationships among the microsystems, also relating closely to transactional theory. For example, the child care providers and parents have a relationship with each other that can affect the parent–child relationship or the teacher–child relationship. When a father brings his baby to Perry saying, "I love seeing the way you are with Marissa, and she is so excited to see you," Perry may feel an increase in her positive feelings toward Marissa. At the end of the day, when Perry hands Marissa back to her mother saying, "Marissa is the most loving baby I have ever known. I enjoy her so much," the mother may leave with an increased sense of pride and affection for her daughter.

The strength of bioecological systems theory, however, is that the circles continue to move outward, illustrating the effect of the wider culture and society on the child's development. The **exosystem** includes settings that do not include children but that affect them. In Perry's case, it is the city council's new restrictions that are about to have an impact on her caregiving. She is hoping that the state administrator might be a more helpful part of this exosystem. Other exosystem examples would include the policies of the parent's workplace concerning flexible work hours or staying home with a sick child.

exosystem
The local social settings that indirectly affect the child.

macrosystem
The culture, values, beliefs, and public policies of the society in which the child lives.

The next circle is the **macrosystem,** the values and laws of the society in which the exosystem exists (Bronfenbrenner, 2004). A society that does not believe in women working will not support policies that give women equal wages and flexibility concerning their responsibilities to their children. In Perry's case, if the city values the service of home family providers, and understands that the economics of this business are quite different from other businesses, the city council might exempt child care from their new requirements.

chronosystem
The changes in all of the systems over time, including aging, structure of the family, moving, death, or shifting social attitudes and public policies.

The encompassing circle is the **chronosystem,** which addresses the element of time as it affects the child. Time elements might mark external events such as the parent's divorce or the birth of a sibling, or they may be internal, describing the growth and maturation of the child.

The bioecological model obliges us to be aware that the well-being of any child is dependent on events and forces far beyond the child's own daily experiences. Programs will use a family-centered approach and become aware of community resources available to families. The teacher utilizing the bioecological systems theory would participate in professional organizations such as the National Association for the Education of Young Children or the Family Child Care Association to advocate for policies that are friendly to infants and toddlers.

Summary of the Major Theories

Our theories help us understand the relationships between past events and predict how events might flow in the future. Our theories of child development tell us that infants and toddlers need strong, meaningful, responsive, nurturing relationships in order to grow and develop well. Relationship-based theory illustrates the aspects of a relationship that make it meaningful. Transactional theory examines how aspects of each individual influence the other in relationships. Bioecological systems theory extends the picture into the many aspects of culture and society that directly or indirectly affect the development and well-being of the child. Each of these theories provides for development as a dynamic experience, responsive to many influences.

Relationship-based theory, transactional theory, and bioecological systems theory all take a broad look at development. In the following chapters, you will also see the influence of theorists who worked more directly with specific domains. The following sections describe theories of emotional development, learning, language, and motor development that are used throughout this book.

THEORIES OF EMOTIONAL DEVELOPMENT: A SENSE OF SELF AND RELATIONSHIPS WITH OTHERS

Emotional development, our feelings, our loves, our motivations and desires, our fears and feelings of safety, and our ability to reflect on our experiences all proceed within the context of our relationships. The theories of emotional development that follow are congruent with relationship-based, transactional, and bioecological systems theory, but they focus our attention on how we develop a sense of self and relationships with others. These are brief descriptions of complex theories, each of which has a rich literature of studies and papers. Although each of the following theories has a different focus, each has contributed to our understanding of how the infant and toddler discover and form a self through a primary relationship with one or more adults.

Theory of Psychosocial Development

Cecil had worked with infants and toddlers for 15 years. When he had newborns, he often thought, "This is my favorite stage!" Then he would have older toddlers and wonder at their competence, thinking, "This is my favorite stage!" Part of what Cecil likes is that at each stage, not only are the children different, but they seem to need different things from him.

Cecil doesn't know it, but his thinking in terms of stages is very much influenced by the work of Erik Erikson, a psychologist who created a framework of stages to explain development from birth through adulthood, which he called the **theory of psychosocial development**. Erikson proposed that children go through eight distinct, predictable stages as they develop their sense of self and their relationships with others, as shown in Table 3.1 (Erikson, 1950). At each stage, as a child

theory of psychosocial development Human development is a series of eight stages characterized by psychosocial crises that derive from physiological development and the demands made on the individual by family and society.

Table 3.1 Erikson's psychosocial stages

Age Range	Basic Conflicts	Developmental Tasks
Birth to 18 months	Trust vs. Mistrust	Infants learn that teachers can be trusted to meet their needs and that the world is a safe, pleasant place to grow up.
18 months to 3 years	Autonomy vs. Doubt, Shame	Toddlers discover that their actions are their own and enjoy independence, but they experience shame and doubt when corrected or criticized.
3 to 6 years	Initiative vs. Guilt	Children work hard to be responsible for their bodies, their toys, and their actions. When they are irresponsible or criticized, they may experience guilt.
6 to 12 years	Industry vs. Inferiority	Children learn schoolwork, sports, household chores, and work toward achievement while dealing with feelings of inferiority.
Adolescence	Identity vs. Role Confusion	Adolescents work to solidify a sense of identity.
Young adulthood	Intimacy vs. Isolation	Young adults struggle to form intimate relationships within which they can maintain their own identity. Failure to create intimate relationships results in isolation.
Middle age	Generativity vs. Stagnation	Generativity means helping the next generation become productive; stagnation means contributing nothing to the next generation.
Old age	Integrity vs. Despair	As older people look back on their lives, they either feel that the various crises were resolved well and that the whole picture of their lives has integrity or cohesion, or they feel that the crises were not resolved well and they experience feelings of despair and doom.

Source: Based on Erikson (1950).

experiences different biological, social, and cognitive needs, a sort of developmental crisis provides an opportunity for that child to discover whether her family, society, and culture can meet those needs. So Cecil sees the young, crying baby who cannot provide for herself as needing a quick response from him. If she can rely on him, she passes through this stage having developed a sense of trust in Cecil's ability to care for her and in her own ability to summon the help she needs. This trust gives her the confidence to begin to explore the world a little more independently.

As you can see in Table 3.1, each crisis or dilemma is an opportunity for increased potential and healthy development and decreased vulnerability. Each stage's crisis reflects a sense of struggle; in the resolution of each crisis, both of the options should be represented. For example, the infant should not feel that everyone could be trusted in every moment to meet every need. The toddler, while achieving increasing independence, must develop an understanding that his actions may have consequences that are hurtful or dangerous and that the feelings of shame and doubt can be good warning signals. The infant-toddler care teacher must be responsive while respecting that there is potential for growth in tolerable levels of struggle.

The Hierarchy of Human Needs

Selma was a perceptive observer of the children in her care. She knew that trying to teach a crying 2-year-old was never a good idea. So when Joseph screamed over being wet and hungry after his nap, she comforted him. Later, in a quiet moment, she talked to him about how he might get up from his nap more comfortably tomorrow.

hierarchy of human needs
Development proceeds in human beings in response both to basic needs being met and to needs for growth, the more basic needs having the priority.

Selma is intuitively responding to Joseph through the **hierarchy of human needs** (Maslow, 1968). In an explanation of development that is somewhat different from Erikson's, Abraham Maslow looked at the research on human motivation and suggested that people are motivated to further their development because of their needs—needs that arise from deficiencies and desire for growth.

In the hierarchy of human needs, as shown in Figure 3.3, the needs that are lower in the figure, forming the foundation, must be met before the person even experiences the needs that are higher in the figure. So Joseph, experiencing physiological discomfort, had to achieve comfort in that area, which led him to feel safe again. Selma used her own ability to comfort him before she even began to appeal to his need for mastery—a way to consider waking up from nap tomorrow without screaming. In one way, the hierarchy does follow a path of human development. Young infants must first regulate their physiological needs, and then they develop a sense of safety in the world. As that sense of safety evolves, they feel a sense of love and belonging with the adult who keeps them safe. During preschool and school years, children work on mastery, gaining the skills and knowledge they will need in life. As people mature, they find self-fulfillment in marital relationships, in work and productivity, and in passing on their legacy to another generation.

However, the levels of the hierarchy may be visited at any time in life. Even very young infants are moving back and forth among physiological needs, safety and security, a sense of belonging, and need to achieve mastery. So a wise teacher, like Selma, responds to each child on the level in which they are experiencing need.

Separation and Individuation

Sam's group of children was just turning 2 years old. He was always fascinated by the way they would insist on being independent, doing things on their own, and then suddenly, desperately, needing to be held and comforted.

theory of separation and individuation
Development is a process of achieving an understanding of oneself as a separate individual.

Sam was noticing an aspect of development addressed in the **theory of separation and individuation** (Mahler, 1975). Margaret Mahler proposed a stage theory of the development of self, or what she called the psychological birth of the infant, shown in Table 3.2. Her main point was

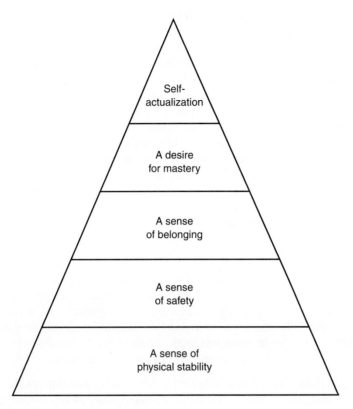

Figure 3.3   Maslow's hierarchy of human needs.
Source: From Maslow, Abraham H.; Frager, Robert D.; Fadiman, James, *Motivation and Personality*, 3rd Edition, copyright 1987. Adapted by permission of Pearson Education, Inc. Upper Saddle River, NJ.

Table 3.2   Mahler's stages of separation and individuation

Stage	Age Range	Characteristics
Normal autistic phase	Birth to 1 month	Achieving physiological homeostasis Unable to differentiate between self and outside world
Normal symbiotic phase	1 to 5 months	Associates relief and gratification with the caregiver Beginning of mother–infant bond "Awakening" as interest in the world increases
Differentiation	5 to 10 months	Need to frequently check in with mother Finds strangers frightening because infant cannot "hold" image of mother
Practicing	10 to 16 months	Can physically leave mother to explore, but returns frequently for "emotional refueling"
Rapprochement	16 to 24 months	Increasing sense of independence conflicts with desire to be engaged with mother
Consolidation and constancy	24 to 36 months	Has stable image of mother in mind and can tolerate her absence and use others as a substitute Has image of self and mother as separate beings

Source: Based on Mahler (1975).

that at birth, the infant does not know the difference between himself and the outside world but, over time, he develops a stable mental image of himself and of his mother, as separate beings. He is able to use that mental image to continue to feel safe and connected to his mother.

Although some of Mahler's image of the very young baby as being unaware of his surroundings or unable to differentiate himself from his mother are contrary to our current knowledge of infants actively engaging with other people, her observations provide a vivid picture of infants and toddlers using an important adult to establish a sense of who they are. Mahler's observations, in fact, are similar to Sam's, in the previous example, as he watches his children on the playground. Mahler would call this age period one of rapprochement. This period presents a sort of crisis for the toddler. On the one hand, he is suddenly quite physically capable—he can walk and run, play on his own, and be exhilarated by his independence. On the other hand, he tries to engage his parent or teacher in everything he does, "wooing" them to be interested. Mahler would describe him as being highly involved in the somewhat scary process of individuation—of becoming a separate, individual person.

Attachment Theory

Aurelia was always fascinated by the differences among her little toddler group in how they played. Ethan was calm and played well alone or with others, as long as she checked in periodically. Meredith was clingy but also resisted being comforted. Alicia seemed to play very independently, rarely looking at Aurelia—but she was distraught if Aurelia ever moved out of her line of sight. What was so interesting to Aurelia was that when these children greeted their parents in the evening, she saw echoes of this behavior.

attachment theory
Children need a relationship that provides safety and security in order for them to attend to learning and exploration.

Aurelia is seeing the three classic forms of behavior described in **attachment theory** (Ainsworth, Blehar, Waters, & Wall, 1978; Bowlby, 1982). Her three children demonstrate how they use her presence to feel safe enough to play and explore. At the same time, they are showing her that they have had very different experiences with being kept safe by the adults in their lives.

John Bowlby described crying and smiling, eye contact, cooing, responding to the mother, following, and clinging as attachment behaviors meant to keep a parent close enough for the child to be safe. Bowlby believed that these behaviors were instinctive and were triggered by events in the environment. Seeing a human face, for example, makes an infant smile. The toddler's ability to wander away and explore, sometimes causing the child to feel in danger, leads to the toddler's responsive behavior of clinging and following for safety. These attachment behaviors of smiling and clinging are not intended to develop a loving relationship so much as to keep the helpless young child safe to promote the likelihood of survival (Bowlby, 1982, 1988). Bowlby was influenced by ethologists' theories that the behavior of animals had meaning and that the purpose of the behavior was ultimately to serve the survival of the species (Darwin, 1859; Lorenz, 1966; Tinbergen, 1951).

Aurelia, as a toddler teacher, sees Ethan, Meredith, and Alicia each using different actions—touching base, clinging, or visual awareness—for the same purpose: They want to stay close enough to her to feel safe. When they are safe, they are able to play and explore freely.

Bowlby proposed that the earliest emotional experiences have a lifelong effect. The baby is an active participant in trying to get her needs met through her early relationships. Through these interactions, the child develops a mental image of herself and of her expectations of relationships. She uses this mental image in all later relationships.

When you look at the picture of the baby and her mother, it is easy to imagine that this little girl has a long history of counting on her mother to keep her safe and to encourage her explorations in the world. Showing a healthy hesitance toward a stranger, she also offers an inviting smile, as if to say, "Most people I know are pretty nice. I'm thinking you might be, too. But until I'm sure, I'm staying close to Mom."

Mary Ainsworth, observing mothers and infants in their own homes over the course of a year, documented the wide array of attachment behaviors and found that she recognized a predictable pattern regarding the order in which they would emerge. More importantly, she documented the behavior of the mothers and tentatively concluded that the securely attached babies, who felt free to explore as toddlers, had warm, responsive mothers. Fretful, worried, clingy children were more likely to have mothers who were highly anxious and distracted. Overly independent children had mothers who were unable to respond to their children's need for assurance and comfort. Aurelia, like so many other teachers, sees all of these attachment behaviors in the children. Attachment theory is further described in chapter 6.

Infants use their favorite adult as a secure base from which they can safely engage a stranger.

Teachers utilizing attachment theory in their work are responsive to infants and toddlers in ways that help them feel safe. They help young infants manage their own feelings and reactions to difficulties and help toddlers feel free to explore while gently assuring them of their safety.

Interpersonal Development Theory

At 6 months, Eli looks from his mother to his infant care teacher, clearly knowing each of them. On some level, he has an ongoing sense of what it is to be Eli with these two people he knows so well.

Daniel Stern (2000), a psychoanalyst and developmental psychologist, offers a theory of emotional development based on the last several decades of infancy research. It differs from earlier theories in significant ways. Stern asserts that infants experience themselves as separate beings from birth and the development of a sense of self is developing along with a sense of self-with-other, always working toward greater connection. He also rejects the stage theory. Instead, the child experiences moments in which he is aware of an internal or external experience, at the same time he is experiencing the sensation of his body (breathing, posture, muscle tone) and a consciousness of the experience combine to give the infant a sense of self having the experience.

These moments become linked as memories or mental images. This *experience of being* occurs with a sense of self-agency (an ability to make things happen), a sense of self-coherence (awareness of being a complete, contained entity) and a sense of continuity (sensation of going-on-being). At the same time, the infant is aware of *being with other*—managing a sense of being a separate self with another person.

Stern suggests that these are layered experiences that support each other. Rather than having stages of emotional development, he calls this layered development. To some degree, the experiences of developing a sense of self and a sense of self with others occur simultaneously.

The infant-toddler teacher utilizing the interpersonal development theory would understand the importance of each moment's experience to the infant. She would be responsive to his cues and know that he is building his model of being with people, in part, from his moments with her (Stern, 2000).

Summary of Theories of Emotional Development

Each of these theories of emotional development describes a process in which infants are trying to regulate their physiological needs, to feel safe and secure in the world, and to develop a sense of themselves and relationships with others. Erikson and Mahler emphasize predictable stages, with tasks that must be resolved before the child can move on to the next stage. Maslow describes motivations for development that derive from needs to address deficiencies and needs to grow and develop. Bowlby and Ainsworth, looking closely at the relationships between infants and their mothers, developed a theory that states that children offer attachment behaviors in order to attract adults and keep them close enough to keep them safe. Children offer different kinds of behaviors in reaction to the ways mothers are able to respond. Stern offers a process by which internalized memories chain together to create a sense of a separate self and a sense of oneself with others.

In these theories, the main points of relationship-based theory, transactional theory, and bioecological systems theory are evident. Each theory focuses on the importance of a relationship for the baby's well-being, on the way infants and parents affect each other, and, at least by implication, the influence of the wider community and society.

THEORIES OF COGNITIVE DEVELOPMENT: LEARNING ABOUT THE WORLD

Just as we have many perspectives on emotional development, there are many theories describing how children learn about the world. Many of these theories echo aspects of the theories of emotional development. They describe a developmental process, they divide that process into stages, and they recognize the importance of interested, available adults in supporting learning. The learning theories most closely aligned with the theoretical basis of this book are constructivist theory and sociocultural theory, each of which is briefly described here.

Constructivist Theory of Learning

Over and over, 6-month-old Jeremiah would bang his little trucks together, suck on them, look at them, and toss them aside. He was always happy to see them on the play mat, but didn't appear to look for them when his tossing landed them behind a larger toy and out of sight. At 9 months, however, if one of Jeremiah's trucks rolled out of his sight, he would crawl after it and retrieve it.

constructivist theory
Children construct an understanding of the world through their play and interactions.

schema
A combination of ideas and actions that babies create in order to learn and explore.

Infant-toddler teachers have many opportunities to observe how very young children keep making new discoveries about how the world works. A Swiss developmental psychologist, Jean Piaget, depicted infants and children as actively constructing their understanding of the world through their play and exploration, in his **constructivist theory** (Piaget & Inhelder, 1969, 2000). The child develops **schemas**, mental structures of his current understanding of the world. At first these schemas are reflexes such as rooting, sucking, and grasping. Next, the schemas are simple motor actions such as banging, throwing, and mouthing. As the child grows older, he experiments more internally and is able to think through possibilities and learn new things through mental processes. Jeremiah at first uses a variety of motor schemas to learn about his trucks, but he does not have a firm mental image of trucks. As Jeremiah grows older, his mental image is firmer, and he is able to understand that his trucks continue to exist even when he does not see them. As he grows a bit older, he'll use his trucks in pretend play that is specific to trucks. He'll "drive" them around on the floor.

McKyle constructs his understanding of the world through work with different materials. Here he rolls, pushes, and pulls on play dough.

assimilation
Using existing schemas to explore and understand new experiences.

accommodation
Developing new schemas to understand information when the established schemas are not adequate.

equilibrium
The point at which the mental image of the world seems to adequately explain the environmental information.

disequilibrium
The point at which the child's existing schemas or mental images are not adequate for understanding the environment.

Piaget suggested that children first try to use their existing schemas to understand new information and new experiences. He called this process **assimilation**. At 6 months, Jeremiah uses the schemas of sucking, shaking, banging, and tossing with almost every object. If the schemas are not adequate to explain the information, the child creates new schemas to use in a process called **accommodation**. For example, when a child who is using grasping and looking as a way of understanding the world is given a small drum and a rounded stick, he may decide to try banging as a new method of exploring the two items together. Piaget used the term **equilibrium** to describe the moments when the child's schemas and the information presented are in balance. When the current schemas are not adequate for exploring or explaining new information, the child's mental organization is thrown into **disequilibrium**. The child then modifies his mental structures to accommodate the new information (Flavell, 1996).

Like several of the emotional development theorists, Piaget described cognitive development as a series of stages, as shown in Table 3.3. Each stage is a very different way of seeing and

Table 3.3   Piaget's stages of cognitive development

Stage	Age Range	Characteristics
Sensorimotor	Birth to 2 years	Child moves from using reflexes to using simple motor actions as means of exploration. Motor actions become increasingly intentional, they are combined into a series of actions, and the child increasingly develops expectations about the effect of his actions.
Preoperational	3 to 7 years	Children replace their earlier sensorimotor actions with symbols such as language and pretend play. The way children think about the world can be magical and illogical—for example, thinking they could float away down the bathtub drain just as the water in the tub does.
Concrete operations	7 to 11 years	Children develop logical understandings of concrete things.
Operational thinking	Early adolescence	A child can imagine a variety of solutions to a problem, can understand the abstractions of higher mathematics, and can begin to grapple with theoretical questions concerning deity or the meaning in life.

Source: From Piaget and Inhelder (1969, reprinted 2000).

understanding the world. Jeremiah is firmly in the sensorimotor stage, but he is moving along from mere motor actions to constructing a mental image of his favorite playthings and developing effective strategies for their use—and retrieval—in play. In the photos on the previous page, McKyle explores clay with his hands—rolling, pushing, and shaping it. He also uses the clay symbolically, creating a snake like one his father has at home.

The impact of Piaget's work on American early childhood education cannot be overstated. Piaget's image of children busily constructing their knowledge of reality has been the driving force in early childhood programs concentrating on creating learning environments to be explored. The assumption that children learn through exploration derives directly from his work. Interest in Piaget's basic theory of cognitive development has led researchers to more closely observe how children begin to think about themselves, how they think about relationships, and how they use different strategies to complete their goals.

Although his work far preceded the current research on brain development and early learning, he did a great deal to establish the image of infants and toddlers as active learners. In fact, he broke down the first 2 years of life into six distinct substages of learning processes, describing the progression of infant learning from the first reflexive reactions to the world at birth, through the use of language and **symbolic representations** by the age of 2, as seen in Table 3.4.

As impressive as Piaget's contribution is to our understanding of children, his work is criticized on two points. First, research on learning and brain development in infancy suggests that Piaget greatly underestimated the young infant's ability to think—even to hypothesize about the possible outcomes of their actions. Second, the children Piaget writes about seem to discover all of their knowledge through their own exploration and construction. The role of culture and the impact of the other people in the children's lives are not identified within the learning process (Sutherland, 1992).

Despite these criticisms, constructivist theory continues to be a strong force in American education. Jerome Bruner forwards Piaget's ideas that learning is an active process in which learners construct new ideas or concepts based upon their current and past knowledge. Bruner's work incorporates the infancy research respecting that the child selects and transforms information, constructs hypotheses, and makes decisions, relying on a cognitive structure to do so. The cognitive structure, whether called a schema or a **mental model**, provides meaning and organization to experiences and allows the individual to go beyond the information given. Jeremiah, for example, constructed a mental model of the truck and was able to plan to use his

symbolic representation
The ability to use a symbol to stand for something else.

mental model
Bruner's term for the cognitive schema, or mental image held by the child to orgzanize and give meaning to information in the environment.

Table 3.4   Substages of sensorimotor development

Substage	Age Range	Characteristics
i. Reflexive actions	0 to 1 month	Responds automatically to outside stimuli
ii. Primary circular reactions	1 to 4 months	Intentionally repeats actions because they are pleasurable, such as sucking a thumb
iii. Secondary circular reactions	4 to 8 months	Repeats actions to achieve goals, such as reaching for an object to put it in his mouth
iv. Coordination of secondary circular reactions	8 to 12 months	Develops more elaborate and goal-directed coordination of actions
v. Tertiary circular reactions	12 to 18 months	Establishes object permanence and uses mental representations to actively explore the environment
vi. Inventive abilities via mental combinations	18 to 24 months	Uses symbolic representation in language and imaginary play

Source: Based on Piaget and Inhelder (1969, reprinted 2000).

body to crawl after the truck when it was out of sight. For Bruner, the role of the teacher is to provide opportunities for children to discover basic principles by themselves, although social and cultural influences are also at play. The teacher structures the information in ways that allow children to grasp it, understanding that they will continuously revisit the same information in greater depth as their capacity to understand deepens (Bruner, 1966, 1996b).

The infant-toddler teacher who utilizes the constructivist theory of learning will provide a variety of interesting materials for infants and toddlers to manipulate and explore. She will understand that the child is motivated to learn, actively building an understanding of how people relate, and figuring out how the objects in the world work.

Sociocultural Theory

> *Morris, at 7 months, also enjoyed playing with trucks. He still sometimes mouthed them and threw them—but he also watched the older toddlers "driving" their trucks on a carpet with roads marked on it. Sophie, his teacher, talked with him about his trucks. "Look at all your trucks Morris! Let's make sounds like trucks—Rrrrr. rrrrr. This truck carries food to the store. Oh, look out the window—there are trucks on the street!"*

The addition of the adult partner, or even the other children to watch, adds an important element to how children construct their knowledge about the world. Morris may be using schemas to learn about trucks, but he is also using the language of his teacher. Lev Vygotsky (1962, 1978), a Russian psychologist, agreed with his contemporary Piaget that infants and children are active learners who construct their mental organization of knowledge and that cognitive development evolves in stages that create different ways of seeing the world at different ages. However, Vygotsky believed that adults and more knowledgeable peers teach culture, language, beliefs, customs, and highly valued activities to younger children. In fact, full cognitive development could not occur without social interaction.

Vygotsky's **sociocultural theory** made a very important contribution to our understanding of development, in emphasizing the role of the adult in teaching or supporting the learning of the child. He describes how learning happens when children get *just enough* help and information from adults to allow them to figure out solutions to problems that are just beyond their reach independently, problems he describes as being in the **zone of proximal development**. For example, a 10-month-old baby who is playing with sounds becomes hungry and makes complaining noises to her teacher. Her teacher knows the baby is not ready to use words, but she is nearly ready. Word use is in her zone of proximal development. So the teacher supplies the word: "Bottle? You want a bottle?" The baby then makes a "Ba-ba" sound, demonstrating more skill in language with help (or *scaffolding,* to use Vygotsky's term) than she could do alone.

A second important contribution from Vygotsky was attention to the role of language in learning. Young children use the language of others—parents, teachers, and peers—to help them develop new concepts. He believed that children also used language to guide and teach themselves in a way similar to that used by adults with children—for example, by naming objects and using words such as *dog* to classify and organize information.

A third, and perhaps most important contribution from Vygotsky was his awareness of how knowledge is created, first in a cultural context on an interpersonal level and then on a personal level. A child's culture influences his belief, use of language, social attitudes and skills, and priorities.

The infant-toddler teacher who utilizes a sociocultural approach will study the cultures of the children in his program and discuss cultural beliefs with the families. He will observe children to determine the children's zone of proximal development and will scaffold children's learning to guide them to learn the tools for how to solve problems. He will use rich, descriptive language to support children's ability to communicate and use language to organize their world.

sociocultural theory Learning is embedded within social events and occurs as a child interacts with people, objects, and events in the environment.

zone of proximal development The difference between what the child can do with help and what the child can do without guidance.

Social Learning/Cognitive Theory

Social learning theory (Bandura, 1977) is now often referred to as social cognitive theory (Bandura, 1989, 2001) to recognize the importance of children's thinking abilities. Imitation is a primary way that young children learn and cultures are transmitted from one generation to another. Albert Bandura emphasized how children decide who and when to imitate, showing that imitation is not a rote action but rather a decision-making process. Children learn through imitation, with reasons for imitating some people over others or objects. For example, 18-month-olds will not imitate an adult's actions if that adult says "Oh, no" after completing the task as this indicates to the infant that the behavior is not one to imitate. In fact, Bandura emphasizes self-efficacy, the ability of humans to set goals, problem solve, and reflect (1997). He also emphasized that what children believe about how effective they are influences how they act.

This ability to make decisions about who and what to imitate is referred to by Gergely, Bekkering, and Király (2002) as "rational imitation." Gergely and Csibra (2006) also emphasize that "human infants are equipped with specialized cognitive resources that enable them to learn from infant-directed teaching" (p. 9). They tune into the cues of an adult; for example, by 15 months they can imitate what an adult intended to do but failed (for some reason) to do (Bellagamba, Camaioni, & Colonnesi, 2006; Meltzoff, 1995). More 9- to 12-month-old children imitated a three-step action by an adult when the adult demonstrated the sequence as compared to control groups of children who saw only the last step or no demonstration. Infants and toddlers are truly "rational imitators."

An infant-toddler teacher who knows social cognitive theory will observe how and what the children in the program observe and imitate. The teacher will recognize that infants and toddlers can imitate adults' and peers' *goals* and *actions*. They will understand that a child's belief about his capabilities will influence how he behaves.

Core Knowledge Theory

Elizabeth Spelke, a cognitive psychologist, bases her core knowledge theory on the research on infant learning. This theory proposes that humans have evolved with inborn systems or brain structures ready to learn about those things necessary to survival. The four core knowledge systems address how infants learn about objects, agents, number, and geometry. The idea of separate knowledge systems refutes the belief that learning happens through one, "general purpose device" (Spelke & Kinzler, 2007, p. 91). Core knowledge also emphasizes the importance of social interactions that provide the content of what and how much children learn in the different systems.

The core system of *object representation* allows human infants to "perceive object boundaries, to represent the complete shapes of objects that move partly or fully out of view, and to predict when objects will move and where they will come to rest" (Spelke & Kinzler, p. 89). For example, a young baby (4 to 5 months old) will react as an object approaches demonstrating an understanding that objects that move toward them may hit them (Schmuckler, Collimore, & Dannemiller, 2007). The core system of *agents* (persons and animals) allows infants to recognize goal-directed actions of living things. If the agent has a face, infants look at the adult to interpret their actions. For example, at 10 to 11 months of age an infant will look where an adult is looking if the adult has her eyes open, but not if the adult's eyes are closed (Brooks & Meltzoff, 2005). The core system of *number* has its own limits and principles. An infant will look surprised if two objects move behind a curtain but only one object comes out the other side (Wynn, 1992). Jordan and Brannon (2006) found that 6- to 8-month-olds looked at a video with the number of adults that matched the number of voices they were hearing. The fourth system is *geometry of the environment*. It allows children and adults to orient themselves in relation to places in the environment. We've all seen infants who quickly learn cxum=...=.

how to crawl down a hallway, into the bedroom through one door and out the other, confidently orienting themselves in the environment.

The core knowledge theory suggests an inborn knowledge and an ability to learn about what is most important for survival. It suggests that different skills are needed for different areas of learning and that humans have developed structures in the brain providing an ability to learn these skills over time.

Summary of Theories of Cognitive Development

Piaget and Vygotsky used their sensitive observation of young children to create an understanding of children as active learners who construct knowledge of the world through play, exploration, and experimentation. Their work influenced the increasing use of learning or discovery centers, like water tables or manipulatives in early childhood classrooms. They also helped define the role of the teacher as facilitator of learning and as a partner in relationships. Spelke offers a picture of the human infant as predisposed to learning about how objects and people function in the world, as well as having some innate understanding of number and geometry. As this theory gains prominence, teachers may become more intentional in the materials and activities they provide to ensure that each system is being engaged.

Go to the Activities and Applications section in Chapter 3 of MyEducationLab to watch *The Puzzle Story,* a sequence of photos about a teacher and child's interactions that demonstrate theoretical perspectives.

THEORIES OF LANGUAGE DEVELOPMENT

The historical debate over language acquisition reflects the age-old, but now obsolete, debate over the effects of nature versus nurture. The behaviorist B. F. Skinner proposed that language is learned as a result of external rewards, such as the attention of a parent. The child was a tabula rasa, a blank slate, ready to learn any language the family taught through a series of positive and negative reinforcements (Skinner, 1957). The nature side was taken by Noam Chomsky who proposed that human beings were born with an innate knowledge of a universal grammar and phonetics. This innate knowledge is present in the brain as a language acquisition device (LAD), develops through maturation, and is triggered by language input (Chomsky, 1975).

Kuhl's Perceptual Mapping Model

Today, a leading researcher in language acquisition, Patricia Kuhl, proposes a model of language acquisition called **perceptual mapping**. This theory is consistent with a constructionist theory of learning and a relationship-based theory of development. The basic premise of how infants learn language is that infants are able to figure out the structure of language in the first year of life before they can speak (Kuhl, 2000). Infants actively use learning strategies to understand the sounds and rules of their language.

perceptual mapping
Capacity for figuring out (mapping) the rules of language

Kuhl emphasizes that in the first year of life, infants are capable of figuring out the structure of language (or languages). They can break down the language they hear to determine the critical aspects of that language and determine patterns. They are able to predict which sounds in their primary language generally follow each other. Infants are able to figure out the likelihood of when words will start and end by attending to how often certain combinations of sounds are likely to occur within words or between words. They learn which syllables in words in the language they are hearing are usually stressed and by 9 months prefer the patterns they hear in their language over patterns in other languages. They "map" the major components of language—sounds, words, intonation, rules for how language is constructed. Infants can also discriminate non-language-related sounds, so this ability may not have evolved specifically for speech.

According to Kuhl (2000), experience with hearing language changes how infants hear language. Infants map the most commonly heard language sounds in their brain. When they hear similar sounds, these are drawn (as though by a magnet) to that same part of the brain to be stored. As infants they are able to hear and discriminate the sounds (auditory processing) of every language in the world, but by 12 months they hear only the differences between sounds they have heard frequently.

Learning to speak a language requires hearing it spoken and hearing yourself making the sounds of the language. Many parents around the world use a high-pitched, exaggerated, simplified form of language called "parentese" in speaking directly to young infants. It includes using new words repeatedly and with many examples. This exaggerated form of language is also called "child directed speech" (Thiessen, Hill, & Saffran, 2005) because it is directed at the child and functions to help the child learn speech and language. Young children need this experience with responsive adults to learn to speak a language.

The infant-toddler care teacher utilizing the perceptual mapping theory will recognize that for the infant, learning language is an active, relationship-based process. She will use parentese (a simplified language) with young infants, speak to the infant or toddler frequently throughout the day, and read to the child, providing rich language experiences.

Social Interaction Theory

Other language researchers emphasize how the social environment interacts with biology to influence language development rather than emphasizing specific innate language structures (Johnson, 2005). *Social interaction theory* of language development incorporates Vygotsky's sociocultural theory, and emphasizes that infants and toddlers need (1) responsive interactions with adults to learn a language and (2) opportunities to communicate. This theory argues that it is important not only for a child to hear language but also that the adults speaking the language are responsive and engage infants in baby conversations—responding to sounds, wiggles, and words as an infant's contribution to a conversation. This helps infants learn *how* to engage in a conversation—with turntaking, pauses, and listening. While Bruner (1983) recognized that children may have a LAD (Chomsky, 1975), he proposed that the child must have a language acquisition support system (LASS)—the child's family, teachers, and peers.

Teachers who emphasize *social interaction theory* will recognize that infants are active learners who co-construct language with adults as they adjust their language in order to be understood. Teachers will constantly listen for children's yawns, sounds, and words and respond in order to engage a young child in a conversation. They will give the child many opportunities to express herself, making mistakes but constantly learning how to engage in human communication. Teachers will understand how children's emotional environment helps make them feel safe to express themselves and how giving children opportunities to use all of their senses also enhances language development.

A THEORY OF MOTOR DEVELOPMENT: LEARNING TO MOVE

> *Niko was a good crawler. He safely crawled around the room, up and down the three steps to the little climbing structure and even up and down the low slide. His teacher was surprised, when he first started walking, that he would step right off the 5-inch platform of the cozy area and fall on his nose! What happened to his good judgment about moving in space?*

The traditional theory of motor development proposes an ages and stages progression of locomotor abilities that flow as the child's neuromuscular system matures (Gesell, 1946). Today, however, movement is understood as a process of learning, or as Karen Adolph (2008), puts it, "learning to learn to move" (p. 217). Movement requires the infant or toddler to overcome gravity, have the strength to support her own weight, and balance and coordinate body parts.

It also requires the child to readjust to constantly changing skills, size, and environments. Adolph suggests that the skills and judgment needed moment to moment in movement requires the child to "learn to learn" rather than to learn one particular solution. For instance, knowing how to maneuver down a small slope while *crawling* does not give the child the knowledge of how to *walk* down that same slope a month later. Niko, in the previous vignette, cannot call upon his knowledge of crawling and slopes to keep him safe as a new walker. He has to take in new information, adjusting it to his current posture and mode of locomotion and learn how to solve the problem of walking down a slope.

Learning to learn to move involves three major characteristics:

1. Responding adaptively to a novel problem (such as slopes) by generalizing past experience (maintaining balance in a posture such as crawling)

2. Developing a "flexible variety of solutions compiled on the fly rather than a fixed solution drawn from an existing repertoire" ("experienced walkers and crawlers find new ways of descending slopes such as sliding down in sitting, backing, and head first positions")

3. Failing to transfer knowledge directly (a confident crawler would avoid a steep slope but, as a new walker, the same infant would plunge off the edge and down the slope, unable to use the perceptual judgment he had as a crawler) (Adolph, 2008)

The idea that motor development is a matter of ongoing learning and adjustment to changing abilities brings new appreciation to the dedication shown by mobile infants and toddlers to mastering movement. Every time they grow longer, gain weight, change proportion or even change clothing, they are facing new challenges in movement. They must learn what adjustments to make moment to moment.

This theory of motor development is also a relationship-based theory because movement is encouraged and informed by the infant's relationship with adults. When an infant's perceptive information tells him a movement will be completely safe or very risky, the infant will trust his own understanding and disregard encouragement or discouragement from his mother. However, when the infant is unable to clearly judge the safety of a movement, he will use the messages of safety or danger from his parent or care teacher as he decides whether to move forward (Tamis-LeMonda et al., 2008).

The infant-toddler teacher who utilizes the learn to learn to move theory understands that each new posture requires new learning on the part of the infant or toddler as to how to move in the world. She would provide lots of opportunities for movement but understand that with each new posture, the child would need to learn again how to move in the environment. She would offer opportunities and encouragement but know that she needed to be vigilant about safety as infants and toddlers are constantly learning new ways to move.

APPLYING THEORIES IN PROGRAMS

Although most early childhood development and education programs in America are based on the theoretical approaches described in this chapter, we are more likely to know them by names such as *developmentally based* or *relationship based*. Each of these programs uses the stage models of development and the constructivist and sociocultural theories, although their applications differ in terms of environments, learning activities, and the role of the teacher. The stage model is evident in the way programs usually group children within a fairly small age range, demonstrating a belief that the developmental and learning needs are related to age groupings. The constructivist and sociocultural theories are evident in the way learning activities are set up to give infants and toddlers many opportunities to make choices, use their senses, solve problems, and initiate interactions with others.

Child Development Programs

Most infant and toddler programs would identify themselves as being developmentally based and would reflect an understanding of attachment theory; of child development theories derived from Erikson, Piaget, and Vygotsky; and of the brain research of the last two decades. If you visited a high-quality, developmentally based program you would see many different things happening. Attachment theory would be evident in that each care teacher would have primary responsibility for a small group of babies and would provide their care for a long period of time, preferably the first 3 years of life. The care teacher and parents would have a close partnership in which each would support the other's understanding of and affection for the baby. Erikson's theory would be most evident in how teachers support the early development of a sense of self. With infants, the teachers would be highly responsive as they support the child's development of trust. With toddlers, teachers may consciously pull back, encouraging children to explore their environment and develop autonomy while still being physically and emotionally available to meet the toddlers' needs.

Piaget's theory of cognitive development would be evident in how teachers follow the interests of the child and provide a variety of books, small toys, mirrors, and appropriate large motor experiences for the infant or toddler to explore. The materials would be likely to offer information on basic cognitive concepts such as object permanence or cause and effect. Vygotsky's theory of sociocultural development would be evident in the way the teacher interacts with the children and families and in the many symbols of the culture in the room. There would be posters showing "our community," and dramatic play materials that replicate the kitchen and workroom equipment used in the children's own households. Teachers would adjust the language they use and the type and amount of help they give children according to the child's ability to accomplish the task at hand.

Relationship-Based Programs

While probably every early care and development program values relationships, programs based on relationship theory would have some recognizable features. A relationship-based program would create a structure of teachers' schedules and group sizes that would provide opportunities for relationships to develop over time. A primary caregiver would be assigned to each child, and small groups of children would stay together with the same teacher from infancy to preschool (Lally et al., 1995). Friendships between children would be nurtured and honored (Wittmer, 2008). Adults would model caring, responsive, thoughtful relationships with children and with other adults (Edwards & Raikes, 2002). Teachers and families would communicate regularly to ensure a consistent caregiving experience for each child.

Early Head Start (EHS) programs have been encouraged to be relationship based, emphasizing close relationships with families as well as children. Environments in EHS programs usually resemble a home setting more than a preschool (Lally & Keith, 1997). Care and attention would be given to the development of secure, affectionate attachment relationships and to the expression and understanding of emotional experiences.

Summary of Applying Theories in Programs

In visiting programs, the philosophical base should be apparent. The role of the teacher will demonstrate whether there is a belief in Piaget's theories about independent discoveries or Vygotsky's scaffolding of learning. Relationship-based programs will emphasize the close, nurturing, and enduring development of emotional connections.

Your observation of children and programs will deepen your understanding of theories, and your study of theories will increase your ability to facilitate child development and assess programs.

SUMMARY

myeducationlab
Go to
MyEducationLab
and complete
the Building
Teaching Skills
and Dispositions
exercise in Chapter 3.

Theories are explanations of information, observations, and life experiences. The theoretical foundation of this book encompasses relationship-based theory, transactional theory, and bio-ecological systems theory.

- Relationship-based theory:
  - Infants and toddlers do not exist as separate entities but as part of social networks.
  - Infants and toddlers require meaningful, supportive, enduring relationships.
  - Relationships differ on a number of dimensions, and intimacy, reciprocity, and commitment are important factors in determining the quality and usefulness of a relationship.
- Transactional theory:
  - Relationships are bidirectional: Adults affect children and vice versa.
  - Transactions include the baby's behavior or appearance as a stimulus, the meaning given by the adult to the baby's behavior, and the adult's response.
  - Relationships that are troubled may be responsive to intervention at any of three points: the baby by remediation, the meaning by redefinition, and the response by reeducation.
- Bioecological systems theory:
  - Development can be affected by many levels of relationships, from close family all the way to national policies.
  - All systems affect one another.
- The theories of emotional development and cognitive development are constantly evolving. Some theories that are important today include:
  - Theory of psychosocial development: Erikson's stages of emotional development characterized by crises that need to be resolved
  - The hierarchy of human needs: Maslow's description of human motivation
  - Separation and individuation: Mahler's process of the child achieving a sense of self as an individual
  - Attachment theory: Bowlby's and Ainsworth's description of organizational systems that allow us to explore and learn while remaining safe and protected
  - Interpersonal theory: Stern's description of how infants develop a sense of self and a sense of self with others
  - Constructivism: Piaget's stages of cognitive development
  - Sociocultural theory: Vygotsky's processes of learning through exploration, relationships, and culture
  - Core knowledge: Spelke's theory of four innate systems of knowledge that form a foundation for learning
  - Perceptual mapping: Kuhl's theory of language acquisition
  - Learning to move: Adolph's theory of movement as a learning process

Key Terms

accommodation
assimilation
attachment theory
chronosystem
constructivist theory
disequilibrium
equilibrium
exosystem

hierarchy of human needs
macrosystem
mental model
mesosystem
microsystem
perceptual mapping
schema
sociocultural theory

symbolic representation
theory of psychosocial
  development
theory of separation and
  individuation
zone of proximal development

REFLECTIONS AND RESOURCES FOR THE READER

Reflections

1. In your own life, using Bronfenbrenner's bioecological systems theory, fill in the circles of the system. It is probably obvious to you that your family and closest friends, your teachers, and your employers affect your life. However, you may see new connections between yourself and the people or groups in the exosystem and macrosystem of your own ecological system.

2. From your readings, observations, and experiences with infants and toddlers, can you describe your own theory of how children develop?

Observation and Application Opportunities

1. Visit an infant-toddler child care program. From your observation of the environment and the interactions, how would you describe the theory of child development being practiced? What do the people in this program believe influences the development of a child?

2. In observing adults and children together, you may see one adult treating children differently. Transactional theory suggests the child's characteristics are affecting the interaction. Are you able to observe differences in infants or toddlers that are influencing the responses of adults?

Supplementary Articles and Books to Read

Pence, K. L., & Justice, L. M. (2007). *Language development from theory to practice.* Upper Saddle River, NJ: Prentice Hall.

ZERO TO THREE. (2008). *Caring for infants and toddlers in groups. Developmentally appropriate practice*, (2nd ed.). Washington, DC: ZERO TO THREE.

Interesting Links

myeducationlab

These and other web links are included in this chapter on MyEducationLab.

http://www.childstudy.net/tutorial.php

Classic Theories of Child Development   ChildStudy.net offers an overview of the classical child development theorists and a month-by-month description of child development, relating each month to the developmental phases proposed by the classic theorists—Freud, Mahler, and Erikson.

http://www.pnas.org/content/97/22/11850.full.pdf+html

Proceedings of the National Academy of Sciences   The article "A New View of Language Acquisition" by P. Kuhl (2000) is available at this Web site.

http://www.ncrel.org/sdrs/areas/issues/students/earlycld/ea7lk18.htm

Theories of Child Development and Learning   The Web site of the North Central Regional Educational Laboratory includes a link to a short paper titled "Theories of Child Development and Learning," describing maturational, environmental, and developmental perspectives.

The Power of Observation
Learning About Infants and Toddlers

Patty thought to herself that if LaNita had one more tantrum she would throw herself on the floor and join her in the screaming! Patty felt as if. LaNita had tantrums almost nonstop. When the behavior consultant from the Child Care Resource and Referral office came in to help, he began by observing and recording the tantrums. To Patty the day seemed like a typical one with LaNita tantruming many times, but to her amazement, there were only four tantrums. Patty realized that she spent the entire day dreading, tolerating, and recovering from the tantrums.

Sometimes our own reactions to events affect our ability to understand the meaning of the event for the child. Patty found LaNita's tantrums so upsetting that she felt they went on all day. An objective observation by the behavior consultant helped her see that LaNita had a limited number of tantrums and that each lasted less than 5 minutes. Together, Patty and the behavior consultant analyzed his notes and discovered that most of LaNita's tantrums occurred when both care teachers in the room were busy responding to the immediate needs of other children and couldn't help LaNita in the moment. When one of the teachers was on the floor where the children were playing, LaNita rarely lost control. Patty and the behavior consultant used the observation to make a plan together to ensure the children always had enough adult attention.

OBSERVING—A POWERFUL SKILL

This chapter will cover why observation has long been a cornerstone of early childhood practice, how findings from observations have influenced the major theories of development, and how theories influence what is important to observe. We discuss ethical considerations that influence how professionals do observations and how they use them. We describe many methods of observing and recording the observations that are available for students of child development, care teachers, and families along with guidance on how to choose the best method for the purpose of the observation. We end the chapter with how effective observation also involves awareness of the observer's own reactions and biases. This chapter sets the stage for the use of strategies that readers can use as they move through the next 12 chapters—to see children in new ways and to be able to interpret their actions and reactions, the exciting ways they learn, their many emotions, and their individual interests.

Why Observation Is Important

Observation is one of the most powerful skills for learning more about infants and toddlers. Observation provides opportunities to learn about an individual child's interests, development, and perspectives. Families use this information to plan experiences at home and teachers use it to plan curriculum that is responsive to the child's interests and goals. Information, shared from observations at home and in a program, guides how a care teacher, early interventionist, or family member interacts with a child as well as needed changes in the child's routines, guidance, and environment.

When teachers and families thoughtfully observe infants and toddlers, and share their observations with each other, they deepen their awareness and appreciation of children's ongoing, meaningful discoveries. For example, when professionals and parents observe an infant's strategies for communicating, they may be in awe of the many gestures, sounds, and facial expressions that the infant uses to communicate. Adults not only begin to see *a* child differently, but they may also see the capabilities of *all children* differently. This knowledge may change the way adults value children's communication efforts and inspire the adults to respond to infants as proficient communicators. Through observation, we understand the process of learning as well as how children may be challenged and when they need special support.

Most important, observation and documentation methods allow care teachers and other professionals to build relationships with children and families. "Observing helps you build relationships by revealing the uniqueness of every child—including the child's temperament, strengths, personality, work style, and preferred mode of expression" (Jablon, Dombro, & Dichtelmiller, 1999, p. 9). When a child feels understood, relationships blossom. When family members know that a teacher understands their child, teacher–family relationships develop as well.

Observation and Theory Have Changed How Children Are Understood

Historically, observation has changed the way children are viewed. Several theorists influenced our thinking about children as worthy of observation. They include Erikson, Piaget, Bandura, Vygotsky, and Hinde (see Table 4.1).

Erik Erikson (1963, 1994), originally from Denmark with training in Montessori education and psychosocial behavior, studied children in order to understand the development of identity. He researched development in natural settings with Native Americans as well as working with children in urban settings in Europe and America. Based on Erikson's work we know that an important focus of observation should be children's emotional and social development.

The Swiss developmental psychologist Jean Piaget's (1952, 1954, 1962, 2002) work focused on the child as a thinking being who interacts with the world differently in sequential, increasing

Table 4.1   The focus of observations based on theory

Theorist	Theory	Focus On
Erik Erikson	Psychosocial	Social and emotional development, trust, autonomy, and initiative
Jean Piaget	Cognitive	Children's interests, goals, strategies, and the ideas they have about how the world works. What challenges the child?
Albert Bandura	Social learning/cognitive	How children learn how to be social, who and how they imitate
Lev Vygotsky	Sociocultural	How culture and the environment influence children's and families' ideas, behavior, and attitudes
		Children's zone of proximal development: What and how do they learn with adult or peer support? What and how do they learn when they are working by themselves?
		What scaffolds development: support by adult or peer that helps a child learn *how* to solve a problem.
Robert Hinde	Relationship-based	Whom does the child relate to in positive, neutral, or negative ways? How does the child show that a relationship is important to him or her? What does the child need to feel safe and experience contentment and joy within a relationship?

complex stages. He studied his own three children with particular interest in how they learned about the world around them. Sometimes, he would set up materials to see what they understood, such as hiding a toy under a cloth from a young baby. Babies as young as 7 months seemed to forget it existed while slightly older babies, at 10 months, would lift the blanket to look for the toy—suggesting the baby understood that the object continued to exist when it was out of sight. Piaget's work shows us that we can learn through observation about how each child constructs her knowledge of how the world works. For example, a teacher might observe that a 6-month-old tosses a block over her shoulder and never looks for it. A few months later, she tosses a toy over her shoulder and she turns to find it. The observant teacher understands that this girl is establishing an understanding that objects continue to exist when they are out sight. The teacher may initiate games of peek-a-boo or provide containers for hiding and then finding objects.

Albert Bandura's social learning/cognitive theory (1965, 1977, 1989, 1997, 2001) highlights the importance of children learning by imitating others. Young children look to the modeling of adults to learn how to behave toward others and in different situations. This view encourages us to observe not only how children learn, but also from whom they learn, such as from peers, siblings, parents, or teachers. For example, we can see this theory in practice when we observe a teacher who sits with toddlers at a family-style lunch. She sets a good example for the children when she uses the meal as a social experience. Her warm smiles and simple language help the toddlers learn about the cultural customs of sharing meals. In the moment, the care teacher can observe how her modeling inspires imitation on the part of the children.

Vygotsky's sociocultural theory (1962, 1978, 1987) reminds us to observe how culture influences children's actions and to observe children in a variety of settings within the home, program, and community; and also to observe children within their zone of proximal development. For example, a 2-year-old may concentrate on solving a 4-piece puzzle but throw the pieces of a 7-piece puzzle on the floor. With the care teacher nearby and offering suggestions, the child may be equally successful with the 7-piece puzzle. The larger puzzle was within the child's zone of proximal development—with adult support. To gauge their zone of proximal development, we observe what children can do when they are receiving scaffolding support from adults or peers and when they are playing independently. This knowledge helps adults know when to scaffold and how to scaffold a child's learning in ways that are unobtrusive and, most importantly, to teach children *how* to solve a problem so that they gain the tools for learning.

Relationship-based theory (Hinde, 1992a, b; 1987) also influences the how, where, what, and why of observing children. This theory requires that a child be observed within the child's

Keaton tries different strategies to place the shapes in the container.

network of relationships at home, in his program, or in the community with family members, teachers, and peers in order to know the child and be able to support him to engage in thriving relationships. For example, a 14-month-old boy knows his mother dotes on him. When she is nearby, he smiles, laughs, and plays freely. However, he is very reserved around his somewhat stern care teacher. He is hesitant to try new things and the teacher worries that his development is delayed. An observer watching the responsiveness, sensitivity, and emotional tone of the two relationships would determine that the child's enthusiasm with his mother and his hesitation when he is around his teacher may be relationship based.

Each of these theories gives us insight as to what is important to observe in young children. Currently, scientists all over the world who have been influenced by these theories are observing infants and toddlers in both natural settings and laboratory situations to better understand learning and development.

THE ETHICS OF OBSERVING

Adults who are with young children want to do the right thing—behave ethically. Ethical considerations influence observation and documentation, as they do every aspect of working with young children and families. These range from the professional guidance on ethical behavior from the National Association for the Education of Young Children (NAEYC) and the Division for Early Childhood (DEC) of the Council for Exceptional Children (CEC) to the basic common sense about being respectful. Ethical considerations include having permission to observe and record observations of a child, the parent's right to see records, maintaining confidentiality, and how the care teacher writes and talks about children.

Observation and recording by the care teacher is a solid tradition of early childhood education. NAEYC's Code of Ethical Conduct (2005) and DEC's Position Statement: Code of Ethics (2008) do not directly name observation but there are specific statements that should guide one's actions in doing observations. The overriding principle in NAEYC's Code of Ethical Conduct (2005) states:

> P-1.1-Above all, we shall not harm children. We shall not participate in practices that are emotionally damaging, physically harmful, disrespectful, degrading, dangerous, exploitative, or intimidating to children. This principle has precedence over all others in this Code.

How could observations be harmful? Observation recordings may attribute unkind intentions to a child's actions or ridicule or demean the child, her family, or her culture. The purpose of observation should always be to achieve a deeper understanding of the child; never to prove there is something wrong with the child.

Conducting observations and sharing them with families can serve the following principles from the NAEYC Code:

> P-1.5-We shall use appropriate assessment systems, which include multiple sources of information, to provide information on children's learning and development.
>
> P-1.7-We shall strive to build individual relationships with each child; make individualized adaptations in teaching strategies, learning environments, and curricula; and consult with the family so that each child benefits from the program.

This principle goes on to describe the possible need for additional supports or another placement. In addition, the DEC Code of Ethics (2008) states:

> III. 7. We shall be responsible for protecting the confidentiality of the children and families we serve by protecting all forms of verbal, written, and electronic communication.

During a program's enrollment process, teachers should inform families that observations are part of the program and explain which recordings will be kept confidential and which might be shared publicly. For example, an observation method called *time sampling* to track biting would be kept confidential, but photo panel documentations with photos and captions are often posted on the wall for the children and families to enjoy and to communicate to visitors what children are learning. The purpose of observation and documentation may be explained through a permission to observe form as seen in Figure 4.1.

WHAT TO OBSERVE

In the book *The Power of Observation,* Jablon and colleagues (1999) define observation as "watching to learn." They go on to say: "We learn about children by watching them, listening to them, and studying their work. Watching and listening to children helps us understand what they are feeling, learning, and thinking" (p. 1).

What else can we learn by watching and listening to children? We can learn about how the child behaves and feels within different relationships. We learn about the stages of development (for example, how a child coos before he says words), but we also learn about the *quality* of development (how a specific child uses communication, to whom he talks, the words he says, and the feelings expressed). We also learn the following:

- How infants and toddlers learn
- What they are feeling and how they regulate their emotions
- When children feel fear, anger, sadness, happiness
- How they think
- How they use their bodies
- Their interests and what they especially enjoy
- How they relate to others
- Their temperament, character, and motivation
- Their challenges
- Their many skills
- On whom and how they bestow affection
- The strategies children use to accomplish their goals
- What children are learning from playing with certain materials such as blocks

Observation Permission Form

Date: _____

Name of Child: _____

*Name of Program, Agency, or Person Requesting Permission: _____

_____

Dear Parent or Guardian, Please complete the remainder of this form and return it to:

_____

I give permission for my child _____
to be observed for educational purposes. These observations can be written, photographic, or electronic (video or computer). I understand that these observations may be displayed or used in the program or in educational settings to provide insight to teachers, parents, family members, and children into how children think and learn. My child's name may be used unless I refuse by writing a note to that effect at the bottom of this page.

I understand that I may decide to refuse permission at any time and I understand that all observations will be available for me to review at any time.

Date Signed: _____

Name of Parent/Guardian (print): _____

Signature of Parent/Guardian _____

Address _____

City_____

Zip _____ County _____

Phone (Home) _____ (Work or Cell) _____

* Review the legality of this form with the program or agency for which you are doing the observation.

Figure 4.1   Sample permission form.

- How to interact with children in a responsive way
- The materials, equipment, and toys to make available to children to encourage engagement, participation, and relationships

As can be seen by the list there are many areas you might choose to observe. Sometimes it is helpful to try to capture everything that a child says and does for a time period, and at other times to choose a behavior, such as smiling, and record evidence of only that behavior. At other times, you may want to observe what the children in a group are learning from playing with certain materials such as water. As you observe you will begin to see infants' and toddler's behavior and interests in new ways.

Observers who study child development learn to observe the intricacies of infants' and toddlers' attitudes and behavior. For example, a classic study demonstrated how toddler hitting may have different meanings depending on how the toddler hits (Brownlee & Bakeman, 1981). An open or low-intensity hit or a swipe at the body of another toddler might mean, "Leave me alone." When a toddler hits another child with an object in the hand in a low-intensity way the behavior could mean, "Hey, wanna play?" A hard hit, on the other hand, seems to mean "I don't like that" and is more likely than other hits to provoke a negative response from the other toddler. Once an observer knows that toddlers may understand hitting differently than adults do, the adults see toddler hitting differently than before. Care teachers need to know that when they observe hitting they will want to observe different types of toddler hits and try to determine the meaning of the hit to both the hitter and the receiver. Reading the child development literature in books such as this, journal articles, or books that summarize research will inspire observers to think about development in new ways. Then the observer can conduct his or her own research and ask, "Does the information about the meaning of hits among toddlers hold true with individual children, at particular ages, and/or in specific settings?"

HOW TO OBSERVE AND RECORD OBSERVATIONS

There are many established methods of conducting and recording an observation. This section presents the steps for the use of anecdotal records and running records, event sampling, charts and diagrams, and documentation with infants and toddlers. Observation may also be used to create a portfolio for each child—a collection of teacher and family observations and the child's own creations such as scribbles on a piece of paper.

With each of the following methods, you will want to begin recording the observation with a cover page that has space for

- The child's name
- Age
- Date of observation
- Setting
- The name of the person conducting the observation

If the observations are placed in a portfolio, then families and other team members will appreciate the additional information.

Anecdotal Records and Running Records

Anecdotal records and running records are written accounts of children's actions and typically include comments that are written after reviewing a number of the observations.

Anecdotal Records

These are short accounts of children's behavior written while or soon after the behavior occurs. They describe what happened in a factual way and include when and where it happened. They are usually brief descriptions that the teacher writes in an objective manner. Descriptions that are objective are factual and do not include the observer's opinions or feelings about the child's behavior. With practice, the adult captures the child's behavior with words that help someone who is reading the record visualize what the child was doing. Often, after capturing the child's actions objectively in the left-hand column of a page the comments based on the observation, called interpretations or **inferences**, are written in the right-hand column.

inferences
Conclusions that an observer draws from interpretation of objective observation.

Inferences are conclusions that the observer draws from the objective observation. For example, if a toddler was observed throwing dandelions into a stream and watching the current carry them away, the observer might *infer* that the child was learning about the properties of water and movement. She could objectively observe his motions, but she is inferring the intentions and mental processes that drive his motions. As a teacher records an observation he may ask, "Is the child watching the current or is he just enjoying the movement of the flowers?" "Is he experimenting or are his actions random?" The teacher may write his questions and/or several possible inferences in the right-hand column. After several observations, the teacher might see a pattern in the child's behavior.

Anecdotal records may focus on behavior that represents the concepts explored by the child, such as how objects fit into containers; specific domains of development, such as the social domain; or behavior that is of special interest, such as challenging behavior. See Figure 4.2 for an example of an anecdotal record. Note how the actions in Figure 4.2 that are written in the left column are objective and the notes in the right column are interpretations of the records.

To use anecdotal records to focus on a particular area of development of a child, such as fine motor development, record a number of short observations over a time period, such as 4 months. See Figure 4.3 for an example of a series of anecdotal records of a toddler's ability to grasp that was observed during lunchtime once a month for 4 months and the inferences drawn from these observations. After sharing the information with the family, both the care teacher and the mother expressed surprise at how LaDon's fine motor abilities had developed in such a short time.

Anecdotal Observation of Nicholas (2y-9m)
Observer: Michelle
Date: 6/1/08
Place: Play yard

Sequence	Inference
Nicholas and the other toddlers in my group took off their socks and shoes to wade in our stream.	
Nicholas watched the water moving downstream in a little current.	Nicholas appeared to notice the movement of the water.
He dropped a dandelion from his hand into the stream and watched as the current took it away.	Dropping the dandelion looked accidental and he seemed surprised by the water carrying it away.
He picked a few more and threw them into the water. Watched.	He seemed to be trying to understand how the water was carrying the dandelions.
Picked up a plastic container and splashed water with it.	
Took container onto grass and half-filled it with dandelion flowers.	He seemed to be very purposeful in collecting the flowers.
Returned to stream and emptied dandelions into stream, watching current take them away. Smiled, pointed, and yelled, "Look. Look."	He seems to be testing his hypothesis about water, currents, and dandelions. His "Look" was a toddler "Eureka!"

Figure 4.2   Sample anecdotal record.

Anecdotal Record Name of Child: LaDon Age of Child: See below Setting: Fine motor development—several observations Observer: Marvin	
Behavior	**Inference**
7/15/08 (7m) High-chair Picks up softened cereal "O's" with raking motion—using all of her fingers without much help from the thumb.	She has an intent look as if she is really working hard.
8/14/08 (8m) High-chair Picks up softened cereal "O's" with a scissors grasp—using her thumb with her fingers.	In one month she moved from using a raking grasp to a scissors grasp. She still looks very intent when she is accomplishing a task.
9/15/08 (9m) High-chair Picks up cereal "O's" with a pincer grasp—using her thumb and first finger only.	Again, in a month she has progressed to using a pincer grasp. She seems to like fine-motor and hand-eye coordination tasks.
10/15/08 (10m) High-chair Picks up cereal "O's" with a pincer grasp. She picks up the cereal one by one and puts each one in her mouth.	She easily picks up the "O's" and as she picks them up she often smiles as if she is really enjoying herself. We will need to provide safe eye-hand coordination activities each day as she really seems proud of herself and very interested.

Figure 4.3   Sample anecdotal record of a child's fine motor development.

Running Records

Running records are written observations that capture the details and sequence of children's behavior. They are typically longer than anecdotal records. Running records could be used, for example, if the observer wants to capture a child's behavior for 10 minutes on the playground. A care teacher used the running record in Figure 4.4 to learn more about Paul's level of play, when he interacted with peers, and how he interacted with them.

When writing running records try to write exactly what the children are doing and saying. Try to describe movements, facial expressions, and gestures. Describe exactly what the children say to each other without making inferences. Inferences are written after reviewing one or more running records.

Running records require practice to write a continuous stream of behavior. Immediately after the observation, the observer can review the record and add more details.

After reading several running records on Paul, the teachers recognized how important active play and movement are to Paul. They expanded the large motor area in the room and the time outdoors. The teachers also noticed that Paul had a great interest in Derrick (and Derrick in Paul), so the care teachers sat them beside each other at lunch.

Care teachers, early interventionists, and students have developed creative ways of observing with anecdotal and running records. They

- Use sticky notes or index cards kept in a pocket of an apron or clothing.
- Use a sheet of address labels on a clipboard writing an anecdote on one or more labels.
- Schedule times during the day when one teacher will observe while other teachers interact with the children.

running records
Observations that require recording a child's behavior as it happens with descriptive language. They are generally longer and more detailed than anecdotal records.

myeducationlab

Go to the Activities and Applications section in Chapter 4 of MyEducationLab to watch the video *Mobile Infant with a Stacking Toy*. Write a running record, paying attention to how the child changes strategies.

Name of Child: Paul	
Date: 12/17/08	
Age of Child: 20 Months	
Setting: Outdoors	
Sequence	**Inference**
At outdoor time, Paul ran out the door to the play yard.	Paul seems intent on running the minute he is outside. He can hardly wait to get through the door.
For 3 minutes, Paul ran all around the yard, looking at his feet or just ahead of his feet as he ran.	He seems to need to run—maybe to burn off energy.
	Paul looked content but serious as he is running.
Derrick (about 2 feet away) called, "Paul" as Paul ran by him. Paul did not look at Derrick. After 3 minutes, with a smile on his face, Paul ran back to Derrick. He said, "Trucks," to Derrick and sat on the hill, joining Derrick. Paul pushed a truck for approximately two feet using both hands while he kneeled on the ground. He then turned to Derrick and said, "Trucks" again. Derrick looked at Paul and began pushing his truck.	He settles down with his friend after he runs, although he still enjoys active play.
	We may need more open, active areas inside or increase outdoor time for Paul.

Figure 4.4   Sample running record.

Event Sampling

Observers, such as care teachers and parents, use **event sampling** to record and analyze the nature of certain events. Usually, the collection of information about events, such as biting incidents, begins with a question, such as "When, where, and how does the child bite others?" (see Figure 4.5). Observers may also question the frequency, or how *often*, a child exhibits a particular behavior. Next, an observer decides when to observe the behavior. Perhaps the biting behavior primarily occurs when the toddler is outside in a family child care setting. An observer might begin to observe in that setting. The observer then describes the incident as soon as possible after a biting event with detailed information to answer the question (of course, after responding to the situation).

After several of these events, the observer(s) might see a pattern of the child biting when other children are moving in too closely to the child or when he is tired or before lunch when he is hungry. In Figure 4.5 a teacher concluded that Grace, who doesn't have language yet, doesn't like it when another child moves in too closely to her and doesn't have words to tell the other child. A care teacher stayed close to Grace for several days to try to support Grace to use sign language for STOP when another child came too close to her. The teacher continued conducting event sampling to see if the intervention worked to decrease biting. Observing before, during, and after an intervention is planned and implemented gives adults valuable information about what intervention might be helpful to the child and reduce the number of aggressive behaviors.

A second type of event sampling is shown in Figure 4.6. An observer may want to study a class of behaviors such as those that intentionally hurt others—often called aggressive behavior— to determine how often they occur (a frequency count). First, the observer (or observers) defines the term *aggressive behavior* in specific terms. An observer might discuss the following questions with teammates:

- Does *aggressive behavior* include hitting, biting, and yelling at another child?
- Does it include the child biting teachers as well as peers?
- Does the behavior need to seem intentional?

Event Sampling						
Child's Name: Grace Child's Age: 19 Months Observer: Tom Behavior to observe: Biting Define the behavior: Placing the teeth over the skin of another person						
Date Time	Setting	What Happened Prior to the Event?	Event	What Happened Following the Event?		Duration
2/18/09 9:10 a.m.	Break fast	Sam pushed his chair close.	Grace bit him on arm.	Tom checked Sams arm-talked to Grace.		1 min.
2/19/09 10:05 a.m.	Play time	Sarah sat on Grace's legs.	Grace bit Sarah's arm.	Tom checked Sarah. Talked firmly to Grace.		1.5 min.
2/22/09 11:06 a.m.	Play time	Matt took Grace's toy.	Grace bit matt's arm.	Tom took care of Matt. Laura talked to Grace.		1 min.

Figure 4.5   A sample event sampling focusing on biting events.

Child's Name: Melikia Child's Age: 22 Months Date: 9/10/08 Observer: Mia	
Behavior/Time Event Occurs	Tally (Object of Behavior)
Hit with open hand	Peer: ||
	Teacher:
Hit with closed fist	Peer: |
	Teacher:
Hit with an object	Peer: ||
	Teacher:
Bite	Peer: ||
	Teacher:
Pushing	Peer: |
	Teacher:

Figure 4.6   Sample event sampling of aggressive behavior.

To obtain accurate observations, observers must be clear about these definitions.

The care teachers who studied this event sampling learned that the child uses aggressive behaviors with peers rather than teachers (at this time); hits, bites, and pushes; and hits with a closed fist, which is more likely to cause the victim to retaliate. The next step would be to observe with the more detailed event sampling demonstrated in Figure 4.5 to learn what might be triggering the behaviors in the immediate context. The care teacher can observe further and discuss the observations with the child's parents concerning the child's experience with trust and feelings of security (Erikson), the child's thinking about how to interact with peers (Piaget), whom the child may be imitating (Bandura), the child's sociocultural experiences (Vygotsky), and what strategies scaffold the child's success in social situations (Vygotsky). Event sampling can be repeated before and after care teachers and families implement strategies that increase prosocial behavior and decrease aggressive behavior to determine whether the strategies used are successful.

Charts

An interesting way to observe and document children's choice of activity and their behavior includes charts. Care teachers and others interested in observing children often use time sampling.

Time sampling involves developing a chart that is used to observe children's behavior at designated times (see Figure 4.7). For example, a care teacher might want to observe to determine how many children are using particular areas of the room and if there are any areas that are not being used by the children. The information will help the teacher develop an environment that infants and toddlers truly enjoy.

After studying the time sampling in Figure 4.7, the care teachers could see that the housekeeping/dramatic play area was not used and the toddlers did not engage in any games that they or the teacher created from 9:00 to 9:30 a.m. Also, a child or different children were wandering in 4 out of the 7 observations. After several time samplings with similar results, the teachers began to watch for children who were wandering to try to help them make a choice of an activity or be with the teacher and they added empty boxes of food to the housekeeping area to see if that sparked any children's interest. Observing provided important information to the care teachers on patterns of behavior that were not easily observed while the teachers were naturally very busy staying near or being with the toddlers. Figure 4.8 provides an example of time sampling with a focus on a child. After reviewing Figure 4.8 the care teachers

Activity/Time	9:00	9:05	9:10	9:15	9:20	9:25	9:30
Wandering—no obvious aim				1	1	1	1
Moving from one area/teacher to another	1	2		1			
Water			2	3	3	1	1
Painting	2	2	1	1	2	2	2
Housekeeping							
Manipulative	2	3	2		1	1	1
Construction							
Active Area	2	1	2		1	3	2
With a Care Teacher	1		1				1
Involved with game—such as musical chairs—created by the children or teacher							

Figure 4.7 Time sampling of toddlers: 8 toddlers/2 care teachers.

Activity/Time	10:00	10:15	10:30	10:45	11:00	11:15	11:30
Playing beside another child	1						
Playing alone—no child within 3 feet			1	1		1	1
With a care teacher with other children		1					
With a care teacher without other children					1		

Figure 4.8   Time sampling: Focus on a child.

realized how often Letty is isolated from both peers and teachers. The teachers asked whether this behavior occurs because the child chooses to play away from others or because the child is being rejected by others. This led to further investigation with running records and event sampling. Note that the time sampling did not reveal how many minutes the child played beside another child or alone. It did reveal what Letty was doing at the designated times she was observed.

Documentation

Documentation is more than record keeping. It is a special way of observing that records children's experiences through a variety of media for use in analyzing and understanding their construction of knowledge (Gandini & Goldhaber, 2001). Often documentation includes a series of photos, video recordings, and other *visual* means that are displayed to communicate the remarkable process of how infants and toddlers learn. Documentation frames your understanding of children and your work as a teacher. When photos or children's drawings are displayed, for example, the children's learning becomes visible to teachers and parents.

documentation
Recording of children's experiences through a variety of media for use in analyzing and understanding their construction of knowledge.

Our current interest in documentation has its origins in Reggio Emilia, an Italian approach to young children's care and education. In the Reggio approach, respect for young children's ability to construct knowledge is central to the organization of the early childhood programs. The key tool used by teachers to understand the child's construction of knowledge is purposeful observation and documentation of the children's activities. This documentation process is not simply recording activities or accomplishments; it is a method of coming to thoughtful, reflective understanding of the children's activities and thinking. It is the basis of the teacher's planning for introducing new activities or materials into the program. The documentation process consists of observing and collecting supporting information (for example, pictures and samples of a child's language), thinking about and talking with the other teachers and the families about the observations, and then planning and responding from one's understandings of the children's knowledge and interests (Gandini & Goldhaber, 2001).

The documentation process usually begins with a question. It may be something general about many of the children in the group, such as "What are the children most interested in right now?" or "In what ways are children showing interest in mathematical concepts?" Or it may be quite specific and individual, such as "What is Mia learning as she takes her first steps?" or "What is Matt discovering when he plays with the blocks?" The question may be posed and one teacher in a center or several may choose to work together on the same question with the same or different children.

Observation within this model is not aiming at objective, detached recording of the children's activities. Teachers are actively involved with the children, trying to "construct a shared understanding of children's ways of interacting with the environment, of entering into relationships with other adults and other children, and of constructing that knowledge" (Gandini &

Goldhaber, 2001, p. 125). The recording of observations, then, includes thoughtful choices concerning what to record and the medium to use for creating the record. Pen and paper, still cameras, video cameras, audio recordings, and the artwork of the children are all used. However, the intention is rarely to capture an event in just one photo. These documented observations record the series of moments that comprise an event—and related events over time.

"The intent of documentation is to explain, not merely to display" (Edwards, Gandini, & Forman, 1998, p. 241). The observations—as text, pictures, or artifacts—are reviewed and organized by the observer and shared with colleagues, parents, and the children themselves. The very act of reviewing the documentation and making choices regarding its organization provides the teacher an opportunity to reflect on the children's experience and of her own way of relating to the children. The observations then are shared with others to create a deeper and more complex understanding of the children's actions and ideas, as well as to plan what materials, environmental changes, and relationships could spark children's discoveries. Documentation can be used to demonstrate how an infant or toddler with special needs is progressing on the goals that were developed by the family and recorded on an individualized family service plan (IFSP).

Example of Documentation

In Figure 4.9, Gabriella seats herself at a tray prepared with materials for bubble blowing. She opens the bottle of soap and pours some into the bowl. She adds water to the bowl from the

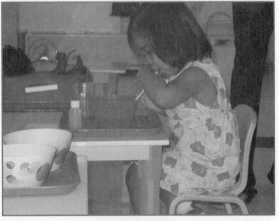
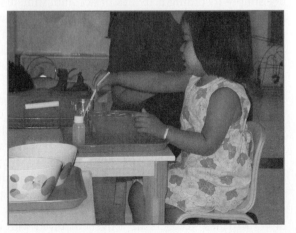

Figure 4.9   Example of documentation.

glass. Using a straw she blows bubbles in the bowl. She pauses and uses her straw to stir the water in the cup.

Gabriella shows great interest in how to make the bubbles. She pauses as if to ask, "Did I do that?" Her goal seems to be to make bubbles. Her strategies include pouring soap into a bowl, adding water, and blowing on one end of the straw with the other end in the water. She may think that she needs to stir the water in the cup in order to make more or better bubbles or she may be experimenting with whether she can make bubbles by stirring the soapy water.

Documentation can be used to plan curriculum that meets the interests and needs of a number of infants or toddlers in a group. If a teacher provides opportunities for children to experience water and several children show an interest, the teacher will want to provide more opportunities related to water play.

Summary of Observation Methods

Anecdotal records, running records, event sampling, charts, and documentation strategies all lead to increased knowledge of individual children's development, thinking, and interests; a group of children's well-being or use of materials; and how children relate to adults' creations of enriched environments and responsive interactions. Another way to gather information about children's development is through developmental profiles and screening instruments. In these methods, observation skills are critically important.

OBSERVATION AS PART OF ASSESSMENT

Group care programs and early intervention programs often use developmental profiles to observe and record children's development and to *plan* for individual children and a group of children. As you read this book you may want to observe children using the Developmental Trends and Responsive Interactions charts at the ends of chapters 6 through 10 or a developmental profile discussed below as well as the other observation and documentation strategies described in this chapter.

Developmental Profiles

A developmental profile lists a sequence of behavior in domains such as communication, emotional, social, thinking, and motor development.

A developmental profile outlines or profiles a summary of a child's development. Care teachers and other observers observe a child over time and in his home or program environment, use the information to learn about his development and, if in a program, to plan responsively for him.

Developmental profiles generally do not capture children's interests: for example, playing with water, dropping objects to see what will happen, fitting small bodies into small spaces, or making a friend. In addition, they often do not capture the nuances or qualities of a child's behavior—for example, the intensity in which a child expresses anger—although teachers' notes do. Nor do developmental profiles capture the variety of strategies that a child might use as he tries to fit objects into a container. These are all important aspects of a child's essence that adults want to observe and document to know a child well.

Developmental profiles do, however, provide valuable pieces of information about how the child is developing and, if completed in concert with the family, provide an excellent point of conversation about the child. They also provide information that care teachers can use to plan an individualized program for the child and that early interventionists might use with the family during a home visit to discuss the strengths of the child and the next developmental steps. They also begin to give the family and care teacher an idea of whether the child is developing as a typical child does.

Let's examine a few of the most commonly used developmental profiles, how they are used, and the information they provide.

The OUNCE Scale

The OUNCE Scale is an assessment that covers from birth to age 3½. The *User's Guide* (Marsden, Dombro, & Dichtelmiller, 2003) emphasizes that "it can be used with children who are at risk, those living in poverty, those with known disabilities, and those who are thriving and developing as expected" (p. iii). There are three elements that make up the OUNCE Scale: the Observation Record, a Family Album, and Developmental Profiles with associated learning standards. Each element is divided into eight age ranges: 0 to 4 months, 4 to 8 months, 8 to 12 months, 12 to 18 months, 18 to 24 months, 24 to 30 months, 30 to 36 months, and 36 to 42 months. For more information on the OUNCE Scale go to the following Web site: http://ags.pearsonassessments.com/group.asp?nGroupInfoID=aOunce

The OUNCE Scale is organized around six meaningful areas of development:

- Personal connections—how children show trust
- Feelings about self—how children express who they are
- Relationships with other children—how children act around other children
- Understanding and communicating—how children understand and communicate
- Exploration and problem solving—how children explore and figure things out
- Movement and coordination—how children move their bodies and use their hands (Meisels, Dombro, Marsden, Weston, & Jewkes, 2003)

The Observation Record provides a focus for center-based child care providers, Early Head Start teachers, home visitors, parent support group leaders, visiting nurses, teen parenting programs, early interventionist specialists, family home providers, or pediatricians and health aides to observe and document children's behaviors in programs or in the home (Meisels et al., 2003).

The Family Album provides a means to learn about the child's development. It creates an opportunity for the teacher "to 'wonder' along with families so you [the teacher, early interventionists, etc.] can learn how they see or experience their child. This wondering and observing together is the foundation for building trusting relationships between caregivers and parents" (Marsden et al., 2003, p. 11).

Developmental Profiles are organized by social and emotional, communication and language, cognitive development, and physical development and give the rater an opportunity to summarize growth and development and compare the development to expectations for that age. Summaries of the results for individuals and groups can be obtained from a Web database.

The authors emphasize that this is a relationship-based tool that improves the teacher–child relationship, family–child relationship, and teacher–family relationship. Families report how the OUNCE has helped them learn about typical child development as well as how they can support their children's learning at home.

High/Scope COR *for Infants and Toddlers*

The purpose of the COR (Child Observation Record) is to provide care teachers a method for observing children's development and determine "whether children are developing as they should be. They use the results to continue what is working and improve what is not; for example, to decide whether to provide more training to caregivers or to redesign infants' and toddlers' play areas" (High/Scope, 2008). Developed by High/Scope (2001), the COR covers these developmental areas:

- Sense of Self
- Social Relations
- Creative Representation
- Movement

- Music
- Communication and Language
- Exploring Objects
- Early Quantity and Number
- Space
- Time

With the COR, teachers write observations that describe children's behavior. The information can be entered into a Web database and summarized to plan for individual children and a group.

The **Creative Curriculum System** *for Infants, Toddlers, and Twos*

This curriculum provides sequential child behaviors in four areas: social/emotional, physical, cognitive, and language. The assessment system helps teachers observe children intentionally and use what they learn to respond to children's interests, strengths, and needs; share information with families; and identify children's levels of development in reaction to 21 objectives in 4 goal areas (Teaching Strategies, 2008, p. 1). The system is also designed to help teachers support the inclusion of children with disabilities.

For examples of these tools go to the following Web sites:

Observation Record—http://www.pearsonschool.com/index.cfm?locator=PSZ5Sz&SubLocator=PSZ28c

Family Album—http://www.pearsonschool.com/index.cfm?locator=PSZ5Sz&SubLocator=PSZ28c

Developmental Profiles—http://www.ounceonline.com/home/tour/developmental_profile.cfm.

These developmental continuum tools supplement the observation and documentation strategies discussed earlier in the chapter. In fact, the strategies described earlier are necessary in order to complete the developmental continuum tools in an accurate manner and to support the results with observations.

Screening Tools

Programs may also use screening instruments to find out if a discussion should occur between the care teacher(s) and a child's family to refer them to an assessment team for a more comprehensive evaluation to determine if the child has a disability. This referral process is described in chapter 15 of this book. One screening tool that is frequently used is the Ages and Stages Questionnaires (ASQ): A Parent-Completed, Child-Monitoring System, Third Edition. The ASQ is a widely used system developed by Bricker and Squires (2009). Parents answer questions at only one point in time or numerous times based on the age of their child. Since the measure is standardized, answers are scored and compared to cutoff scores to determine whether the child should be referred for more in-depth assessment. Chapter 15 describes the ASQ as well as the Denver Developmental Screening Test.

WHAT METHOD TO USE?

As we've discussed, there are many ways to observe and to record observations. These include anecdotal records, running records, event sampling, and time sampling. There are also a number of documentation strategies to use, for example, use of photos or video. Professionals and students of infant-toddler development also use developmental checklists and developmental

Table 4.2   Sample questions and methods of observation

Sample Questions	Methods of Observation
What are the interests of each child and the children in the room?	Anecdotal records Running records
What concepts (space, time, object permanence, light, how to relate to peers) is a child or are the children exploring?	Anecdotal records Running records
When, where, and how frequently does a particular behavior occur, for example, biting?	Event sampling
How does each child spend his or her time when playing?	Time sampling documentation
What does a child or what do the children in the group know about water, for example? What opportunities could be provided to help the children learn about the properties of water?	Anecdotal records of children's conversations, strategies, or concepts explored Documentation of children playing with water
How is a child or how are the children in the group developing?	Developmental checklists
How do we know if a child should be referred to an assessment team for a comprehensive evaluation to determine whether he or she is eligible for special support services?	Developmental screening

screening tools. During assessments to determine whether a child has a disability, a team of professionals may use more formal assessments, but recommended practice advises using many of the described methods in this chapter to observe the child in familiar environments and involve families and teachers in the assessment process.

How does an observer know when to use a particular method of observing? The left-hand column of Table 4.2 lists sample questions that care teachers and other professionals can ask themselves and discuss with team members and families. The right-hand column indicates methods that answer those questions. Each of these methods has been described in detail in this chapter.

BRING INFORMATION TOGETHER: PORTFOLIOS OF OBSERVATIONS/DOCUMENTATIONS

Care teachers and others who are interested in learning about development may compile individual children's observations and creations into individual portfolios. A care teacher, early interventionist, and/or family member accumulates the information in a notebook. Often the notebook is organized by information about the child, photos of the child, family photos, dated observations, planning forms (see chapter 12 of this book), documentation, and results of assessments. Portfolios can be organized by age of child; by topic (drawing, playing blocks); or by domains (emotional, social, cognitive, language, and motor development).

WHAT THE OBSERVER BRINGS TO OBSERVATIONS

Observers bring themselves to an observation—their past experiences, beliefs, values, culture, knowledge about children, their skills in observing, and their relationships with the children they are observing.

Past Experiences, Beliefs, Values

The observer's perspective may be affected by his own past experience, beliefs, and values about child rearing or culture. Care teachers who believe that children should be heard and not just seen may focus on strategies that toddlers use to negotiate with adults. They may interpret a child saying no as a positive step in development, while others may see it as insubordination. To avoid this type of **bias**, observers can discuss their observations with team members and families before drawing conclusions from the behavior. Observers can give the objective piece of an observation to another person, ask for his or her interpretation, and then check to see how well the interpretations match (reliability).

bias
Basing conclusions on partial information or preconceived ideas.

Culture

Culture may provide a frame through which observers interpret behavior. A culture that promotes the independence of children will view a child's shy behavior differently than a culture that values interdependence or dependence of children. Awareness of all of the possible influences on an observer's choice of what, how, and when to observe; the interpretation of the observations; and the use of the observations are key to reducing bias, whether the observer is using more objective or subjective methods.

Presence

Observers try not to change the setting by their presence. If the observer knows the children, then observing is challenging because infants and toddlers have certain expectations for their care teachers to respond to them as they typically do. If observing in a group setting, observe only if the ratio of teachers to toddlers is adequate without counting you. If observing a child or children who do not know you, introduce yourself, encourage the parent or teacher to smile at you to show the children that you are safe, and sit among the children for a period before observing. Once the observer begins to observe, however, it is important to try to remain unobtrusive.

Remaining unobtrusive while observing is not easy. One of the authors thought she was being a low-profile observer of a toddler group when one of the toddlers speedily ran to her sitting in a low chair and hit her as hard as he could on the leg with a block. Obviously, the child had been quite aware that a stranger was present and either he wanted the observer to know that he was not comfortable with her presence or he wanted to check to see if she was alive. However, sitting back, staying low, and being quiet are still the best ways for an observer to create minimal changes in a setting. If a toddler approaches the observer, he can say, "I'm watching you play today" in an enthusiastic voice. After several observations with the same group, toddlers begin to ignore the observer.

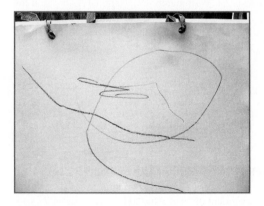 

Deanna's early drawing and a later drawing can be placed in a portfolio to demonstrate changes in development.

SUMMARY

Observing is a skill that a parent, teacher, early interventionist, or someone who is studying about infants and toddlers can use to learn more about child development, children's interests and needs, and how to plan responsively. There are many methods to use to observe and document children to support the learning of infants and toddlers in all domains of development—emotional, social, cognitive, communication, and motor.

Key Terms

bias	event sampling	running records
documentation	inferences	

REFLECTIONS AND RESOURCES FOR THE READER

Reflections

1. What do you think is the most important aspect of a child to observe first to develop a positive relationship with the child?
2. Observation is collaboration among you, the child, and family. How will you improve your observation skills in a collaborative way? How will you build trust among the three participants?

Observation and Application Opportunities

1. Observe two children of approximately the same age using the Developmental Trends and Responsive Interactions charts at the end of chapters 6 to 10 (or other observation technique). How are the two children alike? How are they different?
2. After observing two children of different ages identify their interests and how they pursue those interests.

Supplemental Articles and Books to Read

Dodge, D.T. (2006). *Creative curriculum for infants, toddlers, and twos: Developmental continuum assessment tool.* Washington, DC: Teaching Strategies.

Greenman, J., Stonehouse, A., & Schweikert, G. (2008). *Prime times* (2nd ed.): *A handbook for excellence in infant and toddler programs.* Minneapolis, MN: Redleaf Press.

Jarrett, M. H., Browne, B. C., & Wallin, C. M. (2006). Using portfolio assessment to document developmental progress of infants and toddlers. *Young Exceptional Children, 10,* 22–32.

Koralek, D. (Ed.). (2004). *Spotlight on young children and assessment.* Washington, DC: National Association for the Education of Young Children.

Meisels, S. (2005). *Developmental screening in early childhood: A guide.* Washington, DC: National Association for the Education of Young Children.

Interesting Links

http://journal.naeyc.org/btj/200401/dichtel.pdf

NAEYC. Dichtelmiller, M. L., & Ensler, L. (2004, January) Infant/toddler assessment. One program's experience. *Beyond the Journal, Young Children on the Web,* 1–7.

This on-line article on infant/toddler assessment highlights the challenges and benefits of developmentally appropriate assessment.

http://www.educate.ece.govt.nz/Programmes/KeiTuaotePae/Assessmentforinfantsandtoddlers.aspx

Early Childhood Education Teaching and Learning. Assessment for Infants and Toddlers.

This exquisite site sensitively discusses the meaning of assessment of infants and toddlers and provides specific examples of children's portfolio pages.

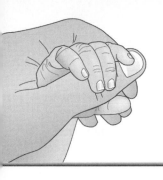

Brain and Prenatal Development, Birth, and the Newborn

5

LaShana smiled to herself as she remembered the morning. As a toddler teacher, she frequently was included in special moments in the lives of the children's families. This morning Alberto's mother was almost dancing as she brought him in. She pulled LaShana aside and whispered, "I'm pregnant!"

This really is beginning at the beginning.

In a book designed to help teachers understand infants and toddlers and care for them in groups, there are two very different reasons for including information on a period of life before infants can possibly be in group care. First, to appreciate the wonder and complexity of early development, it is helpful to be aware of the fascinating new details of how our brains develop, as well as the amazing information we now have on the journey from conception to birth. Development races forward from that first meeting of egg and sperm in ways that illustrate the developmental and ecological theories of our field. In essence, it helps us understand babies if we know about brain development, conception, gestation, and the first weeks after birth.

The second reason we need to understand pregnancy, prenatal development, and the earliest period of life is that either directly, as in home visiting programs such as Early Head Start, or

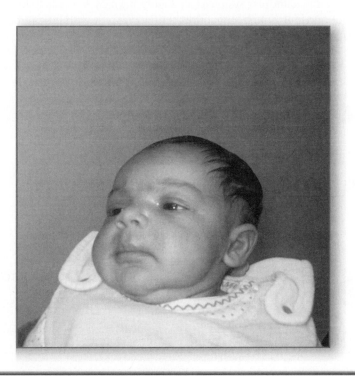

indirectly through serving toddlers whose parents become pregnant with another child, we are often in a position of providing parent education around this very early period of development. Parents recognize teachers as having knowledge and experience with infants and toddlers and see teachers as a source of personal support in parenting issues. Everyone benefits by the teacher being grounded in the details of healthy pregnancy and prenatal development as well as being a resource for information and services.

BRAIN DEVELOPMENT: AN OVERVIEW

The newborn responds to the feel of a nipple on his cheek with a reflex and begins to suck before the nipple even reaches his mouth. Four months later, the baby knows that when his caregiver moves from the cupboard to the sink, she is preparing a bottle for his snack. How much has been learned—and remembered—in these few months!

gestation
The period of pregnancy when the fetus is carried in the uterus.

The development of the brain begins within the first days following conception and it continues to develop throughout our lifetimes. The course of brain development during **gestation** is generally predictable, but it is affected by the mother's nutrition, her emotional condition, and exposures to toxins. Both the nutrients available to the developing brain and its experiences affect the structure of the brain.

The Structure of the Brain

In the first weeks following conception, as cells are rapidly dividing and the amniotic sac and placenta are first developing, the embryo develops three layers of cells: (1) the ectoderm, which will become the brain, sensory organs, and nervous system; (2) the mesoderm, which will become the circulatory, skeletal, and muscular systems; and (3) the endoderm, which will become the digestive and glandular systems (see Figure 5.1). By 4 weeks following conception, the embryo is about one fourth inch long, curled into a crescent with little nubs sticking off the sides; a heart tube forms and begins pulsating; the internal organs are beginning to develop; and

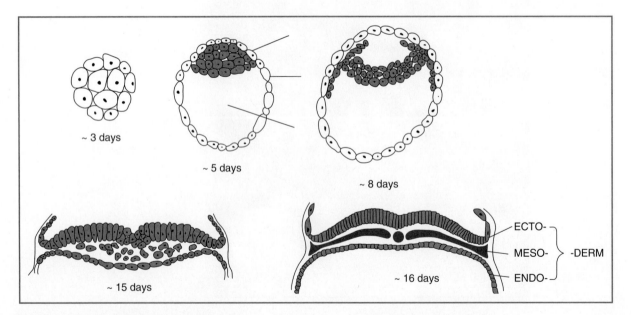

The cells rapidly multiply, the ball shape begins to flatten to a disk, and the embryo develops three layers of cells.

Figure 5.1   Early development of the human embryo.

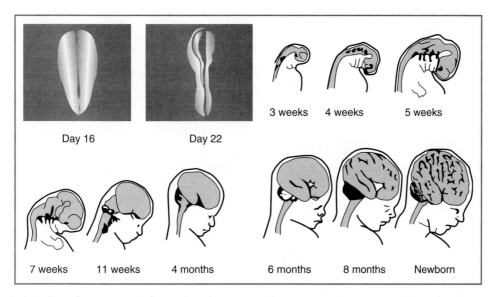

The brain begins to form at the end of the embryo, first as a thin plate. A groove develops, delineating the future hemispheres. The brain rapidly grows into its adult form and then creates many folds as it becomes increasingly differentiated.

Figure 5.2   Prenatal brain development.

the future brain and nervous system become apparent as a spoon-shaped structure, only one cell thick, known as the neural plate. The neural groove runs the length of the neural plate, dividing it into right and left halves, a precursor of the future cerebral hemispheres (Restak, 2001, p. 2).

Over the next several weeks, fetal brain cells, or neurons, are generated at about 250,000 per minute and the brain develops three areas: the forebrain, the midbrain, and the hindbrain (see Figure 5.2). These become larger and more differentiated in the womb and form the sections of the adult nervous system. The forebrain becomes the cerebrum, controlling thinking and language; the midbrain becomes the thalamus and hypothalamus, controlling the passage of sensory information; and the hindbrain becomes the cerebellum and the brain stem, controlling heartbeat, respiration, and motor development ("Fetal Development," 2007).

At about 5 months gestation the brain is growing rapidly but it is relatively smooth. In the last 3 months of gestation, the brain continues to grow quickly, limited by the containing force of the skull. As the surface of the brain continues to grow, the cerebral hemispheres fold in on themselves, packing themselves efficiently into the available space. By the time a baby is born, the brain looks as furled and gnarled as that of an older child or adult, with a visible crease down the middle separating the two hemispheres (Shore, 1997).

It is the large size and complexity of the human brain that makes us different from every other species. Babies are born with about 100 billion brain cells—twice the number they will have as adults. This abundance of cells helps ensure that babies will be born with healthy brains and will be able to learn whatever they need to survive in their unique environment (Restak, 2001, p. 5).

Creating Connections Between Neurons

The work of neurons is to make connections with other neurons, constantly exchanging information. The fetus's, and then the baby's, experiences provide the information that causes the connections to form, therefore literally creating the physical structure moment by moment. Each neuron has an axon (transmitter), a thin fiber that carries information in the form of electrical signals out from the neuron to the dendrites (receivers) in other cells. Each neuron

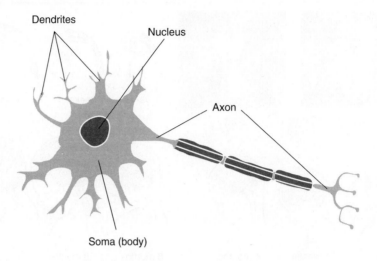

Dendrites

Nucleus

Axon

Soma (body)

A single neuron with one axon transmitting information and many dendrites receiving messages.

Figure 5.3   The neuron.

also has many dendrites, hairlike fibers that receive electrical information from other neurons (see Figure 5.3). When an axon sends out information from one neuron, dendrites from one or more other neurons receive the information through a connection between axon and dendrite called a synapse (Huttenlocher, 1984; Shore, 1997). A neuron may connect to up to 15,000 other neurons, creating the phenomenon known as "wiring the brain" (Gopnik et al., 1999). In order for the transmission of an electrical signal across the synapse, a neurotransmitter chemical such as serotonin, dopamine, or endorphins must be present (Chugani, 1997, 1998) (see Figure 5.4).

The synapses, or connections, that are used repeatedly in the infant's day-to-day life will be reinforced and strengthened. The synapses that form but are never reactivated will be eliminated in a process often called *pruning* (Chugani, 1998). This profusion of synapses followed by a sort of weeding out of unused dendrites is a very efficient way of ensuring that the child learns what he or she needs to.

myeducationlab

Go to the Activities and Applications section in Chapter 5 of MyEducationLab to watch the video *Synaptic Development,* which demonstrates brain development in young children.

The genes are the bricks and mortar to build a brain. The environment is the architect. (Christine Hohmann)

For example, say a very young infant is hungry and crying. He sees a familiar shape moving toward him in a familiar way. The shape is wearing something soft and light blue. It has a familiar smell and it is making familiar sounds: "It's OK, honey, I'm here. Are you sooo hungry?" Synapses begin firing all over the baby's brain: "What do I know about that shape? Sometimes it's Aunt Sherri or a stranger, but it's usually Mommy. It looks like something Mommy often wears. It smells like Mommy, it sounds like Mommy's words and voice."

The infant has information about all of these aspects of "Mommy" stored in synapses in his brain. When he is near Mommy, or probably even just thinking about her, these synapses carrying familiar information are set off and become strengthened. On the other hand, if a stranger passes the infant in the grocery store, the baby registers information but never "reactivates" it. Synapses that are formed in brief, onetime experiences but never reused tend to wither and be eliminated in a process often referred to as pruning. If synapses are activated frequently, they become stable and are preserved from pruning. So, connections that are made and strengthened in the brain in the early years create the physical wiring of the brain of the adult (Rakic, Bourgeois, & Goldman-Rakic, 1994).

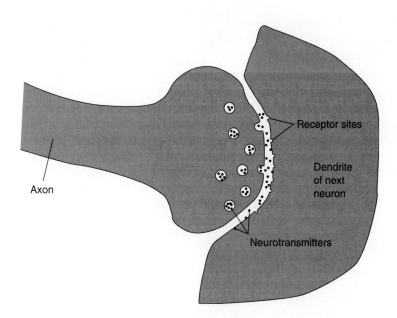

The axon and dendrite exchange information at a point of connection called a synapse, using chemical neurotransmitters.

Figure 5.4   A synaptic connection.

All learning, throughout one's life, follows this pattern of synaptic connection. We continue to have experiences—either physical or conceptual—immediately scan our synapses for stored information, and either pull up the relevant information or create new synaptic connections. In doing this we continuously change the physical structure of our brains.

The Importance of Early Experiences for Brain Development

Some synapses are created in the brain while the fetus is still in the womb. In the last months of the pregnancy, the fetus is able to hear external sounds and see light. The sounds and light, in addition to the proprioceptive information of his own movement and possibly the sense of touch he feels when his mother rubs her expanded belly, all provide information that is conducted through the brain in synaptic connections (DeLoache, 2000). Even the process of pruning synapses begins in the womb. So it is no exaggeration to say that early experiences have enormous and lasting impact on the brain.

During the first year of life, an infant's brain grows to about 70% of its adult size; by age 3, the human brain develops to 90% of its full adult growth and establishes most of the structures that will guide all future emotional, behavioral, social, and psychological functioning later in life.

Newborns are dependent on adults for their survival and to help them have appropriate experiences with the world. However, babies are not passive participants. They clearly express their need for nourishment and comfort, and demonstrate interest in both sensory experiences (sounds, smells, sights, touch) and relational experiences (hugging, cooing, smiling, comforting). For most babies, these sensory and relational experiences occur simultaneously and become transformed into patterned neuronal activity that influences the ongoing forma-

Babies need an emotionally available adult partner for healthy brain development.

tion of the brain in positive ways. An infant's brain is most likely to keep the synapses that are formed through experiences that are repeated *and* that occur within emotionally meaningful relationships.

Long before we knew the specifics of how our brains develop, researchers had understood the importance of an emotionally available adult partner for babies. In studies of very young children in hospitals, orphanages, and other institutions in the 1930s, it was clear that food, clothing, and a bed to sleep in are not enough for young children. Between 25% and 30% of these infants and toddlers, receiving custodial care without human interaction, died. Many who survived were severely mentally retarded (Skeels & Dye, 1939; Spitz, 1945). Bruce Perry (1999), a leading researcher in early brain development, puts it this way:

> The young child's undeveloped brain is trained in a "use dependent" way, mirroring the pattern, timing, nature, frequency, and quality of experiences and interactions. Think of it in terms of nutrition, if an infant or toddler is not fed consistent, predictable messages of love and communication, then those areas of the brain are shut down and the child's capacity to function later in life are compromised. (p. 1)

The Effects of Stress and Violence on Brain Development

Of course, positive experiences are not the only experiences that have impact on an infant's or toddler's brain development. When adults ignore babies' cries or respond to crying with abuse, the infants or toddlers are not having the kinds of experiences they need to build the typical rich and complex neuronal network of the well-developed brain. Infants who repeatedly experience frightening events such as physical or sexual abuse will constantly utilize the parts of their brain that focus on survival and responding to threats. In a similar way, infants who experience the chronic stress of neglect, hunger, cold, fear, or pain will also utilize their brain's resources for survival. This is the "stress-response" system at work.

According to Perry's research (1996), chronic stress in the first years can cause changes in attention abilities, impulse control, sleep, and fine motor control. Chronic activation of the parts of the brain involved in responding to fear can "wear out" other parts of the brain involved in higher level thinking. As an evolutionary function of the brain, when survival is at stake people do not use their more thoughtful, reflective parts of the brain. Instead, cortisol, adrenalin, and other hormones activate the part of the brain that

This little boy enjoys the way his teacher talks to him while they play.

focuses on choosing a survival strategy: fight or flight, or in very young infants, freeze. As these neural connections are reinforced through usage, they become the predominate pathways the brain uses to assess situations. Every event is perceived as a life-or-death situation. The brain that results from these early experiences may be highly adaptive in abusive or neglectful situations, but it is inadequate for the work of healthy relationships. The child who does not experience love, support, and positive social opportunities may not develop the memories—and therefore the neural pathways—needed to recognize and

Toddlers can feel frightened and vulnerable.

understand them when they do occur. "The result may be a child who has great difficulty functioning when presented with the world of kindness, nurturing, and stimulation. It is an unfamiliar world to him; his brain has not developed the pathways and memories to adapt to this new world" (CWIG, 2001).

Children who experience chronic stress in infancy use their brains differently later in life. They may be in a state of hyperarousal, always scanning the environment for signs of danger. These children may even evoke in others the abusive behavior that they fear, just to have some control over it. Therefore, a boy whose mother was raging and frightening may pick fights with other children, or a girl who was sexually abused may act seductively with a teacher. The opposite reaction to early frightening experiences is to feel so powerless that the child just freezes, or dissociates. Dissociation appears to be surrender to the situation, but the child feels as though she is not even present in the moment. During dissociation, the child may not even hear what is said to her, and so she does not attempt to respond. The child may have no memory of the experience. If children do not experience reliable responsiveness in their caregivers, they may later lack the neuronal pathways that would present adult assistance as a possible solution to problems. If children experience extreme deprivation in infancy, little contact with caregivers and little stimulation from the environment, they will develop significantly smaller than normal brains (Perry, 1996; Perry & Pollard, 1997). The brain may incorporate the effects of chronic frightening or neglectful early experiences for a lifetime.

GENETICS AND PRENATAL DEVELOPMENT

The process of brain development begins with conception, and it continues throughout life. The brain is a good example of the value of understanding prenatal development as a foundation for understanding early development. Our knowledge of the brain has increased dramatically in the last decade, as has our knowledge of every aspect of development.

We know more about the composition of our bodies today than at any time in history, and more is being learned every day. For example, your body is composed of about 100 *trillion* cells. Your little toe is made of 2 or 3 billion cells. Each cell is smaller than the diameter of one strand of hair—and yet the material inside each cell makes us similar to all other human beings and, at the same time, our own, completely unique selves.

Our skin is made of skin cells, our liver made of liver cells; about 200 different kinds of cells are needed to create our bodies. Each cell contains genetic information that directs it to be a specific kind of cell doing the work it needs to do in our body. (See Figure 5.5.)

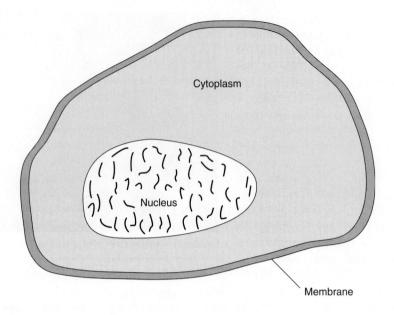

Figure 5.5   A cell.

Each cell is enclosed by a somewhat porous membrane. Within the cell membrane is a watery fluid called cytoplasm—a mixture of water, enzymes, amino acids, glucose, and other molecules. At the center of the cell is the nucleus. Protected by a nuclear membrane, the nucleus holds 6 feet of DNA (deoxyribonucleic acid) tightly packed into 46 chromosomes. Human beings inherit 23 chromosomes from their father and 23 from their mother. There are 22 pairs of autosomes and one pair of sex chromosomes, designated the X chromosome and the Y chromosome, which determine gender. (See Figure 5.6.)

The DNA of the chromosome is a pattern that tells the cell how to make its proteins. Each strand of DNA is a pattern of pairs of nucleotides that link together between two strands like rungs in a ladder. The strand of DNA then has the appearance of a double helix. Human beings have about 3 billion base pairs of nucleotides on our DNA (refer again to Figure 5.6).

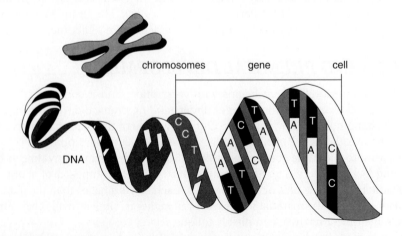

Each chromosome is packed with long strands of DNA, carrying all of the body's genetic information.

Figure 5.6   A chromosome, DNA, and genes.

About 2% of the DNA provides genetic information. Each little section of the pattern of DNA is marked by a starting point and an ending point. The material between those points is a gene. Genes carry the general information on how to create and maintain the body as well as specific information that tells your body to have hair color like your mother's or a nose like your grandfather's (HGP, 2008).

There are around 60,000 different genes in the human genome. The Human Genome Project, described in Box 5.1, has mapped out the entire human genome. At this point we have identified more than 5,000 genes, any one of which, if damaged or missing, can cause drastic changes in the human being. Missing genes are known to cause a variety of diseases and disabling conditions including lactose intolerance, albinism, cystic fibrosis, Tay-Sachs disease, sickle cell anemia, hemophilia, and muscular dystrophy. Disabilities caused by genetic issues are described in chapter 15.

There is not necessarily a direct one-to-one, gene-to-disease correlation, however. Damage to one gene may cause a variety of problems, and many diseases are caused by damage to a set of genes. **Genetic counseling** can be very helpful to families who have concerns about inherited diseases.

genetic counseling
Informing parents of possible birth defects in their children on the basis of chromosomal tests and such medical procedures as amniocentesis.

In sum, the foregoing has been a brief introduction to some of the newest, most complicated, and most compelling information science is currently providing. We are each complex and unique human beings—yet we are each built of single cells that are predominantly exactly like the cells in all other human beings. While the components and functioning of single cells are pretty impressive, when two cells meet and create a new human being, the picture of development is really thrilling!

THE FETUS

The development of the baby from conception to birth takes about 40 weeks. In talking about gestation, or the period of pregnancy, we usually divide those weeks into three parts, or trimesters.

The First Trimester

Fetal development begins when the sperm cell from the father enters the ripe egg (ovum) of the mother. These two cells are very different from all others in the human body. While almost all cells have 46 chromosomes (23 pairs), the sperm and the ovum each have only 23. This enables the genetic material from the mother and father to pair up and begin to create a whole new person.

When the ovum and the sperm combine to create a new cell, this cell quickly multiplies as it travels down the fallopian tube to implant itself in the uterine wall on the 6th day after conception. The placenta develops to keep the fetus nourished and to supply oxygen. (See Figure 5.7.)

During these first 3 months of development, the first trimester, the cells rapidly multiply but they also begin to differentiate into blood cells, liver cells, nerve cells, and so forth. As you can see in Figure 5.7, the external features such as eyes, ears, arms and legs, and the internal organs have begun to form. Although less than 3 inches long, the fetus can make a fist, spontaneously move her arms and legs, begin a rudimentary sleep and waking cycle, and grasp, suck, and swallow ("Fetal Development," 2007; Solchany, 2001).

Box 5.1

The Human Genome Project

This study of the DNA in our cells was designed to tell us:

- How many genes we have
- How cells work
- How living things evolved
- How single cells develop into complex creatures
- What happens when we become ill

The work includes:

- Charting the sequence of the 3 billion letters of human DNA
- Mapping the human genes

Source: Funded by National Institutes of Health and the U.S. Department of Energy.

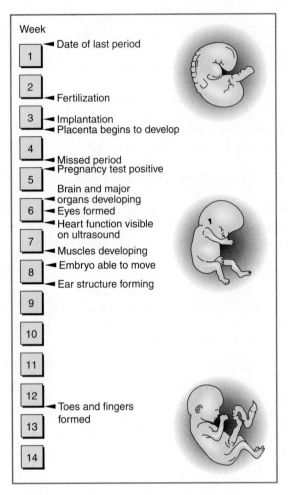

Week

1 ◄ Date of last period

2 ◄ Fertilization

3 ◄ Implantation
◄ Placenta begins to develop

4

◄ Missed period
◄ Pregnancy test positive

5

Brain and major
◄ organs developing

6 ◄ Eyes formed
◄ Heart function visible
on ultrasound

7 ◄ Muscles developing

◄ Embryo able to move

8 ◄ Ear structure forming

9

10

11

12 ◄ Toes and fingers
formed

13

14

Figure 5.7   First trimester of fetal development.

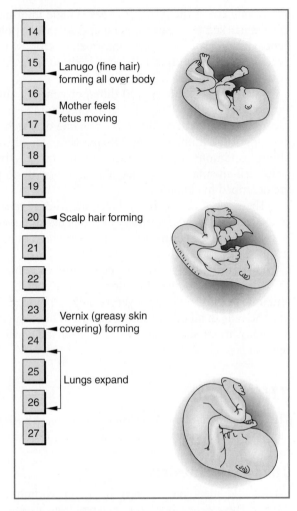

14

15 ◄ Lanugo (fine hair)
forming all over body

16 ◄ Mother feels
fetus moving

17

18

19

20 ◄ Scalp hair forming

21

22

23 ◄ Vernix (greasy skin
covering) forming

24

25] Lungs expand

26

27

Figure 5.8   Second trimester of fetal development.

The Second Trimester

Go to the Activities
and Applications
section in Chapter 5
of MyEducationLab
to watch the
video *Prenatal
Development,*
which captures the
remarkable changes
as a fertilized egg
transforms into
a newborn.

Months 4 through 6 of gestation are a time of growth and development. The fetus grows to about 15 inches and weighs about 2 lbs. 11 oz. (See Figure 5.8.) The fetus is active about half the time and the mother can sometimes feel the movement. The heartbeat, and sometimes even crying, can be heard with a stethoscope.

The Third Trimester

By the beginning of the third trimester, the fetus could survive a premature birth, but the potential for complications is high. The brain is rapidly developing, perhaps in part stimulated by movement, light, temperature changes, and sounds. Listening through the noises of the womb to the voices of her family, she may be learning the sounds of her family's language. After birth, the baby will be able to recognize stories read during this gestational period. The fetus gains body fat and grows quickly to fill the entire uterus. (See Figure 5.9.)

Thus the development of the human being is the predetermined work of the new cell formed by the egg and the sperm duplicating itself over and over. The genetic information encoded in the DNA tells each cell where to travel in the developing embryo and what sort of cell it should be.

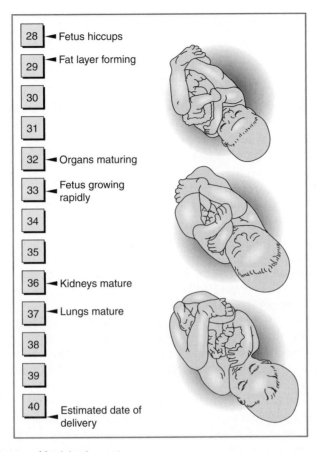

28	◄ Fetus hiccups
29	◄ Fat layer forming
30	
31	
32	◄ Organs maturing
33	◄ Fetus growing rapidly
34	
35	
36	◄ Kidneys mature
37	◄ Lungs mature
38	
39	
40	Estimated date of delivery

Figure 5.9　Third trimester of fetal development.

Over the course of 40 weeks, the human being grows from one cell into a complex, competent human being who is able to hear, react, and learn even while still inside the womb.

THE WOMB AS AN ENVIRONMENT FOR DEVELOPMENT

As Peter entered the center to begin his shift as a toddler teacher, he passed by Trina, who seemed to be taking a minute in the doorway after dropping off her daughter for child care. Peter was surprised to see her smoking, as just a few weeks earlier she had happily announced that she was pregnant with her second child. Peter greeted her, paused, and said, "Trina, I'm a little startled to see you smoking. Do you know about the effects of smoking during pregnancy?" This time it was Tina's turn to be surprised. "No, is it a problem?" she asked. "I know not to drink beer or anything, but smoking . . . What's the problem?"

We used to think of the womb as a safe place for the developing fetus with the placenta as a barrier that kept dangerous things outside of the womb. While the placenta is able to act as somewhat of a filter, we now know that the fetus can be compromised if the mother has inadequate nutrition, that the fetus may be affected by many substances that can harm it, that genetic and other congenital factors can cause the formation to go astray, that the birth process can be dangerous, and that maternal stress and anxiety may directly affect the baby's well-being. Without frightening expectant families, when infant-toddler teachers have ongoing contact with the parents, they can provide information and resources that promote the best outcome for every pregnancy.

Nutrition

Women with a good nutritional diet before pregnancy probably don't need to make big changes in what they eat in order to provide themselves and their baby with the protein, vitamins, and minerals they need. According to the American College of Obstetricians and Gynecologists (ACOG), pregnant women should increase their usual servings of a variety of foods from the four basic food groups to include the following:

- Four or more servings of fruits and vegetables for vitamins and minerals
- Four or more servings of whole-grain or enriched bread and cereal for energy
- Four or more servings of milk or milk products for calcium
- Three or more servings of meat, poultry, fish, eggs, nuts, dried beans, and peas for protein

Eating a well-balanced diet while pregnant will help keep mother and baby healthy. Most physicians agree that the Recommended Daily Allowances (RDAs), except those for iron, can be obtained through a proper diet (NWHIC, 2009).

There are some specific nutrients that pregnant women must be sure they are getting, either through diet or with supplements. Iron is needed in larger doses, especially in the later stages of pregnancy, and it is difficult to consume enough of it through food. This mineral is essential to the formation of healthy red blood cells and will help the mother avoid anemia and being susceptible to infections.

A woman's need for folic acid doubles during pregnancy. Folic acid has been shown to be important in preventing neural tube defects, such as spina bifida and anencephaly and is essential to the formation of red blood cells. Folic acid can be found in many foods, including kidney beans, leafy green vegetables, peas, and liver—or a doctor may prescribe a diet supplement.

Pregnant women need to increase their calcium and fluid intake. Pregnant and lactating adult women require an additional 40% of calcium a day (three extra servings of milk or dairy products). Almost all of the extra calcium goes into the baby's developing bones. Extra fluids, especially water, are needed to support pregnant women's increased blood volume. They should drink at least eight glasses of water each day to prevent dehydration and constipation (NWHIC, 2009).

Many cultures around the world have particular beliefs about nutrition during pregnancy. In India and many Asian countries, women are encouraged to "eat down"—eat less than before the pregnancy in order to keep the baby small and the delivery easier (Brems & Berg, 1988). Many Asian cultures also think generally about health, and particularly about food, in terms of being *hot* or *cold*—not literally hot or cold in how they are served, but as in adding heat or cold to the balance of the body's temperatures. Pregnancy is thought of adding heat, so cold foods are increased to provide balance (Nag, 1994). Young mothers in Latin America avoid hot foods during pregnancy but consume them in the postpartum period as a way of reestablishing heat lost in childbirth (Taylor, Ko, & Pan, 1999). Some cultures believe specific foods have specific effects on pregnancy. The Beng tribespeople in Africa avoid eating large bananas because they would create a fat baby, meat from the striped antelope because it would create striped or patchy skin, and boiled yams because they would make for a difficult delivery (Gottlieb, 2000). Middle Eastern Muslim customs include ensuring that the newly married woman eats foods that are rich in iron to ensure the baby is well nourished. These include a molasses-like grape drink and organ meats (Delaney, 2000). An aboriginal group in Australia's desert believes it is important to avoid meat from animals with sharp, pointed parts to avoid miscarriage (Pierroutsakos, 2000).

Cultural beliefs, habits, and access to healthy foods can all affect a woman's nutrition during pregnancy. Child care programs often keep pamphlets providing nutrition information in their parent information areas because they are helpful and of interest to pregnant women. It is also helpful to keep information handy on what may be harmful to the developing fetus. Women like Trina, at the beginning of this section, may not always know what to avoid during pregnancy.

Toxins and Teratogens

Many substances in the environment may threaten the positive development and cause disabling conditions in the fetus. Some of these conditions and their effect on development are described more thoroughly in chapter 15. In this section, there is information that infant-toddler teachers may want to share with expectant families. For instance, while you may be a little uncomfortable bringing up the use of alcohol or drugs with a parent, general information about substances in the environment that may be harmful to a fetus or threatening to a pregnancy is important information. Having this kind of information as part of ongoing parent education efforts is especially important because harm can occur before the mother even knows she's pregnant.

Because of the rapid division and replication of cells early in gestation, exposure to a toxic substance is likely to cause more damage the earlier it occurs in the pregnancy. Chronic alcohol use during pregnancy often has severe effects on the child, including mental retardation, growth deficiency, and facial abnormalities (Jacobson & Jacobson, 2002). More than 40,000 babies a year are born with alcohol-related damage (AAP, 2000a). Cocaine use appears to be related to spontaneous abortions, stillbirth, and premature births. As many as 1 million children have been born exposed to cocaine in the United States since the 1980s (Frank, Jacobs, Beeghly, Augustyn, Bellinger, & Cabral, 2002). Effects of cocaine—including low birth weight, poor growth, tremulousness, and high muscle tone—all contribute to babies who are difficult to comfort and challenging to engage in pleasant interactions (Chiriboga, 1991; Zuckerman, Frank, Hingson, Amaro, Levenson, & Kayne, 1989). The effects of drug exposure in utero continue throughout childhood. Teachers report that children exposed to drugs in utero are "easily frustrated, hyperactive, impulsive, disruptive, irritable, withdrawn, and have poor initiative and frequent tantrums" (Kim, Sugai, & Kim, 1999). Smoking in pregnancy accounts for an estimated 20% to 30% of low-birth-weight babies, up to 14% of preterm deliveries, and 10% of all infant deaths. Even apparently healthy, full-term babies of smokers have been found to be born with narrowed airways and curtailed lung function. Smoking in pregnancy can cause low birth weight, preterm birth, and even infant death (U.S. Department of Health and Human Services, 2008a). Some 15% to 30% of women in the United States smoke. Only about 30% of women who smoke stop during pregnancy; about 11% of women smoke during their pregnancy (CDC, 2004).

Exposure during pregnancy to environmental toxins such as lead, mercury, arsenic, cleaning products, and chemical solvents may all lead to miscarriage, premature birth, low birth weight, and developmental delays. Lead may be present in drinking water through old lead plumbing pipes. Mercury is stored in the fatty tissue of most fish. Arsenic exposure may occur through industrial workplaces and cleaning products and solvents often used in the home (Perera, Illman, Kinney, Whyatt, Kelvin, & Shepard, 2002).

Pesticides pose similar hazards to the fetus, although unless women are in agricultural areas the risk is not great. Recently, though, health care providers have voiced concerns about insect repellents containing DEET. Given the dangers of West Nile virus or Lyme disease, it is suggested that a pregnant woman use small amounts of insect repellent on her clothing, socks, and shoes and that she wear gloves when applying it (OTIS, 2005).

Child care providers may want to keep informative brochures on hand to help expectant families be aware of substances that could be harmful to their unborn child. Such materials can often be obtained from the March of Dimes or the local public health agency. A program's nurse consultant could be very helpful in obtaining these materials.

Structural/Metabolic Birth Defects and Maternal Infections

Of course, many prenatal problems are not anticipated. Sometimes, for reasons we do not yet understand, malformations occur during gestation. Missing chromosomes, abnormal genes carried by one or both parents, and inaccurate migrations of cells can cause a variety of malformations in the fetus. Cleft palate may be caused by a combination of these factors. Metabolic disorders (1 in 3,500 babies) such as Tay-Sachs or phenylketonuria (PKU) are generally genetic diseases and can be harmful or even fatal.

The term TORCH syndrome—an acronym for Toxoplasmosis, Other agents, Rubella, Cytomegalovirus, and Herpes simplex—refers to a set of maternal infections that can cause harm to a fetus. When maternal infections such as rubella (rare, due to vaccinations) and cytomegalovirus (3,000 to 4,000 babies a year) occur early in the pregnancy, it may result in mental retardation, blindness, or deafness. Sexually transmitted diseases (1 in 2,000 babies) may result in stillbirth, newborn death, or bone defects (MOD, 2009e).

Prenatal Testing

Child care providers are increasingly likely to serve infants and toddlers who are medically complex or have disabilities. Understanding both the normal progression of gestation and birth, and the difficulties that can occur in the process, will help you be a resource and support to expectant and new parents.

Many problems that occur during gestation can be diagnosed through prenatal testing. Doctors are able to test for various conditions as well as the general well-being of the fetus through a variety of methods, from simple tests of the mother's blood to actually inserting a needle into the amniotic sac and removing fluid. The three-dimensional, moving images of the fetus available through ultrasound are so fascinating, that parents sometimes keep the still photographs or videos as their first pictures of their baby.

There is a short description of the most common prenatal tests in Table 5.1. Nearly every pregnant woman hears her baby's heartbeat through the Doppler device during regular prenatal

Table 5.1 Types of prenatal testing

Prenatal Test	Purpose	Performed at
Doppler device	Ultrasound to hear fetal heartbeat	6 weeks to birth
Ultrasound	High-frequency sound waves to provide live-action picture of fetus, track growth and development	5 weeks to birth
Chorionic villus sampling (CVS)	Needle sampling to test for genetic disorders	10.5 to 13 weeks
Magnetic resonance imaging (MRI)	Creates images of soft tissue such as the brain	12 weeks to birth
Fetal echocardiography	Detailed ultrasound for babies at high risk for heart problems	14 weeks to birth
Alpha fetoprotein blood tests (AFP)	Screens mother's blood for alpha fetoprotein assessing risk of Down syndrome, neural tube defects	15 to 18 weeks
Amniocentesis	Tests amniotic fluid for chromosomal disorders	16 to 18 weeks

Source: From *Windows on the Womb,* by Lauren Aguirre. Available at the Web site of Life's Greatest Miracle (http://www.pbs.org/wgbh/nova/miracle/windows.html).

checkups. Medical offices are also sometimes using ultrasound to create a visual image of the developing fetus.

THE MOTHER'S EXPERIENCE AS AN ENVIRONMENT

Luisa came in at the end of the day to pick up her 2-year-old daughter, Anna. Harriet, Anna's teacher, commented on how tired she looked. "It's been hard just being a mom and working," Luisa said, "but being pregnant too—I'm so tired. I have to tell you, though, this morning I was just dragging, but you were so happy to see Anna, and I felt like you cared for me . . . it made my whole day better!"

Sometimes one moment of friendliness or kindness can completely change your attitude. You actually *feel* differently. That is because attitude and feelings have a chemical component. The experience of fear increases the presence of fear-fighting hormones such as cortisone; pleasurable experiences increase serotonin. If emotions are translated into hormonal activity, and hormones can cross the placenta and enter the fetal bloodstream, it is easy to understand that the mother's emotional experience is part of the baby's environment.

Maternal Stress, Anxiety, and Other Factors

Anxiety

Pregnancy can be a joyful time if a family is stable and financially secure, has a good support system, and wants the child. When any of these components are missing—and sometimes even when they are all present—pregnant women can experience stress and anxiety. When the mother is anxious, the baby's heart rate may increase, less blood flows to the uterus, and the result is a baby with decreased birth weight. When a mother has high levels of stress hormones such as cortisol in her bloodstream, the baby is likely to have low birth weight, a small head and poor brain development, and low **APGAR** ratings in the minutes after birth. Certainly home visitors in programs such as Early Head Start need to be aware of the impact of maternal stress on the developing fetus. Child care providers would do well to attend to a mother's reports of stress and anxiety as well, providing information and emotional support as they are able.

APGAR
Scoring system of a newborn's well-being in the areas of activity (muscle tone), pulse, grimace (reactivity to irritation), appearance (skin color), and respiration.

Depression

Some situations during pregnancy are not well known but can be dangerous to the mother and the fetus. Although postpartum depression is discussed in detail in chapter 6, the less well-known condition of prenatal depression is described here because of its potential effects on the baby. Prenatal depression may be very difficult, even for professionals, to diagnose because physical symptoms of pregnancy are so similar to symptoms of depression; poor appetite, fatigue, difficulty sleeping, and mood swings are certainly common to both depression and pregnancy (Matthey, Barnett, Ungerer, & Waters, 2000). Home visitors, child care providers, and health providers should pay particular attention to pregnant women who speak of feeling flat and hopeless. Depression during pregnancy is a strong predictor of postpartum depression. Women who are depressed during pregnancy should be referred for mental health evaluations and counseling.

Domestic Violence

An even harder issue to think about during pregnancy is domestic violence and its impact on the fetus. Although this area is not well researched, the Centers for Disease Control and

Prevention (CDC) report that domestic violence occurs in up to 8% of all pregnancies of women giving birth to live children. Various studies, with different population groups, report as many as 36% of pregnant women experiencing domestic violence (Canterino, VanHorn, Harrigan, Ananth, & Vintzileos, 1999). The National Center for Chronic Disease Prevention and Health Promotion (CDC, 2006) warns that in addition to the immediate dangers, the presence of domestic violence during a pregnancy may result in:

- Stress for the mother, with health implications for the baby
- Delays in seeking prenatal care, with health implications for the baby
- Unhappiness with being pregnant, with implications for the relationship between the mother and the child

Home visitors for Early Head Start may deal with these issues more directly than child care providers. However, child development and education programs could provide staff training on domestic violence, know the community resources, provide parent information brochures, and have a plan in place for helping move a woman and her children to safety if necessary.

Simply reading about some of these issues may feel heavy and difficult. It may seem far out of the realm of working in a pleasant child development and education program and taking care of babies. Most teachers will never deal with these issues with pregnant mothers. Nonetheless, this is good information to tuck away. Simply being aware of these issues, knowing your community resources, and keeping information available to parents could make a significant difference in the lives of children and their families.

Pregnancy is such a natural part of life that it's easy to take it for granted. Reading through all the potential dangers can be a little distressing, especially if you are of childbearing age yourself. So, it is important to remember that most pregnancies proceed without alarm and result in wonderful, healthy, and amazingly capable newborns.

THE NEWBORN

The evidence that very young infants are active learners is compelling. They are born able to find the nipple and suck, thanks to inborn reflexes. They like to look at human faces and hear human voices. They use facial expressions that adults can easily understand, even though they have never seen their own faces. Newborns are ready to learn and ready to engage in relationships.

The first days and weeks after birth are a time of great adjustment for the new infant and the family, especially the mother. The baby is adjusting to life outside the womb, managing breathing, eating, digestion, elimination, and temperature regulation. The newborn infant is experiencing an array of new sensory experiences—touch, sound, light, odors, and tastes. The newborn can see about 8 to 12 inches and is most interested in human faces and human voices.

Adults help the newborn manage these sensations by reading their facial expressions, cries, and gestures to help determine what the infant needs. Adults help the baby learn to coordinate swallowing and sucking, keep diapers clean, and stay comfortably warm. Adults help the newborn fall asleep and maintain short periods of being awake and alert. During this time, mothers are going through hormonal changes as their bodies adjust to a postpregnancy condition. Mother and child may both be discovering the fine points of breast-feeding. Newborns may sleep for very short periods, needing to eat every few hours, so mothers are likely to be extremely fatigued during this postpartum stage.

At 6 weeks, just as mother and infant are each beginning to get their bearings, many mothers have to return to work. The baby may not have sleep patterns established yet. Breast-feeding babies may have little experience with the bottle and their mothers may have difficulty expressing enough milk to send to child care. Babies often go through a growth spurt at 6 weeks, eating frequently and stimulating the production of more milk in the mother. Teachers need to be aware of how vulnerable these very young infants are when they enter group care.

Postnatal Brain Development

The food that is good for the heart is likely to be good for the brain. (Hippocrates)

The first 3 months of life are sometimes referred to as the fourth trimester of gestation. Human babies are born after 9 months in the womb but they still have significant developmental tasks before them. Although the brain has been growing and becoming more complex, at birth it is only 25% of its adult weight. The lower parts of the brain (the spinal cord and cortex) are well developed but the higher levels of the brain are quite immature. The lower brain then controls much of the newborn's activity through reflexes.

The newborn brain has all of its neurons, but there are few connections among them in the cortex, the higher level of the brain. Over the course of the first year, these synaptic connections will begin to form at an astounding rate peaking at 2 million per second (ZERO TO THREE, 2009). Adults protect the newborn brain by maintaining a quiet and calm environment and being reponsive to the baby's needs. The messages the baby receives and processes must be given in ways the baby can understand. Touch and language are two important ways adults communicate with newborns.

Touch

Touch is one of the most powerful sensory experiences for a young infant. In fact, Bruce Perry has said in conference presentations that touch is vital to an infant's ability to grow and develop: "Biologically, it is as critical for a baby to be touched and held as it is to be fed." Very young infants benefit from beng held and carried much of the time they are awake. Teachers and home caregivers may want to use a commercially available infant carrier such as a Snuggly to keep the young infant against their own body while keeping hands free to be with other children.

Infants use touch to learn about the world; sucking on objects, feeling them with their hands, and kicking at them with their feet. They respond with strong cries to physical discomforts such as hunger or wet diapers and are comforted by being held close to their caregiver's body or snug swaddling.

Language

Long before infants are able to utter a single word, they are learning language through their early experiences of listening to the language around them. In order to acquire a specific language, the infant brain has to develop a structure that emphasizes the distinctive sounds in the child's own language and ignores other sounds. A revealing long-term observational study of infants and toddlers showed that children learn the language culture of their families. For example, some families' verbalizations to their children were composed of 80% negative comments. By age 3, these families' children's language was composed of about 80% negative comments to their parents and peers. Children also learn to talk about as much as their families talk. Children with the best verbal skills and highest intelligence scores were active partners in eliciting conversations with their parents and the parents were responsive, used a diverse vocabulary, had a positive tone, talked about the relationship between things and events, and often asked their children to do things rather than telling them what to do (Hart & Risley, 1995). Language learning however, is a resilient process, meaning that even under adverse circumstances children learn some communication strategies (Shonkoff & Phillips, 2000).

Developmental Milestones of the Newborn

In the first weeks of life, the newborn will move his arms and legs in small jerking movements or in wide flailing movements, but none of these actions appear to be intentional. Most babies will move their hands near their face and those who sucked their thumbs in the womb may recover that skill. The newborn keeps his hands fisted and will hold an assymetrical posture on his back, with one arm down to his side and the other raised near his head.

His hearing is good and, as described, he will recognize his mother's voice and the sound of her language. He prefers to hear familiar voices and to look at human faces. Most of his actions, including rooting for the nipple, moving his head from side to side, and grasping his daddy's finger, are actually reflexes. If he is lifted into an adult's arms, his head will fall backward because he does not have control of his head, neck, or trunk.

In these first weeks, the infant depends entirely on responsive adults to help him regulate or manage his reactions to hunger, fatigue, and other discomfort. He needs help in learning how to suck and swallow and to burp up air from his tummy. He may need help to move from waking to sleeping, from sleeping to waking, and from crying to calm. Teachers and home caregivers who care for these very young infants will still be helping with these basic tasks of regulation throughout the day.

As the baby reaches 4 months, he will use his arms to raise his head and chest when lying on his stomach. He can bring his hands together to his mouth and use his hands to hold and shake lightweight toys. He will recognize familiar people and grace them with a smile. His vision is improving and he may recognize his family at a small distance. He is likely to watch faces intently and enjoy playing with people.

At 4 months, infants are likely to be much better regulated and easier to serve in group care. They are likely to be accomplished at bottle feeding, interested in others, and communicating their needs clearly. They are able to play alone for very short periods of time and may take longer naps. Mothers may be physically and emotionally better able to return to work.

UNIQUE BEGINNINGS

premature
Born less than 36 weeks gestation.

Not all babies remain in the womb for the full gestation of 40 weeks. Infants born before 37 weeks gestation are considered **premature**. There are many possible causes and outcomes of prematurity. However, medical intervention has improved so much that

> more than 90% of premature babies who weigh 800 grams or more (a little less than 2 pounds) survive. Those who weigh more than 500 grams (a little more than 1 pound) have a 40% to 50% chance of survival, although their chances of complications are greater. (KidsHealth, 2009)

Infants closer to full term and weighing more usually have better outcomes.

The cause of a premature birth is not aways known, but common causes include external threats to maternal and fetal health including the mother's use of drugs, alcohol consumption, cigarette smoking, poor nutrition and low weight gain, obesity, physical stress, and lack of prenatal health care. Medical conditions that can cause premature birth include maternal hormone imbalances, problems with the uterus, or various illnesses including high blood pressure and diabetes. Women carrying twins or triplets are also at increased risk for premature birth (KidsHealth, 2009; MOD, 2009c). Premature births constitute about 12.5% of all births in the United States. About 25% of the more than half a million premature births are either induced or delivered by Caesarean (MOD, 2009d).

Babies born prematurely are at risk for a variety of problems. The least mature babies, those born at less than 28 weeks gestation, need intensive medical intervention in specialized hospital wards called neonatal intensive care units (NICU). They may stay in the hospital for many months, even beyond the original due date, as they learn to suck, swallow, and breathe on their own. These infants are at high risk for significantly disabling conditions such as cerebral palsy and serious learning and communication disorders.

All premature infants are at risk for these issues:

Respiratory Distress Syndrome **(RDS)** Babies born before 34 weeks gestation do not produce the protein **surfactant** which helps the air sacs in the lungs stay open. Without the surfactant, these babies struggle to breathe. Now, mothers who are in premature labor are given medication to begin the production of surfactant in the baby. Artificial surfactant is then administered directly to the baby. Infants with RDS usually also require additional oxygen and, sometimes, a ventilator for breathing.

Apnea Apnea is a condition in which the brain is too immature to regulate breathing and the infant stops breathing. Most babies born at less than 30 weeks experience apnea. Babies may wear an apnea monitor in the hospital and at home. They may be given medication or use a device that blows a steady stream of air into their nostrils to keep the airways open.

Intraventricular Hemorrage **(IVH)** IVH occurs most often in infants born before 32 weeks gestation. This bleeding in the brain may resolve without damage or may cause severe damage resulting in cerebral palsy or other problems. IVH may be treated with medication or the insertion of a tube to relieve the buildup of fluid.

Retinopathy of Prematurity **(ROP)** ROP is the abnormal growth of blood vessels in the eye which can result in vision disorders or blindness. Severe cases can be treated with a laser.

Jaundice (Hyperbilirubinemia) Jaundice occurs when the liver is too immature to filter a waste product called bilirubin. Infants with jaundice are treated with special lights.

Chronic Lung Disease (Bronchopulmanory Displasia **[BPD])** BPD is a condition caused by extended use of oxygen which causes a buildup of fluid, scarring, and lung damage. These children continue to suffer from a chronic lung disease that resembles asthma.

The following chapters will describe development in each of the domains in detail. The 9 months from conception to birth and the first 3 months of life are certainly a time of enormous growth and development. The next 3 years are even more exciting!

surfactant
A substance produced in the lungs that coats and lubricates the air spaces of the lungs. It prevents the lungs from collapsing between breaths.

SUMMARY

The journey from conception to birth is both hazardous and wondrous. The child and her brain are constantly moving toward increasing complexity and ability—vulnerable to assault but responsive to loving care, good nutrition, and a healthy environment. Early experiences, even within the womb, can have lifelong effects. In the first 3 months of life, the brain continues its rapid growth and the infant is gaining some control of her body. She is also becoming a relationship partner.

The brain begins development within days of conception:

- Rapid cell division follows from the moment of conception.
- At 4 weeks, the neural groove appears, establishing the two cerebral hemispheres.
- Over the next weeks, thousands of neurons are generated, creating the forebrain, the midbrain, and the hindbrain.
- Neurons experience sensory information, transmitting that experience through an axon to dendrites on other neurons at a connection called a synapse.

myeducationlab

Go to MyEducationLab and complete the Building Teaching Skills and Dispositions exercise in Chapter 5.

- A human infant is born with over 100 billion neurons, twice the number he will have as an adult.
- Synaptic connections develop rapidly in the first 3 months of life

Early experiences create the structure of the brain:

- Experiences either reinforce the synapses of the brain or, through lack of use, cause them to be pruned.
- Touch, language, and responsive, loving care create strong, healthy circuits in the brain.
- In the first 3 months of life, infants begin to gain control of their head and trunk and to become relationship partners.
- Hormones associated with stress and violence change the structure of the brain, creating a brain that is attentive to danger but not to affection.

Fetal development is a time of tremendous growth and development:

- Fetal development is directed by the genetic information embedded in our DNA.
- The first trimester of gestation is marked by rapid cell division and differentiation as cells become skin cells, muscle cells, brain cells, and so forth. Internal organs and external features are formed.
- The second trimester is a period of growth and development. The mother can feel movement and, with a Doppler device, hear the baby's heartbeat.
- The third trimester is a period of rapid growth and the formation of synapses in the brain as the baby experiences movement, light, and sound.

Early experiences affect the fetus in the womb:

- Nutrition is key to healthy fetal development.
- Toxins from the environment are harmful to a fetus. These include tobacco smoke, alcohol, prescription and illegal drugs, and chemicals from common household and industrial products.
- Maternal experiences such as illness, anxiety, and domestic violence can affect the health of the fetus. Adults develop relationships with newborns through touch and language. Premature births constitute about 12.5% of all births in the United States.

Key Terms

APGAR   gestation   surfactant
genetic counseling   premature

REFLECTIONS AND RESOURCES FOR THE READER

Reflections

1. The emphasis on the impact of early experiences on brain development has changed some ways we think about being with infants. What would you try to be aware of in a baby's environment because of your knowledge of brain development?
2. The womb is not as safe a place as we once thought. What might you do as an infant-toddler teacher to support parents in having healthy pregnancies?

Observation and Application Opportunities

1. Visit an infant-toddler program. What, if any, information is available for parents on healthy pregnancies? What could be provided?
2. Reading the newspaper and popular magazines, can you find information that is readily available on having a healthy pregnancy?
3. Observe an infant-toddler program. In what ways are the environment and interactions supporting brain development? What would you change?

Supplementary Articles and Books to Read

Kump, T. (2008, December). Testing 1–2–3: The prenatal tests you may receive and what they mean. Available on the Web site of *Fit Pregnancy* magazine (http://www.fitpregnancy. com/yourpregnancy/89).

Nilsson, L., & Hamberger, L. (2003). *A child is born* (Rev. ed.). UK: Delta Publishing Co.

Stanford University Medical Center. (2007, July 30). Severe trauma affects kids' brain function, say researchers. *Science Daily*. Retrieved from http://www.sciencedaily.com/releases/2007/07/070726184910.htm

Interesting Links

http://www.parents.com/pregnancy/

Pregnancy   The links on this site provide a week-by-week description of prenatal development and information on a vast variety of other pregnancy topics.

http://www.pbs.org/wnet/brain/

The Secret Life of the Brain   This series of video clips and text is taken from a PBS television series on the brain. Features include a 3-D brain anatomy and episodes titled "The Baby's Brain" and "The Child's Brain."

http://www.pbs.org/wgbh/nova/miracle/program.html

Life's Greatest Miracle   This film originally aired on the PBS series *Nova* and is available for viewing online. It shows the development of a fetus from the moment of conception through birth and provides a wonderful overview of the information covered in this chapter.

http://www.zerotothree.org/site/PageServer?pagename=key_brain

Brain   This site describes how the brain grows in the womb and through the first 3 years of life, with an emphasis on the importance of relationships. It is made available by ZERO TO THREE and includes links to articles and other resources.

myeducationlab

These and other web links are included in this chapter on MyEducationLab.

6

Attachment and Emotional Relationships

Nora had midwifed hundreds of births. As she watches babies, even in their first minutes out of the womb, she reacts to them as though she believes they have feelings. As the newborn cries out, feeling room temperature air and flailing in space, Nora is sure to say, "Oh, you don't like this, do you? You want to be warm."

THE UNIQUENESS OF EACH CHILD

We react this way because from the first moments of life, babies are using the language of emotional expression to communicate with us. They don't need to be taught that quivering lips, a grimacing face, and a cry are ways to communicate; they are born as effective emotional communicators. We watch them and believe that we can understand their feelings from their expressions. We want to help them be calm and comfortable.

Infants and toddlers babies use our responses to keep them feeling safe. The increasing competence is apparent in the child, but it develops through ongoing, meaningful, consistent relationships with adults.

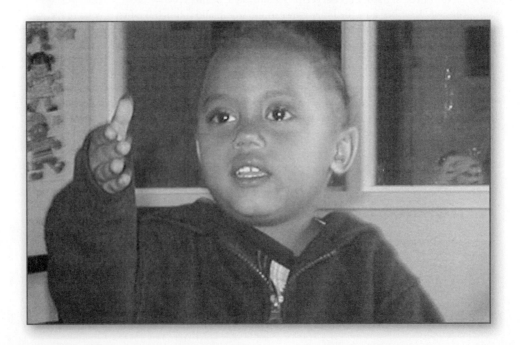

Capacities

Capacities refer to children's innate or biological potential and abilities. "Infants are born highly vulnerable and somewhat competent," said Ron Lally at a 2000 conference (Head Start Child Development Institute). "And over the next few years, the balance changes and they become much less vulnerable and highly competent." Using their inborn abilities to engage with others through nonverbal communication, infants move quickly toward remarkable competency in emotional development. The significant capacities and accomplishments of emotional development are:

- Learning to regulate one's reaction to the environment
- Learning to express emotions and understand the expression of emotions
- Developing an attachment relationship with a caring adult
- Developing a firm sense of self

Infants demonstrate an increasing control over their own reactions, an increasing ability to understand and communicate with others, the development of a deep and meaningful relationship with others, and, through these accomplishments, the development of a coherent sense of oneself as a person. As we explore the aspects of early emotional development, the emphasis on the child's emotional capacities developing within close and secure personal relationships will be clear.

> At 3 months, Henry can't pull his eyes away from his mother's face. She can't pull hers away from him. They gaze at each other with love, sharing little smiles, adjusting to each other's moments of attention and distraction. When Henry becomes hungry and begins making quiet crying noises and sucking on his fist, his mother picks him up, holds him against her shoulder, murmuring, "Are you hungry, little buddy? How about some milk?"

In the moments following birth, as the baby takes his first breath, he lets out a cry. We wait for the cry. We listen for it. It is the sign of health, life, and vitality. It is the infant's first moment of reaction to the world, and is followed quickly by an adult swaddling him in a warm blanket, or laying him on his mother's chest—acts of calming and soothing, acts of regulation.

Regulation is the process that allows the baby to manage sensory and emotional experiences as well as develop interest in the world. The newborn must suddenly contend with lights, sounds, temperatures, textures, touches, tastes, and smells—all of which are very different from the protected environment of the womb. If the immature central nervous system reacted to each piece of sensory information without any discrimination as to importance or any ability to filter the sensations, the world would be confusing and overwhelming. Somehow, the baby needs to regulate his reactions and react only to the information most pertinent for survival.

regulation
The ability to manage one's physical and emotional reactions to internal sensations or events in the environment.

> Your emotions affect every cell in your body. Mind and body, mental and physical, are intertwined. (Frank A. Clark)

In order to survive life outside of the womb, the baby must learn to regulate breathing, body temperature, eating and digestion, elimination, waking, and sleeping—and, later, to regulate his own reactions to both physical and emotional experiences of life. Emotional regulation describes the activities used by the baby (gaze aversion, finger sucking) or by the adult (soothing, rocking, swaddling) to reduce the baby's distress and help him maintain a calm, alert level of arousal (Rothbart & Derryberry, 1981). Greenspan and Greenspan (1994) write about babies having a balance between a regulatory system (physical and emotional aspects that help them stay calm and attentive) and a system of interest in the world (using one's senses to learn from experiences in the world). They describe these two systems as being highly intertwined—as the baby's ability to be calm and attentive allows him to get sensory information from the world, while at the same time the baby is able to use sensory information from the world to become and remain calm and interested. For example, a mother's quiet voice and gentle rocking or a father's heartbeat and firm hands will calm a crying baby and help him reach a quiet, alert state (Greenspan & Greenspan, 1994).

Observation Invitation 6.1 shows a slightly premature baby trying to fall asleep, but failing at his attempts to soothe and regulate himself. Swaddling, holding him close, and helping him use a pacifier eventually relaxes him into sleep.

Hierarchy of Human Organization

To varying degrees, the very young infant must struggle with the immaturity of her own neurological system, her digestive tract, and her relatively unused muscles. The high level of relationship between systems regarding regulation is well illustrated by Als's (Als, Lester, Tronick, & Brazelton, 1982) image of the hierarchy of human behavioral systems, seen in Figure 6.1. In working with premature babies, Als observed that stable functioning begins with the *autonomic system*: regulating body temperature, digestion, and breathing. If that system is not regulated, no other system will work smoothly. If the autonomic system is stable, the *motor system* involving muscle tone, the ability to resist gravity, and the capacity for graceful, controlled movement may function well. The next system in the hierarchy is the *state of alertness system,* regulating whether the infant can achieve a deep restful sleep, an active REM sleep, and quiet and active alert states.

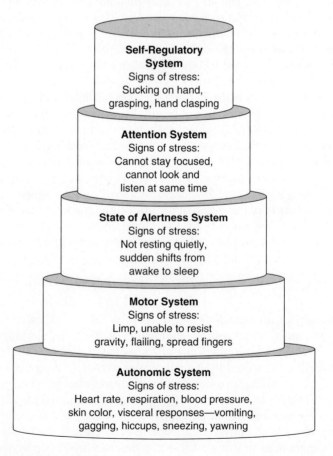

Figure 6.1   Hierarchy of behavioral organization.
Source: Based on Als, Lester, Tronick, and Brazelton (1982).

A well-regulated state system allows the baby's *attention system* to focus and attend to information, to engage in excitement, to calm and rest—and to move between these states without too much difficulty. At the top of the hierarchy is the *self-regulatory system*.

It is important that adults who interact with infants understand these systems. Als also described how babies lose their sense of organization system by system—first losing their ability to self-comfort, then crying or demonstrating other disorganized states of alertness, then exhibiting movements that are jerky and disorganized, and finally losing the organization of their autonomic system by hiccupping, drooling, or gasping for breath. A sensitive adult is more likely to respond when the infant is struggling with self-comforting or showing distress through a fussy state of alertness rather than waiting until the baby has completely fallen apart. The sensitive teacher can quickly help the mildly disorganized baby to recover, calm, and attend to the world.

Observation Invitation 6.1: Emotional Development

Maddox is very tired and trying to sleep. He tries to calm himself with his fingers but can't keep them in his mouth. He yawns, getting quietly but increasingly more distressed. Swaddling, a pacifier, and holding him close help but he startles awake, his fingers awkwardly splayed. He finally settles into a deep sleep, holding his care teacher's finger. How else could you comfort Maddox?

Regulation and Relationships

Emphasizing the role of relationships in emotional development, Robinson and Acevedo (2001) suggest that these moments of distress actually provide parents with opportunities to experience and understand the child's emotional cues. She suggests that infants who opt too quickly for self-comforting strategies may reduce the opportunities for adults to provide help and become their partners in understanding the world. Also, "not signaling adults for help may result in strategies such as aversion or **dissociation** when fear is aroused" (Robinson & Acevedo, 2001).

A recent study relating early emotional regulation to secure attachment suggested that "some infants may be naturally better able to regulate emotions than others" (Braungart-Rieker, Garwood, Powers, & Wang, 2001), perhaps as a result of temperamental style. However, it is possible that a teacher who sensitively meets an infant's emotional needs is helping the baby develop regulation skills, while a disinterested or rejecting teacher may leave the infant struggling to find ways to self-comfort (Braungart-Rieker et al., 2001). Braungart-Rieker and colleagues suggest that at 4 months, some infants who are faced with a less sensitive mother may already be suppressing their emotions and highly regulating their own reactions, developing coping styles that derive in part from their temperament. Other infants faced with similarly less sensitive mothers respond differently, becoming highly emotionally reactive—perhaps reflecting (1) more sensitive temperaments unable to tolerate distress and (2) coping styles aimed at drawing in less responsive mothers.

The adult partner, whether parent or teacher, helps the infant regulate her physical condition by ensuring that the baby is warm, dry, well fed, rested, and in a comfortable position. If a baby is crying, you can soothe the baby by holding her upright against your shoulder, rocking, swaddling, or moving into another room or outdoors. When the baby is calm and awake, you can provide opportunities and support for the infant to focus her attention on interesting things.

Attributes

Attributes are characteristics of a child that make that child unique. Temperament is an attribute. The following example illustrates how two children might react to a parent saying good-bye.

> On entering the toddler room in the morning, Kevin sobs as though his heart is broken as his father leaves. After a moment of comforting, and full of energy, he enthusiastically plays with the rocking horse, leaps off, and runs to the easel. Faron enters the room quietly, kisses her mother good-bye, and settles into the housekeeping area. Terra clings to her mother's skirt, preventing her from leaving in the morning. When her mother finally is able to leave, Terra hangs back and watches the other children play while she sucks her thumb and holds her teddy bear.

Temperament

Each of these children is going through the experience of being welcomed into the child development and education program and separating from his or her parents. However, each of these children brings a very different behavioral style and a very different way of expressing emotion to the experience. Although adult behavior has enormous effect on young children, in a transactional, relationship-based, and bioecological model of development, infants and toddlers bring their own characteristics to expressing emotions and being in relationships.

Since the pioneering work of Thomas, Chess, Birch, Hertzig, and Korn (1963), these differences have been known as temperament, or **temperament style.** Early temperament research looked at the dynamic interaction between characteristics that were inherent to the child and characteristics of the child's environment. Thomas and colleagues identified nine temperament traits, defined in Figure 6.2: activity level, biological rhythms, approach/withdrawal, adaptability, intensity of reaction, mood, persistence, distractibility, and sensitivity. In children, these traits seem to appear in groupings that the researchers called *temperament*

- *Activity level:* Amount of physical movement
- *Biological rhythms:* Regularity of eating, sleeping, elimination
- *Approach/withdrawal:* Comfort in new situations
- *Mood:* Amount of time in pleasant, cheerful mood as opposed to fussing, crying, or resisting others
- *Intensity of reaction:* Energy level of emotional expressions
- *Sensitivity:* Response to sensory information, including light, sounds, textures, smells, tastes
- *Adaptability:* Ability to manage changes in routine or recover from being upset
- *Distractibility:* How easily the child's attention is distracted
- *Persistence:* How long a child will stay with a difficult activity before giving up

Figure 6.2   Temperament traits.
Source: Based on Thomas, Chess, Birch, Hertzig, and Korn (1963).

types: easy, difficult, and slow-to-warm-up. The "easy" or flexible child tends to have regular biological rhythms (eating, sleeping, and eliminating on a predictable schedule), a positive mood, easy adaptation to new experiences, moderate emotional reactions, and low sensitivity to sensory stimulation. The "slow-to-warm-up" or shy child tends to withdraw from new situations and adapt to them slowly. The "difficult" or feisty child is very active, emotional expressions are intense, and attention is easily distracted. These children are very sensitive to changes in light or sound; they tend to eat and sleep without regular patterns; and their moods can change frequently (Thomas et al., 1963; Thomas & Chess, 1977).

Temperament is an aspect of development that resonates for most people. We recognize these traits in ourselves and see them as the source of conflict or ease in our relationships. (It's annoying when someone plays music louder than you like it, or comfortable when the lighting in a room is just as you like it.) However, some temperament traits may be more central than others to successful development. The trait of intensity of reaction, sometimes called emotional reactivity or vitality, combined with the abilities for self-regulation is one trait that may have enormous impact on a child's life (Rothbart, 1989). Emotional vitality or reactivity "can be defined as the lively expression of emotion that is shared with others" (Robinson & Acevedo, 2001). Infants with high emotional vitality are more expressive and more likely to recruit an adult's involvement into whatever interests them. These moments of interaction provide opportunities for babies to develop a relationship with the adult during which they may think, "I know you are interested in me—and you will help me when I need it. I know how to call on you for help."

In a relationship-based model, we think about the effect of the child's temperament on the adult and on the relationship. In their initial work on temperament, Thomas and Chess proposed the idea of "goodness of fit" between child and parents. They proposed that no one temperament was any easier or better, nor that any one parenting style was really better. They proposed that the ease of the relationship between parent and child would, at least in part, depend on how well matched the parent and child were on certain temperamental traits. For example, the highly active and emotionally expressive child would have a goodness of fit with a parent who was also active and expressive. That same child might be difficult for a very quiet, subdued parent. Or, it might not be the parent's own personality but his expectations about children derived from his own history or culture that would apply to the goodness of fit.

While the concept of goodness of fit continues to be useful, we currently tend to think of it in a more complex way. For example, goodness of fit involves at least two individuals, each with their own biological capacities, experiences, beliefs, and expectations. Understanding that the perception of behavior is important begins to link the concepts of temperament and attachment.

DEVELOPMENT AND LEARNING THROUGH RELATIONSHIPS

Lyssa is playing on a blanket when the teacher, Tinnaka, walks past. Lyssa feels pleasure at seeing Tinnaka and smiles at her. Pleasure and happiness comprise Lyssa's feeling state. Lyssa's muscles and nervous system give her information about the smile on her own face and what her body feels like when she is feeling this happiness. To Lyssa, Tinnaka's smile looks somehow similar to the way her own smile feels and assures her about the accuracy of her emotional response to this experience. Tinnaka adds language to the experience by saying, "Lyssa, are you happy to see me? I'm sooo happy to see you today!" as she picks her up and snuggles her. Lyssa is learning that there is language that applies to this feeling state and that she can cause reactions in her environment. Lyssa's sense of self, in this moment, is of a well-loved, easily understood, and welcomed human being.

Every experience that a baby has occurs within a physical experience, a feeling state, and, generally, information from the environment that both inspires the moment and informs it. As memories of these experiences accumulate for the infant, he begins to develop a sense of himself, an internal picture of self, an identity: "This is me when I am happy and playing with my teacher—my body is active, my face is smiling, my teacher has smiling eyes, and her voice sounds like music." Developing an identity is a complex mixture of the baby's own temperament; physical, sensory, and processing abilities; and the physical, social, and emotional environment surrounding him.

In infancy research, the development of a sense of self is understood to occur during interactions with others, through moment-by-moment experiences of emotional communication. Babies learn about themselves as they learn about the feelings of others.

> *Children have never been very good at listening to their elders, but they have never failed to imitate them. (James Baldwin)*

self-fusion
The idea that very young infants do not know they exist as separate individuals from others.

Although some theorists believe that in early infancy babies exist in a state of **self-fusion**, not knowing that they are actually separate beings from others (Mahler, 1975), relationship-based theory points out that from the moment of birth, babies are experiencing themselves as separate beings contained in a boundary of skin. From the first moments, the experience of being held by another person is different from being swaddled in a crib; seeing your own hand and simultaneously feeling the motor information of the movement of that hand is a different experience from seeing another person's hand (Stern, 2000). As described in our chapter on cognitive development, Stern (2000) asserts that the infant's greatest task in emotional development is not learning that they are separate from others but learning to make connections with others.

Cultural Differences and Emotional Development

The two major elements of emotional development discussed in this chapter—emotional expression and attachment—must be considered within a cultural context. Cultural differences in emotional expression are sometimes stereotypical. We think of Italians as being highly expressive, using a full range of emotions, waving their hands, and telling whole stories with their facial expressions. We think of the British as being reserved and never expressing emotion. On the other hand, we talk about a universal set of facial expressions that babies use and seem to understand.

A number of studies suggest that infants around the world use the same facial expressions, with potentially the same meanings, in the same situation—but they may express emotion more or less quickly and more or less heartily. For example, when researchers recorded the reactions of American babies in Berkeley, Japanese babies in Fukushima, and Chinese babies in Beijing to a situation that evoked a variety of emotions, they found that all three groups used the same facial expressions, but with different intensities. Each group consisted of 24 11-month-old infants. They were each seated in a high chair, with their mother next to them, and a female researcher interacted with them for 10 minutes. She then restrained their wrists and held them immobile for up to 3 minutes, inducing frustration. Then, to elicit fear, she placed an animated gorilla head on a table near the baby. The head growled, its eyes lit up, and its lips moved. The experimenter moved the gorilla closer and closer to the baby, until the child cried for 7 seconds. The American and Japanese babies expressed positive and negative emotions with similar intensity, happy to interact at first, crying quickly when restrained or exposed to the gorilla. Chinese babies did not show significant negative feelings, as though they had already learned to mask their feelings (Camras, Oster, Campos, Campos, Ujiie, & Miyake, 1998).

Attachment studies around the world also reflect potential cultural differences. Traditionally, attachment is the close emotional bond between parents (or other adults) and the child, and is measured by how the baby reacts to a series of increasingly stressful separations from the parent. An attachment is deemed secure if the baby goes to the mother for comfort on reunion, as will be explained more fully later in this chapter. However, German babies are more likely to avoid the parent on reunion after a separation, which may be related to a greater emphasis on independence in infancy (Grossman, Grossman, Spangler, Suess, & Unzer, 1985). West African infants, who are always close to their highly responsive mothers and other nurturing women, never avoid but go immediately to their mothers on reunion (True, Pisani, & Oumar, 2001). Japanese infants, who are rarely left with strangers, become very anxious when separated from their mother and continue to be upset upon reunion (Miyake, Chen, & Campos, 1985).

A more thorough discussion of emotional expression and attachment, from an American perspective, follows.

Emotional Expression and Understanding

Emotional expression is the primary form of communication for very young children. Infants make themselves known, and know about others, primarily through emotional expression. Early studies of a baby's emotional expression and understanding reflect the old nature-versus-nurture argument. Some researchers felt that babies were born able to use a universally understandable set of facial expressions to demonstrate a few basic emotions, and that more complex emotions appeared in a predictable pattern over time (Izard & Malatesta, 1987). Others believed that emotional expression and understanding, inborn to some extent, were quickly learned through interactions with adults (Emde, 1998). Our current understanding of the development of emotional expression suggests that many elements are at play: innate reactions common to all humans, what is unique to the child physiologically (including temperament), and what is learned through actual interactions with parents and teachers in a particular culture (Camras, 1992).

Infancy

The innate reactions are seen during the first months of life, but babies are also learning through their interactions with others. Infants begin to respond to others with big, genuine social smiles and to anticipate how their favorite adults will behave. They learn to expect certain patterns of interaction and are surprised when things go differently. They will coo and smile at toys that respond contingently to their actions (Watson, 1972). Emotions become more specific as joy becomes different from contentment, and anger and sadness emerge as separate experiences from distress (Lewis, 1993). Active games such as "I'm going to get you!" followed by blowing on the baby's tummy can bring chortles at 4 months, especially when little variations maintain the sense of suspense and surprise.

In the period from about 4 months through 7 months, there is a shift in emotional development, as infants begin to demonstrate that they are "falling in love" (Greenspan & Greenspan,

1994). They will brighten, smile, and reach for the beloved adult when they see her. A parent or consistent care teacher gets the feeling that the baby recognizes her, enjoys her, and calms and feels safe when she is near.

At 9 to 12 months, babies go through a second shift in emotional development that Stern (2000) calls "the discovery of **intersubjectivity**—the knowledge that the baby's own thoughts and feelings can be known by others and that they can understand the thoughts and feelings of others. They begin to use the facial expressions and emotional tone of others as a way to interpret the meaning of events in their environment. This process, called **social referencing,** allows the baby to use a trusted adult to judge whether a stranger or a new experience is safe. The baby literally looks to the adult to see how to react. Although this visual checking in with an adult to clarify ambiguous events can be easily observed in everyday situations, researchers have found very creative ways to determine how babies use increasingly sophisticated strategies for social referencing. Klinnert (Emde, Butterfield, and Campos, 1986) investigated the idea of babies understanding that an adult's emotional expression had meaning tied to an object or an event. She created a smooth surface for a baby to crawl over, with the mother waiting on the other side. The middle of the surface, however, appeared to have a sudden drop-off; it was a "visual cliff." When the new crawler approached this apparent cliff edge, he would look to his mother for information. If she smiled and nodded reassuringly, the baby would continue crawling across the seemingly empty space. If she looked fearful, the baby would stay on his side of the "cliff" (Klinnert et al., 1986). (See Figure 6.3.)

Other researchers have shown that babies will watch a researcher's reactions to a toy, or to the contents of two boxes, and will willingly explore the objects that were targets of positive adult reactions and will avoid the objects that adults treated with disgust (Repacholi, 1998).

During this period, infants also use information from adults to learn which emotions can be expressed and how and when they can be expressed. These **emotional display rules** may be specific to a particular family or even a member of a family. One parent may encourage the child to experience the full range of human emotions. Another may be uncomfortable with displays of love and intimacy and react in very restrained ways in comforting or showing approval to their baby. Another family may be extremely uncomfortable with the expression of sadness or anger and the family may teach the child to minimize or avoid expression of these emotions (Gottman, Katz, & Hooven, 1997).

Infants are constantly watching the adults in their world for genuine expressions of emotion that appear to be congruent with the events that inspire them. In fact, when infants are taught to suppress negative emotions they may become anxious, they experience physiological hyperarousal, and they may store the negative emotion and the maladaptive response they develop in

---

intersubjectivity
A sense of sharing an experience between two people.

social referencing
The way a baby makes use of an older child or adult's signals to determine the safety of a situation.

myeducationlab

Go to the Activities and Applications section in Chapter 6 of MyEducationLab to watch the video *Social Referencing.* You will see a challenging example and then a positive example of social referencing.

emotional display rules
Culture-specific social rules about how and when to express certain emotions.

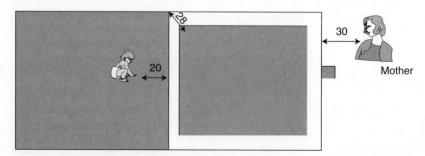

Figure 6.3   The visual cliff paradigm.
In the visual cliff study, an infant is seated on a table. In order to reach her mother, she must cross what appears to be a drop of more than 2 feet—although, in reality, the table is covered in a clear plastic. The mother either encourages the crossing with an inviting expression or discourages it with a terrified facial expression.
Source: Based on Klinnert, Emde, Butterfield, and Campos (1986).

their memory to be used in future, similar situations (Eisenberg, Cumberland, & Spinrad, 1998). For example, if a father is not comfortable with closeness in relationships, he may stiffen and feel awkward as his baby nuzzles in to his shoulder. The infant feels the rigid response, and, over time, learns that to be close to Dad requires being restrained. Because this is not an expectable human reaction, it may feel confusing to the baby and cause anxiety. However, most parents tend to model more positive emotions than negative emotions to their babies, and they facilitate more positive expressions from their babies and discourage negative expressions (Malatesta, Culver, Tesman, & Shepard, 1989). When children suffer abuse or are exposed to marital aggression, their emotional development can suffer. Children who suffer early experiences of abuse or neglect have difficulty even differentiating among emotional expressions (Pollak & Kistler, 2002). Crockenberg, Leerkes, and Lekka (2007) found that aggression among marital partners, especially if the infant is highly reactive, leads to infant emotional and physical withdrawal.

Cultural differences are evident as well in the emotional display rules that babies learn. Different cultures have different norms regarding emotional and social competence (Kitayama & Marcus, 2000). Our individualist, Western culture values assertiveness and independence. We associate inhibited behavior with shyness and isolation. However, the collectivist Chinese culture values interpersonal harmony that requires each individual to restrain personal expressions of emotions for the benefit of the group. Therefore, the more adept Western parent may encourage emotional displays while the more skilled Chinese parent is teaching her baby to inhibit emotional displays (Chen, Hastings, Rubin, Chen, Cen, & Stewart, 1998). Each parent is teaching her baby to win approval and be successful within her own culture.

Toddlers

The third major shift in emotional development occurs as the infant becomes a toddler, between 18 and 20 months. As symbolic thinking becomes established, children are able to use language to organize their thinking. They remember past events and form representations of repeated events that help them anticipate what future events might be like. This is particularly true of the representations they form of what it is like to be in a relationship.

The increased ability to symbolize is accompanied by a more fully developed sense of self. Children begin to recognize themselves in a mirror, use personal pronouns to refer to themselves, and identify themselves as boys or girls. They also begin to express self-conscious emotions such as guilt, shame, embarrassment, and empathy. They are also beginning to control their own behavior in the service of maintaining relationships.

The Attachment Relationship

There is probably no one concept that has been more influential in our field than that of attachment theory. A recent keyword search on Amazon.com for "attachment infancy" returned more than 13,000 book titles on the topic. Attachment theory has been used to explain how we relate to others in our world, from infancy through our adult lives, and it is a serious consideration in the study of child care and parenting (NICHD, 2003).

John Bowlby's Theory

The concept of attachment was introduced by Bowlby (1982). In a theory that described early development in terms of many active systems, Bowlby described an exploratory system that forwards the child's goal of learning about the world. However, the young, vulnerable child also has the goal of survival; and the attachment system motivates the child to stay close enough to an adult who is invested in their well being that the child feels a sense of safety and security. The exploratory and attachment systems thus operate as balance to each other, with infants using the **attachment relationship** as a secure base from which to explore. As they venture out to play and explore, they

myeducationlab

Go to the Activities and Applications section in Chapter 6 of MyEducationLab to watch the video *Self-Awareness*. See how a 12-month-old and a 15-month-old demonstrate self-awareness when looking at their images in a mirror.

attachment relationship
A relationship in which young children use their parent as a source of security when distressed or during exploration.

carefully maintain enough proximity to remain in visual contact with their attachment figure. In the current, casual use of the term *attachment,* we are often referring to feelings of love and affection. Attachment really addresses basic feelings of trust, safety, and security (Bowlby, 1982).

Bowlby described children as developing an internal representation, a constant mental image, of themselves and their relationships to others. A child notices every moment of interaction: each time his father picks him up and soothes him, each time his mother plays with him, each time his sister makes him laugh. If his moments of discomfort and distress elicit sensitive, helpful, soothing responses, he begins to develop an expectation of having his distress noticed, honored, and resolved. He learns that he can count on that one sensitive person to help him when he needs help and leave him feeling safe and secure.

During these moments of interaction, the baby is also learning how to regulate most effectively his own emotional expressions in order to maintain proximity to the mother, father, or teacher from whom he derives feelings of security. He will learn to match his attachment behaviors (touch, proximity, visual connection, signaling distress) to the responses of his attachment figure. If his father responds to a cry or smile, he will actively signal his father when he needs closeness. If his mother resists being touched, he will find ways to be close enough to her to feel safe, without touching her.

Mary Ainsworth's Work

In naturalistic studies of infants and their mothers, first in Baltimore and later in Africa, Mary Ainsworth began to notice patterns in the behavior of mothers toward their infants, and a consistent pattern of responsive behavior from the infants toward certain maternal behaviors. The behavioral goal of the baby at around 1 year of age seemed to be to maintain a feeling of safety and security. Physical proximity to the mother seemed to be the most effective way of achieving this. However, Ainsworth saw babies going about this task with three basic, but differing strategies, each of which related to the mother's usual pattern of being with the baby. These strategies were eventually described as three patterns of attachment: secure attachment, anxious-ambivalent attachment, and anxious-avoidant attachment (Ainsworth et al., 1978).

Most of the mothers Ainsworth watched were sensitive and responsive to their babies' feelings and communications and tended to have babies who experienced a **secure attachment** to them. When the baby was frightened or distressed, he would cry out, mother would pick him up or call to him from nearby, and the baby would be comforted by his mother, feel safe again, and be able to resume play and exploration.

Ainsworth also watched mothers who seemed to attend to or ignore their babies according to their own needs, rather than those of the baby. The baby's cues requesting closeness or distance were not even noticed, or were only occasionally noticed and responded to sensitively. On the other hand, the mother might shower the baby with kisses and attention in a moment when the baby had been quite contentedly playing alone. These babies, when frightened or distressed, might cry intensely, as though their world was ending, but when mother tries to pick them up, they arch their backs and refuse to be comforted. Ainsworth described these babies as having **anxious-ambivalent attachment.**

The third group of mothers seemed unable to respond to their babies in a loving way. They were likely either to ignore their babies' signals or to react angrily to them. These babies learned that the best way to regain a feeling of security was to stay near, or within sight of their mothers, without actually initiating any interaction. When these babies are distressed, they may be seen backing up across a room to sit near their mothers, but not facing them. Ainsworth called this pattern **anxious-avoidant attachment.**

The strange situation. Following her naturalistic studies, Ainsworth found a way to evoke attachment behavior from babies in a laboratory setting. She developed a research protocol called the "Strange Situation," in which babies are first given time to play and explore in a room with their mother or father, then the situation becomes increasingly stressful as a stranger enters, the parent

secure attachment Children are able to use their parent as a secure base for exploration and can be comforted by their parents when distressed.

anxious-ambivalent attachment Children have exaggerated preoccupation with their caregiver's attention but may both solicit and resist comforting when distressed.

anxious-avoidant attachment Children seem to ignore the presence of their caregiver and concentrate on play and exploration, but seem to be working at containing their distress.

leaves and returns, until finally the baby is momentarily alone in a room. The baby's behavior during the exploration and the increasing tension tell quite a bit about the attachment relationship. However, it is the behavior of the infant upon reunion with his mother that most clearly illustrates the attachment category of the child. Securely attached children run to their mothers and allow themselves to be comforted. Children with anxious-ambivalent attachment run to their mothers but resist being comforted. Children with anxious-avoidant attachments will appear to ignore the mother's return while scrupulously regaining proximity to the mother (Ainsworth et al., 1978).

Attachment Research in the Late 20th Century

Attachment theory writing and research exploded in the late 20th century. One aspect of Bowlby's early work generated particular interest. It was the idea that attachment behavior actually signified the mental representations the child held of relationships. If the child did indeed form a sort of mental template for understanding and even seeing relationships, all future encounters with people would be measured against the familiarity of this first relationship (Bretherton, 1985; Sroufe, 1990). Furthermore, because it is the only way an infant knows how to be with other people, the infant (or child or adult) may behave in ways that inspire the other person also to behave within the expectations of the attachment relationship.

For example, Sherri, a teacher, may have a history of secure relationships. In caring for little Ben, who has a history of anxious-ambivalent attachment, she responds to his distress by picking him up and comforting him. Ben, not trusting that this comforting will really be available when he needs it, does not trust this moment and arches away from her, crying harder. Sherri isn't avoiding contact with Ben, but her history of responsive relationships leads her to read his cues and put him back down, believing that is what he wants. Ben's idea that people are not necessarily there for you when you need them is reinforced by being put down when he is distressed. Ben's expectations and behavior essentially create behavior in other people that continually tell him that he is right to be ambivalent about his relationships with others.

As researchers continued to work with attachment theory and the strange situation categories, there were children whose behavior did not fit into the three groups, which were popularly referred to as "B" (secure attachment), "A" (anxious-avoidant attachment), and "C" (anxious-ambivalent attachment). These three categories, although they varied in their effectiveness as methods of healthy adaptation, each allowed the child ultimately to engage the teacher to provide enough care and attention for the child to feel secure. Main (Main & Cassidy, 1988) calls these the *organized* categories. However, not all attempts to elicit care work. Main and Cassidy (1988) introduced a fourth pattern—one in which the children couldn't seem to come up with or settle on a strategy to help them feel secure. They labeled this one "D" (disorganized attachment) (Main & Cassidy, 1988).

Children who demonstrated the disorganized pattern had parents whose behavior was violent, frightening, or frightened, whose own childhoods had been violent and frightening, or who had experienced an unresolved loss. These parents responded to their children's attachment cues in such confusing ways that these children simply could not come up with a strategy that would consistently work to give them a feeling of safety and security. There was no way for the baby to develop any feeling of control over a distressing situation. For example, the mother may ignore her baby's crying and at the same time ask for a kiss. Or maybe the mother would laugh when the baby is distressed. The mother may suddenly change her own affect with no apparent cue or change in the environment to inspire this shift. The mother of a baby using disorganized strategies might increase the baby's attention to attachment issues by expressing her own feelings of need and at the same time clearly signal the baby that she does not want to be approached. The conflicting messages leave the baby without any possible coherent strategies to adopt.

Attachment categories are not permanently fixed once set, but they are likely to stay consistent if the overall stability of the family remains the same. Studies of preschool children and 6-year-olds show high correlations with attachment categories at 12 and 18 months. The secure preschoolers tend to have positive peer relationships and are well regarded by their teachers, who see them as resilient and likely to be leaders. They are neither victims nor victimizers in relationships (Troy & Sroufe, 1987; Weinfield, Sroufe, Egeland, & Carlson, 2002). At 6 years old, secure children are open to a range of emotions and have ideas for actions that would alleviate difficult feelings. A secure 6-year-old is fluent in her conversations with her parents in use of language, addressing feelings, and introducing topics (Main, Kaplan, & Cassidy, 1985).

Avoidant infants tended to harass and victimize their peers in preschool and their teachers tended to reject them—as though children rejected by their mothers elicited rejection by others (Troy & Sroufe, 1987; Weinfield et al., 1999). At 6 years, children who were avoidant in infancy had very restricted conversations, with parents asking questions that led to "yes/no" answers. Topics focused on inanimate objects. Although they were not demonstrative of their own feelings, they could accurately ascribe feelings to pictures of children—however, they could not come up with ideas as to how the children might make their situations better (Main et al., 1985).

Children assessed as anxious-ambivalent at 12 months tend to be "babied" by their teachers, being treated as younger than they are, and they are often the victims of the anxious-avoidant bullies (Troy & Sroufe, 1987). At 6, they tended to welcome their parents with exaggerated affection but then turn away from them. Feelings dominated the conversation and they responded to the pictures of the children with ambivalence: "One described the pictured child as running after the parents but then shooting them" (Main & Goldwyn, 1994).

> *It is easier to build strong children than to repair broken men. (Frederick Douglass)*

Working Models of Attachment

Bretherton stresses that the mental models we hold of attachment relationships are "working" models. That means that if our caregiving or other intimate relationship circumstances change—or more importantly, if our understanding of our relationships changes—our mental models can change as well (Bretherton, 1985). As we note in the previous quote by Frederick Douglass, it is best if healthy working models are established in the beginning, but it is always possible to repair and rework our models of relationships.

Main, working with colleagues in Berkeley, has led the high interest in investigations of how the mother's working model of attachment relationships may be driving her own attachment behaviors and creating an intergenerational pattern of attachment (Main & Goldwyn, 1994).

Main developed the Adult Attachment Interview as a way of learning about the parent's own mental representation of attachment relationships. Parents are asked a series of questions to describe their relationships with each of their own parents, and for five adjectives or phrases to describe their relationship with parents. They are then asked to relate memories or incidents that would illustrate why they chose that adjective. Questions continue regarding which parent they had felt closer to and why, what happened when they were ill or when they were injured or upset, how they had responded if and when someone important to them had died, whether their parents had been threatening to them, or whether any of their experiences seemed like a setback in their development. They are asked why they think their parents behaved as they did and what their relationship with their parent is like now. They are repeatedly asked to describe and evaluate how they understand these early experiences to have affected them (Main, 2000; Main & Goldwyn, 1994).

The narrative material is then assessed on the content that was intentionally shared as well as for material of which the individual seems unaware, such as inconsistencies or incoherence. The three organized classifications are very similar to the three organized classifications of infant attachment. They are secure/autonomous, insecure/dismissing, and insecure/preoccupied. Individuals may also be classified as unresolved if they report attachment-related traumatic loss or abuse that has not been emotionally resolved.

Secure/autonomous adults express "clear valuing of attachment figures and attachment-related experiences, together with an apparent objectivity in the descriptions and evaluations of particular relationships" (Main, 2000, p. 1078). They may have had easy childhoods or difficult ones, but they have come to understand their parents' motivations and have achieved some level of compassion and forgiveness. They reflect on their own feelings and accept their role in current attachment relationships. They were parents of securely attached babies.

Parents of avoidant babies presented themselves as dismissing of the importance of attachment relationships. They deny the impact of early relationships, have difficulty recalling specific events, idealize early experiences ("by ignoring my hurts, my mother made me stronger"), and describe a history of rejection. Their answers are short and terse and often consist of "I don't remember" (Main, 2000, p. 1080).

Insecure/preoccupied adults are continually preoccupied with their own early relationships with their parents—much like their own insecure/ambivalent babies who are so preoccupied with keeping track of their mothers, they cannot settle their attention on play. Preoccupied adults ramble between past and present, relevant and irrelevant information, complaining and angry feelings. They get caught up in their answers, often contradicting themselves, and interviews often run over the allotted time (Main, 2000, p. 1080).

The Importance of Attachment Theory

Attachment theory has been a central point in our understanding of infant development and human relationships in the last 50 years. In many ways, it captures the elements of interaction, temperament, self-regulation strategies, and development. It has also become a fundamental tool in our efforts to improve the mental health and ultimate outcomes of infants and toddlers and their families.

Infants and toddlers rely on the adults in their lives to care for them, keep them safe, and support their development. Supporting emotional development includes helping babies learn to self-regulate, to express themselves emotionally and respond to the emotional expression of others, and to develop attachment relationships.

Impact of Maternal Depression

> Brooke has just given birth to her third child. She took a leave from her job, but is having trouble returning to it. She has always felt good about her life, her marriage, her children, and her work. Since this last birth, however, she can't seem to feel interested in anything. She is tired and bored. She can see her baby trying to have a relationship with her, but just can't respond the way she wants to.

In the last several years, postpartum depression has been recognized as a major element impeding a mother's ability to care for her new baby and as having lasting effects on the baby's abilities.

It is estimated that approximately 50% to 80% of all new mothers experience postpartum blues in the first weeks after giving birth. This usually includes a few days of mild feelings of sadness, fatigue, feeling overwhelmed, and tearfulness. In a survey of new mothers (Brown University, 2006), 19% of mothers reported moderate to severe depression. This may include debilitating symptoms of low mood, sleep and appetite changes, lack of pleasure in daily life, poor concentration, fatigue, irritability, feelings of worthlessness, despair, and thoughts about harming herself or her child. In addition, a very small number of women experience postpartum psychosis, delusions, agitation, paranoia, and, often, thoughts about suicide or infanticide (Clark & Fenichel, 2001). The Early Head Start (EHS) national research reports that as many as 52% of women enrolling in EHS were depressed. For 12% of women, that depression was chronic and lasted through their child's third birthday (EHSREP, 2006).

Although mothers suffering from postpartum psychosis are the ones we see on the news, the less dramatic postpartum depression is being recognized as a serious problem for the well-being of both mother and infant. Although maternal depression often occurs within a cluster of other risk factors such as low income, marital dissatisfaction, prior episodes of depression, mothers' negative perceptions of their neighborhoods, (Campbell, 1995; Cooper & Murray, 1998; Murray & Cooper, 1999; Christie-Mizell, Andre, Peralta, and Laske, 2008), it occurs in all socioeconomic groups. Recently, colic in the baby and maternal depression have been found to be related, but it is not known whether infant colic causes maternal depression or if depression leads to infant colic (Maxted, et al. 2005).

Maternal depression was found to have negative effects on babies as early as the neonatal period, suggesting that there may be effects from prenatal exposure to a biochemical imbalance in the mother's body. Babies of clinically depressed mothers were poorly regulated in their behavior, their physiology, and their biochemistry. Depressed mothers seem to offer one of two interactive styles. They withdraw, or they become very intrusive. Each of these styles has deleterious effects on the infant's ability to organize his state of arousal, to interact, and be responsive to the world (Field, 1998). This poor start in well-regulated interaction is related to children of depressed mothers having poorer cognitive outcomes and more behavior problems in the toddler and preschool years (Murray & Cooper, 1999).

Maternal depression is generally treatable, through both medication and therapeutic intervention (Cooper & Murray, 1998). Mothers of premature babies were less depressed two months after the child's discharge if they participated in a parent empowerment program (COPE) while the child was in the hospital (Melnyk, Crean, Fischbeck, & Fairbanks, 2008). The teacher, the family child care provider, and other infant and toddler professionals can be helpful in warmly accepting the depressed mother, understanding that her lack of vitality does not mean that she does not care about her baby or the child care experience. The infant and toddler professional can also give the infant some very different experiences of interactions, with good opportunities for sharing moments of pleasant, mutual interest. These experiences may buffer the effects on the baby of the mother's depression (Field, 1998).

CHILDREN WITH SPECIAL NEEDS

The emotional system is so basic to the human body that the responders for pleasure and pain exist in the same part of the brain that regulates breathing and heart rate (Damasio, 2003). This may explain why infants and toddlers with even the most significant, multiple disabilities still demonstrate a preference for being with their own family. However, while emotional experience is a common, even defining, aspect of our humanity, it is also the source of each person's completely unique sense of identity and unique relationships.

autism
A disorder that affects a child's ability to engage in social interactions and to communicate. Child may engage in repetitive behavior. Symptoms begin before the child is 3 years old.

bipolar disorder
A disorder of the brain that affects energy, mood, and behavior.

Because emotional development occurs within the brain, conditions that affect the brain may affect emotional development. **Autism** and **bipolar disorder** are two examples of biological aspects of the child that may result in poor emotional development. Autism, even in children of normal intelligence, is often characterized by an inability to understand that other people exist with their own point of view, feelings, and experiences (Gopnik et al., 1999). Bipolar disorder, an emotional illness characterized by severe, often out-of-control mood swings, has a biological basis and may be identified in infancy (Egeland, Weinfield, Bosquet, & Cheng, 2000). These biologically based issues may make it very difficult to develop a mutual, loving, healthy relationship between a child and even the most committed parent or teachers. David Howes (2006) writes that although it may be challenging to parent some children with disabilities, if parents receive support to be reflective and are emotionally tuned in to their children, they are likely to feel secure.

It is important to remember, however, that in the infant and toddler years, the child's emotional development must always be understood within the context of relationships. Adults are expected to provide safety, to see and respond accurately to communication cues, and to be sensitive and responsive. Even when infants or toddlers bring very real challenges such as biologically based emotional illness, it is important to promote parenting relationships that can help the child achieve the best possible development. Further information about the progression of emotional development and how adults can create strong relationships is available in a chart on pages 128–131 called Developmental Trends and Responsive Interactions.

PROGRAMS THAT ENHANCE EMOTIONAL DEVELOPMENT AND LEARNING

Infant Mental Health

As the fields of child development and psychology have developed an increased appreciation for the powerful lifetime effects of early relationships, a new branch of psychotherapy has also been created. In Michigan in the 1970s, Selma Fraiberg and her colleagues were also attending to the early relationships of babies and their parents. Fraiberg was a social worker and psychoanalyst who specialized in working with young children. Her work with infants and parents revealed many situations in which parents seemed unable to see their infants as human beings having their own experiences and reactions to the world. Instead of recognizing the message sent by the baby's expressions and actions, the parent attributes meaning and motivations to the baby that really generate from the parent's own life experiences (Fraiberg, 1996). For example, a woman who has been physically abused, first by her father and then by her husband, sees her baby son as physically threatening to her. A man who was never able to achieve a close relationship with his own depressed mother sees his baby daughter as rejecting him. A woman who was constantly criticized by her own mother as eating too much and being too fat feels that she cannot satisfy her baby's endless hunger—while feeding the baby less than 2 ounces every 4 hours.

STRATEGIES TO SUPPORT EMOTIONAL DEVELOPMENT AND LEARNING

1. Comfort young babies who are stressed or unhappy by swaddling, holding them close to you, rocking them, and speaking or singing quietly.

2. Help young babies learn to regulate themselves by letting them suck on their hands, feeding them on demand, and helping them fall asleep and awaken calmly.

3. Be available for interaction when babies are awake and alert; talk quietly and gaze into their eyes when they are interested; allow them to turn away and collect themselves when they need a break.

4. Mirror a baby's facial expressions, adding words that describe the feeling with a congruent tone of voice.

5. Express your own feelings honestly and clearly.

6. Allow infants and toddlers to express the full range of emotions. There are no "bad" feelings and babies need to learn socially acceptable ways to express their feelings.

7. Use your facial expressions and language to let infants and toddlers know whether a situation is safe or not from a small distance.

8. Be responsive and reassuring when infants and toddlers are fearful about exploring. Let them know you watch them and keep them safe.

9. Encourage infants and toddlers to explore and play, while you remain available when they return to you for moments of contact.

As should be clear from the rest of this chapter, in infants and toddlers, good mental health requires a partner who helps the baby regulate his reactions, express and understand expressions of emotions, and develop a secure base of attachment balanced by an autonomous sense of self. Unfortunately, for some babies a reciprocal relationship with a sensitive, responsive adult partner is not available. When adults are unable to "see" the infant, situations become confusing for the baby. Adults behave in ways that do not make sense and the child's development can be thrown off course.

Infant mental health is a growing field that promotes healthy children and intervenes in the relationship between parent and infant when there are relationship challenges, trying to support the parent in giving accurate, responsive care. The intervention is founded on a supportive relationship built between the therapist and the parent. By compassionately understanding and caring about the parent's immediate or earlier experiences, the therapist may provide a kind of relationship never before experienced by the parent. The actual therapeutic work always includes seeing the parent and infant together. Although the parent's conversation and actions may dominate the session, the therapist is always watching and sometimes commenting on the relationship between the parent and the baby. If a mother is revealing a particularly sad and painful story from her own childhood, the therapist might acknowledge the mother with a comment such as, "I'm sorry, that is really more than such a little girl should have to experience," but she may then add, "I'm really taken with how your baby watched you as you talked about this. She can't understand your words but she seems very concerned about whether you are all right." Awhile later, the therapist might point out, "Your baby seems to watch you a lot. She's so interested in everything you do. And she really reacts to your feelings." The ability of the therapist to genuinely ally herself with a parent while still standing up for the baby may provide an entirely new kind of relational experience for the parent.

Respectful and consistent, the practitioner remains attentive to each parent's strengths and needs. Within the safety of this relationship, parents feel well cared for and secure, held by the therapist's words and in her mind (Pawl, 1995). The practitioner listens carefully, follows the parent's lead, remains attuned, sets limits, and responds with empathy. Within the context of the working relationship, the parent experiences possibilities for growth and change through the relationship with her own infant (Weatherston, 2001).

Traditional infant–parent psychotherapy, in the Fraiberg model, utilized five basic components in creating change: emotional support, concrete resource assistance, developmental guidance, insight-based psychotherapy, and advocacy (Weatherston, 2001). *Emotional support* is the therapist's compassionate acceptance of the parent's viewpoint and experience. *Concrete assistance* may include helping the family secure food, shelter, or transportation. A therapist may even accompany a parent to a doctor's appointment or food store, if doing so seems to be therapeutically useful. *Developmental guidance* includes providing information on child development, perhaps observing the baby together to help the parents appreciate their own baby's growth and help the parents feel more confident in their responses to their baby. Sometimes developmental guidance is provided in anticipation of developmental changes, to help parents prepare for new stages. *Advocacy* refers to the therapist's role in sometimes speaking for the infants' and toddlers' needs for care and the parent's responsibility to provide that care.

Insight-based psychotherapy emerges from exposure to the parent and infant together, as the therapist becomes aware of particularly conflicted moments of interaction. The therapist may ask the parent how she feels when her baby cries, or perhaps if she remembers how someone comforted her when she was little and crying. Questions designed to help parents remember and reflect on their own childhoods, or their immediate feelings in this moment, help them become aware of the discrepancy between their response and the baby's real needs.

For example, a foster mother and her two foster children were in therapy for several years. Initially, the therapist witnessed the foster mother as particularly angry toward the younger 18-month-old sister who had been sexually abused and neglected. This very little girl would be punished harshly, for little accidents or activities that were unnoticeable to the therapist. Punishment would consist of being seated on a tall stool, in the middle of the kitchen, while being either ignored or berated by the foster mother. As the therapeutic visits progressed, the therapist came to understand that the foster mother's own father had sexually abused her as a child. Further, she had had polio as a child and spent several months in an iron lung, being told to be strong and not to cry or she would never be allowed to see her family again. The 18-month-old child, simply by being a victim of sexual abuse, evoked powerful feelings and memories in this foster mother to which she responded by re-creating, as a punishment, the frightening containment and isolation she had experienced in the iron lung. As the woman began to work with her memories, she was able to see the little girl as a separate person and could begin to offer her the tender caregiving she had wished for herself, so many years earlier.

Insight, new understandings, or changes in behavior may derive from the parent gaining new skills in understanding her child's behavior, in reflecting on the moments of parent–child interaction, in the child's representations or images of the parent, in the parent's representations or images of the child, or in the relationship between the therapist and the parent (Lieberman, Silverman, & Pawl, 2000). The therapeutic work may emphasize the remedial effects of the therapeutic relationship and insight, or emotional support and interaction guidance to improve the responsive caregiving skills of the parent. An infant mental health intervention from Canada called "Watch, Wait, and Wonder" (Muir, Lojkasek, & Cohen, 1999) is structured to include a period of parent–infant play followed by a time for the therapist and parent to discuss both their observations of the play and the parent's feelings and experiences.

Each of these approaches concentrates on the relationship between the parent and child, and its adequacy to meet the emotional developmental needs of the baby. This approach has also been used in consultation with child development and education programs. Always be aware that you may also have issues in your relationship history that may play out in your caregiving relationships. Or a child's behavior may be so confusing that you will need support in understanding and responding to the child.

Child Care Experiences and Emotional Development

Given the tremendous importance of deep, meaningful, ongoing, responsive relationships in the first years of life, there has understandably been considerable concern about the effects on infants and toddlers of long hours each day in child care. In 1989 the National Institute of Child Health and Development (NICHD) launched a massive study of the effects of child care on child development. While the study

Children may use dolls and family photographs to help hold an image of their mothers or fathers while at their development program.

Developmental Trends and Responsive Interactions
Attachment and Emotional Relationships

Infants and toddlers develop a strong sense of who they are through increasing self-regulation, learning about effective emotional expression, and developing attachment relationships.

Development	Example
0–4 months (infant)	
· Infants are taking in a lot of information about the world. · Infants can get overwhelmed and begin to yawn, look away, or fuss. · Infants begin to calm themselves by sucking on their hands or listening to an adult talk quietly to them. · Infants gaze into their teacher's eyes as she feeds them. · Infants turn their heads toward a familiar voice. · Infants relax and allow themselves to be comforted by familiar people. · Infants cry when they are hungry, tired, or uncomfortable.	Carlos followed Karen with his eyes wherever she entered the room. When she came close to him, he looked at her as though he wanted her to join him. Accepting his invitation to play, she sat with him on the floor. As he began to tire and fuss, she swaddled him in a blanket, held him close, and spoke softly to him.
4–8 months (infant)	
· Infants like to look at their hands and feet. · Infants wave their arms and kick in excitement when they see a familiar person. · Infants will smile at a teacher expecting her to smile back. · Infants use their faces and bodies to express many feelings: everything from frowning and crying to laughing out loud. · Infants express their feelings more clearly to familiar people and are more reserved with strangers.	Deborah loves being carried in her teacher's arms as they move around the room "talking" about the things they see. Her eyes are wide and bright, she smiles, and she makes cooing sounds as though taking her turn in the conversation. When a visitor enters the room, Deborah gets very quiet and serious, and holds tightly to her teacher's shoulder as she looks at the visitor.
8–12 months (mobile infant)	
· Mobile infants may be fearful with strangers. · Mobile infants will call upon familiar adults to help them when they are upset. · Mobile infants will look at a familiar adult to determine whether a situation is safe or dangerous. · Mobile infants will cling to a familiar adult when they are in a strange situation. · Mobile infants will find humor in silly games and adults making big facial expressions.	Jamie is enjoying his new ability to quickly crawl anywhere he wants to go. He loves the little climber that lets him look out the window. But when the ramp feels a little shaky, he likes to look back at his teacher, Fred—just making sure he's still safe.
12–18 months (mobile infant)	
· Mobile infants will imitate the actions of familiar adults, such as using the phone or caring for a baby doll. · Mobile infants will seek adult attention by pulling on their leg or taking their hand. · Mobile infants will use a favorite blanket or stuffed animal to help calm themselves. · Mobile infants will protest loudly when their parents leave them. · Mobile infants will relax and be comforted by cuddling with a familiar adult. · Mobile infants will let their likes and dislikes be clearly known.	Amelia carries her teddy bear around all morning. Sometimes she copies her teacher Sophia's actions, patting its back or "feeding it a bottle." When she gets tired, she rubs teddy against her ear and sucks her thumb.

Teacher or Parent-Child Interaction	Environment
0–4 months (infant)	

• Keep young babies close to you, in your arms, in a snuggly, or on a blanket nearby. • Recognize the signals that indicate a baby wants to be with you—intent gazing, reaching, a happy look—and respond with quiet, verbal and nonverbal turn taking. • Recognize the signals that indicate a baby needs a break—yawning, drooling, looking away—and sit back quietly and wait while the baby regroups. • Comfort babies whenever they cry.	• Being close to a familiar teacher is best. • A serene, quiet space with gentle lighting limits the information an infant needs to take in. • Avoid playing background music all day. • Limit the number of objects, sounds, color, and movements around a young infant. • The teacher is the most interesting thing for a baby to watch, but other babies, mirrors, and toys within the baby's visual range of focus are also interesting.

4–8 months (infant)	

• Provide opportunities for babies to look in mirrors as they play. • Mirror the emotional expressions of the infant and add appropriate words: "I'm so excited to see you today!" • Respond to babies in a way that helps them be calm and active. If babies are crying, soothe them.	• Mount unbreakable mirrors on walls. • Provide floor time where babies can play with their feet while on their backs, and move around on the ground. • Books and posters of photographs of real faces with different emotional expressions are very interesting to infants.

8–12 months (mobile infant)	

• Encourage mobile infants to move off and explore by reassuring them that you are watching and keeping them safe. • Understand that mobile infants may become afraid of new situations that wouldn't have been frightening a few months ago. Be comforting and reassuring.	• Play peek-a-boo. • Read stories about mothers and fathers who go away and come back. • Read books with flaps to lift to find things. • Keep room arrangements and routines predictable.

12–18 months (mobile infant)	

• Demonstrate your interest in babies' activities. • Show your pride in babies' accomplishments. • Let babies use you as a secure base from which to explore the world. • Let babies know you understand their feelings and respond with respect. • These are still very young children who need lots of cuddling and holding.	• Provide child-size copies of tools adults use: telephones, dishes, keys, etc. • Post photographs of the infants with their family on the wall. • Laminate photos of the infants with their family for carrying around. • Make photo albums of the children at your program and talk about the pictures. • Have adult chairs and quiet, comfortable spaces for holding children.

Developmental Trends and Responsive Interactions (continued)

Development	Example
18–24 months (toddler)	
• Toddlers begin to control some impulses, saying "no, no, no" as they begin to throw blocks. • Toddlers may stop their actions when told to by a teacher. • Toddlers may not want to stop playing when their parent comes to pick them up. • Toddlers may cry when they are unable to master what they are trying to do. • Toddlers know their own names and may use "me" and "mine."	Frankie climbs up onto the table, looking his disapproving teacher right in the eye, and says "no, no, no."
24–36 months (toddler)	
• Toddlers can sometimes be independent, but they like to know the teacher is close by. • Toddlers like to study pictures of themselves, their friends, and their families. • Toddlers listen to your words and the tone of your voice when you talk about them. They want you to be interested in them and proud of their accomplishments. • Toddlers need clear and consistent limits. They will forget rules, or test rules, but feel secure when you remind them and help them follow the rules. • Toddlers may use words to express their feelings, or they may hit or bite. • Toddlers care about the feelings of others and will comfort someone who is sad or bring a band-aid to someone who is hurt.	Kiki carried her baby doll over to the photos of her own family on the wall. She crooned to her baby while looking at her own mother's face.

was a comprehensive look at aspects of quality and child outcomes, the effect of child care on the emotional development of young children was also a primary question. The study does offer some significant information.

Major results of the study revealed that mothering was a stronger and more consistent predictor of child outcomes than child care. There is little evidence that early, extensive, and continuous care was related to problematic child behavior. Among the child care predictors, child care *quality* was the most consistent predictor of child functioning (NICHD, 1998). In terms of the child's attachment to the mother, the child care experience (quality, amount, age of entry, stability, or type of care) did not have a direct effect on attachment security or avoidance. As with children not in child care, maternal sensitivity and responsiveness did have the main effects on security of attachment. There were significant interaction effects when low maternal sensitivity was combined with poor-quality child care, heavy use of child care, and more than one child care arrangement. Boys with many hours of care and girls in minimal amounts of care were somewhat less likely to be securely attached (NICHD, 1997).

The little boy seen kissing his image in the mirror, in Observation Invitation 6.2, appears to be comfortable with himself and at ease with demonstrating affection. His experiences with

Teacher or Parent–Child Interaction	Environment
18–24 months (toddler)	
· Keep your sense of humor. Understand that sometimes toddlers can stop themselves from doing things, but other times they cannot. · Respect the strong feelings of toddlers. Taking turns and sharing come later—now "me" and "mine" are an important part of developing a strong sense of self.	· Provide spaces that allow children to explore without ever being out of sight. · Have enough copies of the same toy for several children to each have one without sharing or taking turns. · Let children bring comfort items like blankets or stuffed animals to your program. Provide a quiet place where they can comfort themselves.
24–36 months (toddler)	
· Establish clear and consistent rules. Be prepared to remind the toddlers frequently of how to follow the rules: "We don't bite. Biting hurts." · Give toddlers enough of your time and attention so that they feel understood. · Echo the enthusiasm toddlers can bring to their play. · Notice and comment on the interactions that toddlers are watching and thinking about.	· Provide many photographs of the children with their family: on the walls, in little books, and laminated to carry around. · Provide protected spaces for quiet play. · Maintain predictable routines and room arrangement. · Provide books that tell simple stories of coming and going, of families, and of friendship. · Sing songs about feelings such as "When you're happy and you know it" and "When you're sad, angry . . ."

child care through Early Head Start have been of high quality and have actually supported his relationship with his mother.

Some of the results reflected differences in the effect of child care on different groups of people. Children from minority and single-parent families were rated as less prosocial by their mothers when in low-quality child care (NICHD, 2002b). More child care experience across the first 3 years was associated with less maternal sensitivity and less positive engagement of the mother for White children, but greater maternal sensitivity and child positive engagement for non-White children through first grade. Positive associations of mother–child interaction with hours of child care similar for both African American and Hispanic children (NICHD, 2003).

Quality of child care consistently related to differences in the children's outcomes. Early experience with higher quality child care benefited children's positive engagement with their mothers through first grade when their mothers were depressed, and seemed to have a positive effect on maternal sensitivity through first grade (NICHD, 2003). Maternal sensitivity and responsiveness and experience in child care both seem to contribute to prosocial skills with peers (NICHD, 2001b).

Observation Invitation 6.2: Emotional Development

McKyle has been exploring his own image. He watches himself giving his mirror image a kiss. If you think of McKyle being in the process of developing a sense of who he is, how do you understand this moment? What might you say?

myeducationlab

Go to
MyEducationLab
and complete
the Building
Teaching Skills and
Dispositions exercise
in Chapter 6.

SUMMARY

Self-regulation, emotional expression, and an attachment relationship create the core of the healthy development of a sense of self and a sense of oneself with others. It provides the attentional and motivational foundations for later relationships, learning, and motor development. It happens internally, but only with a responsive adult partner.

- Each infant and toddler must find a balance between reacting to his experiences and regulating his reactions so that he can be relaxed, alert, and attentive. Adults help babies learn to self-regulate first with swaddling, rocking, and sucking, but later by helping them control their own reactions.

- Responsive adults build their relationship with infants through moments of regulation. Whether they take the opportunity to comfort a baby's distress, or engage in interaction when a baby is alert, this sensitivity to regulation is an opportunity for the relationship.

- Temperament traits are inborn characteristics influencing how a child responds to the world. There are nine traits: activity level, biological rhythms, approach/withdrawal, mood, intensity of reaction, sensitivity, adaptability, distractibility, and persistence.

- Temperament traits are often found in groupings called difficult or feisty; slow-to-warm-up, shy, or fearful; and easy or flexible.

- Within the first year of life, infants learn their cultural norms regarding how intensely people express emotions and the nature of the attachment in infant–parent relationships.

- Infants and toddlers have active emotional lives. They express emotions in similar ways around the world and generally understand emotional expressions, although their ability to interpret expressions is influenced by their early experiences.
- Infants and toddlers use the facial expressions of those they trust to help them judge the safety of a situation through a process called social referencing.
- Over time, through repeated interactions, infants develop an attachment relationship with the important adults in their life. They use the adult as a source of safety and security as they venture out to explore their world.
- Aspects of the level of security a child feels in the attachment relationship (secure, anxious-ambivalent, anxious-avoidant, or disorganized) may provide the mental model for later relationships in the child's life.
- Many women experience postpartum depression to the extent that they are emotionally unavailable to their babies. Postpartum depression is not often identified and it can have very serious effects on the baby and on the mother–child relationship.
- Some parents are unable to establish a relationship with their infants because they have never had close relationships or because of traumatic losses or experiences in their own past. Infant–parent psychotherapy can be very effective during the early years of a child's life.
- Child care can be neutral, beneficial, or harmful to the parent–child relationship. The greatest factor in the effect of child care on the parent–child relationship is the quality of the child care program.

Key Terms

anxious-ambivalent attachment	dissociation	secure attachment
anxious-avoidant attachment	emotional display rules	self-fusion
attachment relationship	intersubjectivity	social referencing
autism	regulation	temperament style
biopolar disorder		

REFLECTIONS AND RESOURCES FOR THE READER

Reflections

1. How do you see self-regulation as being a foundation of healthy development?
2. How could you meet the emotional needs of three or four infants and toddlers in your care at one time?

Observation and Application Opportunities

1. Observe a young baby with an adult. Do the baby's facial expressions become part of his or her language?
2. Visit a library or bookstore and look at some picture books for infants and toddlers. Can you find books that teach babies about emotional expression? About adults who keep them safe in attachment relationships? Share these books in class.

Supplementary Articles and Books to Read

Gillespie, L. G., & Seibel, N. L. (2006). Self-regulation: A cornerstone of early childhood development. *Young Children, 61*(4), 34–39.

Howe, D. (2006). Disabled children, parent–child interaction and attachment. *Child and Family Social Work, 11*, 95–106.

Kim, A. M., & Yeary, J. (2008). Making long-term separations easier for children and families. *Young Children* 60 (5), 32–36.

Sturm, L. (2004). Temperament in early childhood: A primer for the perplexed. *Zero to Three, 24*(4), 4–11.

myeducationlab

These and other web links are included in this chapter on MyEducationLab.

Interesting Links

http://zerotothree.org/

ZERO TO THREE On this Web site click on "Parents." There are many interesting articles on emotional development under Social Emotional Development.

http://www.pbs.org/wholechild/abc/index.html

This site has charts on the PBS: The ABC's of Child Development, Developmental Milestones for your Child's First Five Years, as well as articles on emotional health.

Social Development and Learning with Peers

A 6-month-old lifts up her arms, indicating by her look and gestures that she wants to be picked up by a caring adult. Sitting by herself for the first time, she sees the room from a totally new perspective with other children near, and one is crying. She looks eagerly at the other infant to watch him making such a noise.

In her child care center an 8-month-old pulls herself up to stand, holding tight to a bar fastened securely on the wall. She sees another child near and reaches out to pat him on the head. They smile at each other, but then one, with her awkward emerging motor skills, falls into the other and they both start crying.

An 18-month-old runs to her teacher to dump all kinds of little toys in the teacher's lap. Another toddler notices and soon is imitating the first toddler. Quickly, four toddlers join the others, running back and forth, following each other around the room. They squeal with delight as they move in and out of the group, communicating their joy with the toddler version of follow-the-leader.

THE UNIQUENESS OF EACH CHILD

Capacities

As adults, we know that relationships are a source of joy. They are a fundamental element in the human experience. Infants and toddlers are capable of becoming impressive social partners with adults when they arrive in this world. Social interactions (the moment-to-moment initiations and responses) and positive social relationships (characterized by affection, desire to be with others, and reciprocal warm feelings for each other) are all part of early social development with adults. While a primary focus of investigation has been the parent–child relationship and the teacher–child relationship, we are now "turning the lens" and focusing on peer interactions and relationships (Brownell & Kopp, 2007; Rubin, Bukowski, & Laursen, 2008; Wittmer, 2008).

If you observe closely you will also see just how many capacities infants and toddlers have to interact with peers. Over the infant and toddler years they grow in their motivation and ability to play with other children. They learn to communicate with their peers in effective ways. As toddlers, they can become friends with other children and share moments of glee with them. As they grow from infancy to becoming toddlers, they have the capacity to use positive social skills such as offering, playing beside, approaching, playing with, initiating play or contact, being friendly, forming friendships, comforting, helping, giving, showing a toy, hugging, showing empathy, and defending favorite adults and peers. Infants and toddlers also grow in their capacity to learn how to assert themselves and negotiate conflicts without being aggressive—a very difficult social task. During the infant and toddler years children become increasingly **socially competent** with peers—engaging in social interactions that are mutually satisfying to both partners in a relationship. (See the Developmental Trends and Responsive Interactions chart at the end of this chapter for further information on the capacities of infants and toddlers and the development of social competence during infancy.)

socially competent
The ability to engage in social interactions that are mutually satisfying to all partners.

Interaction among children is a fundamental experience during the first years of life. (Malaguzzi)

Recognizing the significance of quality peer experiences is important for several reasons. First, peer experiences contribute to infants' and toddlers' development. Piaget's (1954) theory emphasizes that young children construct knowledge about *how* to play with peers, cooperate, and negotiate conflicts. Vygosky's sociocultural theory (1978) highlights how children learn about their own and other's culture through peer interaction. Relationship-based theory (Emde, 1988; Hinde, 1988, 1992a, 1992b) emphasizes the importance of the quality of adult–child relationships on how children learn to be in healthy relationships and also stresses that children learn skills in peer relationships that they do not with adults.

Second, the quality of an infant's or toddlers' play experience with peers predicts later social adjustment (Hay, Payne, & Chadwick, 2004). Toddlers who are able to play well (with toddler skills) are more socially competent as preschoolers and less aggressive and withdrawn as 9-year-olds. Children who are more aggressive and withdrawn as preschoolers are more aggressive 9-year-olds (Howes & Phillipsen, 1998). Getting off to a good start in peer relationships, then, seems vitally important for later social relationships. Third, the percentage of mothers who have children under the age of 3 and who are also employed outside the home has increased; therefore, infants and toddlers are experiencing their peers more often in child development and education groups (Capizzano & Adams, 2000). Experiences with peers occur daily for these children and are an integral part of their life. Parents and teachers can all work together to ensure that these experiences are quality experiences.

Interacting and playing with other children facilitates development of language, self-concept, and sensorimotor thinking. (Bodrova & Leong)

We know that young children's capacities for satisfying interactions and relationships, peer play, **prosocial** behaviors, and negotiating conflicts are developed in the context of relationships with family members, teachers, other adults, and peers (Wittmer, 2008). We also know that young children are born with their own unique characteristics that are part of their temperaments, and that these attributes contribute to the nature and quality of their peer relationships.

prosocial
The skills and tendency that a child has to be kind, empathic, caring, helpful, thoughtful, considerate, compassionate, and supportive with others.

Attributes

Each infant and toddler expresses his uniqueness in social relationships. This individuality is a blend of a child's genetic characteristics and his experiences in his home, culture, and community. Attributes such as temperament and gender differences contribute to each child becoming an individual who knows how to relate to others in particular and special ways.

Temperament

The temperament of the child seems to influence play behaviors with peers. Temperament was highlighted in depth in chapter 6, the chapter on emotional development and attachment. Here we emphasize three dimensions of temperament that are related to the identity of the child as it impacts social development (see Figure 7.1). Dimension 1 includes the ability of the infant and toddler to use focused attention, inhibit certain actions when necessary, and control and express intense emotions in a socially acceptable way. Dimension 2 describes the tone of children's emotions or mood, and dimension 3 describes children by their interest and ability to interact with others.

The first dimension, self-regulation of emotions, is a critically important child characteristic that predicts children's social competence—the ability to engage in mutually satisfying relationships with others (NICHD, 2004; Rubin, Burgess, Dwyer, & Hastings, 2003). Among preschoolers, highly regulated children usually (not always) demonstrate socially competent responses to emotionally intensive situations (Fabes, Eisenberg, Jones, Smith, Guthrie, & Powlin, 1999). Socially competent children are also less likely to react negatively to difficult situations. Lack of self-regulation of emotions as demonstrated by negative emotional responses to peer situations contribute to observers and teachers rating children as less socially competent (Fabes et al., 1999). A young child's temperament, it seems, may affect the quality of social interactions if a child has a very difficult time controlling his or her emotions. It is very challenging for toddlers to always control their emotions, though, and adults cannot expect that they will. However, adults can support infants and toddlers to increasingly become self-regulated as they develop throughout the infant and toddler years.

> *The real issue may not be whether children are shy and anxious or overwhelmingly outgoing, but how they learn to regulate how they express who they are. (Shonkoff & Phillips)*

When the research on the second and third dimensions of temperament is examined, it is easy to see how self-regulation comes into play. For instance, the second dimension of temperament is mood; most children express a variety of moods in different contexts, but some children

---

Dimension 1: Self-regulation

Dimension 2: Negative to positive emotions

Dimension 3: Shy to extroverted

Figure 7.1 Dimensions of temperament that affect social development.
Source: Rothbart and Bates (1998).

138 CHAPTER 7

Some infants are enthused and exuberant children.

extroverted
A person who is active, outgoing, and focused on others.

exuberant
A person who is full of life, energetic, enthusiastic, and cheerful.

inhibited
A child who seems very shy, hesitant to interact with peers, and is anxious and fearful of peers.

may be generally more negative or positive. If a toddler has a negative mood much of the time, especially if the toddler doesn't want others near her, then she may have fewer opportunities than other children to learn how to interact with other toddlers. This negative mood could occur for a variety of reasons, including biological conditions and a challenging environment.

Dimension 3, shy to **extroverted**, describes how children are more inhibited or more exuberant. The **exuberant** children (Fox, Henderson, Rubin, Calkins, & Schmidt, 2001)—the Tiggers of the world (Milne, 1926/1991)—are outgoing and demonstrative. Can't you just picture these enthused, happy children bouncing through a room? Their excitement is contagious and they are highly social (Fox, Rubin, Calkins, Marshall, Coplin, & Porges, 1995), but they also can be overwhelming to other children. These vivacious children may actually be slightly more aggressive than others (Gunnar, Tout, de Haan, Pierce, & Stansbury, 1997). Happy toddlers, no doubt, attract a group, are having fun, and are in the middle of everything. And, when a child is in the middle of everything, the chances are higher that the child will bump into other children, take their toys, and boss them around. Again, self-regulation seems important (Shonkoff & Phillips, 2000). If these exuberant children control their emotions when appropriate and necessary, then they are more likely to be the children in the group who attract positive attention from peers (Rubin, 1998). However, once again, we must emphasize that we can't expect toddlers to control their emotions at all times—they are just learning how—and need understanding adults to to express their emotions verbally and to help them calm down when they become too exuberant or upset.

A contrasting temperament to exuberance is *inhibition*. Some young children are very busy and often like to explore and play alone (Coplan, Rubin, Fox, Calkins, & Stewart, 1994; Fox et al., 2001). These busy toddlers who sometimes play by themselves wouldn't be considered inhibited. **Inhibited** children are those children who seem very shy, hesitant to interact with peers, anxious, and fearful of peers. They may also actively withdraw from other children (Rubin & Coplan, 2004). There is evidence that inhibition may have a biological component (Fox et al., 1995; Henderson, Marshall, Fox, & Rubin, 2004; Kagan, 1997). Toddlers with higher levels of social fearfulness had increases in the level of cortisol (a hormone that indicates stress) across the day in child care (Watamura, Donzella, Alwin, & Gunnar, 2003). There are, however, environmental and relationship factors that contribute to whether a child continues to be inhibited or not (Fox et al., 2001; Rubin & Coplan, 2004).

Parents and teachers need to begin early to support infants and toddlers who are inhibited with peers because when toddlers are inhibited they are likely to be inhibited preschool children (Hay, Payne, & Chadwick, 2004). Young children who are inhibited (or withdrawn) need gentle support to enter the social world and learn language, social, and emotional skills to gain self-confidence in engaging in peer interactions. Do not ignore inhibited children or expect them to change quickly. They may not be interacting with other children because of the fear of rejection (Rubin & Coplan, 2004) and when adults are critical or harsh with these children, they are more likely to continue to be withdrawn as they grow older (Rubin, Burgess, & Hastings, 2002). Furthermore, if adults are overprotective and do not encourage with kindness these children's peer interactions, these children may be more likely to continue to think that the world is a scary place (Shonkoff & Phillips, 2000). For instance, you can go with a hesitant child to a block area, engage the child with *one* other child at times rather than with the whole group, and go to the child to encourage him to go with you for a story with several other children.

As children experience these peer relationships, adults can guide children with unique temperaments to try different ways of playing and interacting. New infant and toddler social skills develop through the assistance of helpful, but not intrusive, adults (Honig, 1994; Rubin et al., 2002; Vygotsky, 1978). As these infants and toddlers gain experience, they construct important ideas about how to master the task of interacting with a peer partner (DeVries & Zan, 1996). They have opportunities to imitate more **elaborate play schemes** and try them out within a safe environment (Bandura, 1977, 1989).

elaborate play schemes
The play of children that includes complex themes.

Gender Issues

Children's individuality in social development may also be influenced by gender. The behavior associated with gender may have biological roots, may be influenced by the environment, or may be influenced by a combination of both.

A question that is often asked is, "Do boys prefer to play with boys and girls with other girls?" If they do, is that a problem that should concern us? Moller and Serbin (1996) discovered that among almost 60 toddlers, primarily White, average age 35 months, only 21% of the males but 62% of the females engaged in **same-gender play.** Why do these toddlers seem to prefer **gender segregation?** Three theories to explain why young children might want to play with children of their own gender are presented in Figure 7.2. After carefully observing toddlers in their classrooms and collecting teachers' ratings of child gender behavior, Moller and Serbin (1996) concluded that only one of the theories outlined in Figure 7.2 was supported: the compatible play style explanation. Children of the same sex with similar play styles preferred to play with each other. Girls who preferred to play with other girls rather than boys were seen as the most socially sensitive. Boys who preferred to play with same-gender playmates were seen as more active and disruptive than the other children.

same-gender play
Patterns in which girls play with girls and boys play with boys.

gender segregation
The separation of boys and girls during play or other interactions.

As children develop, their interest in same-sex play increases. Fabes, Martin, and Hanish (2004) conclude from their research that by the time children enter preschool they show a strong preference to spend time with same-gender peers, and this preference increases throughout the elementary years. This tendency occurs across cultures and may be a powerful influence on children learning gender-specific roles in their culture (Fabes et al., 2004). Researchers express concern, however, with the frequency of same-gender play primarily

---

(1) **Cognitive Consonance Theory**
     When children learn to identify their own gender as male or female, they highly value anything associated with their gender category.

(2) **Gender-Types Toy Preference Theory**
     Children segregate according to their toy and activity preferences, and the activities chosen bring children into contact with other peers who also prefer that activity.

(3) **Behavior Compatibility Theory**
     Gender segregation develops out of toddlers' attraction to peers who exhibit play styles that are compatible.

Figure 7.2   Three theories that explain children's desire to play with their own gender.
Source: Moller and Serbin (1996).

because of the compatible play style reason for same-gender play that was beginning to occur among the 2-year-olds discussed in Moller and Serbin's (1996) research.

Fabes and colleagues (Fabes et al., 2004; Fabes, Hanish, & Martin, 2003) summarized Maccoby's (1998) research as well as their own and concluded that preschool boys' play was frequently rougher, more active, and involved more physical contact and taunting. Boys tended to play away from the teacher, engage in less structured play, follow peer direction, and engage in what could be considered math and science activities more than girls. Girls were more likely to emphasize cooperation and use forms of communication that promoted harmony. Girls played more often in the presence of a teacher and received more adult attention and direction from the teacher. They had more opportunities to regulate and control their behavior and emotions. Boys' and girls' different compatible play styles were fostering different behavioral norms and interaction styles, and these play styles were contributing to very different learning experiences for boys and girls in the preschool classroom.

You can observe toddlers during their play experiences to determine whether this type of gender segregation is occurring—and if so, whether the behaviors exhibited are of concern. You should be concerned with same-gender (and mixed-gender) play *if* the behaviors limit the potential of children for learning a variety of skills, if a particular group becomes more aggressive when they are with each other, if a group frequently does not like to have an adult present, or if a child hardly ever wants to play with a child from the other sex. "Although it is important for children to develop a strong sense of self and incorporate what it means to be a girl or a boy, adults must help children see that neither girls nor boys should be limited by gender roles" (Chrisman & Couchenour, 2003, p. 116).

Observe to see if boys and girls are beginning to develop a stereotype that certain toys are only for boys and other toys only for girls. Zoe, a child described by Chrisman and Couchenour (2003) in their article "Developing Concepts of Gender Roles," was likely to deny boys a chance to play with her special toy because she mistakenly thought that only girls could play with that type of toy. If this happens, you would tell Zoe that both boys and girls like to play with the toy (dolls, for example) and then give both boys and girls opportunities and encourage them to do so. Another strategy to encourage children to play with all types of toys is to display pictures of both boys and girls playing with many types of materials and toys (Derman-Sparks & the A.B.C. Task Force, 2003)—and then to talk about them by saying, "Look, that boy in the picture likes to play with blocks and that girl in the picture likes to play with blocks, too." Choose and read books that contradict gender stereotypes by showing girls and boys playing quietly with their toys *and* playing actively on the playground. We do however, want to respect a particular child's temperament for quiet or active play, while gently encouraging that child to try new activities.

DEVELOPMENT AND LEARNING THROUGH RELATIONSHIPS

Letta reached out to touch the nose of her 9-month-old playmate, Carla. Carla, sitting quietly, let Letta softly stroke her nose and then reached out as if to offer a hug. Letta and Carla, ever so gently, touched noses, laughed, and then crawled away to play with some toys next to them.

interpsychological The thinking that occurs between people, such as using language to communicate with others.

intrapsychological The thinking that children do by themselves.

Culture and Peer Relationships

Vygotsky (1978) noted that every behavior of a child occurred first on the social level in the child's culture and then on the individual level; first between people (**interpsychological**) and then inside the child (**intrapsychological**). Letta and Carla seemed to have experienced gentle touches, laughter, and reaching out to be with others on a social level in their culture (interpsychological) and now these behaviors are an integral part of who they are (intrapsychological), thus affecting their behavior in social situations with playmates.

> *It is principally through interacting with others that children find out what the culture is about and how it conceives their view of the world. (Bruner)*

Children's social interactions differ according to their cultural experiences. In Letta and Carla's culture, adults value peer interaction at an early age. This belief influenced their parents, who are friends, to find a child care home where Letta and Carla could be together during the day. The parents and the family child care provider believe strongly that young children need early peer interactions to learn how to play together. Parents in their culture encourage children to "not be shy" and are concerned when infants and toddlers are socially inhibited.

Many families in Italy also believe in the value of early peer relationships. The authors of *Bambini* (Gandini & Edwards, 2001), a book describing Italy's Reggio Emilia approach to early childhood education, state that infant and toddler centers "are viewed as daily-life contexts with the potential to facilitate the growth and development of all children" (p. 25). Parents want early socialization experiences for their children and they want teachers who will support young children's development of relationships.

There may be families, however, in which shyness and social inhibition are *not* viewed as negative traits (Rubin, 1998). These families may want their children to be socialized with family members rather than peers, especially during the infant-toddler years.

Social Development with Peers

Infants and toddlers go through many stages of social development and struggles as they learn how to be socially competent. You will observe, at times, that these very young children are interested in trying to learn how to be social with peers. At other times, the challenges of learning how to negotiate the "me" with the "other" is very difficult and conflicts between peers may seem to erupt often. An infant or toddler might reach out to comfort another child; 5 minutes later, she might bite that same friend, either out of sheer emotional exuberance for the joy of the moment or out of anger because her friend took her toy. However, as they grow from birth to 3 years of age young children learn an incredible amount about social interactions. Let's examine children's development of their motivation and capacity to be and play with other children.

The Developmental Trends chart at the end of this chapter presents a sequence of peer development. Let's take a closer look at many of the milestones highlighted in the chart by examining the development of four capacities of infants and toddlers. Babies, over the first 3 years of life, become increasingly able to:

- Communicate with peers
- Play with peers in increasingly complex ways
- Develop prosocial behaviors
- Manage negative feelings and conflict with peers

At the end of their first 3 years of life, children still have much to discover to maximize their potential in the social domain, but with adults who are knowledgeable of the abilities and motivation of infants and toddlers to learn, children gain a strong foundation of knowledge and skills from which to continue to build that potential.

Communication with Peers

How do infants and toddlers communicate with one another often when they lack the words to express their feelings, needs, and desires? Toddlers have a variety of communication skills that they use to initiate and maintain relationships with other children (Katz, 2004). They inform, direct, and use sounds, words, and laughter to keep other children involved in play with them. Maya Pines (1984a) summarizes the research by Hubert Montagner, a French ethologist, on young children's communication strategies. Noted for his studies with insects, Montagner observed young children's behavior after a challenge from his colleagues in a university in Switzerland to apply his work to children's behavior. As he observed young children for 15 years, he captured their social behavior, particularly the **gestural language** and the individual nonverbal communication styles that affect children's social interactions with others:

gestural language
Movements of the body that communicate meaning.

> Each child spoke a gestural language other children could understand clearly, even if adults could not necessarily decode it, and it affected how others treated the child. (Pines, 1984a, p. 61)

Montagner discovered five major styles of nonverbal communication among children that begin as early as 9 to 12 months of age:

1. Actions that pacify others or produce attachment: Offering another child toys, lightly touching or caressing the other child, jumping in place, clapping one's hands, smiling, extending one's hand as if begging, taking the other child's chin in one hand, cocking one's head over one's shoulder, leaning sideways, rocking from left to right, or vocalizing in a nonthreatening way

2. Threatening actions that generally produce fear, flight, or tears in the target child: Loud vocalizations, frowning, showing clenched teeth, opening one's mouth wide, pointing one's index finger toward the other child, clenching one's fist, raising one's arm, leaning one's head forward, leaning one's whole trunk forward, or shadow boxing

3. Aggressive actions: Hitting with hands or feet, scratching, pinching, biting, pulling the other child's hair or clothes, shaking the other child, knocking the other child down, grabbing something that belongs to the other child, or throwing something at the other child

4. Gestures of fear and retreat: Widening one's eyes, blinking, protecting one's face with bent arms, moving one's head backward, moving one's trunk or one's whole body backward, running away, or crying after an encounter with another child

5. Actions that produce isolation: Thumb-sucking, tugging at one's hair or ear, sucking on a toy or a blanket, standing or sitting somewhat apart from the other children, lying down, lying curled into the fetal position, or crying alone. (Pines, 1984a, p. 63)

The young children differed greatly in the combinations of gestures that they used with their peers. The secret to children's peer success (in fact, becoming a leader among peers) seems to be the children's use of as many of the pacifying gestures as possible, and defending themselves with threatening behaviors only when necessary. Children learn to "read" other children's behavior quickly, avoiding children who use frequent aggressive strategies. Our understanding of young children's remarkable ability to communicate nonverbally with each other opens a window to a fresh view of infant and toddler peer communication.

The magical sequence: head tilted over one shoulder, a smile and outstretched hand. (Pines)

Conversations Between and Among Peers

What do infants and toddlers say to one another when they can communicate with words and how do they develop relationships as they talk with each other? Jane Katz (2004) and Elin Ødegaard (2006) have studied peer conversations among toddlers.

Katz (2004) emphasized the pragmatic skills of toddlers to initiate and maintain a relationship, and Ødegaard (2006) studied the mealtime conversations of nine Norwegian children ranging in age from 1 year to 3 years old attending a preschool program. She found "two-year-olds trying to come to grips with the problems of life" (p. 83) as they talked about problems and expressed feelings such as anger, fear, loss, and desire. For example, one young child engaged his peers in a conversation about a scary event as he related a story about Santa Claus by saying, "Gloomy Santa Claus was there" (at the center of town). These young children also struggled with each other over who would control a story. Ødegaard reports that an almost 3-year-old Ane raised her fist in the air and shouted to another child, "Me talk." Soon the other child responded to Ane with stifled anger, "Ah, Me talk." This conflict between the two children at mealtime continued into their play. The nature of these two children's relationship was apparent in both their words and their play.

Children express, develop, and adapt the meaning of their words and relationships as their conversations continue. Ødegaard (2006) emphasizes that conversations or narratives are coconstructed with the teacher and peers, often in a multiparty discussion. Through thoughtful questions and comments, a teacher often helps a child

Toddlers use the *magical sequence* to comfort one another.

move from talking about the "here and now" (events and objects that are present) to the "there and then" (events and objects not present). Through reflection on children's words and conversations with their peers, the teacher can learn about children's cultures and the relationship experiences with the adults and peers in their lives. These peer conversations with or without adults contribute greatly to children's learning (Shatz, 2007).

Play with Peers

The second capacity of infants and toddlers is to learn to play with peers. As young children develop they participate in more complex interactions. Researchers have tried to capture these developmental experiences by creating scales that identify the important characteristics of each stage of development. Parten (1932, 1933) identified stages of young children's play that included solitary play, parallel play, associate play, and cooperative play (see Figure 7.3 for a definition of each stage).

Howes, Matheson, and Hamilton (1992) observed 48 children from infancy through preschool and revised a peer play scale designed by Howes in 1980. Howes and Matheson's peer play scale started at 12 months and continued, through five stages, to 36 months (see Figure 7.4). Howes' (1980) social sequence, as Parten's did, identified a stage of parallel play but added a stage of "parallel aware play." This stage captured the awareness that one child

Solitary play	Plays alone and independently; different activity; no reference to others
Parallel play	Plays independently but near or among others; similar toys or activities; beside but not with
Associate play	Plays with others; conversation is about common activity, but does not subordinate own interests to groups
Cooperative play	Activity is organized; differentiation of roles; complementing actions

Figure 7.3   Parten's stages of play.

Source: From Johnson, James, E., et al., *Play and Early Childhood Development* (2nd ed.). Published by Allyn and Bacon/Merrill Education, Boston, MA. Copyright © 1999 by Pearson Education. Reprinted by permission of the publisher.

I. 12–15 Months: Parallel Play

Parallel play (playing beside) often includes eye contact and/or exchanges of social behavior (A vocalizes, B smiles).

II. 15–20 Months: Parallel Play with Mutual Regard

Engagement in similar activities is accompanied with turn taking social exchanges (while digging in the sandbox, A smiles to B and B vocalizes back).

III. 20–24 Months: Simple Social Play

Social exchange is marked by each partner taking turns at reversing the actions of the other (run-chase game, rolling a ball back and forth).

IV. 24–30 Months: Complementary and Reciprocal Play with Mutual Awareness

Joint activity has a common plan and the pair's actions are integrated (conversation during joint building of a block structure shows that both intend it for trucks to drive underneath).

V. 30–36 Months: Complementary and Reciprocal Social Play

The social play activity shows differentiation of leader and follower roles (while jointly building a block structure, A directs building construction and B delivers blocks).

Figure 7.4   Howes's peer play scale.
Source: Howes (1988).

has for another as the two children sit near each other. The third stage, "simple social play," describes how young children talk to each other, give each other toys, and sometimes take toys away from each other. Howes, et al. (1992) found that 67% of infants from 10 to 12 months engaged primarily in parallel play, but by 30 to 36 months, 64% of the children engaged primarily in complementary and reciprocal play—playing games like "run-and-chase" or "you bang the spoon then I'll bang the spoon." Starting at 13 months, the majority of children were playing at levels higher than parallel or parallel aware play. In fact, by 30 to 36 months, 25% of the children were engaging in "cooperative social play" and a few (6%) were engaged in "complex social play." Cooperation is a key component of the higher stages of play.

Infants' and toddlers' ability to cooperate with each other on a task improves as they get older and is a remarkable achievement of toddlers (Brownell, Ramani, & Zerwas, 2006). In a research setting, Brownell and colleagues found that the majority of 27-month-old children could cooperate to activate a toy when two children had to pull handles that were strategically placed on opposite sides of the toy so that one child couldn't activate it. However, 1-year-olds (19- to 23-months olds) could not make the toy work by cooperating, even though the adults modeled how to cooperate and reminded the children about the goal of the task. We can wonder, though, and observe how infants and toddlers may cooperate if they know each other well in a program and if they are motivated to do a task such as fill a water table by cooperating to carry a bucket of water.

Vygotsky's work reminds us to see, as in this example, what young children can and cannot do when they are provided models (highest level of the zone of proximal development) and what they can do when they are playing independently (lowest level of the zone of proximal development).

Prosocial Development in Infants and Toddlers

Marissa, 2, runs to Minnie, 18 months, when she cries, patting her cheek as her own mother does to her. When Sam or Mark yells "Help" the other one runs to help move blocks or somehow resolve the crisis. Lenny, only 15 months old, lovingly tries to feed his teacher some of his applesauce. When Jo gets her finger stuck between some blocks and lets out a loud cry, Allison looks concerned, runs to pull on the teacher's leg, and looks back at Jo, as if to say, "Hurry—come help Jo."

We know that infants and toddlers are just learning how to be social—so there can be biting, hitting, grabbing, and pushing when they are together in groups. However, young children can be prosocial. Prosocial behavior includes giving, defending, offering, helping, and showing empathy through facial expressions, words, or gestures. Infants and toddlers hug, pat, look concerned, and often want to give their food to others. You can observe many prosocial moments if you know they exist and if you are watching for them and encouraging them.

In the early research of prosocial behavior in toddlers, Eckerman, Whatley, and Kutz (1975) found that within three age groups of children (10 to 12 months, 16 to 18 months, and 22 to 24 months of age), positive interactions with peers far outweighed negative ones. Howes (1988) concluded that toddlers interact in complementary and reciprocal ways and form stable friendships, and Roopnarine and Field (1983) observed that both infants and toddlers directed positive behaviors toward their peers more frequently than negative behaviors. Murphy (1936) studied sympathy and observed sympathetic behavior among 2-year-olds, including patting, hugging, kissing, picking up another child who fell, or pushing a swing when a child could not make it go. Howes and Farver (1987) studied peer responses to the distress of their peers. Toddlers from 16 to 33 months of age responded to a peer's distress 22% of the time. Of these times, 93% of the responses were prosocial in nature.

The important work of Zahn-Waxler, Radke-Yarrow, and King (1979) focused on the capacity of these very young children for compassion and various kinds of prosocial behaviors. In the researchers' observations in the homes of children between the ages of 10 months and 2½ years, and after reading the records that parents faithfully kept for 9 months, the researchers noted many examples of infants showing empathy for the feelings of others. To their great surprise, as early as 1 year of age, some babies tried to comfort people who were crying or in pain. Infants used gentle touches, snuggles, and hugs to seemingly try to make an unhappy person feel better, or, in a few cases, offered their own bottle or food to an exhausted dad or a sad mom. One baby even tried to defend his mother against a force much larger than himself. When the mother was having her throat swabbed at the doctor's office her infant, not quite a year old, reached out and tried to knock the throat swab from the doctor's hand when his mother made a strangling noise.

As the children moved toward 18 months, Radke-Yarrow and Zahn-Waxler discovered that some toddlers became more inventive at figuring out how to comfort another child. They gave toys and food to the crying child, and urgently pulled an adult over to help the child in distress. Infants' and toddlers' prosocial acts, however, did not always comfort the other person because the offer from the young child mirrored their own needs rather than the needs of the other person. A sticky pacifier, chewed-up food, or an already used baby bottle may not be exactly what the adult or other child wants for consolation. However, these gifts represent a supreme sacrifice on the part of the toddler making such an offer and will ideally be appreciated as such by the receiving party. Figure 7.5 identifies ways that adults can support and facilitate prosocial tendencies.

Toddlers in programs can comfort each other as well. When Lonnie (26 months old) was sad she grabbed her

Two children keep another company outside on his first day in the program.

Parents of toddlers who were most prosocial . . .

- Gave a clear, intense message that their child must not hurt others. A parent might say to the child, "Look what you did. You must never poke anyone's eyes" (said with feeling). The message was given to the child in a serious voice, but these parents did not slap or hurt their child in any way when the child hurt a peer.

- Helped their children see the connection between what they did and how it affected the other child. For instance, "You poked him. That hurt him" (said dramatically).

- Gave explanations for why the child should or should not behave in a particular way. Just saying "No" or "Stop" without giving any additional information did not help children be kind. Instead it taught them to stop any activity when confronted with another's distress.

- Taught their children what to do instead of biting, hitting, etc. A parent might say, "You can say 'Stop,' " or "Pat gently—it feels good when you pat gently."

- Were kind and loving toward their own children. They gave hugs and kisses, soothing words, band-aids, and tissues for gently wiping runny noses. The children modeled after their parents and used the same prosocial behaviors with their peers.

- Helped others when they saw that they were in distress. If the parent couldn't help—for example, if another child cried in the grocery store and that child's mom was already comforting her—then the parent talked to her own child about the event: "Yes, she's crying. She's feeling sad because she hurt herself on the cart. Her mom is making her feel better."

Figure 7.5   Supporting and facilitating prosocial development.

favorite stuffed bunny, sat on the floor, and hugged it tightly. Lukas and two other children saw that Lonnie was sad and sat beside her on the floor—reaching out to gently touch her (see Observation Invitation 7.1). One toddler commented "She sad," while another moved in closer and with a tilt of her head asked Lonnie, "What wrong—you OK?" The third toddler jumped up stating, "She like a sticker," as he ran off to get Lonnie a sticker to make her feel better. These children were growing in their ability to "think of the other" as they struggled to figure out what might make Lonnie feel better. After getting the sticker, Lonnie exclaimed, "All better now." These toddlers had found a way to comfort their friend in distress.

These prosocial strategies were modeled for them by their teachers, with themselves at times the recipient of such caring. The children were able to use the same loving strategies with their peers. It is gratifying to an adult who patiently and gently uses prosocial strategies with young children to see these types of peer-to-peer scenes that mirror the adult responses young children see and receive each day from their favorite adults.

There are strategies that you can use to enhance children's prosocial development—and in the process develop a community in an early care and education program where the small citizens begin to care about each other:

- *Provide continuity of care and groups.* Keeping groups of children together from infancy through toddlerhood promotes familiarity and friendships. Howes (1988), in her research on the social relationships of toddlers, found that peers who are familiar with each other are more likely to initiate play, be more positive, and engage in more complex interactions than children who are unfamiliar with each other. As discussed in the first chapter in this book, continuity of care (when one or more caregivers move to a different room *with* the children as they age from birth to 3) teachers and children develop more trusting relationships, children are more positive with their peers in child care, children are less aggressive and negative at home, and children have increased cognitive and language skills (NICHD, 2001b).

Observation Invitation 7.1

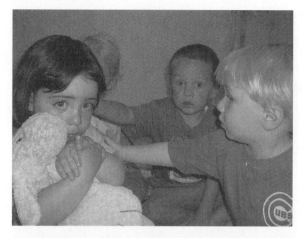

What are the 25-month-old boys trying to do? How are they being prosocial?

- *Give children time together in an enriched environment.* If infants and toddlers can choose their activities then they often choose to be near each other while learning how to help, comfort, and solve problems together.

- *Support positive social behaviors, comment on them, and cheer babies on to continue these caring behaviors.* Use specific approving words when an infant or toddler offers a toy or pats another child to comfort them. Using the words for positive social behaviors, teachers may talk about sharing, caring, giving, helping, comforting, loving, and being generous. Infants and toddlers begin to learn these words and to take the perspective of others. As children begin to understand that positive behaviors are important to adults, those behaviors increase dramatically.

- *Young children need to feel what it is like to have an adult be prosocial with them.* Give them food and toys in a generous way and comfort them when they are distressed. Children need to feel that their emotional and physical needs are met before they can give love and show empathy for another's sadness. Just like a sponge needs to be filled with water before the water overflows, so do infants need to be filled up with love, before they overflow with love and kind attention to others. As babies experience warmth and kindness from adults, this behavior becomes a part of them that they can share with others.

- *In addition to having personal prosocial experiences, infants and toddlers need prosocial models.* Teachers may provide positive models of prosocial behavior at many times during the day. Children see examples of adults being kind to each other and, more importantly, they feel the prosocial atmosphere of the room or child care home. Teachers can model giving to other teachers and to children in the classroom or child care home. Children might hear a teacher say, "I'd like to share this with you," as she gives a book to another adult in the room.

- *Emphasize how being prosocial makes others feel.* Saying things like, "Oh, Ian likes it when you pat him gently. Look, he's smiling." This type of comment helps babies begin to take the perspective of others.

Observation Invitation 7.2

These two toddlers are friends. How are they demonstrating their friendship?

group continuity of care
A group of children who continuously stay together over time in an early development and education program.

Familiarity. Very young children find it easier to play with familiar peers (Howes, 1988, 1996). Time together (Galluzzo, Matheson, Moore, & Howes, 1990) with the same play partner enhances children's ability to play well together, probably as they learn the likes, dislikes, and play characteristics of the other child: "They [peers] are more likely to initiate play, direct positive affect to, and engage in complex interactions with familiar than with unfamiliar playmates" (Howes, 1988, cited in Shonkoff & Phillips, 2000, p. 167).

Because children who have time together and are familiar with each other play more easily with each other, programs should provide **group continuity of care.** A group of children who begin a program fairly close in time to each other can be kept together as a group as they advance in age in the program. The toddlers in Observation Invitation 7.2, who have known each other since they were infants, are happy and comfortable in each other's company.

myeducationlab

Go to the Activities and Applications section in Chapter 7 of MyEducationLab to watch *Friendship Story*, a sequence of photos that demonstrates toddler friendship.

Development of friendships. Is it possible for infants and toddlers to develop relationships? What is a friendship for infants and toddlers? Can they show how they might prefer to be with another infant or toddler and demonstrate more affection toward that other child? How do friendships develop? As Ross and Lollis (1989) note, friendships occur "when two people bring out qualities in one another that are neither exhibited nor elicited in their other relationships" (p. 1083). Toddlers demonstrate their friendships in a number of ways (see Figure 7.6). A 15-month-old's face lights up each time she sees her friend arrive in the child development and education center. An 18-month-old runs to the other side of the living room to greet a friend who has come to visit. Toddlers who are friends may even grieve for each other if one child leaves a program or moves to another room (Whaley & Rubenstein, 1994).

Maria and Lisa had been together in the Boulder Journey School since they were babies. As toddlers they greeted each other, played together often, and obviously enjoyed each other

The relationship is considered a friendship when these conditions are met:

1. Toddlers have opportunities in their daily lives for regular play interactions with a particular partner.

2. Toddler partners are sufficiently well acquainted to have constructed scripted social interactions.

3. Companionship, intimacy, and affection can be inferred from these interactions.

Behaviorally defined, friendships appear some time after children's first birthdays.

Figure 7.6   A relationship is a friendship when . . .
Source: Howes (2000, p. 103).

very much. When Lisa's mother changed her work schedule, Lisa started attending the school on opposite days from Maria. Maria seemed to grieve for her friend. She would often go to the shelf with the "All About Me" books, choose Lisa's book, and lay on the floor looking at pictures of Lisa as a baby, of her first birthday, and as a toddler.

Of course, we also know that when very young children are together in groups, conflict will occur. Young children are learning to regulate their emotions, to gain an understanding of "mine" and "yours," to use language to express their needs, and to understand the meaning of "share" and "take turns." Infants and toddlers can make great progress in their journey toward managing negative emotions and conflict with peers with the support of understanding adults.

Go to the Activities and Applications section in Chapter 7 of MyEducationLab to watch *The Story of the Chair,* a sequence of photos showing two toddlers in a conflict over a chair.

Challenges and Conflicts in Peer Relationships

Charissa toddled up to Ben, her favorite friend in the toddler room, and wrapped her arms around his head in a sweet, comforting way. Ben protested and tried to wriggle out of Charissa's head wrap. Later, Charissa clutched tightly to two toy telephones as Ben tried with all of his might to wrestle one from her grasp. Even later that day, Charissa handed Ben her special doll to hold and then quickly tried to take it back from him.

These scenes happen many times a day at home or in programs where there are two or more infants and toddlers. Older infants who are crawling and cruising and toddlers who are toddling sometimes give and sometimes take away. They often are very good at sharing their teachers, toys, food, and time. At other times, they have no intention of sharing anyone or anything. Words like "mine" and "no" ring out from toddlers. They cling to their special teacher and push other children away. They hang on for dear life to toys that just a moment ago they discarded in a corner. They are learning about social interactions, but they seem to be following the "Toddler Property Laws":

Projects such as "All About Me" books help children who grieve when friends move away.

Toddler Property Laws

If I like it, it's mine.
If it's in my hand, it's mine.
If I can take it from you, it's mine.
If I had it a little while ago, it's mine.
If it's mine, it must never appear to be yours in any way.
If I'm doing or building something, all the pieces are mine.
If it looks just like mine, it is mine.
(*Author unknown*)

myeducationlab

Go to the Activities and Applications section in Chapter 7 of MyEducationLab to watch the video *Aggression.* Think about how conflict may lead to social competence.

Conflict May Be Related to Social Competence

While infants and toddlers are learning to socialize, conflict happens and may actually be related to peer competence. Conflicts between peers include situations in which one person does something and another person objects. Indeed, conflict and aggression initially increase as children try to play together, peaking between ages 2 and 3 before they decline (Brownell & Carriger, 1990). In fact, there are research results indicating that socially competent children may be involved in more conflicts than their less socially competent peers. How can that be?

Conflict is different from mean-spirited aggression and may be related to social competence in two ways. The first involves the fact that socially competent children are not withdrawn or aggressive, but can be rather assertive in their play. They are full of confidence and often right in the middle of the play action, resulting in more opportunities for conflict with peers. Second, young children learn valuable skills during conflict with their peers. The negotiation and self-regulation skills necessary to prevent the conflict from escalating and interfering with play improve as these children gain experience in the art of disagreeing, resisting, or competing. Thus, involvement in conflict may actually play a positive role in peer development (Eckerman & Didow, 2001).

dominant
A person who is controlling or leading another person.

If you've observed toddlers and noticed that some toddlers seem more **dominant** than other toddlers, that they can take toys and the other children won't protest, or that they seem to be the leaders in play, you are noticing an interesting phenomenon. Hawley and Little (1999) describe a prominent characteristic of dominant children: "Dominant children demonstrate facility to interact with the environment unhindered, whereas their subordinate peers decline to do so, at least in the presence of dominant peers." The researchers observed that toddlers who were physically stronger, more mature, more cognitively advanced, more goal-directed, and who had more physical and social experience in a particular group setting seemed to be more dominant than other toddlers. They also observed that girls were dominant more often than boys. Among these children, who ranged in age from 1.4 to 3.2 years of age, the toddler's developmental maturity was the highest predictor of whether a toddler was dominant or not (Hawley & Little, 1999).

It is fascinating that whether or not the toddler was dominant was based on the toddler's play partner. A toddler might behave one way with one partner and another way with a different partner, depending on who was dominant in the group. These researchers' findings—that the behavior of a particular toddler changed based on his partner—were contrary to what was expected of these children. Prior to this, some researchers thought that toddlers acted the same way with all children and couldn't, at that age, adjust their behavior according to the behavior of a peer.

subordinate
A person who is controlled by or led by another person.

Dominant behavior has been observed in children as early as 19 months of age and may prevent aggression (Plusquellec, Francois, Boivin, Perusse, & Tremblay (2007). As a teacher, you can help a toddler who is almost always dominant become an assertive *and* kind leader by using the strategies listed earlier in this chapter, in the section on prosocial development. You can also advocate for and aid a toddler who almost always is **subordinate,** and can help the child become more self-confident in peer relationships. Teachers' strategies that support children's conflict resolution skills are discussed in chapter 14 of this book.

Richness of Peer Development

The richness of peer development is brought to light with thoughtful documentation of the intricacies of peer interactions. When adults carefully observe the behaviors of infants and toddlers for child goals, strategies, and theories (Forman, O'Hara, Larsen, Coy, Gorman, & Stewart, 2003), then the adults' understanding of peer relationships blossoms. Capatides, Collins, and Bennett (1996) captured the nuances of toddler behavior in their observations of six toddlers (18 to 36 months old) one time a month for 6 months. The toddlers' social goal was to be with each other. The strategies they used were to move together. They established and maintained contact with each other through moving their bodies in space, coming together, leaving, holding a conversation with the body rather than with words, moving around the room together, and establishing contacts through physical movement and imitation. The young children's theory may have been "If I follow you, I can continue to be with you." Before playing with objects together, toddlers may need to move around the room together, experiencing and conversing kinesthetically. This social dance is so much more than parallel play. As children take turns being the leader and the followers, they demonstrate complementary and reciprocal interactions with mutual awareness and great enjoyment of each other.

The detailed description of children's moment-to-moment social behavior encourages an appreciation for the social competency of the toddler and an understanding of what leading and following mean to the advancement of toddler social relationships. We all learn from these types of observations. Rather than trying to keep toddlers from moving, wise parents and teachers will provide safe opportunities for toddlers to hold their kinesthetic conversations.

Another detailed observation revealed further capabilities of toddlers. When toddlers from age 2½ to 3 were observed in a child development and education center, they were clearly capable of developing expectations for the behavior of other toddlers. The following vignette clearly demonstrates that some toddlers expect that a peer, Michael, will be hurtful in their play:

> Michael, a 2-year-old in a child care center, picked up a small hammer that accompanied a xylophone. In the small room of approximately 12 toddlers, Michael started swinging the hammer back and forth as he moved quickly around the room. As other toddlers noticed, they scattered to get away from their swinging peer. Michael headed for the wooden lockers that held the toddlers' coats and sat down on the bottom of the locker between two toddlers who were using the lockers as sitting spots as well. As soon as he sat down, the other two toddlers took off, obviously running away from Michael.

At 2 years of age, Michael already had a reputation for aggression, and the other children had learned to stay out of his way. The peers' working model of relationships with Michael seemed to be "Move away fast or get hurt." Michael had learned one way to try to interact with peers. Perhaps this was his working model of relationships, his notion of how to be with others. Unfortunately, this working model won't help Michael make friends and have rewarding peer relationships. Without adult assistance, his negative peer reputation is likely to stay with him if he continues with this group of children, and he would likely behave the same way with a new set of peers. With adult assistance he can learn social skills that will enhance his relationships with peers.

DaRos and Kovach (1998) highlighted an example of how documenting and reflecting on these documentations of peer interaction illuminate the goals of young children:

> Jason, after clutching three plastic bottles filled with colored water, gives them to his peers; after a few minutes, he insists on collecting them. Of course, the toddlers who now possess these coveted, colorful bottles do not want to return them. Jason begins to cry as he reaches for a bottle and turns to his teacher for help. The teacher says to Jason, "That was nice of you to share the bottles with your friends; sharing makes your friends happy." (p. 27)

After documenting this example through written observation notes, DaRos and Kovach decided that Jason wasn't sharing—at least in the same way that adults share. Rather, he was distributing items to others for them to hold for a moment, but to give back to him when he wanted them.

Teachers and parents who observe this type of situation might come to the same conclusion through asking themselves a series of questions: What was Jason's goal? (Make a best guess.) What were the strategies he was using to achieve his goal? What theories did he have about how relationships work? His goal seemed to be to have his peers hold the bottles for a moment and then give them back. His strategies were to give or distribute the bottles among his peers and then let them know that it was time to give the bottles back to him. His theory about relationships may be that when you give someone something, they should give it back if you still want it. This may have happened often in a give-and-take game with his parent who is more willing than a peer to give a toy back to him when he wants it.

These examples demonstrate how documenting the richness of peer interaction and then reflecting on these observations leads to adults "seeing" behaviors with new eyes. Infant and toddler development is fascinating when viewed through the lens of the child's perspective. Young children's behaviors that may have been seen through a negative filter are now wisely understood as progressive developmental steps toward the infant or toddler becoming socially competent.

Learning Through Relationships

The importance of parent–child relationships for children's emotional development was discussed in chapter 6. Adult–child relationships also have an effect on infants' and toddlers' peer relationships.

The quality of infants' and toddlers' emotional experiences with their primary caregivers (parents and care teachers) plays an important role. Infants and toddlers learn behaviors and have feelings in their first emotional relationships with the important adults in their lives. This, in turn, influences how the young child will behave in subsequent peer relationships. Infants and toddlers develop assumptions in their first relationships about how to interact with others and how others will treat them. Infants and toddlers then wisely apply the information they've gained from their first relationships to their subsequent peer relationships.

The children with secure, sensitive, warm, and encouraging relationships with parents seem more competent and more attractive as playmates both in the toddler years (NICHD, 2001a) and as preschoolers (LaFreniere & Sroufe, 1985; Park & Waters, 1989). Ziv, Oppenheim, and Sagi-Schwartz (2004) found that a group of children, average age 7.5 years, who were securely attached as infants expected their peers (those whose behavior was socially acceptable) to be emotionally and instrumentally available to them. These young children have positive social expectations, know the rudiments of reciprocity in relationships, and have a sense of self-worth and self-efficacy (Rubin, Bukowski, & Parker, 1998). They feel safe to explore the environment and interact with peers, building on their experiences to become even more skilled at peer interactions (Rubin et al., 1998). They know that relationships with other adults and peers are rewarding and worth pursuing.

On the other hand, infants and toddlers who are angry and frustrated or experience negativism and rejection in their first adult–child relationships also carry these feelings and expectations to their toddler and preschool relationships (McElwain, Cox, Burchinal, & Macfie, 2003; Jacobvitz & Hazen, 1999). For example, when parents are aggressive toward their toddlers, the toddlers are more aggressive with peers (Brook, Zheng, Whiteman, & Brook, 2001).

It is important, however, to consider that in a relationship-based and bioecological model of human development many factors could be influencing parent–child interactions. An infant's temperament or a toddler's fussiness, for example, may be challenging for a parent or family members may be influenced by the stress of other relationships or challenges in their immediate environment or community. Famiy support can help parents become more sensitive, and this improves children's outcomes. When insecurely attached children at 15 months subsequently received high-sensitive mothering, however, they had better social, behavior, and language outcomes at age 3 (Belsky & Fearon, 2002).

STRATEGIES TO SUPPORT
SOCIAL DEVELOPMENT AND LEARNING

Following is a summary of strategies that teachers and parents can use to enhance the social development of infants and toddlers.

1. Model kindness with infants and toddlers. They learn from adults whether to be calm, exuberant, friendly, and kind or whether they need to be on guard, angry, sad, and aggressive with others.

2. Observe the temperament of each child. Help them self-regulate their emotions with others. Individualize care based on a child's temperament.

   a. Realize that exuberant children may be slightly more aggressive than others just because they are often in the middle of an action.

   b. Help inhibited children by being understanding and supportive—do not attempt to overcontrol, scold, or be critical to get them to be involved with other children, as this undermines their social competence. Support their language and cognitive development and their interactions with peers.

3. Infants and toddlers learn social competence with peers in the company of "expert adults" who are helpful, not intrusive, and who help elaborate play schemes.

4. Help infants and toddlers get off to a good start in peer relationships. Help toddlers who are aggressive become kind and gain a new reputation.

5. Recognize and support prosocial behaviors.

6. Expect conflict as an important part of social development and support children in learning how to resolve conflict with language and negotiation skills.

7. Infants and toddlers with disabilities may need adult encouragement and skills to play with children without disabilities, and vice versa.

8. Set up an environment that encourages peer interaction

9. Include several peers in conversations. Comment on what other children are doing or saying.

10. Provide quality care.

11. Provide primary care.

12. Ensure continuity of peer groups.

13. Maintain appropriate ratios and group sizes.

14. Develop strong, positive adult-child relationships and sensitive, responsive care.

CHILDREN WITH SPECIAL NEEDS

Infants and toddlers with identified special needs often display delays in social interactions and the development of relationships. Parents and infant-toddler teachers can play a significant role in supporting and encouraging these children's social interactions with peers.

> Trevor was the first child with a disability to attend the child care center. Trevor had cerebral palsy. At the age of 18 months he crawled, and he used sounds, but not words, to communicate.
>
> Because of their own ideas about his disability, Trevor's care providers perceived him as fragile and in need of protection from everyone and everything in the environment. They kept him away from the other toddlers, strapped him into an infant seat at mealtimes, and held him on their laps during play times.
>
> Trevor was very lonely in child care. The toddlers in the classroom did interesting things nonstop. They ran from one side of the room to the other, challenging each other with a look to join in or keep up. They copied each other's table banging and joyful sounds, making them louder with each imitation.
>
> As Trevor watched the other children playing, moving, and singing he became increasingly frustrated by the care providers' failure to move him along with the group. Sometimes he would join in the imitative play from a distance. He began to pounce on any opportunity when he was not physically constrained to crawl, and then walk, to where the other children were. His movements became faster and more purposeful. Trevor's moment-by-moment goal seemed to be to get close to the other children and do what they were doing. This interest in watching and imitating proved to be a powerful motivating force for him to try activities he'd refused before. (Wittmer & Petersen, 1992, pp. 55–56)

As illustrated by the previous true example, infants and toddlers who have disabilities enjoy and learn from their peers without disabilities. Other research confirms this idea. In one study (Wittmer, 1991), approximately 70% of the total interactions of the observed toddlers with disabilities in an inclusive setting were with typical peers. In a study of six preschool children friendships occurred between children with disabilities and those without. Similarity in play styles and the opportunities to engage in similar activities contributed to these friendships (Dietrich, 2005).

Adults can encourage social interactions between children with disabilities and children without disabilities. Research has shown that teachers play a crucial role in encouraging peer interactions among all children (Wittmer & Petersen, 1992). Teachers can:

- Document how a child with disabilities likes to be touched or interact with peers so that the teacher can encourage those types of interactions.
- Place infants beside each other on the floor or in supported seats. Infants like to watch each other.
- Provide duplicates of toys to encourage children to play beside and with each other.
- Offer toys and activities that promote social interaction rather than isolated play. Some favorites among toddlers are a large bin full of balls (make sure they are not small enough for toddlers to put in their mouths and choke), water, sand, and coloring or painting on a huge piece of paper that everyone shares.
- Give children with disabilities toys that attract peers to their side, such as a new toy. Then support the child who has disabilities to show typical peers how to use the toy.
- Build on toddlers' inherent desires to imitate others by focusing the attention of the child with disabilities on the behavior of the other children. If other toddlers are patting a table, say "pat, pat, pat" as you show the child how to pat her hand on the table.
- Find a way for the child with disabilities to communicate with words, sign language, or a communication device and interpret the child's subtle cues to the other children. For

example, say to the child without disabilities, "He said, 'Hi.' Say 'Hi' back," or, "She's really looking at the doll. Can you give her the doll?"

- Comment on how children are alike rather than different: "Look, Sarah likes shape boxes, just like you."
- Encourage toddlers to help by pulling another child in a wagon, turning on the faucet for a child with disabilities as the teacher holds her, or bringing toys to a child who has difficulty moving. Then point out how happy that makes the child being helped.

Your use of these strategies builds a harmonious environment where young children learn to see each other for what they can do, not what they can't do.

PROGRAMS THAT ENHANCE SOCIAL DEVELOPMENT AND LEARNING

What will the child learn about relationships "out in the world"? If the infant or toddler attends a child development and education program, will the experiences be positive and enhance the growth of the child? Or will it tax all of the emotional and social efforts of the child to cope?

Quality Child Development and Education Programs

Higher quality child care and education programs result in more competent peer relationships (Howes, Hamilton, & Matheson, 1994; Howes, Matheson; & Hamilton, 1992; Howes, Phillips, et al., 1992; NICHD, 2001a). The quality of the environment and the use of certain types of toys that facilitate play and cooperation among peers will be discussed in detail in chapter 13.

Continuity of Peer Groups

Howes (1988) noted that children who remain together with the same peers over the infant-toddler years in a child care and education home or center are more likely to maintain their friendships and increase their social skills.

Ratios, Number of Adults, and Group Size

Among 2½-year-olds, there is more negative peer interaction and more nonsocial play when group size is larger, when there are fewer adults in the room, and when there is a larger **child-to-teacher ratio.** Conversely, more positive peer interactions occur if there are more adults available, fewer children in the classroom, and a smaller child-to-teacher ratio (Volling & Feagans, 1995).

child-to-teacher ratio
The proportion of children to teachers, in a classroom or family child care home.

Relationship with the Infant-Toddler Teacher

An infant or toddler teacher's relationship with a young child is strongly related to that child's competence with peers. This adult–child relationship can be classified as secure or insecure (see chapter 6 for a detailed description of these concepts). In a secure attachment relationship the teacher is sensitive and responsive to infant cues for food, attention, and play. The infant or toddler feels safe, confident, and expects relationships to be emotionally satisfying. An infant or toddler with a secure attachment relationship is more competent with peers (Howes, Phillips, et al., 1992) and this secure attachment relationship predicts social competence at a later age. Howes, Hamilton, et al., (1994) found that infants who had a secure attachment relationship with their teacher were more likely to participate in complex peer play and were more gregarious (sociable and expressive), less hostile, and less withdrawn at 4 years. Secure, warm relationships with teachers help infants start on a path of positive feelings of self-worth, trust in others, and peer competence.

Developmental Trends and Responsive Interactions
Social Development and Learning with Peers

Capacities: To communicate with peers, be prosocial, play with peers, and manage negative emotions and conflict in peer interaction.

Development	Example
0–4 months (infant)	
· Infants like to look at each other (visual regard). · Infants prefer to look at faces, especially the edges and the eyes. · Infants may cry when they hear other babies cry (contagion).	After the teacher put Tamika by Sam on a blanket on the floor, Tamika stared intently at Sam.
4–8 months (infant)	
· Infants touch a peer, vocalize to each other, get excited, approach other babies, smile and laugh at each other. · Babies may treat other babies like objects—crawling over them, licking or sucking on them, or sitting on them. They are just learning the difference between people and objects. Infants may poke, push, or pat another baby to see what that other infant will do. They often look very surprised at the reaction they get.	Amna crawled over to Nadia who was lying on the floor. Touching Nadia's hair, Amna laughed out loud.
8–12 months (mobile infant)	
· Infants may show a peer an object, sit by each other, crawl after and around each other, play chase-and-retrieve games. · Babies smile and laugh at each other. · Babies make sounds to and with each other—may say first words with peers. · Peek-a-boo is a favorite game as babies explore separation: coming and going, in sight and out of sight. · Infants can learn to touch each other gently. · Because infants become more goal oriented at this age, they may push another baby's hand away from a toy or crawl over another baby to get a toy.	Shamaine peeked around the low toy shelf and saw Carla crawling toward her. Shamaine quickly turned around and crawled away with Carla close behind. Kai crawled over Bridger's legs to get a toy on the other side of Bridger.
12–18 months (mobile infant)	
· Imitation (motor) and interactive turns begin. Toddlers may copy each other—if one gives a toy to another child, the other may imitate. · Mobile infants begin to talk to each other. · Infants may show concern when other babies are distressed. · Mobile infants may take a toy from another child, say "no," push away the other child, clutch toy to self and say "Mine." · Infants are little scientists at this age, experimenting to see how things work. This affects how they get along with peers. They are constantly doing things to other children to see what response they will get. · Biting may appear as infants bite others "to see what happens," to get the toy they want, to express frustration. Infants are on the cusp of communicating well; they may communicate through their mouths in the form of a bite.	Rashida banged her spoon on the table and soon two others tried it. They seemed to be physically following each other's lead (as in a conversation). First, Carmen tried pushing Toby away from her rocking horse. When that didn't work she leaned over and took a bite out of his arm.

Teacher or Parent-Child Interaction	Environment

0–4 months (infant)

- Hold two babies so they can look at each other.
- Place a few babies on a blanket on the floor so that they can look at and touch each other.

- The arms of teachers provide the best environment.
- Blankets on the floor—put two babies beside each other or so their toes are touching each other.

4–8 months (infant)

- Move to music with a baby in each arm.

- While holding one baby in your lap, point out and talk about what another baby is doing.
- Place two babies on their tummies facing a mirror.
- Instead of saying "Don't" or "Stop that" to exploring babies, say "Touch gently." Tell children what you want them to do—model it for them.

- Hang a safety mirror horizontally on the wall, so the bottom is touching the floor.
- Cover an inner tube with soft cloth. Sit two babies in the inner tube so that their feet are touching each other.

8–12 months (mobile infant)

- Name parts of infants' bodies as two infants sit close to each other:
  Here is baby's eyes
  Here is baby's nose
  Touch the part that sees
  Touch the part that blows
- Place a baby with one other baby (pairs), because more frequent, complex, and intense peer interaction occurs than when a child is with many peers.
- Understand that infants are not being "naughty" when they push another child's hand away. Say "Jenny was holding that toy. Let's find you a different toy."

- While feeding, place high chairs so children can see each other.
- Set up cozy corners in the room where babies can "disappear" (but adults can still see them).
- Hang a long wide cloth (so babies won't get tangled in it) from the ceiling. Babies love to crawl around it.
- Place containers with different sizes of blocks in them between two babies. Sit beside them as they begin to explore the materials. Talk about what each one is doing.

12–18 months (mobile infant)

- Show mobile infants how to roll down a small hill together.

- Help mobile toddlers learn each other's names by singing greeting and good-bye songs with the children's names in them: "Here is Tanya, how are you?" and "Here is Henry, how are you?" as you point or touch each child who comes by you or is sitting in your lap.
- Comment on prosocial behavior. Say "You gave him the doll. He likes that!" Babies may not understand your words, but they will be able to tell by your tone of voice that you are pleased with them.
- They will enjoy looking at books together by forming an informal group (this means they move in and out of the group) around the legs, lap, and arms of a favorite parent or teacher.

- Provide a large cardboard box, open on each end. Encourage babies to crawl in and out of the box with each other. Windows on the side encourage babies to peek at each other through the windows.
- Dolls, trucks, cars, and other play materials encourage interactions among peers.

- They love sand and water and playing with different sizes of safe bottles and balls. When each has his own bin or tub of water or sand, play goes more smoothly.
- Outside, large sandboxes or push toys encourage interactive play.

Developmental Trends and Responsive Interactions (continued)

Development	Example

18–24 months (toddler)

Development	Example
• Friendships can develop early. Friends are more likely to touch, lean on one another, and smile at each other than are children who are not friends. • Toddlers imitate each other's sounds and words and talk to each other and begin to communicate with others across more space. • Toddlers give or offer a toy or food to another toddler. • Toddlers may get or pull an adult to help another child or will help another child by getting a tissue, for example. • Toddlers can show kindness for other babies who are feeling distressed. A mobile infant or toddler, however, may assume that what will comfort him will also comfort the distressed child. • Children take turns, for example, with a ball, or jumping up. They may have toddler kinesthetic conversations as they follow a leader in moving around the room—moving in and out of the group, taking turns as leader and follower—as if in a conversation of listening and talking, learning valuable turn-taking skills. • Pushing, shoving, grabbing, and hitting may occur as children struggle over "mine for as long as I want it" and "yours, but I want it, too." Toddlers may fight over small toys more than large, nonmovable objects.	Paulie looked as if he was waiting by the door for Jamie to appear at the beginning of the day. When Jamie and his mom came in the door, Paulie toddled over and took Jamie's hand, a big smile on his face. Tanya jumped (half fell) off a board several inches off the ground. Soon three toddlers were standing on the board and half jumping, half stepping off and on the board, enjoying the activity immensely.

24–36 months (toddler)

Development	Example
• Toddler friendship is "proximity seeking," wanting to be close and to show affection, such as smiling, laughing, and hugging. Friends prefer each other as interaction partners. Friendships continue to develop and deepen. • They exchange information and can imitate past action of others. • Toddlers may congregate and cluster together. When a teacher begins playing with an interesting activity with one child, children often come running from the corners of the room. • Some toddlers are capable of inventing a variety of ways to help others who are hurt or sad. Some may have an impressive repertoire of altruistic behavior, and if one thing doesn't work they will try another way. • Peers work together toward a common goal, with one the leader and one the follower. • Object, personal space, and verbal struggles can occur. Toddlers also engage in playful exchanges—rough and tumble, run and chase, and verbal games. • Some children may gain a reputation with peers for aggressive or kind behavior. • Children become more positive and less negative in their social play between 24 and 36 months. • Dominance of one child over another can occur.	Maria and Sally played on opposite sides of the small shelf of toys for 30 minutes, peeking over at each other every few minutes, and telling each other, "boat," "my boat," "hi," "want juice," "look at me," and saying each other's names over and over. When a fire truck went by outside, several toddlers rushed to the window to look. Josh and Mike pushed, pulled, rolled, and grunted as they worked hard to roll the huge pumpkin from inside to the playground where the toddlers and their teachers were going to cut it open and scoop out all of the seeds.

Teacher or Parent-Child Interaction	Environment

18–24 months (toddler)

- When inside or outside, nurture toddlers as they come and go to "refuel" emotionally with a special teacher, encouraging several toddlers to sit together beside you or in your lap. Allow toddlers to touch each other gently.
- Encourage several toddlers to make animal sounds together and imitate each other as you show them the pictures in a book.
- Ask one child to help another child by getting a tissue, turning the faucet on, opening a door, etc.
- Encourage kindness with one another. If one toddler cries, ask another what "we" could do to help.
- Encourage two peers to set a table together or sponge it off together after eating. Watch them imitate each other.
- Sing songs, encouraging toddlers to take turns with the actions.

- Inside and outside: Provide sand areas large enough for several toddlers and expect them to sit right in the middle of the area.

- Blankets on the floor or ground or over a table provide a spot for peers to play.
- Provide wagons: Pulling or pushing a friend in a wagon will result in squeals of delight.
- Provide balls and pull-toys that encourage interactive play.

- Places to jump safely encourage social exchanges.

- Provide musical toys, several of each kind, so children can make beautiful music together. Sometimes one will lead and another will follow, or vice versa.

24–36 months (toddler)

- Create situations where two toddlers need to work together—for example, to roll a pumpkin from one place to another or carry a bucket of "heavy" blocks from inside to outside.
- Put a band-aid on a doll's arm or leg and encourage toddlers to take care of the baby.
- Ask the toddlers, "How can we help Joey—he's sad—he's crying."
- Try to change the image of a child who is gaining a reputation for aggression. Keep the child close, show her how to touch gently, and comment on her helpful behavior. Give her an interesting toy that might interest other children to engage with her. Stay close and teach her how to play.

- Place hats and easy-to-put-on dress-up clothes in a cozy corner with a big mirror.

- Toddlers will enjoy each other as their friends change appearances under a floppy hat or wearing big shoes.
- Spaces on or under a short loft encourage peer interaction.
- Provide several types of dolls as well as safe feeding utensils, blankets, and small beds. Sit close and watch as toddlers pretend to care for their babies.
- Provide open-ended materials such as blocks, and activities that require cooperation such as painting with big brushes and water on outside walls or filling a big bucket with water from smaller containers.
- Large motor equipment such as climbers or rocking boats encourage toddlers to work together toward a common goal: everyone moving to the top of the climber or rocking the boat with everyone in it.

Another important facet of the quality of teacher strategies is how sensitive and responsive teachers are in their interactions with infants and toddlers. As noted in an NICHD (2001a) study of more than 500 children, summarizing the importance of a positive, responsive teacher for a child's development of social competence: "The most consistent finding for child care experience [for 24- to 36-month-old children] was that more sensitive and responsive behavior by caregivers was associated with less negative, more positive play with other children" (p. 1492).

Socialization Strategies of the Teacher

One aspect of an infant-toddler teacher's behavior includes the specific socialization strategies that you can use to promote peer development. You might use positive, peer-relationship-promoting strategies with toddlers that include physical or verbal help. Take a shy child's hand as you join a group of toddlers playing with blocks. Show a child how to "touch gently." If an infant starts pulling other children's hair, provide a doll with hair that the infant can play with. The strategies for supporting prosocial development for children with disabilities are useful to use with all children, with or without disabilities. These positive, peer-relationship-promoting strategies result in more complex play and fewer behavior problems.

If the teacher uses negative strategies—interrupting peer play without explanation, reprimanding or punishing peer contact, or separating children (Howes, Hamilton, et al., 1994) the children's social competence is affected. When educators use negative strategies, children participate in less complex peer play and teachers rate children as more difficult (Howes, Hamilton, et al., 1994).

myeducationlab

Go to MyEducationLab and complete the Building Teaching Skills and Dispositions exercise in Chapter 7.

SUMMARY

Infants and toddlers have the capacity to learn to enjoy peers, to play and communicate, to become prosocial, to become friends who enjoy each other's company, and to negotiate conflicts with peers. They become increasingly skilled over the first 3 years of life with parents and teachers who use sensitive, responsive strategies to promote these capacities and children's development.

- Children's attributes of temperament and gender influence peer relationships.
  - Children with an inhibited temperament will need support from parents and teachers to develop confidence and skills to play with peers.
  - Exuberant children, the "Tiggers" of the world, may be engaged in more joyous as well as conflictual peer interactions.
  - Toddlers' preference to play with children of the same sex may be explained by the "compatible play styles" theory.
- Culture plays a part in whether early peer interactions are valued by adults.
- Infants and toddlers, over the first 3 years of life, have the capacity to learn to:
  - Communicate with peers
  - Increase their play skills
  - Develop prosocial behaviors and attitudes
  - Manage conflict and negative feelings with peers
- Children with special needs can gain social skills with typical peers.
- There are many strategies that adults can use to support peer development.
- Peer competence is associated with higher quality care in programs, smaller group size, lower child-to-teacher ratios, the nature of the child's relationship with the teacher, and the specific strategies used.

Key Terms

child-to-teacher ratio

dominant

elaborate play schemes

extroverted

exuberant

gender segregation

gestural language

group continuity of care

inhibited

interpsychological

intrapsychological

prosocial

same-gender play

socially competent

subordinate

REFLECTIONS AND RESOURCES FOR THE READER

Reflections

1. Jaheed and Michael often play with each other in the Early Head Start center program. They are becoming increasingly aggressive and try to play away from where teachers are in the room. What would you do if you were a teacher in this room?

2. As a care teacher in a center or family child care home, how would you implement a program that emphasizes prosocial development?

3. How can you promote positive social interactions between children who do have special needs and those who do not? Why is this so important to the children, families, teachers, and program?

4. How does your culture influence how you interact with your peer group?

Observation and Application Opportunities

1. Use the Developmental Trends and Responsive Interactions chart at the end of this chapter and observe infants and toddlers in a center program. What social behaviors do you see at what age?

2. Observe an infant or toddler with a special need who attends a center or family program. What strategies does the teacher use to encourage peer interactions? What else could she do to promote positive peer interactions?

Supplemental Articles and Books to Read

Brownell, C., & Kopp, C. (Eds.). (2007). *Transitions in early socioemotional development: The toddler years.* New York: Guilford Press.

Goldman, B. D., & Buysse, V. (2007). Friendships in very young children. In O. Saracho & B. Spodek (Eds.), *Contemporary perspectives on socialization and social development in early childhood education* (pp. 165–192). Charlotte, NC: Information Age Publishing.

Logue, M. E. (2006). Teachers observe to learn: Differences in social behavior of toddlers and preschoolers in same-age and multiage groupings. *Young Children, 61*(3), 70–76.

Quann, V., & C. A. Wien. (2006). The visible empathy of infants and toddlers. *Young Children, 61*(4), 22–29. Available at the Beyond the Journal Web site, http://journal.nayec.org/btj/200607/Quann709BTJ.asp.

Rubin, K. H., Bukowski, W., & Laursen, B. (Eds.). (2008). *Handbook of peer interactions, relationships, and groups.* New York: Guilford Press.

Wittmer, D. S. (2008). *A focus on peers: The importance of relationships in the early years.* Washington, DC: ZERO TO THREE Press.

Interesting Links

http://www.educarer.com/current-article-relationships.htm

Educarer, Inc.   Social Relationships of Infants in Daycare. Phyllis Porter highlights examples of how very young infants interact.

http://www.nncc.org

The National Network for Child Care   NNCC provides access to articles on a variety of topics including children's social development.

myeducationlab

These and other web links are included in this chapter on MyEducationLab.

Cognitive Development and Learning

The newborn, hours after birth, quietly studies her mother's face.

The 1-year-old repeatedly empties little blocks from a plastic container and then drops them back in. Sometimes he concentrates on the blocks, matching shapes or colors; sometimes he looks to his teacher for her approval.

Bryan, Sherod, and Mikey take the container of musical instruments off the shelf. Each 2-year-old reaches in and takes out a favorite rhythm instrument. Bryan starts to shake his bells. Mikey sings, "Twinkle, Twinkle, Little Star," the song they sometimes sing with their teacher. Within moments the three are parading through the room, playing their instruments and singing.

THE UNIQUENESS OF EACH CHILD

The image we once had of infants doing nothing but eating and sleeping is gone. The word we most often hear used in describing newborns is "Amazing!" Thanks to the recent research on early learning, we know that babies are born with knowledge gained in the womb and that they are actively working to build an understanding of their world in every waking moment.

This chapter will describe the process of early learning—how infants and toddlers learn, how adults support learning, and what infants and toddlers are learning about their world. Early cognitive development includes:

- How infants and toddlers focus, attend, maintain their curiosity, and are motivated to learn
- What infants perceive in the environment through their senses
- How infants and toddlers attempt to make meaning, connections, and patterns from their perceptions
- How infants and toddlers increasingly use language to develop and broaden their ideas
- How infants and toddlers use memories of events to make predictions about their world
- How infants and toddlers solicit and receive the helpful support of adults

Capacities

For the first 8 or 9 months, babies rely primarily on information they perceive through their senses. As they approach their first birthday, they are increasingly able to use language and other symbols as they learn about the world. By their third birthday they use language fluently, engage in elaborate dramatic play, and have important and meaningful friendships. Throughout the first 3 years, they are using their own capacities and the support of their parents and teachers to learn about the world. These are the foundations of learning.

> *Tyler digs in the sand industriously. As he finds small pebbles, he pulls them out and stacks them in a pile. He loads them into a toy dump truck, "drives" the truck across the sand table, and dumps them into another corner. "Build house," he says.*
>
> *Mary also digs in the sand. However, every movement in the room catches her attention. When a stranger enters the room, she stops her sand play and watches the stranger and her teacher.*

Current theories of learning assert that children construct knowledge through their experiences in the world (Bruner, 1996a, b; Piaget, 1954). They learn, in part, through the scaffolding of information and experience provided by adults (Vygotsky, 1978). The theory of core knowledge suggests that infants are born with basic cognitive systems that predispose them to be interested in and to learn about the things that are most important to survival. These include understanding the objects in the world, agents or the goal-directed actions of living things, number, and geometry or the ability to orient oneself in the environment (Spelke & Kinzler, 2007).

Attention

Two aspects of emotional development are pivotal in the infant's and toddler's ability to pay attention to the world: self-regulation and an attachment relationship. Self-regulation helps a child control his reactions and maintain a quiet, alert interest in the people, events, and materials around him. An attachment relationship provides a sense of security that assures the child that an adult will keep him safe as he ventures out to explore the world. By the age of 30 months, Tyler and Mary demonstrate very different abilities in their **executive functioning**— the ability to self-regulate and pay attention to relevant information in the environment; the ability to plan, sequence, and organize behavior (Eslinger, 1996); and the ability to flexibly shift and control one's own behavior (Denckla, 1989).

executive functioning
The ability to regulate, plan, sequence, organize, shift, and control one's own behavior.

In the previous example, Tyler is able to concentrate on his play and use information from the world to make his play very elaborate. As an infant, with responsive parents and teachers, he quickly learned to self-regulate his reactions to the world. He learned to be alert and interested in the world without feeling overwhelmed by information. He also learned that his teacher would keep him safe while he was exploring toys and his environment. He feels free to combine materials such as sand and trucks with his experiences in watching trucks near a construction site. Mary has had a less supportive early experience. As a young infant, no one responded to her cries. No one helped her become calm and attentive when she felt overwhelmed. She was in a child care setting with many children and a teacher who sometimes became enraged. Mary is so busy scanning her environment for signs of danger that she finds it difficult to concentrate on her play. She is wary of strangers and rarely feels safe and relaxed, so she does not pay attention to the world nor remember the things she sees.

The impact of early experience on the child's ability to maintain attention is beautifully articulated in *Heart Start: The Emotional Foundations of Learning* (1992), a report published by ZERO TO THREE. *Heart Start* describes how actively the infant is working to attend to and make sense of his environment:

> It is in the first weeks and months of life . . .
>
> That children first try to understand and master their environment
>
> —or not;
>
> First attempt to concentrate and find it possible
>
> —or not;
>
> First conclude the world is orderly and predictable
>
> —or not;
>
> First learn that others are basically supportive
>
> —or not;
>
> First learn that others are basically caring
>
> —or not;
>
> It is in these years that the foundations for later learning are laid down
>
> —or not.
>
> *Source:* From *Heart Start: The emotional foundations of school readiness,* 1992, Arlington, VA: *ZERO TO THREE.* Copyright 1992 by *ZERO TO THREE.* Reprinted with permission.

myeducationlab

Go to the Activities and Applications section in Chapter 8 of MyEducationLab to watch *Habituation,* demonstrating an infant's habituation/ dishabituation responses.

habituation
A simple form of learning in which an animal, after repeated exposure to a stimulus, stops responding.

Nearly every child is born with the capacity to attend and explore—to try to figure the patterns of activity in the world and understand how one event may affect another. As relationship-based theory states (Hinde, 1988), it is the support, or lack of support, offered by the adults that establishes the foundation of skills as simple as that of paying attention.

Curiosity and Motivation

What is it in the child or in the environment that makes a child curious and eager to explore? Why does one child become fascinated by dropping and picking up objects or making a long string of beads fit into a bottle? Why does another child make a half-hearted attempt to stack cups and then drift off to another toy when the orange cup doesn't fit in the purple cup? How does the spark of curiosity match the sense of confidence the young child has to explore, problem solve, and manipulate the things in his environment?

One interesting insight into early cognitive development is that infants and toddlers like to be challenged by new information. Even though babies show us that they recognize and like familiar things, they are also interested in new things. In fact, when an infant or toddler can *always* accurately predict what will happen, an event is no longer very compelling and the baby will stop looking at it; researchers call this **habituation.** Then if a novel element is introduced, babies will become more alert and pay attention to the event again. Early studies of infant learning provide a good example. Watson (1972) rigged a mobile to a pressure-sensitive pad that responded selectively when an infant turned her head to the right or to the left. An infant would quickly notice that the mobile would turn when she turned her head in one direction but not the other. Or, when the pattern was changed to be more challenging, if she would turn her head in both directions in a certain pattern. Babies would actively work to turn the mobile until they had mastered the required pattern of head turning. When they could absolutely predict how to make the mobile turn, they would lose interest in it. It was the act of achieving understanding that was so compelling. The difficulty and effort, as Malaguzzi and Gandini (1993) point out, are part of the pleasure of learning for infants and toddlers:

> The pleasure of learning and knowing, and of understanding, is one of the most important and basic feelings that every child expects from the experiences he confronts alone, with other children or with adults. It is a crucial feeling which must be reinforced so that the pleasure survives even when reality may prove that learning, knowing and understanding involve difficulty and effort. (p. 174)

The relationship between learning and emotion is well established. Bowlby (1969), in proposing the process of attachment between babies and their parents, described attachment as an internal motivational system that balances another internal system: the drive for exploration. Bowlby even suggests that attachment is necessary in part to protect our vulnerable young from dangers they might encounter as they respond to their strong desire to explore. The child's feeling of attachment keeps her in safe proximity to a caregiver. The evolutionary benefits of attachment are obvious, in promoting the safety of our young so that they may grow up to reproduce. The child's desire to explore may lead her into the path of predators—or traffic. However, the evolutionary benefit of exploration is in the learning and discoveries that are made.

Pruett (1999) states that learning occurs when an event evokes both emotional and cognitive reactions. Learning begins with an event in the environment—maybe a small toy is offered for exploration or a dog enters the play yard. Pruett calls this event an **interactive stimulus.** Then there is a **cognitive process;** the child instantly reviews categories of similar experiences and recognizes the toy as interesting or the dog as familiar. Memories are evoked of other toys or other dogs. The child will experience feeling from the memory. He liked that kind of toy and feels pleasure; or that dog snapped at him and he feels afraid. Finally, he will respond with behavior grounded in his emotional reaction and his cognitive understanding. He reaches for the toy or runs from the dog. The abilities to *perceive information,* to have *emotional reactions,* and to *learn* are inextricably intertwined.

Happiness and excitement are not the only emotions that promote learning. Anxiety also supports learning as children need to learn how to manage their own disappointment, sorrow, and frustration. In fact, young children have limited interest in tasks that are either too easy for them or that seem impossibly hard. They are most engaged by a tolerable amount of challenge (Morgan, Harmon, & Maslin-Cole, 1999; Pruett, 1999).

In recent years there has been rising interest in what infants and toddlers find motivating—what makes them want to explore, understand, and solve the problems posed by their environments. (See Box 8.1.) There is also interest in understanding why some babies appear to lack or lose their motivation to learn. In laboratory studies, infants have been presented with tasks over which they have no

myeducationlab

Go to the Activities and Applications section in Chapter 8 of MyEducationLab to watch the video *Making a Discovery: The Water Table.* How does this demonstrate curiosity and motivation to learn?

interactive stimulus
An environmental event that invites interaction.

cognitive process
Scanning memory, organizing and categorizing information, or thinking.

Box 8.1

Curious Minds at Work

"What's dat?" asked Cara as she pointed to the flower. "What's dat?" inquired Sammy as he played with a toy. Haniya turned her bottle around, trying to suck on the other end, and Jama watched intently as the mechanical train whistled and sped around the track. When it stopped, he tried to push it, pull it, and pound on it to get it going again.

What do these infants and toddlers have in common? They are all curious! They are interested, inquisitive, even nosy. They want to know, learn, and find out how things work. They are busy trying to understand their world.

Curiosity is a disposition that helps adults make new discoveries, try new things, read and write books, and learn how to do their jobs in a better way. One of the greatest traits that we can inspire in children is a sense of curiosity. Without curiosity, children are not motivated to appreciate, perceive, master, and discover. When a healthy sense of curiosity is discouraged or punished in children, they lose the learning sparkle. How does that sparkle—the desire to learn—develop and how can it be lit and kept glowing?

control—for example, mobiles that turn or remain still with no relationship to the baby's efforts. When later presented with mobiles that do respond to their actions, 2-month-olds cannot figure out the right contingent response (Watson, 1972). Toddlers, first presented with unsolvable puzzles, won't even attempt new, solvable puzzles.

Depending on how infants and toddlers experience their efforts at learning and problem solving, they develop internal working models of themselves as people who can—or cannot—effect change in their environment. Infants or toddlers who are overly challenged by the tasks in their environment or young childrens who are always directed to use their toys in a "correct" way may see themselves as helpless in learning situations. When a child's past experiences give him the belief that he has little or no control over the events that affect him, he develops a **learned helplessness** (Seligman, 1992). Other concerns about motivation center on passive experiences such as watching television.

On the other hand, infants with experiences of having influence on their social and physical world begin to demonstrate mastery motivation. **Mastery motivation** includes "(1) attempts to master a task independent of adult direction, (2) persistence in mastering a task even when difficulties arise, and (3) selection of a task that is neither extremely easy nor extremely difficult" (Redding, Morgan, & Harmon, 1988).

Parents and teachers appear to have a strong influence on whether a child is motivated by a desire for mastery or by learned helplessness. The reliable responsiveness of the adult to the infant's cues provides a sense of efficacy in social relationships as well as freeing the child to attend to and explore objects. Parents and teachers are also able to provide responsive environments, with toys and materials that respond to the child's actions, strengthening his sense of competence, and encouraging him to master materials (Yarrow, 1981). When adults use gentle guidance with their toddlers in learning situations—making suggestions such as "Have you tried all the pieces?" or encouragement such as "I think you're getting it!"—children are less likely to avoid challenges. Looking at Observation Invitation 8.1, the child seems emotionally flat and almost dutiful in completing the puzzle when his teacher helps too much. However, when she sits nearby, using only some words of encouragement and suggestion, he turns back toward her and seems to take more pleasure out of completing the puzzle. At 3 years old, children show more persistence in mastery tasks if their mothers offer corrective feedback in affectively neutral ways and praise their children's products and efforts. In addition, mothers who encourage their children's autonomous efforts to master play activities have children who are more persistent and motivated in other mastery activities (Kelley, Brownell, & Campbell, 2000).

As described in relationship-based theory (Hinde, 1988), every aspect of infant and toddler learning is intertwined with the child's early relationships. Adults help young children feel effective and in control; they provide interesting environments to explore; they provide language, gestures, facial expressions, and body postures to communicate information about situations and events; and they help infants sort out the pieces of the environment to which they should attend. Adults bring different levels of skills to these tasks, and so do the infants and toddlers.

Sensory Perceptions

To a great degree, a baby's ability to learn depends on her ability to perceive sensory information and then to process, or make sense of and remember, that information. In fact, Piaget (1954) named the first, newborn stage of learning, the *sensorimotor* period, describing the active perceptual work infants do to study faces, to remember smells, to touch and taste everything they can bring to their lips.

As we know, even in the womb, infants are taking in sensory information such as sounds and light. The synapses in the brain capture and transmit this sensory information—the muffled sound of their parent's voices, the salty taste of amniotic fluid, and the shifting pressures of their mother's moving body—so that they are born with surprisingly well-organized perceptual systems.

Observation Invitation 8.1

Here McKyle is working on a puzzle. He chose this activity himself and started it by taking all of the pieces out and tucking each one under his left arm. His teacher thought that made it difficult for him to work and had him put the puzzle pieces down. She then helped him do the puzzle. When it was complete, he emptied it and began again—his way. His teacher stayed nearby and silently watched.

What does his facial expression tell you about his teacher's involvement?

What do you think his teacher is doing that is helpful for him?

Seeing

The seriousness and intensity of the very young infant's gaze can be surprising. Watching the eyes of very young babies, it is easy to believe that they are intent on drinking in all the information the world has to offer and putting together the information that makes sense to them. Newborns are able to visually follow movement within a distance of 9 to 12 inches, although the focus is a little fuzzy. This provides the newborn with a wonderful ability to look into his mother's eyes as she is feeding him from the breast or his teacher's eyes as she cuddles him with a bottle.

In the first months, the baby sees best out of the corner of his eye, using peripheral vision. He will be most interested in objects that offer high contrasts of light and dark and images that resemble the human face (Bower, 1977; Lamb, Bornstein, & Teti, 2002). By 3 months of age,

168   CHAPTER 8

Go to the Activities
and Applications
section in Chapter 8
of MyEducationLab
to watch *A Story
about Lines*—a
sequence of photos
that demonstrate
how a baby
experiments with
learning about lines.

infants are looking straight ahead and showing interest in their own hands. They enjoy the movement of mobiles twirling slowly above them as they practice using their two eyes together, learning to focus on an object and fuse the images entering each eye. If the eyes are not aligned—some people call them "crossed"—the baby will have "double vision" and will stop using one eye to clear up the image. If one or both eyes do not work properly, the connections between the eye and the brain may not develop. By 6 months of age, the infant's range of vision has stretched to focus on greater distances; by 9 months, he can see as well as an adult at both close range and distances (ZERO TO THREE, 2009). The sequence of visual development is illustrated in Figure 8.1.

Edges and lines. Although infants are highly interested in other human beings, they also spend quite a lot of time sorting out the pieces of the environment. Infants are surrounded by an endless number of colors, shapes, and noises. In order to learn, they must figure out which of these deserve their attention and which can be ignored. One of their first tasks is to organize the images they see and the sounds they hear into a recognizable and understandable order. Using their vision, very young infants study images with high contrasts between light and dark areas, and their eyes travel along the edges of objects as they learn where one object ends and one begins (Haith, 1980; Lamb et al., 2002).

Figure 8.1
Vision milestones.

Age	Visual Ability
Birth to 2 months	Sees best at 9 to 12 inches Sees best out of the corner of the eye Loves to look at your face Likes objects with strong contrasts in light and dark Can follow slow movement Eyes are sometimes uncoordinated
2 to 6 months	Begins to recognize objects as one image Looks at own hands Uses vision to reach for objects May stare at anything interesting Looks in mirror Recognizes bottle
6 to 8 months	Sees all colors Sees as well as a teenager May touch self in mirror Turns head to see object Likes certain colors
9 to 12 months	Can see small objects such as cereal pieces Is developing depth perception Can follow fast movements
12 to 18 months	Can do simple-shape puzzles Interested in pictures and books Recognizes own face in mirror
18 to 36 months	Can focus near and far Points and gestures for certain objects Scribbles, sometimes in imitation

Source: Milestones compiled from Morgan Stanley Children's Hospital of New York–Presbyterian. (nd).
Age Appropriate vision milestones (http://childrensnyp.org/).

Moving objects. Babies combine their interest in edges and lines with an interest in movement to discern what comprises a single entity. They quickly learn that an object that appears to be one single entity—given its visual edges—should move in space in one piece. The movement may be an important part of figuring out what makes a single object. For example, the cover of a book may have a title on a banner (with edges of its own) and a picture of a teddy bear (with its own defining edges). However, when the book is lifted and carried, the edges of the whole book move together. Here, the movement helps define the object (Spelke, Breinlinger, Jacobson, & Phillips, 1993).

Babies understand the rules of movement in the physical world. In research situations, they show great surprise if an object moves in ways that are contrary to the laws of physics. If an object is moving in an arc toward a screen and then disappears behind the screen, the infant's eyes will move to the point on the other side of the screen where the object would appear if it continued in its arc. When the object appears at another point, babies look surprised. In experiments where pieces of objects are placed so as to look like one object, babies are surprised if the parts move away from each other separately. Babies even show some knowledge of gravity. They are surprised when an object appears to stay in the air without support (Baillargeon, 1993).

Hearing

Infants are able to hear even before they are born. Newborns recognize sounds that are already familiar to them. Using particular patterns of sucking on specially designed pacifiers, newborn babies will suck harder and longer to hear voices similar to their mother's voice, which they hear in the last few months of gestation through the walls of the womb. Newborns demonstrate through their sucking that they prefer to listen to the language that they heard prenatally; they even prefer to hear familiar passages of stories that their mothers had repeatedly read aloud during the pregnancy (DeCasper & Spence, 1986; Mehler, Jusczyk, Lambertz, Halsted, Bertoncini, & Ameil-Tison, 1988; Moon, Cooper, & Fifer, 1993).

Hearing milestones, as shown in Figure 8.2, are observed in relation to the baby's attention to language. From birth to 3 months, babies turn toward a sound. They pay attention to sounds in the environment, such as caregivers talking quietly to them. Between 3 and 6 months of age, infants understand a few words such as *bye-bye* or *no*. They will babble and imitate sounds. Between 6 and 12 months, they begin to intentionally use simple words such as *mama* or *dada* (ZERO TO THREE, 2009).

Touch

Infants are very sensitive to touch. They respond with strong cries to physical discomforts such as hunger or wet diapers. They are comforted by being held close to their caregivers' bodies or within snug swaddling. Infants use touch to learn about the world; they suck on objects, feel them with their hands, and kick at them with their feet. Early studies of babies in institutions demonstrated that although babies may be fed adequate nutritional matter, if they are not held and touched they may actually die (Spitz, 1945). Lack of experience with being touched is identified as one of the factors that cause the brains of maltreated children to be underdeveloped (Perry, 1996).

Touch is being utilized in some intensive care nurseries with premature infants. In a practice called *kangaroo care,* parents hold their premature infant in skin-to-skin contact on their chests for several hours a day. Studies show these babies regulate their heart rate and breathing sooner, sleep longer, grow faster, maintain their body temperature, and have brain activity that looks identical to the brain activity of contentment and the creation of synapses (Richardson, 1997). They score higher on developmental tests at 6 months (Feldman, Eidelman, Sirota, & Weller, 2002). Earlier studies showed that premature infants given gentle massage for 10 days, while still in the neonatal care intensive unit, increased their weight gain by nearly 50% over babies not receiving massage (Field & Brazelton, 1990). Mothers and fathers benefit as well.

Figure 8.2
Hearing
milestones.

Age	Hearing Ability
Birth to 2 months	Can hear many sounds Prefers human speech Startles at loud sounds Can be soothed by soft sounds Turns head toward familiar voice
2 to 6 months	Looks toward new sounds Responds to different tones of voice Enjoys toys that make sounds May babble repeated sounds "ba-ba-ba" Frightened by loud noises
6 to 8 months	Is very interested in human voices Looks for the source of a sound Babbles Responds to own name Recognizes simple, common words
9 to 12 months	Shows interest in telephone Understands many words Looks at pictures as adult describes them Points to pictures when named Sometimes follows one-step directions
12 to 18 months	Enjoys playing with sounds Uses a few words, maybe a few words in a sentence Points to body parts when asked Follows directions without being shown
18 to 24 months	Understands yes/no questions Understands simple phrases Enjoys hearing stories Will understand your use of color words
24 to 36 months	Understands size words Understands action words

Source: Milestones compiled from Spectrum Health. (2009). Hearing Milestones. Retrieved
March 10, 2009, from https://www.spectrumhealth.org.

They are more sensitive to their baby's cues and at 3 months provide a better home environment (Feldman et al., 2002).

Smelling and Tasting

The sense of smell develops quickly in the newborn and seems to be used to help the baby recognize his mother. In a series of studies, 2-day-old babies could not differentiate a pad soaked with their mother's breast milk from a clean pad or one soaked with another mother's milk. By 5 days, babies show significantly more interest in the pad with their mother's milk than the clean pad. On the sixth day of life, babies turned their heads to keep their faces near their mother's milk-soaked pad rather than that of another new mother (McFarlane, 1975). It is possible that smell has some role in the development of attachment in both the baby and the adult's experience. Babies quickly learn the shampoo or cologne scents of their parents and are more easily comforted by blankets or stuffed animals that carry familiar smells (Mennella & Beauchamp, 2002).

At birth, babies are able to taste sweet, sour, and bitter. They prefer sweet tastes and will bring their hands to their mouths when given something sweet in the first weeks of life. Some cultures—such as Egypt, Mexico, Jamaica, and India—give newborns sweet-tasting liquids to help them calm and sleep. Breast milk is also very sweet (Rochat, 2001). Although most babies do not taste salt until about 4 months, recent studies show that babies with a family history of hypertension are able to taste salt at 2 days—and they prefer it to other tastes (Zinner, McGarvey, Lipsitt, & Rosner, 2002). These studies suggest that salt sensitivity may be related to a predisposition to hypertension.

Babies show highly individual differences in their taste preferences. Some infants welcome the introduction of new foods at about 6 months of age; others demonstrate very clearly their preference for staying with the familiar. It is unclear if these differences are related to how babies taste differences, or whether it has more to do with their temperament and a desire to take risks versus keep everything pretty much the same.

Amodal Learning

Although we tend to separate the senses in trying to understand how they develop over time, babies use their senses in a very coordinated way—or in a way that transcends the use of any one mode of taking in information. Babies are capable of this *amodal* learning from birth (Bahrick, 1995; Lewkowicz & Lickliter, 1994). They are able to take in information through one sensory mode and translate it into usable information for another sense, even when the second sense had never been exposed to the object, proving that this is an innate coordinated skill, and not learned through experience.

Meltzoff and Moore (1977) found evidence that infants can translate or transfer information from one sensory mode to another. They gave babies a rubber nipple to suck without letting the baby see the nipple. Some babies were given a smooth nipple; some were bumpy. After a few minutes of sucking, the baby was shown both the smooth and bumpy nipples. The babies consistently chose to look at the nipple that they had just felt in their mouth, as though recognizing it, although they had never seen it.

Babies also have expectations that their senses will provide them with coherent information. They want the information from their eyes to match the information from their ears. At 3 months, babies will look with interest at a video of their mother speaking while they hear her voice. However, they are distressed at the sight of their mother's face with someone else's voice coming from it or a picture of another woman with their mother's voice coming from it (Spelke & Owlsley, 1979). This coordinated use of senses has not been well studied, but it may be one of the most powerful tools babies use as they explore and master their environment.

Attributes

The relationship between gender and play style was discussed extensively in chapter 7. There also seem to be differences at birth between boys and girls in regard to their looking preferences, which relates to our discussion of attention in the first part of this chapter. One-day-old boys looked longer at mobiles and girls looked longer at faces (Connellan, Baron-Cohen, Wheelwright, Ba'tki, & Ahluwalin, 2001). At 12 months of age, boys looked longer at a video of cars moving, while girls looked longer at a moving face (Lutchmaya & Baron-Cohen, 2002).

While researchers have found gender differences in looking preference and in the size of various regions of the brain, there are no definitive answers in regard to how these differences affect learning, cognitive development, and behavior and what differences are genetically and environmentally influenced (Cahill, 2005). Research on this topic is expanding exponentially and we can expect many more answers in the near future.

DEVELOPMENT AND LEARNING THROUGH RELATIONSHIPS

"Where's your nose?" asked Terri, showing great delight as Jeremy gleefully pointed to his nose. "Where're your eyes?" "Where's your mouth?" If she'd stopped to think about it, Terri would have imagined that teachers all over the world would be playfully asking these questions of 1-year-olds. But adults around the world have many different ways of helping babies learn.

Culture and Relationships

Piaget, from his observations of his own children as described in chapter 3, helped us recognize how infants move from learning about the world primarily through sensorimotor experiences to the use of symbols as toddlers. Piaget believed that the processes of learning (reasoning, classification, logic, and memory) were general across all humanity (Rogoff, 2003). Cross-cultural studies, however, would argue that Vygotsky's sociocultural theory of learning provides a better basis for understanding the differences in cognitive development within different cultures.

Vygotsky (1978) suggests that cognitive skills develop not from a child individually interacting with materials in the environment, but through participation in sociocultural activities. Cultural tools, such as literacy or mathematics, are used by people to think about tasks within their own culture. Thinking and learning occur within social relationships and cultural experience. Cognitive development describes the learning a person does to participate in his or her own culture. For example, an American mother may unintentionally teach the category of "animal" to her infant by always pointing out and naming the animals in pictures, but not the plants, tools, machines, or buildings. The infant learns to attend to this particular grouping of individual objects and see them as a category. A mother in another culture might group horses and elephants with cars and trucks as part of the category of "things that take us places."

The questions asked by Terri, the teacher in the previous example, seem perfectly natural to most Americans. Our culture is filled with situations in which a person demonstrates competence by answering direct questions. Jeremy is actually learning to be a test-taker in America. Some cultures respond very differently to direct questions. A study in North Africa found children unwilling to answer direct questions, because in their culture people do not ask questions to which they know the answers. This kind of question would be seen as a challenge or a trick (Irvine, 1978). In some cultures, where a 1-year-old might well know where her nose is, she would not be asked such a question because the role of children is to listen and obey adults, not to converse with them (Super & Harkness, 1997).

Our appreciation for children who quickly learn words and concepts might not be shared by Ugandan villagers who equate intelligence with words like *slow, careful,* and *active* (Wober, 1972), or Navajo families who value reflection and planning (Ellis & Siegler, 1997). Kenyan parents might describe intelligence in terms of being trustworthy and participating in the family's life (Super & Harkness, 1997). Many cultures emphasize values of social responsibility over personal knowledge in describing intelligence.

The following descriptions of how children learn, how adults support learning, and what we expect children to learn should be considered more meaningful and accurate for children in the United States and Europe than as a general description of learning across cultures.

Tools of Learning

At 21 months, Sudie already loved books. She would stroll over to the book corner, browse through the shelves, and choose a book about dogs. She had favorite books about dogs but welcomed new ones. It fascinated her teacher that she could choose with such purpose.

If learning is built on the foundation of attention to perceptual information, curiosity, and mastery motivation, it is built with the mental tools of memory, categorization, and problem solving. Each of these abilities is apparent in the earliest months of infancy, but through the toddler years they become established as the tools we continue to use for learning throughout our lives. (See Observation Invitation 8.2.)

Memory

We know infants have the ability to develop memories from their ability to recognize stories heard in the womb and to differentiate their mother's breast milk from another woman's. In laboratory studies, newborns recognized sounds 24 hours after first hearing them (Swain, Zelazo, & Clifton, 1993). Three-month-old babies, taught to move a mobile by kicking their feet, repeated the kicking motion several days later when shown the mobile again—even though they were unable to make it move the second time (Rovee-Collier, Sullivan, Enright, Lucas, & Fagan, 1980).

One of the most interesting questions about memory is how the child develops a memory of himself—a personal history, a sense of "This is me . . . and I go on being me." Toddlers demonstrate in their pretend play their memories of routines such as preparing meals or going to sleep, or social scripts such as answering the phone by saying "Hello." How do these memories of the activities of life contribute to the child's sense of himself, his relationships with others, and his growing depth of knowledge about the world?

Observation Invitation 8.2

Marisol is "reading" her favorite book out loud to herself. She often goes to the bookcase, takes a book, and makes herself comfortable to read. She turns the pages, points, and names the pictures.

What learning tools would you say Marisol is using?

Categorizing

Memory alone is not knowledge. If an infant or toddler stored every individual memory but had no way to organize the information, the world would be chaotic. The ability to recognize similarities and differences is a good one to use as an example of how infants understand the world in increasingly sophisticated and complex ways. Recognizing similarities is a precursor to the skill of *categorization*: sorting, matching, comparing, and contrasting. As infants have more experience with the world, between 3 and 5 months of age, they can create categories or representational groupings of objects. These categories are initially created to group objects with observable, physical similarities. For example, presented with a series of figures of cats, at first babies will look longer at "new" cats, figures they are seeing for the first time. Before long, new pictures of cats are no longer interesting. Babies begin to look less at new cats, even if they haven't seen that particular cat before, but perk up and pay attention when shown figures of other kinds of animals (Eimas & Quinn, 1994).

As children continue to interact with objects in the world, their ability to create categories becomes increasingly sophisticated as they include **invisible information** such as the function or purpose of an object. They understand that bottles, cups, and glasses are all for drinking. They group toys that *make noise when shaken* or toys that *roll when thrown*. These more subtle categories of invisible properties of objects go beyond what the child can see into a generalized mental representation called a *concept*.

Fourteen-month-old toddlers demonstrated their increasingly complex conceptual understanding of how the world works. Researchers showed a toddler an activity such as pretending to give a toy dog a drink from a cup. The toddler was then given three toys to use in reenacting the activity: a cup, a bird, and an airplane. Toddlers would offer the cup to the bird but not to the airplane. Activities such as eating or sleeping were reenacted with the figures of animals; trucks and airplanes were chosen for activities such as using a key (Mandler & McDonough, 1996).

invisible information
Properties of objects that can be known but not seen.

Problem Solving

myeducationlab

Go to the Activities and Applications section in Chapter 8 of MyEducationLab to watch the video *Cognitive Development: Infant & Toddler—Part 1* and observe all of the strategies that the child uses to explore the object.

Memory and categorization are tied, to some extent, to sensory information and real experiences. Toddlers are certainly engaged with the world in a concrete way but they have a growing ability to manipulate information and possibilities in their heads. Even babies, working out the rules of making a mobile move, seem to be developing and testing hypotheses. Toddlers are not limited to knowing what they can actually observe. For instance, 18-month-olds watched a series of intended, but not completed, acts such as pushing a buzzer with a block, hanging a loop on a protuberance, and fitting beads into a container. Toddlers who watched the successfully completed acts and toddlers who watched the intended but failed acts were equally successful in performing the acts successfully when given the materials. Toddlers who watched random movement around the objects, or who were given the objects with no demonstration, did not often attempt the intended actions. The toddlers somehow translated their observation, through mental constructs, into an understanding of the intention of the act and were not tied to the concrete reality of their observation (Meltzoff, 1995).

Symbolic Play

Over the first 3 years of life, infants and toddlers have countless day-to-day experiences with language, with family photographs and picture books, with television, and with toy replicas of houses and cars and other real-life objects. They are constantly exposed to symbols of objects (or of feelings) being used by adults and older children as meaningfully as they use real objects. By the age of 3, most children have mastered the use of symbols themselves. They use language fluently and creatively. They follow stories told in pictures and they can incorporate models of household objects into their pretend play. It is our use of symbols that allows human beings to communicate, learn, and create.

Greenspan (1997) describes infants as initially being in a *behavior mode,* where being hugged by Mom or actually eating dinner are sources of contentment. As infants become toddlers and move into a *symbolic mode,* they can begin to feel satisfaction from the *knowledge* that "Mom loves me" or *knowing* that dinner is being prepared (Greenspan, 1997). As with every aspect of development, the key is in the relationship between the baby and the caregiver.

> The shift in modes therefore requires the long-term participation of someone who promotes interaction, who supports ever greater use of signals, who joins in the child's pretend play, who helps the child link the pleasures of relating to the skills of communicating symbolically. The sheer enjoyment of being listened to, the satisfaction of gaining attention through the use of images, motivates the first step in this epochal move. The child delights not only in getting what he wants or having his expectations confirmed, but in letting others know what they are. (Greenspan, 1997, p. 77)

Researchers have tracked how infants move from interest in looking at a picture, to understanding that a picture represents a real thing and, yet, is different from that thing. Five-month-olds were given time to study a doll. They were then shown pictures of that doll and of a new doll. As in other habituation studies described in this chapter, the babies demonstrated their familiarity with the real doll by losing interest in its picture. They treated the picture of the real doll exactly as they would have treated the doll itself; they looked longer at the new doll (DeLoache, Strauss, & Maynard, 1979). Nine-month-olds, presented with realistic picture books of objects, tried to touch and pick up the object, as though not recognizing that this was a *symbol* of the object. However, by 15 months, American infants with lots of experience with picture books would point to pictures and name the objects, demonstrating some idea of the representation (DeLoache, Pierroutsakos, & Troseth, 1997; DeLoache, Pierroutsakos, Troseth, Uttah, Rosengren, & Gottlieb, 1998).

Namy (2001) looked at how infants use a variety of types of symbols. At 12 and 18 months, infants were equally willing to accept words, gestures, pictures, or nonword sounds as the names of objects. After 18 months, the age at which toddlers generally show increased interest in language, they preferred to use words as names of objects.

Within a study of the development of social play, solitary pretend play, and social pretend play in toddlers, Howes, Unger, and Seidner (1989) describe a progression of increasingly complex use of symbolization. From about 12 to 15 months, a toddler will use auto-symbolic schemes in which they perform a pretend act aimed at themselves, such as pretending to drink from a cup (Howes et al., 1989). Toddlers love to pretend to sleep, smiling and looking at the teacher much of the time, while the teacher says, "Goodnight. Shhhh. Quiet everyone. Jacob's sleeping." Then Jacob jumps up laughing and the teacher says, "Jacob, you're up! Good morning!"—at which Jacob is likely to immediately repeat the routine, over and over (Gowen, 1995). It is easy to see how a responsive adult can support this play and this desire to learn in a young child.

> *The important thing is not so much that every child should be taught, as that every child should be given the wish to learn. (John Lubbock, 19th-century astronomer and mathematician)*

At around 15 to 20 months, in **decentered symbolic play,** the toddler directs the pretend action to a toy but with no intention assigned to the toy in the play (feeds the doll but doesn't say the doll is hungry). At 20 to 25 months, toddlers begin sequencing pretend actions such as waking the doll, feeding her, and bathing her, playing repetitions of familiar routines, such as preparing a meal, eating it, and cleaning up afterward using realistic replications of household objects (Westby, 1980). At 24 to 30 months toddlers engage in internally directed symbolic play where they ascribe agency or intention to the toys (the doll is hungry) and then interact with the toy through a sequence of pretend actions. Over the next several months, the child is increasingly able to simply pretend—to use an object such as a block or a stick to be first a coffee cup and then a set of keys. Less familiar and frequent events may also appear within the stories of

decentered symbolic play Play in which children, instead of performing an act themselves, move the action to a toy or object, performing the action on a symbolic level.

pretend play. At 30 to 36 months, in behavioral role-play, toddlers assign roles to their dolls and toys such as being the father or the dog, and the play incorporates the roles.

As they achieve greater use of language, the play becomes more filled with detail and the children have greater capacity to share their interests. Mastery of language and other symbols frees the child to think beyond the concrete experience of the moment (Gowen, 1995; Howes et al., 1989; Westby, 1980).

Learning Through Relationships

> *Sarah, as a young baby, tries to suck on her caregiver's cheek. The caregiver laughs warmly, makes eye contact with her, and says, "Sarah, you're sucking on my cheek! Are you ready for a bottle?" Following a series of experiences similar to this one, Sarah begins to understand that sucking works better with nipples and bottles and that looking, nuzzling, and smiling are good ways to connect with people.*

Infants have enormous abilities to observe, learn about, and predict the behavior of the people around them. They develop mental representations, or understandings, of what they know, and when evidence convinces them that their beliefs are wrong, they change their beliefs to match the evidence. For example, the young infant above may begin relating to others by sucking on the cheek or finger of any available adult. Through the warm interaction with her caregiver, she learns more effective ways of being with others.

Adults have endless opportunities to support early learning. "Our instinctive behaviors toward babies and babies' instinctive behaviors toward us combine to enable the babies to learn as much as they do" (Gopnik et al., 1999, p. 169). Some of the most effective strategies used are *modeling, imitation,* and *scaffolding.* Infants and toddlers are such active learners that adults rarely need to teach so much as they need to be available to support learning. Adults intuitively support cognitive development, helping toddlers become aware that other people have thoughts and feelings as they develop a *theory of mind.*

Modeling and Imitation

Literally from the first moments of life, babies are able to imitate the facial expressions of adults (Meltzoff & Moore, 1977). **Modeling** on the part of the adult, and **imitation** on the part of the child, may be the primary conduit for passing information from one generation to the next. By 14 months, toddlers can repeat the actions of peers and adults in different settings (Hanna & Meltzoff, 1993) and after a one-week delay (Meltzoff, 2005). Toddlers imitate facial expressions, vocal intonations, body movements, and routines of their parents and teachers.

However, adults also imitate infant and toddlers. When adults repeat the expression, vocalization, or movement of a very young child, they are demonstrating to the child some understanding of the child's actions and experiences and a desire for connection and communication. Stern (2000) calls the adult's imitation of the baby **mirroring.** When adults do not directly imitate but match the emotional tone and vitality of a baby's expression, Stern calls it **attunement.** The adult's action of matching or imitating the infant or toddler increases the child's sense of being an active partner in reciprocal interactions. This often leads to the toddler making small changes or elaborations in the movements or sounds that make up the imitation, heightening the creative learning experience.

Scaffolding

A second and equally important way that adults support early learning is identified by Vygotsky (1978) as **scaffolding.** As described in chapter 3, Vygotsky saw the role of the teacher as one of recognizing not only the child's current developmental accomplishments but

---

modeling
The adult's demonstration of actions for the child.

imitation
The child's attempt to learn from the adult by repeating the action or sound that the adult performed.

mirroring
An adult's imitation of facial expression made by the infant.

attunement
An alignment of the internal states of an adult and baby through the adult's matching of the intensity, timing, and shape of the baby's behavior without actually imitating the behavior.

scaffolding
The adult's continual adjustment of the level of her help in response to the child's level of performance, to help the child achieve what he could not do alone.

understanding the next steps in development, or the *zone of proximal development (ZPD)*. The adult then creates a scaffold that will support the child's movement from the current point in development to the next point of development. In the example of symbolic play described earlier, the teacher might scaffold Jacob's symbolic play of sleeping and waking by asking if he wants the teddy bear to sleep—and then supporting his movement into symbolic play with the teddy bear.

Adults scaffold learning by adding and elaborating language during conversations, by suggesting variations in the usual pattern of play, or by introducing new materials or new combinations of materials. The concept of scaffolding will be discussed further in chapter 13.

Theory of Mind

Along with their increasing capacities to think and talk and symbolize, toddlers are becoming aware of their own thinking and talking and symbolizing. The awareness and understanding that children develop concerning ideas, beliefs, thoughts, feelings, and desires is called **theory of mind.** Theory of mind describes the ideas an infant, toddler, or preschooler may have about how invisible forces such as feelings or thoughts affect their behavior or the behavior of other people.

This connection between activities of the mind and behavior is a major developmental step in understanding oneself and others. It begins with the understanding that "people act to fulfill their desires in light of their beliefs" (Astington & Barriault, 2001, p. 2). Therefore, the baby who is hungry but has learned not to cry out in a dangerous and chaotic home, will "act to fulfill his desire" for food "in light of his belief" that it is dangerous to make noise. He will quietly suck on his hand until he falls asleep. The infant who has a loving, responsive caregiver, however, will cry out lustily in the belief that the adults in his life want to keep him safe, happy, and comfortable.

Theory of mind, say Astington and Barriault (2001), grows through ongoing exposure to "people talking about what they and others want, like, think, feel, and so on. Our understanding of one another, indeed all of our social interaction, is based on a theory of mind" (p. 2). They continue:

> There are two things we should make clear at the outset. First we think, know, want, and feel things; that is, we have beliefs, desires, intentions, and emotions, and we can ascribe beliefs, desires, intentions, and emotions (i.e., we can think about people's thoughts, wants, plans, and feelings). It is this latter aspect—thinking about thinking—that is the theory of the mind. . . . Second, we do not expect children to be able to explain their theory of mind. . . . We have to infer their theory from what they say and do in both naturalistic and experimental situations. (p. 2)

The infant or toddler, then, creates a picture of himself as a person with thoughts, ideas, feelings, knowledge, memories, and predictions about things that will happen. Within rich, complex, reciprocal relationships, the child also begins to learn that other people have equally multifaceted internal lives.

Concepts Infants and Toddlers Learn

> *Arman yelled "In!" as he pushed hard to make a large puzzle piece fit in the hole in the puzzle. He first tried a schema that had worked many times in the past: After tasting the piece, he placed it near the hole and pounded it with his fist. He then turned the piece one way and then another until it finally dropped in the hole. With a big sigh of contentment he looked at his great accomplishment. Then he pulled out the piece and started all over again.*

This little moment of activity is filled with learning. Arman is using and learning language, practicing cause and effect in pushing the puzzle piece, working on spatial relationships between the puzzle piece and the hole, hypothesizing and trying strategies to make the piece fit, and demonstrating how his curiosity and his image of himself as a learner contribute to his ability to persist in the task even when it is hard. According to Piaget, the major discoveries of infancy are

theory of mind
The cognitive ability to understand others as intentional agents, having beliefs and desires of their own.

Box 8.2

Early Learning Guidelines for Infants and Toddlers (ELG/ITs)

In 2002, the presidential intiative for early childhood, *Good Start, Grow Smart,* required the states to write early learning guidelines describing what preschoolers should know in language, literacy, and mathematics. Many states found these documents so beneficial that they chose to create guidelines articulating what infants and toddlers are learning as well.

ELG/ITs help parents and teachers understand what infants and toddlers should know and be able to do during specific age ranges. As adults understand and appreciate what infants and toddlers are learning, they can better support the chidren's natural curiosity, exploration, and discoveries. ELG/ITs are becoming a foundational element of professional development systems for state child care systems.

There are several new resources available that track the ELG/ITs being developed by states and that analyze their content and their usefulness. The National Infant and Toddler Child Care Initiative has a paper that describes the structure and content of ELG/ITs (NITCCI, 2009). The National Child Care Information Center maintains a list of links to the ELG/ITs (NCCIC, 2009). A thorough analysis of the content of existing ELG/ITs, *Inside the Content of Infant-Toddler Early Learning Guidelines: Results from Analysis, Issues to Consider and Recommendations* (Scott-Little, Kagan, Frelow, & Reid, 2008). ZERO TO THREE has issued a policy paper on the topic with 17 recommendations for states considering developing or revising the ELG/ITs (Petersen, Jones, & McGinley, 2008).

object permanence, cause and effect, use of tools, and *use of space* (Flavell, 1977). These are huge concepts but only part of what babies are learning through their moments with people and their interactions with the objects in the world. Infants are making Piaget's discoveries—and they are learning language and literacy, developing mental concepts and categories, and beginning to understand numbers. In the last several years, many states have taken on the task of articulating what infants and toddlers learn and how they are learning through early learning guidelines (see Box 8.2).

Object Permanence

An early discovery babies make is that people and things continue to exist whether or not you are with them and can see them—they are making discoveries about the permanence of objects and persons (Krøjgaard, 2005). Experiences with parents, siblings, and teachers are likely to have the greatest emotional impact and develop the strongest sets of generalized, stored information. Infants have numerous experiences with their parents and teachers coming and going, but always reappearing, helping babies develop an understanding of the permanence of the existence of these people. The classic demonstration of object permanence involves hiding a toy under a cloth as the infant is watching. Very young babies behave as though the toy has disappeared and make no attempt to retrieve the toy. Somewhere around 8 months, however, the infant will lift the cloth with every expectation that the toy will be waiting (Uzgiris & Hunt, 1975).

Object permanence involves more than simply knowing that people or objects continue to exist when they are out of sight. Babies learn that a teacher who is so close that only her face is visible is the same person whose entire body they can see across a room. They learn that the teacher's cheek and eye, visible to the baby leaning on her shoulder, is part of the same full face they see when having diapers changed. All of these experiences build a set of information about how people and things exist as whole entities, how they continue to exist through time, and how they continue to exist despite changes in setting or in the emotional tone of the moment.

myeducationlab

Go to the Activities and Applications section in Chapter 8 of MyEducationLab to watch the video *Object Permanence* and observe the infant's lack of understanding of object permanence.

Cause and Effect

Infants learn that people cause things to happen and that they can cause people to do things. Infants have numerous intrapersonal and interpersonal experiences with cause and effect. For example, an empty tummy makes a baby cry. The cry brings a caregiver with a loving cuddle and a warm bottle. Sucking the milk in the bottle causes the baby to feel comfortable and happy again. One event follows another in such a predictable way that the baby begins to have a sense of one event causing another to happen.

Toys also provide numerous opportunities for infants and toddlers to discover and practice cause and effect. Babies need toys that respond in a contingent manner to their actions. Toy pianos that play notes when a key is pushed or a pad is kicked, jack-in-the-box toys that pop up when a button is pushed or a lever flipped, balls that roll away when pushed, blocks that make sounds when squeaked all teach the baby about cause and effect—and give her a sense that she is someone who can make things happen! Many of the new electronic toys are not contingent—once turned on, they essentially provide a light and sound show to a passive baby. It might be entertaining, but infants and toddlers will not be learning about their own efficacy in the world from that kind of toy.

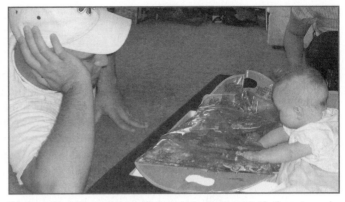

Use of Tools

This 7-month-old is engrossed with the activity she is causing in the water pad. Her dad and teacher stay nearby, encouraging her and using language to describe her actions—and the reactions they cause.

Infants learn some things about the use of tools through their interactions with people. They watch people use tools and see that people can be used as tools. If you cry, someone will come and comfort and feed you. If you point, someone will reach the stacking rings for you. Toddlers learn to ask adults for help in tasks they find frustrating by pointing, looking from the person to the object and back again, and using sounds and language.

Toddlers use tools when they use forks and spoons to feed themselves, when they climb on a chair to reach a shelf, or when they use paint brushes or markers to create pictures. They use tools when they use a wooden spoon to bang on a pot or use a push toy to help them take their first steps.

Use of Space

Babies learn that people have spatial relationships with each other and with the things in the world. People move through space in predictable ways, their bodies exist as a single entity, and they appear bigger when they are close and smaller when they are far away. Babies also have many opportunities to watch adults move objects around in space, put wallets in purses, cups in cupboards, and milk cartons in refrigerators. Babies bring this experience of watching adults to their own explorations of the world. The process of putting one thing into another can be endlessly fascinating to babies. Any collection of objects can become interesting when they are put into and dumped out of a bucket. Shape boxes that allow infants or toddlers to put a toy through a hole shaped like the toy (or coffee cans with a slit cut in the plastic top) will keep them trying over and over. For infants and toddlers, crawling, walking, and climbing are constant lessons in spatial relationships.

Language and Literacy

Language and literacy learning are such important aspects of development that they have their own chapter in this book, but in any list of what infants learn from and about others, it is essential to include language and literacy. As mentioned earlier, babies hear the sounds of language even before they are born. Infants quickly learn to use the sounds of language in turn-taking interactions with adults. They recognize and begin to understand words by listening to all of the exchanges around them—but best of all, by their parents and teachers responding personally to them in little one-on-one, face-to-face "conversations."

Numbers

Just as infants seem to understand some aspects of individual objects in the world, they may have an inherent—or very early—understanding of numbers. The National Council of Teachers of Mathematics (NCTM, 2000) includes references to infants in its standards for

myeducationlab

Go to the Activities and Applications section in Chapter 8 of MyEducationLab to watch the video *Cognitive Development: Infant & Toddler—Part 2* and observe the infant's understanding of object permanence.

pre-K to Grade 2. It points out that the foundation for mathematical learning is established in the earliest years, through ordinary experiences such as a parent counting crackers or cutting a sandwich into squares or triangles. Everyday life can provide infants and toddlers with many casual, offhand opportunities to understand the basics of mathematics.

Researchers find the study of early number understanding, such as counting, to be a controversial one. Wynn (1992) had 5-month-old babies look at a screen. She showed them a little toy Mickey Mouse and placed it behind the screen. If she removed the screen and two Mickeys appeared, the babies were surprised. If she showed the babies the hiding of two Mickeys, they were surprised if removal of the screen revealed only one Mickey Mouse doll. If the babies watched two Mickeys being hidden and saw one being removed, they would show surprise if two Mickeys were still revealed at the removal of the screen.

In other experiments, infants further demonstrated their understanding of numbers. Researchers showed a baby a ball and then put it in a box, out of sight. They added a second ball and told the baby, "Get the ball." Babies would reach into the box two times and retrieve both balls. They never reached in just once, never more than twice (Xu & Carey, 1996).

Could a lot of this just be memory? Some researchers think that infants are not really counting but are using perceived information such as overall size and surface area to understand differences in numbers (Feigenson, Carey, & Spelke, 2002). Nonetheless, infants do demonstrate a variety of early mathematical skills. Xu and Carey (1996) report that 6-month-olds can discern one set of many items from another if they have a 2-to-1 ratio. Brannon (2002) finds that 11-month-old infants can tell the difference between visual displays of items that increase or decrease in number. See chapter 13 for ideas for promoting children's understanding of numbers.

CHILDREN WITH SPECIAL NEEDS

Infants have enormous inborn capacities for learning, but there can also be enormous challenges to their ability to learn. Healthy development can be threatened by developmental disabilities having wide variation in their effect on development.

Biological risks, such as prenatal or postnatal insults to the central nervous system, may cause delayed or impaired development in learning, social relationships, communication, or motor development. Some infants have biological risks from exposure to drugs or alcohol in utero. Other babies suffer from ingesting dangerously high levels of lead from old paint or plumbing pipes (Guralnik, 2000). Sensory impairments may also challenge a child's ability to perceive information from the world. Established conditions such as Down syndrome, cerebral palsy, autism, premature birth, or low birth weight may affect the child's ability to process or use the information in the environment (Guralnik, 2000; Shonkoff & Phillips, 2000).

Because the areas of development are so interrelated in infancy, very young children are particularly vulnerable to the effects of environmental difficulties such as exposure to violence, a parent's mental illness, poor nutrition, and low educational achievement in the home (Shonkoff & Phillips, 2000, p. 338). Large numbers of young children in our society are subject to abuse and neglect, are born to adolescents, or experience family disruption and/or foster care placement.

The issue of motivation in children with physical or developmental delays has not been well studied, but some researchers have found that infants and toddlers with and without disabilities demonstrate about the same level of persistence on tasks (Hauser-Cram, 1996). However, by preschool age, children with disabilities begin to work and play with less intrinsic motivation toward mastery (Jennings, Connors, & Stegman, 1988). The highly directive interaction styles often observed between young children with disabilities and their parents and teachers may have a negative effect on motivation (Mahoney, Fors, & Wood, 1990).

These children may be particularly well served by early intervention. Programs that deliver carefully designed interventions with well-defined goals can affect both parenting behavior and the developmental trajectories of a child whose life course is threatened by socioeconomic disadvantage, family disruption, or diagnosed disability. Programs that combine child-focused educational activities with explicit attention to parent–child interaction patterns and relationship building appear to have the greatest impacts (Shonkoff & Phillips, 2000, p. 379).

People's beliefs about their abilities have a profound effect on those abilities. Ability is not a fixed property; there is a huge variability in how you perform. People who have a sense of self-efficacy bounce back from failures; they approach things in terms of how to handle them rather than worrying about what can go wrong. (Albert Bandura)

Teachers are able to provide rich learning environments for each child by individualizing the way activities are offered. Strong observation skills help the teacher understand how the child perceives and processes information. In addition to always attending to your own interactions and relationship with the child, here are some considerations for planning how to individualize learning activities for each infant or toddler:

Which materials best meet the needs and interests of each child involved?

How can I arrange the materials and equipment to encourage each child's participation?

How can the activity be more accessible to each child?

What can I do so children can come and go from the activity at their own pace? (Mulligan, 1997)

A more detailed description of what infants and toddlers learn, and what adults can do to support that learning, can be found on pages 184–187 the Developmental Trends and Responsive Interactions chart.

PROGRAMS THAT ENHANCE COGNITIVE DEVELOPMENT AND LEARNING

Just as each adult, infant, and toddler bring their own skills and styles to learning, early childhood education and development programs have different approaches to supporting learning. Following is a description and discussion of several approaches, chosen for their diversity and not in an attempt to provide a comprehensive picture of methods and approaches to learning. Specific curricula will be described in chapter 12.

Child Care: Rich Environments and Responsive Relationships

High-quality child care actively promotes children's learning. The results of the NICHD study on child care demonstrated that child care quality matters (NICHD, 2002a, b).

Caregivers with higher levels of education and who worked in settings with fewer children per adult were more sensitive and responsive to children and provided a more stimulating environment. When care environments were more stimulating and well organized, children had better vocabularies, exhibited more advanced attention and memory skills, and got along better with peers. In contrast, children who spent more time in front of the TV showed more behavior problems, had smaller vocabularies, and did less well on math problems (Todd, 2001). High quality care for young children is eloquently described by Carlina Rinaldi (2001) of Reggio Emilia:

Our image is of a child who is competent, active, and critical; therefore a child who may be seen as a challenge and, sometimes, as troublesome. . . . To us, the child is a producer of culture, values, and rights, competent in learning and competent in communicating. . . . We have to try to organize a school, an infant-toddler center for this child. (p. 51)

STRATEGIES TO SUPPORT COGNITIVE DEVELOPMENT AND LEARNING

Infants and toddlers will learn about themselves, about being in relationships with other people, and many of the basic concepts they need to learn about the world. You can assist them with the following strategies:

1. Help infants maintain a quiet, alert state of attention by keeping them in comfortable positions, talking quietly, and looking at things together.

2. Help toddlers keep focused and attentive by limiting distractions and interruptions. Express interest in their activities and try to observe and reflect on what you believe they are trying to accomplish.

3. Spark curiosity by offering materials in new ways, such as setting the dolls up in the book corner "reading" books, or the farm animals on a green cloth over blocks creating a gentle hill.

4. Spark curiosity by noticing things and suggesting, "Let's go see what that is!"

5. Support mastery motivation by offering materials that are challenging enough to be interesting but not impossible, by offering a few choices, and by expressing your interest and encouragement.

6. Support mastery motivation by sharing the joy children feel as they show you their accomplishments.

7. Support sensorimotor learning by offering play and exploration experiences that provide a variety of sensory modes: sand, water, cornstarch, smelling bottles, and so forth.

8. Help children develop memories by keeping the routine and room arrangement predictable; keep toys where children know to find them.

9. Talk with children about what they did earlier in the day or the day before.

10. Provide many opportunities to categorize, match, sort, compare, and contrast with toys and activities.

11. Encourage problem solving by not stepping in immediately when a problem occurs—for example, if a child can't reach the ball that has rolled behind the slide, ask, "What can we do?" and let the child try to figure it out.

12. Play games like peek-a-boo, read stories about mommies being gone and coming back, read books with pictures hidden under flaps to encourage the development of object permanence.

13. Provide toys that respond contingently to a child's actions, such as balls, busy boxes, or push lights to encourage the understanding of cause and effect.

14. Provide toys and materials such as stacking cups, rings on a post, little houses, or tunnels to crawl through to encourage understanding of use of space.

15. Provide markers, paint, water, replicas of household tools, play telephones, keys, and so forth, to promote understanding of use of tools.

16. Provide language, ideas, and materials in ways that make the child's play just a little more elaborate and complex, scaffolding the child's play to the next level.

17. Provide toys and language to introduce awareness of shapes, comparative sizes, amounts, numbers, and one-to-one correspondence. Talk about concepts of time such as today, now, later, before, and after.

Programs for Infants and Toddlers at Risk

Early Head Start (EHS), a federally funded program for infants and toddlers in poverty and at risk for poor development, has adopted many of the aspects of quality identified by ZERO TO THREE and PITC (Program for Infant-Toddler Caregivers) in their Head Start Program Performance Standards (HSPPS) for infants and toddlers. The HSPPS require EHS programs to promote the development of trust and security by having a limited number of consistent teachers over a long period of time in out-of-home settings. EHS also requires both center- and home-based programs to promote children's cognitive development by providing opportunities to explore their environments with a variety of materials and activities that support all areas of development. However, because it is a more comprehensive program, with broader goals than child care, EHS emphasizes working with families and cognitive development.

Early Intervention

Early intervention services are available to infants and toddlers with disabilities through Part C of the Individuals with Disabilities Education Act (IDEA). As a field, early intervention has developed rapidly in the last 30 years or so. For many years, behaviorally based interventions were used to promote learning. Elaborate assessments were developed to break down cognitive development into distinct, small skills that could then be taught sequentially. It was assumed, or hoped, that as the child mastered each small part of a task, the knowledge would generalize to new situations and broader challenges.

Currently, however, learning activities in early intervention tend to be more holistic and more child directed, although they continue to be planned in correlation to specific goals and objectives developed for the child from an assessment. Activity-based intervention (Pretti-Frontczak & Bricker, 2004) represents contemporary efforts to combine some important elements of traditional early intervention teaching strategies with our understanding of all infants' desire to explore, learn, and master the environment. Activity-based intervention contains four elements:

1. Uses child-initiated transactions
2. Embeds children's goals and objectives in routine, planned, or child-initiated activities
3. Uses logically occurring antecedents and consequences
4. Develops functional and generative skills (p. 11)

This approach utilizes the natural motivation of the child's interest in the toys and materials in the environment as a way to engage the child in learning. The interventionist then follows the child's lead, is highly responsive to vocalizations and behavior, but always keeps in mind that child's current developmental goals. The interventionist looks for opportunities to introduce challenges that would prompt the child to gain skill in areas of concern. This approach combines current knowledge of infant learning with subtle but intentional direction to support development in children who otherwise might not challenge themselves.

Early intervention services use a variety of professional knowledge bases to support early learning. Infants and toddlers with disabilities may be at risk for delays in cognitive development because of motor problems, sensory problems, health problems, language problems, or processing problems. Professionals such as physical therapists, occupational therapists, speech therapists, and nurses may all be part of a team, with an early childhood special educator who will help design learning strategies for an individual child.

Developmental Trends and Responsive Interactions
Cognitive Development and Learning

Infants and toddlers learn about themselves, others, and the world through their own unique capacities and attributes, by utilizing the cognitive tools of learning and basic concepts.

Development	Example
0–4 months (infant)	
• Infants follow a moving object visually. • Infants cry to bring an adult to comfort or feed them. • Infants will look around the room with interest. • Infants begin to reach for a toy. • Infants notice that their arms or legs made something happen and will repeat the movement. • Infants recognize familiar people and objects. • Infants begin to bring objects to mouth.	Megan lifted her head, resting on her arms as she lay on the blanket. With a serious expression on her face, she watched the teachers and children around her. Willie kicked the mobile hanging over him and made it wiggle. He stopped, looked at it, and then kicked some more, watching the mobile to see if anything might happen.
4–8 months (infant)	
• Infants like to examine toys. • Infants like to make toys do something—make a sound, put one inside another. • Infants imitate adult expressions and gestures. • Infants turn toward a sound to see where it came from. • Infants look for toys they dropped.	Angela is interested in everything. She watches her friends and then looks at the teacher and smiles. Roger reaches out to touch a dangling toy. When it swings, making a sound, he reaches out to do it again.
8–12 months (mobile infant)	
• Mobile infants like to take the pieces of a toy apart and put them back together. • Mobile infants like toys that do something when you touch them, pull them, bang them. • Mobile infants begin very simple pretend play, such as lifting a cup to their mouth. • Mobile infants like to find small toys hidden under a cloth or cup. • Mobile infants like to pick up and examine a tiny item like a Cheerio. • Mobile infants point to objects, knowing you can also see them.	Charlie loves to take each plastic animal out of the bucket and look at it. When the bucket is empty, he tosses it aside. Aliya likes the push button and the swinging doors on the busy box, but can't work all the mechanisms yet. Her teacher expresses surprise with Aliya when the doors pop open, and every once in a while shows her how to work another of the knobs.
12–18 months (mobile infant)	
• Mobile infants like to use their mobility to explore—crawling, walking, climbing, running. • Mobile infants enjoy playing with sand, water, and dough with different kinds of tools. • Mobile infants are interested in spatial relationships in puzzles and pegboards. • Mobile infants use tools such as keys or telephones in their pretend play. • Mobile infants enjoy looking at books and naming objects, animals, or body parts.	Alexis and Dan are gleeful about being on two feet. They follow each other around, one daringly balancing his way up the sloping surface with the other right behind. Sometimes they both try to squeeze into the area under the slide. Meredith loves to cuddle on her teacher's lap, pointing at pictures in books while her teacher names the animals, or asks her to find a certain animal.

Teacher or Parent–Child Interaction	Environment

0–4 months (infant)

- Slowly move a small toy from one side to another while the infant follows it with his gaze.
- Respond quickly to the baby's cries.
- Provide quiet time for infants to look at what is happening around them. Talk about what they see.
- React to infants' expressions with clear, even exaggerated facial expressions and language.

- Arrange the space so that infants can see some activity but still be protected.
- Provide a few interesting things to look at—small toys on the floor during tummy time, dangling toys when infants are on their backs.
- Provide nonbreakable mirrors.

4–8 months (infant)

- Hold the infant in your arms as you walk around, looking at things and talking about them.
- Sit nearby and talk to the baby about the toys she is looking at.
- Call the baby by name from a short distance to reassure her you are nearby.

- Provide a variety of small toys to handle and examine.
- Provide toys that make sounds when an infant moves them, fit inside each other, or dangle and move when touched.
- Offer board books.

8–12 months (mobile infant)

- Help the infant focus on what is interesting to him, using your presence, your interest, and your enthusiasm to support his attention and exploration.
- Use your emotional expressions and words to show the mobile infant that you delight in his discoveries.
- Use words to describe the child's activity: "Look, you found a Cheerio. You're picking it up with your fingers."

- Provide toys like stacking cups, rings on a post, pop-beads, and tubs full of small, interesting objects such as toy animals.
- Provide child-size replicas of dishes or household tools.
- Provide toys that respond to children's actions—busy boxes, water-filled pads.
- Provide sensory materials such as water and sand with a variety of tools.
- Provide board books with photographs.

12–18 months (mobile infant)

- Allow mobile infants protected time and space to explore.
- Stay nearby to express interest, provide words, and make the activity more elaborate and complex.
- Help mobile infants express their interest in each other gently.
- Express enthusiasm for the things that interest mobile infants.

- Provide simple puzzles, pegboards, shape forms, wooden beads with thick strings.
- Provide small climbers, tunnels, interesting pathways.
- Provide toys that respond to winding, turning on and off.
- Provide simple props for pretend play.

Developmental Trends and Responsive Interactions (continued)

Development	Example
18–24 months (toddler)	
<ul><li>Young toddlers enjoy the ease of their movement and like to use their hands to carry things around.</li><li>Young toddlers understand they can cause things to happen.</li><li>Young toddlers understand and remember the details of routines.</li><li>Young toddlers use objects as substitutes for other objects in their pretend play.</li><li>Young toddlers enjoy increasingly challenging materials that suggest activities such as building, sorting, matching shapes.</li></ul>	Lynn and Matt build little towers of blocks and then drive play trucks into them and knock them down. Before breakfast, Chris puts out his hands for the little song of thanks. When a child arrives and joins the table late, he reaches out for everyone to sing again. Fran takes out the box of 1-inch blocks and makes one pile of red blocks, one pile of blue blocks.
24–36 months (toddler)	
<ul><li>Older toddlers begin to understand concepts such as color, size, shape, time, size, and weight.</li><li>Older toddlers are interested in the story and pictures in storybooks.</li><li>Older toddlers create new stories in pretend play or new structures in block building, becoming more imaginative and creative.</li><li>Assign roles to toys and other children in pretend play; use chairs, blankets, and bookcases as substitutes for items in pretend play.</li></ul>	Erick is feeling a little sad and carries a picture of his mommy around with him, saying, "After nap." Sara takes charge of the dramatic play corner, handing out dolls and stuffed animals. She puts on a hat and says, "Mommy going shopping."

myeducationlab

Go to MyEducationLab and complete the Building Teaching Skills and Dispositions exercise in Chapter 8.

SUMMARY

Infants and toddlers are active learners. They explore, pursue information, organize information, and use it in increasingly sophisticated ways when they have adults in their lives who help them understand the world. Learning in infancy is a complex endeavor.

- Learning in infancy is grounded in the tasks of emotional development. Self-regulation allows the infant to be alert and attentive. A secure attachment relationship provides a sense of safety that allows a child to explore.

- Curiosity about new things seems to be an inherent quality in young infants—but mastery motivation, the ability to persist in learning tasks through some frustration, requires a supportive adult partner and an engaging environment.

- Young infants use their senses with great competence, long before they have motor control or language to learn about the world.

- The content of learning varies by culture, as cognitive development is not so much an objective set of knowledge as a way of learning what you need to know in your own culture.

- The tools of learning used by infants and toddlers include memory, sorting, categorizing, matching, comparing and contrasting, problem solving, and symbolic play.

- Adults help infants and toddlers learn through mutual modeling and imitation, and through scaffolding—providing just enough support for the child to move to the next level of understanding, which Vygotsky called the *zone of proximal development*.

- Mobile infants and toddlers begin to develop a theory of mind, an understanding that other people may have thoughts, feelings, and experiences that are different from their own.

Teacher or Parent–Child Interaction	Environment
18–24 months (toddler)	
• Maintain predictable routines, reminding children of the order with questions like, "It's time to eat. What do we do?" • Keep materials in orderly and predictable places. • Provide scaffolding as toddlers think about their activities, with questions such as "What will you do next?" or "What will you buy at the store?"	• Have toys and materials arranged so that toddlers can make choices, reach them, and put them away (with reminders). • Frequently review the materials you have available to ensure that you are keeping a balance between what is familiar and what is a little challenging.
24–36 months (toddler)	
• Ask children how they might solve problems that occur and let them figure out answers. • Support children working together with materials to share ideas. • Use language that describes time ("now, later, before nap, after lunch"), weight ("heavy, light"), size ("bigger, smaller"). • Count things during the day.	• Provide play opportunities that promote comparison of sizes, weights, colors, shapes, and quantities. • Have books available in all areas of the program. Have several copies of old favorites and bring in new books. • Allow children to combine materials from different areas in creative ways. • Present new materials or new combinations of materials.

- Infants and toddlers make cognitive discoveries about how the world works, such as object permanence, cause and effect, use of tools, and use of space. They learn concepts about how their culture organizes and communicates information, such as language, literacy, and numbers.

- Programs take different approaches to supporting learning. Child care is often based on a developmental model supporting relationships and discovery. Programs for children at risk often include more direct services to the families as well. Programs for infants and toddlers with disabilities may take a more structured approach to learning.

Key Terms

attunement
cognitive process
decentered symbolic play
executive functioning
habituation

imitation
interactive stimulus
invisible information
learned helplessness
mastery motivation

mirroring
modeling
scaffolding
theory of mind

REFLECTIONS AND RESOURCES FOR THE READER

Reflections

1. If infants and toddlers need to be able to have an effect on toys, what qualities would you look for in toys and which would you avoid?
2. If an infant had all the interesting toys in the world, do you think the infant would learn without an interested, engaged, and helpful adult?

Observation and Application Opportunities

1. Visit an infant-toddler program. How does the teacher set up an engaging, responsive learning environment that facilitates cognitive development? What would you change?
2. How does the teacher use herself to support the learning? Does she seem to understand and anticipate that the infant or toddler is making new discoveries in his play?
3. What kinds of experiences might encourage a toddler's learning of object permanence, cause and effect, use of tools, or use of space?

Supplementary Articles and Books to Read

Geist, K., & Geist, E. A. (2008). Do re mi, 1-2-3: That's how easy math can be—Using music to support emergent mathematics. *Young Children, 63* (2), 20–25.

myeducationlab)

These and other web links are included in this chapter on MyEducationLab.

Interesting Links

http://www.sciencentral.com
   Sciencentral   On this site search for "infant cognitive" to view articles and video clips related to infant and toddlers cognitive development.
http://zerotothree.org/
   ZERO TO THREE   The section "School Readiness: Birth to 3" provides information and video clips on thinking skills as well as other areas of development.

Language Development and Learning

Kareem danced around, half hopping and half jumping, as he chanted, "oo, me jump, me dance." His dad, who knew that Kareem was communicating his joy through sounds and words, chimed in too: "You're jumping, you're a jumper." Kareem danced and jumped higher and higher, around and around, saying, "Me jumping." This young boy and his wise father were engaged in a language dance, learning from each other as they took turns with the chant.

THE UNIQUENESS OF EACH CHILD

In the opening vignette, when the father modeled the word *jumping*, the toddler immediately said, "Me jumping" instead of "Me jump." Infants and toddlers engage in a remarkable process of learning to listen, talk, communicate their needs to others, make marks and scribbles on paper, and enjoy books—all aspects of language and literacy development. As relationship-based theory would predict, babies need adults as interactive partners as they make spectacular progress from producing soft *cooing* sounds (sustained production of single vowel sounds

such as "ooo" and "aaa" that sound like a pigeon's coos) as newborns, to using single words by 1 year, and then progressing to fairly complex sentences by 3 years of age.

Language is used for communication with others and is affected by the quality of children's relationships, the social context, and the environment. Infants and toddlers desire human connection, and communication is a primary way for them to learn to socialize. The social experience is also how the child learns language—"it can be acquired only through social interaction with other human beings" (Tomasello, 1992; Vygotsky, 1978). It is through meaningful social interactions that babies, using their biological linguistic capacities, begin to understand that sounds form words, that words go together to form sentences, and that gestures and words communicate meaning.

As Bronfenbrenner (2004) would predict in his bioecological theory, the ecology or system of support for the infant or toddler contributes greatly to whether or not a child will learn language. Infants and toddlers are affected not only by their immediate social environment, but also by the systems of emotional and physical support available. For example, as discussed later in this chapter, the quality of the early childhood care and education program and the relationship between the family and program affect young children's language development. To study language development and relationships, however, it is important to know the definitions of common terms used.

communication
Giving information through talk, signs, cues, gestures, and writing.

language
The ability to use words or signs to communicate.

Let's start with the basics. **Communication** is the giving of information through talk, signs, cues, gestures, or writing. An infant may communicate with eye gaze ("I'm interested in you"), arching the back ("Let me out of this situation"), sounds, or words. **Language,** as defined by Damasio and Damasio (1999), is "the ability to use words (or signs, if the language is one of the sign languages of the deaf) and to combine them in sentences so that concepts in our minds can be transmitted to other people. We also consider the converse: how we comprehend words spoken by others and turn them into concepts in our own mind" (p. 29). The word *language* can also be used to describe the particular way in which a group of people form words through sounds and convey messages to others.

Table 9.1 includes other typical terms used to describe various features of language development. There will also be more examples for these terms throughout the chapter.

Overview of Language Capacities

"Daddy, come here," a young child yells to her daddy, who has wandered from the grocery cart where the 2-year-old sits. "You getting losted." As children learn to speak they create wonderfully unique and innovative words and sentences based on their understanding of the principles of language. There are many questions that one could ask about young children's ability to learn to communicate. How do most children learn the complex rules of language and communication? Why and how do they construct words and sentences that they've never heard rather than just imitating? Why do most infants and toddlers progress in a fairly orderly fashion to learn language by making sounds, then words, then sentences, and then sequences of sentences to tell stories? How do most children learn so much in such a short time period?

The answer to these questions is that they are using their biological linguistic capacities in interaction with others to develop their language skills, as noted by Mei-Yu Lu (2000): "During the early years of language learning, children also create, test, and revise hypotheses regarding the use of language" (p. 3). Indeed, infants and toddlers are born with an amazing capacity to learn language to communicate with others: "They learn grammar and how to apply language across various contexts, audiences, and purposes" (Lu, 1998, p. 1).

The Capacity to Be Communicators

Infants are born with the capacity to be communicators. The Developmental Trends and Responsive Interactions chart at the end of this chapter lists capacities that infants and toddlers have. Refer to this chart often as you read the chapter. From birth they can hear the differences in speech sounds, such as "m" and "n"; are motivated to listen to the sounds of language; strive

Table 9.1   Language terms and definitions

Term	Definition	Example
Expressive language	Speaking or communicating to others through words, signs, or symbols	When Tonya speaks or writes, she is using expressive language. Matt used language well, both speaking and writing.
Morphemes	The smallest meaningful units of a word, whose combination creates a word (in sign languages the equivalent of a morpheme is a visuomotor sign) (Damasio & Damasio, 1999)	"Run" is one morpheme and "running" is two morphemes. "Run" is a unit of meaning and the "ing" is a unit of meaning. The "ing" indicates that the action is happening now and changes the meaning of the word "run."
Phonemes	The individual sound units (such as "s," "n," "m") that when spoken in a particular order produce words	The word "run" is comprised of the individual sound units of "r," "u," and "n."
Prosody	The vocal intonation that can modify the literal meaning of words and sentences (Damasio & Damasio, 1999); includes the tone, rhythm, tempo, and pace of language	A parent may use a higher tone and a slower rhythm when talking with her baby.
Pragmatics	The social features of language including how, where, and when language is used	These skills include taking turns in a conversation, adjusting the level of talking to the level of the listener, following the cultural rules of conversation such as where it is appropriate to talk, and listening when someone is speaking.
Receptive language	The act of attending, listening to, and comprehending language	Charlie listened carefully to his mother and then went and picked up his shoes that she asked him to find.
Semantics	The meanings that correspond to all words, parts of sentences, and all possible sentences	Alana's teacher responded to the semantics of her language rather than to the incorrect syntax.
Syntax	The rules governing the sequence of words and the relationships among parts of a sentence	In English we can say "How are you?" but it is not allowable (if a person wants to be understood) to say "Are how you?"
Lexicon	The collection of all words in a given language; may also refer to a specific person's lexicon of words that the person can understand and/or use	Tamara's personal lexicon included many words for animals.

to communicate through body movements and vocalizations; and thrive when listened to by caring adults. Throughout the first 3 years, infants and toddlers learn to make the sounds of the language spoken to them; combine sounds into words and then combine words into sentences; learn the syntax, pragmatics, and prosody of language; learn the meaning of an astonishing number of words; and communicate in a variety of ways—the furrowing of a brow, a loud screech, whining, pointing, talking, and shouting.

The language learning process in the first 3 years is remarkable. When infants and toddlers are learning to speak English, they learn to add morphemes such as "s" or "es" to words to make them plural and "ed" to words to indicate past tense. They create sentences that they have not ever heard before and learn to use words and sentences for different purposes—to request food, to demand attention, to inform, to express sadness or joy, and to tell an adult "No." Development is generally similar across children, and yet each child finds a unique way of attempting to learn the complex language or languages being used around and with them.

Babies communicate through their facial expressions.

Interaction Between Brain Development and Language

Infants' brains are designed to learn a language. The capacity to learn a language or languages is a part of a child's biological makeup. As discussed in chapter 5, when an adult names objects ("That's your cup"), describes what the adult is doing ("I'm changing your diaper"), sings songs, teaches a baby how to say "bye-bye," or talks about what the baby is doing ("You're playing"), the axon on a neuron in the brain sends an electrical signal and connects that neuron's dendrite with another neuron's dendrite, creating another synapse. Synapses connect the neurons to enhance the child's ability to use language with ease for a variety of purposes, including thinking with language. However, infants and toddlers need responsive adults to learn a language well.

Researchers describe a synergy between early brain development and language experience that actually affects the capacity of a person to learn languages throughout life. When pleasant language experiences are repeated—a song is sung over and over, a book is read many times to a delighted 8-month-old, or a word is used in a variety of ways (for example, "a *cup,* where's the *cup,* you've got a *cup*")—the connections or paths between neurons are made stronger and shape how easily the infant or toddler will continue to learn language. In the first year of life, as infants hear adults talking with them, a cluster of neurons begins to fire when a particular phoneme is heard. By 12 months, an auditory map has been created because of responsive language experiences with adults, with infants' brains already programmed to be able to distinguish the particular sounds in the language being spoken with them (Damasio & Damasio, 1999).

Early experiences with language are essential for the young child's development of this unique characteristic of human beings—the ability to share information, categorize knowledge, and play with words and ideas through verbal language. A baby needs to hear adults talking *with* her and have an opportunity to *respond* in order for the neurons and synapses in the brain that are related to language to develop. A toddler says "ttttt" while playing with a truck, the adult says "Yes, that's a truck," and the toddler responds "tuk." Placing an infant or toddler in front of a TV to hear a language doesn't work for language development because the child is not receiving the necessary auditory and visual feedback required to learn a language.

Attributes

Just as adult interaction and responsiveness affect the quality of language development, so does the gender of the child.

Do girls talk earlier than boys? Generally, researchers conclude that infant and toddler girls talk earlier and speak more than boys (Holdgrafer, 1991; Huttenlocher, Haight, Bryk, Seltzer, & Lyons, 1991; Van Hulle, Goldsmith, & Lemery, 2004). For both vocabulary and frequency of two-word combinations among toddlers, language assessment scores were higher for girls than for boys (Van Hulle et al., 2004).

Researchers suggest a variety of reasons for why girls talk earlier than boys. There may be biological differences, and these early differences then expand language opportunities for girls.

Environment plays an important part, however, in influencing differences in the rate of language development. Several researchers found that the quality and quantity of adult talk with infants and toddlers affect young children's language development much more than characteristics such as gender (Hart & Risley, 1999; Van Hulle et al., 2004).

You will want to focus on providing equal opportunities for boys and girls to engage in language interactions with responsive adults. Now let's examine some other differences that might occur in how young children develop and use language.

DEVELOPMENT AND LEARNING THROUGH RELATIONSHIPS

In order to fully understand the language development of young children we must view it through a family and cultural lens in a social context.

Culture and Language

Language is a major medium for transmitting culture across generations. Through language socialization, adults convey to children, from infancy onward, culturally valued beliefs, behaviors, and processes. (Katz & Snow)

Embedded within a language is a culture, and embedded within a culture is a language that communicates that culture's values, beliefs, style, and purpose for speaking. "**Communicative-linguistic parameters** such as the language used in the home, the communication patterns, and the values underlying those patterns affect every aspect of how we learn about ourselves and the world around us" (Barrera & Kramer, 1997). Language is a powerful medium, then, for infants and toddlers to learn about their own value within their culture and what is of value to learn. Children learn to understand their own culture through the language that is used by and that describes that culture.

communicative-linguistic parameters Cultural factors that influence how children and adults use language and communicate with others.

In all cultures, language is one of the most powerful symbolic systems through which children learn to understand and interpret human behavior. (Harwood, Miller, & Irizarry)

Differences in When and How Language Is Used

When we observe children's language development through a cultural lens we can see that culture is revealed in the content of talk and in how language is used in social contexts. See Figure 9.1 for a list of the aspects of language that may differ based on family and cultural values.

- When talk is appropriate.
- Who a child can speak to, and what are the appropriate ways of addressing people of different status or age.
- What is the acceptable volume or tone of voice for speech and when talk should be brief, discreet, or dispassionate.
- When the use of language can be unguarded or emotional, and how this varies by situation.
- Where you can talk and where is it important to be quiet.
- How much time you wait for someone to talk after you have stopped talking.
- How much eye contact you should give when you are talking to someone and the person is talking to you.
- How much personal space you allow between yourself and the listener when you are talking.
- What constitutes a "good" story and who can tell it.

Figure 9.1   Features of language that may differ based on family and cultural values.

Ritual and System Constraints

Ritual and system constraints are another reason why there may be differences in how young children use language and may be represented in how young children communicate to their teacher that they are hungry. The following scenario describes how Jamie, Cara, Mary, Tamika, and Carmen communicate their hunger differently to their teacher:

> *Jamie looks directly at her infant and toddler teacher as she demands "Eat," to tell her teacher very clearly that she is hungry and expects to be fed. Cara looks at the teacher with a longing look to tell her she is hungry. Mary moves in closely to the teacher, takes the teacher's face gently in her hands, and asks for milk by saying "Milk" in a quiet voice, waiting up to 30 seconds for her favorite teacher to respond. Tamika waits until the teacher approaches her and asks her if she is hungry. Carmen starts to wail when she gets a hungry feeling in her tummy.*

As we can see by the foregoing examples, language use among children and families may differ because of system constraints and ritual constraints (Goffman, 1976). "**System constraints** in conversation are such universal systems as the opening, the closing, the turn-taking, and the rerun related to handling conversations in different languages and culture" (Pham, 1994, p. 5). In the previous example, Mary opens a "conversation" with her infant and toddler teacher by moving close to her and holding the teacher's face in her hands. She waits quietly for the teacher to respond before she takes her turn in the conversation. Jamie, on the other hand, opens the conversation about her rumbling tummy by approaching the teacher and telling her, in no uncertain terms, that she wants to eat. "**Ritual constraints** are the conversationalist's strategies to regulate communication and protect feelings" (Pham, 1994, p. 5). Tamika, in the example, may be regulating her communication and feelings by waiting until the teacher approaches her. Carmen uses a different style and openly, loudly, and with a great deal of feeling expresses her hunger to her understanding teacher. We can view ritual and system constraints as windows into different cultural and individual language styles rather than as limitations.

Children as Conversational Partners in Different Cultures

Cultural differences exist in how children are viewed as conversational partners. The authors of *From Neurons to Neighborhoods* (Shonkoff & Phillips, 2000) summarize research by noting that "in some cultures, children are commonly spoken to directly as *participants* in conversation; in other cultures, children primarily *overhear* talk that is directed toward others" (p. 128). In these cultures, infants and toddlers learn language mostly by listening, or there is more of an emphasis on nonverbal communication. Other researchers conclude that when adults follow children's leads and adopt the topics and activities of interest to the child, they reflect the "Western [countries including the United States and western Europe] notion that children—even from infancy—can be treated as conversational partners" (Pan, Imbens-Bailey, Winner, & Snow, 1996, p. 262). The preponderance of child-centered talk in many interactions reflects a Western model for interacting with children that has been referred to as **infant-directed speech.** In other words, many adults in Western cultures *adapt* their talk with children to a developmental level that is slightly above the child's level of talk, involving the very young child in conversations such as in Box 9.1.

In these interactions the adult treats the child as a person who is capable of taking a conversational turn, even if that turn consists of a sound, a sneeze, a word, or a short sentence. Adults in the Western world who use infant-directed speech to speak with the infant or toddler think that the child learns the rules of conversation in that culture, such as how to wait for the other person to take a turn, take her turn, and then wait again for the other person to speak. These adults believe that the child is learning language by being a conversational partner in a social situation.

system constraints
The opening, closing, turn taking, and rerun related to handling conversations in different languages and cultures.

ritual constraints
The conversationalist's strategies to regulate communication and protect feelings.

infant-directed speech
An adult (or older child) directing speech at infants or toddlers that is on or slightly above the young child's level of language use.

As you work with children and families, it will be important for you to observe the particular patterns of communication of children and families, so that you can appreciate how, why, when, and where a child communicates to peers and adults.

Language Content and Culture

The content of adults' language with children may also differ by families and cultures. For example, families can differ in how they talk about past events with their children. One parent or family may engage their child in lengthy conversations: describing, elaborating, reminiscing, and extending information about the past event. Other parents do not elaborate, but rather tell the more practical aspects of the past experience, prompting their child to remember, and asking many questions (Reese & Fivush, 1993). Reese and Fivush surmise that both of these styles may have their cultural value and purpose and prepare a child for styles of language use that prevail in their particular culture.

Box 9.1

An Example of Infant-Directed Speech

Infant:	Mommy.
Parent:	I'm right here. Your mommy's right here.
Infant:	Mommy.
Parent:	Yes, I'm Mommy. Where's Daddy?
Infant:	Aaaahhh.
Parent:	Yes—he's over there.

Bilingual and Bidialectical Children and Families

Bilingual language acquisition is the norm in many parts of the world and has fueled a prevailing belief that young children can effortlessly acquire two or more languages. (Petitto et al.)

In addition to learning different styles of language, children may also be learning two or more languages—which prompts the question: Are infants and toddlers able to effortlessly learn two languages at the same time? Most infants and toddlers do have the brain capacity not only to hear the differences in the sounds and sequence of different languages, but also to learn the vocabulary of both languages and to speak two languages simultaneously. In fact, certain parts of the brain are dedicated to detect the different patterns in the languages that they hear; this allows the infant or toddler to learn multiple languages at the same time (Petitto, Katerelos, Levy, Gauna, Tetreault, & Ferraro, 2001).

Yet, both parents and professionals are asking many important questions about the benefit or challenges inherent in children learning more than one language during their infant and toddler years. Addressing these questions is essential because the population of the United States is quickly becoming more culturally and ethnically diverse, and many families have the opportunity to raise their children to be bilingual. Does it harm or benefit infants and toddlers to learn more than one language during the infancy period?

Before delving into questions and concerns about young children learning two or more languages simultaneously, a few definitions are needed:

- *Simultaneous bilinguals* are children who acquire a second language before 3 years of age (Katz & Snow, 2000, p. 51).
- *Bilingual* children may be learning a verbal and sign language, or two different verbal languages.
- *Monolingual* children speak one language only.
- *Trilingual* children are learning three languages.
- *Bidialectical* children are learning two or more dialects. (A *dialect* is a particular version of a language, and while children who are bidialectical are learning basically the same language, such as English, they are learning two forms of that language.)

A Second Language: Harm or Benefit?

There are a number of questions and concerns that parents and teachers have about infants and toddlers learning two languages:

- Are language milestones achieved at the same time in each language?
- Do children use words in both languages for the same object?
- What about pragmatic skills?
- Do children learning two languages simultaneously have smaller vocabularies in each language?

Let's examine these issues.

One concern that adults have is related to the timing of language achievement: Are language milestones achieved at the same time in each language when young children are simultaneously learning two languages? Are milestones reached at the same time in bilingual children as for monolingual children? Petitto and his colleagues (2001) conducted a unique study with exciting findings. They videotaped, regularly over a year, three children learning both **sign language** and French, and three other children learning both French and English. The researchers asked questions about whether children learning two languages would reach milestones such as first words at the same time in each language, and whether they would reach milestones, such as combining words, at the same age as monolingual children. "The results revealed that both groups achieved their early linguistic milestones in each of their languages at the same time (and similarly to monolinguals)" (p. 453).

sign language
A structured language using specific hand and arm movements to communicate with others.

Another question is whether, when children are learning two languages, they use words in both languages to label the same object. In the study of the three children learning sign language and French and the three children learning French and English, the researchers concluded that beginning when the children learned words or signs, they would use the appropriate word from each language (or the word from one language and the sign from the second language) when they were using that language (Petitto et al., 2001). This means that very young children used, for example, a word in each language for "ball"—rather than choosing just one word from one language and using that word exclusively. It seems that the infants and toddlers were truly learning the two languages "simultaneously."

Another question concerns pragmatic skills: Can infants and toddlers really learn to differentiate between their two languages and speak the appropriate language to the correct person, considering the language that the listener speaks and understands? If infants and toddlers could use one language with one parent and another language with the other parent, then this would demonstrate that the children have learned the sociolinguistic rules concerning when and where to use each language (Nicoladis & Genesee, 1996). Amazingly, researchers (Genesee, Nicoladis, & Paradis, 1996) discovered that only 4% to 7% of the phrases and sentences that bilingual 2-year-olds used were mixed. Mixed utterances were ones that used words from two languages in the same sentence or phrase—for example, a child might say "doggy dodo," which is a mix of French and English words and means "doggy sleeping." Overall, the young children used English with the English-speaking parent and French with the French-speaking parent by 2 years of age. Another study discovered that children learning both French and English began to keep their two languages separate and speak the correct language with the correct person between the ages of 1 and 2½ (Nicoladis & Genesee, 1996).

When young children do mix words from two languages that they are using, they may be modeling after the adults in their environment. Many adults who know two or more languages may mix words in a sentence. Or, given that the primary purpose of learning language is to communicate with others, children may use all of their language knowledge to get their message across. This is an important concept and has implications for parent-child and teacher-child interactions. If parents and teachers want young children to learn to communicate, then they must respond much more to young children's desire to communicate and their message than to the exact use of certain words. Also, adults should not become upset when a very young child mixes the words from two languages. Children will learn each language as a distinct language if adults *model* each language separately. If children do continue to mix words from two languages, then it is probably because the children, just like many adults, mix two languages in order to communicate better with others.

Also, children may mix languages because they don't know the word in the second language, so they use a word that they do know (Nicoladis & Genesee, 1996), even if the person listening speaks a different language. Young children mix languages with people who they know can understand both languages and who won't get upset with them for mixing the two languages (DeHouwer, 1999). Again, the social context influences how a child uses the language skills that they know.

Finally, we address the issue of vocabulary. Specifically, parents and professionals are concerned about whether children who are learning two languages will have smaller vocabularies in each language than children learning only one language. One study showed that infants and toddlers learning two languages simultaneously do have smaller vocabularies in either language than monolinguals, but they have larger total vocabularies than monolingual age-mates (Pearson, Fernandez, & Oller, 1993). But, in research completed several years later, these same researchers (Pearson, Fernandez, Lewedeg, and Oller, 1997) concluded that, because there is such a wide range of development for monolinguals, the vocabulary of the children who were learning two languages did not differ significantly from the vocabulary of monolinguals.

Does the amount of language input from adults in a particular language contribute to differences in children's vocabulary learning? Does it matter how much we, as adults, talk with infants or toddlers? Researchers have found that it matters significantly. After studying 25 simultaneous bilingual children from 8 to 30 months of age, researchers discovered that children who were talked with more learned more vocabulary from 1 to 2 years of age: "We have been able to show that the number of words learned in each language is, to a large extent, proportional to the amount of time spent with speakers of the language" (Pearson et al., 1997, p. 51). However, there were exceptions. Some young children, it seems, may be better at learning, so may need less language input from adults. These, however, are the exceptions. Most children's language use is related to how much adults talk with them and the quality of the relationship that the child has with the adult.

Infants may not learn a second language with just anyone. If the infant has a positive, loving relationship with an adult, then the child will be more likely to learn the language that the favorite adult speaks with the child. Also, infants and toddlers will learn more of a particular language if the adult uses active and responsive language teaching strategies: "The relative child-centeredness of the adult speakers of each language and the strategies adults employ to guide children's language choices are crucial for getting children to accept input in both languages" (Pearson et al., 1997, pp. 53–54). So, what are some strategies that adults can use to support infants and toddlers while they learn two languages?

Strategies for Adults with Infants and Toddlers Learning a Second Language

From an infant's or toddler's perspective it may be easier to learn two languages if one adult, such as the father, primarily speaks one language with the child and a second adult, such as the mother, speaks a second language with the child. This allows the child to consistently hear the differences in the sounds and words of the two languages, and although children may first confuse sounds and words in the two languages, they soon begin to keep the specific sounds, words, and sentence structure of each language separate and use the appropriate language with the right person who speaks that language with them. DeHouwer (1999) recommends that parents of children learning two or more languages can support their children's language development if they use the strategies identified in Figure 9.2.

- Make sure that children hear both languages frequently and in a variety of circumstances.
- Create opportunities for your children to use the languages that they hear.
- Read books to and with your children in each of the languages that are important to their lives.
- Talk to all your children in the same way. For instance, don't use one language with the oldest child and another language with the younger. Language is tied to emotions, and if you address your children in different languages, some of your children may feel excluded, which in turn might adversely affect their behavior.
- Avoid abrupt changes in how you talk to your children, especially if they are under 6. For example, don't suddenly decide to speak French to them if you have only been using English.
- Be aware of doctors and teachers who tell you to stop speaking a particular language to your children.
- If you feel strongly about your children using one particular language with you, encourage them to use it in all of their communication with you.
- However, do not punish or criticize your children for using or not using a particular language. Instead, encourage them or offer them the appropriate words in the language you want them to speak.
- If a child is not learning either language well, ask a doctor for a hearing test in order to rule out medical problems.

Figure 9.2
Strategies for supporting children who are learning two languages.
Source: Based on DeHouwer (1999).

Honoring the Home Language

Many educators believe that infants and toddlers who attend infant and toddler programs need teachers who speak the child's native language in order to provide the child a firm foundation in the home language before the child learns a second language (Garcia, 1992; Sánchez & Thorp, 1998a, 1998b, 1998c). With so many languages spoken in the United States, however, administrators of programs may find it difficult to find teachers to speak the languages of the babies in their programs. But even if you don't know a child's home language, you can learn words and songs in that language to use frequently—especially words of endearment that help the infant or toddler feel safe and loved. Both the children and the families will benefit if you make an attempt to honor the child's home language.

Whether the teacher is bilingual or only speaks English, the parent should be encouraged to continue speaking the home language to the infant or toddler. Infants and toddlers deserve "linguistic continuity" (Sánchez & Thorp, 1998a, 1998b, 1998c). Programs that try to impose "English-only" rules on families may be doing great harm. "In fact, the abrupt end of the use of the home language by a child's parents may lead to great emotional and psychological difficulties both for the parents and for the child. After all, language is strongly linked to emotion, affect, and identity" (DeHouwer, 1999, p. 2). Also, if the parent doesn't have a great command of a language other than the home language, the language models as well as the emotional interactions may be limited for the child. Another language that is gaining in importance as a form of communication for all young children is sign language (Acredolo & Goodwyn, 2002).

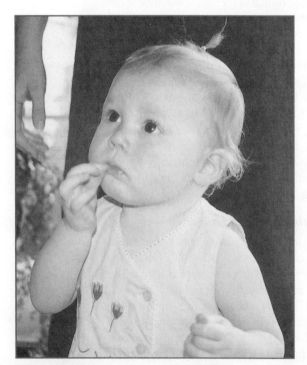
Very young children can learn to use the sign for "eat."

Using Sign Language

Just as with a second verbal language, young children are capable of learning a sign symbol system to communicate. Infants can sign before they can speak because the fine motor development in their hands matures before the body parts needed to speak words, giving them a way to communicate prior to using words.

> *Dawson, at 1 year of age, could sign "more" and "down" because his parents modeled the sign "more" when he wanted more juice and the sign "down" when he wanted down from his high chair. Now Dawson, an 18-month-old, signs "more" and says the word as well. Learning sign language when he was younger helped him communicate with his parents and did not interfere with learning verbal language and won't as long as his parents use words with him as well as sign language.*

Parents and teachers are discovering that when 11-month-olds sign words like "more" and "drink," the adults can use this powerful tool to help them be responsive to the infants' needs. A baby who learns signs may be less frustrated, as he can communicate his needs (Grabmeier, 1999). Signing with an infant does not interfere with later verbal development; rather, it *contributes* to a child's language development (Goodwyn, Acredolo, & Brown, 2000; Grabmeier, 1999), and young children's first words are likely to be the ones they've learned to sign first (Grabmeier, 1999).

Summary of Bilingual Learning

The following statement provides an excellent summary to this section concerning children learning two languages:

> (1) A bilingual environment is most often a necessity, not a choice; (2) hearing two or more languages in childhood is not a cause of language disorder or language delay; (3) children's use of two languages within one sentence is not a sign of confusion; and (4) children do not just "pick up" a language; they need a strongly supportive and rich environment. (DeHouwer, 1999)

In the next section, we will consider the stages of language development and describe, in more detail, the strategies that adults can use to provide a strongly supportive and rich language environment.

Language Development in Relationships

What a remarkable journey we take with infants and toddlers who so seriously and competently listen to the sounds, words, and sentences, figuring out the complex rules of language (Kuhl, 2007). Think about how you learned your first language. You probably can't remember, because it happened so early in your life, and it now seems that the process was effortless. In reality, infants and toddlers are using a number of different strategies to become a conversational partner with others, such as recognizing the voices of the special people in their lives, learning to predict when one word ends and another begins, or using words in the correct order to convey meaning. As we still do as adults, infants and toddlers learn to use nonverbal gestures and facial expressions to communicate their thoughts and feelings. Let's travel with infants and toddlers as they move through their language learning journey.

Prior to Birth

Infants are practicing listening to sounds while still snug inside their mothers' wombs. More than 20 years ago, some ingenious researchers (DeCasper & Fifer, 1980) found that newborns can distinguish between their mother's voice and another female's voice, almost immediately after birth. The infants, at 3 days old, were asked to do something they could already do very well: to suck on a pacifier-like nipple. The nipple was connected through wires to a tape recorder. If a baby

Babies communicate in myriad ways. This little girl's face tells us a story.

sucked on the nipple at a fast rate, for example, she could hear her mother's voice, and if the baby sucked the nipple at a slower rate, she would hear a stranger's voice. The babies quickly learned which rate of sucking would produce their mother's voice and consistently produced the rate of sucking to generate that sound. How did the infants know how to do this incredible feat? Did they immediately learn their mother's voice after birth, or were they eavesdropping prior to birth? To answer this question, researchers DeCasper and Spence (1986) tried a different variation on the first research study. They asked pregnant women to read a particular children's story (such as Dr. Seuss's *Cat in the Hat*) aloud each day for the final 6 weeks of pregnancy. After the infants were born, the researchers played recordings of the mother reading this same story or a previously unheard story. The newborns again used sucking patterns to demonstrate that they clearly preferred the sound of the story they heard in utero. Infants seem to be paying attention and discriminating between complex patterns of sounds even before birth.

Birth to 2 Months

"Infants are 'citizens of the world' at birth and early in life they can hear the differences between all the consonants and vowels used in any language" (de Boer & Kuhl, 2003). They can hear the differences in the sounds in words and are ready to begin to learn any language in the world (McDevitt & Ormrod, 2002). By 1 month of age, and probably earlier, infants prefer to hear talk that is directed toward them (higher pitch, sounds more articulated, simplified, repetitions in sounds and words) rather than adult-directed talk (Cooper & Aslin, 1990).

Babies communicate in a variety of ways, one of which is to cry when they are in pain, hungry, or distressed. They yawn, scrunch up their face, turn away, look peaceful and calm, and communicate in myriad ways to the adult who pays attention to all of the verbal and nonverbal signals of the infant. Important caregivers in infants' lives begin to interpret the burps, quieting, and looking as forms of communication (see Box 9.2). By 2 months of age, infants begin to have different cries for hunger and pain, and an astute parent can hear these differences and respond accordingly, meeting the infants' needs and helping them begin to communicate successfully in different ways.

2 to 4 Months

From 2 to 4 months of age, infants engage in a *language dance* with their parents and other important adults in their lives. Josh, 3 months old, looks into his language partner's eyes. As he makes soft cooing sounds, his language partner patiently waits and then coos or sings or speaks softly to Josh. The partners, adult and infant, share the magic moment when a language connection is made and they are emotionally connected with each other.

Expressive language continues to progress. Babbling (repetition of consonant-vowel sounds, such as "ma" or "da") may begin toward the end of this age period and is enhanced when the infant's language dance partner imitates the infant's sounds. Infants are providing consistently different signals to express to their caregivers that they are hungry, distressed, or feeling pleasure.

Box 9.2

Babies' Nonverbal "Talking"

Mom to baby: "Oh, you're feeling tired. I can tell by those yawns. Oops, your tummy is growling. Are you telling me you're hungry?"

When adults treat infants' nonverbal behavior as forms of communication, babies begin to understand what it is like to be an interactive partner in a conversation.

Observation Invitation 9.1

Language Development

Child's name: *Damika*

Parent's or professional's name: Sharon Nauen

What am I doing? What am I feeling?	**What am I learning?**
(2 months old) She said "ah" as she looked into my eyes.	I can make sounds and get a response.
(4 months old) I am making many sounds when I wake up in my crib. I'm feeling content.	To practice sounds and enjoy them.
(6 months old) I have started to babble "da" when I'm on my back on the floor. I'm happy.	I'm learning to put several sounds together to babble.
(8 months old) I babble to my mom and she babbles back.	I'm learning how to communicate to my mom.

What developmental milestone would you expect to happen next during the 8- to 12-month age period? Read the next section to find out.

4 to 8 Months

Seven-month-olds can remember Mozart music passages, and can still recall these passages after 2 weeks of not hearing them (Saffran, Loman, & Robertson, 2000). Remarkably, they prefer to listen to passages that they've heard before and that are played in the same sequence. (What a wonderful way for the infants to demonstrate their long-term memory as well as their receptive skills!) Infants, during this age period, also begin to turn their heads toward a noise or someone speaking their name—again demonstrating their recognition of the sound of their own name. They also communicate in a variety of ways without using words.

Expressively, infants begin to demonstrate through their movements and facial expressions that they anticipate that their sounds and nonverbal communication (such as reaching up with their arms to be picked up) will get a reaction from an adult. They vocalize to get adults' valued attention. They are learning the social function of language before they learn words (Lu, 1998). As Katz and Snow (2000) note, "Children engage in conversation with adults and with each other before they have acquired their first conventional word" (p. 5).

In addition to communicating nonverbally, they also begin to babble. They are babbling monosyllables ("ba"; "da") and toward the end of this age group are using reduplicative babbling ("bababa"; "dadada"), repeating the consonant-vowel combinations. These first repeated babbling sounds are often interpreted by parents as infants calling them by name. The sound for mother and father, in many cultures, are babbling sounds that the infant first makes, such as "pa-pa," "ma-ma," and "da-da." At 6 months babies are biologically ready to speak any language that they hear frequently, as they can distinguish and make all sounds used in all languages (de Boer, & Kuhl, 2003). This skill seems to be genetically programmed, as all babies babble these sounds, although the babbles of infants with hearing impairment may be qualitatively different from babies who can hear well. Observation Invitation 9.1 describes the sounds that Damika has made at different ages. What developmental milestone would you expect to happen next?

8 to 12 Months

Infants have added listening abilities that contribute to learning a language well. Eight-month-olds show some ability to divide a continuous stream of speech sounds that they hear into individual words (Aslin, Saffran, & Newport, 1998). For example, they can begin to divide "Hereisthemilk" into "Here is the milk." Demonstrating their receptive skills, infants can perceive common sequences of sounds that form words. For example, they won't listen as well when sounds are embedded in nonsense words as when they are used within familiar words in English. By 1 year of age, infants are learning that certain sounds go together to form words in English, and that other sequences of sounds are not combined in English, based on the language patterns they are hearing from adults (Saffran, 2002). Infants are learning that certain sounds are likely to follow other sounds—such as in the word "baby," the "by" is more likely to follow the "ba" than are other sequences of sounds.

In an interesting research study Pruden, Hirsh-Pasek, Golinkoff, and Hennon (2006) found that the 10-month-olds they studied understood a new word after an adult named it five times, but they applied the new word to an interesting object, not a boring one, even though the adult looked at the boring object. The interesting object attracted their attention and they ignored the adult's eye gaze. At 12, 18, and 24 months infants tune into the adult's social cue of looking at an object and understand that the label the adult uses is for that object. Brooks and Meltzoff (2005), however, studied whether 9-, 10-, and 11-month-old infants were more likely to turn and follow the gaze of an adult when the adult's eyes were open rather than closed. They found that the 10- and 11-month-olds who turned and followed adults with eyes open had higher language development scores at 18 months. It is important, then, during this age period for adults to watch where the infant is looking when they label or talk about an object.

All of this information about the capabilities of infants demonstrates how important it is to talk *with* babies during their first 8 months and definitely not wait until they say their first words to talk with them. If adults wait to talk with little babies, their language development may be compromised, since infants need to hear language and engage in the language dance with a responsive language partner during their first months of life. It is also important to be responsive and to talk about what interests the infant.

Additional receptive skills that appear around the child's first birthday include beginning to understand simple directions and the language in games. An adult or sibling might give a direction such as "Wave bye-bye" or "Give Mommy a kiss." Again, demonstrating the desire to be social, infants love it when adults play familiar games such as peek-a-boo, pat-a-cake, or "How big are you?"

Intentional communication increases as infants learn a repertoire of gestures (shaking head "no," holding hands up to be picked up, waving bye-bye), sounds, and first words to communicate their needs and desires. A responsive communication partner teaches an infant that gestures, sounds, and words get results, so that the infant does not need to cry to get his needs met. As described in the following example, when adults respond, infants enjoy communicating with a language partner:

> *Mika, 9 months old, sat in the bathtub with her mother on the floor beside the tub. Playing with the sound of her voice, Mika said "Da-da." Her mother said "Da-da" in a different tone. Mika said "Da-da" in a still different tone, putting emphasis on the second syllable. Her mother said "Da-da" in a higher tone. On they went, taking turns with different sounds bouncing off the wall of the bathroom, until many turns had been taken and "Da-da" had been exclaimed in as many melodies as possible.*

Mika was learning that communicating is fun, that language has prosodic features (pitch, tempo, pauses, and emphatic stress on parts of a word), that she could *initiate* a "conversation" (about "da-da"), and that she could *sustain* a conversation by continuing to take her turn. She was learning that she could be an important and effective conversational partner.

Babbling continues to develop with combined syllables such as "dada," "mama," "nana," and "tutu," but now the infant may be using these sounds to name the mother or father. These words are music to the ears of parents who feel special when their infant repeats these sounds especially and primarily for them.

By the young age of 8 to 12 months, infants are beginning to lose the ability to make all of the sounds of all of the languages in the world, as they listen to and practice the sounds of the familiar language spoken to them in their immediate social interactions (Werker, Pons, Dietrich, Kajikowa, Fais, & Amano, 2007). For example, the English language distinguishes *R* from *L*, and the Japanese language does not (de Boer & Kuhl, 2003). Infants are now hearing the differences in sounds and words that are used in their own language, and losing the ability to hear all of the sounds of all of the languages in the world. So, Japanese children lose their ability to hear the differences in the sounds of *R* and *L* (de Boer & Kuhl, 2003; Kuhl, Williams, Lacerda, Sterens, & Lindblom, 1992). "However, if exposed to a second language at this remarkable time of learning, infants can keep the brain open to the sounds of foreign language" (de Boer & Kuhl, 2003). When 8- to 12-month-old children, who usually lose their ability to hear sounds in a foreign language at this age, were exposed to a second language through inter-acting with an adult for a total of 5 hours, they could distinguish the sounds of that language at 12 months. When infants looked at and heard a DVD or listened to a second language on a tape, though, they did *not* retain their ability to distinguish the sounds of the second language. It takes interacting with adults in a social context to "keep the brain open to sounds."

12 to 18 Months

Receptively, toddlers again demonstrate their beginning language sophistication by paying attention to different things when an adult uses a noun as opposed to an adjective (Waxman & Markow, 1995). They can follow simple directions, such as "Go get your coat" and can cor-rectly point to their nose, eyes, hair, foot, tummy, and other body parts when a parent or teacher playfully asks "Where's your nose?" and "Where's your tummy?" Young toddlers between the ages of 13 and 18 months heard a word just nine times in 5 minutes and then were able to demonstrate that they understood what the word meant, even after a 24-hour delay (Woodward, Markman, & Fitzsimmons, 1994). For example, an infant hearing the word "ball" for the first time will go after the "ball" a day later when an adult uses the specific word (if "ball" has been used frequently during the previous day). Clearly, young toddlers can compre-hend the meaning of words quickly during this age period.

Infants are likely to begin pointing at objects and people with their tiny index finger by the time they are 12 months old, although some children begin earlier. In their attempt to *share attention*, infants may intentionally point at a person or object with a squeal of delight to direct another person's attention toward that object (Legerstee & Barillas, 2003). When an infant points, she is aware that objects are separate from her and that she can direct an adult's attention to some event or object—an observable and exciting step forward in cognitive lan-guage, motor, social, and emotional development. The infants are now sharing experiences with others as they "tune into others and get others to tune into them" (Legerstee & Barillas, 2003, p. 108). When caregivers tune in to the infant's pointing and respond with, for exam-ple, "You see a ball, don't you?" or "Ooh—a ball—I see it," infants enthusiastically continue to point and then progress to using words to focus *joint attention* on an object or person. You can still expect to see many gestures for a while, however, since in the 12- to 18-month age period 85% of infants continue to use gestures as well as words to request and label objects and people (Acredolo & Goodwyn, 1985). The growth of a young toddler's vocabulary,

myeducationlab

Go to the Activities and Applications section in Chapter 9 of MyEducationLab to watch the video *An Infant's Language and Literacy Experiences.* Listen carefully to what you hear.

Lamar, at 16 months, was very busy learning language.

- "Sirt" (shirt) he exclaimed, while also pointing to a shirt his mom was holding.
- "Kitty," he said, as he looked at the kitty.
- "Buses teeth,"as he pointed to his father who was brushing his teeth.
- "Mama, mama, porch," Lamar called out.
- Lamar joyfully practiced a new word: "Back, back, back," as he ran through the kitchen.
- The next day he said "juice" when his dad took the juice container out of the refrigerator.
- Other words that Lamar used over the next few days included "feet," "eye," "boke-boke" (broke) after breaking a plastic cup, "sut" (shut), and "pease" (please).

Figure 9.3   Language characteristics of a 16-month-old.

though, is miraculous during this age period. Through *joint attention conversations* with adults, mobile infants learn that every action has a name and they can use these wonderful new words. When adults respond to mobile infants' pointing, they are moving children toward a language explosion.

This rapid word learning between 12 and 18 months is often referred to as a *language explosion* or *productive naming explosion* (Woodward et al., 1994), a very surprising increase in language development that demonstrates a toddler's desire to learn to label people, places, and things in a social context. Just as fireworks explode with a variety of colors and in many different surprising directions, the language explosion delights adults who are in awe of the sudden increase and variety of words spoken by the toddler. The adult may wonder how these words can suddenly appear, but we know that the infant and growing toddler has been participating in a rich language dialogue since birth. Carey (1978) noted that at 18 months, toddlers were learning as many as nine new words a day. Phrases with two or more words are heard at the end of this age period, such as "more mik" (milk), "more juice," and "Mama, bush (brush) teeth." Figure 9.3 lists some words and phrases that a 16-month-old boy could use and that are characteristic of that age. Notice that Lamar says many words and is beginning to put two words together ("buses teeth").

Mobile infants continue to communicate in a variety of ways—using gestures, words, phrases, and simple sentences to reject, request, comment (Holdgrafer & Dunst, 1990), refuse, demand, and inform—and may, at times, be difficult to understand. For example, you will still hear toddlers *jargoning*—a sequence of sounds with intonation of an adult, such as "ba bad a da tu le?" with the rising intonation at the end to indicate a question. They may seem to be telling you a piece of very important information with a great deal of emphasis on different sounds, but it is difficult to understand what is being said. Parents and teachers often have to be mind readers in order to understand young toddlers who are intent on communicating something quite important, and who may get very frustrated when adults don't understand them. Encouraging a young toddler to take your hand and show you can often help diffuse the situation.

myeducationlab

Go to the Activities and Applications section in Chapter 9 of MyEducationLab to watch the video *Two-Year-Olds Playing with Toys—Part 1*. Observe the language development of each child.

18 to 36 Months

Toddlers demonstrate that they can detect slight mispronunciations in words by looking at the objects when the researchers used the correct pronunciation (Bailey & Plunkett, 2002), such as "doll" instead of "dole" (for *doll*). They have accomplished what is called *fast mapping*, attaching a name to an object very quickly. At 18 months, toddlers easily learn both gestures and words as names for objects, but by 24 months they interpret only words as names for objects, unless they are given additional practice with gestures. Their ability to use both words and gestures as symbols for an object becomes refined as they learn that, in most social situations, words are primarily used to name objects (Namy & Waxman, 1998). It is impressive that most toddlers become more focused on learning words rather than gestures, simply because they *observe* that people around them use mostly words rather than mostly gestures. Because of this ability to focus on learning words to name people, places, and objects rather than learning just gestures, toddlers are able to participate in their social group more effectively.

Listening to toddlers talk is a joy because they try so hard to communicate their excitement about all of the new things that they are learning. They want to tell their special adults what's bothering them, where to look, what to feed them, and how to dress them. They want to share what they've found with you and want you to share in the moment with them—to really be there emotionally and linguistically. As they develop autonomy, they demand, request, inform, and describe their world. Their language is a window—sometimes clear and sometimes foggy—into what they are thinking.

From saying sounds to saying words to putting words together, infants and toddlers try to make sense of the language they are hearing. Toddlers make linguistic mistakes, but they are developmentally appropriate mistakes and tell us that toddlers are not just imitating what they hear, but are also applying some rules that they've discovered all by themselves. They may think that the word "dog" applies to all four-legged creatures, so the next cat, horse, or pig they see will enthusiastically be called "dog." This mistake of *overgeneralization* tells us that toddlers are listening to what we are saying and that their minds are very busy fast mapping the words to an object, animal, or person. They may also *undergeneralize* a word and not use it for all of the cases to which it applies. For example, to them, a cat is only a cat if it is a black cat. So, when they see a white cat, they think that it is named something else. After all, objects that they drink out of are strangely called cups, glasses, thermos, or bottles, so shouldn't there be different names for a black, white, spotted, gray, or furless cat? During this age period, as before, toddlers work very hard to figure out all of the names of things, the characteristics that differentiate them, and how to talk about them. We can help them by engaging them in conversations about all of the exciting things in their environment, such as their red shoes, the large refrigerator, cheddar cheese, how a puppy is different from a kitty as well as talking with them about their emotions—anger, sadness, worry, fear, and joy.

> At 18 months, Carmen could say the words "up," "meow," "open," "down," "door," "diaper," "pretzel," and "neck." She also could use sentences such as, " go kitty," " go car," and " go Mommy"—open-pivot sentences, so labeled because different words pivot around one word, such as "go."

Toddlers progress from saying mostly one-word and some two-word sentences at 18 months to multiword sentences at 36 months. As noted in the previous example, they begin to use *open-pivot* sentences. They also use *telegraphic speech.* Spoken sentences such as "Kitty eat food" are called telegraphic because, just as a telegram leaves out words for the sake of brevity, the toddler leaves out words and uses the essential parts of speech that communicate meaning. Soon, Carmen was saying "Dada, dada, I boke (broke) eggs," adding the "s" on words to indicate that they are plural. Next, she added "ing" to say "I jumping" rather than "I jump." Again, mistakes are made because of a toddler's active mind. Applying the "s" rule to indicate plurals, some exceptions in the English language, such as "deer," may be called "deers" by the learning toddler (Brown, 1973). By 3 years of age, Carmen was saying wonderfully creative sentences, such as "People pee in the potty and puppies pee in the now (snow)," "Why you are crying?" or "It's too louder" (the music was playing at a high volume).

The language learning journey continues for many years, but what incredible progress Carmen and other children make from birth to age 3. There are a variety of strategies that adults can use to support and enhance children's language development.

Strategies to Encourage Language Learning

The teacher's voice was warm and caring as she soothed Katrina after a fall. Katrina, 9 months old, crying intensely, stopped and looked up at the teacher. The teacher continued comforting Katrina with calm words. The teacher then stopped and waited expectantly for Katrina to take a turn in the conversation. Katrina started babbling, as if telling the teacher all about the nasty fall. This communication exchange seemed emotionally satisfying to both Katrina and the teacher, as Katrina stopped crying, gave a big sigh, and began babbling excitedly.

The teacher in this example is using responsive language. She is empathic and waits for Katrina to take a turn in the conversation. We have identified a dozen strategies like those represented in the scenario with Katrina that parents and teachers use to support children learning to express themselves, to hear and understand language, and to become competent communicators.

1. Build Relationships—Be an Empathic Language Partner

When a person cares about another person, he or she usually wants to communicate with that person. An infant or toddler will want to communicate with you when she feels safe and cared for in loving ways. Infants and toddlers communicate when it is pleasant to communicate, when the affect or feeling of the communication is warm and loving, and when they understand that their communication attempts will get a response.

2. Respond and Take Turns—Be an Interactive Language Partner

conversational dance
A conversation of sounds, words, or sentences, much like in a coordinated dance, in which an adult follows the lead of the child.

Through your interactions with the infant or toddler you are helping the child learn to use language to communicate. When a toddler asks for a drink and a parent or teacher responds, then the toddler learns that communication is an effective way to get his needs met. When an infant makes sounds or a toddler uses words, respond and then wait for the child to take a turn with sounds, words, or sentences. This **conversational dance** with each partner taking a turn helps the child learn the pragmatics of conversation—that people take turns exchanging ideas in a social context. These adult–child conversations build young children's vocabulary as well as their ability to take language turns—a skill that helps them become a *conversational* partner and a *capable communicator*. Try not to dominate the conversation with an infant or toddler (Girolametto, 2000) by taking more turns than the child or bombarding the child with language. Instead, focus on reciprocal and responsive interactions with equal give-and-take conversations.

3. Respond to Nonverbal Communication

Can babies that can't talk try to tell you something? Yes, they can. A yawn can mean the baby is tired or bored, snuggling in to an adult's body tells you that the infant feels safe and relaxed, a toddler running to you tells you she wants to connect with you, and kicking feet say "I'm uncomfortable." When babies turn away, they may be communicating that they need a break from the interaction. When infants or toddlers use a strong communication cue, such as arching their back, it means "that hurts," or "stop what you are doing." When adults understand and respond to infants' and toddlers' nonverbal communication they let children know that they are communication partners. With responsive adults, infants and toddlers are soon using sounds and words, while still maintaining many nonverbal ways to communicate.

4. Use Self-Talk and Parallel Talk

Self-talk is talk that adults use to describe what they are doing while with the infant or toddler. For example, a teacher who is diapering a baby might say, "I'm getting your diaper. Now I'm lifting your feet. I'm putting the diaper on. All done." **Parallel talk** occurs when an adult talks about what a child is doing. For example, while the child is playing or eating the adult might say, "Mmm, you're eating your toast" while pointing to the toast. These strategies tie language to an act or object manipulation, making words come alive and have meaning for the child.

5. Talk Often with the Child, Using a Rich and Varied Vocabulary

Does it matter how much you talk with an infant or toddler, sing, and look at picture books together?

Research shows that the number and quality of the conversations that adults have with infants and toddlers directly affects how they learn to talk (Hart & Risley, 1999; Honig & Brophy, 1996; Shonkoff & Phillips, 2000). The number of total words and different words that the parent uses with the child daily, the number of conversations, and the positive affirmations from the parent are all related to infants' and toddlers' language development (Hart & Risley, 1999).

Researchers have found astounding differences in how much parents talk with their children. Some infants and toddlers hear an average of 600 words an hour while others hear as many as 2,100 words an hour. Some children hear 100 different words an hour while others hear 500 different words an hour. These differences in the amount of language that children heard made a difference in their language development. By age 3 the children with talkative parents were talking more and with a richer vocabulary. They were averaging three times as many statements per hour and twice as many words per hour than the children of quieter parents. "The more time that parents spent talking with their child from day to day, the more rapidly the child's vocabulary was likely to be growing and the higher the child's score on an IQ test was likely to be at age 3" (Hart & Risley, 1999, p. 3).

Use language-rich routines and many interactions with infants and toddlers to build their vocabulary. Diapering, for example, is a perfect time for a parent or teacher to talk about "first" we get a clean diaper, "second" we take off your diaper and so forth. Talking about hands, nose, ears, and toes enlightens the baby about body parts and makes diapering an easier job for you.

6. Use Joint Attention Strategies

> Adults in Western cultures often point to the people or objects under discussion when talking with their young children, thereby directing their children's attention . . . and the mother of a young deaf child is most likely to sign to her child when she knows that the child can simultaneously see both her signs and the objects or events she is talking about. (Harris, 1992, reported in McDevitt & Ormrod, 2002, p. 240)

As noted, infants and toddlers learn best if the adult labels or talks about an object or person when the infant or toddler is focusing on it. Joint attention occurs when both the adult and the child are focusing on the same thing at the same time. Adults who point at the object of discussion or wait until the infant or toddler is looking at an object to talk about it ensure that the child will attach the language label to the correct object. This type of shared attention enhances language development (Adamson, Bakeman, & Deckner, 2004).

self-talk
Talk that adults use while with an infant or toddler to describe what they are doing.

parallel talk
Talk in which an adult describes to a child what the child is doing at the present time.

7. Use the Four E Approach

Encourage children to communicate by listening, responding, and not correcting their language. *Expand* on both the semantics and the syntax of a child's words and conversational turns. *Elaborate* on (make more complex) and *extend* (lengthen) the sounds, words, and sentence—for example, by adding a different sound, a new word, or a slightly longer sentence. Imitating and then expanding on the language of the child models the next step in development. The child hears your expansion and is likely to begin to use the newly modeled language forms. An added benefit of using the four Es is that infants and toddlers feel *effective* and a language *equal,* promoting further use of language to communicate.

8. Use Semantically Responsive Talk

When adults took language turns with toddlers and stayed on the same topic, children were significantly more likely to reply than if the adult responded but changed the topic (Dunham & Dunham, 1996). While a conversation made up of cooing sounds may seem as if it would be boring to an adult, the delight in an infant's eyes, the emotional connection, and the continuous development of the infant's language is reward enough to the caring adult. The adult's **semantic elaboration** supports the child's tendency to stay on the topic, as well. If a toddler is talking about the "airplane" and the listening adult responds semantically with information about the shape or color of the airplane, then the toddler is likely to stay on the topic and say something more about the airplane.

semantic elaboration
Conversations with children in which the adult stays on the same topic that the child is discussing but expands the meanings that the child is expressing.

9. Use Infant-Directed Speech

> *Janna, 13 months old, played quietly with a ball, rolling it and scrambling after it, only to roll it again across the carpet. When she tired of rolling the ball, she looked at her grandfather. Her grandfather sat on the floor beside her and said, "Ball, let's roll the ball." Janna smiled as she rolled the ball in Grandpa's direction. "Ball," she said quietly, imitating her grandpa's word.*

In 1985, Anne Fernald discovered that 4-month-olds prefer infant-directed speech. Most parents and grandparents use infant-directed speech and babies like Janna learn from it (McDevitt & Ormrod, 2002; Thiessen, Hill, & Saffran, 2005). As parents and teachers generally try to *simplify* language in order to maintain the infants' attention and teach them to use language, they use speech with a child that is significantly different from speech with an adult. For example, parents might stress a key word such as "jumping" in the phrase, "You are *jumping.*" Adults using infant-directed speech also point or direct the child's attention to the focus of the conversation—for example, pointing to a cup while saying "cup." Adults repeat words—for example, they might say to an infant or young toddler, "Look, a *bird.* The *bird* is flying." But, isn't the term *infant-directed speech* just another term for "baby talk"?

We've all heard that we shouldn't talk **baby talk** to an infant, but parents and teachers *do* use a special language when they interact with their infants because young children are more attentive when adults use it. Adults in most cultures use these practices, and in so doing, they are a communication partner and language model for infants and toddlers. Parents who use infant-directed speech are modeling bite-size pieces of language that infants and toddlers can digest and practice. Examples would include the following strategies:

baby talk
A special language that adults and older children use with younger children, in which the adult uses shorter sentences and decreased vocabulary.

1. Use responsive talk.
2. Use shorter sentences and decreased vocabulary.
3. Exaggerate the pitch and intonation of your voice.
4. Direct your communication at the infant or toddler.

5. Use longer pauses between words and utterances.

6. Frequently repeat words.

7. Don't be afraid to be redundant—for example, say, "A *bird*—a blue *bird*," repeating the word *bird*.

8. Elongate the vowels in words ("Oooh, whaaaat is that?").

9. Use diminutive words ("blanky," "piggy," "doggy").

10. Use frequent paraphrasing or recasting of previous utterances (toddler says "We go" and parent recasts by saying "Yes, we're going").

11. Talk about what is immediately present.

12. Use frequent phrases and parts of sentences in isolation ("in the car").

13. Use questions and attempts to elicit speech.

14. Label words—nouns and actions—in context.

Many adults also simplify their speech pragmatically when speaking directly to an infant or toddler. For example, we use language for a variety of social goals: to inform, question, promise, request, refuse, play, and to direct others (functions of language). Parents use fewer functions when infants are young and gradually increase the number and types of functions as the infant grows to become a preschooler and can better understand the intentions of language.

Newman and Hussain (2006), however, suggest that by 13 months, mobile infants may need more than infant-directed speech. They will need adults who responsively talk about past events, future events, feelings, and reasons for actions as well as adults who use sentences that are slightly above the child's level of language.

Infant-directed strategies, however, also build the affectionate relationship between parent and child. While most adults stop using these strategies as infants become toddlers and preschoolers, some words are like emotional glue that binds an adult and child together across time and space. Some special words a parent and child will use forever when they are together. A mother of a 30-year-old might ask her grown child if she would like some "pasgetti" (spaghetti), reminding them both of the early years when the child could not say "spaghetti" and the close attachment between them. A grandmother's name may become "Ta-ta" forever, because those were the first sounds that the infant made when lying peacefully in the grandmother's lap.

10. Use Questions and Control Carefully

Questions are often used by adults to start a conversation with a child, to take a conversational turn, or to gain information. Some questions are **true questions** that are asked because the teacher doesn't know the answer. Other questions are asked to test children—for example, "What is that?" as they point to a toy on the floor. These questions are often referred to as **closed questions** because they usually have only one correct answer. There are thoughtful **open-ended questions** that have more than one acceptable answer, such as, "What song do you want to sing next?" **Choice questions**—for example, "Do you want juice or milk?"—are perfect questions for toddlers who are exerting their independence from adults.

Infants and toddlers enjoy and benefit from interactions with teachers who use a **conversation-eliciting style** characterized by conversational turns, maintenance of a mutually interesting topic, and infrequent use of directives. This style is in contrast to a **directive style,** which is characterized by frequent directives and monologues, infrequent

true questions
Questions for which the asker does not know the answer.

closed questions
Questions that have one correct answer.

open-ended questions
Questions that allow for more than one correct answer.

choice questions
Questions that give the responder options.

conversation-eliciting style
Conversation that is characterized by conversational turns, maintenance of a mutually interesting topic, and infrequent use of directives.

directive style
Conversation that is characterized by frequent directives and monologues, rapid topic changes by adults, and a low level of topic maintenance.

210   CHAPTER 9

Observation Invitation 9.2

These children are teaching each other about how to use a flashlight to make "the sun." What strategies could the teacher use to support their language development?

questions, rapid topic changes by adults, and a low level of topic maintenance (Katz & Snow, 2000).

Use *behavior control* carefully. Behavior control refers to statements that are used by teachers to elicit group participation around a common activity or to manage safety concerns. Frequent prohibitions from adults (for example, "stop that," "don't") result in less favorable child outcomes than when adults use more active listening strategies of repeating, paraphrasing, and extending infants' and toddlers' statements (Hart & Risley, 1992).

11. Listen with Your Eyes

> A 3-year-old child's mother picked her up from child care and took her home immediately, so that the mother could prepare dinner. As the mother was pulling food out of the refrigerator, the little girl tried to tell her mommy about something that had happened during the day. The mother, focused on her task, commented, "Hmm, oh, that's nice." The little girl, obviously very frustrated with her mother's lack of response, said, "Mom, listen to me with your eyes."

Infants and toddlers—in fact, all human beings—love to be listened to with another person's full engagement and focus. The little girl described in the previous example wanted her mom to look at her and "listen with her eyes." Infants and toddlers thrive, learn to listen, and take language turns, when adults in their lives do the same with them. (See Observation Invitation 9.2.) They learn that holding a conversation means taking turns with listening and talking, so they will look at you intently, waiting as patiently as they can for you to finish what you want to say. If a child or family member from a particular culture believes that it is disrespectful to "look into your eyes" while talking, he may prefer for you to listen carefully with your ears and voice, acknowledging that you've heard.

12. Read, Sing, Use Finger-Plays and Social Games Like Peek-a-Boo

Playful activities are crucial to enjoyable language learning. Chapter 13 will discuss these topics, including literacy development and experiences, in great detail. On page 213 you will find a summary of strategies to support language development in infants and toddlers.

CHILDREN WITH SPECIAL NEEDS

Individual infants and toddlers differ in how they develop and use language. Some children talk continuously and others are quieter; some talk to themselves as they are playing and others talk mostly with other people. As you observe infants and toddlers you will also see differences in the ages at which babies begin to speak. Most developmental charts indicate that typically developing infants will say their first word around 12 months, some two-word sentences by 18 months, and *many* single words and two-word sentences by 2 years. However, some babies may say their first word as early as 8 months and some as late as 15 months of age. A child that we knew spoke 100 words at her first birthday (this is extremely rare), while other children that we've known were making many sounds but had no words at age 1. While the average number of words that infants speak at 14 months is 10 words, the individual differences in development among children are quite significant. Knowing when to become concerned about a child's **language delay** (children not saying words and sentences when most other children do) may require discussing your observations with other professionals. Keep in mind that language delay at an early age may predict later language and reading challenges (Scarborough & Dobrich, 1990). Scarborough and Dobrich found that children who later had difficulty in reading in elementary school had shorter sentences and less sentence complexity at 2½ years of age and difficulty understanding language and naming objects at age 3. It is very important, then, to identify language delay early in a child's life, so that the child and family receive support in developing language skills.

> **language delay**
> When children do not use words and sentences by the age that most other children do.

Differences may occur for a variety of reasons including biological and environmental. One primary reason is that there are differences in how much children are exposed to language (Huttenlocher et al., 1991). Some children hear many words from adults and some do not. Usually, the more descriptive and kind words that infants and toddlers hear, the more words they will use. Use the strategies discussed on pages 206–211 in this chapter. Another reason for language delay may be hearing impairment. Children with hearing challenges may develop receptive and expressive language in a different way from other children. The pronunciation of sounds, as well as a child's vocabulary and syntax development, will all be affected by hearing challenges.

Hearing Impairment

Hearing loss is one of the most common abnormalities present at birth. Significant hearing loss is present in 1 to 3 per 1,000 newborn infants in the healthy nursery population and 2 to 4 per 100 in the intensive care nursery population. The average age of detection of significant hearing loss is 14 months. Unfortunately, by this time, infants have missed a wealth of language and learning experiences. Hearing screening by a pediatrician for babies between birth and 3 months is recommended and intervention must be in place before the baby is 6 months old for maximum benefit (AAP, 1999). Infants, who are diagnosed before 6 months of age are likely to develop better language skills than children diagnosed after 6 months of age (Yoshinaga-Itano, Sedey, Coulter, & Mehl, 1998).

It is often difficult for parents to read the sometimes subtle signs of hearing loss in their infant, especially if the hearing loss is mild. An infant who is hearing impaired may not turn her head toward a voice, smile in response to a person's voice, or look around when her own name is called (by 5 months of age). Older infants may babble, but the quality is different from typically developing children and babbling may diminish between 8 and 12 months, when the infant begins to practice just those sounds in the language that she is hearing. Infants and toddlers with hearing impairment may watch adults' gestures very carefully and have a hard time following simple directions from words alone, without the additional information from the gestures. They may also be delayed in saying their first words and sentences. It is important that infants and toddlers with hearing impairment be exposed to a communication system early in their lives during the sensitive period for language development.

Not only does learning a communication system, such as sign language, enhance communication, but it also supports that child's developing cognitive abilities—thinking, problem solving, and categorizing. Mayberry, Lock, and Kazmi (2002) discovered that deaf adults who had experienced sign language as infants had higher levels of performance on English learned later in life than adults who had not experienced sign language in their first 4 years.

PROGRAMS THAT ENHANCE LANGUAGE DEVELOPMENT AND LEARNING

As many infants and toddlers venture outside the home environment to participate in child care centers, family child care homes, or early intervention programs such as Early Head Start or programs for children with disabilities, they develop relationships that can enhance or discourage language development. A review of how these community programs influence infants' and toddlers' language development will shed light on specific factors that have positive effects.

Child Care: Relationships and Responsive Interactions

The results of the NICHD (2000b) study, following 500 to 800 infants and toddlers in 10 different sites in the United States attending a variety of types of child care programs as well as those at home with a parent most of the time, found that the overall quality of child care and language stimulation in particular was related to children's language development at 15, 24, and 36 months. Also, the quality of the environment is correlated with the language outcomes for infants and toddlers, both receptive language and expressive communication skills (Burchinal, Roberts, Nabors, & Bryant, 1996).

Early Intervention Programs

Early intervention programs include programs for infants and toddlers at risk for learning challenges because of their socioeconomic status and programs for young children identified as having disabilities by assessment teams. The parents of a child at risk or with a disability may receive home visits from a family support program or attend a family-centered child care center or intervention play group.

The communication enhancement strategies in Figure 9.4 acknowledge the strengths of each child, ensure the child's success, emphasize adult–child interactions as crucial for the language achievements of the child, and promote language development in the environments where the children use language.

1. Facilitating parent–infant language interactions during routines, such as bath time, feeding and eating, and trips to the grocery store

2. Accepting the child's communication bids by showing affection, attention, and verbal feedback

3. Using a facilitative (encouraging) versus a directive style (demanding)

4. Contingent responding through expansion of the child's sounds, words, and sentences

5. Using augmentative communication devices for children who cannot speak (picture symbols that the child uses or computer-like devices that speak for the child)

Figure 9.4   Effective strategies for improving language development in young children with disabilities.
Source: From Prizant, Weatherby, and Roberts (1993).

STRATEGIES TO SUPPORT LANGUAGE DEVELOPMENT AND LEARNING

1. Recognize the capacities of infants and toddlers to understand language and communicate using gestures, facial expressions, sounds, and words.

2. Identify language delay early in a child's life so that the child and family receive support in developing language skills.

3. Follow DeHouwer's (1999) recommendations for parents of children learning two or more languages during the infant and toddler years.

4. Honor a child's home language by encouraging parents to continue using the language, employing native language speakers in the program, and using words and phrases from the child's home language during routines and interactions with the child.

5. Use a dozen strategies to support children's language learning:

   a. Build relationships—be an empathic language partner.

   b. Respond and take turns—be an interactive language partner.

   c. Respond to nonverbal communication.

   d. Use self-talk and parallel talk.

   e. Talk often with the child using a rich and varied vocabulary.

   f. Use joint attention strategies.

   g. Use the four E approach.

   h. Use semantically responsive talk.

   i. Use infant-directed speech.

   j. Use questions and control carefully.

   k. Listen with your eyes.

   l. Read, sing, and use finger-plays and social games like peek-a-boo.

6. The quality of the environment and teachers' use of responsive and sensitive language strategies are related to children's language development.

7. Use routine-based intervention strategies.

Developmental Trends and Responsive Interactions

Language Development and Learning

Infants and toddlers develop the capacity to understand, express, and use language.

Development	Example
0–4 months (infant)	
• Infants may startle if they hear a loud sound. • Infants hear the differences in sounds. • Infants may stop crying when they hear a familiar adult's voice. • Infants prefer to hear talk that is directed toward them. • Infants listen when an adult talks or sings to them while looking at them. • Infants cry when they are in pain, are hungry, or are distressed. • By 2 months of age babies have different cries for hunger and pain. • Infants "coo" (make soft vowel sounds). • Infants smile and laugh toward the end of this age period. • Infants will stare at interesting pictures in books.	Brenda held Jordon so they could gaze into each other's eyes. Jordon cooed softly and Brenda cooed back. Then she waited for Jordon to take another turn. Erica gave her father a big smile when he picked her up out of her crib.
4–8 months (infant)	
• Infants turn their head toward a noise or someone speaking their name. • Infants enjoy adults talking, singing, and laughing with them. • Babies vocalize with intention to get a response from the adult. • Babies make high-pitched squeals. • Infants practice their sounds when exploring and with favorite adults. • Infants begin to babble—at first with one consonant and then by combining two consonants. • Infants engage in turn-taking conversations with adults. • Babies will look at different pictures in a book and get excited at a favorite one or at the enthusiastic tone of an adult who is reading to them.	As Danielle, the infant teacher, was holding Donovan on her lap, she pointed to the pictures in the sturdy board book. "Look," she said, pointing to the picture, "a ball. There's your ball," as she pointed to a ball on the floor. Donovan looked at the picture, then at the ball on the floor, and back to the picture. "Tt" said Afi as he lay in his teacher's arms looking up at her. "Tada" exclaimed his teacher back to him. "Tt" repeated Afi as he took his turn in the conversation.
8–12 months (mobile infant)	
• Mobile infants are beginning to play social games such as peek-a-boo or "so big." • Infants enjoy listening to sound play (rhymes), songs, and finger-plays. • Babbling continues to develop with combined syllables such as "dada," "mama," "nana," and "tutu," but now the infant may be using these sounds specifically for mom or dad. • Infants will use sounds consistently for an object or person or animal. • If they hear another language *with* an adult through interactive conversational strategies, then infants can "keep the brain open to the sounds of a second language." • Infants may begin to use single words. • At the end of the age period, infants may begin to point to engage an adult. • They are using facial expressions and gestures such as shaking head or arms out to be picked up to communicate to adults or peers.	One of Dana's first words was "mama," which she said over and over again when she saw her mother. One of Trishanna's first words was "dada," which she excitedly said over and over again when she saw her father.

Teacher or Parent–Child Interaction	Environment

0–4 months (infant)

- Use infant-directed speech.
- Hold and talk to babies. Engage in long eye gazes while having conversational dances. Respect the baby if he needs a break and turns his head away.
- Read books with rhythmic phrases and books with one picture on a page with 2- to 4-month-olds.
- Interpret babies' burps, cries, yawns, stretching, and sounds as forms of communication. Say, "Oh, you're telling me you're sleepy."
- Sing lullabies and other songs.
- Be an empathic language partner—comment on the baby's feelings.
- Use words and sounds to comfort babies.

- The best environment is in the arms of a caring adult who holds the baby and talks softly.
- Provide toys that make pleasant sounds. Gently hold the toy and share the sounds with the baby.
- Provide interesting materials to touch while you comment on the textures.
- Add mirrors low along a wall. Babies will look and possibly make sounds.

4–8 months (infant)

- Use infant-directed speech.
- Talk with babies often. Show them new objects and people and name them.
- Repeat the sounds that infants make and wait for the infant to make the sound again (turn taking).
- Use sign language for several familiar items such as "milk" or "dog."
- Sing songs and say finger-plays.
- Use words to describe children's feelings expressed through gestures, body postures, and sounds.
- Read simple books with one to two pictures on a page. Point to the pictures as you say the name of the picture.
- Read the same books over and over.
- Use joint attention strategies—point at a toy or picture in a book when you say the name or talk about it.

- Provide interesting toys and materials for babies to handle and explore.
- Provide cardboard books with handles so that babies can crawl to them and pick them up.
- Books with handles encourage babies to hang on to them.
- Make a peek-a-boo picture book by gluing a piece of cloth over each picture.
- Create a cozy book corner where teachers can be comfortable and read to babies.
- Provide sound boxes (safely sealed) with different objects in them that make different sounds when shaken.
- Add puppets to the environment. Use them at times to "talk" to the child. Put the puppet on the child's hand and wait to see what the child says or does.

8–12 months (mobile infant)

- Play familiar games such as peek-a-boo, pat-a-cake, or "how big are you?"
- Respond to infants' nonverbal communication with words.
- Look at and wait for infants to initiate sounds or words.
- Imitate the sounds and then expand, elaborate, and extend the baby's language.
- Model the next step in language development.
- Use self-talk and parallel talk.
- Talk often in a responsive way using a varied vocabulary. Don't bombard the child.
- Read books with enthusiasm—changing the tone of your voice with different characters.
- Talk about the pictures and the story as you read it. Engage babies in the story with your voice and gestures.
- Wait while looking at a picture for babies to initiate with sounds, pointing, or facial expressions.

- Create a cozy book corner where babies can easily reach and handle books.
- Create an "All About Me" book—small photo albums for each child with pictures of themselves, their family, their favorite toys, peers, teachers, and the family pets. Make them available to the children. Change the pictures as the child grows.
- Musical push toys encourage infants to handle them and make sounds.

Developmental Trends and Responsive Interactions (continued)

Development	Example
12–18 months (mobile infant)	

Development	Example
• Mobile infants can follow simple directions such as "Come here" or "Go get your shoes" without you gesturing. • Mobile infants can play a social game without you demonstrating the action—for example, when you say "Wave bye-bye" they wave even though you don't show them how. • Mobile infants will point to engage adults and peers. • Rapid word learning—a language explosion—may occur with the children learning many new words. • Mobile infants will combine words toward the end of this age period. • Mobile infants will jabber (stringing many sounds together) using the intonation that adults use. • Mobile infants will use gestures and language to reject, request, comment, refuse, demand, and name objects and people. • Mobile infants use language to maintain an interaction or conversation with an adult or peer.	Janeika's teacher said, "Let's play pat-a-cake," and Janeika started clapping her hands together. Ross looked up expectantly at his teacher, jabbering many sounds together as if asking her a question.

Development	Example
18–24 months (toddler)	

Development	Example
• Toddlers can go get familiar toys from another room in the house when an adult asks them to and can follow directions such as "close the door." • Toddlers combine words to name things ("that cat"), to deny ("no bite"), and to reject ("no more"). • Toddlers are combining two to three words with meaning. • Toddlers use language for a variety of purposes, including asking "What that?" • Toddlers point to an increasing number of pictures in books when an adult talks about the picture.	"Hi, Kitty," "open door," and "hat on" were just a few of the two-word combinations Cheral used at 20 months of age. Tyra moved quickly over to the bookshelf, picked up a book with a bright cover, and rushed back to his teacher. After sitting comfortably in her lap, he opened the book and enthusiastically started pointing to the pictures as his teacher named them.

Development	Example
24–36 months (toddler)	

Development	Example
• Toddlers understand more complex directions and remember words to short songs and finger-plays. • Toddlers are using many two- to four-word sentences. • Toddlers can point to and name many body parts. • Toddlers add "ing" to words. • Toddlers begin using prepositions such as "on" and "in." • Toddlers add an "s" to words to indicate plurals. • Toddlers may begin to ask "Why?" • Toddlers will begin to tell you stories about what they did or what they saw. • Toward the end of this period, a toddler can use the pictures to tell you what is happening in a story.	Mindy started to add "ing" to words she had been saying for several months. She said, "I running" and "I eating" rather than "I run" and "I eat." "Look, he's playing," exclaimed Treat as he pointed to a picture in his favorite book.

12–18 months (mobile infant)

Teacher or Parent–Child Interaction	Environment
• Stay on topic in a conversation with a mobile infant. See how many turns the child will take. • Respond to the intonation of the child's jabbering. For example, if it seems as if the child is asking a question, answer what you think the child might be asking. • Respond to mobile infants' pointing and other nonverbal communication with language. • Use words that describe and compare sizes, shapes, and sounds. • When a mobile infant uses words such as "I jump," model the next step in language development by saying "You're jumping," adding the "ing" to the word. Do this with both the content of the words and the structure of the words or sentences. • Read books with longer stories, pausing as you go through the book to encourage mobile infants to talk about the pictures and the story.	• Introduce art materials such as play dough, clay, and paint. • Add paper towel rolls for mobile infants to make sounds. • Musical pull toys entice mobile infants to walk and pull objects behind them or push them. • Sturdy music boxes encourage mobile infants to push buttons to "make music." • Drums and other musical instruments can be made available. • Add a sturdy CD player with a story from a parent taped on it. • Use a tape recorder to tape mobile infants' voices and play it back to them. • Provide bubble-making materials. • Provide spaces for two or three children to encourage peer conversation.

18–24 months (toddler)

Teacher or Parent–Child Interaction	Environment
• Read books with longer stories, pausing as you go through the book to encourage toddlers to talk about the pictures and the story. Ask open-ended questions such as "How does the bear feel?" • Wonder often with the child: "I wonder what will happen to the bear." • Engage toddlers in conversation, trying to stay on the same topic as the child. • Introduce new conversations about interesting objects and events.	• Set up an elaborate obstacle course and use words such as "in," "out," "over," "through," "around," "up," and "down" as the toddler goes through the course. • Provide new books each week but keep children's favorites available. • Provide a wider variety of art materials. • Provide sensory materials.

24–36 months (toddler)

Teacher or Parent–Child Interaction	Environment
• Answer their "why" questions with patience and enthusiasm. This is how children learn and engage in social interactions. • Listen with your eyes to toddlers' "stories" that they tell. • Model saying words that are plurals, such as "dogs," "elephants," and so on. • Use descriptive words such as "mozzarella cheese" rather than just "cheese," or "bluejay" rather than just "bird." • Have long conversations with toddlers, following their lead. • Read books to small informal groups or to individual children.	• Provide pictures for children to match. • Puzzles of animals, people, vehicles, and food are important. • Books with many pictures and short stories can be added to the environment. • Dramatic play materials encourage conversation.

myeducationlab

Go to
MyEducationLab
and complete
the Building
Teaching Skills
and Dispositions
exercise in Chapter 9.

SUMMARY

Infants and toddlers have the capacity to become proficient language learners in the first 3 years of life.

- Language is used for communication with others and is affected by the quality of the child's relationships, the social context, and the environment.
- Throughout the first 3 years, infants and toddlers learn to make the sounds of the language spoken to them; combine sounds into words and combine words into sentences; learn the syntax, pragmatics, and prosody of language; learn the meaning of an astonishing number of words; and communicate in a variety of ways—the furrowing of a brow, a loud screech, whining, pointing, talking, and shouting.
- Girls do seem to talk earlier and speak more than boys in the first 20 months of life. However, differences in language development between boys and girls didn't seem to last, and after children were 20 months old fewer differences were found in the vocabularies of boys and girls.
- Hearing loss and prematurity are two factors that affect language development in young children.
- Cultural differences exist in how children are viewed as conversational partners.
- Young children do have the capacity to learn two languages simultaneously and there are strategies to support infants and toddlers as they are learning.
- Young children progress through clear stages of language development.
- There are 12 major strategies that adults can use to support language development.
- When infant and toddler teachers are more responsive and sensitive, then the language development of the children increases.

Key Terms

baby talk	conversation-eliciting style	ritual constraints
choice questions	directive style	self-talk
closed questions	infant-directed speech	semantic elaboration
communication	language	sign language
communicative-linguistic	language delay	system constraints
parameters	open-ended questions	true questions
conversational dance	parallel talk	

REFLECTIONS AND RESOURCES FOR THE READER

Reflections

1. What are the key strategies that adults can use to support children as they learn two languages?
2. Identify the important features of a child care and education setting that support infants' and toddlers' language.

Observation and Application Opportunities

1. Jeff is 2 months old and his parents want him to learn to speak both English and Spanish. His dad speaks Spanish and English quite well and his mom speaks English. What advice would you give them?
2. Choose one stage of language development and expand on the concepts highlighted for that age group. What are the implications of the information for parents and teachers?

3. Choose one of the 12 strategies for promoting language development and give examples of a conversation between an adult and a child, with the adult using the strategy.
4. Observe infants or toddlers in a child development and education setting. Identify the skills that two children of different ages have in receptive and expressive language.

Supplementary Articles and Books to Read

Selman, R. (2001). Talk time: Programming communicative interaction into the toddler day. *Young Children, 56*(3), 15–18.

Weitzman, E. (2000). *Learning language and loving it. A guide to promoting children's social and language development in early childhood settings.* Toronto, Ontario, Canada: The Hanen Center.

Interesting Links

http://www.deafness.about.com
   About Deafness/Hard of Hearing   This Web site provides excellent information on causes of hearing impairment. Also covered are topics such as medical issues, deaf culture, and sign language.

http://www.pitc.org/cs/pitclib/view/pitc_res/34
   PITC *Early Messages: Facilitating language development and communication.*   View the video clip on language development and strategies that caregivers can use to support language development.

http://www.zerotothree.org/site/PageServer?Pagename=key_/language
   ZERO TO THREE: Early Language & Literacy   This site offers articles, handouts, and instructional materials.

myeducationlab

These and other web links are included in this chapter on MyEducationLab.

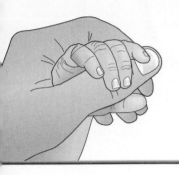

10

Motor Development and Learning

Joella flapped her arms and ran around the yard with glee. Every inch of her body spoke to her energy and excitement.

Michael froze in place, a serious, uncertain look on his face. His body was slightly hunched as he listened intently to the distant sound of a barking dog.

Raj squatted to study a bug moving across the play yard, a picture of concentration.

Helen, their teacher, watched them and thought, "I know so much about what they feel and think by watching their little bodies."

THE UNIQUENESS OF EACH CHILD

In so many ways we think of infants and toddlers in terms of their motor development. We even name an entire stage of development after the toddling, balancing gait of the beginning walker. Our first thoughts of milestones, aside from smiling and sleeping through the night, tend to be motor milestones—rolling over, crawling, standing, and walking. It's not just the

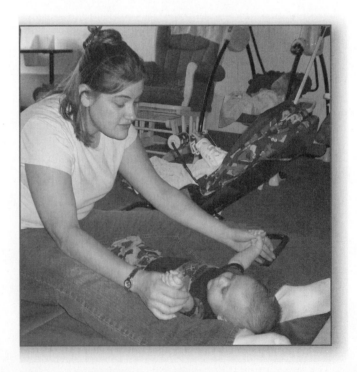

adults who think about motor development, either. Motor development occupies much of a baby's time and effort: moving her body to get where she wants to be, and reaching and holding to bring objects to look at and taste.

Capacities

Current theories of motor development propose that it is a complex, ongoing process of learning and not a simple process of maturation (Adolph, 2008). Throughout the first years of life, and even prenatally, infants and toddlers are constantly adjusting their movements to changes in height, weight, proportion, and posture. While the earliest movements are determined by reflexes, the process of learning quickly takes over and becomes the driving force in motor development.

Infants are moving long before they are born. Using ultrasound, doctors have observed extension-like movements of the upper spine as early as 5 to 6 weeks of gestation, and movements of arms and legs by 8 to 9 weeks (Malina, 2004). The motor activity of the fetus is part of the developmental process, as the body and brain develop and store information about movement patterns. These movements help the fetus develop muscles and move through the birth canal.

Newborns are physically active, and reflexes that are an extension of prenatal movements drive much of their activity. Reflexes are the body's automatic reaction to certain physical events. The primitive motor reflexes of the newborn operate at the brainstem level: protecting the baby, helping him find food, and keeping his head, arms, legs, and trunk organized. In fact, reflexes are checked by physicians as a way of making sure that messages are passing between the body and the brain. Of the nearly 75 reflexes present in the newborn, the most well known support feeding, gazing, and grasping—as you can see in Figure 10.1.

The **rooting** and **sucking reflexes** help the newborn find the nipple and begin to eat, although babies also root and suck on their own hands to comfort themselves. When the baby feels a slight pressure against his cheek, he turns his head toward the pressure, "rooting" around for the nipple. When his lips come in contact with a surface, he begins sucking. Newborns are already practiced at sucking; it is reflexive and does not need to be learned. However, newborns also have a reflex that protects them from swallowing anything other than liquids. They have a tongue-thrust reflex that pushes everything out of the mouth. It's a good idea to wait to begin spoon feeding until this reflex disappears.

The **Moro reflex,** or startle reflex, is a physical response to a loud sound or the sense of falling. The baby throws back her head, extends her arms and legs, and then pulls them back in. The posture also seems to act as communication to parents and teachers that the baby is stressed and needs to be picked up and comforted. The **tonic neck reflex** moves the arms in response to the baby's head turning in supine (lying on his back) position. When the baby's head is turned to the right, his right arm will thrust out, his left will be raised straight up. If he turns his head to the left, the arms will adjust. This may help the baby keep one hand in front of his eyes. This reflex begins to disappear as the baby begins to bring his hands together in the midline, in front of his eyes. The **palmar grasp reflex** causes the baby to close her fingers around something placed in the palm. She will grasp an adult's finger or hair, or a toy. Her feet will also curl when lightly brushed. When a baby is held upright, with her feet touching a solid surface, the **step reflex** makes the baby appear to be walking.

These primitive reflexes are very effective for the first few months and then begin to fade. As the primitive reflexes fade, another set of reflexes begins to emerge. *Postural reflexes* help the baby deal with gravity and provide the basis for developing balance, posture, and voluntary movement. The postural reflexes become integrated into the central nervous system and function throughout life. These reflexes help a person turn his head or shift his weight to regain lost

rooting reflex
A newborn's response, when stroked on the side of the face, to move its face in the direction being stroked, open its mouth, and search for a nipple.

sucking reflex
A newborn's response to suck when an object brushes across the lips.

Moro reflex
A newborn's startled response when experiencing a loud sound or the sense of falling.

tonic neck reflex
A newborn's response of maintaining an asymmetrical posture, with the head turned toward one arm extended upward and the other extended outward to the side.

palmar grasp reflex
A newborn's response to grasp and hold an object placed in the palm.

step reflex
Reflex that makes a baby appear to be walking when the baby is held upright with feet touching a solid surface.

Figure 10.1
Primitive reflexes.

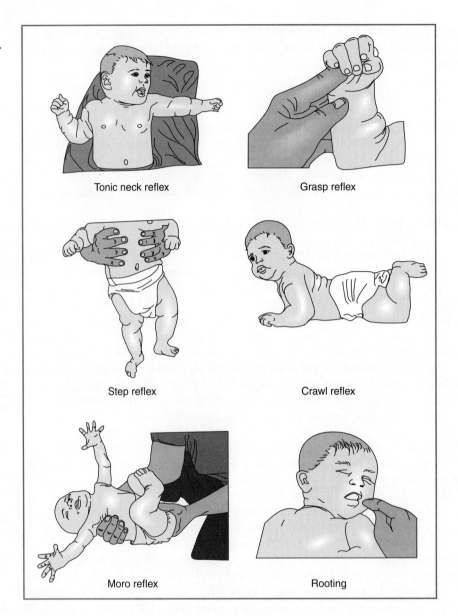

Tonic neck reflex

Grasp reflex

Step reflex

Crawl reflex

Moro reflex

Rooting

myeducationlab

Go to the Activities
and Applications
section in Chapter 10
of MyEducationLab
and watch the
video *Reflexes* for
a demonstration of
reflexes in infants.

balance. They also help modulate the muscle tone so that a person may move his head without throwing his entire body into a reaction.

Even though reflexes are dominant for several months, the baby's interest in her parents and teachers, and in the play opportunities they provide, are very important factors in early motor development. Being supported in various positions (tummy, back, snuggly, on the hip or shoulder) provides many opportunities to practice head and trunk control, using arms for support, and legs for kicking.

With a healthy brain and muscles, babies make remarkable progress in their ability to use their bodies to perceive sensory information and move toward or manipulate the source of the information. Within the first 3 years, babies make the journey from almost no voluntary movement to running and jumping, and they advance from sucking on a hand to calm themselves to using buttons and zippers to get dressed.

Attributes

Attributes, motor abilities, and interests certainly vary within a wide range from person to person. To what extent are these differences related to gender and to what extent are they simply individual differences?

Gender

The bodies of men and women certainly differ. Men tend to be bigger and stronger, with bodies evolved to be hunters. Women are smaller, with bodies evolved to reproduce. But are these differences present in infants and toddlers? It is difficult to sort out whether the gender differences we see in motor development are a result of inherent differences, different environmental experiences and expectations, or simply stereotypes.

Adults are likely to bring stereotypical images of boys and girls to their interactions with babies, and probably do engage boys in more physical play. Mondschein, Adolph, and Tamis-LeMonda (2000) found that mothers of 11-month-old boys overestimated their boys' ability to

Observation Invitation 10.1

The little boy in the white shirt is a confident walker, but the incline is challenging. He holds his arms out for balance. His friend is a newer walker and when his attempt to follow failed, he crawled up in front. Now the older child is stopped, unable to turn back and unable to move forward. What do you think will happen next?

crawl down steep and shallow slopes (set up by the researchers) while mothers of girls under-estimated their girls' ability. However, research is showing that boys appear to be more active than girls in infancy as measured by instruments and not just by parental report (Campbell & Eaton, 1999). This is likely due to biological differences, particularly a surge in testosterone in boys between 30 and 60 days after birth (Bancroft, 1989). An Australian study found differences in the actual arm and leg coordination of spontaneous movements of boys and girls in the supine position at 6, 12, and 18 weeks (Piek & Gasson, 2002).

"The typical boy differs little from the typical girl on activity level, but the most and least active children in a group are likely to be a boy and a girl, respectively" (Eaton, 2009). Of the two toddler boys on the incline in Observation Invitation 10.1, one is a little older and far more adventurous. However, on the day they were observed, only boys were trying to climb the incline.

Temperament

Temperament may affect motor development more directly than gender. The motivation of an active child to move, or the inhibition of a more fearful child, would certainly affect the competence a child achieves in motor skills. Brenda Hussey-Gardner describes some children as "motor driven," wanting to try everything and highly motivated to learn and practice motor skills. Others are described as "motor cautious," needing time to watch others before trying new activities (Hussey-Gardner, 2003).

Activity level is one of the elements measured in determining temperament (Thomas & Chess, 1977). Clearly, temperament as a determining element of a child's willingness to try motor activities would be a huge factor in opportunities to practice and become proficient in motor skills.

DEVELOPMENT AND LEARNING THROUGH RELATIONSHIPS

Infants and toddlers learn through their bodies and express themselves with their bodies. They use their bodies to come close and connect to others or to move away, as they develop their relationships.

Culture and Motor Development

As in nearly every aspect of child rearing, cultural beliefs and practices differ in approaches to motor development. Comparing cultural differences in opportunities for movement and the resultant differences in both the timing and the quality of mastering motor movements has led to a number of questions about the timing and progression of motor development. Are certain early experiences necessary for motor development? Is the time line of motor development genetically predetermined? Or do children develop the motor skills needed for living effectively in their own culture?

Adults provide very different motor experiences for babies around the world. They vary from carrying the baby at all times to using play to encourage sitting, crawling, and walking. The developmental milestone time lines used in the United States may be relevant only for babies in our own culture.

The Zinecanteco Indians of southeastern Mexico carry their babies in a *rebozo*, a sling across the mother's belly. The infants are quiet and alert but not very exploratory. However, they develop motor skills in the same order as children in the United States, even though their environment has been very different. The time line of acquiring these skills is about a month later than children in the United States (Brazelton, 1972).

The Ache mothers of eastern Paraguay carry their babies all of the time. An Ache baby is in a sling on his mother's body 93% of the daylight hours and on her lap all night. Even at 1 year their mothers will hold them 40% of the day. At 18 months, toddlers are taught to ride in baskets or piggyback on their father's back (Kaplan & Dove, 1987). Ache children begin walking about 9 months later than children in the United States.

The !Kung San, known as the Bushmen of the Kalahari Desert, have infants and toddlers with very advanced motor skills compared to babies in Western countries. San mothers carry young infants positioned vertically in a sling. San parents invest time in promoting motor skills and encourage babies to explore by 7 months. San children achieve motor skills earlier and better and concentrate harder than American toddlers (Konner, 1977).

Some cultural practices may seem at odds with promoting motor development (Thompson-Rangel, 1994). When adults dress and feed older toddlers and even preschool-age children, it serves the cultural values of the Latino tradition. The Hopi and Navajo practice of keeping babies in cradleboards serves their traditional mother–infant relationships. When your cultural background differs from that of the family, it is important to remember that children from all cultural practices do achieve the same motor milestones eventually. Cultural practices and beliefs affect motor development, and cultural values need to be considered in the child development and education program's curriculum for motor development.

Motor Development Through Relationships

If simply the position and amount of time we carry our babies affects their motor development, then imagine the impact of the opportunities we provide for movement or the handling of objects, of our comfort with movement, and our attitudes toward safety and risk taking. While teachers are not making a genetic contribution to a child's motor abilities, they are certainly having an influence at the environmental level.

Observation Invitation 10.2 is intended to be provocative. The first impulse of most teachers would be to tell this toddler to keep her feet on the steps and to hold on to the sides. We try to keep our children very safe. But she is safe. She has wonderful balance and a good sense of where her body is in space. She is practicing her motor skills. Luckily, her teacher was able to tolerate this little bit of risk taking, and Lucia is developing a sense of herself as being physically competent.

Principles and Progression of Motor Development

There are some common trends in motor development that seem to be fairly constant across cultures or relationships. First, development is **cephalocaudal,** meaning that voluntary muscle control progresses from the head down. The baby first achieves neck control, then trunk control, then leg control—control moving from the head (cephalo) to the tail (caudal). Second, development is **proximal-distal,** beginning with the midline (proximal or near) and progressing outward and downward (distal or distance). Third, control begins with the large muscle groups and proceeds to the small muscle groups (Appleton, Clifton, & Goldberg, 1975). The infant and toddler's major goals for motor skills are moving around, using tools, and coordinating perceptual and motor experiences.

cephalocaudal
Moving from head (cephalus) to tail (caudal).

proximal-distal
Moving in the direction from close (proximal) to distant (distal).

Typical milestone charts are organized in ways that separate large and small muscle skills, but development is more interactive than that. For example, as a 3-month-old is gaining head and neck control, she will enjoy being on her tummy and looking around. As the control strengthens, she will be able to use a hand to hold something while she holds her head up. When she is able to sit with stability, not using her hands to balance, both hands are suddenly free to handle and play with objects. It is only after she has mastered stable sitting that she will develop the ability to pick things up, move them from hand to hand, put them into containers, and throw them. The Developmental Trends and Responsive Interactions chart at the end of this chapter lists the motor milestones.

Observation Invitation 10.2

Lucia climbed the stairs to wash her hands. She turns on the faucet and holds one hand under the running water. With the other hand, she holds the side of the stairway. She balances on her left leg while raising her right leg in space.

What might Lucia be learning about her body? About movement? How would you react if you were standing nearby watching?

Movement

For infants and toddlers, motor skills are a way to achieve their goals in relationships (staying close to the teacher) and in learning (figuring out how rings fit a stick). Most importantly, achieving new motor skills is a goal in itself. Infants and toddlers work tirelessly, attempting a new skill and practicing it over and over until they are proficient. However, they may go about their motor tasks in very unique ways:

> I've always been impressed by the different paths babies take in their physical development on the way to walking. It's rare to see a behavior that starts out with such wide natural variation, yet becomes so uniform after only a few months. (Kutner, 1993)

Researchers who study the development of motor skills in babies see the progression of development as a dynamic system rather than a genetically preordained series of accomplishments. Karen Adolph (2008), for example, sees motor development as a flexible response to new and challenging situations. When a baby achieves a new posture, such as moving from lying face-up to sitting or from sitting to crawling, her perspective on the world changes so much that she needs to figure out motor control all over again. Each new posture brings the baby into contact with new aspects of the world, new perceptual information. The new perceptual information presents new goals for the baby. Being able to see and touch the bottom book shelf presents the goal of emptying the shelf of its books. Being able to see and touch the cupboard door presents the goal of opening and closing it. Each new posture then requires practice in reestablishing balance and control in pursuit of other interests (Adolph & Eppler, 2002).

This view of babies developing motor skills as solutions to problems posed by the interplay between perception and action is called the *dynamic systems approach* by researcher Esther Thelen. Rejecting the idea that motor development is purely maturational, Thelen describes motor development as an ongoing problem solving of the tension between a child's goals or desires and the constraints of his body's mechanics. The baby is constantly trying to reach or move and constantly correcting his efforts to adjust for his changing body weight, proportions, and postures (Thelen & Smith, 1996; Thelen, 2000).

Head Lifting and Rolling

A constant developmental theme of the first 3 years is the large muscle work of moving around independently. This is a good example of the cephalocaudal and proximal-distal direction of development. The ages given in this section should be taken very loosely as a way of showing the general trend of development.

Babies begin life with large, heavy heads and soft, curled bodies. As their bodies change size and proportion, and as they have opportunities for movement in the environment, they gain control of their bodies and begin to move, as seen in Figure 10.2. Over the first few months of life, a baby develops control of her head and neck, so that she can look around when held in her teacher's arms. With time to practice on her tummy, she begins to use her arms for support as she lifts her head and chest at about 2 months. With "proximal" control of the neck and trunk, she will begin to develop "distal" control of her arms and hands. Sometimes, in the next several months, when playing on her tummy and reaching for a toy, she will accidentally roll over on her back. At around 5 months, rolling will be intentional and she may use rolling as a way to get from place to place. The ability to roll purposefully comes in part from the stronger muscles the baby is building in her abdomen and back. She is developing trunk control that helps her sit upright with support, or keep her legs in the air while she enjoys the spectacle of her own dancing feet.

Just this simple sequence of movement development can be seen from the perspective of a learning opportunity. Imagine the baby lifting her head at 2 months. As a teacher, sitting near her on the floor, exclaims with joy, "Look at you! You're lifting your head way up! You're looking at me, Sweet pea!" Knowing that this is a new, emerging skill, later in the day the teacher places the baby on her

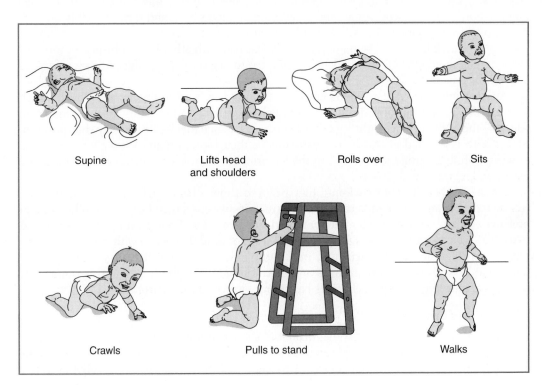

Supine   Lifts head   Rolls over   Sits
                and shoulders

Crawls   Pulls to stand   Walks

Figure 10.2
Progression of movement.

Claire has mastered lifting her head and using her hands to play with what she sees.

tummy to play in front of a wall-mounted mirror. Now, every time she lifts her head, she gets to see herself. The teacher continues to stay close by and talks to the baby about how hard she is working to lift her head. The next time she places her on the floor to play, she places a few simple, brightly colored toys in front of her, giving the baby more reasons to keep working at this new skill. It brings her teacher pleasure; it allows her to see more things; and it seems to induce her teacher to enrich the environment. When the next steps of development occur, such as rolling over, even if they happen accidentally, they set off a whole new cycle of encouragement, connection, enrichment, and inherent value.

Rocking and Sitting

As the baby grows cognitively, and in muscle strength and control, movement becomes increasingly voluntary. Between 4 and 6 months the baby can sit with support. By 7 months, he can sit alone and by 8 months he can move in and out of a sitting position on his own. (The same trunk control that supports these movements allows him to lift his abdomen and rock on all fours.) A baby may begin moving around while sitting, sort of hitching himself around. Moving toward the first birthday, many babies begin to lift themselves to stand by holding on to a table or the side of the crib. A baby, who wakes up, pulls himself up to stand, and can't figure out how to get back down, often awakens parents during the night at this stage.

Creeping and Crawling

myeducationlab

Go to the Activities and Applications section in Chapter 10 of MyEducationLab to watch the video *Crawling* and observe the differences in how two children begin to creep and crawl.

One baby may use a variety of crawling postures on the way to walking. Many belly crawl or creep, using their arms to pull them forward. As the baby is able to move into and out of a sitting position, he may spend some time on all fours, rocking back and forth. Possibly on purpose, possibly by accident, he will rock a little harder one time and push off from his knees, propelling himself forward. The more practice he has had with other less sophisticated forms of crawling, the more likely he is to seize this moment to begin to crawl efficiently with purpose (Adolph, Vereijken, & Denney, 1998).

Another milestone that supports efficient crawling is related to the flexibility with which infants move in and out of a sitting position. Babies are able to use their "diagonal interlimb pattern" (their left arm and right leg or vice versa) to balance themselves as they shift position. This pattern is adopted in crawling as babies move their right arm and left leg forward in the same motion, balancing their weight on the left arm and right leg to keep themselves upright (Freedland & Bertenthal, 1994).

Actually, babies do not crawl until they begin to show a hand preference. While they are still bound to using both hands together, they rock in place. As they begin to develop a hand preference, they also have greater freedom to orient the head without postural constraints, and to use a kicking motion with weight on the legs. It is not until they reach with one hand, falling forward on the other, orient their head freely, and kick with weight that they begin to crawl (Goldfield, 1989). Because their arms are often stronger than their legs at this point, first attempts at crawling often propel babies backward—much to their surprise!

Standing and Cruising

Using those stronger arm muscles, the infant will soon pull himself up to a standing position. This new perspective on the world, and the similarity to the way he has always seen adults moving, may inspire a whole new round of concentrated practice. A baby is likely to use low tables, sofas, shelves, and even an adult's leg for pulling to a stand. This is a time to be very sure that nothing the baby is likely to pull on can fall back down on him. Most infants figure out how to stand up before they understand how to sit back down.

Standing with support soon becomes cruising, as baby takes a few tentative steps along the edge of a sofa or coffee table. Babies make good decisions about using support in their movement. In a set of experiments, 16-month-old toddlers crossed bridges of different widths in the presence or absence of a handrail. They attempted wider bridges more often than narrow ones, and attempts on narrow bridges depended on handrail presence. Toddlers examined the bridge and handrail and modified their gait when bridges were narrow and/or the handrail was unavailable. Toddlers who explored the bridge and handrail before stepping onto the bridge and devised alternative bridge-crossing strategies were more likely to cross successfully. They used the handrail as a means for augmenting balance and for carrying out an otherwise impossible goal-directed task (Berger & Adolph, 2003).

Walking

All of this preparation and practice, of course, is leading up to those most important baby steps—the moment in which we see almost every baby echo the transition of all humankind from all fours to an upright posture. The first steps may be unaware, as the baby's interest in something distracts her attention from holding on to a support as she lets go for a moment—and is walking! The first steps are usually wide-legged, with arms outstretched for balance and protection. There may be only one or two steps before she falls. When a baby has been encouraged and appreciated, he knows this is a huge accomplishment. In fact, the first steps have come to have such great meaning to families that teachers often choose not to tell parents when they have witnessed them. They leave this moment of discovery for the family to savor. With experience in walking, the child's gait becomes longer, narrower, straighter, and more consistent (Adolph & Vereijken, 2003). As an infant learns to walk, she may even take an occasional step that is longer than her own leg, demonstrating balance and strength (Badaly & Adolph, 2008).

Toddling

As Lois Barclay Murphy (1994) describes so beautifully, the first steps are not the end of the locomotive adventure for the baby:

> As I sat on a bench at the side of the road in the zoo, watching the children brought by their mothers or fathers, I rarely saw a little boy walking quietly beside his parent. One was hopping, another was jumping. Others were leaping, or skipping, or loping, raising each foot higher than it needed to be lifted for ordinary walking. Some children waved their arms. Each one seemed to savor the feeling of the moment, wanting to discover the possibilities of locomotion. (p. 1)

Once babies have mastered their first steps, they turn to moving around in earnest. The uneven, unsure gait that gives this age period its name becomes a driving force in the toddler's activities. Simply toddling from place to place is satisfying. Using their suddenly free hands to carry things from place to place or to push or pull toys becomes a favorite activity. As the toddler gains confidence in his ability to stand up and get down, he adds the motion of *stooping*, bending his legs without really sitting, to examine small objects on the ground.

As walking becomes more secure, running, jumping, and climbing become the new challenges. Motor games like ring-around-the-rosy that combine walking with falling down and getting back up evoke laughter and many repetitions.

Using Tools

Moving around is only one of the large goals of motor development in the first years of life. Just as they are working to control their bodies to move through space, infants and toddlers are working to control their arms and hands in order to manipulate the objects in the world. Being able to use tools involves using the fingers and hands in increasingly sophisticated grasps and releases, reaching for objects, and ultimately manipulating tools for a purpose such as using a spoon to eat. This small or fine motor development follows the same trends of all motor development, cephalocaudal and proximal-distal. Fine motor development is also related to opportunities in the environment and to the support and interest of adults.

Even in the womb, a fetus puts her hand to her mouth and sucks her thumb. This simple movement that appears prenatally illustrates the increasing complexity and accuracy of motor skills over time. In a study of hand-mouth movements of infants between 2 and 5 months old, it appeared that young infants were bringing their hands to their face, but not to their mouth with much accuracy. At 4 months of age, touches on other parts of the face diminished, and there was a focus on the mouth. Only after the arm and finger movements became more precise did the babies begin to open their mouths in anticipation of a finger or object's arrival, possibly demonstrating a relationship between the motor and cognitive developments in the same activities (Lew & Butterworth, 1997).

Grasping and Releasing

myeducationlab

Go to the Activities and Applications section in Chapter 10 of MyEducationLab to watch the video *Infant Putting Blocks into Container.* Watch how he changes strategies as he grasps and releases the blocks.

palmar grasp
A very young infant's hold on objects achieved by pushing fingers against the palm.

raking grasp
A young infant's use of open fingers to "rake" an object into the palm.

pincer grasp
A child's more refined grasp of index finger and thumb to pick up an object.

The baby's ability to pick up an object, hold it, and release it at will is as interesting as the development of walking, albeit on a much smaller scale. The development of efficient grasping and releasing combines all of the elements of a natural physical progression, the requirement of environmental opportunities, and the involvement of an interested adult. It is a foundational skill for writing, drawing, self-feeding, and the use of all sorts of tools.

The grasp is one of the primitive reflexes present in the newborn. If someone's finger is pressed against the newborn's palm, the newborn will automatically grasp it. This reflex controls much of the baby's hand activity for the first 2 months. In fact, the newborn's hand is usually clenched in a fist, and it is the gradual opening of the fist, followed by the voluntary opening and closing of the fist, that signals a shift in the maturation of the brain. As the hands begin to come under the baby's control, he will "discover" his hand visually and show some interest in looking at it.

At 3 to 4 months, as the primitive reflexes begin to fade, using his hands and arms becomes a very interesting activity. He can't actually grasp much on purpose, but swipes at objects to bring them closer and enjoys using his hands and arms to bat at dangling toys when he's on his back. As Figure 10.3 portrays, at around 5 or 6 months, the baby may pick up objects with both hands together or use a **palmar grasp** to pick up objects. He presses the object into his palm and then closes his fingers around it. As he begins to control his fingers, he uses them to close around an object with a raking movement called the **raking grasp**. In the raking grasp, he is still using all of his fingers together. Between 7 and 9 months, sitting independently, with improved vision and able to focus on small objects, he will begin to point with one finger, or use one finger to push a key on a toy piano. This independent use of the fingers is utilized in a fine **pincer grasp** of the pointer and the thumb to pick up small objects such as pieces of cereal.

Handling Objects

The changes in the way infants and toddlers handle and use objects provide insight into their motor development, although the handling of objects is also a prime way we look at cognitive development in the first 3 years. At first, reacting to an object with the palmar grasp and bringing it to her face, the baby's handling of an object is almost purely reflexive. Soon, the hold on the object becomes more intentional and is used to help examine the object by mouth and visually. By 4 months, the baby is reaching to secure a toy and can transfer toys from one hand to another. The baby will finger toys to explore them as well. Teachers may provide dangling toys for reaching, small light toys that can be grasped in one hand, and toys of different textures that promote fine motor exploration.

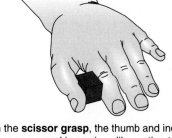

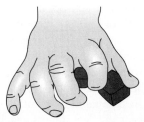

The palmar reflex becomes a simple, but controlled **palmar grasp** using the fingers to hold an object against the palm.

In the **scissor grasp**, the thumb and index finger are used in a scissorlike motion to pick up an object.

Each finger and the thumb work together in the **raking grasp** to pull an object against the palm.

By 1 year, the baby will use the same thumb and index finger **pincer grasp** as an adult.

Figure 10.3
The developmental progression of grasping: palmar, raking, scissor, pincer.

At about 6 to 8 months, as grasping and releasing are coming under the baby's control, she is likely to begin using objects as tools. She may hold her own bottle while drinking or want her own spoon to hold while being fed. She may hold a toy in each hand and bang them together to make noise. She may use her pointer finger to poke, push, or hook objects. She will enjoy toys that invite fine motor activity such as banging, shaking, mouthing, rocking, or creating reactions such as pop-ups.

As the baby approaches his first birthday, he can use his hands as tools to feed himself finger foods, or drink out of a bottle or a lidded cup with handles. Just as he is enjoying moving his own body around in space, he will enjoy filling containers with little objects and dumping them out again. This exploration of spatial relationships and the beginning use of tools are cognitive discoveries with very strong motor components. Children with motor impairments can make the same discoveries, but may need specifically planned opportunities.

Between 18 and 24 months, as his coordination increases, markers, paints, turning pages in books, using utensils, and buttons and zippers all become interesting as cognitive development provides increasing opportunities for using tools. The baby may enjoy simple pretend play with small cars that he can manipulate as though to make them drive. He may enjoy the challenge of simple shape boxes and puzzles that require fine motor manipulation as well as planning and problem solving.

From 24 to 36 months, fine motor tasks such as large pegboards, bead threading, scissor cutting, and drawing and painting will engage the baby's fine motor skills, learning, and also her emerging sense of creativity and artistic expression. Her new competence in handling objects and using tools will be evident as she pours milk from a small pitcher at the snack table, dresses herself to go outside, or wraps a baby doll in her blanket for a nap. This new competence in self-help should also be expressing itself in an interest in toileting. We will discuss the guidance issues related to toddlers learning how to use the toilet in chapter 14.

Perceptual-Motor Coordination

Theoretically, there is a clear connection between motor development, environmental opportunities, and supportive relationships. Exactly how, though, does the infant or toddler perceive sensory information and link it to motor actions? Thinking along the lines of Adolph and Thelen, researchers James and Eleanor Gibson proposed that for movement to be planned and executed in an effective way in a particular moment, the actions need to be informed by perceptual information in the environment. In turn, the movement of the head, body, and limbs generate perceptual information such as changes in light, sounds, the feel of muscles, and the proprioceptive information of movement. Perceptual information and motor actions are inextricably linked (Gibson & Pick, 2003).

Reaching

Several laboratory studies have attempted to determine exactly what sensory information infants use to plan the motor act of reaching. In one study, 6-month-old infants were presented with objects that gave off sounds under three conditions of illumination: in full vision, in the dark with the object glowing and making a sound, and in the dark with the location specified by sound alone. The babies used the same reaching motions with the same frequencies for objects in the light and for glowing objects in the dark. The reaches for the sound-emitting objects in the dark were faster, of shorter duration, and had more errors compared to the other conditions. These findings indicate that vision of the hand did not appear to affect infants' reaching in this situation, whereas vision of the target did (Clifton, Rochat, Robin, & Berthier, 1994).

A second study set up a more complex problem that required accommodating to somewhat challenging visual information, being able to predict an object's trajectory, and use the proprioceptive information of their own muscles to anticipate how and where to reach to capture the object. Infants were presented with a moving object under two lighting conditions to investigate the role of vision in early reaching. Infants were tested twice, at 5 and 7½ months of age, with a moving object in the light and the same object painted with luminescent paint in the dark. Infants successfully contacted the glowing object on about half of their attempts at both ages, although 7½-month-olds reached more often. Infants took into account the motion of the target object by aiming their reaches ahead of the object. These results suggest that proprioceptive feedback of their own arm and the sight of the target allow for successful reaching with limited visual information, even in relatively complex reaching tasks. The infants' success also demonstrates their ability to adapt their movements and reaching strategy to the speed and trajectory of the target object in order to reach predictively (Robin, Berthier, & Clifton, 1996).

Sensory Integration

The relationship between perception and motor experience makes sense. Even if we were unable to use vision and hearing in a meaningful way for movement, touch, vestibular, and proprioceptive information speak directly to our motor systems. The **vestibular system** controls the sense of our body's balance or equilibrium. The **proprioceptive system** controls information coming from muscles, tendons, joints, and the inner ear, and detects the motion or position of the body or a limb by responding to sensations arising within the body. This sensory information is part of the motor system.

When infants and toddlers are unable to integrate sensory information to use their bodies effectively in the environment, they may need particular supports. For example, a baby who cannot stand to be touched because she is hypersensitive may find it difficult to bond with a parent or teacher. She may be hungry but unable to tolerate a nipple in her mouth. The proprioceptive experience of being lifted and put down again can be overwhelming. All of the caregiving activities that are meant to soothe and comfort may feel like assaults. Adults caring

vestibular system
Affects balance, muscle tone, equilibrium responses, the ability to use both sides of the body together, and coordination of the head, neck, and eye movements.

proprioceptive system
Gives the nervous system input on the position of muscles, joints, and tendons.

STRATEGIES TO SUPPORT MOTOR DEVELOPMENT AND LEARNING

Infants and toddlers are highly motivated to use their bodies to move and to use tools. These skills do not develop automatically, though. Some strategies you can use to support motor development follow.

1. Provide opportunities for young babies to play on their tummies. Tummy time helps babies strengthen their trunk and neck control.

2. Limit the use of swings, infant seats, bouncers, or other furniture that restrains infants. When caring for several children at once, offer toys on the floor for tummy time, space for crawlers, or hanging toys for reaching from supine. Restraining babies makes them passive and discourages active exploration. Think of using their bodies as active, learning opportunities.

3. When young babies are playing on the floor on their backs, offering toys a little off to the side and above the head encourages reaching and turning, which develops into rolling over.

4. Create an environment that encourages movement at every stage of motor development. Think about how you can help babies develop an active lifestyle from the beginning, countering the possibility of childhood obesity.

5. Firm, washable cubes, pads, and inclines can be arranged to create interesting and challenging surfaces for crawling, creeping, walking, and climbing.

6. As mobile infants begin cruising, they need long, low, stable surfaces to hold. In homes they use sofas and coffee tables. In centers, if they are using shelving units, be sure they are bolted to the wall.

7. Small stairs with platforms, climbing bars bolted to walls, and sturdy structures encourage toddlers to climb. If the stairs and platform provide access to a window or the climbing bars face a mirror allowing the toddlers to see themselves, there is even more motivation for climbing.

8. Use music for movement, not just as background sound. Infants love being held while you dance with them, swooping and spinning to the rhythm. Toddlers love singing and playing instruments while dancing or marching.

9. Spend as much time outdoors as the climate allows.

10. Be aware of the child's changing abilities to handle objects and offer materials that match these abilities. Young infants need lightweight rattles, older infants need small objects they can pick up with a raking grasp but large enough to prevent choking when they mouth them.

11. New walkers enjoy carrying objects in each hand. Older toddlers enjoy the precision of fitting rings on sticks, stacking cups, or fitting pegs in pegboards.

12. Use small chairs and tables for meals, allowing toddlers to sit and rise by themselves.

for hypersensitive babies need to develop a firm and gentle touch. They need to use gentle pressure around the mouth to make feeding more comfortable. And they need to stay calm and limit the variations in position and handling used with the baby.

CHILDREN WITH SPECIAL NEEDS

The progression of motor development consumes the interest of infants and toddlers as they practice the skills they have and undertake new ones. Healthy motor development is dependent on the brain, the central nervous system, the muscles, the bones, and the opportunities infants have for practice. Motor development, while often taken for granted, is vulnerable.

Motor Concerns

Injury, prenatal substance exposure, poor nutrition, and disease can all affect motor development. Motor disorders may have a variety of symptoms, as described in Figure 10.4.

The most common motor disorder in infancy is **cerebral palsy (CP).** Cerebral palsy is a nonprogressive disorder of the motor (muscle) control area of the developing brain. "The diagnosis is dependent upon two findings: evidence of nonprogressive damage to the developing brain and the presence of a resulting impairment of the motor (neuromuscular) control system of the body; the latter usually accompanied by a physiological impairment and functional disability" (UCP, 2009). Next to mental retardation, CP is the most common disorder of the developing brain; 70% of cerebral palsy occurs prenatally, 20% in the birthing process, and 10% in the first 2 years of life.

Cerebral palsy is a somewhat general term for a variety of different conditions. Infants and toddlers with cerebral palsy may not be able to inhibit their primitive reflexes and so they continue to be subjected to reflexive reactions rather than developing voluntary actions. Because of central nervous system injury, infants may have **spastic cerebral palsy,** with muscles that constantly remain so tight that they proscribe voluntary action. This could affect the legs, one side of the body, or the whole body, depending on the location and severity of the injury to the brain (MOD, 2009a). **Athetoid cerebral palsy** affects the entire body with fluctuating muscle tone that may result in uncontrolled movements and difficulty speaking or eating. **Ataxic cerebral palsy** affects balance and coordination, creating an unsteady gait or difficulty with fine motor tasks (MOD, 2009a). Physical therapy can help children achieve the maximum possible control of their bodies within these conditions.

Effects of Motor Disorders

Motor disorders may affect more than movement. When a child is unable to participate in his part of the attachment relationship, the parent–child relationship may suffer. If the child is unable to smile at parents, to follow their movements visually, to reach out to be lifted, or to cuddle when held, the adults may be confused as to the child's feelings. Teachers and early interventionists are often most helpful by pointing out the ways the child does signal his pleasure and comfort in being with familiar, well-loved people.

Emotional and cognitive development may proceed despite a motor disorder. Sometimes adults need to learn to read the unique cues of the child, whereas other times adaptations need to be made to materials in the environment. One of the side effects of a motor disorder is that the baby or toddler may be inaccurately assessed as having cognitive delays because so many developmental assessments rely on motor skills to demonstrate cognitive understanding. For

---

cerebral palsy (CP)
A group of motor, postural, and physical disorders that result from a brain injury or abnormal brain development.

spastic cerebral palsy
Muscles are stiffly and permanently contracted; affects 70% to 80% of patients.

athetoid cerebral palsy
Characterized by uncontrolled, slow, writhing movements of the hands, feet, arms, or legs and, in some cases, the muscles of the face and tongue, causing grimacing or drooling.

ataxic cerebral palsy
A rare form of cerebral palsy that affects the sense of balance and depth perception.

Figure 10.4
Warning signs of motor disorders.

- The child's limbs are stiff.
- The child's muscles seem floppy and loose.
- The child doesn't walk within expected parameters.
- The child walks on her toes.
- The child favors one hand or one side of his body.
- The child seems very clumsy.
- The child is constantly moving.
- The child has trouble grasping and manipulating objects.
- The child drools and has difficulty eating.
- The child's motor skills are regressing.

Source: From Baby Center (2008).

example, we expect a baby to pull a cloth off a hidden object to demonstrate object permanence or to stack several blocks to demonstrate the ability to imitate. Children who lack the motor ability to perform these actions may be unable to show that they understand the concepts being assessed. Unfortunately, because of the limits of the testing situation, these children may have no way to demonstrate their knowledge.

PROGRAMS THAT ENHANCE MOTOR DEVELOPMENT AND LEARNING

Opportunities that invite movement, interesting materials to handle, and attentive and engaged adult partners can be part of any program or experience for infants and toddlers. In this section, we discuss three kinds of programs with the potential to enhance motor development. Child development and education programs, serving more than 6 million infants and toddlers, have the potential to either support or impede motor development. Physical and occupational therapy, professional services included in early intervention for children with disabilities, will be briefly illustrated. Then, in a change of perspective, we examine a relatively new and still unestablished form of psychotherapy used with infants and toddlers: movement-based psychotherapy, a method of using the movement patterns of infants and toddlers as a way of understanding their experiences. Each of these approaches has the potential to significantly impact the quality of movement patterns of infants and toddlers.

Child Development and Education Programs

With more than half of America's infants and toddlers in out-of-home care, the program environment is influencing the quality of life of America's children. If teachers understand the process and pattern of early motor development, they can support it with minimal effort. Infants and toddlers need opportunities to move freely, balanced with holding, cuddling, and rocking. The strategies listed on page 233 provide many ideas for activities that support motor development. This section contains some broader guidelines.

Understanding a child's current developmental capacities allows you to provide developmentally appropriate activities. Very young babies, working on head control and functioning within the grasp reflex, need "tummy time"—time to play on a firm surface while practicing lifting their heads and shoulders off the ground. The surface should not have any coverings that could cause suffocation if the baby got caught up in them. On her back, she might enjoy turning her head slowly to visually track a toy the teacher moves from one side to another. Throughout the first year of life, infants enjoy playing on the floor, rolling, sitting, and crawling—with an adult nearby talking to them and playing with them. Selections of small toys to hold or put in and take out of containers, pop-up boxes, and shape boards are available at different times.

The important part of the environment, though, is a sense that physical activity is fun and encouraged. Oftentimes, teachers with too many babies to care for use a variety of swings, bouncy seats, and other equipment for containing babies. When this is the baby's experience hour after hour, he learns that he is not supposed to move and use his body to explore. He becomes passive and bored. Losing the ability to become interested in the world, he finds that nothing but being contained is comforting. Not only is the baby losing valuable opportunities for motor development and learning, he may be setting lifelong patterns of inactivity that lead to obesity and disease. In addition to the constraint, many of these pieces of equipment vibrate and play sounds at the same time. This can be simply too much stimulation for a baby.

Any equipment used to restrain babies may have harmful effects, but next we describe one piece of equipment that is truly dangerous.

Box 10.1

Baby Walkers Are Dangerous!

Even when babies are supervised, they can be injured while using baby walkers. Documented injuries include:

- Rolling down stairs: Most common accident causing broken bones and head injuries
- Burns: Higher reach and mobility leads to burns from coffee cups, pots on stoves, radiators, fireplaces, and space heaters
- Drowning: Falls into pools, bathtubs, or toilets
- Poisoning: Higher reach for access to household chemicals
- Pinched fingers and toes: Caught between walker and furniture

Source: AAP (2004).

Baby Walkers

Child development and education programs often use baby seats, swings, and other equipment to provide a variety of postural and motor experiences for babies. While any of these pieces of equipment should be used with discretion, the mobile baby walker should not be in any program. A mobile baby walker is a piece of nursery equipment that holds a baby, who is too young to stand and walk, in a standing position. When the baby's feet touch the ground, small pressures of weight cause the walker to roll. The American Academy of Pediatrics (AAP, 2004) and the National Association for Children's Hospitals and Related Institutions have urged the Consumer Product Safety Commission to ban their manufacture and sale in the United States. The Canadian government has already banned the sale, advertisement, and importation of baby walkers in Canada.

According to the U.S. Consumer Product Safety Commission, baby walkers send more than 21,300 children under 15 months of age to the hospital every year (2001). Most of these injuries happened when adults were watching but were unable to respond quickly enough (a mobile walker can move more than 3 feet in 1 second!). The AAP further urges parents not to leave their child in care anywhere that mobile baby walkers are utilized (see Box 10.1).

While it seems as though the early experience of walking would be beneficial and enriching, a study on the effect of early experiences with walkers (Siegel & Burton, 1999) finds the opposite is true. The authors describe the use of walkers as early deprivation because walkers are designed in a way that deprives the baby of visual access to his own moving limbs. In a study of 109 infants from 6 to 15 months, the researchers found that babies with walker experience sat, crawled, and walked later than babies who didn't use walkers. The walker babies also scored lower on the Bayley Scales of Mental and Motor Development, a widely used assessment of cognitive, language, and motor development. The authors concluded that the risks far outweigh the benefits of walker use.

Physical and Occupational Therapy

neuromuscular
The interrelationship between the central nervous system and the muscular system.

tonicity
The strength, tension, or health of a muscle.

low muscle tone
Hypotonia; muscles that are loose and floppy, limiting motor skills and postural support.

high muscle tone
Hypertonia; muscles that are tight and contracted, making movement constrained.

Infants and toddlers identified with disabilities, or at risk for disabilities, may receive special therapies for their motor systems. Physical therapists tend to work with head and trunk control, the limbs, the large muscles, stability, balance, and locomotion. Occupational therapists work with the limbs and fingers, feeding and swallowing, adaptive and self-help skills. In fact, their work often overlaps. Both work with the **neuromuscular** system, comprised of the central nervous system (brain and spine), as it learns and stores memories of movement patterns, and the muscles, changing **tonicity** or learning new motor patterns. Conditions such as Down syndrome often cause muscles to be weak and floppy—**low muscle tone**—making it difficult to achieve control of movement. Conditions such as cerebral palsy cause muscles to be too tight to move easily—**high muscle tone**—also limiting control. Neurological issues such as cerebral palsy or seizures may cause the primitive reflexes to remain in action, driving the body's movements. An additional group of infants and toddlers apt to receive occupational or physical therapy services are children with sensory impairments such as visual or hearing impairments. Given the strong connections between sensory perception and motor development, the benefits of motor intervention are obvious.

The most beneficial time to intervene in the neuromuscular or perceptual-motor domain is during the first 3 years of life. The central nervous system and muscles are still forming and able to learn patterns or sometimes find alternate routes.

Approaches to intervention involve observation and assessment of the baby's movement patterns, muscle tone, and postures. They attend to the child's **mobility** (the ability to move his limbs), to control his **stability** (posture), to bear his own weight, and to manipulate objects. Many therapists also observe children's ability to tolerate and integrate sensory experiences in their motor actions. Treatment generally involves the therapist exercising or working the body and providing movement opportunities to stimulate the use of new patterns. Various sensory experiences such as ice, brushing, vibration, or weight packs may be introduced to stimulate the muscles. Swinging, rocking, and swiveling experiences may be used to reach the proprioceptive and vestibular senses. Treatments are incorporated into the daily routines, activities, and even settings of children's lives in the hopes of having the greatest generalization of skill development.

mobility
The ability to move freely, independently.

stability
The ability to maintain a posture.

Movement Psychotherapy

This chapter has described the developmental progression of the motor system and suggested ways to support it. In a shift of perspective, we describe a relatively new and not yet established form of psychotherapy called *movement therapy*. The premise of this work is that the way we move our bodies is an expression of our experiences, our relationships, and our understanding of the world. For infants and toddlers, in particular, whose lives are experienced in the sensorimotor realm, "nonverbal behaviors are expressions of self and have potential to be used for meaningful communication" (Tortora, 2004, p. 6). The movement psychotherapist is not trying to change the quality of movement so much as using the quality of movement as communication. The therapist "must always look through, behind, under, and over nonverbal behaviors, thinking, "What might this child be trying to tell me through these actions?" (Tortora, 2004, p. 6).

The movement psychotherapist is observing the movement for its coherence, its ease, its rhythm, and the relationship between personal space and general space. A child who starts and stops actions, changing direction or intention, may have little experience with complete, satisfying circles of interaction. The freedom or lack of freedom shown by the child in moving through space, using the different areas of a room, may reflect his ability to safely relate outside of his own body. The ability to expand movement and contain it again may speak to the child's sense of safety in emotional expression.

The movement psychotherapist "tries on" the child's movement patterns, imitating them to see how they feel. Is there discomfort? Is there a feeling of constraint? No sense of control? The therapist then uses her ability to imitate the child's movements, with variation, to begin a nonverbal dialogue with the child. Suzi Tortora (2004) describes beginning her work with a child with autism by touching his outstretched toe with her own—creating their own nonverbal language. As their work progresses, she is able to support the child's discovery that he can maintain a sense of relationship with her, and with his mother, even as he is lost in the terror of a tantrum. Using their bodies, the therapist and the mother are able to communicate their emotional connection to the little boy as he finds his way back to some sense of control.

Developmental Trends and Responsive Interactions

Motor Development and Learning

Infants and toddlers develop motor skills for locomotion, for using tools, and for coordinating perceptual information and motor actions.

Development	Example
0–4 months (infant)	
· Infants lift head when held at shoulder—hold head steady and erect. · On tummy, infants lift their head and shoulders off the ground and can hold a toy in hand. · Infants turns head toward a familiar voice. · Infants hold body still to pay attention; wiggle and move to encourage continued interaction. · On back, infants thrust arms and legs in play. · Infants turn from side to back. · Infants hold finger, light toy with reflexive grasp. · Infants suck on own fingers and hands, objects. · Infants move arms and legs.	Rosie held her head up and looked around at the other children as Sharon held her against her shoulder. Robert, on his tummy on a blanket, lifted his head to see himself in the mirror mounted at floor level on the wall. Jen held a rattle placed in her hand, but seemed unaware it was there. Filipe brought his fingers to his mouth and sucked on them, while looking intently at the toddlers.
4–8 months (infant)	
· Infants turn from back to side, later roll from back to front. · Infants sit—first with support but steady alone by the end of this period. · Infants reach with one arm. · Infants use raking grasp. · Infants crawl. · Infants shake, bang, hold, let go of objects. · Infants move objects from hand to hand. · Infants can hold their own bottle. · Infants can bring objects to their mouth.	Micky rolls from his back to his tummy to reach a toy, then rolls back over to play with it. Erin, sitting steadily alone, loves using both hands to pick up objects and study them. Freddy loves being held while he has his bottle, but he insists on holding it himself.
8–12 months (mobile infant)	
· Mobile infants pull to stand. · Mobile infants cruise. · Mobile infants stand alone. · Mobile infants walk with help and then alone. · Mobile infants sit in a chair. · Mobile infants finger-feed. · Mobile infants use spoon, tippy cup. · Mobile infants use pincer grasp.	Hershel crawls to his teacher's side, then holds her leg as he pulls up to stand. Jem sits at the lunch table, alternating between using her spoon and her fingers to enjoy her meal.
12–18 months (mobile infant)	
· Mobile infants stack and line up blocks. · Mobile infants can dress and undress self, arm into sleeve, foot into shoe. · Mobile infants can walk. · Mobile infants walk while carrying objects in each hand. · Mobile infants climb stairs.	Gary stood at the table, carefully using both hands to build a tower with colored blocks. Michelle toddled across the room, with her teddy bear in one hand and her blanket in the other.

Teacher or Parent–Child Interaction	Environment

0–4 months (infant)

- Change the baby's position; sometimes on his back, sometimes on his tummy. Even when holding the baby, sometimes cradle him in your arms, sometimes hold him upright against your shoulder.
- When baby is on the floor, lie down face-to-face with him.
- When baby is on her back, reaching for toy a little beyond her head, support her trunk as she rolls over.

- A stiff blanket (to prevent the danger of suffocation) on the floor provides space for early movements.
- Small, interesting toys, pictures, and books to look at will encourage babies to lift their heads. A mirror bolted to the wall at floor level always provides something interesting to look at.
- As babies begin to reach, they enjoy stable bars that dangle toys for them to bat at or reach and grasp.

4–8 months (infant)

- Stay near the baby who is just beginning to sit alone.
- Know the progression of motor development; emotionally encourage and physically support new attempts.
- Believe in the lifelong health benefits of an active lifestyle.

- Provide safe places for rolling, sitting, and crawling. Protect babies from anything that might fall on them.
- Provide small, washable lightweight objects (too large for choking) for handling and tossing, and provide containers for objects.

8–12 months (mobile infant)

- Stay alert to when practicing walkers need a little help—and when to let them keep trying.
- Allow time for older infants to practice feeding themselves.

- Safe places to pull up to stand.
- Push and pull toys to help support practicing walkers.
- Busy boxes.
- Board books for turning pages, lifting flaps, and poking fingers through holes.

12–18 months (mobile infant)

- Imitate baby's growing variety of movements.
- Introduce songs with little dances and movements.
- Provide time and patience while a toddler practices putting on his own jacket.

- Stable, low-to-the-ground riding toys.
- Stable, low-to-the-ground rocking toys.
- Skill-based manipulatives such as stacking cups, rings on a stick.

Developmental Trends and Responsive Interactions (continued)

Development	Example
18–24 months (toddler)	
· Toddlers point to objects to communicate. · Toddlers make marks on paper. · Toddlers pound, shape clay. · Toddlers run. · Toddlers sit on and get up from small chairs alone. · Toddlers are developing spatial confidence—explore their body in space.	Mindy rolled the dough with her hands, then used tools to make designs. Joseph sat down at the table to eat, then took his dirty dishes to the tub.
24–36 months (toddler)	
· Toddlers thread beads, use scissors, paint with fingers or brushes, do simple puzzles. · Toddlers throw and kick a ball. · Toddlers stand on one foot. · Toddlers stand and walk on tiptoes. · Toddlers walk upstairs with one foot on each step. · Toddlers climb, slide, jump. · Toddlers eat with spoon and fork. · Toddlers can dress self. · Toddlers can pour milk from small pitcher.	Robert doesn't even have to think about his body as he runs to greet his dad at the end of the day. Peggy and Misha make a game out of imitating each other's tiptoe steps, postures, and gestures. Lawrence and Evelyn use the dress-up clothes for their game, struggling a little to pull on the pieces.

myeducationlab

Go to
MyEducationLab
and complete
the Building
Teaching Skills and
Dispositions exercise
in Chapter 10.

SUMMARY

The work of motor development is compelling for infants and toddlers and an ongoing source of interest and pleasure to the adults in their lives.

- Infants practice motor skills in the womb and use a repertoire of reflexes to guide their actions while they develop the strength for control and voluntary movement.

- Motor development generally follows the trends of cephalocaudal and proximal-distal direction and moves from large muscle to small muscle control.

- Different cultures approach motor development differently, and early experiences seem to affect the time line and quality of development more than the progression of development.

- Motor skills are not mastered independently from other areas of development. Adult partners promote locomotion by providing opportunities for movement, keeping infants and toddlers safe, and encouraging and enjoying each new attempt. Infants and toddlers use increasing cognitive skills, as well, as they plan how to use their bodies to move around.

- Infants and toddlers progress from head and neck control, to trunk control, rolling, sitting, rocking, crawling, pulling to a stand, cruising, walking, and finally running, jumping, and climbing.

- These processes are echoed as infants and toddlers use their small muscles for handling objects and using tools—progressing from random movements of the hand to the face, to reaching, manipulating objects for exploration, and gradually using objects with purpose. The ability to plan and execute efficient motor actions is connected to the sensory information perceived by the body.

Teacher or Parent–Child Interaction	Environment
18–24 months (toddler)	
• Provide materials that challenge toddlers' growing use of their fingers. • Stay present with toddlers as they try new skills and support them. • Provide opportunities for climbing, walking, running.	• Art materials with thick paint brushes and markers, large surfaces for painting. • Smaller, skill-based manipulatives such as connecting beads and pegboards. • Lots of space for movement—dancing, balls, riding toys, climbing, slides.
24–36 months (toddler)	
• Be aware of the balance of time between active and quiet activities. • Watch for increasing accuracy in fine motor skills, as subtle issues may begin to be apparent. • Be available with encouragement and patience as toddlers increasingly feed, dress, and toilet themselves.	• Provide a variety of materials to practice fine motor skills: simple puzzles, shape boxes, threading beads, table blocks, clay, art materials. • Space, opportunity, and structures to encourage movement— outdoor time, obstacle courses, dancing, and riding toys.

- Child development and education programs can encourage motor development by providing many opportunities for active play and the purposeful handling of objects. However, if programs use constraining equipment for infants and toddlers—such as bouncy seats, high chairs, and swings—they may hinder motor development.
- Child development and education programs should never use baby walkers.
- Physical and occupational therapy may be utilized for children when motor development is not proceeding in a typical course.

Key Terms

ataxic cerebral palsy	neuromuscular	spastic cerebral palsy
athetoid cerebral palsy	palmar grasp	stability
cephalocaudal	palmar grasp reflex	step reflex
cerebral palsy (CP)	pincer grasp	sucking reflex
high muscle tone	proprioceptive system	tonicity
low muscle tone	proximal-distal	tonic neck reflex
mobility	raking grasp	vestibular system
Moro reflex	rooting reflex	

REFLECTIONS AND RESOURCES FOR THE READER

Reflections

1. Does your image of an ideal infant or toddler include a child who is always active and on the move? Our inactive lifestyles are contributing to childhood obesity, but some of our child development and education programs are designed to keep children sitting quietly. How does your image of a healthy child affect how you would set up your space?

2. Are you naturally active? Would your personal preferences for activity or inactivity contribute to the kinds of motor activities you make available to the infants and toddlers in your care?

Observation and Application Opportunities

1. Observe an infant or toddler. How does she use her body to achieve some personal goal?
2. Notice how an infant or toddler handles objects. What sort of grasp does he use? Does he manage the objects well? Can he move them from hand to hand? Can he throw or release at will? Can he carry objects while moving around? Do different children use different ways of handling objects?
3. What materials would you offer infants and toddlers at different stages to support their increasingly effective grasps? Make a poster of the grasp and the materials that would support it. Share it in class.

Supplementary Articles and Books to Read

Davis, M. M., Gance-Cleveland, B., Hassink, S., Johnson, R., Paradis, G., & Resnicow, K. (2007). Recommendations for prevention of childhood obesity. *Pediatrics, 120*(Suppl. 4), S229–S253.

Pica, R. (2008). Learning by leaps and bounds. Why motor skills matter. *Young Children, 63*(4), 48–49. Retrieved from http://www.journal.naeyc.org/btj/200807

Smith, L. B. (2006). Movement matters: The contributions of Esther Thelen. *Biological Theory, 1*(1), 87–89. Retrieved September 23, 2008, from http://www.mitpressjournals.org/doi/pdf/10.1162/biot.2006.1.1.87?cookieSet=1

Interesting Links

http://www.zerotothree.org/site/PageServer?pagename=key_childdevt

ZERO TO THREE   The link "On the Move: The Power of Movement in Your Child's First Three Years" discusses how movement activities are critical not just for children's physical development, but for their overall development.

http://www.zerotothree.org/site/PageServer?pagename=ter_key_childdevt_crawling

ZERO TO THREE   The short article "Jeepers Creepers: Your baby Is Learning to Crawl" focuses on the variations in crawling and signs for concern about motor development.

http://www.psych.nyu.edu/adolph/publications1.php

Motor researcher Karen Adolf makes dozens of publications available in PDF format.

Responsive Programs
Quality, Health, Safety, and Nutrition

Sheila wanted to be responsive to each baby. But she could barely get through feeding and diapering. She was alone with six babies—and there was no way to do anything but run from one crying infant to another. She understood the importance of quality, but quality depended on more than her good intentions.

The issues of quality, availability, and funding of infant-toddler child care are inextricably intertwined. Given our current understanding of the effects of early relationships and environments on the development of the brain, or simply our own compassion for another human being's experience, we should ensure that the hours infants and toddlers spend in group care are filled with safe, loving, responsive, and enriching experiences. The quality of care that young children receive is directly related to their well-being, developing skills, and subsequent adjustment (Phillips & Adams, 2001).

Unfortunately, the high cost of providing quality care and ambivalent attitudes toward working mothers have left more than half the parents of infants and toddlers in America using child care that is of mediocre or poor quality. As mentioned in chapter 1 of this textbook, a study of more than 400 centers in the United States rated only 8% of infant classrooms as being of good or excellent quality (CQO Study Team, 1995). Studies of infant and toddler child care

have helped clarify which elements are most important to ensuring quality. Low ratios, small group sizes, and well-trained teachers are necessary for the focused, warm, enriched relationships babies need for good development (NICHD, 2001b). These factors, of course, make for an expensive service. At the same time, some Americans believe that mothers should be at home raising their children and will not support public funding that ensures quality child care services for all children (Sylvester, 2001).

Major research studies have helped define the elements of a child care program that contribute to high quality. This chapter will describe the components of quality, the effects of these components on infants and toddlers, how quality is evaluated, and the policies, laws, and systems that support quality. Health, safety, and nutrition are primary components of quality and discussed in detail within this chapter.

WHAT IS QUALITY . . . AND WHY DOES IT MATTER?

In its simplest perspective, every description of quality includes these three items:

- The safety of the child
- Communication between the family and the teacher about the child
- A warm, responsive relationship between the teacher and the child (Kontos, Howes, Shinn, & Galinsky, 1995)

The definition of *quality,* however, is not that simple. Each of these items—safety, communication with families, and a warm relationship—has its own defining elements, established by research. Safety includes keeping the environment clean and free of hazards, preventing the spread of infection, and promoting healthy practices and good nutrition. Communication between families and teachers includes having clear policies that families are able to understand, respect for differing cultural beliefs and child-rearing practices, and ways to resolve conflicts that may arise. The quality of the relationship between the teacher and the baby is affected by the teacher's own training, knowledge, and skills, as well as the program's curriculum, variables such as ratios and group sizes, and individual characteristics of each baby such as the clarity of her cues or ability to be calmed.

This teacher knows the importance of quiet, focused time with just one toddler.

ZERO TO THREE: National Center for Infants, Toddlers, and Families expands the list of elements that must be addressed to achieve high quality in infant and toddler care with the following eight components:

- Health and safety
- Small groups for infants and toddlers, with teachers responsible for no more than three young or mobile infants and no more than four children 18 months to 3 years old
- Primary teacher assignments
- Continuity of care
- Responsive caregiving and planning
- Cultural and linguistic continuity
- Meeting the needs of the individual within the group context
- The physical environment (Lally et al., 1995)

While it is true that all of these elements need to be considered in creating a high-quality program, in some ways it seems like a mix of apples and oranges. Some are concrete and easily observable; others are subtle, subjective, and relationship based. So, in order to really examine the elements of quality, we will separate them into *structural variables* and *process variables.*

Structural Variables of Quality

The **structural variables** of quality provide the foundation on which responsive relationships can be built. The variables include low child-to-teacher ratios, small group size, primary caregiving, continuity of care, and a well-educated, well-compensated, stable workforce. Comfortable, safe, healthy, and enriching environments are also important structural variables. Management structures within a program that support the smooth running of the program and support the efforts of teachers and families alike are also part of the underlying structure. In looking at this set of variables, it is clear that providing the foundation for high-quality infant-toddler care is an expensive endeavor. Therefore, adequate financing is also a structural variable.

Let's explore some of these variables more deeply.

structural variables
Measurable aspects that affect quality in child care, including ratios, group sizes, caregiver training, and health and safety standards.

Ratios and Group Sizes

Infants and toddlers need adult partners who attend to their feelings, their communication, their interests and understanding of the world, and their physical needs. Caring well for only *one* baby can be a full-time job. In order for teachers to provide the emotional connection and caregiving that promotes healthy development, one teacher cannot be responsible for more than a few babies. Very young children, in turn, are easily overwhelmed by the noise and activity of large groups of people, and in order for them to focus and learn, they need to be in groups of limited size.

Lower ratios in infant-toddler rooms were associated with more secure attachment to teachers in a study of 150 centers (Howes & Smith, 1995). These researchers also found that better ratios were related to more complex play with peers and objects, more proficient adaptive language, and fewer behavior problems such as aggression and anxiety.

The NICHD Early Childhood Research Network (2000a) study of over 1000 children found that better ratios were also related to more positive caregiving for 1 to 3 year-old children. A study of 79 African American infants found that lower ratios and small group sizes were associated with better communication skills in 12-month-olds and higher scores on the Bayley Mental Development Index (Burchinal et al., 1996).

The funding challenges of child care make it difficult to keep group sizes small and ratios low, although the benefits have been known for a long time. Ratio and group size tend to be determined by licensing regulations—and states vary widely in their legal requirements for child care programs, from 3 to 12 infants per teacher in regulated centers. The NICHD study of early child care found adult-to-child ratios ranging from 1:1 to 1:13 (Phillips & Adams, 2001).

Early Head Start defines the ratios and group size requirements in the Program Performance Standards and several national organizations have weighed in with recommendations for best practices, as shown in Table 11.1.

Small group sizes and low ratios promote a sense of belonging within the community of the program.

Table 11.1 Recommended ratios/group sizes

Children's Age	Early Head Start (required)	American Academy of Pediatrics	NAEYC	ZERO TO THREE
Birth to 12 months	1:4 / 8	1:3 / 6	1:3 or 1:4 to 15 months / 6–8	1:3 / 6
13 to 30 months	1:4 / 8	1:4 / 8	1:3 or 1:4 for 16 to 28 months / 6–12	1:3 for 12 to 18 months / 9
30 to 35 months	1:4 / 8	1:5 / 10	1:4 to 1:6 for 28 to 36 months / 6–12	1:4 / 12

Primary Caregiving

Primary caregiving is the practice of assigning responsibility to one teacher for each baby. This promotes consistent caregiving, allows the teacher and the child to develop a predictable and always deepending relationship, and provides the family with one person to depend on for ongoing sharing of information. Primary caregiving does not mean exclusive caregiving. Generally, more than one teacher is in a room with a group of infants or toddlers, and all teachers strive to have warm, affectionate relationships with all of the babies.

The emphasis on primary caregiving comes from the ever-deepening understanding of the importance of caregiving relationships for healthy development. Attachment theory demonstrated the importance of caring, sensitive, emotionally nourishing relationships as a necessity for an infant's secure and positive development (Ainsworth et al., 1978). Emotionally available, attentive teachers help infants and toddlers understand what is expected of them, what feels right in the world, as well as the patterns of social reciprocity, turn taking, and cooperation (Emde, Biringen, Clyman, & Oppenheim, 1991). Consistent relationships can promote interest in exploration, pleasure in play, and abilities to manage stressful and challenging situations (Emde, 1994; Zahn-Waxler & Radke-Yarrow, 1990).

A relationship with a primary teacher allows the intimacy and mutual knowledge for a relationship to grow in depth. It takes time to develop an attachment to a teacher, and babies are less likely to form attachments if their teachers change frequently (Raikes, 1993). When infants and toddlers have to adjust to many new teachers, they may not even try to know the new teacher but just try to re-create the character of the relationship with the last teacher (Howes & Hamilton, 1993). Having a focused relationship with one teacher over time, providing continuity of care, appears to be helpful for every aspect of a child's development.

When young children are constantly going through adjustments to new situations, they often feel unsettled and irritable.

Continuity of Care

Continuity of care extends the assignment of the primary teacher over a long period of time, preferably from the time of enrollment until the child is at least 3 years of age. By allowing the caregiving relationship to exist over years, the child is able to experience the time and intimacy needed to learn about himself and form meaningful relationships. When teachers change frequently, the baby may experience both the grief of losing a valued friend and the stress of having to learn a new person's expectations. When relationships are repeatedly disrupted early in life, an infant or toddler may stop investing the effort needed to develop new relationships, and life can become very distressing for the toddler.

Continuity of care, between a child development and education provider and a baby, may be achieved in several ways. The two most important elements involved in continuity of care approaches are:

1. The day-to-day interactions between the primary teacher and the baby that give the baby a sense of predictability in their daily experiences
2. The deepening relationship and shared memories created through the enduring, year-after-year relationship between the primary teacher and the baby

Extended time together supports children's sense of history of themselves with the teacher. It helps babies believe that people remain in their lives in caring, meaningful ways—that they can rely on and safely love other people. For families experiencing multiple challenges (e.g., unstable housing leading to multiple moves, unstable employment, or numerous adults or other individuals rotating in and out of the home), continuity in the caregiving environment is especially beneficial for the young child.

When continuity of care is provided by a primary teacher, there are also many opportunities for the teacher and parents to develop a caring relationship. Teachers may learn from parents how the infant or toddler expects to be handled and any cultural or personal care practices the family utilizes. The teacher, in turn, may inform the family on the thinking behind some of the care practices in the program. Open, genuine communication between parents and teachers increases the continuity of the baby's experiences between home and child care.

Different structures for continuity of care include mixed age groups of infants and toddlers, nurtured by primary teachers throughout their first 3 years, similar to the design of family child care. Another model is remaining with the same children in a close age group, and as the children grow older moving to a new, age-appropriate space with the same teacher, thus providing the teacher and child with the opportunity to form long-lasting bonds. As time progresses, teachers in this arrangement work with various age groups over several years. A third method is to maintain a close age group with the same teacher but modify the environment as the children's abilities and interests change.

While some teachers may feel more competent with specific age groups and prefer to work, for example, only with young infants or only with 2-year-olds, the teacher and baby will reap mutual benefits from a more long-term relationship spanning the duration of the child's enrollment. Teachers can feel confident of their ability to *really know* a child, to be able to read each baby's cues, and to know how to individually comfort and challenge each baby. The teacher avoids the stress of constantly "learning" new babies.

Teacher Characteristics

Personal characteristics such as warmth, comfort with intimacy, a sense of humor, and enjoying children are important for infant and toddler teachers. However, other factors such as general education level and specific training in child development (Burchinal, Howes, & Kontos, 2002), compensation and stability in the workplace, and the structure for ongoing supervision by the director consistently correlate to better child outcomes in studies of early care.

Teachers with either a bachelor's degree or specialized training at the college level are more sensitive and less harsh with children, are warmer, more enthusiastic, and more developmentally appropriate in their communication (Whitebrook, Howes, & Phillips, 1998). In child-care homes caregivers who were better educated and had higher and more recent levels of training demonstrated more positive caregiving (Clarke-Stewart, Vandell, Burchinal, O'Brien, & McCartney, 2002). Teachers with as little as two courses at the community college level are less authoritarian than those with no training at all (Arnett, 1989).

Teachers with more education maintain cleaner, healthier environments and reduce the number of accidental injuries in their classrooms (Ulione, 1997). Their classrooms are likely to receive higher scores on global quality rating scales such as the Infant Toddler Environmental Rating Scale (ITERS). (ITERS and other rating scales are discussed later in this chapter.) However, most health and safety practices are best maintained when a program has established ongoing monitoring of its own practices (Ulione, 1997).

The stability of teachers in their positions is also related to their education. Teachers with more education are more likely to remain in the field (Whitebrook et al., 1998). Family home providers participating in initial training tend to seek out additional training and increase their commitment to their jobs (Galinsky, Howes, & Kontos, 1995). A study in Alabama found that preservice training reduced the turnover rate among child care employees, with 68% still employed in the field 1 year after graduation (Shirah, Hewitt, & McNair, 1993).

Of course, whereas education tends to improve both the performance and stability of the teacher, the low wages and lack of benefits in most child care jobs make it difficult to recruit and retain people who have invested in their own education. In 1999 only 15 occupations earned less than child care workers. Gas station attendants, food service workers, animal trainers, and messengers all earned more than the average $7.42 an hour of child care workers. Family child care providers earned even less, averaging about $4.82 an hour in a 55-hour work week (CCW, 2004). Benefits such as health insurance are rare, and wages are so low that workers often cannot afford to pay their share even when employers pay a portion of the cost (CCW, 2004). The low wages result in a poorly trained workforce with a turnover rate of nearly 40% (CCW, 2004). These factors directly affect the quality of care available to infants and toddlers.

The most important predictor of the quality of care . . . is staff wages. (Lombardi)

These structural variables—low ratios, small group sizes, primary caregiving, continuity of care, and well-trained and supported teachers—provide an environment that makes possible the kind of caring, responsive interactions by which we can ultimately judge the quality of a child's experience in child care. Without the foundation of these structural variables, the following process variables will not possibly contribute to quality.

Process Variables of Quality

process variables
Actual experiences that occur in child care settings, including children's interactions with caregivers and peers and their participation in different activities.

The moment-by-moment experiences of children in child care are the dynamic processes that must be observed to really understand quality from the child's perspective. These **process variables** include the interactions between children and teachers, among children, and the play, learning, and health activities in which the children participate (Vandell & Wolfe, 2001).

The process variables of greatest importance to infants and toddlers are responsive caregiving and planning, cultural and linguistic continuity, meeting the needs of the individual within the group context, and the physical environment. These topics are covered in depth in chapter 12 as part of the discussion of the teacher's role in a responsive, caring curriculum, and additionally in chapters 13 and 14 as responsive teaching relates to promoting children's social, emotional, cognitive, language, and motor development. A very brief summary of the definition of these items as related to the broader concept of quality follows.

Responsive teaching, of course, describes the process of understanding the child's experience and knowing how to respond appropriately. Lally (2001) writes of seven gifts that good child care and early education programs offer infants and toddlers, described in Box 11.1. These gifts provide a clear description of responsive teaching. The gifts of nurturance, support, security, and predictability help children believe that they will be loved and cared for in the child care setting. The gifts of predictability, focus, encouragement, and expansion support the child's intellectual engagement and understanding of the world.

Cultural and Linguistic Continuity

Babies develop expectations of how they will be cared for in their first days of life. They become familiar with the sound of their family's language, even in the womb. Teachers, ideally, would be of the same culture and home language as the family, thereby being most likely to intuitively offer continuity in the child's experience and avoid cultural clashes with families. However, in today's diverse communities, it is unlikely that all children will have a teacher from their native culture. Teachers can, however, learn the words of caregiving and education from families and try to match the family's practices. They can include pictures, toys, or artifacts of a specific culture in their environment, and they must always speak of the child's culture with respect. In chapter 12 of this book we will discuss specific strategies for developing relationships with families from diverse cultures.

Meeting the Needs of the Individual Within the Context of the Group

Teachers need to find ways to respect the individual temperament, moods, preferences, and routines of each child in their care. This includes feeding on demand, being helped to fall asleep, and diapering or toileting as needed. Low ratios and small group sizes are critical factors in whether a teacher will be able to attend sensitively to the individual and the group.

Box 11.1

> ## The Seven Gifts of Caregiving
>
> *Nurturance:* Individualized, responsive giving of comfort, attention, warmth, food, and protection.
>
> *Support:* Helping children achieve developmental shifts of trust, exploration, and learning about themselves by acknowledging their feelings, encouraging curiosity and independence, and, at the same time, teaching and enforcing the rules that allow children and adults to live in harmony.
>
> *Security:* The very young child's sense that she is safe.
>
> *Predictability:* Social interactions, sequences of routines, and orderly environments that are both reliable enough for comfort and flexible enough for reaction to learning or play opportunities.
>
> *Focus:* Helping children increase their ability to attend and explore by focusing meaningful activity and attention on what interests the child, protecting the child from too much stimulation, and being a calm, reliable presence who frees the child's energy for learning.
>
> *Encouragement:* The teacher letting the infant or toddler know he understands exactly what the child is trying to learn and communicating through words and interest that he has every confidence in the child's growing competence.
>
> *Expansion:* The teacher's addition of rich, meaningful words or small elaborations in materials or play to help children grow through their experiences.

Source: From "The Seven Gifts of Caregiving," by Ron Lally, 2001, *The Art and Science of Child Care* (unpublished document). Sausalito, CA: The Program for Infant/Toddler Caregivers. Copyright 2001 by WestEd. Reprinted with permission.

Physical Environment

The environment must be kept particularly clean, given the immature immune systems of infants and toddlers, and especially safe for young children who will mouth and swallow anything and are constantly developing new abilities in movement. The play spaces must offer interesting opportunities for exploration without being overwhelming with too many choices. Above all else, the environment must be set up and monitored to ensure the health and safety of the children in care.

AN EMPHASIS ON HEALTH AND SAFETY

Although no one would challenge the idea that the most basic responsibility of child care is to keep the children safe and healthy, our limited licensing regulations and ambivalent attitude toward regulating child care do not ensure that the best health and safety practices are always followed. In fact, although national health and safety standards for child care were first

Box 11.2

Caring for Our Children: National Health
and Safety Performance Standards:
Guidelines for Out-of-Home Child Care
Programs: Second Edition

Caring for Our Children was created by the American
Academy of Pediatrics and the National Resource Center for
Health and Safety in Child Care to provide the most current,
evidence-based information on health and safety practices
for group care. Standards describing best practices, scientific
rationales, and comments address these areas:

· Staffing
· Program: Activities for healthy development
· Health promotion and protection in child care
· Nutrition and food service
· Facilities, supplies, equipment, and
  transportation
· Infectious diseases
· Children who are eligible for services under IDEA
· Administration
· Licensing and community action

Specific procedures for handwashing, diapering, cleaning
and sanitizing, food handling, and every aspect of maintaining
a safe and healthy environment are included.

The entire document is available online and updates are
regularly posted as the current science provides new information for our decision making. The document and updates are
available at http://nrc.uchsc.edu/CFOC/

published in the United States in 1992, when the second
edition was published in 2002 (APHA & AAP, 2002)
most states had still not officially adopted the standards in their regulations. However, because *Caring for
Our Children: National Health and Safety Performance
Standards: Guidelines for Out-of-Home Child Care
Programs* (APHA & AAP, 2002) is the most thorough,
well-researched, and reviewed material available, the
practices in this section come from that source and we
highly recommend that every teacher use the original
document, as well.

While keeping children safe and healthy in child
care is a foundation of quality, it is not enough, as
expressed in the introduction to *Caring for Our
Children:*

> Health involves more than the absence of illness and
> injury. To stay healthy, children depend on adults to
> make healthy choices for them and to teach them to
> make such choices for themselves over the course of a
> lifetime. (Chang & Aronson, 2002)

Health and safety practices in infant-toddler child
care include a range of activities for the purpose of
avoiding injury and infection and promoting health.
They include:

• Sanitizing and preventing the spread of disease
• Promoting safety and preventing injuries
• Adopting policies that promote and protect health

Sanitizing and Preventing the Spread of Disease

Babies are vulnerable. In the first weeks of life, they cannot even support their own heads
when being held. They cannot take action to keep themselves dry, warm, fed, or safe—and
they cannot, at the end of a day of care, tell us whether they were treated kindly. As parents,
we are so aware of this vulnerability that we watch their breathing as they sleep, to reassure
ourselves. And the most basic demand we make of nonparental care is that our babies will be
healthy and safe.

This vulnerability is not simply our perception of babies. In the last 2 months of gestation,
the mother's immune system creates enormous amounts of immunoglobulin, the protective
agent against most infections, and sends it to the baby across the placenta. At birth the newborn has a higher immunoglobulin count than his mother. However, at birth, the baby stops
receiving the immunoglobulin from his mother and the protection slowly decreases. The baby's
immune system does not begin producing its own immunoglobulin until around 7 months,
and by 2 years of age is still offering only about 80% of the average adult protection (Collier &
Henderson, 2000). So babies are considerably more prone to infection, and less resilient in
recovering from infection, than people at any other stage of human development.

When we understand the vulnerability to infection in the infant and toddler and then add
the risks of repeated exposures to infection that are inherent in group care compared to being
at home with one parent, it is clear that teachers have a responsibility to maintain a very

sanitary environment. See Box 11.2 for ways to find more information on health and safety practices for group care. For teachers of infants and toddlers, preventing the spread of disease depends on scrupulous attention to the following:

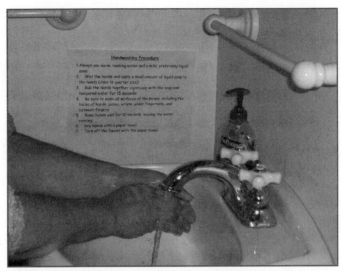

- Handwashing
- Diapering
- Sanitizing toys, furniture, and bedding
- Excluding children who are ill

Following written procedures for handwashing, diapering, and food handling will protect the health and safety of everyone in the program.

Handwashing

Handwashing is the primary defense against illness in child care. It is such a basic step in hygiene that it is amazing how often it is either not done when it should be or is done improperly, and thus ineffectively. Unwashed or improperly washed hands spread infection and may be the cause of diarrhea outbreaks among both children and staff. Centers that have implemented handwashing training programs have decreased the incidence of diarrhea by 50%. Handwashing also reduces the spread of colds and respiratory infections and protects the children, as well as the teacher, from illness.

According to the National Health and Safety Performance Standards, all teachers, volunteers, and children should wash their hands when they arrive for the day or when they move from one care group to another. They should wash their hands *before and after* eating, handling food, feeding a child, giving medication, and playing in water that is used by more than one person. They should wash hands *after* diapering, using the toilet or helping a child use the toilet, handling uncooked foods, handling animals, playing in sandboxes, cleaning, handling garbage, and handling bodily fluid from sneezing, wiping, and blowing noses, from mouths, or from sores (APHA & AAP, 2002).

Teachers should receive training in proper handwashing procedures and be monitored for the accuracy of their use of the procedure and whether they are handwashing in every required situation. Programs should post proper handwashing procedures above sinks. Specific procedures need to be in place describing how teachers will wash the hands of infants too young to do it themselves, or assist toddlers in washing their own hands.

Diapering

A second important area of hygiene in group care is diapering. The National Health and Safety Performance Standards caution that fecal contamination of objects or the hands of teachers or children can cause serious gastrointestinal diseases—so the first requirement concerning diapers is that they absorb liquid and hold solids tightly. Three kinds of diapers meet the standards for use in child care: disposable diapers with absorbent gelling material, one-piece reusable diapers with a cloth lining attached to a waterproof outer covering, or reusable cloth diapers worn with a front-closure waterproof cover. It is also important to use diapering procedures that prevent diaper dermatitis (irritation of skin that has been in contact with urine or feces).

Safe and healthy diapering procedures include changing diapers whenever it is obvious from the feel of the diaper through the clothing that it is wet, or from the smell that there are feces. Diapers should be checked with a visual inspection at least every 2 hours. Diapers should always be changed as soon as they are found to be wet or soiled. A specific area set aside for

myeducationlab)

Go to the Activities and Applications section in Chapter 11 of MyEducationLab to watch the video *Diapering.* Think about the health and safety procedures that the care teacher follows.

Box 11.3

Diluted Bleach Sanitizer

First clean the surface with detergent and rinse with water. Mix ¼ cup of household liquid chlorine bleach in 1 gallon of water (or 1 tablespoon of bleach to 1 quart of water). Sprayed onto a cleaned surface, the sanitizer requires 2 minutes of surface contact to kill the usual infectious agents found in feces.

diaper changing will reduce the risk of contamination of other parts of the child care environment. Children's access to this area should be limited to the times when they are being changed. Diapers should not be changed on areas used for other purposes, especially not on any surface that is used for food preparation or mealtimes. If cloth diapers or training pants are used, they must never be carried through the child care area to place the fecal contents in the toilet. Soiled cloth diapers must be kept in a sealed plastic container and removed each night by the family or a commercial laundry service.

The changing table that is used must also be diligently sanitized using a solution such as the one described in Box 11.3. Changing tables must be made of a nonporous material, cleaned and sanitized after each use to remove visible soil, and followed by wetting with a sanitizing solution such as the diluted bleach solution. The sanitizer must be left on for the required contact time. Some sanitizers need to be wiped off afterward with water, but bleach does not as the chlorine evaporates, leaving only water on the surface (APHA & AAP, 2002, Standards 3.012–3.019).

Sanitizing Toys, Furniture, and Bedding

In addition to careful diapering procedures and frequent handwashing, the National Health and Safety Performance Standards provide directions for the overall routine cleaning and sanitation of all aspects of the child care area. Infants and toddlers are likely to touch any surface they can reach, thereby both spreading infectious agents and coming in contact with contaminated surfaces anywhere in the environment. One precaution in the standards that is only for infant rooms is the requirement that people either cover their street shoes or replace them with slippers before walking on the infant room floor (APHA & AAP, 2002, Standard 3.035).

Infants and toddlers will sneeze and cough without covering their noses or mouths, they will mouth any toy or object, and they drool when they are teething. The potential for spreading disease is impressive. A routine for cleaning and sanitizing all surfaces should be established and implemented by all programs.

Excluding Children Who Are Ill

The National Health and Safety Performance Standards suggest that children who are ill be excluded from child care for a short period of time. Each state's licensing standards may have specific regulations regarding when children should be excluded from care, and health consultants or health advisory committees should also be consulted. However, the basic guidelines from the National Health and Safety Performance Standards include specific conditions for exclusion from the program. For instance, a child should be excluded if the illness prevents the child from participating in the activities or the illness requires teachers to provide a higher level of care than they are able to do without compromising the other children. A child with any of the following conditions should be excluded from group care: fever; symptoms and signs of severe illness such as lethargy, uncontrolled coughing, persistent irritability or crying, difficulty breathing, wheezing, or other unusual signs; diarrhea; blood in stools; vomiting; persistent abdominal pain; mouth sores with drooling; rash with fever; purulent conjunctivitis (pink eye); pediculosis (head lice); scabies; tuberculosis; impetigo; strep throat; chickenpox; pertussis; mumps; hepatitis A virus; measles; rubella; respiratory tract illness; shingles; or herpes simplex.

Excluding children with mild infections has only a small effect on limiting the spread of infection because many viruses are spread before the child actually exhibits any symptoms of the disease. So programs should also consider the child's comfort and the needs of the staff when they create policies for excluding children who are ill (APHA & AAP, 2002, Standard 3.065).

Administering Medication

When children with mild illnesses or chronic conditions require medication, the child care program may be involved in medication administration. The National Health and Safety Performance Standards, the Head Start program performance standards, and most state licensing regulations require programs to have a written policy and procedures for medication administration. The best option is that medication be prescribed in ways that allow parents to administer it before or after the hours the child is in care. However, young children are prone to illnesses and it is sometimes necessary for programs to take on the responsibility.

When programs must administer medications, the National Health and Safety Performance Standards have several standards concerning this issue, including Permissible Administration of Medication (3.081), Labeling and Storage of Medications (3.082), and Training of Teachers to Administer Medication (3.083). These standards limit the administration of medications to prescribed medications ordered by a health care provider with written permission of the parent or legal guardian and nonprescription (over-the-counter) medications recommended by a health care provider for a specific child or for a specific circumstance for all children, with written permission from the parent or legal guardian. So, a health care provider could write a standing order for the use of sunscreen or acetaminophen for use in specific circumstances (exposure to sun or fever over 101°. Parents must be notified of each application of any medication and each application should be logged.

Prescribed medications brought into the child care facility should be in their original containers, dated, labeled with the child's first and last names, the date the prescription was filled, the name of the health care provider who wrote the prescription, the expiration date, the instructions for administration, and the name and strength of the medication. Over-the-counter medications should be brought in their original container and labeled by the parent with the child's name and instructions from the health care provider. All medications should have child-resistant caps, be stored away from food, and be kept inaccessible to children.

A child care teacher who administers medication may be required by state licensing requirements to have specific medication administration certification. Teachers are trained to check the match between the name on the medication and the child's name; to read and understand the directions in relation to dose, frequency, and circumstances such as in relation to meals; to administer the medication; to observe any side effects of the medications; and to document the administration of each dose (APHA & AAP, 2002).

Promoting Safety and Preventing Injuries

In addition to the vulnerability of very young children to disease, infants and toddlers are quite susceptible to injuries through accidents. They are just developing the ability to move around and do not automatically understand how to keep their balance, how to avoid falling over steep edges, or how to get themselves out of tight places they have somehow managed to squeeze into. Infants and toddlers who are so interested in the ideas of "in" and "out" apply those ideas to tiny objects that can choke them or to interesting openings in walls where adults plug in lamps and radios. The world can be a dangerous place for the curious explorer who brings limited experience to his movements, or the consequences of his actions. It can be challenging to find a balance between keeping the child care area safe and still providing an environment that invites children to play, learn, and explore.

Accident Prevention

Teachers who care for infants and toddlers are constantly scanning the environment for anything that may cause injury to their charges. A key to keeping the environment safe for infants and toddlers is to see the area through their eyes. Getting down on the floor and taking a child's-eye view can alert the teacher to dangers she might not see from an adult height. Are tall shelves bolted to the wall so they can't fall down on a climbing child? Are outlets covered? Are more remote parts of the carpet vacuumed as frequently as the open spaces? Accident prevention requires an awareness of potential hazards, eliminating known hazards, knowing what to do in an emergency, and teaching children about safety (Watson & White, 2001).

With infants and toddlers, the teacher's vigilant observation of the children and the space is the most important factor in preventing accidents and injuries. Teachers arrange furniture to allow visual access to children at all times. Furniture is checked for stability, door edges are protected to prevent pinched fingers, electrical cords are not dangling or within reach of children, and outlets are covered. Infants and toddlers are never left unattended in high chairs, infant seats, or swings. Choking hazards such as small objects, broken parts of toys, curtain cords, balloons, popcorn, peanuts, hot dogs, grapes, gum, and hard candies are kept out of the environment. Infant and toddler toys should be greater than 1¼ inches in diameter to avoid choking. Toys are chosen for their age-appropriateness, checking the labels for age recommendations. Toys should be nontoxic, wooden toys kept free of splinters, and cloth toys should be flame retardant.

All cleaning supplies and medications should be kept locked and out of the children's reach. Other potentially toxic substances include poisonous plants, small batteries, salves used in diapering, and even art materials. Colored inks used in magazines may contain lead.

Outdoor play must also be well supervised. Children should be dressed appropriately for whatever weather is present, with children kept well hydrated and safe from the sun. Playgrounds should be designed for infants and toddlers and provide surfaces that provide protection from the inevitable falls. You will read more about how to set up an interesting outdoor environment and how teachers can provide responsive outdoor care in chapter 13.

Despite all precautions, accidents may still occur. Teachers need to have current first aid and infant-toddler CPR training, fully stocked first aid kits kept handy, and written plans for reacting to emergencies. Programs should practice evacuation drills for fires, hurricanes, and tornados. Infant programs should have evacuation cribs to provide for quick transport of a group of infants.

Adopting Policies That Promote and Protect Health

All programs serving young children need health and safety policies that are written out, approved by a health consultant or health advisory committee, and understood by staff. Teachers should receive training on the policies and be monitored for their adherence to the policies and procedures. Handwashing, cleaning, sanitizing, diapering, and accident prevention are all areas that should be covered by those policies. Schedules that promote a balance between active and quiet play and rest times, good nutrition, and the constant presence of a responsive, caring adult all promote health.

There are two more areas that are important to emphasize in a discussion of infant-toddler programs: safe sleep positioning and child abuse reporting.

In 1992, the American Academy of Pediatrics Task Force on Infant Positioning and SIDS (sudden infant death syndrome) made the strong recommendation that young infants be placed to sleep supine (on their backs) to reduce the risk of SIDS. Their public awareness effort became known as the "Back to Sleep" campaign. Between 1992 and 2001, the SIDS rate had been reduced by 53%. All child care programs should ensure safe sleeping positions as a policy. The most recent AAP (2005a) policy statement on SIDS makes these recommendations:

1. Place infants on their backs to sleep.
2. Use a firm sleep surface.

3. Keep soft objects and loose bedding out of the crib.

4. Do not smoke during pregnancy.

5. Provide a separate nearby sleeping environment (recommended).

6. Offer a pacifier at naptime and bedtime.

7. Avoid overheating. (pp. 1251–1252)

Child abuse and neglect are sensitive, emotionally charged issues for everyone. Parents fear for their child's safety when left in group care, with abuse sometimes being one of those worries. Teachers are often the first to recognize and identify signs of parental abuse and then have the difficult task of reporting the abuse or neglect to authorities. The National Child Care Information and Technical Assistance Center (NCCIC, 2009) defines child abuse as a "nonaccidental injury or pattern of injuries to a child for which there is no 'reasonable' explanation." Abuse may include:

- Nonaccidental injury
- Neglect
- Sexual molestation
- Emotional abuse

Teachers are required to report all suspected cases of abuse and neglect. It is important to have training in recognizing signs of *possible* abuse and characteristics of child abusers. It is also important to understand the legal mandate for reporting in your state, as well as the procedures for reporting suspected abuse or neglect. Programs should have policies in place to ensure that abuse never occurs within the program and should have a method for investigating any accusations of abuse that could be filed. Although this topic requires greater depth of training than can be given here, a short description of each of these issues will help in achieving some understanding. If a teacher recognizes an indicator of abuse or neglect, it should be considered within the context of explanations given by the family, the medical history, and the ability of the child to participate in the activities said to cause the accident.

The indicators of abuse or neglect are as follows:

- *Indicators of physical abuse:* Any injury on an infant such as burns, fractures, bruises, welts, cuts, scrapes, head injuries, fear of adults, appearance of pain
- *Indicators of emotional abuse:* General unhappiness, reacting without emotion to unpleasant statements or actions, delayed emotional development, or for infants an appearance of freezing as though withdrawing completely from the present moment
- *Indicators of sexual abuse:* Difficulty in walking or sitting; torn, stained, or bloody underclothing; pain when urinating; bruises or bleeding in vaginal or anal areas, mouth, or throat, or vaginal infections; unwillingness to have clothing changed; being fearful of a particular person; or unusual interest in or knowledge of sexual matters
- *Indicators of physical and emotional neglect:* Infants or toddlers left in the care of other children, dressed inadequately for the weather, poor hygiene, not getting regular well-baby care, no weight gain, or always hungry

Characteristics of child abusers include these traits:

- Isolated, under stress, mental health issues
- Alcohol or drug influence
- Unfulfilled needs for nurturance and support
- Feel that their failures are greater than their successes

- Lack of supports in marriage, extended family, or jobs
- Likely to feel that violence is an acceptable way of dealing with problems

Reporting suspected child abuse is one of the most difficult things teachers may have to do, but it is not a choice. If you suspect abuse or neglect, you are legally required to report your suspicions to authorities. Each state has its own definition of what constitutes abuse or neglect. You are never required to have proof before reporting and must report an incident as soon as it is noticed. Part of your program's policy should include knowing which agency to call in your community. Many states will take an anonymous report over the phone, but it is useful to provide your contact information.

Teachers may also need to consider how their program's discipline policy may be seen in light of issues of abuse and neglect. Corporal punishment may never be used in child care. Discipline must never interfere with a child's schedule of eating, sleeping, or toileting. However, a responsive teacher will not use discipline with infants and toddlers. Her own good skills, an engaging but serene environment, and positive interactions with children will provide the guidance very young children need as they learn to control their own behavior. In chapter 14 you will find very specific strategies in regard to guidance for infants and toddlers.

THE IMPORTANCE OF GOOD NUTRITION

The nutrition infants and toddlers receive directly affects the ability of the brain to form and develop and may have a lifelong effect on the child's ability to learn, to cope with difficult circumstances, and to grow and have strong bones. Mothers who are severely malnourished in pregnancy produce babies with smaller head circumferences and smaller brain weight. The enormous spurts of growth in the last months of gestation and the first years of life require sufficient amounts of food and sufficient quantities of particular nutrients. Cell growth and division occurs only during childhood. The nutrients available to each cell may determine which cell type becomes dominant within tissue, how large or small each cell becomes within each body part, and how efficiently each cell performs in the future (Roberts & Heyman, 2000).

Child care and education programs may play a very important role in assuring that infants and toddlers in care have adequate nutrition and establish healthy eating habits. By being knowledgeable about the foods babies need in order to grow and be healthy, helping them get used to a variety of healthy choices, and using proper food-handling techniques, programs can influence the patterns children set early in life. Teachers must establish healthy eating habits, good sleep routines, a balance between active and quiet play, and some time outdoors every day to lay the foundation for good growth and development.

Nutritional Needs of Infants and Toddlers

Human breast milk is the best food for young human babies. The composition of the mother's milk changes as the baby grows, giving the baby exactly what she needs at the time. The protein is easily digested and the vitamins and minerals are almost entirely absorbed, compared to only 10% of iron and vitamins from formula. Certain fats found in breast milk, but not in formula, are used by the developing central nervous system and the photoreceptor rods in the retina (Lazarov & Evans, 2000; Meyers & Chawla, 2000). The American Academy of Pediatrics strongly endorses breast-feeding, in part because of the significant immunological benefits. More than 50 immune agents are transferred through breast milk, giving babies protection from otitis media (middle ear infections), lower respiratory infections, and gastric infections causing diarrhea (AAP, 1997). Breast-fed babies have a lower incidence of SIDS, allergies, childhood lymphoma, childhood-onset diabetes, and obesity (Lawrence, 1997). Infant and toddler programs can support mothers in their breast-feeding by encouraging them to visit their child during the day to breast-feed or to express milk to use in bottles. Infants weaned before 12 months of age should be fed iron-fortified formula.

Bottles of breast milk, formula, milk, or juice should never be propped for a baby to use without being held. The nurturing, social aspect of feeding is nearly as important as the nutrition for babies. Bottles should also never be used as a way to help a baby fall asleep because the prolonged contact with the natural sugars in the liquids can cause tooth decay. Even very young babies should have their gums wiped with a moist cloth after feeding to remove any remaining liquid which could turn to plaque and cause tooth decay (APHA & AAP, 2002, Standard 3.010).

Certain micronutrients (vitamins and minerals) are essential for healthy growth and development. Iron, iodine, and zinc are all necessary for proper cell development. Babies are born with enough iron for the first 4 to 6 months; babies get iron from breast milk, iron-fortified formula, iron-fortified cereal, beans, vegetables, and meats. Iron is used by the body in the development of red blood cells and in brain tissue, including the network of neurotransmitters used for information processing (Beard, Connor, & Jones, 1997). Toddlers with iron deficiency have lower scores on both the mental and psychomotor indices of the Bayley Scales of Infant Development and are more wary, hesitant, easily tired, and less attentive, involved, and playful than children with adequate iron (Lozoff, Klein, Nelson, McClish, Manuel, & Chacon, 1998). Iron deficiency is often associated with poverty, but iron-fortified formulas or iron supplements can prevent anemia (Meyers & Chawla, 2000).

Micronutrients affect the child in utero and postnatally. Iodine deficiency has been associated with hypothyroidism and cognitive deficits (Huda, Grantham-McGregor, & Tomkins, 1999). Zinc deficiency occurs in children with malnutrition and poor diets and results in a variety of cognitive and behavioral problems (Golub, Keen, Gershwin, & Hendrickx, 1995). Zinc is available in oat cereals, meat and poultry, wheat germ, egg yolk, and cheddar cheese. Vitamin B-6 influences mother–infant interactions and behavior (McCullough, Kirksey, Wachs, McGabe, Bassily, & Bishry, 1990).

Between 4 and 6 months, babies begin to supplement breast milk or formula with foods such as rice cereal or unsweetened applesauce—foods that are unlikely to trigger allergic reactions. Solid foods should be introduced one at a time, with a few days passing before introducing the next new food so that any reactions to the food can be easily identified. The introduction of these soft solid foods coincides with the baby's developing abilities to move the food in his mouth and swallow it.

From 6 months to the first birthday, babies continue to rely on breast milk or formula for most of their nutrition, but they are increasing the amount and variety of solid foods they are eating. At this time babies eat pureed cereals, fruits, vegetables, and meats. They learn to eat a wide variety of healthy foods, incorporating more solid foods as they have teeth for chewing. Foods that are likely to cause allergies or choking should not be introduced. Water is offered to quench thirst. Babies begin to finger-feed themselves toward the end of the first year and enjoy holding their own spoon while they are being fed. Important habits are being developed during this time. Babies should be fed when they express their hunger through crying, sucking on their fist, fussiness, or pointing to places where food is kept. They eat quickly when hungry and will begin to slow down and explore or socialize as the hunger abates. When the baby signals through a closed mouth or turning away that she is full, the teacher should end the feeding. One of the lessons the baby is learning is to understand her own body's signals of hunger and fullness.

Babies cannot eat a great deal at a time, and they need food that is packed in healthy calories to assure their growth and development. Babies need fat in their diet but they do not need salt or sugar to flavor their foods, and both salt and sugar should be kept to a minimum in their diets. High salt intake can lead to hypertension in adults and it is not necessary to teach a baby to develop a desire for it. Sugar is linked to hyperactivity, diabetes, tooth decay, and other chronic diseases later in life (Meyers & Chawla, 2000).

Breast-fed babies may continue nursing after their first birthday if it is working well for the mother and the baby. However, formula-fed babies usually switch to cow's milk at about 1 year of age. Between 1 and 2 years, a toddler's daily nutritional needs are for about 16 to 24 ounces of milk; ½ to 1 cup of fresh fruits and vegetables; 1 or 2 one-ounce servings of meat, poultry, fish, or eggs; about 200 to 500 calories worth of other good foods such as fortified cereal, breads, and legumes; and water for thirst. Between 2 and 3 years, toddlers need 16 to 24 ounces of milk; ¾ to 1¼ cups of fresh fruits and vegetables; 1 to 3 servings of meats, poultry, fish, or eggs; about 400 to 800 calories worth of foods such as fortified cereal, breads, and legumes; and water for thirst (Roberts & Heyman, 2000). Teachers must be sure to avoid serving foods that cause choking, such as hot dogs (whole or cut into rounds), raw carrot rounds or sticks, whole grapes, hard candy, or nuts. Other foods that present choking dangers include seeds, raw peas, popcorn, marshmallows, spoonfuls of peanut butter, and chunks of meat (APHA & AAP, 2002, p. 168).

As toddlers are becoming skillful eaters with increasing appetites, teachers and parents can be teaching and encouraging healthy choices. Toddlers enjoy feeding themselves, having some choice in what they eat, eating when they are hungry, and being allowed to determine when they are through. Child care programs should not even have unhealthy salty or sugary foods available as possible choices. Children should see child care as a place where only healthy foods are available. As toddlers naturally use their mouths to explore during the second year of life, give them opportunities to explore a wide variety of foods. By the age of 2, children can have a repertoire of as many as 200 foods that they enjoy. Toddlers may want to eat the same food day after day for every meal and then suddenly get bored and refuse to touch those very foods at all. As long as children are getting a well-rounded diet that meets their nutritional needs, with ongoing opportunities to broaden their tastes, it is all right to allow them to make choices about what they eat at any one meal.

Child Development and Education Programs Supporting Safe and Healthy Nutrition

When providing foods for infants and toddlers in child care, the changing nutritional needs are only part of what teachers need to know. The National Health and Safety Performance Standards recognize the importance of the emotional and social environment of snacks and meals, the safe handling of foods and the utensils used in meal preparation and eating, and the policies in place that assure each infant or toddler has an individualized diet plan including how to respond to family preferences or allergic reactions to food.

The Social Environment of Feeding

myeducationlab

Go to the Activities and Applications section in Chapter 11 of MyEducationLab to watch the video *Infant Feeding,* which you may recognize from Chapter 1. This time focus on health and safety issues.

It is almost impossible to separate the importance of nutrition from the importance of being held, touched, and talked to while being fed. In child care, as well as with parents, babies should always be held during bottle-feeding. Bottles should never be propped in a crib or carried around by the child. Teachers should also feed infants on demand, and a consistent adult, preferably the primary teacher, being the one to feed the child as often as possible. The primary teacher develops the ongoing relationship with the baby that allows them each to understand each other's cues and develop expectations about the rhythm and pattern of the feeding. The consistent adult partner will recognize signs of hunger before the child is so distressed that he is crying (APHA & AAP, 2002, Standards 4.013, 4.014). As older infants begin to eat solid foods, they may at first be spoon-fed in the teacher's arms as part of the meal, which is still primarily bottle-fed. However, as the child is able to sit, and the amount of solid food is increasing, the baby should be in a supported chair. The teacher should be talking with the child and creating a pleasant tone for the feeding and always communicating a positive attitude toward the food, with words such as, "Oh yummy. These peas are soooo good. Green beans are so good for you! You really enjoy this, don't you?" Older toddlers will begin to have meals and snacks in small groups, the adult sitting with them, promoting the social aspects of mealtime such as passing foods to one another and having conversations.

Teachers should never force children to eat nor prevent them eating. Food may not be used as a punishment and should not be used as a reward (APHA & AAP, 2002, Standard 4.039).

Safe Handling of Food and Utensils

As in all areas of health and safety, the recommendations for the safe handling of food, eating areas, and utensils are thoroughly described in the National Health and Safety Performance Standards. Some of the most important points include having seating arrangements for infants and toddlers during meals in which they can sit comfortably, with tables coming between stomach and midchest levels, on seats that allow their feet to rest on a firm surface while eating. This provides the most comfort and increases the developing independence of the child. Seats that attach to the side of a table leaving little feet hanging in midair would not meet this recommendation (APHA & AAP, 2002, Standard 4.028).

Utensils and eating surfaces must, of course, be kept clean and sanitized to prevent the spread of disease. Eating utensils should enable children to eat at their developmental level and should never have sharp edges that could cut the tissue inside a baby's mouth; plates and utensils must be free from chips; single-use materials such as paper plates or napkins must be discarded after one use; washable bibs, placemats, napkins, or tablecloths must be washed and sanitized after each use; imported dishware must be certified to be free from lead or other heavy metals; and all surfaces in contact with foods must be lead free. Table surfaces and even high chair trays appear to be much more likely to be contaminated by microorganisms than single-use or washed and sanitized dishes (APHA & AAP, 2002, Standard 4.029).

The food preparation areas must be kept separate from areas of the program used for eating, play, laundry, toileting, bathrooms, and any area where animals are permitted. Sinks used for food preparation may not be used for handwashing or any other purpose, and sinks used for handwashing and diapering may not be used for food preparation. Refrigeration must be able to keep foods at 40°F or lower, and freezers must maintain 0° or lower at all times. No staff with symptoms of illness should handle food. Food that was unfinished on individual plates or family-style serving bowls should be discarded. The storage of foods, washing of dishes, and transporting of meals purchased from off-site food services should follow the regulations of the National Health and Safety Performance Standards and the Child and Adult Care Food Program of the U.S. Department of Agriculture (APHA & AAP, 2002, Standard 4.7).

Policies Supporting Safe and Healthy Food Services

In a role similar to that of a health consultant to a program, each child care program should have a nutritional consultant. This nutritionist can help determine how to meet individual requests from families (e.g., vegetarian, kosher), how to train and plan for food-related emergencies such as allergic reactions or choking, and how to be sure that feeding plans for individual children are meeting their nutritional needs. A program might develop policies regarding the consistent feeding by one adult for bottle-fed infants or limit the number of children per adult during a small group meal. Program policies can articulate the training and monitoring of staff for safe food-handling practices.

An additional role for a nutrition consultant may be to provide nutrition education for families or help teachers plan nutritional learning activities for toddlers. The consultant may help educate staff and parents about programs that can support their ability to provide healthy foods such as the Child and Adult Care Food Program (CACFP) described in Box 11.4.

Box 11.4

The Child and Adult Care Food Program (CACFP)

CACFP is a federal program that provides healthy meals and snacks to children and adults receiving day care. It plays a vital role in improving the quality of day care and making it more affordable for many low-income families. CACFP reimburses participating centers and day care homes for their meal costs. It is administered at the federal level by the Food and Nutrition Service (FNS), an agency of the U.S. Department of Agriculture. The state education or health department administers CACFP, in most states. Independent centers and homes and sponsoring organizations enter into agreements with their state agencies to operate the program.

In order to participate in CACFP, homes and centers must agree to meet the nutritional meal and snack requirements of the program. In turn, the program receives reimbursements for each snack and meal served.

Child Care Centers. Public or private nonprofit child care centers, Head Start programs, and some for-profit centers that are licensed or approved to provide day care may serve meals and snacks to infants and children through CACFP.

Family Day Care Homes. CACFP provides reimbursement for meals and snacks served to small groups of children receiving nonresidential day care in licensed or approved private homes. A family or group day care home must sign an agreement with a sponsoring organization to participate in CACFP. The sponsoring organization organizes training, conducts monitoring, and helps with planning menus and filling out reimbursement forms.

To learn more about CACFP, contact your state agency. If you have questions about any of USDA's nutrition assistance programs, check the information on the other pages of the USDA FNS Web site.

Source: Child and Adult Care Food Program, http://www.fns.usda.gov/cnd/Care/CACFP/aboutcacfp.htm.

EVALUATING QUALITY IN CHILD CARE PROGRAMS

Given the aspects that contribute to quality already described in this chapter, it should be clear by now that assessing quality is anything but clear. When we walk into a child care program and find infants and toddlers quietly and intently engaged in their play and learning and looking to teachers for a moment of emotional connection, the teachers calm and interested in the children, we know we are looking at high quality. Understanding each child's experience is, of course, the most important way to assess quality, but it is very subjective. The evaluation tools available for infant-toddler programs use both structural and process variables as researchers develop increasingly sophisticated measures of quality.

There are several different reasons to assess the quality of care. Researchers are continuously trying to determine which elements of quality have most impact on the developmental outcomes of young children. Policy makers use that information to determine where to invest resources. Parents use quality indicators to help them choose the best care possible for their own child. Large public programs such as Early Head Start use program evaluation as a measure of accountability for the use of public funds. Measurement tools can be used by programs to assess their own quality and develop their own plans for improvement. Here are descriptions of some of the most frequently used measures.

Infant-Toddler Environmental Rating Scale (ITERS)

The ITERS–Revised (Harms, Cryer, & Clifford, 2006) is one of the most widely used measures of quality in the United States. It is part of a series of measures used for specific age groups or settings, including preschool, family child care, and school-age care. In its new revision, the ITERS–Revised consists of 39 items organized into seven subscales: space and furnishings, personal care routines, listening and talking, activities, interaction, program structure, and parents and staff. The observer has to observe materials or interactions taking place. Each item is measured on a 7-point scale ranging from inadequate to minimal to good to excellent. Each subset is scored and a global score is given. The information available from the measure can be very helpful for a program working on improving quality.

The ITERS–Revised is often used in research as a reliable, valid measure. Many states have adopted its use as one factor to provide higher child care reimbursement rates to programs that offer higher quality. The ITERS–Revised and its related scales are sometimes criticized as overemphasizing the structural variables and not being sensitive to the subtleties of responsive caregiving.

Observational Record of the Caregiving Environment (ORCE)

The ORCE (NICHD, 1996) was developed on the theoretical basis of the overriding importance of the child's earliest experiences with teachers on his well-being and development. The focus of this tool is on the actual interaction between the teacher and the child. Four 44-minute-long observations are done over the course of 2 days. At the end of each 44-minute period, the teachers are rated on individual items, from 1 point = "not at all characteristic" to 4 points = "highly characteristic." Higher scores describe a teacher who is sensitive, responsive, warm, positive, and cognitively stimulating and neither detached nor hostile. This measure can be used across settings and ages, and across types of teachers.

Teacher Interaction Scale

The Teacher Interaction Scale (Arnett, 1989) was one of the earliest attempts to evaluate the teacher's sensitivity during interactions. Two separate observers, in two separate 45-minute observation periods, use the 26-item scale to develop three scores: sensitivity (warm, attentive, engaged), harshness (critical, punitive), and detached (low levels of interest, supervision, interaction).

Program Review Instrument for Systems Monitoring (PRISM)

The Office of Head Start Monitoring Protocol (Head Start, 2008) is a very complex system for reviewing Head Start and Early Head Start programs. A federal program officer and a team of reviewers spend several days reviewing every aspect of the program's services and management systems. The questions, checklists, and observational tools in the PRISM all derive from the Head Start Program Performance Standards, the federal regulation that describes the requirements of virtually every aspect of a Head Start or Early Head Start program.

POLICIES, LAWS, AND SYSTEMS THAT SUPPORT QUALITY PROGRAMS

The Head Start Program Performance Standards (HSPPS) are a good example of how government uses regulations to influence quality. The HSPPS provide detailed descriptions of what is required of every aspect of the program; a system of technical assistance is available to help programs achieve the standards, and the programs are reviewed every 3 years against the full set of standards. Whenever public funds are used for programs, some set of regulations provides the limits within which those funds may be used. The Head Start Bureau, the Child Care Bureau, state and city governments—all have policies and regulations ranging from minimum standards of safety to standards of quality. Public money and private institutions also provide a wide network of programs to support and encourage quality. Although this is not a comprehensive list, it will give students of child development an idea of the wider system in which they will be working.

Child Care Development Fund (CCDF)

The federal government provides funding for child care through the Child Care Bureau in the Administration for Children and Families (ACF) within the U.S. Department of Health and Human Services (HHS). CCDF provides each state with funds to subsidize the cost of child care for families who are in work or education programs as they transition from welfare assistance. A portion of each state's CCDF funds is to be used for increasing quality, and a specific portion has been earmarked for infants and toddlers. States use their infant-toddler earmarked funds to make infant-toddler specific improvements in facilities, such as appropriate playgrounds or bathrooms. They support infant-toddler specific training for teachers and infant-toddler specialists in the resource and referral networks. Some states use these funds to raise public awareness of the importance of the early years and the impact of good or poor quality child care on later development. CCDF is used to promote quality in child care, but there is not sufficient funding or authority to ensure quality care from the federal government. The overall quality of a child care system depends on the licensing regulations and initiatives of the individual state.

Licensing

Every state requires programs providing child care to be licensed. The actual licensing requirements, and the range of settings that are exempt from licensing, vary widely from state to state. At the minimum, a state has minimal safety requirements for a setting and age requirements for teachers. Many states have detailed regulations determining group sizes, ratios, training requirements for staff, health and safety practices, and even plans for learning activities. Most states have specific licensing requirements for programs serving infants and toddlers. However, even the most minimal requirements are not always enforced because of the many programs that may be exempt from licensing or may be operating illegally without a license. The licensing regulations for each state are available on the Internet, either on the state government Web site or on the Web site of the National Resource Center for Health and Safety in Child Care (http://nrc.uchsc.edu/).

Each state has an office administrating the CCDF and child care licensing. These may not be the same offices, or even the same departments of state government. Nonetheless, each of these groups would like to be able to ensure safe and high-quality child care for every infant and toddler who requires out-of-home care. If it were possible, each state would set licensing requirements that ensure low ratios, small group sizes, highly trained staff, and strong health and safety policies at every program.

Unfortunately, high-quality child care is expensive, and states fear that by requiring expensive child care and highly trained workers, they would reduce the availability of care—as private owners and nonprofit organizations would be unable to meet the cost of providing child care on the basis of the tuition they can collect. The states themselves are struggling with terrible deficits and are unable, or unwilling, to commit precious funds to supporting child care when their public schools and colleges are struggling for survival.

Unable to ensure high-quality child care by legislation, states and national organizations are trying a number of other strategies to promote and inspire quality. States are developing quality rating systems wherein they rate the quality of particular programs, either as a way of informing consumers or as the basis of providing differential subsidy reimbursements. National child care organizations offer accreditation to programs as a statement of recognized quality. We examine these two strategies next.

Quality Rating Systems and Tiered Reimbursement

tiered quality systems
Graduated sets of criteria developed to rate the quality of early childhood programs.

Tiered quality systems are one way for states to inspire, recognize, and reward quality. As of a review conducted in June 2004 (NCCIC, 2004), 36 states have implemented a strategy of tiered quality ratings. In tiered reimbursements, states give higher subsidy payments to child care centers and homes that demonstrate quality beyond the requirements of licensing. These may include having a national accreditation, or may include a variety of factors such as group size, ratios, teacher training, compensation, family involvement, and ratings on standardized tools. Some states have only two tiers, licensed and above. Other states have more complex systems, often symbolized by a rating of 1 to 4 stars. Quality rating systems, sometimes called star rating systems, may be tied to higher reimbursement rates or they may be aimed primarily at getting consumers to demand higher quality. These systems are a sort of report card for programs. When they are most effectively used, programs are able to receive increased funds for better quality, but are also able to receive technical assistance and support to help them make improvements (NAFCC, 2009).

Accreditation

Many national early childhood organizations offer program accreditation as a way of promoting and recognizing high quality in child care. The two major national accreditation programs are from the National Association for the Education of Young Children (NAEYC, 2006b) for centers, and the National Association for Family Child Care (NAFCC, 2009) for home and family programs. The NAEYC has more than 8,000 accredited child care programs around the country serving more than 700,000 children and families. In 2006, the organization introduced a revision of its accreditation process and criteria (NAEYC, 2006a, 2006b). Both NAEYC and NAFCC require an in-depth self-study by the program. The self-study report is validated by a team of trained visitors to the program (or individual to a home). The validated self-study is then submitted to a national commission, judged to be in compliance, and granted accreditation for a limited number of years. In order to maintain accreditation, the program must submit yearly reports on progress and its responses to suggestions from the national organization. Accreditation carries considerable respect within the field of child development.

SUMMARY

The potential of child care to have either positive or negative effects on infants and toddlers depends entirely on the quality of the program involved.

- For infants and toddlers to experience warm, nurturing, ongoing relationships, child care programs need:
  - Low child-to-teacher ratios and small group sizes
  - Continuity of care—children staying with the same teacher over the course of years
  - Teachers who are warm, comfortable with intimacy, and enjoy children, as well as being well educated specifically in infant and toddler development, well compensated, and well supported in their work
  - Cultural and linguistic continuity with the home
  - Structure that meets the needs of the individual within the group
  - A comfortable, homelike environment with daily exposure to family-like routines as well as engaging learning experiences
- For infants and toddlers to be safe and healthy in child care, teachers must maintain good procedures for:
  - Sanitizing and preventing the spread of disease
  - Handwashing
  - Excluding children who are ill
  - Administering medication
  - Promoting safety and preventing injuries and accidents
  - Meeting the nutritional needs of infants and toddlers
  - Providing safe handling of food
- Quality in child care programs may be assessed with a variety of tools that examine the environment and the interactions.
- Quality is supported by structures at the federal government, the state government, and through national professional organizations offering accreditation.

myeducationlab

Go to MyEducationLab and complete the Building Teaching Skills and Dispositions exercise in Chapter 11.

Key Terms

process variables   structural variables   tiered quality systems

REFLECTIONS AND RESOURCES FOR THE READER

Reflections

1. If our greatest concern for quality, after the basics of health and safety, is the responsiveness of the teacher, why do we measure quality by the structural variables of group size and ratios?
2. Infant and toddler programs can be very busy places. What can a program do to ensure that care is always being taken with health, safety, and nutrition?

Observation and Application Opportunities

1. Visit an infant-toddler program and ask to review its health, safety, diapering, and food-handling policies. Do you see the policies as thorough enough to provide guidance to the staff? Is there a system for monitoring how the policies are implemented? Would you make any changes?
2. Contact a program in your community that has been accredited by the National Association for Family Child Care or the National Association for the Education of Young Children. Interview a staff member about the process of accreditation.
3. Contact a child care licensing agent in your community and interview him or her about the role of licensing in supporting quality.

Supplementary Articles and Books to Read

American Academy of Pediatrics Committee on Early Childhood, Adoption, and Dependent Care. (2005). Position paper on quality early education and child care from birth to kindergarten. *Pediatrics, 115*(1), 187–191. Electronic copy available at the Pediatrics Web site, http://pediatrics.aappublications.org/cgi/content/full/115/1/187

NAEYC. (2006). NAEYC accreditation. Assessment in the new NAEYC accreditation system. *Young Children, 61*(3), 60–62.

NAEYC. (2008). NAEYC accreditation. Program administrators on the NAEYC accreditation process. *Young Children, 63*(1), 56–57.

Interesting Links

myeducationlab

These and other web links are included in this chapter on MyEducationLab.

http://nrc.uchsc.edu/CFOC/
National Resource Center for Health and Safety in Child Care   This Web site includes the full text of *Caring for Our Children: National Health and Safety Performance Standards for Out-of-Home Child Care* (2nd ed.). It also has links to each state's licensing standards.

http://www.healthychildcare.org
Healthy Child Care America   The Web site for Healthy Child Care America, a joint project of the Child Care Bureau and the Maternal and Child Health Bureau, is a great source of information on healthy practices in child care.

http://www.naeyc.org/accreditation/next_era.asp#standards
National Association for the Education of Young Children   The NAEYC Web site has information on many interesting topics, but this link takes you to the new accreditation criteria for programs, providing background information on the reasons for the criteria as well.

Creating a Relationship-Based Curriculum

Hours in infancy have more power to shape us than months in middle age. The relative impact of time—time lost or time invested—is greatest early in life. Indeed, humanity was created in childhood. (Perry)

This chapter will discuss a framework for designing and evaluating curricula for infants and toddlers. In chapter 11, we began to investigate the importance of quality in early child care and education programs. In this chapter, we delve deeper to analyze what curriculum means to children, teachers, and families in an infant-toddler development and education center or a family child care home. The major elements of a child-centered, responsive, relationship-based curriculum for infants and toddlers will be described.

The curriculum roots are in Developmentally Appropriate Practice (age, individually, and culturally appropriate) (Copple & Bredecamp, 2009) and Division for Early Childhood's (DEC's) Recommended Practice (Sandall, Hemmeter, Smith, & McLean, 2004), both of which provide extensive guidelines for quality practice in early childhood programs.

The curriculum that we describe in this chapter and chapter 13 has as its philosophical foundation a focus on the importance of relationships and planning strategies that are responsive to individual children's needs, interests, and strengths (in collaboration with families). The philosophy of a child-centered, responsive curriculum is inherent in many published curricula and approaches for infants and toddlers, such as the the *Creative Curriculum for Infants, Toddlers, and Twos* (Dodge, Rudick, & Berke, 2006), the High/Scope approach to caring for infants and toddlers in group settings (Post & Hohmann, 2000), the Program for Infant/Toddler Caregivers (PITC, 2008), and the responsive approaches recommended by Gandini and Edwards (2001), Gonzalez-Mena and Eyer (2009), and Szanton (2001). A focus on relationships as the core of the curriculum is recommended by ZERO TO THREE in its book *Caring for Infants and Toddlers in Groups*, second edition (ZERO TO THREE, 2008)—a must-read for infant and toddler professionals working with young children in group settings.

The relationship-based approach discussed in this book fits well with most infant and toddler curricula and approaches and adds a planning process of *respect, reflect,* and *relate,* planning guides, and further detailed illumination of a relationship-based approach.

A responsive, relationship-based curriculum has as its primary focus the mental health of infants and toddlers (see chapter 1 for a definition of mental health). The curriculum is based on the perspective and needs of infants and toddlers and is focused on the responsive, caring, moment-to-moment and day-to-day experiences that lead to valuable, enduring relationships in each child's life—family–child, teacher–child, and peer–peer relationships. The moment-to-moment responsive interactions of the teachers with the children are the ingredients that together create nourishing relationships with them. Relationships are created over time, and they require a teacher's emotional commitment to each child's well-being as well as reciprocal emotional connections. In a program using a caring, responsive curriculum, the more enduring relationships—between the children and their families, the teachers and the children, and the teachers and families—provide the foundation for children to love and learn and experience joy.

A relationship-based curriculum for infants and toddlers considers everything that happens to them from the moment they are carried or walk into the child development and education program until they leave to go home. Teachers create the environment and then vary it as indicated by the changing developmental levels and interests of the infants and toddlers. The adult–child interactions are also responsive to the moment-to-moment, daily, and life needs of the children and families in the program. The teacher is empathic with children's joy and pleasure and responds to children's unhappiness and distress with tender care (Weil, 1993). Teachers are kind, caring, considerate, and compassionate with young children's and their families' feelings, needs, and learning goals and know how to develop an enriched environment that supports important relationships in children's lives. The curriculum is truly "day to day the relationship way."

Table 12.1 describes the eight components of curriculum planning that are considered in chapters 12, 13, and 14. Components 1 through 4 are discussed in this chapter and components 5 through 7 will be highlighted in chapter 13. Component 8 is covered in chapter 14.

Janelle, a family child care provider, enjoys reading to her group.

Table 12.1   Important components of a curriculum

1. *The Foundation—A Way of Thinking About Infants and Toddlers*

   What are the beliefs and assumptions about the nature of infants and toddlers?

   What are the needs of infants and toddlers?

   What is important for infants and toddlers to learn?

   How do infants and toddlers develop and learn?

2. *The Teachers' Roles in a Relationship-Based Program*

   What is the program's view of the nature of teacher–child interactions, the importance of teachers' emotional connections with the children, and the teachers' roles and responsibilities?

3. *Relationships with Families and Culturally Sensitive Care*

   How does the program view partnerships with families?

   How do program teachers respond to a child's and family's culture?

4. *Responsive, Relationship-Based Planning*

   How do teachers plan for each child and the group?

   How do teachers individualize the curriculum for each child (including children with disabilities)?

5. *Transitions and Routines—A Time for Relationships*

   What is the value placed on transitions, routines, rituals, and schedules?

6. *Responsive and Relationship-Based Environments and Choosing Materials for "Day to Day the Relationship Way"*

   How is the environment developed, created, and adapted to individual children and groups?

7. *Responsive Experiences and Opportunities*

   How are materials and experiences chosen and provided?

8. *A Relationship-Based Approach to Guidance*

   What is the philosophy and what are the strategies used to guide infants and toddlers?

Go to the Activities and Applications section in Chapter 12 of MyEducationLab to watch the video *Infant and Toddler Setting,* which you may recognize from Chapter 6. What is a curriculum for infants and toddlers?

COMPONENT 1: THE FOUNDATION—A WAY OF THINKING ABOUT INFANTS AND TODDLERS

Influencing factors for determining the foundation of the curriculum—a way of thinking about infants and toddlers—include teachers' beliefs and assumptions about the nature of children, children's emotional and social needs, *what* is important for children to learn, and *how* children develop and learn. Let's begin with the beliefs and assumptions about the nature of children.

What Are the Beliefs and Assumptions About the Nature of Infants and Toddlers?

A framework for an infant-toddler program is based on certain principles and beliefs regarding the nature of infants and toddlers. There are two questions regarding the nature of babies: Do infants and toddlers have human rights and responsibilities? Are they capable learners?

Most adults think that young children have rights—the right to be protected, to learn, to be loved and to love, and to be treated with respect. They have the right to belong and participate in their family, culture, and social life. The United Nations developed the Convention on the Rights of the Child in 1990:

> [The] Convention on the Rights of the Child is a universally agreed set of non-negotiable standards and obligations. It spells out the basic human rights that children everywhere—without discrimination—have: the right to survival; to develop to the fullest; to protection from harmful influences, abuse, and exploitation; and to participate fully in family, cultural, and social life. Every right spelled out in the Convention is inherent to the human dignity and harmonious development of every child. (UNICEF, 2009)

In addition to believing that children have rights, many adults also believe that infants and toddlers are capable learners—that they enter this world as active learners, discoverers, and problem solvers. When they are offered empathic care and an enriched environment they quickly construct their knowledge in interaction with caring adults, family members, and peers. Jerome Bruner (1996a) emphasizes this point: "The child is *not* merely ignorant or an empty vessel, but somebody able to reason, to make sense, both on her own and through discourse with others" (p. 57).

Adults' belief about the nature of children influences the attitudes that they have about their role in children's lives. If children are viewed as having rights and as being capable learners, then they are treated with respect for their "personhood" (Honig, 1993). In a relationship-based, responsive program adults trust that very young children need and want to belong to a social group, that they strive to develop well and to be healthy, and that they would like to and can master their environment if given the opportunity and responsive care. Adults trust that meeting infants' and toddlers' basic needs for protection and nurturance will result in children who are more likely to be competent, caring, and courageous.

What Are the Needs of Infants and Toddlers?

As discussed in previous chapters, infants and toddlers need strong, positive, emotional connections with their families, teachers, and peers in order to thrive. Children have a neurobiological expectation for nurturance (Shonkoff & Phillips, 2000). This means that children are biologically programmed to expect to be protected and cared for in loving ways—and if they are, then they are more likely to develop optimally. As highlighted in chapter 5, brain development occurs best when children receive tender care, when adults take the perspective of what it is like to be a baby and respond sensitively and perceptively to the children's needs. Babies need protection. They need to feel safe; they need adults whom they can count on to be emotionally and physically available to them. Ideally, there is one person who is "just crazy about him" (Bronfenbrenner, 1994), thinks he is precious, and knows him well—the funny way he wriggles his nose when he is hungry or the way he feels sad if the teacher looks sad.

All infants and toddlers need affection, compassion, gentle holding, and kind touch. They need responsive, sensitive interactions and interesting things to do. Most of all, infants and toddlers need adults who are willing to invest emotionally in their well-being—to have a healthy relationship with them, develop a loving bond, and have an emotional commitment.

How can the basic needs of babies be met by parents and teachers? As Gonzalez-Mena and Eyer (2001) have said, "infants and toddlers need attention to their physical and psychological needs" (p. 6). They state that one of the most important needs of an infant is the pacing of care—a thoughtful, unhurried, finely attuned dialog between the infant and teacher. Lally, Torres, and Phelps (1994) stress that settings for infants should offer "security, protection, and intimacy" (p. 2) to meet babies' needs.

We can see that infants and toddlers feel securely attached if:

- They can generally be comforted by the teacher and relax in the teacher's arms
- They can engage in long, mutually satisfying gazes and conversations of sounds and words with the teacher

- They show that they feel valued and loved by the teacher
- They are generally happy to see the teacher
- They can experience joy with the teacher
- They (mobile infants) move away from and explore the environment but hurry back if they sense danger or need a hug
- They (toddlers) can focus and engage with toys, materials, and the environment, but often need the teacher for assistance, nurturing, scaffolding, and guidance.

Some teachers may become concerned about becoming *too attached* to an infant or toddler in their care. Yet, as we learned in chapter 6, children who are securely attached to the important, special people in their lives at home are more resilient, more trusting, and more likely to develop positive relationships with others. As we might expect, infants and toddlers in child care or early intervention programs who are securely attached to their teachers are also more likely to be socially and emotionally competent (Howes, Phillips, et al., 1992) than children who experience insecure attachment with their teachers. Three criteria identify attachment figures other than the mother: (1) provision of physical and emotional care, (2) continuity or consistency in the child's life, and (3) emotional investment in the child (Shonkoff & Phillips, 2000).

> Securely attached children have a more balanced self-concept; more advanced memory processes; a more sophisticated grasp of emotion; a more positive understanding of friendship; and greater conscience development. (pp. 236–237)

Teachers must acknowledge that even when young children spend a significant amount of time in child development and education programs, the parents are the most influential adults in their lives (NICHD, 2002b), and teachers should do everything possible to support children's primary relationships with their families: It is critical that infants and toddlers have a secure relationship with their parents. At the same time, teachers should not underestimate the importance of their own relationship with the child. Children cannot thrive in the absence of secure relationships with both parents and teachers. Relationships are one of the most significant needs of infants and toddlers, influencing healthy growth and psychological well-being. Each child who experiences healthy relationships carries within him the parallel hope for the universe.

What Is Important for Infants and Toddlers to Learn?

> *Children's motivation toward mastery, self-regulation and social commerce and their reliance on relationships with trusted teachers for support and guidance [are] seen as central to program planning. (Gandini & Edwards)*

Gandini and Edwards (2001) emphasize that teachers should consider what children learn about themselves and what they learn about how to relate to others when creating the curriculum: The capacities described in detail in chapters 6 through 10 are summarized in Table 12.2.

> *How is the child viewed—what needs, competencies, desires, are determined by the adult to need nurturing or to be squashed? (Szanton)*

Szanton (2001) lists the following in answer to her question: readiness for change, flexibility with decisions, the ability to get along, competence with language, a belief that they can make a difference in their own lives and those around them, the ability to speak out, a use of words and logic instead of violence, a profound sense of the importance of equal opportunity and the dignity and rights of each individual, and the ability to be gifted parents. These are competencies that develop in children in a relationship-based program that emphasizes the attachment (emotional connections) between parents and children and between teachers and children.

Table 12.2   Areas of learning for infants and toddlers

1. Emotional Development

- Self-control (self-regulation) and expression of feelings: They develop the ability to modulate and control their own actions in age-appropriate ways—a sense of inner control. They learn to express feelings in socially acceptable ways.

- A sense of self and identity as a person of worth who deserves to be treated well: They develop an identity as a unique person, a sense of worth, and expect others to treat them kindly.

- Relatedness: They develop the ability and desire to engage with others based on the sense of being understood by and understanding others (this includes culture). They feel that they belong to a family, culture, and community. Children learn that relationships with others are satisfying and fun. They learn to feel secure and trust important adults to take care of them. Toddlers will show that they have the confidence and courage to go away from their special teachers and explore the room, but also know that they can come back to the protective arms of a teacher and "refuel emotionally" (Kaplan, 1978).

2. Social Development

- Children begin to balance their own needs with those of others in a group.

- As infants develop, they become generally affectionate, friendly, loving, and kind with others.

- They are motivated to be with peers and develop in their ability to play with peers in cooperative ways.

- During the second and third years of life, children are increasingly aware of the feelings of others, which leads to empathic responses to another in distress. They develop a sense of "I can care for others as well as myself."

- As they grow, they become better able to handle conflict with others.

3. Language Development

- Children have the wish and ability to exchange ideas, feelings, and concepts with others.

- The desire to communicate is related to a sense of trust in others, and of pleasure in engaging with others, including adults.

4. Cognitive Development

- Children are curious and sense that finding out about things is positive and leads to pleasure.

- They are intentional—they wish and have the capacity to have an impact, and act upon that with persistence.

- They sense that they are more likely than not to succeed at what they undertake, and that adults will be helpful.

- They sense that they can contribute and make decisions and truly believe "I am a capable and competent person."

- They become more proficient at using the tools of learning, and the concepts that they know increase each day.

5. Motor Development

- Children become increasing able to use their large and small muscles to accomplish what they attempt to do.

- They become more stable and can use their bodies effectively.

---

working sense of self
The child's ongoing development of a sense of self.

Lally (1995) discusses how teachers must focus on helping infants and toddlers develop a sense of identity as a person of worth—what he calls a **working sense of self**:

> Preschoolers have formed a somewhat well-developed "working sense of self," with likes and dislikes, attitudes, and inclinations. [In contrast] infants and toddlers are in the process of forming this preliminary sense of self. Part of what infants and toddlers get from teachers are perceptions of how people act at various times in various situations (seen as how the infant should behave), how people act toward them and others (seen as how they and others should be treated), and how emotions are expressed (seen as how they should feel). The infant uses these impressions and often incorporates them into the self she becomes. (p. 59)

In addition to learning about themselves and others, infants and toddlers are learning about how the world works. What is grass, how does applesauce taste, where do caterpillars go when they crawl away, how many blocks can fit in a basket, what are the properties of water, and what is a friend are among the important things that babies learn about the world. There is so much for infants and toddlers to learn in the first 3 years of life, and there are so many exciting opportunities for nurturing adults to help these children to enjoy being in and learning about the world.

How Do Children Develop and Learn?

In addition to the question of *what* is important for infants and toddlers to learn, there is the question of *how* they develop and learn. We know that only when a child is secure in his relationship with the important adults in his life is there freedom to be independent in play with toys and peers (Honig, 1993). The way infants and toddlers develop and learn can be summarized as follows:

A dandelion sparks Alex's interest.

1. Learning is integrated.
2. Learning is developmental.
3. Children learn through play.

Let's start with integrated learning.

Learning Is Integrated

> Marilee crawled across the carpet with great speed, making babbling noises to the cat. Her mother commented to her, "You are so fast!" Marilee picked up a colorful soft toy and turned it upside down, studying it carefully. She looked at her mother to see if she was still there sitting on the floor. Marilee smiled and crawled toward her mom.

As all children do in almost any experience, Marilee is developing in emotional, social, cognitive, language, and motor domains in one sequence of behavior. She develops emotionally and socially as she learns to trust her mother. She learns language as she practices babbling and hears her mother match words to her actions. As she studies the toy, her cognitive development is enhanced as she learns about how an object looks from another viewpoint. Her crawling is an important aspect of motor development. As she crawls toward her mother she is establishing an emotional bond with her as well as improving her motor skills. Marilee is growing in all domains, not just sequentially, but simultaneously. Her learning is integrated with all developmental domains in use and affecting each other: "In infants and toddlers, all domains of development are interrelated. Each is a thread in the same cloth; pull one, and the others follow" (Parlakian, 2003, p. 4).

Adults divide children's development into the different domains to help them observe and learn about children, but children are including and applying all of their skills together to accomplish their goals. Development in one domain also affects development in another domain.

Learning Is Developmental

A child care and education program looks different for infants (0 to 8 months of age) than it does for mobile infants (8 to 18 months) or for toddlers (18 to 36 months). Children of these different ages have distinct needs and learning goals that develop as they grow (Mangione, Lally, & Signer, 1990), although we also know that they exhibit a broad range of individual differences. If we

dance the
developmental
ladder
How adults can
respond to
children's differing
developmental
levels in all
domains.

listen, infants and toddlers tell us what they are experiencing and how we can respond to these changing needs. Teachers learn how to **dance the developmental ladder** (Honig, 2000).

The physical changes as children grow from infants to toddlers are easily seen. It is more difficult, however, to detect the changes in a child as he grows from a dependent baby to a more independent person—and the significance of this development can only be understood by caring, observant adults who provide for both the group and the unique individuals within the group.

Infancy: 0 to 8 months. Infants rely totally on parents and teachers to meet their emotional and social needs; to provide nurturing, sensitive care, calm and interesting environments; and to present opportunities for the infants to move and explore objects. Ideally, during the first 8 months of life, infants will become emotionally attached to their parent(s) as well as to primary teacher(s)—wanting to be with these special persons in their lives, receive comfort from them, and learn from them. The baby will turn to the sound of this person's voice, brighten when spoken to, and give a special smile just for the person(s) they are growing to love. The infant learns what to expect, how that person will treat her, and the tone of that person's voice. As early as several weeks of age, infants feel more comfortable when they are with their special person(s) and can become distressed when they are not. The most important thing that babies this age are learning is that they can trust adults to take care of them rather than having to defend and protect themselves most of the time. They need adults who can hold, rock, sing, and talk quietly to them, and who can play "follow the leader" by imitating the baby's eye-blinks, sounds, and facial movements and then waiting for baby to take a turn.

The environment must be tailored for infants. Infants need safe places to be on the floor to practice their "tummy" moves. They need quiet, calm places to sleep and places to sit (without being knocked over), to bang objects on the floor or together in their hands. As they approach 8 months of age, many of the infants are ready to pull themselves up to a standing position. This requires that there be space for an adult on the floor; the infant can then inch himself up the trustworthy adult's body to look her in the eye or collapse safely in her arms.

Mobile infants: 8 to 18 months. Mobile infants (8 to 18 months old) are on the move. They are often crawling, walking, and fitting their bodies into a variety of spaces.

Infants who are on the move need nurturing adults who provide the emotional and social base from which they explore their world. They are often dashing back or fussing when an emotional connection to a caring teacher is needed. The most important thing that mobile infants learn in your care is that they can "make things happen" with both people and objects. This is what Cawlfield (1992) calls **Velcro time** with language, when mobile infants stick like Velcro to the teachers' responsive words, finger-plays, and book reading as their language bursts forth. The environment also changes as mobile infants develop.

Velcro time
How mobile infants
stick like Velcro to
the teachers'
responsive words as
their language
bursts forth.

The environment requires open spaces and cozy corners to encourage both *interaction time* with teachers and peers and *alone time* to gather energy for the next adventure. For mobile infants, life is truly an adventure as they make exciting discoveries with toys and peers. Open-ended toys (with no correct product) encourage stacking, pulling, pushing, throwing, and filling. As mobile infants reach 18 months they are ready for fat crayons, art materials, large beads and string, and more challenging motor activities. Mobile infants thrive in a room or family child care home that has space to explore, interesting materials to investigate, peers to imitate, and caring adults who admire their blossoming skills.

Toddlers: 18 to 36 months. Toddlers need loving, understanding people in their lives who think they are very special with all of their new skills and antics. As stated by Lerner and Dombro (2000), "For babies, the world is a banquet to be gobbled up with eyes, ears, nose, mouth, and fingers" (p. 20). The light in a toddler's eyes when he discovers a bug, listens with his ears to the bathtub drain to hear where the water goes, or sees a kitten for the first time recharges an adult's sense of wonder and delight in learning about the world and in turn provides emotional energy for the child to continue learning. Experienced teachers even love when toddlers say "No" because they understand the emotional struggles of very young children who are so brave to stand up to a person more than twice their size. Living with toddlers requires that parents and teachers be ready for anything, as toddlers experiment with what happens when they poke a friend or when they continuously pull tissues out of a tissue box. It helps parents and teachers to remember that toddlers are learning with all of their senses and that their experimentation is their enthusiastic way of learning about their world.

Martina is learning through her play.

Toddlers are little scientists who are inventing, taking apart, creating, and exploring on their way to figuring out the ways of the world. They have to touch to learn. They can't just look at an object—they have to investigate it. They can't just watch—they have to manipulate objects. They are prob-lem solvers and it is the teachers' and parents' role to give them a physically and emotionally safe environment in which to explore and learn. It is also easier to be a teacher of toddlers when you understand that they are not purposely trying to frustrate you, but rather that they are experiencing important internal struggles on their way to becoming good decision makers and problem solvers.

Toddlers need materials to pound, squeeze, and cut (with safe scissors with rounded points). Puzzles with a variety of pieces and pictures are challenging and interesting for devel-oping muscles that will soon try to write. Pasting, painting, and coloring are messy but fun for toddlers, as they love to "make their mark" on the world. Longer and more complicated stories and songs (but not too complicated) delight toddlers, and they love to move their hands and carry objects while walking and running.

For all of these ages—infancy, mobile infants, and toddlers—play is the way to learn.

Children Learn Through Play

Many theorists and researchers strongly believe, based on their observations and the results of research, that children learn through play and active exploration of their environment (Bettelheim, 1987; Perry, 2001; Pratt, 1999). Bettelheim (1987) defines play as a child's activi-ties characterized by freedom from all but personally imposed rules (which are changed at will). Play is an opportunity for pure enjoyment and is also important for many other reasons.

Why is play so important? Perry (2001) discusses why play is vital for the developing child: "We learn best when we are having fun" (p. 24). Play enhances "verbalization, vocabu-lary, language, comprehension, attention span, imaginativeness, concentration, impulse con-trol, curiosity, more problem-solving strategies, cooperation, empathy, and group participation" (Smilansky & Shefatya, 1990, p. 220). Caruso (1988) states that "it is only through acting on the world using developmentally appropriate skills during exploratory play that infants build a meaningful understanding of the environment" (pp. 67–68). Howes and Phillipsen (1998) conclude from their research that complex play as a toddler predicts a child's prosocial behav-ior as a preschooler and less aggressive and less withdrawn behavior as a 9-year-old. It seems that as young children play they learn many cognitive and social skills that result in social com-petence later in their childhood. As described in Box 12.1, from the view of the child, play is definitely the way to learn.

What will infants and toddlers do when they are playing? This will vary according to a child's developmental level. Generally, they are trying to figure out how the world works. Infants will

myeducationlab)

Go to the Activities and Applications section in Chapter 12 of MyEducationLab to watch the video *Two-Year-Olds Playing with Toys— Part 2.* What are these toddlers learning as they play?

Box 12.1

Letter from a Toddler

For young children, play with others and by themselves is a way to learn. If toddlers could, they might describe what goes on in a good child care and education setting that encourages play in the following way:

Dear Teacher of Mine,

You looked a little tired and discouraged when the parents were coming to pick all of us up today. Then, when that one dad said, "Did they learn anything today or did they just play?" I thought you'd just about had it. I'm writing to cheer you up and tell you that I'm learning lots because you help us play.

Tonight at supper my big sister said that she learned "the nines table" in school today. I'm not sure what the "nines table" is but everyone seemed pleased and excited that she'd learned it.

I learned a lot today too. Unfortunately, I can't talk enough to describe what I learned about how the world works. I know that dumping out bins of toys, climbing, knocking over blocks, and squashing bananas on my feeding tray doesn't sound as mysterious as "the nines table" but I'm sure grateful that you know how important it all was.

Thank goodness you know I have to play to learn. For example, remember today how every time you'd kneel down and open up your arms, I'd run to you for a big hug? We were playing a game, of course, and we'd both laugh—but just the act of running was learning for me. Babies and toddlers learn through their big muscles, you know. When I ran into your arms it not only made me feel loved and happy, it gave me a chance to practice the movements of using my arms and legs together. I'm brand new at that. Running strengthens those muscles too. It was fun. I wanted to do it over and over. I'm glad you had time to play so that I could learn. Thank you.

And I'm glad you noticed today how much fun I had tapping with the xylophone hammer, remember? I tapped the xylophone for a while, then the table, then the floor and lots of other objects. I discovered so many different sounds—metallic, strong, soft. Oh, by the way, sorry about Robby's head. It sure scared me when he cried so loud. Thanks for finding all those boxes and pans for me to tap. I am beginning to understand so much more about the world now because you realized I was learning, not "just playing."

I heard you say, "Tappers need things to tap!" You must believe that "dumpers need things to dump" too, because you filled up that coffee can with clothespins over and over and let me dump it out as much as I wanted to. You must have realized that I wasn't trying to make a mess when I dumped out all the tubs of toys yesterday. I need to dump things out. I'm so curious about how something can be full one minute and empty the next—and that I can make it happen. Dumping things out makes me feel big. After lots of play at dumping, I'll want to try filling. It's really the very first step toward being able to put things away neatly—when I'm older.

Thanks to your helping me play, I'm learning that it's good to be curious, it's good to explore and learn and understand. I get the feeling you think my play is pretty valuable. My play is all my own idea, you know. You must think that my ideas are pretty valuable, too. Hey, that must mean you value *me*, too. I'm important, and what I learn is important—even if it isn't "the nines table."

Please don't be discouraged. You helped me play today. You gave me gifts of learning and self-worth that nobody can ever take away.

See you tomorrow!

A Toddler in Child Care (author unknown)

mouth, bang, shake, and pound on toys to learn about them. They will watch other children with great interest. They vocalize and responsive caregivers respond. Mobile infants will imitate each other during play, turn objects around, put objects in and take them out of containers, and pull and push objects to see out how they work. They engage in games such as peek-a-boo with their favorite caregivers, who they trust will not really disappear. Toddlers will try many strategies to learn—change strategies, adapt strategies, try another strategy, go away from the problem, come back eons later (2 minutes or 2 days) and try again with toys, materials, and people. Older toddlers will begin to pretend as their understanding of symbols progresses (for example, using a toy telephone as if it were a real telephone) and, as we learned in chapter 7 on social development, play becomes more reciprocal with peers. We can begin to appreciate how children work hard while playing when we see them move a large toy, position a block on top of a tower, or gain the attention of special adults and peers, not because they have to, but because they want to learn.

How to Encourage Play

> *Once we understand that toddlers learn by active involvement with people and by manipulating objects, it becomes clear that such activities as coloring books, worksheets, and models made of clay or other materials that children are expected to imitate are inappropriate. (Lally, Provence, Szanton, & Weissbourd)*

Infants and toddlers learn by active involvement. To support infants' and toddlers' active involvement and play, first provide long play times where they can make choices with comforting and challenging materials, persist at activities, explore, and even have conflicts with peers that provide a foundation for future social relationships. This builds a child's confidence, sense of competence, and motivation to learn. When infants are kept in car seats, swings, walkers, and other containers and not allowed to move freely, they can feel trapped and become inactive and passive. Rather than all toddlers doing the same thing at the same time—such as everyone going first to the puzzle table, then a circle time, then an art activity, then back to a large group story time—they need time to explore alone, with peers, and with their favorite adults. When young children are not allowed to make choices during play we have seen them become passive and sad. From the outside looking in, it may even seem that these toddlers are quiet and "well behaved," but a closer look at their faces tells us that they are not engaged in the activities—and when toddlers (or adults) aren't engaged and interested, they are not learning. Infants and toddlers need to move their bodies, explore sensory materials, manipulate toys, and experience the consequences of their decisions in order to learn. The program where children are provided a rich array of materials in a well-organized environment can, in fact, be noisy at times with the sounds of children learning through choice and initiation. Provide opportunities for children to explore materials on their own in their own way, with a favorite teacher close by for emotional support.

COMPONENT 2: THE INFANT-TODDLER PROFESSIONAL'S ROLE—CREATING A RELATIONSHIP-BASED PROGRAM

Developing a relationship-based program requires professionals who are special people who value emotional connections.

A Special Kind of Person

Because of the type of empathetic care—kind, concerned, and compassionate—that infants and toddlers need, the profession of teaching young children can be quite demanding emotionally and physically. It can also be very rewarding. It is satisfying for teachers to experience emotional connections and relationships with the children and families, as they must if they are to meet the social and emotional needs of babies. As a professional working with infants, toddlers, and their families you must be concerned and must invest yourself emotionally in the infants, toddlers, and families you will serve. At the same time, to do a good job, you must maintain an objective view of the needs of babies and families. Effective teachers, then, facilitate children's learning about themselves, others, and the world while meeting their needs through responsive interactions and relationships.

> *Your work is not merely what you do, but how you are as you do it. (Pawl & Dombro)*

Box 12.2

The Top Eight Responsibilities of an Infant-Toddler Teacher

Whether in an education and development center or family child care home, the responsibilities of an infant-toddler teacher include the following eight components:

Component 1: Develop the foundation for a relationship-based program.

Component 2: Structure the program to emphasize the importance of relationships—provide primary care and continuity of care to the children. Take care of children's physical needs—keep children safe and healthy. Provide responsive and reciprocal interactions—give/take, engage/break, negotiate, and cooperate. Care for the spirit of the child—meet the emotional and social needs of children.

Component 3: Build caring, responsive relationships with families, diverse cultures, and the community.

Component 4: Use a responsive planning process—day to day the relationship way. Facilitate individual child development.

Component 5: Create a flexible schedule with responsive routines.

Component 6: Set up the environment for routines, nurturing, playing, learning, and relationships.

Component 7: Provide toys, materials, and opportunities that are individually, culturally, and age appropriate.

Component 8: Use a relationship-based approach to guidance that involves family members and other staff.

Teaching infants and toddlers is an important profession. Teachers are helping build the character and identities of children through responsive interactions and relationships. An infant-toddler teacher is a person who nurtures, guides, and facilitates children's development in an emotional blanket of caring that warms the spirit of the child.

Box 12.2 highlights the roles of the infant-toddler professional in a program. Notice how these roles relate to the eight components of a curriculum. Teachers' relationships with other teachers, an encouraging administrative staff, and a supportive community are keys to teachers' successes with all of these roles. This topic will receive in-depth coverage in chapter 16. Let's begin here by discussing how teachers can develop a community of caring for infants, toddlers, and their families.

Creating a Relationship-Based Community

Communities are places where a group of people work and play together. Programs are communities where infants and toddlers and their teachers often spend many hours together. Carter and Curtis (1998, p. 71) recommend that programs for young children and the staff, who spend many hours at work, resemble a home more than an institution to reduce staff and children's stress and to develop a physical environment and structure to the day that "connects and nurtures people." The authors recommend the creation of an environment that includes interesting colors, a variety of textures and natural elements such as plants and rocks, cozy lighting, framed pictures of children and families, and inviting aromas.

Center programs are often housed in buildings that have separate rooms that look like classrooms. Because of this classroom arrangement, teachers and children are often isolated from each other. Greenman, Stonehouse, and Schweikert (2008) recommend using the term **homebases** rather than *classrooms* in center-based programs where "classrooms" are considered homes and there are common areas such as playgrounds where children and teachers from the different homes gather at times. Honig (2002b) recommend organizing children into **attachment groups**—small groups that emphasize continuity of care for children with their special teachers throughout their years in a center program. Whatever arrangement is chosen, babies need to feel safe, nurtured, and have a sense of belonging.

homebases
"Classrooms" in a center-based program for infants and toddlers.

attachment groups
Small groups that stay with a special teacher throughout the infant and toddler years in a program.

Adult-Child Interactions and Relationships in a Relationship-Based Program

Teachers Are Intentional

Infant and toddler teachers are deliberate in how they support children's development. Sometimes when a person who doesn't understand a responsive curriculum peeks into a child care and education home or center and sees babies playing or sitting on teachers' laps for a snuggle, the person may think that not much teacher planning occurs. Indeed, we know that teachers of young children carefully plan a responsive environment that meets the developmental needs of each child in the room. They also know how to *use the moment* to support children's development in emotional, social, language, cognitive, and motor development. They are purposeful in how they develop strong and positive relationships with families.

Teachers Follow Children's Lead for What They Need

Adults follow children's leads for what they need in both moment-to-moment adult–child interactions and in weekly planning for changes in adult–child interactions and the environment. In the moment-to-moment responsive interactions, the professional or parent observes the child, reads the child's cues, tries to determine what the child is thinking, and then responds by continuing to observe or by responding to the child in a way that encourages further action on the part of the child. A 1-year-old, for example, may cover an adult's foot with a blanket, the adult wiggles his foot under the blanket, and then the infant laughs and pulls the blanket off of the foot. The adult shares the delight of finding his own foot under the blanket. The infant covers the foot again as if to ask "Will the foot wiggle again?" It does! Again, the infant is delighted. This 1-year-old is not only sharing an emotionally gratifying moment with the adult, but he also is exploring cause-and-effect principles. He is learning how to learn and will likely explore different ways to make that foot move. At times, following children's lead may mean that the adult observes that the child is ready for the adult to initiate an opportunity for the child to use strategies to learn.

For example, after the adult offers a toy, rolls a ball to the child, or sits on the floor with a book, the adult then watches to see if the baby is interested in these opportunities. Does the baby begin to use strategies to pursue his own goal—starting to play with the toy, rolling the ball back to the adult, or showing delight in listening to the book? As Lerner and Dombro (2000) state so well, when the infant-toddler professional or parent sometimes leads and sometimes follows, the interactions feel like a satisfying dance to both the adult and the child:

> Learning and growing together is like dancing. Step by step, day by day, you and your child learn about each other and how your relationship works. Sometimes you lead, and sometimes you follow your child in the dance you create together. (p. 1)

Teachers Are Responsive to Children's Emotional Needs

Because children's emotional development is the foundation for children to love and learn, teachers think about the well-being of the child from the child's perspective and ask, "What's it like to be an infant or toddler in this program?" and "What can I, as the adult, do to support this baby emotionally?" Teachers' interactions must care for the spirit—the emotional health and vitality—of the baby by demonstrating a profound respect for each child's emotional experiences. When you are a teacher in a center or family child care home for infants and toddlers, always ask the question, "How would it feel to be an infant or toddler in this setting?" and then respond to help babies feel loved, safe, and competent.

Figure 12.1 includes examples of responsive care and education practices that focus on supporting the emotional capacities of infants and toddlers through recognizing cues of communication and responding in ways that are satisfying to the infant or child. Teachers are not only responding to infants and toddlers, but also watching and learning from the children about what those children like and how those children think. Many of these concepts were introduced in earlier chapters in this book, but we discuss them now as they apply to teacher–child interactions and relationships in a program setting. Let's examine how these responsive teacher and parent strategies support emotional development, the foundation for learning.

Keep children safe and healthy. The responsive care and education provider consistently protects children—keeps them safe and healthy.

1. Protect children and keep them safe and healthy.

2. Develop strong, positive, secure relationships with children.

3. Be attuned (read, reflect, and respond) emotionally and physically to children's cues and communication attempts, reflect on their meaning, and respond *as needed by child*.

4. Interact by following a child's lead in a way that is satisfying to the child—take balanced turns (reciprocal interactions) and match the pace of interactions with the child.

5. Be approachable, accessible, and available to children, both emotionally and physically.

6. Maintain a pleasant and positive emotional tone throughout the day.

7. Respond to children's distress and intense emotional outbursts and other displays of displeasure calmly and in a way that comforts them and helps them regulate themselves physically and emotionally.

8. Notice, identify, encourage, and show admiration for strengths, interests, and new skills in each and every child in the group.

9. Appreciate development and differences—help children feel appreciated for their uniqueness.

**holds and
enfolds**
Holding a baby and
surrounding that
child with a caring
and supportive
personal and
physical
environment.

Babies must feel protected and safe in order to love and learn. Sometimes we say the adult **holds and enfolds** the baby. Holding babies is, of course, a familiar idea. The concept of "enfolding" means to surround each child with a caring and supportive personal and physical environment. A teacher can reflect whether she uses any of the following strategies during the day:

- Holds a crying infant
- Puts her arm around a toddler who is sitting near to her
- Responds helpfully to an infant or toddler who becomes upset when another parent comes into the room

Develop strong, positive relationships with children. The responsive care and education teacher is kind, affectionate, warm, empathic, caring, and compassionate with children. The teacher helps each child feel safe, secure, lovable, loving, worthy of love, and cherished.

Babies must know that they can trust and count on the people who take care of them. Significant emotional connections and secure attachments are reflected in the happy eyes of infants and toddlers and their teachers. Babies demonstrate attachment by looking to special teachers when they are startled or afraid, by being comforted more easily by their special adults, and by looking happy to see their special teacher each day. Toddlers will show that they have the confidence to go away from their special teachers and explore the room, but also know that they can come back and be reassured of their teacher's attention. To support parent–child attachment, teachers can continually communicate with families about the children's day, while also asking and listening to parents concerning their children's interests, development, and unique personalities.

Babies need affection, kindness, and encouragement to flourish and to learn how to be affectionate and kind themselves. They need touch—people hugging, holding, and sitting near them—for healthy mental and social development. Infants and toddlers need adults who will hold them when they need to be held, are positive with them when they choose or need to be close, and are

Darron is thriving with a responsive teacher.

always kind to them. Teachers' frequent smiles result in young children's affectionate responses (Zanolli, Saudargas, & Twardosz, 1997). Without affection, children learn to be on the defensive, to protect themselves, to be on guard, and to generally distrust people. With affection, they learn that they are worthy of being loved.

Teachers show affection and warmth to children through smiles, gentle touches, and mutual gazes. Honig (2002c) and Lally and colleagues (1994), emphasize that teachers need to be intimate with babies and have a relationship of genuine caring and commitment to the child's well-being. Being intimate with a baby means that there is a warm, friendly relationship that includes an emotional connection of caring between an adult and child. *While adults in group care may not cherish each child, each child needs to be cherished by at least one adult in the group and all adults need to be warm and affectionate with all children.* A teacher can ask herself whether she does any of the following in a day:

- Uses frequent responsive, caring touch
- Uses kind words with children
- Shows affection for children
- Empathizes and shows compassion with children's feelings ("Ooh, that must hurt," or "I can tell you are feeling sad")

Be attuned to children's cues. The responsive care and education teacher is consistently attuned emotionally and physically to children's cues and communication attempts, reflects on their meaning, responds *as needed by the child,* and interprets children's cues and communication attempts.

Babies need teachers who are attuned to their obvious and subtle communication signaling and who notice and understand the intentions and feelings of the child. **Attuned** means that a teacher is sensitive to and understands what infants and toddlers are trying to communicate with facial expressions, sounds, gestures, or words. For example, the teacher might say "You want up" in response to a child's upraised arms, or say "It seems like you are feeling sad" to a baby with a sad expression on her face. When a caregiver is well attuned to a baby, she will mirror the baby's experience in observable ways. A teacher might reflect on whether she does any of the following during the day:

attuned
To be sensitive to and to understand what infants and toddlers are trying to communicate with facial expressions, sounds, gestures, or words.

- Shares a child's delight
- Asks children what they want or how they are feeling and helps them express feelings
- Focuses on what the baby is trying to communicate
- Actively listens with eyes and ears to the infant or toddler's facial expressions, gestures, body movements, sounds, and words

Magda Gerber, an early infancy expert, would say to a baby, "I don't know what you are trying to tell me, but I want to figure it out" (Mangione et al., 1990). She believes that when an adult responds to a baby's communication attempts, the baby gains a positive concept of self and others as communication partners. The children will learn to use words to express their thoughts and emotions rather than crying, yelling, or whining much of the time.

When adults cannot respond physically to a child, they can respond verbally. For example, while the teacher is changing one baby's diaper, he might respond in a reassuring voice to an infant who is crying, "I'm changing Jareem's diaper. I'll be there soon." A teacher might reflect on his own responses to children's communication and reflect on whether he uses any of the following strategies during the day:

- Looks for and reads both clear and subtle communication cues
- Uses words to identify feelings
- Responds *quickly* and *positively* to children's questions and other bids for attention

Follow the child's lead in your interactions. The responsive care and education provider interacts by following the child's lead in a way that is satisfying to the child, takes balanced turns (reciprocal interactions), and matches the pace of interactions with the child.

A reciprocal interaction is one in which there is a sense of give and take, of shared moments, and of joint attention. This important teacher skill not only promotes communication skills in young children but also meets their emotional need for "making things happen." If the infant coos, the teacher coos back. If the infant rolls the ball to the teacher, she rolls the ball back. The teacher may initiate the interaction by picking up a book and offering it to the toddler. The toddler then takes the book, sits down beside the teacher, and holds up the book to be read.

These are examples of balanced, reciprocal turn taking. While all interactions may not be quite this even, taking balanced turns promotes a child's sense of confidence and skills as an interactive partner. Reciprocity helps a child feel some control over what happens to him or her—which is important if the child is to have motivation to learn. This sense of control and efficacy helps infants and toddlers become more engaged in an activity (Lussier, 1994) and tolerate small frustrations.

A teacher might watch for moments like these to reflect on her abilities to follow the infant or toddler's lead and promote reciprocity:

- Being sensitive to a baby's cues in interaction
- Taking balanced turns in play, eating, and communicating
- Waiting to approach a young child without interrupting or disrupting his activity (noticing that Henry is concentrating on stacking blocks, so waiting a few minutes to change the toddler's diaper)
- Approaching children from within their visual range, rather than swooping them up from behind (leaning down or getting on the floor with the child and telling him what is happening next: "After you finish playing with your toy, I'm going to change your diaper.")
- Asking the child what he wants, how he is feeling, and/or what he would like to do next, either with gestures or verbally (rather than *assuming* that the child wants to be picked up, asking the child and then waiting for the child to respond with a look, a gesture, or words)

Be available, both emotionally and physically. The responsive care and education provider is consistently approachable, accessible, and available both emotionally and physically to children.

Infants and toddlers develop a sense of security when an adult is emotionally and physically available to them. Reciprocal interactions are more likely to occur when a teacher is physically on the child's level; infants and toddlers learn to maintain focus and attention when emotionally available adults engage them in longer turn-taking exchanges through games such as peek-a-boo or through conversational interactions. If infants and toddlers approach an adult and are rejected (often because teachers mistakenly don't want the children to become *too* dependent on them or attached to them) infants and toddlers may actually become *more* dependent and clingy because they are not feeling safe and secure (Sears & Sears, 2001).

A teacher might use these strategies to ensure her emotional and physical availability to children:

- Spends time with children by sitting on the floor with them—allows them to come close, to move away, and then come back to sit in or near her lap at their discretion
- Spends one-on-one time with each child each day
- Limits talking time with other adults so that infants and toddlers feel her emotional presence
- Sits on the infant or toddler's physical level to encourage eye contact and touch

Maintain a pleasant emotional tone. The responsive care and education provider consistently maintains a pleasant and positive emotional tone throughout the day.

"When adult voice tones are hurried, sharp, critical, or upset, babies pick up the emotional tone of any adult worry. They may cry, become distracted from play, and show tension in body and facial muscles. The calmer your voice tones, the more peaceful your classroom will be" (Honig, 2003b). Infants and toddlers pay considerable attention to the moods and emotions of the adults who care for them. Teachers have an impact on each child in their program all of the time, not only when they are in direct interactions. The teachers need to provide a sense of calm, comfort, and joy as they encourage the children to approach life with a sense of hope and optimism.

The teacher creates a positive atmosphere in the room or family child care home when she uses these strategies:

- Finds ways to reduce her own stress
- Creates a peaceful environment by playing soft music and making the room beautiful
- Remains calm and reassuring throughout the routines of the day

Respond to children's distress in a calm, comforting way. The responsive care and education provider consistently responds to children's distress and intense emotional outbursts and other displays of displeasure calmly and in a way that comforts children. The teacher tries a variety of strategies to comfort children and helps infants and toddlers regulate and express a range of emotions in socially and culturally acceptable ways. The teacher reduces stress and distress in the room or child care home.

Maintaining a sense of calm in an infant-toddler program may be a challenge when children express their feelings intensely. Teachers can encourage children to express feelings in appropriate ways. Even infants need to hear comments such as "You seem tired" or "You don't like it when I have to change your poopy diaper. I'll hurry so I can rock you and make you feel better." When parents and teachers encourage infants and toddlers to express feelings, there are fewer tantrums because they feel heard and acknowledged, and over time they learn to *use their words*. Dr. Honig often acknowledged the feelings of a friend's toddler, Dana, who could then say, "Me so mad and me so sad" when her mother said good-bye to her at her child care center (Honig, personal communication, January 6, 2005).

Teachers might try these strategies for supporting self-regulation in moments of distress:

- Being willing to comfort a child to help her regulate her behavior
- Trying different strategies with individual children to calm and be calming
- Responding to initiations from a child for comfort (an infant may crawl over to you and want you to hold him for a minute; a toddler may want you to put a Band-Aid on a boo-boo)
- Responding to emotional outbursts and other displays of displeasure calmly and with a kind, understanding voice; trying to soothe the child, staying close rather than abandoning the child emotionally; saying things like (choose words appropriate to the age and experience of the child) "You seem angry," "You feel like stomping your feet," "You wanted the toy," "You can tell me what's wrong—I'd like to help you," or "Do you need a hug?"

Encourage the developing skills in every child. The responsive care and education provider consistently notices, identifies, encourages, and admires the strength, interests, and new skills in each child in the group.

Young children gain a sense of self-worth when they are noticed in positive and caring ways. Young children thrive when adults share "joy and true delight" (Honig, 2002c) in their efforts and accomplishments. Say things like "You jumped up" or "You picked up the blue toy" rather than just giving praise, such as "Good" or "That's nice." Specific encouragement gives children more information than vague, general praise and encourages their sense of intentionality.

Teachers might use these strategies to encourage and show admiration for the infants and toddlers in their care:

- Affirming the worth of each child by noticing and identifying the strengths of each child; saying things like "You are such a helpful person" or "You can make people smile"
- Being specific and avoiding phrases such as "good," "nice," "wonderful," and "cute" that have a different meaning to each person
- Showing admiration for new skills such as climbing, walking, jumping, talking, and helping
- Identifying at least five strengths of *each child* and talking about them often

Appreciate developmental differences. The responsive care and education teacher consistently appreciates children's developmental stages and differences and helps each child feel appreciated for his or her uniqueness.

Just as adults appreciate when others accept them for who they are, infants and toddlers develop a sense of identity as a unique person with special skills and attributes. A sound background in child development helps the teacher accept children's behavior that is developmentally appropriate—including thumb sucking, spilling food (because the wrist movement isn't fully developed), falling into another toddler, or saying "No" as often as possible when they start to develop autonomy and want to do things by themselves.

Teachers can demonstrate their understanding of child development and individual development by using these strategies:

- Showing approval for children attempting and mastering new skills without being critical or scolding
- Helping children enter play if they need the support
- Staying with children in new situations until they feel comfortable
- Checking in frequently with quiet children and providing active children with opportunities to use their energy
- Helping children negotiate challenges when they need help
- Accepting developmental stages (sucking thumb, needing blanket, trying to use spoon but spilling)

Teachers Imitate the Child in an Interaction

> When an adult imitates a child, the child, in turn, is stimulated to imitate the adult by increasing his output in the task at hand. (Forman & Kuschner)

Imitating children not only helps the adult tune into their developmental level, but also stimulates children to continue their play and discoveries. An infant will bat at a musical toy and it will make a jingly sound. The adult bats at the toy and looks at the infant. The infant is likely to bat the toy again and may bat it in a different way. She will be discovering that the different ways to bat the toy result in different sounds. She is exploring cause and effect and is more motivated to continue because of a partner in the exploration. Providing a model for the children to imitate is another effective teacher strategy.

Teachers Scaffold Learning in All Domains of Development

Teachers and other adults, as well as peers, can support children's learning through *scaffolding* (as discussed in chapter 3, under Vygotsky's theory). Just as a scaffold holds a painter to keep the painter from falling, a teacher figuratively holds the infant or toddler while the child learns. Rather than painting *for* the painter, the scaffold helps make it possible for the *painter* to paint—to figure out *how* best to paint. Scaffolding a young child's learning in all developmental domains is similar. For example, if a toddler is challenged while trying to put together a three-piece puzzle, the teacher could do one of several things to scaffold the child's goal of mastering the puzzle. Toddlers often have a theory that pushing hard on the pieces will make them "work" in the puzzle. Rather than tell the toddler that pushing doesn't work, it is important to provide teacher support while the toddler experiments. The teacher could hold the frame of the puzzle so the toddler could "push" the pieces in to see how they fit. The teacher could suggest that they take out one piece of puzzle at a time and look carefully at each piece. This helps the toddler see the colors or pictures on the puzzle pieces and then the toddler can more easily put the pieces back in the puzzle frame in the right places. If the toddler is getting frustrated, a teacher might suggest that the toddler turn the piece slightly so that it will fit, thus helping the child *learn a strategy* for how to put puzzles together.

Or, to scaffold for the future, a teacher might add several two-piece puzzles to the environment or three-piece puzzles with handles on each piece to support the toddler when he experiments with strategies for putting a puzzle together. The teacher is providing a supportive personal and physical environment to help the child experiment and learn *different* strategies to achieve his goals. While completion of a task provides satisfaction to the child, the most important goal is not that the toddler completes the puzzle, but rather that the toddler learns different *strategies* for how to put a puzzle together.

The secret to scaffolding is to support children's thinking about *how* to use a tool for learning—initiating to a peer, learning how to express emotions, building, dumping, filling, or asking—and to take the next step in development. Another aspect of scaffolding is to provide the materials to support children's learning. When a teacher observes that a toddler is trying to learn how to jump off a short platform, she can provide a mat on the floor. An environmental prop often is just the thing to encourage a tentative child to try something new.

One of the most important ways to scaffold young children is to develop an emotional climate for exploration. Show an interest in what a child is trying to learn. Your smiles and attention will encourage him to continue his "work." Listening demonstrates that you value what the child has to say. Holding the hand of a child learning to jump or a toddler learning to climb (when they want you to) scaffolds a next step in development. Do not worry that you will make the child dependent on you—a child who is motivated to learn won't always want your hand. For now, your hand provides the emotional and physical support the child needs to have the courage to try.

COMPONENT 3: RELATIONSHIPS WITH FAMILIES AND CULTURALLY SENSITIVE CARE

Considerations for families and culture were covered in chapter 2. Here we discuss very specific strategies that teachers and other infant and toddler professionals can use to create relationships with families in the context of a child development and education program.

Strategies for Developing Relationships with Families

Teachers' relationships with families and the community weave a network of support for infants and toddlers that provides for their well-being. Positive relationships and interactions with families begin at the first telephone call or visit of the family to the child care center. An intake form is usually completed with a program director or family child care provider and parent together. Not only is crucial information collected from the family that supports the child's development, but budding relationships are formed that provide a firm foundation for all future interactions with the family. Information is exchanged—teachers provide information

A family bulletin board includes pictures of the families in the program.

about the program and parents provide information on how to best meet the child's needs. Table 12.3 highlights some strategies for developing a family-centered program: one that recognizes and respects the child's need for a strong, positive relationship with his family and that provides as much consistency as possible for the child across the two settings.

Strategies for Developing Relationships with Families from Diverse Cultures

Each family has a culture. As *culture* pertains to child-rearing practices, it is a set of beliefs about how children should be viewed and the role that parents and teachers should play in a child's life (Copple, 2003). Teachers will have their own cultures as well. Child care providers, Early Head Start teachers, or family child care home providers may agree or disagree with parents about how to care for a child. Areas of agreement or difference may include when children should start feeding themselves, when and how children should learn to use the toilet, what types of food children should eat and when, to what degree children should be kept clean, or whether a baby should be placed on the floor (or on a blanket or mat). These varying convictions about children's behavior are supported by conscious or unconscious beliefs about the meaning of what happens, for example, when babies start feeding themselves (Barrera, Corso & Macpherson, 2003; Gonzalez-Mena, 2008). For *many* families, the child's ability to feed himself means that he is no longer as dependent on the parent. For *some* families, this is a good thing and means that the child is on the road to independence, a valued trait in those families. Other families might believe that children need to be dependent longer in order to develop strong family bonds, so it is not a positive thing if a child is feeding himself with his hands or a spoon at 1 year of age. For some families, food should not be wasted, so the parents feel strongly that they must spoon-feed their 1-year-olds rather than let them pick up food from a high chair tray and, more than likely, drop some precious food on the floor as well as smear it all over their faces. How can early care and education teachers be responsive to parents' wishes and cultures?

With healthy dialog, teachers and families can negotiate an agreed-upon practice in the child care and education program. And, as always, a *relationship of mutual respect*—of asking and listening—can be developed between parents and teachers in regard to the most important issues about child rearing. Gonzalez-Mena (2001) states wisely that "no matter what culture a person comes from, a goal should be to develop a person-to-person relationship. Treating people with respect solves many cross-cultural problems" (p. 16).

Whereas the items in Table 12.4 are important, it is the *relationships* between teachers and families that are most important. Developing healthy relationships with families involves listening *to* them and dialoging *with* them on key issues of potential conflict. Gonzalez-Mena (2001) recommends that teachers dialog with families rather than trying to convince them that the teacher is right. Arguing involves trying to win somebody over to your side by persuading them, she says, while in dialoging everyone tries to understand the other's perspective. She summarizes the difference between arguments versus dialoging as follows:

- The object of an argument is to win; the object of a dialog is to gather information.
- The arguer tells; the dialoger asks.
- The arguer tries to persuade; the dialoger tries to learn.
- The arguer tries to convince; the dialoger tries to discover.
- The arguer sees two opposing views and considers the valid or best one; the dialoger is willing to understand multiple viewpoints. (2001, p. 4)

Table 12.3 Characteristics of a family-centered program

1. *Support the relationship between each child and his family.*
   - Display photographs of each child's family around the room and place them where children can easily see them. They may be laminated and held to the wall with Velcro, so that an infant or toddler can take the picture of his family and carry it around. Or, the children's family photos could be displayed on a large poster board with a piece of fabric over each picture, so that mobile infants and toddlers can play peek-a-boo with their own and others' family pictures.
   - Be sure books or photograph albums with pictures of the children and their families are available to the children.
   - Ask family members to make tape recordings, telling a story or singing a song.

2. *Make family members feel welcome in the program through your own welcoming attitude and through a friendly classroom environment.*
   - Institute an open-door policy for families. They can be with their children at all times of the day and for as long as they like, visiting and interacting with the children.
   - Have a family-friendly bulletin board that describes opportunities for families to visit and volunteer and that includes notices and announcements.
   - Provide a private area for family members who want to give their child a bottle or breast-feed their babies or spend some moments alone with their children.
   - Have a "family information" space (filing box or cabinet, for example) with information on resources, discipline, reading to children, etc., where parents can add to it or help themselves to articles, pamphlets, and brochures that build family–child relationships.

3. *Involve families in the program. While certain strategies will fit one type of program more than another, as well as one type of family more than another, the important factor is creating a feeling of partnership between the program and the child's family.*
   - Survey families concerning the different ways that they would like to be involved.
   - Include families in policy decisions by inviting families to serve on a board of directors or policy council for the program.
   - Plan social events, with family input, that include the whole family.
   - Invite parents into the program to take pictures of children or record language samples that can then, for example, be made into a display of children's interests and learning.
   - Develop a sense of community by including parents in the planning and writing of a monthly newsletter that includes interesting information about the program, monthly events, children, and families.
   - Involve parents in fund-raising activities.
   - Provide opportunities for family members to help at home by making homemade toys (sock puppets, "feely boxes," beanbags, lotto games) for the program.
   - Provide opportunities and information about resources for family support—for example, learning a second language, divorce support groups, teenage parenting, and learning about Medicaid and Medicare.

4. *Develop a system for daily exchange of information between families and child care staff.*
   - Create a friendly place inside the room or family child care home, where information concerning a child's needs for the day can be written by a family member and shared with the teacher.
   - Create a friendly place inside the room or family child care home, where information about each child's day is kept so that families can easily pick up the information and talk to teachers about how the day went.
   - Create a friendly "Conversation Corner" somewhere in the center or family child care home so that teachers and families can have a private place to talk.

5. *Be sure families have ample opportunity to continually express preferences, beliefs, values, and concerns regarding the practices of the child care and education center (for example, routines, feeding, holding, naps, play, holidays, and language). Be sure the teachers are responsive to families' requests.*
   - Develop a process for communicating with parents who speak a different language from the teachers. If necessary, obtain a translator to assist in communication with children and/or families.
   - On a regular basis, ask parents to share information indicating their own and their child's needs, interests, developmental history, and any other relevant information that will help make the program more responsive to the child's individual needs.

Table 12.4   Providing culturally responsive care

Families

- Always take time to talk to families about their beliefs about child rearing.
- Include questions about routines (separation, feeding, diapering, sleeping) and time for the teacher and family to dialog about routines when the child enters the program and again frequently throughout the year.
- Invite families to share a day in play at your education and development center or family child care home.
- Invite families to help redecorate the room; discuss the important aspects of a diversity-rich and stereotype-free environment.

Language

- Use important words from the infants' and toddlers' home languages whenever possible.
- Ask the families for words of endearment in the home language and use them with children.

Eating and Feeding

- Encourage families to let you know what their children like to eat.
- Encourage families to let you know how and when their children like to eat.

Toys

- Ask families what the child's favorite toy is and try to provide it.
- Select toys and dolls that represent different cultures (and not just the cultures represented in the classroom).

Books

- Select books that demonstrate a variety of cultures in positive roles.
- Select books that show women and men in a variety of roles.

Songs

- Ask families to share their favorite cultural songs, CDs, and other music.
- Ask a family member to come in and sing with the infants and toddlers as they play.
- Play and sing a variety of music from a variety of cultures including your own.

Posters, Pictures, and Wall Hangings

- Display pictures of children's families (including pets), laminated and adhered to the wall with Velcro, at the child's level. Allow a child to pull off a picture and carry it around.
- Provide small pillows with a picture of the family tucked inside a pocket. Let infants and toddlers carry them around.
- Display posters of a variety of cultures.
- Display quilts, cloths, paintings, and wall hangings from a variety of cultures (always ask your licensure person what is safe).

Dramatic Play

- Include clothing, shoes, and accessories from a variety of cultures.
- For toddlers, include clothing, hats, shoes, tools, and other items from different types of jobs and roles in the community.

When teachers and parents take time to dialog, then issues about feeding, schedules, whether the child should wear pull-ups or pants while learning to use the toilet, and what the infant or toddler could be learning become opportunities to build relationships. These relationships are built on trust that the other will listen, try to understand, and problem solve to find the best solution at that moment in time.

Teachers must be able to self-reflect about their own cultural values and how those are represented in their behavior. Something as simple as whether a teacher sits on the floor with a child illustrates that teacher's cultural values regarding the role of children.

> *The very act of sitting down on the same level with the crawling baby or toddling child is symbolic of a more equal relationship between the adult and child. It levels the playing field. Whether an adult is sitting with feet spread apart and rolling a ball back and forth with a toddler or watching what the child is playing with and talking about it with her, that adult is giving the message, "You are as important as I am. Your interests are my interests." (Szanton)*

To become more culturally self-aware teachers can:

1. Engage in conversations with other teachers and families about cultural issues
2. Read books such as *Skilled Dialogs* by Barrera, Corso and Macpherson (2003)
3. Engage in discussions with professionals and parents from diverse cultures to learn their points of view on child rearing and education issues
4. Attend conferences or sessions at conferences about diversity
5. Keep a private journal of thoughts about cultural issues and reflect on beliefs and bias

Providing culturally responsive care is a skill that teachers can learn. Table 12.4 provides some ideas for how to honor children's and families' cultures in a child care and education program.

COMPONENT 4: RESPONSIVE, RELATIONSHIP-BASED PLANNING

> *Curriculum planning is a continuous circle of energy that flows from the children through perceptive teachers and returns to the children with the power to motivate, recharge, and inspire them. (Wittmer)*

At the heart of a responsive curriculum is the ability of the teacher to astutely observe children, perceptively document their learning, and use the information for planning supportive environments and interactions with children. In a responsive, relationship-based curriculum the moment-to-moment, day-to-day, and weekly needs and interests of the *children and their families* guide teachers' planning process. The teacher does not start planning the curriculum with a list of activities, but rather starts planning for the day or week by *observing* what the children are doing and learning in all developmental domains. (See the Developmental Trends and Responsive Interactions charts at the end of chapters 6 through 10.)

> *We believe infant care should be based on relationship planning—not lesson planning—and should emphasize child-directed learning over adult-directed learning. Rather than detailing specific lessons for caregivers to conduct with infants, the PITC approach shows caregivers ways of helping infants learn the lessons that every infant comes into the world eager to learn. (Lally)*

The teacher observes, documents her observations, and uses the information to plan interactions and changes in the environment and experiences provided for the child that support the child's learning. For example, the teacher observes and documents that Hiawanda is starting to walk. She also considers that starting to walk influences Hiawanda's development in the social, emotional, and cognitive domains because he will be seeing and experiencing the world in new ways. Based on her *respect* for Hiawanda's internal motivation to walk, her *reflections* on how his efforts influence his development in all domains, the teacher *relates* (communicates, shares feelings, observes with interest) to the child. She responds by frequently sitting on the floor to provide a secure base for Hiawanda's walking adventures. She also responds by examining the environment to ensure that he has space to take his first steps. The teacher has thought about changes in the environment and her responsive interactions based on her observations of Hiawanda's goals that

Box 12.3

What Teachers Can Do to Be Responsive

Respect: Value what the child is trying to do and how the child feels. Admire the child's feelings, goals, and how the child is learning.

Reflect: Observe, think, and feel. How is the child showing you how he or she feels? What are the child's goals? What is the child learning? How is the child trying to learn it? What does the child need?

Relate: Be responsive by observing with interest, interacting, communicating, sharing feelings, or changing the physical environment.

---

he is setting for himself. She has used the 3 R approach to curriculum planning—respect, reflect, and relate. Box 12.3 defines these terms.

The process begins with *respect*. At the beginning of the chapter, we discussed the concept of respect for the personhood of infants and toddlers. As Emde (2001) puts it: "Each child is valued as a child, not just for what adults want the child to become" (p. viii). Children will pursue their goals in an emotionally supportive and physically interesting environment. A child who is figuring out how to stack blocks will often work on it for a long period of time. A child who is learning to walk will practice until she "gets it right" (p. xi). No one has to say, "Now it is time to practice your walking—start walking." A teacher who *respects* the internal motivation of young children to work at goals that they set for themselves and their ability to "figure things out" will then be intentional about *reflecting* on the children's goals, feelings, what the child is learning, how the child is learning it, and what the child is "telling" you he needs. Reflecting includes both observing and thinking about what you are observing. It also is a *self-reflective* process because you consider how you (the adult) are feeling and what you are thinking. Often, reflection takes place in a split second when you have to respond to a screaming baby, but may also take place over time as you ponder the meaning of observations and interactions with the child. *Relating* includes the actions that you take after you respect and reflect. Relating includes being responsive by continuing to observe with interest, interacting, communicating, sharing feelings, or changing the physical environment for and with the child with a focus on healthy relationships—again, both in the moment and over time.

We have provided individual and group planning forms that teachers can use to plan a curriculum that is responsive to children's individual and group needs and interests. See Appendix D for full-page ready-to-use planning forms. The individual planning forms are completed by the teacher(s) responsible for planning for a few specific children. If the primary group system is used, then each teacher is responsible for completing guides on a small number of children each week. Infant and toddler professionals who conduct home visits in a family support or early intervention program could complete these forms with the family. Teachers should try to complete two individual guides a week to document the child's feelings, discoveries, and explorations.

There are two versions of individual planning forms. Version 1 (Box 12.4) and Version 2 (Box 12.5) allow for documenting children's interests with photos or anecdotal records. Both guides ask you to think about what the child is doing as well as what the child may be feeling (inference) and also what the child is learning (concepts and developmental milestones). Under the Respect and Reflect sections, Version 1 asks teachers to write what the child is learning in each developmental domain, while Version 2 asks teachers to write a response that integrates learning. For a brief list of possible concepts that the child might be exploring, see Table 12.5. Teachers and parents can add more to the list as they observe children. They could also use an observation system such as the OUNCE (Meisels et al., 2003) to describe behaviors, knowledge, and developmental steps (such as beginning to use two words together or beginning to crawl). They could use additional observation systems to describe the goals, strategies, and theories of each child. Teachers in center programs or family child care homes can ask the family members to share information about what they have observed at home.

On the individual planning guides, the teachers and/or parents use the observation to plan for the changes that could be made in regard to responsive interactions (teacher–child, parent–child, peer–peer, and teacher–family), including routines, and a responsive environment

Box 12.4

Individual Child Planning Guide: Version 1

Child's Name: <u>Sophie</u>

Plans for Week of (Date): <u>March 9–13, 2009</u>

Person(s) Completing the Guide: <u>Matt and Carla</u>

Respect: Child's Emotions, Effort, Goals, Learning, and Relationships

Write an observation or use a photograph or other documentation here—date all notes: 3/9/09

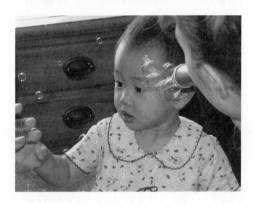

Respect and Reflect	Relate

What am I doing?
- I am trying to catch (or pop) a bubble that is between the teacher's fingers. I am focusing intently on the bubble. I am imitating the teacher saying, "Pop."

How am I feeling?
- I am feeling safe to focus on the bubbles with my teachers. I feel confident that I can pop the bubble.

What am I learning?

Emotional
- I am learning to trust that my teachers will have fun with me. I am gaining self-confidence in my ability to make things happen. I am learning how to focus (self-regulation).

Social

Cognitive
- I am learning that bubbles pop when I touch them.
- I am learning about cause and effect (I can do something that will have an effect).

Language
- I am learning new words and that people can have fun with words.

Motor
- I am learning to control my body so that I can catch a bubble.

What will you do to support my development and learning?
Responsive Interactions
- You like to learn new words so we will continue to talk with you and name objects and people.
- We will put the bubble bottle on a tray on the floor and see if she is interested in trying to blow bubbles yourself.
- We will see if next time another child wants to join us.

Environment, Toys, Materials, and Experiences
- We will bring in more challenging cause/effect toys.
- We will continue to provide bubble experiences.

Box 12.5

Individual Child Planning Guide: Version 2

Child's Name: <u>Sheila</u>

Plans for Week of (Date): <u>March 9–13, 2009</u>

Person(s) Completing the Guide: <u>Chloe</u>

Respect: Child's Emotions, Effort, Goals, Learning, and Relationships

Write an observation or use a photograph or other documentation here—date all notes:

3/9/09: Sheila is on the floor and she is lying on her back shaking a ring toy up and down. She has a smile on her face. She is making sounds such as "ba," "ma." She rolled over and crawled crablike across the floor.

3/10/09: When Dad came to pick her up today she was sitting in Chloe's lap. She squealed loudly and smiled when she saw her dad.

Reflect

What am I doing?

- I have started to crawl. I put my hands forward, bunch up, and crawl crablike across the floor. I squeal with a big smile on my face when I see my dad at the end of the day. I hold the plastic ring toys when I am on my back and make them jingle loudly—shaking them quickly up and down. I am starting to make sounds like "ba," "ma."

How am I feeling?

- I seem to feel very happy when my dad comes. I enjoy making noise with the ring toys.

What am I learning?

- I am learning that Dad will respond happily when I squeal in delight when I see him and that I can make things happen (jingly ring toy). I'm also learning that I can make the jingly noise (cause and effect) when I shake the ring toy and that toys can make noises. I'm learning to communicate by babbling.

Relate

What will you do to support my development and learning?
Responsive Interactions

- I will ask her father what you likes to do at home.
- The teachers will babble back to you and then wait for you to take a turn.
- Martha will be her primary care teacher. She will try to be the one to feed you and rock you to sleep.

Environment, Toys, Materials, and Experiences

- I will bring in some different ring toys for you to shake.
- We'll add other cause-and-effect toys to several of the cozy corners.
- We'll make sure that there is a clear space to crawl.

(environmental arrangement, equipment, materials, and experiences offered to children) to support the child's learning in all domains of development. We have discussed responsive interactions, but routines, environment, and experiences will be described in chapter 13. After reading chapter 13 and seeing several models of individual planning guides, you will be ready to complete the Relate section of the individual planning guide.

Many of these changes are implemented immediately, in the moment-to-moment interactions with the infant or toddler, and some may be implemented over time. The Developmental Trends and Responsive Interactions charts found at the end of chapters 6 through 10 provide

Table 12.5   "I'm exploring and learning . . . "

Emotional/Attachment	Social/Peers	Cognitive	Language/Literacy	Motor
Whether I am worthy of love	What peers will do	How to solve problems	How to communicate my needs with gestures	How to move
Who will protect me and keep me safe	How I can play with others	What will happen when I'm curious	How to talk	How to control my body
How to get my needs met	Who will play with me	How I can use tools to do what I want them to do	How to understand what another is saying	How to crawl
Who I can trust to take good care of me	Who will treat me kindly and who will hurt me	How to dump objects out of a container or fill a container	How to get others to understand what I am communicating	How to "pull to stand"
How others feel about me	How I can get another person's attention	The properties of objects and materials	How to take language turns with another person	How to walk
How to get adults to pay attention to me and be with me	How I can comfort or help a peer	Cause-and-effect: How I can make things happen	Who will respond to my sounds, words, and language	How to jump
How to express my feelings	How to protect myself and my things	Cause-and-effect: What causes what	How to ask questions	How to jump off something
How others express feelings	How to handle conflict	How to fit objects into a space (spatial relationships)	How words fit together to make a sentence	How to move objects around
How to express myself without falling apart (self-regulation)	How to make a peer laugh	How to get glue, tape, dirt, paint, etc., off my hands	How to add endings to words to express meaning	How to climb
How to wait	How to make a peer go away	Time	How to hold books	How to get down
How to separate from my loved ones	How to share space	Putting objects in sequence based on height, etc.	What pictures in books tell me	How to crawl or walk up stairs
How should I react to strangers	How to share the special adults in my life	How to sort objects	How to open and close books	How to wiggle my body into spaces

many ideas for responsive interactions and changes in the environment. Figure 12.1 earlier in this chapter also has ideas regarding responsive adult–child interactions.

There are two forms for group planning as well. The form shown in Box 12.6 is to be used at the end of a week to plan special opportunities for the following week. When teachers develop the group plan together, they bring the individual planning guides and share information so that all of the teachers can contribute to the recommended changes in interactions and the environment. As you plan, you build on the concepts and developmental steps, interests, and strengths of the children in the group.

The second group planning form (Box 12.7) provides space for teachers in center or home programs to reflect on routines of the day and develop a community of caring, and should be completed at least once a month. The group planning guides could also be used by home visitors to plan with families to make routines, such as bath time, more successful for everyone involved.

Box 12.6

Individually Responsive Group Planning Guide

Name of Group: <u>Robins</u>

Week of: <u>March 16–20, 2009</u>

Person(s) Completing This Guide: <u>Matt, Carla, Chloe</u>

Respect and Reflect

(Use information from the individual planning guides.) The children in my group are . . .

Exploring cause and effect

Gaining self-confidence as they learn new things and make things happen

Trusting adults to respond to them and have fun with them

Learning to express themselves through squealing and words

Relate: Plans for the Week to Meet Children's Interests and Needs

Songs/Finger-Plays

Continue singing songs with children in a responsive way.

Sit on the floor and start singing several children's favorite songs.

Bring in pictures or real objects to accompany the songs.

Sing the bubble song while playing with bubbles.

Stories/Books

Build on Sophie's interest in cause and effect.

Sit on the floor and invite children to listen to a story several times a day.

Respond when a child wants a story read.

Responsive Interactions

Be sure to follow children's lead in interactions.

Be sure to comment on children's feelings.

Respond to children's language:

> Respond to Sheila's babbling by babbling back and saying words to her.

> Use new words with Sophie and other children.

Environment, Toys, Materials, and Opportunities

To build on Sophie's interest in cause and effect add flashlights to the cozy corner to provide opportunities for children to explore turning them on.

In the middle of the week add colored cellophane.

Make sure there is room for Sheila to crawl.

Add a cause-and-effect toy (a waterwheel) to the water table. Add "tubs for two" with water to encourage social interactions. During the middle of the week add bubbles to the water table and "tubs for two" for opportunities for them to learn more about bubbles.

Develop an obstacle course outside.

Add different sizes of balls to the active area with baskets of various sizes.

Add more ring toys to provide opportunities for cause-and-effect play.

Experiences with Families

Exchange information with families about how their children explore cause and effect and make things happen at home and in the program.

Ask families for ideas about what toys, materials, experiences their children might like during the day in the program.

Special Experiences

Silvio's dad will visit on Tuesday and will play his flute.

Box 12.7

Group Planning for Routines

Name of Group: Robins

Week of: March 16–20, 2009

Persons Completing This Form: Matt, Carla, Chloe

Developing a caring community: Think about what is happening and what could happen to develop a relationship-based program for children, families, and teachers.

Routine	What is going well for the children and teachers?	What could we do to improve the experience for children, families, and the teachers?
Greeting time or good-bye time	A teacher is greeting each parent and getting information on how the child's night was.	Place the forms for parents to write on about their child's night or any special information closer to the door. Provide a comfortable adult chair by the door.
Feeding infants and toddler eating times	The toddlers are enjoying the songs that we are singing when they are seated and are waiting for the food.	To make the atmosphere more pleasant we could provide placemats and some flowers on the table for the toddlers.
Infant sleep and toddler nap time	The toddlers are falling asleep easily after we read stories to those who want a story read to them.	To make the transition from lunch to nap time easier, we will give each toddler a special hug before going to sleep.
Diapering	We are talking to them and they are talking to us.	No change.
Toileting	The older toddlers are beginning to use the toilet. There is no pressure, but when one starts to sit on the toilet several others do as well.	Remember to encourage them but not to ever force them. We want to emphasize that they are learning how rather than that we are training them how.
Play times	Most of the toddlers are engaged in play most of the morning.	Continue to plan based on what we are observing are their interests and needs.
Outdoor times	We created some shade so that the toddlers can sit in the shade while outside.	Ask families to help build a sandbox with a lid.
Transitions	Singing the "cleanup" song has helped establish a routine for cleanup.	Put pictures of several items on the shelf so that they can match the object to the picture
Other routines		
Other routines		

SUMMARY

The emotional development of infants and toddlers creates a foundation for the child to learn and love. Teachers' responsive strategies promote children's sense of well-being; meet infants' and toddlers' emotional needs for affection, love, and encouragement; and help them learn. Scaffolding is an adult strategy that can be used to promote emotional, social, language, cognitive, and motor development. Teachers observe and document children's learning and use the information for planning to develop a responsive curriculum.

myeducationlab

Go to MyEducationLab and complete the Building Teaching Skills and Dispositions exercise in Chapter 12.

- A curriculum for infants and toddlers is responsive to individual children's needs, interests, and strengths (in collaboration with families) and focuses on the development of children's healthy relationships. A curriculum is everything that children experience from the beginning to the end of the day—they are constantly learning.

- There are eight components to a curriculum, with components 1 through 4 discussed in this chapter. The eight components are:
    1. The foundation
    2. The teachers' roles
    3. Relationships with families and culturally sensitive care
    4. Responsive, relationship-based planning
    5. Transitions and routines
    6. Responsive and relationship-based environments
    7. Responsive experiences and opportunities
    8. A relationship-based approach to guidance

- The teachers' beliefs about the nature and needs of infants and toddlers, what is important for them to learn, and how they best learn form the philosophical foundation for a curriculum. Play is an important way that infants and toddlers learn.

- One of the most important roles of the teacher is to create a relationship-based community to ensure that babies feel safe, nurtured, and experience a sense of belonging. Teachers are intentional in how they scaffold children's emotional, social, language, cognitive, and motor development and follow children's lead for what they need. There are nine dimensions of adult–child interactions that promote children's emotional development, the foundation for all learning.

- When teachers develop strong, positive relationships with families from a variety of cultures, they weave a network of support for the well-being of infants and toddlers. To create respectful relationships, teachers and parents must take time to dialog.

- In a responsive, relationship-based curriculum the moment-to-moment, day-to-day, and weekly needs and interests of the children and their families guide the planning process. A responsive planning process that includes *respect, reflect,* and *relate* will ensure that the curriculum is truly "day to day the relationship way."

Key Terms

attachment groups
attuned
dance the developmental ladder

holds and enfolds
homebases

Velcro time
working sense of self

REFLECTIONS AND RESOURCES FOR THE READER

Reflections

1. What are the key components to planning a curriculum for infants and toddlers? Which are most important?
2. What do you think are the most important goals for infants and toddlers?
3. What does it mean to respect an infant or toddler?
4. What are the nine responsive strategies that teachers can use to promote infants' and toddlers' emotional development—a foundation for learning? Why are these strategies important for children, families, and teachers?

Observation and Application Opportunities

1. Use the items in Tables 12.3 and 12.4 to observe an infant and toddler program and to interview the teachers to determine how they develop responsive relationships with families in general and also families from diverse cultures. Write a summary of your observations and interviews and make recommendations for improvement.

2. Analyze the following: Abria is 28 months old. Abria's parents want the teachers to feed her with a spoon and do not want her to play with her food at lunchtime. In the program that Abria attends, the toddlers sit together at a table and feed *themselves* with a spoon, even though it is often messy. Sometimes they get tired and pick up food with their fingers. The teachers in the program think that it is important for children to learn to feed themselves. How would you dialog to discuss this issue with the family?

Supplementary Articles and Books to Read

Baker, A. R. (2003, Spring). Communicating big projects and moments of wonder in your infant/toddler classroom. *Focus on Infants and Toddlers, 15*(3), 1–2, 4–7.

Britt, D. R., & Gillespie, L. G. (2008). *Rocking & rolling. Supporting infants, toddlers, and their families.* Retrieved September 25, 2008, from http://journal.naeyc.org/btj/200801/BTJRockingRolling.asp

Friedman, S., & Soltero, M. (2006, July). Following a child's lead: Examples of emergent curriculum for infants and toddlers. *Beyond the Journal,* 1–5 Retrieved February 3, 2009, from http://journal.naeyc.org/btj/200607/Friedman706BTS.

Lally, J. R., & Mangione, P. (2006). The uniqueness of infancy demands a responsive approach to care. *Young Children, 61*(4), 14–20.

Interesting Links

http://www.pitc.org/cs/pitclib/view/pitc_res/182

    PITC   This site includes video clips from pitc's video—*The next step: Including the infant in the curriculum.*

http://www.unicef.org/crc/

    UNICEF   This Web site includes a link to the Convention on the Rights of the Child. Available on this link is the full text of this international human rights treaty, which articulates a new world vision committed to protecting children's rights.

myeducationlab)

These and other web links are included in this chapter on MyEducationLab.

Routines, Environments, and Opportunities
Day to Day the Relationship Way

In this chapter you will find information about how to establish responsive routines and create an enriched environment in a responsive curriculum. You will learn how to provide opportunities for very young children to develop within the context of relationships, and you will see examples of the *respect, reflect,* and *relate* (3 R) planning process. At the end of the chapter we describe other infant and toddler curriculum approaches to use in group settings. But first, see Box 13.1, where you can peek into an infant and toddler classroom that focuses on responsive interactions and relationships. The infants and toddlers in the program described in Box 13.1 are having profound experiences that will influence how they view themselves, relationships, and the world. Considered alone, each experience may not seem important, but when they are combined they are transformed into who a child is and will become. How do we give these young children the experiences they deserve—day to day the relationship way? One of the most important experiences for infants and toddlers is how they transition into a program and the routines that they experience each day. As you will remember, this is component 5 of a curriculum, as described in chapter 12.

Box 13.1

> ## A Responsive Classroom
>
> Every infant in Angie Hicks's classroom shares the attention of a teacher with just one or two other children. Designated teachers have primary responsibility for three or four children. These teachers spend the bulk of their day with their children and monitor their basic needs. On the day of our visit, this arrangement is evident in the children's behavior. When one of the teachers goes to get a bottle, Samantha's eyes trail after her, then start to tear up. The other teacher, seeing Samantha's concern, says comfortingly, "Are you getting sad because Jeannie is leaving?"
>
> The large infant rooms are very calm. Soft music plays for the children who are awake. Two additional rooms contain cribs as well as a quiet area where mothers can breast-feed. Teachers rock children to sleep in their arms and often sing lullabies before placing the babies in a crib.
>
> The room is well organized and well labeled so teachers do not have to spend time searching for supplies. Personal belongings, including diapers and pacifiers, are all kept in labeled locations. Food allergies and sunscreen requirements are posted in large letters on the wall. The providers are fastidious about health precautions, maintaining clean facilities, washing their hands between feedings and diaper changes, and using rubber gloves while wiping children's noses. The room has a voice-activated speaker phone that picks up in the active part of the classroom, so that no teacher has to lift a telephone receiver. Parents frequently call to check on their children.
>
> Most important, the infant teachers have worked consistently with babies for many years. As director Burroughs says, "The teachers in this room prefer to work with very young children and have not experienced the burnout" so common in the infant care profession. Their devotion to the children is apparent. One teacher lovingly hugs a child who had just awakened, then rubs his back, allowing him to transition slowly into the activities of the day. Conversations are filled with encouraging and caring comments. "Keep crawling—you are almost there!" "Thank you for handing that to me!" Teachers convey their excitement to parents, proudly reporting on the children's activities.
>
> The teachers follow the children's lead. When one child carries a book to one of the teachers, the gift prompts a group reading session. When an infant pushes back on the pillows supporting him and begins to cry, a teacher takes the cue to move him onto his back, where he becomes immediately content. Another teacher asks a toddler, "What are you trying to tell me, Jenny? Do you want me to blow the bubbles?" Jenny gives an enthusiastic "Bubba ba ba." The teacher helps Jenny blow the bubbles herself, then encourages other children to come join the activity.
>
> Since toddlers learn to communicate verbally, most of the conversation in the toddler room develops out of the children's ideas. Astar holds out a plastic ice cream cone and says, "Daddy." The teacher responds, "Does Daddy buy ice cream?" When Astar then picks up a milkshake cup, she asks, "Is that a milkshake you are making? Let's all go and get some ice cream." In the house area, the toddlers play ice cream scenarios. After a while, a boy excitedly announces that he has made a cake. The teacher and the children start to sing "Happy Birthday."

Source: Kinch and Schweinhart (2004).

COMPONENT 5: TRANSITIONS AND ROUTINES—A TIME FOR RELATIONSHIPS

Transitions and routines are important opportunities for strengthening a child's relationships and learning with teachers, families, and peers. *Transitions* are times of change that occur in a child's life, such as when an infant or toddler enters an education and development center or family child care home or when an infant changes rooms in a center as he grows and has new needs (hopefully with a favorite teacher moving "up" with him). Daily transitions occur when a child or group moves from one experience to another—for example, from indoor play to outdoor play. *Routines* are regularly occurring events that the child experiences during a day, such as diapering time, feeding time, or moving from play into nap time.

Transition of Entering a New Child Care and Education Program

One of the more difficult times for babies may be when they enter a program or child care home for the first time. Teachers and parents can work closely together to support the child during this time of separation and adjustment to a new environment, new adults, and new experiences. Notice how difficult it is for Tim in the following example reported by Pawl and St. John (1998):

> Tim stood just inside the entrance to the big playroom. He was sturdy for two and a half years, but short. The noise was jarring, and he looked around for the woman his mother talked to when they came in. She had said to his mother, "He'll be fine—I'll get him started," and she had taken his hand. But now, just as fast, she was gone. It scared him as much as the other time. This was not a good place to be. He wanted his mother, and he wanted to go home. A boy running past bumped him hard and Tim nearly fell, but he caught himself and made his way to the corner of the room. He still couldn't see that big person or the other one—just lots and lots of small kids. He sat down and fingered some colored blocks on the floor. A big boy came and grabbed one and stepped on Tim's hand. Tim yelped and cried and looked around. He held his hurt hand in the other, and the tears ran down his cheeks. No one saw. (p. 12)

What could have made it easier for Tim, his mother, and the teacher? Remembering how hard it is for us to separate from a loved one helps us take the perspective of the child and parent. The parent may feel anxious, guilty, and as if she is giving up a part of herself. T. Berry Brazelton, pediatrician and child development expert, noted that some parents may express their feelings openly, others seem distant as they prepare themselves to separate from their baby, and others seem angry as they attempt to maintain control but really feel out of control (Griffin, 1998). Babies like Tim can be confused and sad.

Transitions During the Day

At the beginning of the day parents and teachers could use *ciao* time—a word that means both "hello" and "good-bye" in Italian—instead of *dropping off*. The morning is "good-bye" time from the infants' and toddlers' perspectives, as the babies say good-bye to their parents. However, it is also "hello" time, as the infant or toddler and the parents say hello to the child's teacher. Thus, it is both good-bye and hello if we think about this transition time from the child's perspective.

An infant's or toddler's "good-bye to the parent and hello to the teacher" time must be handled with care, as it is an emotional exchange of the child between the parent and teacher. Although a baby is held emotionally through time and space by the physically absent parent, an infant or toddler will not be able to think about how the parent still loves her after the parent disappears (according to the child's perspective). The child has to *transition her trust* from the parent to the teacher—not an easy task unless the relationships with both are positive.

A routine provides child, parent, and teacher predictability—a sense of expectancy—about ciao time, leading to smoother transitions for all.

> As an infant, Kia's mom made sure she was comfortable in the child care home and sang her one song before saying good-bye. The teacher always greeted Mom and Kia and asked how the baby's night had been and if there were any special needs for the day. As a mobile infant, the teacher did the same thing, only now she greeted Kia with a special hug. Kia's mom sang one song and read one story and then said good-bye with hugs and kisses, telling Kia that she would be back after Kia's nap in the afternoon. The teacher made sure she was near and ready to pick up Kia, hold her, or read a story to help Kia settle in for the day. In the toddler room, the teacher sat at a table near the door with interesting things like play dough, books, or new toys. When a child came in the door with a parent, the teacher could be right there asking the parent about special needs and greeting Kia with a smile.

Kia took off her shoes and put on her special slippers for the day. This routine helped her make the transition into the center and she was able to say good-bye to her mother with a big hug and a kiss.

These transition times at the beginning of the day are repeated at the end of the day in a similar way to smooth the child's transition from program to home.

Transitions during the day are important times for building teacher–child relationships. Inform children before individual and group transitions occur and give them time. For example, to an infant who needs to have a diaper change, says things like, "It is time to change your diaper. . . ." *before* you pick up the child. Help them finish a task before toddling toward the diaper table. Snatching mobile infants and toddlers from their play for diaper changes can result in child defensiveness and anger. Remember, when you transition to another part of the room or out of the room, it is also a change for the children. To help children feel more secure, you can tell infants and toddlers when you are leaving to change another child's diaper or fix food, *and when you will be back.* Transitions from one room to another in a center are very difficult for infants and toddlers unless there is continuity of care. This concept was discussed in chapter 11.

Responsive Routines

"Family routines are patterned interactions that occur with predictable regularity in the course of everyday living" (Kubicek, 2003, p. 4). Caregiving routines are important opportunities for strengthening teacher–child relationships and child learning and include diapering and toileting, feeding and eating, and sleeping times. Infants and toddlers learn to expect that they will be fed when they are hungry and helped to sleep when they are tired. From a baby's perspective a routine is a time for physical and *emotional* needs to be met. Routines are incredibly intimate and emotional times when infants and toddlers gain a sense of self-worth, learn about the kindness of others, and develop relationships with those who meet their needs in responsive, kind ways. With responsive routines, babies become self-regulated (a sense of inner control) rather than, for example, out of control because they are crying frantically for food. They learn whether adults are trustworthy. Their brains become organized as they experience the patterns of routines (Butterfield, 2002).

Routines are times for teaching the important lessons in life—how to feel about oneself and others. They are social, emotional, cognitive, language, and motor experiences that provide teachable moments for the child and teacher. Talking softly to infants and toddlers who are eating, naming pictures on the wall for babies being diapered, and patting the backs of toddlers transitioning to nap time while singing their favorite lullabies are only a few ways that teachable moments become moments of relationship building. As always in a family-centered program, teachers and parents constantly coordinate routines; they share information each day and they negotiate differences in how routines are achieved so that babies experience as few changes between home and program as possible (Griffin, 1998).

For infants, routines are individualized and responsive to their needs. Babies know they are hungry or overwhelmed and usually let you know. The teacher reads the cues of the baby concerning an empty or full tummy, a need for interactions, or a diaper change. These interactions form the core of relationship-building between the infant and teacher—and begin the formation of the infant's identity as someone who can trust others and who feels lovable. For mobile infants, routines are times for shared relationships as they participate in conversations (cooing, babbling, and first words) with teachers during diapering, eating, and rocking time for sleep. Infants and toddlers are included in the diaper changing process. When a teacher says, "It is time to take your diaper off. I'm putting on a clean diaper" the routine is completed *with* the child, not *to* the child. Toddlers share routine times with teachers and peers as, over time, diapering time turns into toilet

myeducationlab)

Go to the Activities and Applications section in Chapter 13 of MyEducationLab to watch the *video Diapering,* which you may recognize from Chapter 11. Pay attention to the responsiveness of the care teacher.

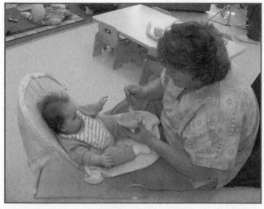

This baby enjoys her feeding routine with her favorite teacher.

time, feeding turns into eating with peers at small tables, and helping infants fall asleep becomes supporting toddlers as they transition to nap time. Teachers can use Table 13.1 to determine how responsive their routines are for the infants and toddlers in their program.

Routines happen continuously in a program and there is a danger that they will become routinized (montonous). Teachers may wonder why they are wiping noses, cleaning bottoms, and feeding toddlers. They may wonder what routines have to do with teaching.

When we recognize that these times represent opportunities for learning and emotional connections, then we will treat them for what they are—perhaps the most important part of the day.

myeducationlab

Go to the Activities and Applications section in Chapter 13 of MyEducationLab to view *Mobile Infant Environment—* a series of photographs of an Early Head Start environment.

COMPONENT 6: CREATING RESPONSIVE, RELATIONSHIP-BASED ENVIRONMENTS

Another role of the infant-toddler professional is to set up a relationship-based, responsive environment with equipment, materials, and opportunities that support children's development. Torrelli and Durrett (2007) describe many elements of a quality environment that infants, toddlers, and their teachers would enjoy:

> A developmentally-designed environment supports children's individual and social development. It encourages explorations, focused play, and cooperation. It provides choices for children and supports self-directed learning. A developmentally designed environment also supports the teacher-child relationship. It minimizes management and custodial activities, allowing teachers more time for interactions, observation, and facilitation of children's development.

A Quality Environment for Centers and Child Care Homes

Other elements of a responsive environment include:

- innovations that are responsive to children's and adults' sensory needs, and "our need to gather, be comforted, rest, and explore" (Carter & Curtis, 1998, p. 75)
- spaces that encourage play
- aspects that support children's development of trust and security, their ability to make choices, and their sense of mastery.

Greenman (1988) discusses how developing a learning environment begins with recognizing what babies need to *do* and determining how to maximize their opportunities to have the appropriate experiences. He asks, "What do babies do for a living?" He answers:

> Most simply, it is to make sense of the world of people and things and to develop their capacities to the fullest. Babies are explorers and scientists; they test and discover their own properties, the properties of objects and people, and the relationships between the elements of the world. (p. 99)

And, of course, we can't forget babies' needs for environments that promote relationships—both adult–child and peer relationships. With all of these purposes in mind, teachers can set up an environment that is a home away from home. See Figures 13.1 and 13.2 for examples of floor plans for an infant room and a toddler room. For babies to feel both safe and motivated to learn, a quality environment needs the elements found in Table 13.2. Environments need cozy spaces and special places for infants and toddlers to delight in their surroundings.

Table 13.1 Responsive routines

1. *Responsive Daily Routines*

   • Provide a daily routine that follows each infant's need for feeding and sleep.

   • Implement a flexible routine (eating, sleeping, inside–outside) that the toddlers learn to predict.

   • Use routines as opportunities for emotional interaction and learning.

   • Provide primary caregiving.

2. *Responsive Routines for Infant Feeding and Toddler Eating*

   • Provide a private place for parents to feed an infant, if parent desires.

   • Respect the mother's wish to breast-feed or not.

   • Ask families about their cultural and family preferences for the child's eating habits, needs, and food preferences.

   • Sit with toddlers for eating rather than hovering above.

   • Respond to young children's requests and comments while feeding and eating with the children—name foods; use words that describe the color, shape, size, texture, and taste of foods; and talk about pleasant events while feeding and eating with the children.

   • Hold infants gently for bottle-feeding. Babies need to be held for feeding to ensure safety and to meet babies' emotional needs. Talk softly, hum, sing, or remain quiet according to the infant's needs.

   • Speak in a soft, kind, friendly, gentle, encouraging, and positive way to the children during feeding and eating activities.

   • Respond when infants or toddlers indicate that they are hungry or want more food, and respect children when they indicate that they are satisfied or want to stop eating.

   • Use plates and place mats instead of napkins or paper plates to serve toddlers.

   • Provide opportunities for toddlers to begin to serve themselves, pour milk out of a small pitcher, and clean the table with a sponge.

   • Provide a system for giving daily information to families concerning how, when, what, and with whom the child ate.

   • Provide a system for documenting families' wishes on issues related to weaning from the breast or bottle.

3. *Responsive Routines for Diapering and Toilet Learning*

   • Provide pictures of family members or other interesting pictures on the wall at the baby's eye level in the diapering area.

   • Make diapering a special time for adults to talk, sing, and be with infants.

   • Use encouraging and positive words and self-talk such as "first," "next," and comforting words.

   • Coordinate toilet learning with the parents to provide continuity from home to program.

   • Help toddlers and talk gently to them when they use the toilet.

   • Never force toddlers to use or stay on the toilet.

4. *Responsive Routines for Sleeping*

   • Provide long, luxurious holding times for infants and toddlers.

   • Gently rock or pat babies who need help to get to sleep, watch and listen for infants to signal when they want to be picked up from a crib, and respond positively and quickly when they signal that they want out of crib or bed.

   • Provide each toddler with a cot that is labeled, both with her or his first name and a special symbol or picture. Label sheets, pillows, and blankets in the same way.

   • Plan and implement a transition time from play to sleep with a predictable sequence for toddlers. To build positive relationships, read stories, talk gently, and/or pat a child gently to sleep according to the child's needs. Toddlers may pick a special book or have their own stuffed toy or blanket if needed.

   • Allow toddlers to sleep only as long as they need. Plan a quiet activity for toddlers who wake up.

   • Help toddlers transition from nap to wake time.

   • Prepare the nap area for toddlers before lunch, so that if a toddler is tired or falls asleep during lunch the teacher can help the child transition to nap time.

5. *Responsive Greeting and Good-Bye Times*

   • Greet each infant, toddler, and parent warmly in the morning. Help children transition from home to the program at the beginning of the day. Give family members a chance to communicate needs, priorities, and concerns.

   • Greet each family member warmly when the family picks up the baby. Help children transition from the program to parent at the end of the child's day. Talk about the daily record with the family. Give each infant and toddler a special good-bye.

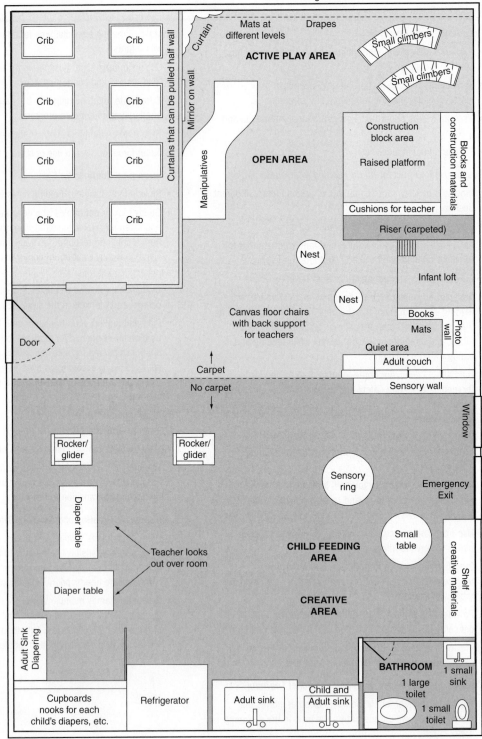

Figure 13.1

Floor plan for an infant and mobile infant room (2 months to 18 months).

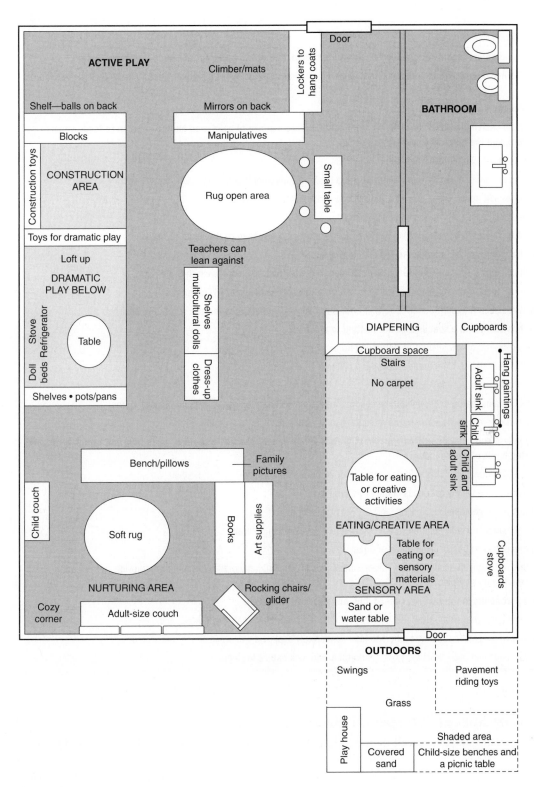

Figure 13.2
Floor plan for a toddler room (18 months to 3 years).

303

Table 13.2   Environment observation guide

1. **Environments for children are clean, safe, properly lighted, ventilated, and provide appropriate temperature regulation.**
   - The environment is free of materials or conditions that endanger children's health and is constantly monitored by the teachers for hazards.
   - The environment is clutter-free.

2. **Environments contain design elements that reduce stimulation, create a sense of calm, and enable children to focus on each other, their teachers, and the materials they are exploring.**
   - The environment is bright, cheerful, and beautiful.
   - The environment is not overstimulating with paint that is too bright or wallpaper that has too many figures on it.
   - The environment has soft items—small couches and pillows, and a variety of textures.
   - The environment offers spaces for teacher–child interactions.
   - There are spaces for one child or several children to be alone (but can still be seen by the teacher).

3. **The environment has furniture and equipment that is child-size.**
   - The environment includes short toddler chairs so that toddlers' feet can touch the floor when they are sitting.
   - The environment includes short tables so that toddlers can sit in toddler chairs and easily eat or play.
   - The environment has short and sturdy shelves so that babies will not knock them over, but can reach toys easily.

4. **The environment has comfortable spaces that are inviting to children.**
   - Spaces are clearly divided by low shelves or cloth hung from ceiling.
   - The environment is divided into clear areas for play and children can delineate.
   - The environment feels organized—not cluttered.
   - The environment contains features that encourage children to interact and develop relationships with each other.
   - There are spaces at different levels, for example, platforms, lofts, and mats

5. **Teachers provide indoor and outdoor environments that provide a rich variety of activity choices, materials, and toys that respond to children's varying levels of development.**
   - Materials and toys are attractively displayed on shelves (not dumped into a toy box).
   - Materials can be used in a variety of spaces in the environment.
   - Materials and toys are in good shape, working, and are not broken or dirty.
   - Materials and toys can be used by children who are at different developmental levels.
   - Materials and toys encourage active exploration and play.
   - Materials and toys are changed according to children's interests, while the majority of the toys remain to provide stability and consistency for the infant or toddler.

6. **Environments support adults in interacting, supervising, and observing children.**
   - There are "camping" type chairs that allow teachers to sit on the floor with their backs supported.
   - There are pillows and bolsters that allow teachers to lean comfortably against a wall while sitting on the floor.
   - There are rocking chairs that allow teachers to sit comfortably and rock babies to sleep.

Cozy Spaces and Special Places

Learning spaces are well-defined places with materials that support relationships and learning. Integrated learning in all domains (emotional, social, language, cognitive, and motor) occurs in all areas of the room. As teachers set up these corners, nooks, cozy spaces, and special places, they can think about all of the opportunities for children to laugh and learn. All of the equipment and materials are not available at one time, but instead the teachers alternate materials based on the interests and developmental levels of the children. As a teacher sets up these areas she can think about each child in her group and how that child might use these materials. Remember, play is the way for children to learn—and they will play, explore, experiment, eat, and rest if enticing spaces are created (Sawyers & Rogers, 2003). The teacher is physically and emotionally available to promote children's emotional well-being, their feelings of safety, enduring relationships with adults and peers, and learning in all of the developmental domains.

Spaces invite, entice, and engage children. Table 13.3 describes a variety of spaces that could be created in an infant and toddler room in a center and adapted for a family child care

Table 13.3　Creating cozy spaces

A Quiet Space

- A space away from active play
- A space with
  - a mat or layers of mats with a low mirror on the wall beside it
  - family photograph books, dolls and blankets, soft toys, quiet toys, puppets, and books
  - a nest (*Kaplan Early Learning Company Catalog*, 2008); or create one with an inner tube with a blanket over it
  - boxes large enough for child to crawl in and out

Special Places for Nurturing Children

- A comfortable space away from active play for teachers to sit on the floor (with back support) and hold a child
- A loft
- An adult-size couch
- A mat on the floor against the wall with pillows with washable covers
- A rocking chair/glider

A nest provides a special place to nurture infants and toddlers.

Spaces for Delighting the Senses

- Short tables for toddlers for play dough and other creative materials
- A space with
  - small tubs, other containers, or water tables with water for infants and toddlers (always monitor children very carefully with water—children have drowned in an inch of water in a container)
  - containers or tables for sand and other natural materials
  - a light table (see Reggio materials)
- Wading pools filled with different textured balls or other safe materials
- A space to use feeling and sound boxes and bubbles with various sizes of wands
- A sticky wall (Isbell & Isbell, 2003, p. 67)

Sand delights children of all ages.

A Space to Use Materials to Create

- A space without carpet for painting on paper on the floor
- A space to use nontoxic paint; thick crayons; clay; play dough; large pieces of paper to tear, draw, and paint on; brushes; short easels
- A table for toddlers to use materials to create

A table for toddlers to create with crayons.

(continued)

Table 13.3   Creating cozy spaces (*continued*)

A Space for Peek-a-boo and Other Social Games

- A space made with a cloth hanging from ceiling with a mirror on the wall
- Boxes of various sizes with holes cut out of the sides—add cloth over the holes for variation and "peek-a-boo" games
- Lofts with a Plexiglas panel in the floor so babies that are up can look down and babies that are down can look up and enjoy one another

A Space for Active Play

- Floor space so that children can move freely with
  - balls of all sizes
  - couches to walk around and climb up on
  - ramps and short climbers to climb
  - rocking boats
  - tunnels to crawl through
  - mats at different levels for climbing
  - objects that can be moved such as child-size shopping carts, doll strollers, and riding toys
  - a bar fastened to the wall on various levels so that children can pull to stand
  - large empty appliance boxes with windows cut out of it and/or the end off of it so that children can crawl through the box

Mats at different levels provide a place for mobile infants and toddlers to climb.

A Space for Toys and Other Manipulatives

- Short shelves and space in front of shelves to play on the floor with
  - a child-size table and chairs for mobile infants and toddlers
  - toys that move, make noise, and change shape
  - toddler nesting blocks, ring towers, large beads, cause and effect and "take apart" toys, blocks, shape sorters
  - wooden animals, little houses, multiethnic play people, trucks and cars
  - small balls, blocks of various sizes, large pegs, large beads for stringing, puppets, puzzles, dolls, toy telephones
  - tubes of varying lengths and sizes

A puzzle with a handle on each piece is perfect for infants.

A Space to Build and Construct

- A platform for building
- Blocks of all sizes, shapes, and textures
- Wooden animals, little houses, play people, trucks and cars

A Space for Dramatic Play With

- mirrors, low pegs to hang clothing, scarves, purses, safe kitchen untensils, hats, pots and pans, containers of various sizes, dress-up clothes
- multiethnic dolls, doll blankets, baby bottles, baby bed
- puppets of varying sizes and shapes
- child-size tables, stoves, sinks, refrigerators, pots and pans, dishes (for mobile infants and toddlers)

Toddlers pretend with a child-size stove and sink.

A Space for Reading to Children

- A special place that is designed for older infants, mobile infants, and toddlers to choose books from an attractive, easily reached display and "read," or be read to, in comfort
- Also place books around the room (any space is a great space for reading to a child)

This attractive book holder shows the covers of the books.

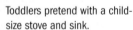

Feeding and Eating Spaces With

- comfortable floor chairs for adults to feed infants sitting in infant seats
- rocking chairs/gliders for feeding bottles to infants
- child-size chairs and tables for toddlers to eat
- a refrigerator
- a sink at children's level for mobile infants and toddlers
- an adult-size sink

Sleeping, Diapering, and Toileting Spaces

- Sleeping
  - cribs for infants
  - cots for mobile infants and toddlers
- Diapering
  - a diaper table with storage space
  - sturdy stairs with sides for toddlers to climb to diaper table
  - an adult-size sink
- Toileting
  - child-size toilets for toddlers who are learning to use the toilet
  - a child-size sink

home. Provide the equipment, toys, and opportunities based on children's individual interests and developmental level.

> *No space is marginal, no corner is unimportant, and each space needs to be alive, flexible, and open to change.* (Malaguzzi)

How the space is organized, the equipment, and the materials all provide opportunities for relating and learning. As Greenman (1988) states, "Teachers are sure to think about how to creatively use each corner in the room to entice and tempt babies to explore." Teachers also provide special opportunities for learning in each of the cozy corners.

COMPONENT 7: RESPONSIVE OPPORTUNITIES

Don't think in terms of activities; think in terms of each child and the group's interests and levels of development. Think of providing opportunities for learning from which children choose—and then *respecting, reflecting,* and *relating* to children as they experience these opportunities. As noted by Maria Montessori:

> *It is not the quality of the object that holds a child's interest, but the opportunity it affords the child for action.* (Torrence & Chattin-McNichols)

Planning Opportunities

There are many activity books that teachers can buy—some include activities that are responsive and that provide a rich array of opportunities to entice infants and toddlers to explore, problem solve, and discover. Some, however, are much too structured for infants and toddlers and require enforced group time, which is not appropriate for children so young. The questions in Figure 13.3 will guide you as you think about whether the *opportunity* is appropriate for the children in your group.

Figure 13.3
Choosing
materials and
opportunities.

1.	Does it meet one or more children's needs and strengths?
2.	Does it provide for a variety of developmental levels (infants, mobile infants, toddlers)?
3.	Is it safe? Durable? Washable? Nontoxic?
4.	Does it support learning in a variety of developmental domains (motor, communication, thinking, social, emotional, and cultural)?
5.	Does it spark the interest of a child or a number of children?
6.	Does it support a child doing a number of different things with the toy or material (for example, with a ball a child may chew on it, bounce it, roll it, put it in a container, etc.)? A toy may lend itself to one response (such as a puzzle); however, a child could explore the toy in a variety of ways.
7.	Does it support non-gender-biased, multicultural thinking, and nonviolent-prosocial behavior?
8.	Can I use the materials or the activities by offering them as *opportunities* for children rather than a forced activity?
9.	Can the material or experience be adapted for children with special needs?

Following is an example of how a teacher used the guidelines to decide whether an experience was appropriate for the children in her group:

> Mara, a teacher in a room for children 18 months to 3 years old, had several children in her room who loved to play with balls. She read about an experience that she might provide in her room in a book, Infant and Toddler Experiences *by Hast and Hollyfield (1999, p. 133). The experience entailed bringing balls of different textures, sizes, and qualities into the room as well as baskets or containers to put the balls in. The activity recommended that she fill the room with all of the balls and let the toddlers discover them. After thinking about the questions in Figure 13.3 she decided that she would try it. She decided, however, that instead of filling the room she would place the balls and containers in the active area so that the children would not be overstimulated. For Tommy, who couldn't walk yet, she would place a small basket and small balls near him to explore with other children.*

Let's explore some wonderful opportunities (see Figure 13.4) for children that could be provided in the cozy corners. Not all of these experiences are available at one time and the environment, materials, and opportunities change in response to children's needs and interests. Teachers may *plan* for opportunities to occur in specific cozy places, such as the ball experiences described previously in the active area or literacy experiences in the corner where books are available. Opportunities for creative activities with crayons or paints will likely take place in the creative arts cozy corner. However, we want to emphasize that most of the following opportunities can take place in *all* of the cozy spaces described in Table 13.3—for example, opportunities for nurturing; social, prosocial, language, cognitive, and motor development; delighting the senses, music, and learning about literacy and numeracy, happen in *all* of the cozy corners. If teachers are *reflective* of the possibilities for learning in all of the areas, they will *respect* infants' and toddlers' choice of equipment, toys, materials, and cozy corners, and will *relate* to children based on the opportunities for learning inherent in all of children's experiences. (Petersen & Wittmer, 2008).

Quiet and Calm Opportunities

Quiet spaces create opportunities for children to calm themselves, suck their thumbs, gather their energies, and rest either by themselves or with another peer, the teacher, or a parent. These spaces have softness in them—quiet, visually pleasing toys, and pillows for mobile

Quiet and calm opportunities

Nurturing opportunities

Social opportunities

Prosocial opportunities

Opportunities for social experiences for and with children with disabilities

Language opportunities

Cognitive opportunities

Delighting-the-senses opportunities

Creative opportunities

Writing and drawing opportunities

Music, song, and creative movement opportunities

Numeracy, space, and shape opportunities

Opportunities for active play and motor development

Outdoor opportunities

Figure 13.4
Opportunities for infants and toddlers.

infants and toddlers. A large inner tube with a blanket that covers the inner tube creates a nest inside where an infant or two can be placed or where a toddler can relax. Boxes with pillows in them for mobile infants and toddlers provide a place to hide away from the group, slow down, and unwind.

Nurturing Opportunities

Opportunities for children to experience nurturing can also happen in many spaces and at many times throughout the day. Nurturing children is one of the most important roles of the infant or toddler teacher—for example, when a toddler falls and cries and an adult finds a band-aid (the magic cure). Examine a room. Are there places for teachers or parents to nurture their children? Quiet spaces may double as nurturing places, but rooms will also need rocking chairs, a stuffed chair, or a comfortable corner for two or three. A soft blanket to wrap an infant or a small quilt to cover a toddler adds a sense of comfort to a nurturing space.

1. Create areas where the adult and children can be cozy together and the teacher can hold and comfort children.

2. Create comfortable areas where the adult can sit with his back supported—then infants and toddlers can sit close, lean on the adult, or plop on a lap.

3. Create spaces where the teacher can see eye-to-eye with children.

4. Provide a firm mattress on the floor in front of a safety mirror hung low on the wall, so that infants, toddlers, and teachers can enjoy looking in the mirror, patting the images they see, singing songs to their reflections, and making faces at the faces looking back at them.

5. Provide pictures of families that teachers laminate so that the children can carry them around.

6. Provide peek-a-boo pictures of children and family members on a board with a piece of cloth over each one so children can lift up the cloth and see the picture.

Social Opportunities

As discussed in chapter 7, infants and toddlers show great interest in peers very early in their lives. Teachers can support children's very early interactions and developing friendships by:

- Supporting infants' interest in each other by laying or sitting children near each other. For example, place infants close to each other so they can touch each other.

- Providing long periods of play where infants and toddlers can imitate, approach, follow, and try to engage other children.

- Sharing the strategies that infants and toddlers use to engage others. Continually document through pictures or video how young children enjoy each other. Share the information with parents. Encourage parents to share their pictures and examples of their child's interest in other children. See Box 13.2 for an example of how a teacher might plan for a child based on a photograph of a social interaction.

- Seting up cozy areas for several children—for example, a box for one or two or more, a small couch, and a nook under the loft.

- Providing two or more of each favorite toy or similar toys so that children can enjoy them together. Sometimes the best "friendships" develop for toddlers when they each have their own materials, but can easily see and interact with one other child (parallel and reciprocal play).

- Using large motor equipment that promotes social play, such as a climber or a rocking boat. Conflict between peers occurs less often with large pieces of equipment than with small toys (although those are necessary as well).

- Providing places for infants and toddlers to have alone time to promote emotional and social development. Private spaces, such as a box on its side that one mobile infant or toddler can fit into, allow for emotional refueling. Too much togetherness, and no opportunity for alone time, *for some babies* can contribute to their feelings of stress.

Language Opportunities

Teachers of infants and toddlers play a significant role in facilitating infants' and toddlers' language development. There are opportunities for children's language development in each interaction and experience that the child has with teachers and peers. Review the 12 strategies for language learning in chapter 9 and use them often throughout the day. As a child climbs on the climber you can use *parallel talk* and say, "You are climbing up. Now you are climbing down." When you are responding to an infant or toddler's sounds or words you can use *semantically responsive talk* and you can *elaborate and extend* the child's language. When a child climbs into your lap, you can ask him how he is feeling today. An astute teacher doesn't bombard children with comments and questions, but rather uses *responsive talk* at all times so that infants and toddlers experience the joy of communicating.

Miller (1999) describes materials that teachers can add to the environment to encourage language development and communication between children. Large, empty gift-wrap tubes provide opportunities for children to experiment with how their voices sound different when they talk through the tube. Mobile infants and toddlers will use pretend phones to "talk" to Mommy or Grandma. Picture cards of favorite people, animals, toys, and babies that teachers laminate and place in a box provide opportunities for children to name the pictures. Miller suggests putting a different object in a hinged box each day to provide an opportunity for naming and conversing about the "surprise" object.

Box 13.2

Day to Day the Relationship Way

Individual Child Planning Guide

Child's Name: Tom

Plans for Week of (Date): Sept. 7–11, 2009

Person(s) Completing the Guide: Torren and Nicole

Respect: Child's Emotions, Effort, Goals, Learning, and Relationships

Write an observation or use a picture or other documentation here—date all notes:

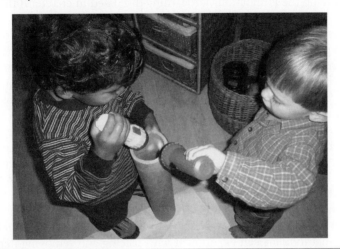

Respect and Reflect

9/7/09

What am I doing?
I'm in the orange shirt (on the left) and I'm holding a flashlight and pointing it down a cardboard tube.

How am I feeling?
I am enjoying playing with my friend.

What am I learning?
Emotional
• I am learning how to focus (self-regulation).

Social
• I'm learning how to play with a friend and take turns.

Cognitive
• I am learning how flashlights work.
• I am learning about light.
• I am learning about cause and effect (I can do something that will have an effect).

Language
• My friend said to me, "Look, point it down the hole." I'm learning the names of objects and how to give directions.

Motor
• I am learning to use my hands and eyes together.

Relate

What will you do to support my development and learning?

Responsive Interactions
We will continue to provide a long play time during the day to provide an opportunity for peer play.

Environment, Toys, Materials, and Experiences
We will bring in more challenging cause-and-effect toys to enjoy with friends.
We will continue to provide more containers and tubes for you to experiment with light.
We will bring in an overhead projector to provide an opportunity for you to experiment with light.
We will provide at least two items (such as flashlights) to encourage social interactions.

Cognitive Opportunities

Cognitive activities occur every day in every way. With cognitive development, the environment, toys, and materials facilitate children's development of the learning sparkle. The materials in the environment and the adult-child interactions will facilitate each child's sense of wonder, joy, interest, and discovery in all areas of the room. It is this sense of wonder that leads to learning and the love of learning.

Provide toys that adapt to changes in the child's development. For example, a stacking toy can usually be chewed and examined and passed from hand to hand by an infant. It can also be stacked, at first incorrectly and then correctly (after much experimentation) by a toddler. *The toy hasn't changed, but the way that the child plays with the toy has changed.* This toy is adaptable and can be used by children who are at different developmental stages in their ability to play with this toy and by the *same child* as he develops. Adults also provide opportunities for children to develop the foundations for learning discussed in chapter 8 through the materials that they provide and their responsive interactions.

Infants and toddlers gain confidence in their ability to initiate, be intentional, persist at tasks, and problem solve when they are given opportunities to discover what they can do with toys and materials. This may include tasting, sucking, banging together, tapping, moving, dumping, building, and tasting again. To help them gain confidence and the desire to problem solve give them many opportunities to succeed by providing materials that interest them and that are at or slightly above their developmental level.

Infants and toddlers often gravitate toward different and interesting materials, such as using crayons with corrugated cardboard—two materials that often aren't used together. The cardboard provides a challenge that sparks the child's problem solving and initiation. Mobile infants and toddlers like surprises. Provide a container with a hole in the bottom or a slotted spoon in the water table, a solid block in with the stacking rings, or a toy that doesn't make music with a small basket of musical toys. Toddlers enjoy and are surprised by contact paper with the sticky side up. Tape it to a wall or the floor. Place toys, feathers, and other material nearby so that toddlers can experiment with placing and removing items on the paper. These materials create *disequilibrium*—a concept discussed in chapter 3.

Also, create and share the "wow" moments with infants and toddlers. Create and look for the moments when an infant seems puzzled by a wobbly toy or when a mobile infant has the look of surprise when she discovers how balls sound different from blocks as they are dumped from a basket. Share those wow moments with your own surprised looks to build an emotional feeling of excitement about learning. When teachers support children's learning dispositions, they support children's desire and confidence to learn *and* build positive relationships with the children.

Delighting-the-Senses Experiences

Infants and toddlers are using all of their senses—hearing, seeing, feeling, tasting, and smelling—in all areas of the room. When children delight their senses they are learning about object permanence, cause and effect, and attributes of objects and materials. With a responsive teacher and peers, infants' and toddlers' language development grows by leaps and bounds. As they play with sand and water they are also developing their small motor skills.

Sand provides a delightful sensory experience. Sand in a short sand/water table indoors and outdoors encourages mobile infants and toddlers to feel the texture, pour sand through their fingers, and experiment with filling and emptying cups and other containers. Waterwheels, funnels, sifters, containers of different sizes, and plastic animals encourage toddlers to experiment. Create a sandbox beach (Cryer, Harms, & Bourland, 1988) inside for toddlers, with a small swimming pool full of sand, safe low beach chairs, large plastic sunglasses, beach towels, and magazines.

Provide water in a variety of containers for mobile infants and toddlers (always watch carefully to prevent drowning). (In Box 13.3, Vernon [2003] provides a wonderful example of how toddlers enjoyed water in her program.) Provide small basins of water for mobile infants and water tables for toddlers. Add different materials each day or week to encourage exploration. Refill the containers of water often to reduce the spread of infection. Water tables have drains on the bottom for ease of emptying. Squeeze bottles and paintbrushes encourage toddlers to use water outdoors to "paint" a fence.

Provide infants with materials of different textures to touch. Feelie bags (cloth or paper bags) with different objects in them delight mobile infants and toddlers as they cautiously put their hands in the bags.

Think about how to offer opportunities for children to explore with their other senses in addition to touch. Listening boxes can be made by placing different items in each box (be sure to tape them up well). Stop and have the children listen when there is a new noise. Use *loud, soft, noisy, quiet,* and other descriptive words to enhance language development while exploring sound. Provide visually pleasing materials such as bottles (again, taped closed very carefully) with oil and food coloring combined in them.

Box 13.3

Sink Play

When it is too cold for water play outside, we invite the children to immerse themselves in water at the sinks [standing, with only diapers on, in front of low sinks filled partially with water and toys]. I always find it interesting to observe the different ways children play even while standing right next to each other. Kevin and Trent stood side by side, each engrossed in his own task. Trent concentrated intently on filling the large bucket and carefully pouring it out again into the sink. He poured water on a single washcloth, and then would hold it up and watch the water drip steadily down into the sink.

Kevin was interested in filling many small containers with water and then pouring them into each other. He also used a bottle with a squeeze-lid to spray the water into the containers. He used the bottle to "feed" his baby doll and also to wash the baby's hair. He experimented by filling a container to the top, pushing his hands and arms into the container, and watching the water pour out.

The children were using many words to describe what they were doing: "pour," "top," "wash baby," "water," "my baby," "mine." Not only do the children enjoy playing in the water, it seems to soothe them, and they learn many things about their world. They also learn about such concepts as cause and effect, size, shape, and quantity. And, they get to share a pleasurable experience with their classmates and learn from each other.

Source: Vernon (2003, p. 5).

Creative Opportunities

Serena was excited. She hurried over to the paints and large pieces of paper that the teacher had placed carefully on the low table. Serena's teacher helped her put her smock over her head and then adjust it, Serena grasped a wide-handled paintbrush in a hammer grip, dipped the brush part into the short-side containers of paint, lifted the brush, and watched as the beautiful yellow paint dripped off the end. As she started to move the pretty paintbrush toward her mouth to taste it, the teacher said, "Here, put the paint on this paper," and helped guide Serena's hand toward the paper on the table. Serena was fascinated by the yellow mark that appeared.

Infants and toddlers love to create—make messes, invent new sounds, make a toy move in a surprising way, or put two or more items together in an innovative manner. When watching young children, adults can see the joy and wonder expressed when toddlers make marks on paper with crayons or when they glue two pieces of wood together. When young children are making messes, dumping, mushing, exploring, discovering, inventing, collecting, imagining, observing, and playing with materials, they are creating.

Being a creative person begins in infancy. An infant reaches out to touch his parent's face, the parent's eyes open wide in delight, and the infant has created an emotional connection. The infant squeezes a toy and creates a funny, squeaky noise. She plays with her mouth and creates new sounds. He bats at a musical toy and creates a beautiful tune. A mobile infant, who is just beginning to walk, creates a stir as adults marvel at this new development. Toddlers throw toys into a box and create crashing noises. They place one block beside another and begin to create

Kyanne created this painting at only 15 months of age.

a row. One day they stack a block on top of another and create a tower. A toddler will accidently stick his finger into the neck of an empty soda bottle and create a new toy that waves around when he moves his finger. Turning the pages of a cardboard book creates a new scene to enjoy. Colorful marks made with crayons and nontoxic paints are masterpieces to a toddler budding artist. Groups of toddlers with colorful scarves create a kaleidoscope of colors. As infants and toddlers create in this way they learn that they can *produce, build, generate new ideas,* and *construct*—all aspects of being a creative person. They also develop a healthy sense of mastery, a positive self-concept, and a feeling of being effective, capable, and competent.

Honig (2003a) notes that "working with art materials gives sensory joy to toddlers as they knead play dough or watch in awe as cornstarch goop stretches in their fingers" (p. 22). Creative, sensory, open-ended materials engage children and often reduce stress. Open-ended materials are those that allow the child to use them in a variety of ways. Teachers make the materials available and young children experiment *rather than try to make a product.* The *process* of feeling, pouring, dumping, lifting, examining, turning over, and testing is what is important for very young children—not the end product.

Offer play dough and clay, then stand back and watch the wonderful exploration and investigation that occurs. As they delight their senses, children are learning about the composition of materials, how to shape and reshape them, number, quantity, and mass. All of these activities provide perfect opportunities for teachers to support the language development of infants and toddlers. Toddlers are also learning social skills as they negotiate space and share the materials.

Create a cozy corner where children play with play dough on the floor or on a short table. Place separate piles of play dough on the table or provide one large ball of play dough in the middle of the table. If the materials are available for lengthy periods of time and almost every day, infants and toddlers will relax as they trust that the materials will be available and have time to test their theories about how the material works.

One of Kyanne's first pictures (shown at the top of this page) demonstrates how young children enjoy painting. Nontoxic paint that is especially made for young children and purchased through catalogs or in a teacher supply store can be offered to toddlers with large pieces of paper on a table or on the floor. Toddlers can use their hands or large paintbrushes with the paint to test their theories on how to make a mark on a page. Short easels for toddlers spark their creativity with crayons and paint. Smocks (aprons) can be purchased to cover toddlers' clothing if parents or the children are concerned about getting paint on their clothes. Toddlers can learn to go get their smocks before they begin to paint, but often need help from a teacher or peer to get them on correctly.

Ditto sheets to color or requiring toddlers to create products such as egg carton caterpillars are not appropriate tasks for mobile infants and toddlers because they stifle creativity. Toddlers are *making something happen* rather than *making something.* Be open to all of the possibilities for what children do with the materials. Materials should always be offered as a *choice* and children should not ever be forced to touch or play with them. Let them wash their hands as soon as they would like, to build enjoyment in the experience of being creative.

Finger painting is always a popular creative activity.

Writing and Drawing Opportunities

Infants and toddlers make their mark on the world through drawing with nontoxic crayons, magnetic boards with an attached large pen, and markers (without the lids, which are a choking hazard). Mobile infants like Dawson (as shown in Box 13.4) grasp the big pen, with an overhand grasp, using the large muscles in his arm to make big circles on the paper. Infants will bang or jab their crayon on the paper, but soon they will make straight lines. Vertical lines usually appear before horizontal lines. Dawson has had quite a bit of experience using crayons and other writing materials, so he is already making circles with his pen on his magnetic board.

Provide comfortable small chairs, such as Dawson is using, or create a cozy corner with a small table where mobile infants and toddlers can

Almost anything can serve as a toddler's canvas.

use nontoxic crayons and large pieces of blank paper. Opportunities to use crayons on sandpaper and other unusual materials, chalk outside, and finger painting spark a mobile infant's or toddler's interest in writing and drawing.

Opportunities with Blocks

Blocks may be small or large, plastic or wooden, of various sizes and shapes. Hirsch (1996) has identified six stages of block development: carrying, stacking and placing in rows, bridging, building enclosures, creating patterns, and representational play. An infant will mouth the blocks, a mobile infant will carry them around and begin to explore their properties, and a toddler will begin to stack them one on top of the other. Soon rows of blocks will appear, and then varying forms of bridges. You may see a toddler creating an enclosure with blocks on all sides to contain a zoo full of wooden animals. Patterns may appear—for example, a toddler may use four blocks of the same size to support a large unit block. Toward the end of the toddler period, children may begin to use the blocks as symbols for another object, such as a firefighter's hose, and may begin to pretend—for example, to be a firefighter.

Blocks provide opportunities for learning at all ages and provide opportunities to support development in all domains. As infants and toddlers manipulate the blocks and then play with them in a purposeful way, they are developing self-regulation. Playing with blocks is often a social experience and provides opportunities for children to learn to play together and resolve conflicts. Creativity blossoms as toddlers build with blocks. Toddlers will also knock down a block tower that they have built, to *create* a noise and to *create* a mess. Knocking down blocks, as well as building with them, is about learning about the properties of materials. They are also using many of the problem-solving strategies, as described in this example cited by Reindle (2004):

> Tyrone, 2, discovered that the teacher had built a bridge out of three blocks and had placed it on a short table next to the block area. He pushed a little car he found under the bridge and soon it came tumbling down. He picked up the blocks and stacked them one on top of the other, because that was the schema that he used to build. After realizing, on his own, that his blocks did not have a space under them, he moved two blocks so that they were apart by a few inches. He then took the other block and placed it across the two base blocks to make a bridge. Tyrone had figured it out. (p. 3)

Box 13.4

Day to Day the Relationship Way

Individual Child Planning Guide

Child's Name: Dawson

Plans for Week of (Date): Sept. 7–11, 2009

Person(s) Completing the Guide: Torren and Nicole

Respect: Child's Emotions, Effort, Goals, Learning, and Relationships

Write an observation or use a picture or other documentation here—date all notes:

Respect and Reflect

9/7/09

What am I doing?

I am making large circles on a magnetic board. I am holding the large attached pen with my left hand and holding the board with my right. This is called holding and operating. I am using an over-hand grasp which is typical for my age and allows me to use the large muscles in my arm to draw.

How am I feeling?

I am feeling very focused. I am intent on what I am doing.

What am I learning?

I am learning how to use the large muscles in my arms and the small muscles in my hands to write and to create. I am learning to focus and attend when I want to accomplish something. I am learning, "I can do it," and I am learning about cause and effect.

Relate

What will you do to support my development and learning?

Responsive Interactions

We will talk with your parents about how much you enjoyed this experience and we will ask them what you like to do at home. We will use words to describe what you are doing (parallel talk).

Environment, Toys, Materials, and Experiences

We will provide other creative experiences such as play dough, finger paints, and crayons as as well as other "cause and effect" toys.

When an older toddler pretends to build a house, a fence around a pretend playground, or a birthday cake he is building a foundation for literacy development (Stroud, 1995). Stroud identifies ways that block play supports success in literacy development:

1. Children learn about representation and symbols as they pretend with blocks and block structures. When children begin to reproduce and name their buildings, for example, block builiding becomes representational and serves as an introduction to symbolization; "the blocks themselves become symbols for other objects, just as printed letters and words are symbols for objects and ideas" (p. 9).

2. Visual discrimination—a skill necessary for distinguishing similar letter and word formations during the reading process—is enhanced by block play. Children are continually looking at, comparing, and matching blocks of varying shapes and sizes. Cleanup provides another opportunity to sort and return blocks to a labeled position on storage shelves.

3. Fine motor strength and coordination used for writing are developed with blocks. Writing skills needed to manipulate crayons and pencils are developed through grasping, carrying, and stacking blocks.

4. Oral language develops as young children label the toys as "blocks," describe them, and talk about them with others.

Stroud also recommends adding books and writing materials to the block area to encourage literacy experiences.

Children's receptive and expressive language develops as adults and peers name the blocks, describe their attributes, and talk about spatial concepts. An adult says, "You put the red block on the blue block," and then waits responsively for the infant or toddler to respond with a sound, a gesture, an action, or words. The adult listens for these language expressions and responds by observing, imitating, expanding, elaborating, or extending the child's language.

Motor capacities develop as babies handle the blocks with their hands (small motor), pick up blocks and carry them around (large motor), and explore how they feel and listen to how they sound when they fall (sensory development).

When infants and toddlers play with blocks of all sizes and shapes, have a cozy corner where they are displayed and easy for babies to reach, room for floor play with the blocks, and responsive teachers, then the possibilities for learning in all of the developmental domains is endless. Place blocks on a low shelf with each shelf clearly labeled. As children "clean up" after play time, they learn to classify as they replace the blocks on the shelves in their designated places.

Music, Song, and Creative Movement Opportunities

Sarah, just a year old, laughed as her teacher played pat-a-cake with her. As her teacher began singing the song, Sarah clapped her hands together repeatedly with delight. After the song ended, Sarah's teacher pointed to Sarah's hands with delight and said, "You clapped your hands." Sarah looked joyfully at the teacher as if to say, "Do it again."

While diapering Jamika, her teacher sings, "You have ten little *fingers,* and ten little *toes,* two little *arms,* and one little *nose.*" As her teacher touches her fingers, her toes, her arms, and her nose, Jamika wriggles in delight at hearing this familiar tune. Soon Jamika will start chiming in with her teacher as she sings this song.

Teachers can sing songs throughout the day. A good-morning song helps infants and toddlers transition from home to child care. A good-bye song signals that a parent is here to pick up his child. Songs sung throughout the day comfort children or help them transition from one activity to another, such as from indoor play to outdoor play. As Jamika waits for her mom and dad at the end of the day, one teacher sings to Jamika, modeling how to clap and tap: "Two little hands go clap, clap, clap. Two little feet go tap, tap, tap." Soon, several toddlers are sitting with the teacher. Jamika watches her friends intently as they clap and tap in all different and unique ways. These familiar activities are opportunities for young children to enjoy music and learn concepts in fun, responsive, sensitive ways. Teachers don't have to have the best singing voices in the world to sing to infants and toddlers. Babies love to hear songs and it doesn't matter to them how a teacher sings them—children love the warm feelings that are conveyed (Honig, 1995; Ilari & Johnson-Green, 2002). There are many benefits to children of singing, listening to music, making rhythms, and moving their bodies. These experiences:

- Provide opportunities for pure joy
- Provide opportunities to move, practice crawling, pull to stand, jump, run, experience rhythms, and feel comfortable with their bodies in space
- Increase self-awareness and worth
- Provide opportunities for children to learn concepts such as "up" and "down"
- Provide opportunities for children to interact and learn prosocial behavior
- Help children make transitions and makes routines and learning times fun
- Provide opportunities for children to learn words and longer sentences in their own and other languages
- Encourage children to listen and follow directions
- Encourage creativity and problem solving
- Provide opportunities for representational and symbolic play—for example, when toddlers sing "Twinkle, Twinkle, Little Star" they use their hands to represent stars
- Music can comfort and soothe children and help them fall asleep

Go to the Activities and Applications section in Chapter 13 of MyEducationLab to watch the video *Individual Story Time: Toddler.* Think about the importance of literacy experiences for young children.

Literacy Opportunities

Literacy experiences are among the most important that a teacher can provide to young children. What is literacy? How does it develop? What is the relationship between talking, social experiences, and learning to read and write? McLane and McNamee (1991) define literacy as "the notion that writing and reading are ways of making, interpreting, and communicating meaning" (p. 1).

Becoming literate is about learning to read and write—and *becoming* begins in infancy when an infant hears the sounds of language and begins to make sounds herself. Bridges to literacy (McLane & McNamee, 1991; Rosenkoetter & Barton, 2002) built during the infant and toddler years provide pathways to the more formal process of learning that letters form words and that sentences contain meaning that can be deciphered and understood.

Language is a strong bridge that connects to later reading and writing because infants and

Cory enjoys a book by experiencing it with his body.

toddlers learn how to communicate—the ultimate purpose of reading and writing. Play is a necessary bridge—playing with sounds and words, and making marks on a page. Learning about symbols is also a connecting bridge to literacy as toddlers learn that a picture or an object (a plastic apple) can represent something real that is seen and touched. This leads to a later understanding that squiggly lines called letters have meaning. Experiences with water, sand, toys, animals, and people are essential bridges because the child can bring a wealth of understanding to written concepts and when they are older, they can write stories based on their many rich understandings. And certainly, one of the most important bridges to becoming literate is the love of books—a foundational bridge that provides a link to later reading and writing. Positive relationships with special adults and peers are the supports that strengthen the bridges to literacy.

Learning to Love Books

When a child learns about books and writing she is inherently involved in social activities. Infants and toddlers quickly learn that books have interesting pictures and stories (Honig, 2007). As infants and toddlers listen to books they learn new words and ways to communicate. Throughout infancy, when read to often, infants and toddlers begin to learn about representations—a picture of a duck is not a real duck, but they can talk about it as if it were a real duck. They learn about symbols—that letters make up words and that words (squiggly lines to them) have meaning. When teachers read books, they are developing relationships with children and encouraging peer interaction. As infants try to turn the pages of cardboard books and toddlers the pages of paper books, they are developing their motor skills. As usual, infants and toddlers are learning many things through one activity. We hope they will also learn to love books.

> *Ezra, 26 months old, snuggles against his teacher's arm as she reads a book to him and two other toddlers who are sitting together on the floor. He likes turning the brightly colored pages with the pictures of familiar toys, and he especially likes to hear his teacher's animated voice as she reads the story aloud. Ezra loves books and often finds books in the room and runs to his teacher holding out the book for her to read.*

When does this interest in books start and why do most babies love books? Most young infants adore looking at visually interesting images found in books. They tune into the reader's voice and learn about the rhythms, tones, and sounds of language. Nursery rhymes and poetry can soothe a baby with their reassuringly rhythmic sounds. Books with one word and picture on a page spark a baby's interest as the adult "reads" the pictures. Cloth and soft vinyl books allow infants to grasp, chew, suck, and crinkle books as they learn through all their senses. Sitting in a teacher's lap is the perfect way for an infant to see the pictures and enjoy a fun, colorful book.

Mobile infants love to look at books as they sit, walk, and toddle around. For mobile infants, books are playthings that can be touched and turned, and they reveal a world of surprises with every flip of the page. Because mobile infants are absorbing language and learning new words every day, they're beginning to relate the pictures in books to objects in real life. A book about toys or animals is a great choice for this age group. Choose short books with simple stories. Books made of heavy cardboard allow mobile infants to use newly developed motor skills to turn pages.

Toddlers love stories about familiar animals, objects, and people. Pictures with a few printed words on every page can keep a busy toddler's attention as she points to the pictures and asks, "What's that?" Interactive pop-up books, with their hidden surprises, trigger grins of delight from curious toddlers.

Allow toddlers to choose from books displayed on shelves with the cover showing—rather than thrown in a box, where they're hard to identify. Even toddlers are beginning to learn how books work: that you start at the front and read from top to bottom, that the story is usually about the picture, and that some of those strange squiggles sound the same each time an adult reads them.

Here are some ways you can help infants and toddlers have fun with and learn to love books:

- *Create cozy "reading" corners.*   Schickedanz (2003) talks about creating a book nook for infants and toddlers. Equip these corners and nooks with a small, soft-covered mattress, a cloth-covered inner tube, and for toddlers a short couch just their size. Make sure that the corner is comfortable for teachers to lie on their backs while holding up a book with a baby by their side, who is looking up as well. Or, create a place where teachers can sit with their backs supported by the wall or pillows (no pillows for infants for safety reasons). Mobile infants and toddlers will enjoy looking at books together.

- *Place books around the room.*   That way, they greet and tempt a child at every turn. Be creative. Putting a book about bears right next to a stuffed bear makes that book hard to resist!

- *Read throughout the day.*   Infants can look and listen when teachers hold them in their comfortable laps. Toddlers like one-on-one time with a teacher as well, but also enjoy clustering together around a favorite teacher on a couch, in a cozy corner, or wherever books are in the room. Take your cues from the children and read whenever they ask you. Instead of having a structured reading time for toddlers, teachers can entice them to listen to a story by sitting down where toddlers can join together. Don't be surprised if other toddlers come running to hear the story as well. Let them come and go—they will soon learn to sit for a whole story. When toddlers are forced to sit in groups to listen to a story, they often become disinterested quickly and their love of books can be jeopardized. Toddlers learn to love books when they are shared with an adult who makes them feel safe, loved, excited, soothed, or important, depending on the child's need at the time.

- *Choose books carefully.*   Cloth and heavy cardboard books (sometimes called board books) are sturdy and can be transported, carted, stashed, put in containers, and "read" by curious infants and energetic toddlers. Choose books with rhythmical language, touch-and-smell books, and books with clear pictures (Kupetz & Green, 1997). Select books with pictures of children and families from a variety of cultures and books that show both boys and girls in a variety of activities.

- *Read responsively.*   Use interactive storybook reading strategies (Whitehurst, Zenvenberger, Crone, Schultz, Velting, & Fischel, 1999). Notice which pictures children seem to enjoy, point to them, name them, and when possible, point out the real objects they represent. Interact with children as you read the story and encourage their engagement. Encourage infants to makes sounds and toddlers to discuss their experiences as you read a story. Answer their questions. Avoid pestering children with too many one-right-answer questions such as "What's this?" and "Who's that?" Have fun reading, use lots of feeling, exaggerate sounds, and wait for infants and toddlers to respond with their own sounds, words, and gestures.

- *Exchange information with families through home visits, book bags to borrow, and information about the importance of reading as well as how to read to infants and toddlers.*   The ZERO TO THREE Web site (http://www.zerotothree.org) and the National Center for Family Literacy (NCFL) Web site (http://www.famlit.org) provide tip sheets, activities, and research related to supporting families. Ask families what books their infants and toddlers like at home and what secrets they have for sparking their children's interest in books.

- *Provide a literacy-rich environment.*   Books and printed words should be found in all parts of an infant or toddler room. Photograph albums of family members, friends, and pets are available with the name of the pet, for example, written at the bottom of the page. Add their names and photos to their cubbies. Rather than quiz children, comment with excitement when a child is looking at a word.

Math, Space, and Shape Opportunities

All of the materials in an infant-toddler room or home offer opportunities for learning about numerals (the symbols that represent numbers, such as the numeral 2) and numbers (the concept of amount—there are two blocks) as well as other math concepts. As an infant holds one block in one hand and another block in another and looks back and forth from one to the other, he is learning about numbers—that he now has more blocks than he did before when he was holding one block. "More" becomes evident as the infant feels what two are like compared to one.

Teachers and parents can nurture infants' and toddlers' understanding of mathematical concepts (Geist, 2003). An adult's role is to set up a rich menu of math *opportunities* for young children and to support their interest and exploration through math interactions. Teachers and parents can promote children's ability to process information—how to think. To support mathematical understanding, toddlers are not given worksheets and they are not drilled in their numbers and shapes by adults. Rather, possibilities for learning about math concepts in a play environment are found everywhere that children go in their home, center room, or family child care home and in many interactions that occur daily with teachers. Adults who are knowledgeable about mathematical concepts and see the possibilities for supporting mathematical understanding every day in relaxed and informal ways take advantage of playful moments and the environment to help young children learn. Here each concept is defined and a list of materials and interactions that promote mathematical understanding are described. Understand though, that most materials and interactions have the possibility of promoting many concepts—for example, a finger-play with a toddler (such as "Round and round the garden, like a teddy bear, one step, two steps, tickle you under there") uses concepts of shape (round and round the garden) and counting (one step, two steps), as well as builds relationships. (Use your finger to trace a circle around and around the palm of a young child's hand. Walk your fingers up the baby's arm as you say "one step, two steps" and then *if the baby is enjoying the finger-play* gently tickle the baby under the arm. Wait at least 5 seconds to see if the baby puts out her hand for another turn. If so, repeat the finger-play. If not, try again another time.)

Opportunities for Learning About Counting

Infants and toddlers learn to count in myriad ways if the adults in their lives are aware of the many daily opportunities for counting. *Model* counting during play as you point to and count children, toys, and books. For toddlers, start counting "1" and then point to the next item and wait to see if the toddler counts the next item. If not, continue modeling in a warm tone of voice. Routines provide opportunities as adults count babies' fingers and toes in playful and responsive ways. Snack time provides many opportunities for counting pieces of food, cups, plates, and silverware. Once adults are aware that it is important that they model counting for children, then they will see many opportunities during the day to count. As always, count when the infant or toddler seems receptive and the counting doesn't interfere with a goal that the child is attempting to achieve, such as carefully stacking blocks.

Opportunities for Learning About One-to-One Correspondence

One-to-one correspondence occurs as babies begin to understand that there is a number for each item that is counted. Provide an environment that contains a variety of objects that work together in a one-to-one relationship: cars and garages, containers with lids, and dolls with beds. Provide opportunities for toddlers to put the plates on the table for a snack or meal—one for each child in the group or one for each member of the family. You can say, "One plate for Daddy, one plate for Mommy, and one plate for you," as you point to the plates.

Opportunities for Learning How to Classify

Infants and toddlers are also learning concepts about classifying people and objects. Classification is a concept that describes a child's actions of comparing similarities and differences, sorting by various attributes, putting objects into different categories, and arranging objects by various characteristics. Infants, for example, begin to categorize which adults are friendly and which aren't. Mobile infants figure out which items make a noise when shaken or which items roll. Use responsive planning and provide the child with objects that make noise and objects that don't to encourage further discoveries. Table 13.4 includes a number of opportunities that teachers can provide to encourage infants' and toddlers' exploration of classification, spatial relationships and shapes, quantity, patterning, and seriation.

Table 13.4   Learning opportunities: sorting, numeracy, space, and shape

Opportunities to Learn About Classification (Sorting)

- Compare objects—point out similarities and differences in color, shape, and size.
- Provide an environment that includes a variety of manipulatives (parquetry blocks, unit cubes), collections (pebbles, plastic animals), dramatic play props (variety of clothing, dishes, dolls), and art materials (fabric samples, tongue depressors) in different colors, shapes, and sizes to offer classifying and sorting experiences throughout the day.
- Provide opportunities for children to assemble collections (walk to the park to collect pinecones or fallen leaves) and talk about why the children sort, classify, and order objects in a certain way.
- Use language and point out similarities and differences in, for example, toys and blocks, as toddlers put them on the shelf during cleanup time.
- Compare collections one-to-one to determine "more," "less," and "same as."
- Provide opportunities for toddlers to sort objects according to two characteristics at the same time (big red, small red, big yellow, small yellow). Understand, though that this is challenging for toddlers.

Opportunities to Learn About Spatial Relationships and Shapes

- Provide opportunities for mobile infants and toddlers to explore spatial relations (next to, above, below, inside, outside) during the day. You can say as you point, "Sarah is sitting *next to* Amanda." "Oh, you're putting the block *in* the basket." "Put the puzzles on the shelf *above* the blocks."
- Provide opportunities for children to build complex 2-dimensional and 3-dimensional shapes by putting simple shapes together (pattern blocks, tangrams, unit blocks).

Opportunities to Learn About Quantity

- Provide different sizes of containers during water and sand play.
- Provide opportunities for mobile infants and toddlers to experiment with full and empty.

Opportunities to Learn About Patterning

- Provide opportunities for children to notice patterns (visual pattern in bricks in the sidewalk, auditory pattern in the melodies of music, repetitive language of predictable stories, physical patterns in exercise).

Opportunities to Learn About Seriation (Ordering by One or More Dimensions)

- Provide materials for toddlers to explore seriating (various sized cups in water table to sort by size, paint-chip samples to seriate by color hue, fabric squares to sort by texture from softest to least soft).
- Use terms such as *short, tall, high, low, wide, thin* to compare objects.

Opportunities for Active Play and Motor Development

Large Motor and Active Play

Provide spaces for infants and toddlers where they can use their large muscles to crawl, pull to stand, stand alone, walk, climb, toddle, and run. They will need space away from the quiet, nurturing, and creative areas. The equipment in this indoor area usually includes mats stacked to create different levels, a rocking boat, a short climber, a large tube to climb through, or a few steps to a loft area. These large pieces of equipment promote social as well as motor development (Honig, 2001). For small spaces, these pieces of equipment can be shared with other homerooms in centers and teachers can alternate these exciting opportunities.

At various times, depending on the interests and needs of the children, balls of various sizes and shapes, large containers and boxes, push and pull toys, small "grocery" carts, riding toys, wagons, and blankets with toys on them for pulling can be introduced. Miller (1999) describes large motor opportunities; for example, place large boxes with the ends cut out end to end and cover them with blankets to create box tunnels. Punch a hole in the ends of shoeboxes and tie them together, end to end, to make a little train. Leave a string about 10 inches long on one end so that the child can pull the train. Children will place various toys from around the room into the boxes to give them a little ride. These open-ended materials (no one correct way to use them) provide numerous opportunities for infants and toddlers to problem solve, exploring their multiple uses (Segatti, Brown-DuPaul, & Keyes, 2003).

Small Motor and Manipulative Opportunities

Toys and items for infants to grasp, shake, and bang develop the small muscles in their hands and give them opportunities to manipulate objects. With all small motor and manipulatives make sure that there are no small parts or that the toy or material doesn't present a choking hazard. Provide natural materials such as rocks, shells, and pine cones. Mobile infants and toddlers usually love to model after an adult and blow on a bubble wand. They can use the small muscles in their hands to hold the wand and wave it, and then fit the wand back in the bottle so that they can create more bubbles. Large wands can be created out of clothes hangers and dipped into a tub of soapy water. Easy puzzles, large beads for stringing, shape formboards, and other manipulatives can be placed on low shelves with space between each item so that mobile infants and toddlers can see them easily.

Outdoor Opportunities

> *Joshua looked with anticipation at his teacher when she announced, "Time to go outside." This was the time of day that Joshua seemed to like best. When the door to the outside opened, Joshua was the first to toddle outside. He put his face to the sun and then scurried to the sandbox to bury his hands deep into the cool sand. It was all his teacher could do to keep up with him as she carried a big box of sand toys to the area.*

Outdoor time brings opportunities for infants and toddlers to poke and dig in the sand and dirt, push and pull wagons, touch everything in sight, and feel the soft breezes on their faces. They savor the scent of flowering trees, learn new outside vocabulary, and gain a spark in their eyes from invigorating and challenging physical experiences such as walking in sand and climbing over safe obstacles.

Outdoor time also brings challenges for teachers as they strive to provide interesting and exciting experiences for infants and toddlers, allow them to explore with all of their senses, and yet provide a sense of security and safety that infants and toddlers need so much, indoors or outdoors (see Table 13.5).

Infant and toddler professionals can challenge themselves to think about the potential for children's learning in all of the equipment, materials, and experiences available in a center, a family child care home, or in a family's home environment. Children choose from these opportunities and learn from each experience that they have in a carefully planned environment and in teacher and peer interactions that happen moment to moment and day to day the relationship way.

We have described the experiences that can be offered as opportunities for learning. Teachers are very intentional about setting up an environment that engages infants and toddlers and they choose from the opportunities. Almost any opportunity that they choose offers possibilities for children to learn in all domains of development.

CURRICULUM APPROACHES

We have shared information on seven components of planning a responsive, relationship-based curriculum. Many of these components are shared by the curricula and programs available to purchase, although some emphasize the importance of relationships more than others.

Table 13.5 Security and safety issues for outdoor time

Age	Activities (Delighting the Senses)	Security and Safety Issues
Young Infants (Birth to 8 Months)		
During this age period infants will begin to turn over, then roll, and crawl. Grasping improves and soon everything in sight, including grass and bugs, may go to the mouth.	Place babies on a soft blanket to allow them to practice their physical skills. Bring each baby's grasping and biting toys outside. Small plastic swimming pools in the shade (without water in them) provide a separate and safe place for young infants. Continue activities like "reading" picture books, repeating sounds, and providing responsive toys.	Young infants need to know that their special teacher is near and nurturing. Infants need particular care when outdoors to protect them from the sun and extreme temperatures.
Mobile Infants (8 to 18 Months)		
Crawling, toddling, and running are skills that may emerge during this period. Walking backward and climbing up and down a low set of stairs are challenging tasks for this age. Small motor skills improve greatly during this period. Many very small and large items go straight to the mouth. Infants like being near each other, exchanging looks, touches, and sometimes even toys. Older infants in this stage may learn to say "Mine" and clutch items closely.	Provide equipment that is safe for cruising infants to pull themselves up on and walk around. Gather push-and-pull toys such as small trikes and wagons for the walking crowd. Balls and stacking toys are great outdoors as well as inside. Fill small plastic pools with balls or safe manipulatives. Large boxes with doors and windows cut out are the perfect places for mobile infants to play peek-a-boo and crawl-in-and-out. Small individual tubs of water are perfect for this age, but need one-on-one attention for safety reasons. Language develops as teachers comment on walking, jumping, climbing, in, out, up, down, over, and around.	Children tire easily and need a lap to sink into to regroup and gain energy for the next physical tasks. "Watching them like a hawk" has special meaning at this age to prevent unwanted and unknown objects from finding their way to the mouth. Provide shady spots for all sun-sensitive infants. Watch water play, even in very small containers, because infants and toddlers have drowned in pails or small pools of water. Provide nutritious safe snacks and plenty of fluids.
Toddlers (18 to 36 Months)		
This age delights in practicing all of their physical skills. They will challenge themselves to climb and jump higher and farther. Imitating an adult or a peer occurs frequently. Toddlers may become frustrated easily because they want to do more than their physical skills allow. Some toddlers may begin to "pretend" to be firefighters or other characters that they have experienced live or on TV. They want to be with peers and will play beside or with others. Toddlers alternate between wanting to "do it myself" and wanting adults to help them. They need special teachers who understand how they struggle between wanting to be grown up, but still need loving, nurturing, and holding (on their terms, of course).	Sand and water are favorites. Provide sand areas, large enough for several toddlers and expect them to sit right in the middle of the area. Bring *many* sand toys for pouring, digging, and poking safely. Pulling or pushing a "friend" in a wagon will result in squeals of delight from both. Expect squabbles over toys, just as indoors. Paintbrushes and water go together for an outdoor art experience. Set up other art materials such as crayons, paints, and a variety of paper on the ground or a low table. Dolls, trucks, cars, and other play materials encourage interactions among peers. Blankets on the ground or over a card table for puzzles, stories, and manipulatives provide a spot for a quiet break from large motor activities. Provide a nurturing place with soft blankets and pillows for a toddler to "refuel" emotionally with a special teacher.	Remember, toddlers need time to experiment, problem solve, and explore materials alone and with peers. When they tire they will need to be near an adult whom they trust and like. Try to accumulate many toys for toddlers outdoors. Otherwise, they will become bored and fight over the few toys available. Provide nutritious, safe snacks and plenty of fluids. Survey the playground for sharp objects and broken equipment before allowing children outside each day.

With any of the following that we describe here, however, a teacher's emphasis on the importance of relationships and responsive interactions and planning can complement the materials available. Let's start by discussing a program that has lead the way in promoting a relationship-based approach to curriculum planning.

The Program for Infant/Toddler Care (PITC)

We begin by describing *The Program for Infant/Toddler Care* (PITC), a comprehensive training program for infant-toddler teachers, because this program has greatly informed the authors of this book. The goal of PITC is to help teachers recognize the crucial importance of giving tender, loving care and assisting in the infants' intellectual development through an attentive reading of each child's cues. The PITC videos, DVDs, guides, and manuals are designed to help child care administrators and teachers become sensitive to infants' cues, connect with the children's families and cultures, and develop responsive, relationship-based care. The training materials provide the foundation for teachers to study the children in their care, reflect on and record information about the children's interests and skills, and search for ways to set the stage for the child's next learning encounters.

As a relationship-based approach, PITC particularly emphasizes the importance of primary caregiving, continuity of caregiving, small group sizes, low ratios, and responsiveness as foundations of child care settings where infants and toddlers are able to learn and thrive. PITC holds an image of the child as an active learner who will make important discoveries about the world through her own exploration, if supported by a responsive adult in an engaging environment.

Videos and training materials for PITC are available from http://www.pitc.org.

High/Scope

High/Scope is an approach to preschool and infant and toddler education that highlights key experiences to frame early learning and development. These include sense of self, social relations, creative representation, movement and music, communication and language, exploring objects, early quantity and number, space, and time. The environment is organized to promote child initiation and choice among a variety of interesting materials. Teachers assess children for key experiences using the *Child Observation Record* (COR) for infants and toddlers and then use the information for planning changes in the environment and experiences for children.

The Creative Curriculum for Infants, Toddlers & Twos

The Creative Curriculum for Infants, Toddlers & Twos provides extensive information for planning a responsive curriculum (Dodge, Rudick, Berke, & Dombro, 2006). Table 13.6 describes the main components of this well-known curriculum. Also see www.teachingstrategies.com for information on the philosophy, goals, strategies, assessment tools, and resources available.

Reggio Emilia

"For the last three decades, certain Italian regions and localities have been sites of extraordinary efforts by educators and public officials, working together with parents and other citizens, to build high-quality public systems of care and education to serve families with young children" (Gandini & Edwards, 2001, p. 1). The fundamental points of the Reggio philosophy can be summarized as follows:

> One of the fundamental points of the Reggio philosophy is an image of a child who experiences the world, who feels a part of the world right from birth; who is full of curiosities, full of desire to live; a child who is full of desire and ability to communicate from the start of his or her life; a child who is

Table 13.6   Five components of *The Creative Curriculum for Infants, Toddlers & Twos* curriculum

1. Knowing infants, toddlers, and twos
   Describes development and the unique characteristics of children

2. Creating a responsive environment
   Describes how to set up an environment that is responsive to individual children

3. What children are learning
   Describes relationships, interactions, materials, and experiences that are building blocks of learning

4. Caring and teaching
   Describes the diverse roles of teachers including how to use ongoing assessment

5. Partnering with families
   Describes how to partner with families in a respectful and responsive way

Sources: Berke, Rudick, & Dodge (2007); Dodge, Rudick, Berke, & Dombro (2006).

fully able to create maps for his or her personal, social, cognitive, affective, and symbolic orientation. Because of all this, a young child reacts with a competent system of abilities, learning strategies, and ways of organizing relationships. (Rinaldi, 2001, pp. 50–51)

Bambini: The Italian Approach to Infant-Toddler Care by Gandini and Edwards (2001) describes the Reggio Emilia approach in detail. The Italian approach to early childhood education grows from their well-articulated image of the child. The image of the infant and toddler as highly capable of making discoveries and constructing knowledge is, of course, congruent with research findings on early learning. This image drives the organization of the infant-toddler centers in Reggio Emilia.

Respect for very young children's ability to construct knowledge from their relationships and their environment is central to the organization of the early childhood programs and the environments, relationships, and experiences they offer in supporting learning. The key tool used by teachers is purposeful observation and documentation of the children's activities. This documentation process is not simply recording activities or accomplishments—it is a method of coming to thoughtful, reflective understanding of the children's activities and thinking, and it is the basis of the teacher's planning for introducing new activities or materials into the center. The documentation process consists of forming a question or hypothesis; observing, recording, and collecting artifacts; organizing observations and artifacts; analyzing and interpreting the observations and artifacts, which leads to building theories; possibly reframing the original questions; and then planning and responding from one's understandings of the children's knowledge and interests (Gandini & Goldhaber, 2001).

myeducationlab

Go to
MyEducationLab
and complete
the Building
Teaching Skills and
Dispositions exercise
in Chapter 13.

SUMMARY

- Responsive routines that provide stability, consistency, and opportunities for learning for infants and toddlers are a key component of a relationship-based program.

- An environment set up with cozy spaces and places and the opportunities provided within this environment entice children to choose, play, develop, relate to others, be nurtured, and learn.

- Every experience offers an opportunity for children to develop their capacities in the emotional, social, cognitive, language, and motor domains.

- A variety of infant and toddler curricula are available to purchase and each offers unique possibilities for child development.

REFLECTIONS AND RESOURCES FOR THE READER

Reflections

1. How do responsive environments support infants' and toddlers' relationships with adults and peers?
2. How would you interact with a toddler during diaper time to help him or her feel safe and enjoy the time with you?

Observation and Application Opportunities

1. Use the environment guide (Table 13.2) at the beginning of this chapter to observe an infant or toddler environment. What components does the environment include? What do you think needs to be added or changed in the environment?
2. Observe an infant or toddler program. What literacy and math opportunities do you see provided for children (interactions, environment, materials, and experiences)? Are children able to choose among these literacy and math opportunities?
3. Choose one curriculum described at the end of this chapter and report to other students on the eight components of a curriculum described at the beginning of chapter 12.

Supplementary Articles and Books to Read

Birckmayer, J., Kennedy, A., & Stonehouse, A. (2008). *From lullabies to literature: Stories in the lives of infants and toddlers.* Washington, DC: NAEYC.

Friedman, S., & Soltero, M. (July, 2006). Following a child's lead: Examples of emergent curriculum for infants and toddlers. *Beyond the Journal,* 1–5.

Knapp-Philo, J. (2008). *Celebrating language and literacy for infants, toddlers & twos.* DVD. Disc includes user's guide for professional development and family workshops. Rohnert Park, CA: Sonoma State University.

Lally, R., & Mangione, P. (2006). The uniqueness of infancy demands a responsive approach to care. *Young Children, 61*(4), 14–20.

Petersen, S., & Wittmer, D.S. (2008). Relationship-based infant care: Responsive, on demand, and predictable. *Young Children, 63*(3), 40–42.

Zambo, D., & Hansen, C. C. (2007). Love, language, and emergent literacy: Pathways to emotional development of the very young. *Young Children, 62*(3), 32–37.

Interesting Links

http://nccic.org

National Child Care Information Exchange   The NCCIC has several Web pages of helpful information about literacy development.

http://www.pitc.org/

PITC Demonstration Programs: Virtual Tours!   To get ideas for an infant and toddler environment, take a virtual tour through five California community college children's centers that are implementing the PITC approach to infant-toddler care.

myeducationlab
These and other web links are included in this chapter on MyEducationLab.

Respect, Reflect, and Relate

The 3 R Approach to Guidance

At the beginning of this chapter we discuss the eighth component to planning a curriculum: a relationship-based approach to guiding infants' and toddlers' behavior while meeting their emotional needs. In planning the guidance component, we use the 3 R approach (respecting, reflecting, and relating)—a way of thinking about children's development, the reasons for their behavior, and how adults can respond in ways that build children's social and emotional skills and relationships with family, teachers, and peers. The 3 R approach to guidance builds on the relationship-based model presented in chapter 1. This model reminds us to consider how the individual child's attributes, capacities, and uniqueness as well as the child's family, culture, and ecology affect the quality of the child's relationships, which then influence a child's development and behavior.

We will apply the 3 R approach to developmental issues—topics such as separation anxiety, biting, tantrums, and toilet learning. These are everyday challenges that teachers, family specialists, and early interventionists experience with children at home and in programs. Adults, who have increased knowledge of what the child is experiencing during these times of emotional change, and sometimes turbulence, are more likely to use empathic responses that promote children's capacities.

Unfortunately, sometimes children who are experiencing problems in their lives engage in challenging behaviors to get their needs met. In the last part of the chapter we discuss ideas for understanding and helping children who are angry, aggressive, sad, anxious, or who have experienced **traumatic events.** Let's begin with a discussion of the difference between guidance and discipline and why we use the word *guidance* in this chapter.

THE DIFFERENCE BETWEEN GUIDANCE AND DISCIPLINE

Jose takes off his diaper during playtime. William starts playing with his food. Lynn bites peers who get too near to her when she is tired. Laura grabs toys from other children when she wants them. Before the teacher can stop them, Deanna and John quickly jump up on a chair in order to see better, but the chair topples over and they tumble to the floor.

What do these examples have in common? They are *opportunities* for adults to *socialize* children to the ways of a culture, to *guide* them to try different strategies of relating and getting their needs met, and to *teach* them in order for them to be successful in a world that requires social and emotional competence.

The term **discipline** has traditionally been used to mean adult control, restraint, and authority as well as child obedience—but another meaning of the term discipline is *to teach* infants and toddlers new behavior. Because of the confusion between the two meanings of the term *discipline,* we will use the term **guidance** to indicate a developmental, relationship-based, problem-solving approach to supporting young children's social and emotional competence.

A guide shows the way and supports those she guides on the journey. A guide encourages, models, and structures a journey so that everyone can be successful. *Guiding* means that infants and toddlers are supported as they learn an enormous amount of information in such a short period of time—how to use a spoon or why they shouldn't take off their own diaper in the middle of the room in the middle of the day. They learn the important guidelines for their culture, such as when it is acceptable to laugh and how to help another person in distress. They can also learn how to get what they need without using aggression. *Guidance* implies the use of a positive philosophy and strategies for supporting children as they become **socialized** in the cultures in which they live. Guidance includes assistance, facilitation, and setting limits. It is ongoing throughout the day and doesn't occur just when children "misbehave." In fact, it describes a way for teachers and parents to help children become capable and caring human beings who can guide their own behavior.

COMPONENT 8: A RELATIONSHIP-BASED APPROACH TO GUIDANCE

Respect

Respect for infants and toddlers includes respect for their emotional needs, respect for individual differences and strengths, and respect for the power of development.

Respect for Children's Emotional Needs and Their Goals

When developing an approach to guiding young children's behavior we begin with an understanding that infants and toddlers need protection, secure and caring relationships, responsive interactions, and a sense of self-worth. The importance of adults meeting these needs has been discussed in previous chapters, and we mention those needs here to remind you that they are the foundation for how we think about guidance as well as how children learn in all domains of development.

---

traumatic events
Events that are upsetting, distressful, and emotionally or physically painful.

discipline
1: *(n)* Adult control, restraint, and authority. 2: *(v)* To teach.

guidance
The act of helping and assisting.

socialized
Made social; able to live in one's society, culture, or group.

Infants and toddlers need to *feel* that you really care about them. If they are securely attached and feel a positive emotional connection to you, they are more likely to be cooperative with you. They need to know that you care enough to stop them if they are hurting themselves or others. They trust that they can bury their head in your shoulder when they are sad. They know that you will comfort them when they are hurt. They know that you are emotionally present when they are struggling to learn to walk or climb or talk, empathizing with them. They know that you are there to protect them when they run into your arms when a stranger comes into the room. They trust that you will respond with affection so that they can see their own self-worth in your eyes and voice. They feel as if you are there *for them*.

Respect for Individual Differences in Children

Respect for infants and toddlers also entails appreciation for what children bring to a relationship in terms of capacities, attributes, and individual styles of interacting and learning. When we recognize that each child is unique, we will reflect on how their temperament, personality, needs, and strengths influence what and how we are guiding them. We will *individualize* our guidance strategies for each child's unique personality.

sensory challenges
Difficulty with any of the senses—touch, vision, hearing, taste, or smell.

Tune into children's illness, temperament, energy levels, fatigue, and **sensory challenges.** This concept has been emphasized throughout this book, and the following example demonstrates how a teacher is accepting of Tim sucking his thumb, knowing that he uses it to self-regulate before he courageously crawls into the midst of play.

> Tim sat on the floor sucking his thumb contently while watching all of the action in his child care home. Martha, his teacher, watched Tim and reflected on how Tim liked to observe before crawling into the midst of the other infants playing on the floor. She admired his ability to regulate and calm himself by sucking his thumb. Martha smiled at Tim, Tim smiled back, and he began to crawl toward another baby.

Tim has found a unique way to ready himself for peer play by jumping into the fray *only* after he is ready, and sucking his thumb helps him self-regulate and gain strength and confidence. Martha's respect for Tim's style of playing allows him to develop at his pace and in his own way.

Perceptive adults also focus on children's strengths and what they *can* do rather than what they *can't* do. Build on what the child can do and think of each child in terms of his or her competencies. Avoid labeling a child as, for example, an "aggressive child," which defines the very essence of who this child is. For example, Sal is a helper, builder, or a climber rather than a biter. He happens to be biting right now, but biting doesn't define his character. When teachers think of the strengths of each child, they are building the identity and spirit of the child. Thinking about strengths also provides a road map for strategies that will help the child focus on what he can do rather than what he can't do.

Gonzalez-Mena (2006, 2008) emphasizes that we need to show respect for cultural differences in children's families, and that recognizing these differences will influence the strategies we use. Some children require more personal space around them while others require less; some children smile to be friendly while others smile only when they are happy. Some children may have learned that they convey respect by looking downward rather than into an adult's eyes. If we recognize these differences in ourselves and others we can value them rather than misinterpret them.

Respect for the Power of Development

We understand that children are developing their emotional and social skills, that it takes time to learn new skills and ways of being. During some periods of their life, for example, when they are first separating from their parents or when they are using to learn the toilet, life is even more challenging for them. What do we need to understand about child development in relation to guidance strategies?

> *An infant cries when he sees someone new, and a mobile infant sucks her thumb when she gets tired. A young child just learning to use a spoon will get tired and start picking up food with his hands. A toddler suddenly starts saying "No" to everything and has to have his bib tied just the right way to be happy.*

As discussed in previous chapters, as infants and toddlers mature in all domains of development—emotional, social, cognitive, language, and motor—they go through different stages. These stages of achievement can also be times of disquiet and disequilibrium for both infants or toddlers *and* their parents and teachers (for example, when an infant begins to experience stranger anxiety). If teachers don't understand the forces of development, they may have unrealistic expectations that contribute to demanding too much of children (such as expecting a toddler to eat without spilling food). When this happens, infants and toddlers become very frustrated or feel increasingly *incompetent*. Conversely, if a teacher does not notice a certain behavior, such as a 9-month-old patting his hands together, the teacher may not provide interesting, developmentally appropriate interactions such as playing pat-a-cake. Teachers can use the Developmental Trends and Responsive Interactions charts at the end of chapters 6 through 10 and in the appendices in this book to observe the development of the child, gain realistic expectations, and provide experiences that are responsive to child development.

If an infant or toddler has a developmental delay or disability in one area of development, a second area of development may be affected as well. You will remember from previous chapters that a *developmental delay* is a lag or difference in development that is caused by a variety of genetic or environmental factors. Several researchers have discovered that when young children, especially toddlers, are experiencing language delay, they are more likely to also be experiencing social and emotional delays (Carson, Klee, Perry, Muskina, & Donaghy, 1998; Irwin, Carter, & Briggs-Gowan, 2002). Teachers and parents must give infants and toddlers with language delay extra support to help them learn to communicate their needs in socially appropriate ways. Observe for these types of connections between delays in other domains of development.

Respect for Self

Know yourself. What has your culture taught you about how children should behave? How does this influence the way you guide young children? Think about what makes you angry, sad, frustrated, and anxious when you are with children. The more you know yourself and why you respond as you do, the more you will use reflective practice—a concept that we will discuss in chapter 16.

Reflect

Reflection includes thinking about what an experience is like for a child, observing what children are communicating through their behavior, and deciding what you would like the child to do instead. The following reflection strategies pave the way for relating in a way that meets the child's emotional needs and teaches them a new behavior.

1. Ask: "What is the child experiencing? What is the child's perspective on the situation?" Tasha cries every morning when her mother says good-bye and Richard has a hard time transitioning from lunch to nap time. What is each child experiencing? It may be difficult to think about what they are experiencing rather than what we, as adults, are experiencing with them. When we understand what the experience is like from the child's perspective, then we are much more likely to empathize and offer support in ways that are helpful to

myeducationlab

Go to the Activities and Applications section in Chapter 14 of MyEducationLab to watch the video *Stranger Anxiety*. Notice how the child tries to disengage from the stranger.

the child. Tasha may really miss her mother, and Richard may be afraid to be alone on his cot when he can't see his favorite teacher.

Take the example of Serena, cited by Van De Zande (1995). Although her thought processes are not this sophisticated, she is experimenting with what happens when she spits in various places and at different times with different people:

> *"How interesting," Serena seems to think. "Mommy gets mad if I spit on the table! . . . Was that just at breakfast or also at lunch? . . . What about dinner? . . . Just yesterday, or also today? . . . It seems okay to spit in the bathtub. . . . She made me spit out a bug . . . what if I spit on these papers on her desk?" (p. 15)*

After thinking *with* Serena and taking her perspective, an understanding adult will give Serena more information about where and when it is okay to spit rather than punish her without explanation.

2. Ask: "What, when, where, how, and with whom does the behavior occur?"
Observe frequently to try to understand when, where, and with whom a child may be behaving in a certain way. For example, after observing that Peter, a toddler, seemed upset on Mondays, the teacher realized that when he came into the toddler room on those days, he needed several hours to readjust to the room, his peers, and his teachers after a weekend with his mom, who was experiencing stress in her life. Tara, the teacher, tried to make him feel welcome to stay by her side as she checked the classroom pets. Soon, Peter was off playing and checking back with her occasionally when he needed a hug. The information that the teacher gathered was a guide to the strategies she chose.

3. Ask: "What is the child communicating that he wants or needs? What is the purpose of the child's behavior? What is the meaning of the child's behavior?"
Young children communicate their needs in a variety of ways. Infants yawn or turn away when they need a break from an interaction. When they are extremely upset, they may arch their back or kick their feet. Mobile infants may crawl away or cling to you to tell you they are upset or afraid. They may throw a toy down on the floor to tell you that they are frustrated. Toddlers fall into a heap crying when they are trying to tell you that they intensely want something or are trying to assert their independence and separateness from you. Some children may try to distract you with cute faces and antics to avoid having to do something they don't want to do, and some children may hit other children to either get what they want or to tell you, "I'm not feeling safe and I have to protect myself." Some children may even want you to leave them alone—they have learned that adults aren't to be trusted. Children can't usually tell us verbally, but they tell us with their behavior what it is they need or want. We can often decide what they need or the purpose of their behavior by using the observation system depicted in Table 14.1.

4. Ask: "What do I want the child to do?"
What do the family and teachers and peers want the child to do *instead* of the behavior the child is using to communicate her needs? Will the new behavior help the child meet her needs? Once you have determined what it is that you want the child to do, then you can begin to support the child to learn new ways to meet her needs. In the example in Table 14.1, the parents and teachers decided that they wanted Julie to learn to say "Stop" to other children when they try to take something away from her or interfere with her play.

Relate

Respecting and *reflecting* may give adults insight that needs no further response on their part to support the child. However, they will often *relate* (use strategies) to help children learn and

Table 14.1   Observation of Julie

Date	What Happens Before	The Child's Behavior	What Happens After	Possible Purposes of the Behavior
12/1	Tasha took Julie's crayon out of Julie's hand.	Julie hit Tasha with an open hand on Tasha's side.	Tasha cried and dropped the crayon. Julie picked it up and started using it.	To get her crayon back
12/5	Dale stepped on Julie's block structure.	Julie hit at Dale's leg when Dale went by her.	Dale left the area and Julie continued playing.	To get Dale to leave her alone

express their individual personalities and develop positive and healthy relationships. Box 14.1 summarizes the relate strategies that are described in detail in this section.

For each of the three general ways to relate that are listed in Box 14.1, there are specific guidance strategies that can be used to meet children's emotional needs and support them as they become competent and caring individuals. These strategies create children who have internal guides to behavior and who can uniquely contribute to the well-being of themselves and others through engaging in positive relationships. Let's start with building relationships.

(1) Relate: Support Children's Healthy Relationships with All of the Important People in Their Lives

In other chapters we have emphasized the importance of teachers supporting the family–child relationships as the key ongoing foundation in a child's life. We also know that the quality of other relationships that the child might observe or experience affects the relationships that the child has, for example, with teachers or peers. In their studies of aggression in toddlers, Brook and colleagues (2001) found that there were associations with parenting style and marital relations. When the relationships between the mother and father were strained, toddlers were more likely to exhibit aggressive behavior with their peers. This is a good example of how important it is to consider the ecological and relationship factors that influence a very young child's behavior. Let's think about how a teacher might support the parent–child relationship.

- **Support the child's relationship with his or her family.**

  Karin seemed happy all day at the care center, but when her father came to the door each evening, she fell apart.

In this example, how can teachers use a relationship-based approach as a framework to think about solutions to this challenge for Karin? The teacher wonders how to handle it so that her relationship with Karin *and* Karin's relationship with her father are both strengthened. It is tempting to think that Karin likes her teacher better than her father, but this could be a mistake. Brazelton (1992) talks about how children can "hold it together" emotionally during the day, but that they can literally "fall apart" as the day ends and transitions occur. The teacher can acknowledge how hard the end of a day is for both Dad and Karin and do what she can to support them both. She decides to ask Dad if he could call ahead when he left work and then the teacher could prepare Karin that Dad was coming and help her get ready to go. This strategy of respecting the importance of *all the relationships in Karin's life* influences how the teacher promotes and supports parent–child relationships as well as the teacher's relationship with Karin. Also, if an infant or toddler is unhappy, aggressive, or fearful, the teacher can reflect on how to build a better relationship with the child using all of the strategies for building emotional development that we have been discussing so far. The teacher can also partner with everyone

Box 14.1

A Summary of Relate Strategies

1. Support Children's Healthy *Relationships* with All of the Important People in Their Lives:
   - Support the child's relationship with his or her family.
   - Constantly communicate with families and other staff to learn about their culture, wishes, and guidance practices.
   - Use a problem-solving approach with families.
   - Build a strong, positive relationship with each child—a truly caring relationship.
   - Use primary care and continuity of care systems to promote ongoing, secure teacher-child and peer relationships.
2. Focus on Adult–Child *Responsive Interaction* Strategies That Promote Children's Capacities:
   - Empathize with the child's goals, struggles, and feelings.
   - Build emotional vocabulary—acknowledge and help children express strong feelings.
   - Patiently guide children toward controlling their own impulses and behavior.
   - Recognize behavior as communication, and teach children to communicate.
   - Explain and teach the child what to do. Make clear, positive statements to children.
   - Provide limits that keep the child safe, others safe, and materials safe.
   - Help children take the perspective of others through other-oriented guidance.
   - Help children learn how to problem solve and handle conflicts.
   - Give children choices that you can live with.
   - Create routines to provide security for mobile infants and toddlers.
   - Gradually build toddlers' ability to wait or to handle disappointment.
   - Use time-in rather than time-out.
3. Create and Change the Environment:
   - Create an environment that contributes to children's engagement and relationships—cozy corners, private spaces, spaces for two, and interesting things to do.
   - Change the environment as needed to ensure positive behavior and help children be successful.

who has a relationship with the child—including parents, siblings, grandparents, and other teachers.

- Constantly communicate with families and other staff to learn about their culture, wishes, and guidance practices.
- Use a problem-solving approach with families.

Bromwich (1997) recommends a six-step problem-solving approach that teachers, home visitors, and other infant-toddler professionals can use when talking with families about guidance issues:

1. *Listen Empathetically to the Parent* (pp. 114–115). Try to see things from her perspective, and try to understand her perceptions of her child and of herself in the context of the family. Listen carefully and convey that what she says, does, and feels is important to you. Comment on the parent's feelings—for example, to a parent who is concerned about her child screaming, say, "It must have felt pretty frustrating to have him continue screaming after you picked him up and tried to cuddle him." However, be careful about not encouraging the parent to talk about issues and feelings before she indicates that she wants to talk about them. Try not to become involved in highly personal matters for which you do not have the knowledge and skills to help the parent. Discuss with other staff when to refer the family to a therapist or human services agency.

2. *Observe* (pp. 114–115). Help the parent become a sensitive observer in order to read his infant's or toddler's cues and respond to them. Observe with the parent to call the parent's attention to the details of behavior that reveal important developmental changes in the child, no matter how small. Observing *with* the parent means that parent and staff share with each other what they have observed.

3. *Ask* (pp. 118–119). Ask the parent to share what she knows about her child that you do not know, recognizing that the parent knows the child best. Build on the parent's strengths by asking her to describe her successful handling of the child in one situation. For example, ask a mother how she calms her child so successfully when he is fussy on weekends. These ideas can be applied to other times when the parent is having difficulty with her baby when she fusses and also when you are trying to

calm the baby. Ask parents specific questions as a first step in the cooperative problem-solving process, such as, "What situations seem to happen right before the child has a tantrum?" or "When did the behavior start?"

4. *Comment Positively*   (pp. 116–117). Comment positively on what you see that the parent is doing that seems to work with her child. Be specific—for example, "Your baby really lights up when she sees you smiling at her."

5. *Discuss*   (pp. 117–118). Discussion usually includes sharing information on typical development. For example, you might say to a parent who is concerned because her child drops things off her high chair, "Many children in this age range drop things from the high chair to experiment with what happens to them and to play." Focus on the observations of the child's current behavior and relate the discussion to those observations. The developmental information may help the parent respond more effectively or anticipate the next stage in development.

6. *Experiment*   (p. 122). Problem solve with the parent to determine a variety of ways to interact with the child. With the baby who was fussy, the parent may notice that the baby is calmer when wrapped snugly in a blanket. You may have noticed that the baby is calmer when it is quieter in the room. One solution will not work forever and some may not work at all. If you talk with the parent about experimenting, then you don't set up the parent for failure. This encourages both you and the parent to try new things and share information about how the solutions worked. If they don't work, then you can begin the six-step process over again—all in the spirit of collaboration.

- Build a strong, positive relationship with each child—a truly caring relationship.
- Use primary care and continuity of care systems to promote ongoing, secure teacher–child and peer relationships.

These recommendations for strengthening the relationship between the professional and child have been discussed in previous chapters, but are important reminders to professionals to recognize the power of these relationships for the child.

(2) Relate: Focus on Adult–Child Responsive Interaction Strategies That Promote Children's Capacities

All of the strategies discussed in chapter 12 on how to support infants' and toddlers' emotional and social development—such as "noticing and encouraging strengths and positive behavior" or "showing affection"—provide the foundation upon which guidance interaction strategies are based. Now would be a good time to review those strategies, as they are critical to remember as the underpinnings to building children's capacities. Approaches that you can use to guide children are discussed here, but they are not likely to be effective if you are not using the basic strategies. Following are the 12 additional strategies that teachers and parents can use to guide adult–child interactions with mobile infants and toddlers.

- **Empathize with the child's goals, struggles, and feelings.**

    Eight-month-old Marku seemed tired and crabby all day. He cried easily and wouldn't sit by himself on the floor. He wanted to be in the teacher's lap and sobbed whenever she had to put him down to help another child.

What is Marku feeling? We don't know for sure, but we can tell that he is not happy. The teacher said to Marku over and over, "I can tell you are unhappy today. What can I do to make you feel better?" Although Marku couldn't understand all of the teacher's words, he could feel that she really cared and empathized with him. She didn't think he was spoiled or "just trying to get attention." Instead, she trusted that Marku had special emotional needs today and that there was a reason, which she didn't understand yet, for why he was clingy. She knew that today was a "care for the spirit of Marku" day, that her special care would help him learn to trust her, and that their positive relationship would provide a foundation for Marku both to feel safe to express and regulate his emotions.

Always start by trying to state what you think the child may be feeling, trying to communicate to you, or trying to achieve. This will help you "tune in" to the child and take the child's perspective in the situation. Then ask, "What can I do to help?"

Honig (personal communication, January 6, 2005) recommends saying, "You wish . . . " to the child to help yourself tune into the child's feelings and acknowledge that you are listening to the messages that the child is communicating to you. For example, you could say, "I know you wish you could have that toy. Tina Marie has it now."

- **Build emotional vocabulary—acknowledge and help children express strong feelings.**

This strategy is similar to the first one, but focuses on helping children describe their own emotions. For infants, teachers describe the emotions that they think the child *might* be feeling. Teachers are making their best guess as they read the child's facial expressions and body movements. For mobile infants, teachers frequently use emotion words to describe the child's feelings and encourage the child to say a word—for example, "You can tell me you feel *sad*." Teachers continue describing a broader range of feelings for toddlers—for example, "You look disappointed"—and continue encouraging the child to express his feelings in a variety of situations.

- **Patiently guide children toward controlling their own impulses and behavior.**

Nate stood at the sand table, gleefully throwing sand on the floor and then listening to the sounds he could make. Cara, the teacher, got down on his level and said, "Sand stays in the sand table. Let's see if we can make noises with the shovel in the table," recognizing his interest in cause and effect and making different sounds.

Because of the teacher's patience, Nate is learning that he can control his own behavior as he starts making noises with his shovel in the table.

- **Recognize behavior as communication, and teach children to communicate.**

The toddler who runs over and kicks another toddler's blocks is possibly communicating that he wants to play but doesn't know how to do so. He needs help learning new strategies of communication for entering play with another child, because his present strategy certainly isn't working very well!

In chapter 9, sign language was discussed as a useful means of communicating with infants and toddlers. Parents and teachers are reporting that when they use a few signs, such as those for *milk* or *more,* then infants and toddlers learn these signs from the modeling of the adult, begin to use them around 9 months of age, and are less frustrated because they can communicate their needs. Michigan State University (nd) provides a demonstration of many signs an older infant or toddler might learn.

"Use your words" is a phrase that is often repeated by teachers of toddlers as they try to teach children to use words rather than aggression to obtain a prized toy from another child, or protect themselves or a toy that another toddler covets (de Hann & Singer, 2003). Saying "use your words" is helpful only if the mobile infant or toddler knows the words to use. It is more helpful in the beginning to tell the mobile infants or toddlers the *specific* words that can be used, such as "please" (often said as "peas") when they want a toy, or "no" or "later" when they don't want someone to take a toy from them. When words are modeled by adults, then mobile infants and toddlers soon begin to use them—a step toward becoming a communicator in social situations.

- **Explain and teach the child what to do. Make clear, positive statements to children.**

Give short reasons and explanations to help young children begin to internalize the rules and their reasons. To help infants and toddlers begin to understand why they should touch a breakable item very gently, give simple explanations such as "Touch gently, it is fragile."

To Verina who just bit Sarah, say, "No biting; that hurt Sarah. Look, she's crying. You can say, 'No' to Sarah instead."

Make positive statements about what to do—for example, instead of saying "Don't run," say "Please walk." When a teacher says "Don't run," a young child may just hear the word "run."

When Mario, 28 months old, picked up an interesting piece of dirt and started putting it in his mouth for a taste, he said aloud to himself, "I put it in my mouth. I shouldn't do it. It dirty."

The words that he heard by his teachers and parents now became an internal guide to behavior. At the moment and more likely in the future, he will not need someone telling him not to put strange things in his mouth. When infants and toddlers hear the reason for doing or not doing a certain behavior, then that reason becomes a part of them. They will then have self-control rather than always needing external control from adults.

- **Provide limits that keep the child safe, others safe, and materials safe.**

Dina climbed up on the chair and looked at the teacher to see what she would do. The teacher helped Dina down, held her in her arms, and said, "I will keep you safe. I don't want you to climb on the chair because you could get hurt." After several days of this, Dina seemed more relaxed and could concentrate on playing in a more focused way.

Follow through when a child hurts himself, another child, or materials.

Andrew, 18 months old, pushed Julie hard on his way to get the box of blocks. The teacher took him gently in her arms and said firmly, "You pushed Julie. That hurt Julie. I want to keep everyone in the room safe. You can go around her like this . . . ," taking his hand and showing him the way.

- **Help children take the perspective of others through other-oriented guidance.**

Joshua stepped over Jerry as he toddled fast to the new blocks. The teacher walked over to Joshua, bent down to Joshua's level, and helped him look back at Jerry, who was crying. "Look, he's crying. You stepped on him. That hurt his hand. Let's go help Jerry," as the teacher gently took Joshua's hand and led him over to Jerry.

When teachers use **other-oriented guidance,** they steer children to begin to think about how others feel. Guiding mobile infants and toddlers to look at the face of another child, interpreting the feeling of the other child, and then thinking aloud about how to help a child who is hurt, for example, starts a child on the challenging and often bumpy road of taking other people's perspective.

- **Help children learn how to problem solve and handle conflicts.**

Thirty-month-old children of mothers who used **justification** (use of reason), **resolution** (trying to bring the conflict to a solution agreeable to all), and **mitigation** (trying to lessen the conflict) during conflict with their children had higher levels of social and emotional development at 36 months of age (Laible & Thompson, 2002). Conflict is inevitable; for example, a toddler might decide that he doesn't want to get dressed or put on a coat. When teachers and parents talk with toddlers and negotiate solutions, toddlers learn important lessons about the give and take of making decisions (Laible & Thompson, 2002).

other-oriented guidance
Guidance that helps children take the perspective of others.

justification
Use of reason.

resolution
Trying to bring the conflict to a solution agreeable to all.

mitigation
Trying to lessen the conflict.

Toddlers and twos can learn to problem solve. When a teacher asks, "What could we do to help Amy?" or "What could you do if you want the toy?" then toddlers *begin* to understand the nature of problem solving. They will need continuous help to think of possible answers, but if teachers keep asking and modeling answers, then toddlers become great problem solvers as they grow.

- **Give children choices that you can live with.**

Give more choices to mobile infants and toddlers with each passing month. Carmen, the toddler teacher, knows that Lulu's diaper needs to be changed, but Lulu is very busy putting blocks in and out of a can. The teacher approaches Lulu, bends down to her level, and asks, "I see you need to have your diaper changed?" Lulu loudly says, "No!" "I can see that you are enjoying your blocks," replies Carmen. "I'll be back in a few minutes to change your diaper." After a few minutes, Carmen approaches Lulu again. "It is time to have your diaper changed; would you like to walk or would you like me to carry you?" Lulu holds her hands up to be carried.

- **Create routines to provide security for mobile infants and toddlers.**

A routine becomes a habit and provides emotional security to the child. Children can predict what will happen when routines are consistent. Details of how to proceed do not have to be explained each day. Use a cleanup song when it is time to put away toys: "It's cleanup time. It's cleanup time. It's time to put our toys away." Use routines for saying good-bye and a routine for going outside. Sing songs if you have to wait for lunch to arrive. Use a routine for moving from lunch to nap time, so toddlers know that when they are done eating they can get their "blankie" or "lovie" and a teacher will read to them on their cots.

- **Gradually build toddlers' ability to wait or to handle disappointment.**

> Toddlers who don't learn gradually about disappointment lose their resilience through lack of practice in give-and-take with other people's needs. They can become self-centered, demanding, and difficult to like or to be with. (Lieberman, 1993, p. 52)

As infants become toddlers they can *gradually* learn about waiting for the food to be warm enough to eat or to go outside, for example. Children are more likely to learn patience and to take the perspective of others if adults talk in a soothing voice to children while they are waiting. Disappointment may occur when children can't go outside because of the weather or because a favorite teacher is absent for a day. Thinking about how you feel when you are disappointed will remind you of how important it is for adults to explain what is happening, acknowledge toddlers' disappointed feelings, and demonstrate coping strategies for how to handle frustration and sadness.

- **Use time-in rather than time-out.**

Time-out is a strategy that has often been used by parents and teachers to punish children by placing them in a time-out chair, a cubby, or a place alone away from everyone else after the child has "misbehaved." Schreiber (1999) discusses the issue of time-outs for toddlers and asks, "Is our goal punishment or education?" When teachers use time-out it is often in a punitive way; the teacher angrily places the child in a separate place and tells the child to stay there until he can "learn not to bite." The child usually focuses on protecting himself in a time-out situation rather than focusing on what happened, why it happened, how he and the other child feels, and what else he could have done instead. **Time-in** is a strategy that involves a parent or teacher spending time with a child who, for example, bit another child—calming the child and teaching the child what to do instead of biting. If a cozy area of the room with soft toys and pillows is always available as a "cozy corner," toddlers, when upset, may go there by themselves to calm themselves or they may ask or pull a teacher to come with them to the cozy corner.

time-out
A brief period during which a child is removed from the action or situation when the adult thinks that there is a "discipline" problem.

time-in
Time that children spend with an adult teacher after the child feels challenged emotionally and socially.

(3) Relate: Create and Change the Environment

The mobile infants in the child care home began to crawl up the stairs, so Melissa put a baby gate across the bottom of the stairs. The toddlers were continually running at full speed through the room until the teachers placed a small climber in the center. Instead of blaming the children for the challenges, the teacher examined what she could do to change the environment to be more developmentally appropriate.

These toddlers are enjoying play with clay on a light table.

Create an environment that contributes to children's engagement, self-regulation, and relationships—cozy corners, spaces for two, and interesting things to do. If the environment includes caring people and interesting equipment, toys, and materials with which the child can be successful, then children are more likely to be engaged. If an environment is attractive and calm, then children are more likely to be able to self-regulate.

Change the environment as needed to ensure positive behavior and help children be successful. Always ask, "How can I change the environment to help this child be successful?" For example, if an infant seems to have difficulty falling asleep, try creating a more private space in the room so that you can rock the infant to sleep without distractions. A small change in the environment can make a big difference for a child.

RELATIONSHIP REALIGNMENTS

Separation Anxiety

For months, Karin's dad had been dropping off his 10-month-old daughter at the same family child care home without seeing so much as a tear from her. But lately, after the usual good-bye hugs and kisses, Karin has started wailing, clinging fast to Dad's leg. Martha, Karin's special teacher, was surprised by this sudden change in behavior and tried to distract the baby with a favorite toy. As the crying continued, however, she and Karin's dad wondered, "What are we doing wrong?"

myeducationlab

Go to the Activities and Applications section in Chapter 14 of MyEducationLab to watch the video *Separation Anxiety* and see an example of an infant demonstrating separation anxiety.

> *With new knowledge comes the fear of being abandoned, unloved, or physically damaged. (Lieberman)*

A young baby may cry when a parent leaves, but at about 7 months of age infants may actively show **separation anxiety,** searching for their loved one, scowling, crying, pushing away others who offer comfort, and having difficulty saying good-bye. Knowing that a person exists when out of sight (person permanence), a cognitive understanding contributes to the infant's growing awareness of "out of sight, but not out of mind." Often infants don't want their favorite teacher to disappear, even behind the bathroom door. Separation anxiety can occur for several months, but the length of this stage varies in children. There are children who by 18 months feel very comfortable saying good-bye to parents, but there are also children who have difficulty with separation all of their life. Teachers can hold an infant, allow her to stay as close as she wants, talk to her in nurturing tones, and appreciate the emotional struggle that the infant is experiencing.

When children enter an early care and education program between 1 and 2 years of age, they may take several weeks to several months to adjust to the new situation. The first several days may go smoothly, but as the toddler begins to realize that the new setting is where he is

separation anxiety
A child's fear and worry about being separated from favorite adults.

Tory is upset when her mother leaves.

going to be each day, he may begin to protest more. Other children are frightened from the beginning of this new separation from parents and they protest vehemently, yet they don't have the language skills to express themselves clearly. Children of this age have a difficult time cognitively understanding where the parent is going and when he or she will return. Many children this age seem very sad after their parents leave and in the midst of their play, they may turn to the door with a hopeful "Mommy?" when they hear someone enter, only to get sad all over again when it isn't their loved one returning. When adults understand that cognitive development affects social and emotional development, and vice versa, they can help young children during this scary time by being emotionally and physically available and commenting on the child's (even a young baby's) feelings—for example, by saying, "I know you thought that was Mommy. Mommy will be here after your nap."

A child can also experience separation anxiety as she leaves the program at the end of the day—crying and fussing at having to make another transition. Teachers can support children and parents in as many ways as possible to ease the transition from program to home with the parent. Teachers can make sure the child is ready to transition with a clean diaper and a full tummy, or if the parent wants to feed the child, the teacher supports the parent–child relationship by timing the feedings (while still being responsive to the child) so that the parent can experience bonding time with the child. If a baby fusses at leaving his favorite teacher, it is important that teachers help build the parent–child relationship through interpreting the feelings of the baby. Teachers can say to the parent, "She is happy to see you; she just wasn't ready to have her coat put on" or "She just seems tired today—I think she needs some cuddle time with her dad."

Toddler Resistance

Teachers and parents of toddlers often feel as if they are on an emotional roller coaster with their children, who are sometimes pushing for independence and at other times want to be taken care of as if they were still infants. A toddler is learning how to be autonomous, or self-directing. They often attempt to gain control, but become frustrated at their lack of control. A toddler can feel mixed up, sometimes wanting to be a grownup and the next minute feeling scared, lonely, or just out of energy and wanting to sit in your lap. Toddler teachers often experience the full range of emotions that toddlers feel in the course of a day—from pure delight and contagious giggles to overwhelming frustration.

Toddlers can get frightened when a parent or teacher doesn't stop them from doing something dangerous; they can feel that there is no one there to hold, help, restrain, or contain them (Lieberman, 1993). They say "No" to tell you that they are a person who can express feelings and to test the safe limits and boundaries of the world. It helps teachers and parents if they appreciate that developmental changes can occur rapidly between 18 months and 3 years of age. It is the teacher of this age group who masterfully gives toddlers opportunities to be self-directing while providing the boundaries for behavior that keep children feeling safe and emotionally secure.

Tantrums

Mobile infants and toddlers may have what adults call **tantrums**—times of distress when they literally seem to fall apart. Some children cry loudly, scream, whine, flail, fall to the floor, stomp their feet, or become stiff or floppy. A teacher may not have put a bib on a child in quite the right way or the teacher may have denied a child a second banana. It is difficult to predict when a young child might have a tantrum. They are very taxing and challenging to both the child and the teachers. Let's now take a look at Keri, who has started having tantrums, to see how many of the guidance strategies discussed in this chapter can be applied to a real-life situation, one that teachers often face in their work with children aged 15 months to 3 years:

> Keri, 2 years old, is in a family child care home for 3 days a week. She eats her banana with great delight. After swallowing the last [delicious crumb, and with banana still dribbling out of her mouth], she gestures to her care provider that she would like another one, only to hear, "I'm sorry, Keri, just one banana today. It sometimes gives you a tummy-ache if you eat two bananas." Keri scowls, jumps up from her chair, stomps her feet, and puts her hands on her hips. As her teacher approaches, Keri suddenly falls to the floor in a heap, crying as loudly as she can.

As toddlers begin to assert themselves, strong emotions and resistance—**negativism**—can occur out of the blue. As Lieberman (1993) explains, "When toddlers are unable to speak about urgent matters, they must resort to crying or screaming. This happens even with adults. The voice is the carrier of emotion, and when speech fails us, we need to cry out in whatever form we can to convey our meaning. Often, what passes for negativism is really the toddler's desperate effort to make herself understood" (p. 38).

What is Keri feeling, and what is she trying to say? Is she more likely to have a tantrum on certain days or times of the day? What are Keri's language skills? Very young children are starting to use words and voice intonation to express strong feelings—but since their language skills are still developing, they often fall back on using tears and tantrums. Recording the observations of Keri can result in strategies that meet her needs. The strategies that adults use in these situations can either set up negative communication patterns between adults and children or support children emotionally as they learn new ways of expressing strong feelings.

Accentuate the Child's Strengths

Instead of thinking of Keri as the little girl who has tantrums, think of Keri's strengths and what she loves to do. She is enthusiastic about everything that she does and she loves it when she can make a choice. Keri's teachers decided to build on this enthusiasm and Keri's desire to make choices by offering her more choices throughout the day—for example, asking her if she would like a blue bib or a white bib as they move toward the table, or if she wants to have her diaper changed before or after a favorite puzzle.

Use Responsive Interactions: In the Moment

Will responding to children's tantrums encourage their negative behavior and spoil them—or can we, as adults, respond to tantrums in a way that helps children learn to use words to communicate their feelings? When deciding how to react, think of outbursts as part of a developmental stage most toddlers go through. Your job is to teach children new ways to express strong emotions, not to discourage these feelings by ignoring them. Your support through this difficult stage will help children learn to communicate more maturely. Following are some ways that you can encourage this process:

1. Validate children's feelings. Even though you won't give Keri another banana, you can let her know you understand why she's upset. By saying in a soothing voice, "Keri, you seem

tantrums
Times of distress when children literally seem to fall apart emotionally.

negativism
Attitude of refusing, or resisting.

very frustrated. I realize you want another banana," you're sending the message that she's been heard and that it's okay to have strong feelings.

2. Build children's emotional vocabulary. Children can learn, from you, the words to express how they feel. So, when you comment on a child's emotions, model words she can use. You might say, with feeling, "Keri, you seem sad. You're crying. You can tell me, 'I'm sad.' "

3. Share children's books about emotions. As you read together, discuss what the characters are feeling, and make connections to events in the child's life. You might read *Miss Spider's Tea Party* by David Kirk and then say, "Keri, Miss Spider was sad because she thought nobody would come to her party. You were sad the other day because you wanted two bananas. Let's see what she did when she was sad." Use books as springboards to discussions about emotions and different ways people handle them.

4. Observe facial expressions, gestures, and body movements to learn when a toddler might be getting ready to tantrum. Catching the toddler *before* she tantrums is one of the keys to preventing tantrums and helping her learn new ways to express disappointment, frustration, and anger.

5. Encourage problem solving by offering choices. Providing options helps toddlers discover new solutions to old problems. For example, giving Keri a choice of more juice or more milk (instead of another banana) will help her feel as if she has some power in the situation. It will give her a sense of control over herself and her environment, while letting her know that a loving adult is watching out for her well-being.

6. Model ways to express strong feelings. To let Keri know she isn't the only person who has feelings, share how you feel with her. You might say, with the appropriate expression, "Keri, it makes me worried to see you upset. I feel upset, too, when you scream at me."

Discussing feelings is neither *giving in to children* nor *giving them everything they want* (common adult fears). Rather, when you show children how to communicate through words and gestures, you're helping them take the next developmental step toward becoming good communicators and problem solvers while providing them safe and healthy boundaries in which to build relationships and learn.

Build Relationships: Beyond the Moment

While many toddlers tantrum because they are overwhelmed in the moment, there may be events that happened at home or in the child care and education program that have affected Keri. Teachers and parents should aim to have a strong, positive relationship so that there can be an open discussion about whether there has been any change in Keri's life that may be affecting her emotionally, such as sudden changes in who is taking care of her at home.

Create and Change the Environment in Responsive Ways

If adults find themselves saying "No," "Stop that," "You can't do that," or constantly removing children from dangerous situations, then the environment *definitely* needs to be improved so that children, peers, and adults are safe and engaged in many fulfilling, interesting activities together. When there is a "No" environment, toddlers will feel quite frustrated and confused concerning what they can and cannot do. The environment can be changed to be more interesting, less stimulating, or more supportive of the child's emotional and social development.

Children Who Bite

One of the biggest challenges in group programs is children biting each other and the teacher. So let's explore the topic of why children bite and the strategies that adults can use to deal with the problem.

Jaheed's mother is coming to the door of the child care center to pick up Jaheed and take him home. About an hour ago, Jaheed bit Aaron. Jaheed didn't break the skin, but Aaron cried for a long time after Jaheed bit him. What are you going to say to Jaheed's mother? What are you going to say to Aaron's mother?

Before babies have teeth, they gum, mouth, and suck on any object they can get into their mouths. Babies are encouraged to "bite" their food and try new oral delights. It is no wonder that as they become motorically active and enter the stage of "true experimentations" between 12 and 18 months, people become one of the new objects that must be tested and tried to see how they taste.

Biting, then, provides babies with comfort (as they suck their fists, fingers, and food) and opportunities to learn (as they discover out what is soft, hard, chewy, tasty, or yucky). Yet, biting, which is so enjoyable and so necessary, can get the toddler into trouble when it extends into the world of adults, children, and animals.

Children may bite other people for various reasons. It will help you handle a biting child if you think about the many possible reasons toddlers bite others. You can then try the solutions based on the particular reason a particular child is biting people. Table 14.2 presents the reasons children bite, as well as possible solutions.

When an infant or toddler bites another person, show the biter with your voice and facial expression that you are very concerned. Speak in a serious voice with the child. Look directly into the child's eyes. Hold the child gently by the shoulders if necessary. For example, you might say, "You bit Candace" (state the behavior). "She doesn't like it. She's crying" (pointing out how the bite's behavior affected the other child). "You can bite this cloth" (food, biting toy, etc.), or "You can tell Candace how you feel" (what the child can do instead). Use words appropriate to the child's developmental level and try to restore relationships between the two children. With toddlers and twos, an adult can ask the victim to tell the biter what would make him feel better.

Help the victim of the biter. Keep ice packs on hand to place on the bite. If the skin is broken, wash it well with soap and water. If possible, bring the biter along to assist the victim (however, the victim may appropriately want the biter to stay far away). Call the parent of the child who received the bite. If the skin is broken, then the parent must take the child to a doctor.

Often the biter is as frightened about what happened as the victim. If punishment for the biter is too harsh, the young biter nurses her own hurt rather than concentrating on and helping the victim of the bite. If you punish or yell at the child or put her in time-out, she will try to protect herself, think only of herself, and will not be open to learning about alternatives to biting others.

If one child's biting continues after several days of repeating these techniques, meet with the family and other teachers to determine what might be causing the child to bite and plan together to provide consistency across home and the child education program. The infant or toddler deserves our best planning, caring, and teaching. Implement a more intense program of time-in and emotional connection with an adult. An adult stays near the child, meets the child's emotional needs, shows the child affection and encouragement, catches her *before* she bites, teaches her alternative behavior, and teaches her how to be gentle or use sign language or words to express her needs.

Keep in mind the following points:

- When adults hit or bite children for biting others, the child learns that biting is OK if you are bigger and stronger than the other person. The child will be *more* likely to bite peers (especially smaller ones).

- Observe when the biting and attempts to bite occur. Keep records. The biting may occur before lunch or when the child is crowded by others.

Table 14.2   Why children bite: relationship-based solutions

Why Children Bite Others (Reflect)	Program Solutions (Respond)
A. "Holding On and Letting Go"	
As children's muscles mature, toddlers experiment with two simultaneous ways of handing experiences: *holding on* and *letting go*. Toddlers are learning to both hold on and let go of (1) parents and other adults, (2) toys, (3) bowel movements, etc. Thus, they are also learning to hang on/let go with their mouths. Often young children are not fully in *control* of their walking, running, handling small objects, bowel movements, urine, or speech. Sometimes the skin of the other child can "just happen" to get between the child's teeth.	Help ease infant or toddler separations (letting go) from their parents. If the baby cries when the parent leaves, then say to the baby, "You're feeling very sad that Mommy/Daddy has to leave. It's hard to say good-bye. Mommy/Daddy will come back after lunch/nap" (some concrete event). Give toys to baby for hanging on/letting go, such as blocks to put into containers. Don't pressure toilet training. Wait until the child shows that he or she can "let go" in other areas of life. Study your environment carefully to ensure opportunities for infants and toddlers to practice blossoming motor skills.
B. Autonomy	
Toddlers are developing autonomy: doing things for themselves, making *choices*, needing to *control*, making demands of adults and the environment, wanting power, moving out and away from adults. Biting can be an expression of a toddler's separation from the adult; infants and toddlers are no longer one with adults if they can bite the adult. Infants and toddlers are showing control of the other person and the situation when they bite. Biting gives children power over others. Toddlers may be allowed to get "out of control" by loving adults who are hesitant to set limits for them.	Toddlers must be helped to achieve a balance between their need for control and their need for loving, firm limits to be placed on their often uncontrollable urges. Because there are so many situations in which adults must control toddlers, allow and provide as many situations as possible when they can *choose* and have *power:* "the red marker or the blue marker," "the Cheerios or the Rice Krispies," whether to have "milk or no milk" on their cereal. Set up the environment so that infants and toddlers can have long stretches of time to explore and learn in a relaxed manner.
C. Exploration	
Biting is a part of sensorimotor exploration. Toys, food, and people must be touched, smelled, and, of course, tasted if the toddler is to learn. Babies are sensuous creatures who learn through their senses and their motoric actions on things and around things.	Provide a variety of sensorimotor experiences. Infants and toddlers should experience closely supervised play with water, paints, play dough, and sand. Infants and toddlers can crawl and tumble over a variety of hard, soft, rough, and smooth surfaces. A colorful array of toys that can be mouthed and easily washed should be available.
D. Teething	
Teething can cause an infant or toddler's mouth to hurt. Babies often need something or someone to gnaw on to comfort them.	Provide infants and toddlers with teething toys, frozen bagels, and chewy foods that disintegrate in the mouth and will not cause choking. Older toddlers can be *encouraged* to bite on apples and firm teething toys. Clean frozen cloths provide cooling relief for teething toddlers (and for the child who has been bitten).
E. Peer Interaction	
Infants and toddlers are just beginning to learn how to engage peers in positive ways. Infants usually do not understand they are hurting others when they bite them (older toddlers may). Infants and toddlers do not know how to approach their peers in acceptable ways. They often express their interest by biting, pulling hair, pushing, etc.	Children need lots of social experiences in order to learn how to interact with others. Take their hand as they reach out to others roughly and say, "Touch gently—that makes her feel happy." Acknowledge their interest in other children by saying, "I know you like Darin—you can give him a toy." Provide enough age-appropriate materials and equipment so children can play beside each other (parallel play). Notice positive peer interaction such as one child hugging another, giving a toy to another, and smiling to another.

Why Children Bite Others (Reflect)	Program Solutions (Respond)

F. Cause and Effect

Infants and toddlers truly investigate cause-and-effect relationships beginning at approximately 12 months. It is as if they are saying, "What will happen if I bite Susie? What reaction will I get?" Biting gets a reaction—usually a very strong one! Baby often receives a loud scream from the other baby, and a yell of protest from an adult.	Provide extensive time for play. Provide toys that "do something" when the child acts on the toy. For example, when a button is pushed, a figure pops up, or when a knob is turned, music plays. Sand, dirt, water, paints, blocks, and crayons allow for creative, open-ended experiences that offer many opportunities for the child to make something happen. Help them notice the positive reaction they get when they pat, hug, or give a toy to another child.

G. Imitation

Babies learn by imitating others, and biting is one behavior that is often learned from other young persons. After 15 months babies can observe a behavior (such as biting), store it in their memory, and perform the act later when conditions are right (this is called *deferred imitation*). Research has shown that children who are physically punished are much more likely than their peers to be aggressive with both adults and peers—especially younger, smaller peers. They learn that hitting and biting others is an acceptable way of handling their anger if they see adults responding in that way.	Model loving, nurturing, sharing, polite, positive behavior for young children to imitate. Develop a repertoire of responses for handling children's negative behavior: redirecting to a positive activity, acknowledging their feelings (e.g., "You are feeling angry at Sarah—she took your toy and that made you feel angry"). Teach the child alternative positive behavior. Positive techniques do work! Children comply more readily and they learn positive ways of interacting with others.

H. Attention

The young child may bite to get attention from others; it is true that "negative attention seems to be better to many toddlers than no attention at all." Everyone hates to be ignored, and children under 3 are no exception. Some children may actually be receiving more negative attention from teachers and peers than positive attention, thus continuing the cycle of negative behavior.	Saturate the biter with positive, warm, nurturing attention. This can be difficult for infant-toddler professionals, especially when they are feeling exceedingly frustrated with the little biter. Remember, however, that when children's positive, busy, curious, helpful, productive behaviors are noticed and rewarded, the children are much more likely to continue those behaviors and behave that way more often. Break into that negative cycle of child behavior with adult positive comments and hugs for desirable infant-toddler behavior.

I. Frustration

Young children may bite others due to feelings of anger and frustration because of unmet needs or because of harsh discipline techniques. A child who cries or whose more positive bids for attention go unheard, or a child who is hit, slapped, yelled at, or bitten by adults may become an angry, biting child. Too many children, too high adult-to-child ratios, or not enough space can lead to frustrated, biting children.	Help young children to develop their own repertoire of behaviors for handling frustrations and angry feelings. Help children learn to say "Not now!" to another child who grabs a toy. Teach children to say "I feel angry (sad, happy, etc.)" to adults and peers. This is not "smarting-off" to adults—it is a healthy sharing of feelings. If infant-toddler professionals or parents are using punitive techniques, they need opportunities to *learn* about the effects of positive versus hostile discipline techniques. Children who have been severely punished will need time to develop trust in adults who use positive strategies. The environment for the young children may need to be changed before biting will be decreased. Smaller numbers of children can make a big difference in a classroom.

J. Anxiety

Young children may be experiencing generalized anxiety about events happening to them or around them (such as parents' divorcing or fighting, the loss of or separation from loved ones, etc.). Anxiety may lead to biting others to relieve tension (just as adults smoke cigarettes, chew gum, or bat a ball around).	Work with parents to determine the source of anxiety. Provide calming activities such as water or sand play. Allow children to suck a thumb and/or hold transitional objects (such as blankets or stuffed animals). Provide time for one-on-one with a special adult. Pat backs and sing songs at nap time to quiet toddlers into sleep. Use infant massage strategies to calm a child. Play soothing lullabies. Stay close to nurture children and explain and help them through transition times.

Box 14.2

Readiness for Toilet Learning

Parents

- are willing to collaborate with teachers to provide consistency for the child.
- are willing to be encouraging and not punitive with the child.
- respect the child's timetable (for example, a child may start the process and then stop for a period of time).
- agree that the child is ready to learn.

Teachers

- have an adult-to-child ratio that is conducive to a teacher being available to the child learning to use the toilet.
- have a trusting relationship with the child.

The child

- has an interest in imitating adults when they use the toilet.
- can communicate his or her needs to adults.
- is not in a resistant stage of development.
- is willing to sit on the toilet with and without diapers.
- can pull pants off and on fairly easily.
- has sphincter (anal) muscles that are sufficiently developed to hold on and let go of a bowel movement.
- has a dry diaper for longer periods of time indicating that the child's bladder is maturing.

- Explore with the parents what the reasons for biting may be. Try a solution based on the possible reasons. Work with the parents of the biter so that the guidance techniques used at home and at the center are consistent with each other.

- Have a staff meeting. Review all the reasons that toddlers bite and all the techniques that can be used. Individualize strategies for each child and then work together to provide *consistency* for that child. Staff can help each other be consistent in the use of the techniques.

- *Before parents and family members become upset* about a biting problem, hold a parent meeting or send a newsletter home to let parents know what techniques they and the staff can use. Parents need to know *why* toddlers bite, that it is a *common* problem whenever toddlers are brought together in a group, and that the name of the biter will not be revealed. Tell parents that the staff will do *everything* possible to ensure the safety of the children.

If a solution works, give yourself a big pat on the back. If a solution does not work, provide the time-in approach. If the child continues biting, bites viciously, or bites and then smiles, seek professional help. Too many parents are asked to take their child out of a center for biting. This solves the problem for the program but not for the child or the family. In collaboration with the parent you can seek support for the child from professionals in the local early intervention team in your school district (see chapter 15). These professionals will provide an assessment and ongoing support if needed to parents and teachers. Children can learn that infant-toddler teachers are there to help them learn new positive ways of interacting with peers and adults.

Toilet Learning

Here's what children do in order to use a toilet. Children must (1) feel the urge to eliminate; (2) understand the urge is a signal to eliminate—"Hey, I gotta go, NOW!"; (3) suppress the immediate urge; (4) get to the toilet (quickly!); (5) pull clothing out of the way; (6) situate and balance on the potty; and (7) relax urinary or sphincter muscles to eliminate (Stephens, 1999, p. 78).

And, those are just the *physical* skills necessary for toddlers to be successful using a toilet. There are also emotional issues. As mentioned in our discussion of toddler resistance, toddlers do want to be grown up—but they often want to grow up on their own timetable.

Most child development specialists who have written about toilet learning recommend waiting until the child shows signs of readiness (see Box 14.2). They use the term *toilet learning* rather than *toilet training* to indicate that children are learning on their own terms, rather than adults training them on the adult's timetable. Learning to use the toilet is a "step up to independence" (Stephens, 1999). It is an opportunity for

Ailana at home involved in toilet learning.

the toddler to express his autonomy. If forced, he will express his autonomy by resisting the adult. We want the child to feel as if it is his idea, not ours, for him to use the toilet and it is his accomplishment, not ours, when he does.

Brazelton and Sparrow (2004) have written a book outlining Brazelton's method for helping toddlers learn to use the toilet. They recommend a relaxed method of taking the child to the toilet and letting him sit on it with his clothes on. If there is no resistance then take the child to the toilet without a diaper on. Always let the child get up and leave if he wants to. At some point you will "catch" the child's urine or stool and the child will begin to get the idea of how to use the toilet. If the child resists or the process does not seem to be working, wait at least a month before trying again. Be encouraging but be careful not to praise too loudly or too much. The child is doing this for himself, not just for you. To provide consistency for the child at home and in a program, it is best if the parents and teachers meet to discuss the toilet learning process.

Toddlers may touch their own genitals while they are learning to use the toilet, and infants may during diapering. This is typical behavior and should not be punished. If you ignore this normal behavior, their curiosity will be satisfied.

Toilet learning can be a frustrating time for parents if they would like to complete the process quickly to eliminate the costly expense of diapers and not have to clean up the sometimes "big messes" that toddlers can make in their diaper. In some cultures, parents may "train" children early (in the first 2 years of life) by learning to read the signs that a child gives when he is going to urinate or defecate and will ask you to do the same in the program. This can be challenging in a program where a teacher often has at least three infants to take care of, and even more if the teacher works with toddlers. Use the dialog methods recommended in chapter 12 for listening to parents and negotiating strategies with them. When they share their observations of the child, parents and teachers can usually agree on methods and a cooperative plan of action—especially if a relationship of mutual trust has been established.

The goal is that toddlers end up with a sense of pride in using the toilet—a very grown-up thing to do—rather than a sense of shame due to failure, or anger because he is being forced against his will. And finally, as Stephens (1999) cautions: "Anticipate accidents by asking parents to provide at least three pairs of extra LABELED underwear, pant/shorts, and an extra pair of shoes. When accidents occur, don't spank, threaten, ridicule, tease, or otherwise punish a child. Reassure them that every boy and girl has accidents when learning to use the toilet" (p. 80).

CHALLENGING BEHAVIOR AND MENTAL HEALTH ISSUES

Managing challenging behaviors in infants and toddlers is just that—a challenge! Infant and toddler teachers and parents have listed children's behaviors that are challenging to them: sadness; flat affect; distress or crying frequently; continuously hurting others (biting, pushing, grabbing, hitting); hurting self; *frequently* having tantrums and falling apart; not sleeping; excess clinginess; noncompliant, defensive, angry, anxious, or fearful behavior; and a general lack of response to guidance strategies. Note that these behaviors *more seriously affect and disrupt infants' and toddlers' sense of well-being, long-term behavior, and sense of self-worth.* They represent a more serious challenge for the child, family members, teachers, and peers and are beyond typical development issues that respond to socialization and guidance strategies. These expressions of a child's need engender intense feelings on the part of everyone involved and are often difficult to understand. Challenging behaviors can leave adults feeling powerless as they try to problem solve to help the child toward well-being and away from distress. In this section we will again emphasize that behavior is a way for young children to communicate their joys, needs, and frustrations. If we can "read" the behavior, then we have a key for unlocking the meaning of the behavior for the child. The child is clearly telling us that he or she needs help.

When adults talk about challenging behavior they usually mean that the child is challenging them—typical guidance strategies just aren't working. However, the *child* is feeling challenged, too. Infant mental health specialists have helped teachers and parents understand that infants and toddlers can and do have strong feelings in response to their experiences in life and that it is very important to intervene early.

What do children with behavioral challenges have in common? Often they are communicating their distress through their behavior rather than using language. They may be ill, tired, or overwhelmed by stimulation. A child who "doesn't listen" may not be hearing well. A child who falls apart frequently and with intensity when there is too much stimulation may be sensitive to noise. A child may be delayed in language development, which then affects how well she can communicate her needs. Children may not be able to tell you with their words, but they are telling you with their behavior that something doesn't feel right.

A child who is feeling challenged may feel overprotected or underprotected. If adults are watching every move and constantly warning the child of dangers, then the child may feel as if the world is a scary place. The child then feels afraid to venture out and explore the environment. This child may feel *overprotected*. Alternatively, if an adult is not setting limits for the toddler—such as "hitting hurts" or "jumping off of high furniture is not safe"—a toddler may feel as if he has too much power and thus will not feel safe. This toddler may do "daring" things as if to say "Doesn't someone care enough to stop me?" In these cases children may feel *underprotected*. Let's examine some emotions that infants and toddlers may express, what they mean, and what teachers can do to support the child and family.

Anxious, Fearful, Vigilant

A child who is anxious, fearful, or vigilant (on guard) may have multiple or specific fears; become agitated easily; or display uncontrollable crying or screaming, facial tics, and tension. The child may be easily upset, not explore, cling to an adult, or run and hide when something fearful happens. Children who are anxious may seem to be constantly watchful of others and the environment. Anxiety is increased by helplessness and lack of knowledge, which makes babies very prone to it (Lieberman, 1993, p. 124).

The child may have had overwhelming, frightening experiences or be experiencing sensory overload—too much stimulation for this particular child's temperament and ability to process information through several senses at once.

You can help these children by doing the following:

- Offer challenges gradually.
- Speak in a calm voice.
- Keep your promises to read a book or to help the child.
- Do not *send* the child over to a new situation. *Go* with her and draw her in. Stay with her until her mood has changed.
- Say often, "This is a safe place. I will keep you safe."
- Provide a primary caregiver model where at least one caregiver "moves up" to the next classroom with the child.

Work closely with families. Researchers Crockenberg, Leerkes, and Lekka (2007) studied how families' marital relationships influence infant behavior. They found that aggressive marital conflicts predicted infant withdrawal at 6 months. The results of this study demonstrate how important it is for early educators to think about children's behavior within the context of the family from a bioecological perspective and provide as many family friendly policies and opportunities as possible. When talking directly with families use the 6-step problem-solving approach discussed earlier and the 10-point problem-solving guide at the end of this chapter.

Angry and Defiant

Infants and toddlers can feel very angry. Infants may cry loudly and their faces may scrunch up and turn red as they express their rage. An angry mobile infant may throw things such as toys or scratch another child who gets too near, and an angry toddler may even throw chairs. Many angry words are screamed by a very upset toddler—words that you didn't know a young child could say. A defiant toddler might destroy materials or toys, throw things, and threaten others.

What might contribute to this behavior? Perhaps this child is easily overstimulated and has difficulty with self-regulation. Perhaps an adult in the child's life doesn't understand development, so scolds or punishes typical behavior. This child may have difficulty trusting others because she hasn't experienced predictable, kind, understanding, or responsive relationships. A child who is angry may have experienced a traumatic event or events. If you look closely you may actually see a very fearful child who is lashing out to protect himself—before someone hurts him.

An angry child can make the adults around her angry, too. It is hard to stay calm in the face of so much feeling from a child so young. Your anger, though, is not helpful to the child. The child may be trying hard to trigger your anger, because that is what the child expects from adults. When we understand the intention of the child we then can respond with the message (through words or actions) that "I'm not going to respond to you the way you have come to expect." Instead, value the feelings of the child. Help identify the child's feelings by saying, "You are very angry!" in a tone that tells the child you understand. You may need to repeat this several times. Tell the child what he can do instead of hurting others or destroying property. Say, "You can stomp when you are angry" and then show him how. Figure out what the child is trying to communicate and what the child needs; help the child learn appropriate ways to get those needs met. Adapt your solutions to the needs of the individual child. Some possible responses may include:

- Take time to be emotionally available—be a respite in the storm. Sit on the floor near the child. Hold and comfort the child as often as possible. Give the child one-on-one time each day.
- Be firm about not expressing anger through aggression. Say (depending on what the child can understand), "Hitting hurts and we need to keep everyone safe. You can say, 'I'm angry.' "
- Help the child feel safe.
- Be responsive so the child feels he can "make something happen" in socially acceptable ways.
- Give choices—for example, say, "Do you want juice, or milk?"
- Provide a quiet area (cozy corner) in the room where the child can go when he is angry. Do not force him to stay in that area, but rather encourage him to use it when he is angry.
- Provide places for boisterous play such as climbing and running.
- Provide a calm environment with places for cuddling, comforting, and caring.

Meet together with the family in a supportive way. The family may be experiencing stress that they do not want to share. Again, use the 6-step problem-solving approach and the 10-point problem-solving guide.

Children Who Behave Aggressively

An adult in an infant or toddler room may experience children, who bite, scratch, hit, kick, spit, or pull hair. Observe these children so that you can understand what they are communicating to you through their behavior. They may be communicating that they don't want other children to be near them or that they need to feel powerful. A toddler may have learned that she gets her needs met (attention, noticed, out of an activity) when she is aggressive or she is experimenting with new behaviors that she observed other toddlers' use.

Aggressive children may feel "out of control" and frightened because there are no clear or consistent rules or boundaries and they are not learning to regulate their behavior. Children who have delayed language development may not be able to communicate their needs, so they resort to physical aggression. Your observation and discussions with family members will help you determine what the child is trying to communicate.

In a longitudinal study of 10,658 Canadian children, one sixth of the children demonstrated a consistent pattern of high levels of aggression from toddlerhood to preadolescence. These children were primarily boys from low-income families whose parents used "hostile/ineffective parenting strategies" (Cote, Vaillancourt, LeBlanc, Nagin, & Tremblay, 2006, p. 71). This research supports the importance of listening and supporting families. Use the 6-step problem-solving approach, including referral of the family for extra assistance if needed. If parents are using hostile/ineffective parenting strategies provide them opportunities for home visits, parent-to-parent stress reduction classes, and guidance classes.

You can help these children by doing the following:

- Work hard to develop the child's trust in you and a positive relationship. Greet the child warmly each day and provide one-on-one teacher–child cozy, comforting time.

- Make 10 times more positive remarks than negative ones: Notice, notice, notice positive behavior.

- Keep teaching prosocial behavior. Help the child get his needs met in more positive ways.

- Talk to the child about his character in a positive way. Say, "You are the *kind of child* who helps others."

- Give the toddler a toy or stuffed animal and say, "This is your toy, and you can hold it all day if you'd like—you don't have to share it. The other toys are for all of the children to share and use."

- If the toddler hits you, hold the toddler's hand and say, "I don't like to be hit. It hurts. You can tell me, 'I'm mad.' "

- Help the child take the perspective of the other child. Say, "No biting, that hurt him—look, he's crying."

- Say "I know you are angry, but I do not want you to kick him."

- Reduce stimuli, create a calm and safe environment, provide cozy corners and a private place for the child (can be a box), so the child can be alone when needed (this is not a time-out spot).

- Create an interesting environment with cause-and-effect toys so the child can feel more powerful.

- Reduce spaces for running in a classroom, but provide places for large motor activities.

posttraumatic stress disorder Anxiety and fear caused by experiencing a traumatic event.

Posttraumatic Stress Disorder

Unfortunately, some infants and toddlers experience extremely unpleasant events such as a car accident, hospitalization, abuse, or witnessing domestic abuse or even murder. **Posttraumatic stress disorder** can occur after an infant or toddler experiences a traumatic event. Gaensbauer

(2004), a professor of psychiatry who helps children who experience trauma in their lives, reports that young children usually relive the trauma through their actions rather than verbally. He reports that a child placed in foster care at 4 months of age had been severely traumatized by a mother with mental illness. She would undress him and wrap him in cold towels. At 9 months of age, when he was reunited with his mother for a supervised visit, she started to undress him. At that moment the infant started to scream and the visit was stopped. He seemed to have a memory of the trauma from when he was 4 months old.

A person, object, or event may trigger memories of the painful. disturbing, or upsetting experience. These memories of the experience may cause fear, anxiety, withdrawal, aggression, crying, or shock. The infant or toddler may become still with vacant eyes or hyperactive with frantic looks. A toddler who experienced cockroaches in his diaper while suffering neglect in his home became frenzied when he felt a prickly or crawling sensation on his skin (Lieberman, 1993). It may seem as if the toddler is having a tantrum, but he is expressing fear. A mobile infant may cling to a blanket or piece of clothing the reminds her of her deceased mother. A child may begin to panic when she sees a pair of scissors because this is what her mother used to protect herself during a domestic violence incident. An open hand raised to help a toddler may cause a child to "freeze" or panic because of parental abuse with an open hand. These children may want to over-control their environment and people *or* may withdraw in order to keep themselves safe. *The overwhelming feelings that a child (or an adult) seems to experience during the traumatic event is one of helplessness, inability to control the situation, and feelings of not being safe or protected.* Adapt your strategies to the individual child's temperament and experience. The purpose of your strategies is to assure the child that you will keep him safe. You can do the following:

- Talk with a mental health specialist for support and strategies that meet this particular child's need.
- Observe and document the child's behavior.
- Help the child learn strategies when lost in a flood of anxiety—for instance, go to the teacher or a safe place at home or in classroom.
- Always tell when you are going out of the room—and say "I'm back" when you return.
- Help the child feel competent with toys and materials at her developmental level.
- Acknowledge the child's feelings—say, "It looks as if you are feeling afraid. I'm here, I'll keep you safe." Say, "This is a safe place."
- Use contingently responsive strategies—for instance, when a child pops up out of a box, say, "Oh, there you are." The child may replay the scene over and over to feel as if he is "making something happen."
- Provide a primary caregiver, continuity of care, and a consistent routine.
- Provide a cozy corner or "safe place" with boundaries and comforting toys (could be a box).
- Simplify things for the child—provide her own bin of water instead of a bin for two, so the child doesn't have to share for a while.
- Provide water—it *may* be soothing to a child.
- Take obnoxiously loud toys out of the environment.

Work with a mental health specialist as you support the family. If the child has been removed from his home, you may be working with the foster parent(s). Help families understand, and learn *from* families how the child is expressing his or her reaction to trauma. Problem solve *with* the family on how to comfort the child. And, of course, if you suspect abuse you obviously must report it.

What Philosophy Will You Use?

A responsive care, relationship-based model that includes a family- and culture-centered approach works very well for helping us think about how to help a child who is challenged and challenges parents, teachers, and peers. Ask: "What strategies promote healthy relationships and are responsive to the child's needs? What strategies make the child feel safe, secure, and able to express emotions in a healthy way? What helps him regulate his own behavior, problem solve, and want to be prosocial? How can you win the heart of a child with challenging behavior?"

Are the important adults in the child's life working together to improve *all* of the child's relationships? If the child is to be helped, it isn't enough to improve only the relationship between the teacher and the child, although that can certainly help the child emotionally. The child's relationship with his or her parents, siblings, or grandparents must also be improved for long-term results. There is no place for blaming the child (as in "He's mean")—but rather, it is the responsibility of adults to positively support the child and work toward the child's mental health and well-being.

Following is a 10-point process for helping children with challenging behavior. The key people in the child's life *work together* to answer the following questions that then lead to a relationship-based approach with the child. Only after all of the key people reflect on the questions can appropriate strategies be developed that truly meet the child's needs.

1. Ask: "Who is this child? Who has positive relationships with this child? What are his strengths? Who likes what about this child?"

   It is important to see the "whole" child with strengths, interests, and needs rather than defining the child only by the challenging behavior.

2. Clearly define the behavior that is challenging the child, the teacher, or family members.

   Before deciding on strategies, the behavior must be clearly defined. Write down the behavior (he bites other children), not an attribute of the child (the child is aggressive). What is the challenge for the child? For example, "The child bites peers." How often does it occur? How long has it occurred? Who does it happen with? Where does it happen? Is it developmentally appropriate?

3. Why is the behavior a challenge?

   Why is the behavior a challenge for the child, the parent, the teacher, and peers? How are the parents and teachers feeling about it? (Angry, sad, rejected, proud, frustrated?) How is it affecting the child and others? Who is it a problem for? What's the meaning for the family and teachers? What are the cultural issues?

4. Why does the family and teacher think the child does the behavior?

   Brainstorm several possibilities. Always rule out any medical problems first. Then observe the child. Observe for temperament, developmental level, delay, disability, coping style, sensory needs, imitation, anxiety, fear, anger, stress, hypersensitivity, sleep deprivation, grief, depression, need for positive attention, recent loss or transitions, trauma, or abuse. Think about how the child is keeping himself safe. Has he learned to avoid adults to protect himself or has he learned to "make himself heard" and use more intense ways of getting the attention of the adult in order to be protected (Crittenden, 1995).

5. What's the purpose of the behavior? What is the child trying to communicate?

   The behavior is working for the child and helping her cope. What does the child gain from the behavior? (If child hits, the child gets a toy away from a peer.) After observing, complete the following chart:

Date	What Happens Before	The Challenging Behavior	What Happens After	Possible Purposes of the Behavior

6. What is the child feeling and experiencing? What's the emotional need being expressed by the child? How is the child feeling challenged? Look at behavior from the child's perspective.

7. What are the child's short-term and long-range social and emotional needs?

8. What do the family, teachers, and peers want the child to be able to feel and do instead of the challenging behavior? Is it developmentally appropriate? Will it help the child meet his needs? Does the child possess the skills to meet the need in a more appropriate way?

9. Think about the strategies you've tried: What's worked, what hasn't? How did these make the child feel? How did they work? How did they make the adult feel? Were the strategies consistent with achieving the goal(s) for the child? Were they consistent with your beliefs about what infants and toddlers need and how they learn?

10. What support do the adults and peers need to help this child? Who can help the child, the family, peers, and the teachers? Whoever has a strong, positive relationship with the child should be the key ones to help. What are some strategies that meet children's needs, help children achieve their goals, guide children to use a more positive behavior, and are developmentally, individually, and culturally appropriate?

SUMMARY

myeducationlab

Go to MyEducationLab and complete the Building Teaching Skills and Dispositions exercise in Chapter 14.

This chapter completed our discussion of the components of a curriculum by examining component 8 (a relationship-based approach to guidance). In planning the guidance component, we applied the 3 R approach: *respect, reflect,* and *relate.* If your guidance strategies include respect for child differences and development; reflection on why, when, and where a behavior occurs and what you want to teach the child; and relating through responsive interactions, building the child's relationships, and considering how the environment affects children—then you are on your way to using guidance well.

- The 3 R approach to guiding infants' and toddlers' behavior includes respecting, reflecting, and relating to meet their emotional needs. When adults guide young children they are teaching them in order for them to be successful in a world that requires social and emotional competence.

- Respect for infants and toddlers includes valuing their emotional needs, individual differences and strengths, and the power of development. Teachers must also respect themselves and know how their culture and past experiences affect their beliefs about how children should behave and become socialized.

- When adults reflect, they think about what an experience is like for a child, observe what the children are communicating through their behavior, and decide what they would like the child to learn to do instead.

- When adults relate with infants and toddlers they support children's healthy relationships with all of the important people in their lives, focus on adult–child responsive interactions that promote children's capacities and development, and create a supportive environment.

- Separation anxiety, toddler resistance, challenges with learning to use the toilet, tantrums, and biting peers and adults are behaviors that are sure to happen with infants and toddlers. When adults understand that young children experience times of emotional turmoil as they develop and learn new behaviors, they can be more understanding and supportive.

- Some infants and toddlers may feel anxious, fearful, and vigilant; angry and defiant; aggressive; or may experience posttraumatic stress disorder. Use a relationship-based philosophy to collaborate with all of the adults in a child's life to support the child's emotional and social development when the child is feeling challenged.

Key Terms

discipline	other-oriented guidance	socialized
guidance	posttraumatic stress disorder	tantrums
justification	resolution	time-in
mitigation	sensory challenges	time-out
negativism	separation anxiety	traumatic events

REFLECTIONS AND RESOURCES FOR THE READER

Reflections

1. Elaborate on the 3 R approach (respect, reflect, and relate) for thinking about guidance. What would you add to each step of the process?
2. What is the child experiencing when he or she is having a tantrum? How do you or other adults you know usually handle toddler tantrums? What would you do to support a child who is having a tantrum and help the child learn new ways to express emotions?
3. Trishanna is 20 months old, in a family child care setting, and feels very angry much of the time. She bites her peers, kicks furniture, and resists any efforts on the part of the child care provider to comfort her when she is distressed. What would you do if you were the provider?

Observation and Application Opportunities

1. Observe an early development and education program. How do the adults guide young children's behavior? Are the strategies supporting the infants' and toddlers' social and emotional development and helping them learn new appropriate behaviors?
2. Choose one of the challenging behaviors and read more about why children may be experiencing anxiety, fear, anger, or posttraumatic stress disorder.
3. Choose one of the developmental issues discussed in this chapter. Develop a guidebook for parents on strategies that they can use when their children are experiencing separation anxiety, biting, tantrums, or learning to use the toilet. Help them understand the issue from the child's perspective.

Supplementary Articles and Books to Read

Brazelton, T. B., & Sparrow, J. D. (2004). *Toilet training: The Brazelton way.* New York: Da Capo Press.

Gaensbauer, T. (2004). Telling their stories: Representation and reenactment of traumatic experiences occurring in the first year of life. *Zero to Three, 24*(5), 25–31.

Honig, A. S. (2007). First fears. *Scholastic Parent & Child, 14*(5), 67.

Ramming, P., Kyger, C. S., & Thompson, S. D. (2006). A new bit on toddler biting: The influence of food, oral motor development, and sensory activities. *Young Children, 61*(2), 17–23.

Szamreta, J. M. (2003). Peekaboo power: To ease separation and build secure relationships. *Young Children, 58*(1), 88–94.

Wiggins, C., Fenichel, E., & Mann, T. (ZERO TO THREE). (2007). *Literature review: Developmental problems of maltreated children and early intervention options for maltreated children.* Retrieved March 4, 2009, from http://aspe.hhs.gov/hsp/07/Children-CPS/litrev/index.htm

Interesting Links

http://www.challengingbehavior.org
Technical Assistance Center on Social Emotional Intervention   The center promotes the use of evidence-based practice to meet the needs of young children who have, or are at risk for, challenging behavior.

http://ceep.crc.uiuc.edu/poptopics/biting.html
The Clearinghouse on Early Education and Parenting   CEEP provides an article on biting and other resources on biting for parents and teachers.

http://www.childtrauma.org
Child Trauma Academy   This site offers educational materials and articles concerning child trauma, including sections for caregivers and interdisciplinary teams.

http://www.vanderbilt.edu/csefel/
Center on the Social and Emotional Foundations for Early Learning   This national center focuses on strengthening the capacity of child care and Head Start programs to improve the social and emotional outcomes of young children.

myeducationlab

These and other web links are included in this chapter on MyEducationLab.

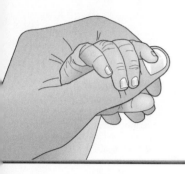

Including Infants and Toddlers with Disabilities in Child Development and Education Programs

Diane stopped in the doorway of the toddler room in the child development and education center as she entered to pick up her daughter Lucy at the end of the day. She couldn't stop the tears that were welling up. Pat, Lucy's teacher, rushed over to her, concerned. "I'm OK," Diane said. "It's just that for a moment, when I looked around the room, I didn't know which one was Lucy. They're all busy and playing. I've never seen her just blend in before."

Moments like this for Diane are possible because community-based child care programs are increasingly likely to include children with special needs. Just as the use of child development and education programs for infants and toddlers has been steadily increasing over the years, parents of infants and toddlers with special needs are using these programs in greater numbers (Buell, Gamel-McCormick, Hallam, 1999). As recently as 10 years ago, most infants and toddlers with disabilities would not have been served in many child development and education programs (child care centers, family child care homes), and most infant-toddler teachers did not have experience with children with disabilities. This has changed dramatically in recent

years. Teachers should now have every expectation that they will be serving infants and toddlers with a variety of disabilities as part of any group of children—and serving them well! These programs serve the needs of parents employed outside the home and can provide a variety of benefits for the infant or toddler with disabilities (Bruder & Brand, 1995). Children are most likely to benefit from the increased opportunities for socialization with peers (Odom & Diamond, 1998). However, the benefits to the child with disabilities, or to any child, depends on the quality of the program (Diener, 1992).

Throughout this book, we have included information on infants and toddlers with disabilities because most of their needs will be met through the same knowledge and strategies used with typically developing children. We include that information throughout the book to illustrate our own commitment to the full inclusion of children with disabilities in child development and education programs. However, there is further, specific information teachers need about children with disabilities.

This chapter provides a description of types of disabling conditions and challenges to development found in infants and toddlers. The early intervention system is described, particularly in regard to supports available to child development and education programs. Finally, although in most cases the aspects of high-quality infant-toddler care that have been described earlier in this book will translate into high-quality care for all children, we will discuss some specific strategies teachers can use to help infants and toddlers with disabilities really participate in activities and develop friendships with other children.

WHAT DISABILITIES DO WE SEE IN INFANTS AND TODDLERS?

Before naming a list of disabling conditions, it is worth pointing out that terms such as *disability* or *special needs* are so general they are almost meaningless. Yet, for each individual, these words can be fraught with meaning. In addition, the diagnosis of a disability can never fully describe a particular child. The disability is only one aspect of the child. There is no meaningful way, for example, to describe "infants with Down syndrome." Any one infant with Down syndrome is born into a particular family with their unique resources and stressors, as well as their own understanding and meaning of the disability. The child may be born relatively healthy or with complicating health issues. The child has his own personality and temperament, and quickly establishes his own history, a sense of who he is, and his own expectations of the world. He may be an only child, a new child among siblings, or live within an extended family. The surrounding culture may contribute particular beliefs about Down syndrome, a wealth or lack of supporting resources, and a welcoming or rejecting attitude.

Thus, because no child can be described fully by the name of his disability, we use person-first language: We say "a person with a disability" or "a child with a disability" or "a child with Down syndrome," *not* "a disabled child" or a "Down's child." The child is a person first with all of the differing individual characteristics, strengths, needs, interests, and desires that all children have. The disability is a part of who that child is, but only a part.

Groups of Disabilities

Nonetheless, we do classify disabling conditions. The disabilities most often identified in infancy tend to be relatively significant, including genetic syndromes, sensory disorders, and central nervous system disorders. These conditions tend to have serious impact on a child's ability to take information from the world, to process and understand that information, and to control the movement of the child's own body. Causes may include circumstances around the birth such as intrauterine substance exposure, prematurity, or low birth weight (Fattal-Valevski, Leitner,

Kutai, Tal-Posener, Tomer, & Lieberman, 1999; Watemberg, Silver, Harel, & Lerman-Sagie, 2002). They may be established conditions such as Down syndrome, cerebral palsy, or seizures (Besag, 2002). Language and communication impairments are often secondary disabilities caused by the primary condition, because producing speech requires considerable muscle control, and learning language requires both sensory and processing abilities (Parkinson, 2002).

It is impossible to name each potential disability and explain its effects. There are thousands of genetic syndromes alone. Nonetheless, young teachers frequently request some overview that would help them understand the kinds of disabling conditions that may present themselves. In this section, we will describe some disabling conditions that would fit under the category "established biological risk," some of their potential effects on development, and some interventions that support development for children with these conditions. Remember, children with each of these conditions have been successfully included in child development and education programs.

Chromosomal Abnormalities and Genetic Syndromes

As described in chapter 5, the gene is the basic component of inherited information, carrying traits from parent to child. The gene reproduces at each cell division and produces exact copies of its DNA and proteins. Normally, each cell in the body, except the egg and sperm, has 23 matching pairs, or 46 chromosomes. Each gene is located on a specific spot of a particular chromosome. **Genetic syndromes** occur when the genes are damaged in cell division or when sets of genes from the mother and/or father carry defective information. *Chromosomal abnormalities* occur when there are too many or too few chromosomes, or when a chromosome has missing pieces, extra pieces, or pieces attached to another chromosome (HGP, 2008).

Chromosomal abnormalities are often identified prenatally, at birth, or soon after birth. Some common chromosomal and genetic abnormalities include:

genetic syndromes Abnormalities caused by information within the genetic material.

- *Down syndrome:* Caused by an extra, or third, 21st chromosome. Because of the cause of the syndrome, it is also known as *trisomy 21*. This occurs most often when the 21st chromosome duplicates in either the egg or the sperm as a pair, rather than as a single chromosome. Down syndrome has a number of visible characteristics such as an upward slant to the eyes, a small mouth and facial features, small stature, a flattened back of the head, and small hands with a single crease across the palm. Children with Down syndrome may have congenital heart defects, poor muscle tone that can delay motor development, and varying degrees of mental retardation. Although children with Down syndrome eventually develop speech, they often begin communication very successfully by using sign language (NDSS, 2005).

  <u>Supporting development</u>: Given low muscle tone, infants and toddlers with Down syndrome may need support in sitting and in being carried to stay near the other children. During the first year of life, they will benefit from using sign language or other communication systems as they have much to communicate but are likely to be delayed in language. Teachers use play as a way to help these infants and toddlers focus and maintain their attention (Kumin, 1998).

- *Fragile X syndrome:* Caused by a partially broken area (fragile) on the X chromosome. Because girls have two X chromosomes and boys have only one, the damage usually has more impact on boys. Children with fragile X syndrome are likely to have mild to severe mental retardation, although they may also have normal intelligence. They may have a large head with noticeably large forehead, nose, jaws, and ears. Some children with fragile X syndrome have attentional problems and some have autistic-like tendencies (NFXF, 2008).

  <u>Supporting development</u>: Children with fragile X syndrome have traditionally been identified at or later than the age of 3 years, but amniocentesis and newborn screening are providing early identification (Cassels, 2008). Infant-toddler teachers may need to help overcome feeding difficulties and promote social interest and language and motor imitation.

- *Cystic fibrosis:*   A disorder in which genes lack the enzymes to break down and absorb fats, causing malnutrition. Thick secretions cause chronic lung damage; teachers may be involved in performing exercises to help the infant or toddler clear his lungs (CFF, 2009).

    Supporting development: Teachers may learn to position the infant or toddler with cystic fibrosis and tap the chest and back in ways that help loosen the mucus so that it may be coughed out (Lewis, 2007).

- *Sickle cell anemia:*   An abnormality in which some red blood cells are crescent or sickle-shaped. Sickle cell occurs primarily in African Americans, causes fevers and enormous pain in joints and the abdomen, and is incurable (ASCAA, 2007).

    Supporting development: Infants and toddlers with sickle cell anemia must have an individualized health care plan that informs teachers what symptoms are of concern and steps to be taken from notifying parents to initiating transport to an emergency medical facility (WSDOH, 2006).

- *Rett syndrome:*   Usually characterized by typical development for the first 6 to 18 months of life, followed by a rapid loss of cognitive, language, motor, and self-help skills. The progressive loss of skills quickly deteriorates to severe or profound mental retardation; obsessive, repetitive movements such as hand wringing; and often the development of seizures. Rett syndrome occurs almost exclusively in girls (IRSF, 2009).

    Supporting development: Teachers may spend additional time with feeding or even use nasogastric or gastrointestinal feeding tubes, if allowed by the state. Each child is different but the skill development is limited and regression is common, so teachers need to be prepared to maintain a high intensity of caregiving (Kantor, 2006).

Sensory Impairments

Sensory impairments describe the categories of problems that can occur with receiving or processing information through the senses. Sensory impairments can occur prenatally or as a result of illness or injury, ranging in severity from mild to total. Hearing impairment, for example, may range from a mild loss of ability to hear to complete deafness. Visual impairment also includes a range from easily correctable issues to complete blindness. Tactile defensiveness, or hypersensitivity to touch, is a less well-known disorder. It involves a child's difficulty in receiving information from his body and results in poor motor planning and poor body awareness (Coleman, 1999).

sensory impairments
Problems affecting hearing, vision, or other senses.

Supporting development: Teachers will work with early intervention teams and families to meet the needs of infants and toddlers with sensory impairments. Teachers may change the environment, adding a darkened space with light-oriented activities for infants and toddlers with visual impairments. Teachers will provide tactile-rich and language-rich experiences. They may learn and use sign language with all of the children, if there is a child with a hearing impairment. Teachers may learn to do exercises with tactily defensive children to help them become more comfortable with touch.

Metabolic Disorders

Metabolic disorders result from inherited deficiencies of particular enzymes. The enzymes are not available to break down materials such as amino acids, which then build up and cause damage to the brain. Some metabolic disorders can be diagnosed and treated, such as phenylketonuria (PKU). Others, such as Tay-Sachs, cannot be treated and are fatal.

PKU is a condition in which children cannot break down the enzyme phenylalanine, which is present in almost all foods. Without treatment, phenylalanine builds up in the bloodstream and causes brain damage and mental retardation. PKU is a genetic disease. Newborns are now tested at all U.S. hospitals and it is recommended that babies tested within the first 24 hours be retested at 2 weeks (NIH, 2000).

Tay-Sachs is also an inherited metabolic disorder, caused by the absence of a vital enzyme called hexosaminidase A (Hex-A). Without Hex-A, a fatty substance (or *lipid*) called GM2 ganglioside accumulates abnormally in cells, especially in the nerve cells of the brain. There is progressive damage to the cells and children do not live past early childhood. People of European Jewish descent are most likely to be carriers of the defective gene (NTSADA, 2009).

Supporting development: Because this is a severe medical condition usually resulting in death in the first 4 years of life, program staff must carefully consider how they will provide emotional support to the teachers, parents, the child, and the child's peers.

Central Nervous System Disorders

The brain and the spinal cord make up the central nervous system. They receive information from the body through a network of nerves. The brain and spinal cord can be malformed in the womb due to exposure to toxic substances, poor nutrition, maternal infections, or poor migration of cells. Neural cells may also be damaged during the birth process if the baby is deprived of oxygen. The nervous system may not develop well after birth if the child is in a chaotic or barren environment, if nutrition is poor, or if the child is exposed to environmental toxins such as lead. The central nervous system may also be damaged by high fevers, disease, and injury.

Some commonly seen **central nervous system disorders** include:

central nervous system disorders
Damage to the brain, spine, or the nerve network that affects learning, sensory, or motor abilities.

- *Cerebral palsy:*   A disorder of motor and postural control from nonprogressive damage to the brain. The type and severity of the disorder depend on the area of the brain that is affected and the degree of damage. Cerebral palsy ranges from a mild motor impairment to almost no voluntary control of movement. Intelligence is not necessarily affected by the damage, but seizures often occur with cerebral palsy (UCP, 2009). This condition was described in chapter 10.

  Supporting development: Children with cerebral palsy are included in group care very successfully, with the support of the family and the early intervention team. Teachers will have to learn the individual child's strengths and needs for support. Supports may include physical positioning, feeding, individual learning capacities, and alternate communication systems.

- *Spina bifida:*   A birth defect that occurs because the neural tube did not close entirely while forming prenatally. The effect of spina bifida depends on which vertebra are exposed and can range from almost no effect to complete paralysis below the spinal opening and severe mental retardation. Some 70% of the cases of spina bifida could be prevented with adequate intake of folic acid during pregnancy (SBA, 2008).

  Supporting development: Most children with spina bifida have normal intelligence and should be responsive learners and relationship partners. They are likely to have significant problems with mobility and bladder and bowel problems. Special services are likely to concentrate on these issues.

- *Attentional disorders:*   Hyper-reactivity, hypersensitivity, hyposensitivity, and attention deficit disorder—a group of disorders probably caused by small abnormalities in the brain. Symptoms include difficulty in maintaining focus and attention, being easily distracted, difficulty controlling impulses, and being overly sensitive and reactive to sensory information (Coleman, 1999).

  Supporting development: Maintaining attention is a basic developmental task of infancy. Teachers support development by helping infants regulate their reactions to the events around them. Limiting distractions is helpful, although sometimes difficult in group care.

- *Shaken baby syndrome:* A set of symptoms found when a baby has been violently shaken. Symptoms include bleeding in the brain and the retinas of the eyes. It can result in cognitive and motor damage, and often results in death (NCSBS, 2009). If the child survives the shaking, he may develop these symptoms over time: lethargy, vomiting, poor sucking or swallowing, lack of smiling, unequal pupil size, and an inability to focus visually or to lift his head (KidsHealth, 2008).

  Supporting development: The teacher may be the one to recognize the symptoms of this head trauma. Every program must have a plan in place for how to report suspected child abuse.

Congenital Infections

Congenital infections are diseases that affect the baby prenatally. As briefly described in chapter 5, maternal infections do cross the placenta and can cause harm to the fetus. The most commonly seen infections, grouped under the acronym STORCH or TORCH-S, are syphilis, toxoplasmosis, other infections (such as HIV or hepatitis B), rubella, cytomegela virus, and herpes. These infections, when transmitted in the womb or at birth, can cause mental retardation, growth retardation, sensory impairments, and even death (MOD, 2005e).

Disorders Secondary to Exposure to Toxic Substances

Toxins that the mother actively inhales or ingests, such as tobacco, illegal drugs, and alcohol, as well as toxins to which the mother is passively exposed, such as cleaning solvents, lead, and pesticides, are all able to cross the placenta and harm the developing nervous system of the fetus. Damage to the nervous system can cause cognitive impairments and diminished growth. The range of effects depends to some extent on the timing and dosage of exposure. These conditions are described more fully in chapter 5.

Chronic Illness

Chronic illnesses requiring some use of medication or medical technology are increasingly common in child development and education settings. Asthma and allergies are very common chronic conditions. Hemophilia is less common but is often reported by caregivers in workshops on disabilities (Coleman, 1999).

- *Asthma:* A chronic respiratory disorder causing wheezing, coughing, and difficulty breathing. Teachers sometimes administer medication for asthma with a machine called a nebulizer.
- *Allergies:* Sensitivity to normally harmless substances. Allergic reactions may include rashes, irritability, vomiting, swelling, difficulty in breathing, or even shock. Individualized health care plans include instructions for how to respond to known allergic reactions.
- *Hemophilia:* An X-linked disorder caused by a lack of proteins needed for blood clotting. Children may spontaneously bleed or be unable to stop bleeding from minor cuts.

  Supporting developments: Teachers must have plans in place describing how to recognize and respond to symptoms. These conditions are episodic and may be emergencies; nonetheless, on a day-to-day basis teachers should be using their well-developed skills of responsive caregiving, individualized planning, and relationship building.

Conditions of Risk for Poor Development

In addition to the disorders already listed, *pervasive developmental disorders* (PDD) comprise another group of developmental disorders, including autism, Rett's disorder, childhood disintegrative disorder, Asperger's disorder, and pervasive developmental disorder that are characterized by impairment in social interaction and communication skills, extreme reactions to change, and obsessive, repetitive behaviors. PDD can have moderate to severe effects on a child's ability to function. NICHCY (2003), a Web site, includes detailed information on these disorders.

Autism has become a national and growing concern. In 2007, the U.S. Centers for Disease Control and Prevention reported that autism is on the rise with a prevalence rate of 1 in every 150 American children and 1 in 94 boys. The Autism Society of America Web site *http://www.autism-society.org/* contains valuable information for parents and professionals on the definition of autism, the prevalence, causes, research, and intervention strategies. It is important that parents and teachers of infants and toddlers know that early diagnosis (ideally within the first 2 years) is critical for better child outcomes. Ozonoff, Macari, Young, Goldring, Thompson, and Rogers (2008) found that autism can be diagnosed earlier than others have thought. Atypical object exploration (spinning, rotating, and repetitive behaviors) at 12 months of age was associated with a diagnosis of autism at 3 years of age.

The Autism Society's home page on "About Autism" states the following:

Autism is treatable. Children do not "outgrow" autism, but studies show that early diagnosis and intervention lead to significantly improved outcomes.

Here are some signs to look for in the children in your life:

- Lack of or delay in spoken language
- Repetitive use of language and/or motor mannerisms (e.g., hand-flapping, twirling objects)
- Little or no eye contact
- Lack of interest in peer relationships
- Lack of spontaneous or make-believe play
- Persistent fixation on parts of objects

Above all, it is important to remember that with children with special needs there is a little person with whom the teacher has all the necessary skills and compassion to develop a meaningful and loving relationship. This child is part of a family that is quickly learning a great deal of new information, dealing with a shock, perhaps becoming new parents, and very possibly worrying about how they will be welcomed anywhere. Early childhood programs can serve infants and toddlers with disabilities well. A program can provide wonderful opportunities for learning and relationships and can be welcoming and reassuring to the family. If the early childhood program conveys a message that "we are a program, a community, and a society that has room for all children," it will always be deeply appreciated by families.

EARLY INTERVENTION: PART C OF IDEA

Although child development and education programs play a very important role in the lives of families, they do not have the primary responsibility for providing therapeutic services to infants and toddlers with disabilities. Since 1986, the federal law providing special education services in the United States has also provided for early intervention services for infants and toddlers. The *Individuals with Disabilities Education Act* (IDEA) requires all states to provide special education services to children between 3 and 21 years of age. The Program for Infants and Toddlers with Disabilities (Part C of IDEA, PL 105-17) was designed to:

- Enhance the development of infants and toddlers with disabilities
- Reduce the educational costs by minimizing the need for special education through early intervention
- Minimize the likelihood of institutionalization and maximize independent living
- Enhance the capacity of families to meet their child's needs (NECTAC, 2005)

The Program for Infants and Toddlers with Disabilities is a grant program from the federal government to the states to help them provide early intervention services for infants and toddlers through age 2 and their families. The state has to meet a set of 16 components, as shown in Box 15.1, and must ensure that they will meet the needs of every eligible child and family.

Eligibility

Part C requires each state to determine its own criteria for eligibility. States are required to provide services to children who have conditions of established risk, "a diagnosed physical or mental condition which has a high probability of resulting in developmental delay." This includes many of the conditions described previously, including "chromosomal abnormalities, genetic or congenital disorders; severe sensory impairments, including hearing and vision; inborn errors of metabolism; disorders reflecting disturbance of the nervous system; congenital infections; disorders secondary to exposure of toxic substances, including fetal alcohol syndrome; and severe attachment disorders." Many states add to this list biological conditions that increase the likelihood of, but do not necessarily result in, developmental delays. These would include low birth weight, intraventricular hemorrhage at birth, chronic lung disease, and failure to thrive. Some states also choose to provide services to children who are considered to be at environmental risk for development because of factors like parental substance abuse, parental mental illness, and child abuse or neglect.

Box 15.1

Required Components of a State's Part C (IDEA) System

1. A rigorous definition of developmental delay
2. Appropriate early intervention services based on scientifically based research, to the extent practicable, available to all infants and toddlers with disabilities and their families, including Indian and homeless infants and toddlers
3. Timely and comprehensive multidisciplinary evaluation of needs of children and family-directed identification of the needs of each family
4. Individualized family service plan and service coordination
5. Comprehensive child find and referral system
6. Public awareness program
7. Central directory of services, resources, and research and demonstration projects
8. Comprehensive system of personnel development
9. Policies and procedures for personnel standards
10. Single line of authority in a lead agency designated by the governor
11. Policy pertaining to contracting for services
12. Procedure for timely reimbursement of funds
13. Procedural safeguards
14. System for compiling data on the early intervention system
15. State interagency coordinating council
16. Policies and procedures to ensure that to the maximum extent appropriate, early intervention services are provided in natural environments except when early intervention cannot be achieved satisfactorily in a natural environment

Source: NECTAC (2005).

Individualized Family Service Plan (IFSP)

If a child is eligible for services under Part C, the child receives a thorough developmental evaluation from two or more professionals, and the family and the early intervention team develop an *individualized family service plan* (IFSP) that determines the goals for development and the services and supports needed to achieve them. See Figure 15.1 for a sample page of an IFSP. Ideally, each IFSP looks quite different from any other and takes into consideration the priorities, strengths, and needs of each family and child. If a program is providing child development and education services, the director or teacher should be included as a member of the intervention team; she can provide valuable information about how the child manages his interactions with other children and can offer her own expertise on typical development. As summarized by O'Brien (1997):

> Unlike many educational documents . . . the IFSP presents developmental information in a way that encourages parents' understanding and contribution. . . . The IFSP contains a narrative description of the child's current level of performance in each of the major developmental domains, and both family members and professionals can offer descriptions to be included here. (p. 57)

Early Intervention Action Plan	
What we see now: *Sierra is very active and able to raise her head when on her tummy and to turn over at will.*	What we want to see for baby/family: *Sierra is starting to eat more solid foods, so her mom wants her to be able to sit up.*
Our strategies to get there: • *Continue using supported sitting positions.* • *Increase exercise through play that will increase muscle tone and trunk control.*	Services and supports we will use: • *Jen, our OT, will continue weekly visits and provide drawings of current exercises.* • *Mom and Dad will work with Sierra in the evenings.* • *Shirley, her teacher, will include exercise in diaper changing and play times.*
How we will know we are there: *Sierra will be able to sit independently during mealtimes and to play.*	Comments: *We want to encourage Sierra's becoming stronger in her trunk and neck—but not to push her if she's not ready.*

Figure 15.1   Sample individualized family service plan (IFSP).

Early Intervention Services

Under Part C, infants and toddlers with disabilities may receive services from early childhood special educators, speech-language pathologists, physical therapists, occupational therapists, or psychologists. A service coordinator manages the variety of services and often coordinates many sources of funding. Part C requires states to "have policies and procedures in place to ensure that to the maximum extent appropriate, early intervention services are provided in natural environments." The steps in the intervention process are as follows:

1. Family contacts Part C provider with concerns.
2. Multidisciplinary assessment of child's development is made.
3. Eligibility is established.
4. Service coordinator is assigned.
5. Individualized family service plan (IFSP) is developed.
6. Services are delivered.
7. Evaluation and plan are reviewed at 6-month intervals.

In many states, the early intervention services are offered within the child development and education program, or, at the very least, with ongoing consultation to the staff. Early interventionists may provide advice on how to physically position a child to maximize his ability to control and use his body, they may offer strategies for adapting toys and materials, they may have tips to make feeding more efficient and satisfying, and they may offer a variety of communication alternatives to help adults understand the cues and signals of the infant or toddler with disabilities. The families of the children receive support as well from the early interventionist and the teacher—family and early interventionist(s) work as a team. O'Brien (1997) describes how the child's skills and abilities may be discussed:

> Even the way developmental domains are described on IFSPs is different from the way most educators have been taught to talk about them, because the labels used need to be focused on the types of skills and abilities cared about by families. Rather than cognitive development, an IFSP label might read as

thinking and *problem solving*. Similarly, gross motor development could be listed as *muscles and movement;* fine motor development as *reaching and playing;* communication as *talking, listening, and understanding;* social and behavioral development as *getting along with others;* and adaptive or functional skills as *daily living.* When presented in these terms, the discussion about the child's development can be shared equally between parents and professionals. (p. 57)

States have different rules limiting the medical procedures that can be performed by anyone other than a nurse. These rules are outlined in each state's Nurse Practice Act. The program's health consultant should be involved in planning care for a child who requires a feeding tube, nebulizer treatments, or any other actions that might be construed as practicing medicine.

The requirement for offering services in natural settings was designed to take full advantage of the benefits to the child with disabilities that are inherent in an inclusive environment. The natural interest of any infant or toddler in her peers provides motivation for children with disabilities to actively work to join their friends in their very compelling activities. The play and exploration of typically developing children can be highly engaging for the child with disabilities and can provide models of a variety of ways to play. All children benefit when they learn to create friendships with children with differing skills.

Making Referrals

Children may come to your program already identified by Part C and receiving services, or your program may have some developmental concerns about a child you are already serving. It is important for every infant and toddler development and education program to understand how to access the Part C program in their community and how to talk to families about making a referral. If the family is concerned about the child's development, Part C must provide a timely, multidisciplinary evaluation to determine whether the child is eligible for services.

There are many ways to assess child development. Many programs routinely review development with a brief assessment called a *screening.* Screening tools (see Box 15.2) are usually comprised of a few items describing typical development in each domain. Teachers may set up situations in which to observe whether a child is performing the task or may answer the items from ongoing observations. Some screening tools ask families to use their experience with the child to report on development. Screening tools are not diagnostic, but can help identify areas of potential concern. All child development and education programs could use screening tools periodically as part of their continuous system of observing and recording development. When each child's development is part of the ongoing conversation between families and the program, concerns can be addressed quickly and with mutual understanding.

If a program and family are sufficiently concerned about a child's development in one or more areas, the family may request an evaluation from the Part C program in the community. The results from regular screening in the child development and education program can provide useful information to the early intervention team. Besides the tools presented in Box 15.2, ongoing assessments such as the Ounce (Meisels, et al. 2003) may also be used to document children's development. An example of the Ounce Scale and how it is used was discussed in chapter 12.

Box 15.2

Screening Tools

The Ages & Stages Questionnaire is filled out by parents every several months. Teachers then code the results to track children's development. The pamphlets utilize parent observations while they help inform parents of the predicted course of development. They can be used with children from 2 months to 5½ years (see http://www.brookespublishing.com/ for more information and samples).

Ages & Stages Questionnaires®, third edition (ASQ-3)
Squires, J. & Bricker, D. (2009)
A parent-completed, child-monitoring system
Baltimore: Brookes.

The Denver Developmental Screen is used by professionals or trained paraprofessionals to track development. A few items in each developmental domain are scored at each observation to see if the child's development is within the normal range. It can be used from birth to 6 years and is known as the *Denver II.*

The Denver Developmental Materials (http://www.denverii.com)

Box 15.3

Child Care and the Americans with Disabilities Act (ADA)

1. The ADA applies to privately run and publicly run child care centers; in the program's interactions with children, parents, guardians, and potential customers as well as in their employment practices. Child care centers run by religious organizations may be exempt.

2. The ADA has these specific requirements for child care centers:

   - Centers cannot exclude children with disabilities from their programs unless their presence would pose a *direct threat* to the health or safety of others or require a *fundamental alteration* of the program.

   - Centers have to make *reasonable modifications* to their policies and practices to integrate children, parents, and guardians with disabilities into their programs unless doing so would constitute a *fundamental alteration.*

   - Centers must provide appropriate auxiliary aids and services needed for *effective communication* with children or adults with disabilities, when doing so would not constitute an *undue burden.*

   - Centers must generally make their facilities accessible to persons with disabilities. Existing facilities are subject to the *readily achievable* standard for barrier removal, while newly constructed facilities and any altered portions of existing facilities must be *fully accessible.*

Source: U.S. Department of Justice (1997).

Child Development and Education as a Natural Environment

Even now, in the 21st century, despite laws such as the Americans with Disabilities Act (ADA) designed to prevent discrimination, some teachers, directors, and home family providers routinely turn away any child identified as having a disability (see Box 15.3). In studies and workshops on this topic, teachers frequently voice concerns about not having the knowledge to care for children with disabilities, about children with disabilities requiring one-on-one care, and about the discomfort other children and families may feel (Kontos, 1988). Family care providers are concerned that the child with disabilities will require so much attention that they will have to serve fewer children, and thus reduce their income (Buell et al., 1999). While that may be true for an infant with multiple disabilities—for example, on a respirator and gastrostomy tube, with visual and hearing impairment—that description would match only a very few of the thousands of infants and toddlers identified each year with disabilities. (See Observation Invitation 15.1.)

Teachers and families who have experienced inclusive services describe them as having many benefits. Teachers with positive experiences in serving infants and toddlers with disabilities enjoy their jobs more and have more positive attitudes toward serving other children with disabilities (Soodak & Erwin, 2000). When they were given opportunities to prepare themselves, learn additional strategies, and establish the supports they felt they needed, teachers were very positive about supporting a child's membership in their community (Cross, Traub, Hutter-Pishagi, & Shelton, 2004). Those teachers who approached the challenge with confidence believed that inclusion promotes gains in socialization among all children (Diamond, 2001).

myeducationlab

Go to the Activities and Applications section in Chapter 15 of MyEducationLab to watch the video *Inclusion.* How does a care teacher develop an environment where all infants and toddlers can be successful?

TEACHER ATTITUDES AND STRATEGIES IN THE CHILD DEVELOPMENT AND EDUCATION PROGRAM

Maintain a Positive Attitude

Nothing is more important for the successful inclusion of an infant or toddler with disabilities than the attitudes of the adults involved. Teachers should reflect on their own feelings about disabilities and discuss any concerns they might have about serving a child with disabilities—concerns, for example, about possibly harming the child through lack of knowledge or skills or being unable to manage the regular ratios when the group has a child perceived to have high needs, as well as their own personal feelings about disability. Program directors or early intervention team members may be helpful in participating in this conversation.

Observation Invitation 15.1

When Antonio came into the classroom, it was breakfast time. Gabriella followed him to the handwashing sink. Gabriella took a quick turn and then joined him as his teacher helped him walk to the table. She took his hand and they walked together. For a moment she held his hand as the teacher lifted him into his supportive seat. Then she immediately claimed the seat next to his at the table.

Consider these pictures for signs of toddler friendship. What does their relationship tell you about the benefits of inclusion of infants and toddlers with disabilities—for all children?

Ask for Information Sharing

Teachers need adequate information in order to serve every child. Teachers should have the opportunity to form their questions and have them answered by the family, health professionals, or early intervention providers. Families should also feel free to ask questions regarding the program's ability to provide any specific services or adaptations needed by their child. If Part C is serving the child, the service coordinator can be helpful in facilitating what might be an uncomfortable conversation. Inclusion is most successful when teachers and parents have frequent opportunities to exchange information, when they are open to each other's suggestions and ideas, and when they value each other's contributions to the children and the success of the experience (Cross et al., 2004).

Document Children's Competence

Documentation can be very useful in helping teachers maintain positive attitudes toward children with disabilities. When teachers use documentation with infants and toddlers with disabilities, it can reflect images of active, productive, and social experiences back to the child, as well as help keep positive images of the child in the teacher's mind. While it is easy to see how this sort of chart (see Table 15.1) would be nice for any child, it can be particularly helpful in keeping the child's strengths, rather than needs and disabilities, in the teacher's mind. The chart shown in Table 15.1 describes the interests and abilities of an 18-month-old girl with Down syndrome.

Adapt Materials and Activities

The large list of disabling conditions described at the beginning of this chapter demonstrated that disabilities might have all sorts of functional effects. Some children have normal or high intelligence but are unable to control their bodies. Some move well but have difficulty processing and understanding information. Some have difficulty focusing attention. Some have difficulty in social relationships. Some have poor sensory abilities. Obviously, different strategies serve different children.

Without question, there is no easier age group for full inclusion than infants and toddlers. Infant and toddler services are already highly individualized. In fact, early childhood educators are constantly making unconscious little adjustments to particular needs: Riley needs protected space to play, Freddie won't eat foods of a certain texture, Rachel needs lots of warning before a transition, and Li needs moments of quiet connection and cuddling throughout the day. Teachers make these adjustments without thinking about them. High-quality programs have low ratios and small groups. The typically developing infants and toddlers haven't lived long enough to greet their peers with disabilities with any preconceived biases. Still, there are a number of considerations and strategies to ensure that inclusion results in a successful, meaningful experience for everyone involved:

> One of the roles of teachers in inclusive child care settings is to serve as *inclusion facilitators*. Facilitating inclusion simply means making sure that children with special needs are incorporated into all of the ongoing activities of the classroom, including daily living activities as well as play activities. An emphasis on facilitating inclusion ensures that children who have disabilities are not set apart from the other children, such as by eating separately because they need individual care, being kept indoors when the other children are on the playground, or being entertained by one teacher while other children are involved in group activities. (O'Brien, 1997, p. 35)

Table 15.1   Sarah's favorite things to do!

Toys	Meals	Outdoors
Sarah loves hugging and carrying her doll, being just like her own mommy. Sarah can put the rings on the stick and the shapes in the box—and she likes to practice that a lot!	Sarah is a good friend at the table. She drinks from a cup and feeds herself "finger food" snacks. She smiles and laughs and is interested in her friends. Sarah signs to Miss Rose to tell her what she wants at mealtimes.	Sarah stays close to Miss Rose outdoors. She likes pulling the "horsie" riding toy around the playground as much as riding it. Sarah loves playing in sand and water.

Friends	Grown-ups	Nap Time
Sarah looks for Ona and Peter when she gets to school. She likes to be near friends and to give hugs.	Sarah loves her mommy, daddy, and grandmas. She especially likes to be with Miss Rose during the day. Sometimes Sarah likes grown-ups to help her when she gets frustrated with a toy or a puzzle.	Sarah gets tired at school and sleeps heavily at nap time. She likes to listen to stories, quiet music, and have her back rubbed as she falls asleep. Cuddling in the rocking chair is a big treat!

Table 15.2   Principles of adapting toys and materials

Stability	Usefulness of Information	Achieving Goals Through Play
Increases baby's control of objects, ability to explore and learn	Provides information through senses and use of body most effective for the baby	Naturally engages baby to attempt goals such as bringing hands together at midline, isolating fingers, or making sounds
• Use Velcro or tape to hold items to table. • Large handles make an item easier to pick up or move. • A weighted bottom makes the item less likely to tip over. • Use thicker materials (e.g., board books rather than paper).	• Simplify materials by offering fewer pieces. • Use sharp contrasts for child with visual impairment. • Take out sound-makers for children who are sensitive to too much stimulation.	• Offer toys that require both hands to hold them. • Blow bubbles to pop when hands are clapped together. • Poke at bubbles with one finger. • Offer toys that require an isolated finger such as a little piano or telephone.

As shown in Table 15.2, adapting toys and materials for infants and toddlers with special needs is a three-step process: (1) understanding what the children are learning and how they learn, (2) providing materials that contain the information in a relevant form, and (3) ensuring that the materials are stable. One of the first considerations in planning learning activities for infants or toddlers with disabilities is to understand what concepts and skills are currently emerging for them and what kinds of toys and materials they find interesting. For example, infants who are just beginning to learn that they can hold on to an object and move it enjoy rattles that are light, fist-size, and make noise. Infants who are beginning to explore spatial relationships enjoy putting objects into containers and dumping them out again. Infants and toddlers with disabilities are making the same cognitive discoveries as typically developing infants, although possibly not on the same time line or through the same sources of information. They need materials that are responsive to the actions they are capable of producing. Infants and toddlers with disabilities do well when the materials they use are stable enough to stay in one place and not be easily knocked over or roll away. The information must be available to them in ways that make sense—for example, simplify the information in stacking cups by offering fewer at a time, or use a light table as the playing surface for a child with visual impairment.

Arrange the Environment

As older infants become mobile, it might become necessary for the teacher to move the young child with physical impairments to be able to stay close to her friends. Supportive seating that allows the toddler to sit at the snack table with everyone else is more conducive to participation than a seat with its own tray. Children with visual impairments, in particular, need the furniture and pathways in the environment to remain unchanged so that they are able to learn how to get from one area to another on their own.

Use Group Affection Activities

In so many ways, we encourage infants and toddlers to be kind to each other. We remind them to be gentle in their touch and give them the general advice to "Be nice." We can be specific in our directions to children as to how they can be most helpful to a child with a disability. It might be "Take her hand," or it might be "Just wait—he'll get it." Teachers can reinforce the toddler with special needs, using positive descriptive words, when he stays close to the other children and observes or imitates their social play: "You really like watching Andre with those trucks. Andre has a good time playing cars and trucks." A further step would be to help the typically developing child invite the child with special needs into the activity: "Andre, would you please give this truck to Jack?" (Lowenthal, 1995, p. 22).

Meet Therapeutic Goals

Infants and toddlers with disabilities should have an early intervention team working with them and an IFSP defining their therapeutic goals. Teachers can promote the mastery of these goals through well-chosen play activities, where the toys and materials inherently suggest the therapeutic actions. Children with nervous system and motor disorders are often working on goals such as using both hands at midline, loosening their fists to use their fingers, using fingers in isolation, and using increasingly sophisticated grasps. Play activities that promote these goals would include offering toys large enough to require both hands be used together, toy pianos, tape players, and other single-button-activated toys. Small toys (but not so small as to be a choking hazard) and foods like bits of bananas or cereal pieces all encourage grasps. One of the best materials for promoting these actions is bubbles. Smashing bubbles with both hands clapping is a great way to bring the hands to midline. Poking bubbles promotes the use of isolated fingers.

Teachers may use a variety of positioning techniques to support children with motor issues to maximize their use of their bodies. Therapists may show teachers how to use simple material such as rolled-up towels to support positions or may provide standing boards or special chairs. Children with severe motor issues may be introduced to toys that run on switches, devices that direct battery-operated toys through the use of whatever part of the body has most control. Switches may be operated through touch, sound, head position, sucking, or blowing. The early intervention team should provide these materials to child development and education programs.

Many therapeutic goals for infants and toddlers require only the same materials and teacher interactions as typically developing children. Teachers create environments that encourage focus, attention, and exploration. They expand play and language. They provide an emotional tone of calm interest to support learning and joyful celebration to support accomplishment. They respond to vocalizations from infants as though they were words spoken with meaning. They promote kindness and empathy toward other children. These actions all support the achievement of therapeutic goals by infants and toddlers with disabilities.

myeducationlab

Go to MyEducationLab and complete the Building Teaching Skills and Dispositions exercise in Chapter 15.

SUMMARY

Infant and toddler teachers today routinely serve children with disabilities in their community settings. High-quality practices serve children with disabilities well, but there are some additional things it is helpful for teachers to know:

- Although there are thousands of potentially disabling conditions, no condition or diagnosis defines a child. Early childhood educators need to learn about each child, her likes and dislikes, her personality, her routines and expectations, and the effects of the disabling condition. No one needs to know about all disabilities and their effects; a teacher simply needs to know how to understand one baby at a time, how to read her cues, and how to develop a relationship with that one child.

- The Program for Infants and Toddlers with Disabilities (Part C of the Individuals with Disabilities Education Act) provides early intervention services including service coordination, physical therapy, occupational therapy, speech therapy, and educational services.

- Early intervention teams serving infants and toddlers with disabilities should be able to support the child in child development and education. Teachers may have a copy of the individualized family service plan (IFSP), which describes the developmental goals and strategies to help the child achieve the goals. The early interventionists may provide special equipment needed to support the child. Early intervention services may actually be provided within the child development and education setting.

- Teachers use many strategies to adapt materials and activities for their successful use by the infants and toddlers with disabilities. Toys need to be stable, match the child's current interests, and provide contingent responses to the child's actions. Teachers need to promote the close physical proximity of infants and toddlers with disabilities to typically developing children as well as the social and emotional connections among children.
- Well-trained infant-toddler educators have the ability to serve all children well because the elements of quality are the same for all children. It is the willingness of the teacher to include a child with disabilities that is the greatest indicator for success.

Key Terms

central nervous system
   disorders

genetic syndromes

sensory impairments

REFLECTIONS AND RESOURCES FOR THE READER

Reflections

1. Our own life experiences, or lack of experiences, around people with disabilities may influence our comfort with inclusive services. Reflect on your experiences and how they influence your feelings about serving infants and toddlers with disabilities in a child development and education program.
2. If you were designing an inclusive infant-toddler environment, would you do anything differently from what you would do only for children without disabilities?

Observation and Application Opportunities

1. Contact the Part C coordinator in your community and see if you could talk to a parent of an infant or toddler with a disability about their child's disability, their use of a child development and education program, and their early intervention experiences.
2. Observe an inclusive infant-toddler program. What works well? What would you change?
3. If you were preparing a parent handbook for an infant-toddler program, what would you include to let families know that you serve all children? Have a parent review the handbook and give you feedback on the relevance and completeness of the document.

Supplementary Articles and Books to Read

Danaher, J., Shackelford, J., & Harbin, G. (2004). Revisiting a comparison of eligibility policies for infant/toddler programs and preschool special education programs. *Topics in Early Childhood Special Education, 24*(2), 59–67.

NAEYC. (2003). FYI: "Using what we know about infants and toddlers with disabilities." *Young Children, 58*(3), 67.

Interesting Links

http://www.cec.sped.org/
   Council for Exceptional Children   Here you will find the Individuals with Disabilities Education Act (IDEA) reauthorization bill of 2004.

http://www.theARC.org/
   The Arc of the United States   The Arc of the United States makes many helpful documents available at this Web site. For instance, *All Kids Count: Child Care and the Americans with Disabilities Act* (ADA) is a resource manual published by the Arc that can be downloaded from this site.

http://www.ccplus.org/
   Child Care Plus   Child Care Plus (the Center on Inclusion in Early Childhood) publishes a wonderful newsletter for teachers—and site has interesting and practical articles on adapting materials, environments, and activities for children with special needs.

http://www.circleofinclusion.org/
   Circle of Inclusion   This is another attractive, very practical Web site full of information for the service provider and for families.

myeducationlab)
These and other web links are included in this chapter on MyEducationLab.

16

The Infant-Toddler Professional

Identity, Relationships, and Resources

THE INFANT AND TODDLER PROFESSION

We end the book by coming full circle in our quest for quality experiences for infants and toddlers. We began the book by discussing how important the infant and toddler years are as a foundation for the development of children's capacities to learn and love. We have endeavored for you to *always* consider the experience of the baby—from the baby's perspective. In many chapters we have detailed *respect for the child*: what the individual child brings to a relationship, the uniqueness of each child, and how active, curious, and motivated a child is to learn. We have emphasized the importance of *responsive and loving relationships* in the home and in a program for the child's sense of well-being and his or her future as a capable and caring human being. We have stressed that we cannot underestimate the importance of *quality early experiences* for infants and toddlers and their families.

All of this information leads us to the importance of the infant and toddler **professional** who creates the opportunities for infants and toddlers and their families to thrive. As defined in chapter 1, infant and toddler professionals are teachers or administrators in child development and education centers, family child care providers, and early intervention specialists. This

professional
A person who is qualified, skilled, or trained.

chapter is about the importance of developing an identity as an infant and toddler professional; becoming reflective; creating and nurturing relationships for professional development; and advocating for yourself, children, families, programs, and your community to move the profession forward.

This chapter encourages infant and toddler professionals to make choices about their own professional path. Professionals are decision makers; they take an active part in determining the quality of their work and the quality of the program where they work.

Greenman and Stonehouse (1996) define *professionalism* as "the ability to accept responsibility and to commit to a standard of performance that sets an example and earns respect of others" (p. 302). But how do we know that there is an infant and toddler profession?

Professional Identity

> *When Jeffrey, an infant teacher at Wee Care Child Care, walked out into the sunshine on the first day of the National Early Childhood Conference, he felt like a professional for the first time. After attending several sessions he realized that he really did have some specialized knowledge about how to work with infants and their families. He felt good about his chosen profession.*

Carter and Curtis (1998) describe the early childhood (birth to 8 years) profession as follows:

Over the last 25 years the early childhood profession has come of age. Early childhood caregivers and teachers have now become a full-fledged workforce with regulations, training systems, professional organizations, conferences, and a huge selection of resources. (p. 14)

Katz (1987) identified the attributes of a profession. A profession has:

1. Specialized knowledge
2. Agreed-upon principles and ethics
3. Knowledge based on the practical rather than the academic (e.g., the precedents in law versus in philosophy)
4. Theoretical knowledge that is not known to laypersons
5. Membership in professional associations or in societies that publish journals, give conferences, and promote continuing education
6. Required, prolonged, specialized training
7. Standards of practice
8. A code of ethics, as the client [the children] is in a "lower power" position
9. Work performed with some autonomy on the part of the client (i.e., professionals are not supervised every moment of the day)
10. An altruistic mission or vision

With respect to the last attribute, a profession sees itself as altruistic—that is, doing work that is essential to society. Professionals identify their goals with the good of humanity. This altruism can mean working longer hours on occasion and inhibits professionals from slipping into customer/sales language.

The infant and toddler profession has all of the attributes listed and we will be discussing them in this chapter. Several of the criteria relate to a profession having specialized knowledge base. This specialized knowledge base is reflected in the **professional standards of practice** developed for a profession.

professional standards of practice
Knowledge, skills, and dispositions needed by the professional.

Professional Standards

Standards ensure that infants and toddlers will experience high-quality interactions and environments and set high expectations for the preparation and performance of early childhood professions—the knowledge, skills, and disposition that all professionals should possess.

Let's examine the standards for professionals who work with children from birth to 8 years old developed by national organizations, and then we will explore the specific standards set for infant and toddler professionals.

Standards Set by Professional Organizations

The National Association for the Education of Young Children (NAEYC, 2006 a, b) has written standards that are intended for early childhood professionals who are being prepared at the undergraduate or graduate level to work with children from birth to 8 years old (Hyson, 2003). Early childhood professional standards include the values of the profession as well as a vision for the preparation of early childhood professionals. As you can see in Table 16.1, the NAEYC standards identify the knowledge, skills, and dispositions (attitudes and values) that research has identified as crucial for professionals to have to perform their work with young children well. The NAEYC standards are taught in an approved college or university that is recognized by NAEYC as an accredited institution.

Advanced programs, such as master's degree programs in early childhood education, must meet additional standards to prepare students for leadership roles (see http://www.naeyc.org/ for more information).

The Council for Exceptional Children (CEC, 2009) has also developed standards for professionals working with children with disabilities from birth to 8 years of age. These standards represent the knowledge, skills, and dispositions that all beginning early childhood *special education* teachers should have and include standards related to the development and characteristics of learners, individual learning differences, instructional strategies, learning environments and social interactions, language, instructional planning, assessment, and professional and ethical practice. The CEC Web site (http://www.cec.sped.org/) contains detailed information concerning the standards.

NAEYC and CEC have collaborated in writing the standards for each organization to ensure that *all* early childhood professionals are prepared to work with children with a range of abilities and disabilities. There are also specific established standards for infant and toddler professionals.

This teacher knows how to implement experiences that promote positive development and learning for children.

Specific Standards for Infant and Toddler Professionals

One example of standards specific to the infant and toddler professional is the Child Development Associate (CDA). The CDA credential is a nationally recognized credential awarded to early childhood teachers and caregivers who demonstrate competencies related to nurturing children's physical, social, emotional, and intellectual growth in a child development framework. Only the Council for

Table 16.1   NAEYC standards summary

1. Promoting Child Development and Learning

Candidates use their understanding of young children's characteristics and needs, and of multiple interacting influences on children's development and learning, to create environments that are healthy, respectful, supportive, and challenging for all children.

2. Building Family and Community Relationships

Candidates know about, understand, and value the importance and complex characteristics of children's families and communities. They use this understanding to create respectful, reciprocal relationships that support and empower families, and to involve all families in their children's development and learning.

3. Observing, Documenting, and Assessing to Support Young Children and Families

Candidates know about and understand the goals, benefits, and uses of assessment. They know about and use systematic observations, documentation, and other effective assessment strategies in a responsible way, in partnership with families and other professionals, to positively influence children's development and learning.

4. Teaching and Learning

Candidates integrate their understanding of and relationships with children and families; their understanding of developmentally effective approaches to teaching and learning; and their knowledge of academic disciplines, to design, implement, and evaluate experiences that promote positive development and learning for all children.

4a. Connecting with Children and Families

Candidates know, understand, and use positive relationships and supportive interactions as the foundation for their work with young children.

4b. Using Developmentally Effective Approaches

Candidates know, understand, and use a wide array of effective approaches, strategies, and tools to positively influence young children's development and learning.

4c. Understanding Content Knowledge in Early Education

Candidates understand the importance of each content area in young children's learning. They know the essential concepts, inquiry tools, and structure of content areas including academic subjects and can identify resources to deepen their understanding.

4d. Building Meaningful Curriculum

Candidates use their own knowledge and other resources to design, implement, and evaluate meaningful, challenging curriculum that promotes comprehensive developmental and learning outcomes for all young children.

5. Becoming a Professional

Candidates identify and conduct themselves as members of the early childhood profession. They know and use ethical guidelines and other professional standards related to early childhood practice. They are continuous, collaborative learners who demonstrate knowledgeable, reflective, and critical perspectives on their work, making informed decisions that integrate knowledge from a variety of sources. They are informed advocates for sound educational practices and policies.

Source: NAEYC (2008).

Professional Recognition in Washington, DC can award a CDA credential. There are four types of CDA credentials:

- Center-Based Preschool
- Center-Based Infant/Toddler
- Family Child Care
- Home Visitor

The CDA Competency Standards are the core of the CDA program. Composed of Goals and Functional Areas, they are statements of the skills needed to be a competent teacher and the basis upon which teachers are assessed. While the Competency Goals establish the framework for caregiver behavior, the 13 Functional Areas describe the major tasks or functions caregivers must complete in order to carry out the Competency Goals. The goal areas and functional areas are the same for each type of credential, but the content varies with each credential. The Competency Goals are:

Goal I: To establish and maintain a safe, healthy learning environment

Goal II: To advance physical and intellectual competence

Goal III: To support social and emotional development and to provide positive guidance

Goal IV: To establish positive and productive relationships with families

Goal V: To ensure a well-run purposeful program responsive to participant needs

Goal VI: To maintain a commitment to professionalism

If a professional does not have a degree in early childhood education or early intervention, then earning a CDA credential is important (see Table 16.2).

A state may require a specific infant and toddler credential as well. New York, for example, provides the New York State Infant Toddler Care and Education credential to formally recognize a professional's specialized knowledge of infant and toddler care and development. This credential is one of the options required of child care providers to be head of a group in a center program.

All of these standards have similar content and define the knowledge base of the infant and toddler profession, and by doing so, advance the recognition of the profession as legitimate and important. These standards are based on research that provides evidence for particular professional knowledge, skills, and dispositions that result in optimal infant and toddler development

Table 16.2   The CDA credential

Why is it important to earn a CDA credential?

Working with children is an important career requiring specialized skills and knowledge in early care and education. Head Start must currently have at least one employee in each classroom with a CDA credential. Forty-eight states and the District of Columbia incorporate the CDA into their licensing regulations. The number of child care providers applying for the CDA credential each year has grown to nearly 15,000 as a result of increase in demand from many public and private employers for trained, qualified staff. By earning your CDA, you will:

- Become more knowledgeable about children's development and about planning appropriate learning environment and activities for nurturing children's growth needs
- Enjoy salary incentives from many employers

What are the requirements of earning the CDA credential?

To receive a CDA credential, candidates must have:

- 120 clock hours of formal education training/CDA coursework within the past 5 years
- 480 hours of experience working with children within the past 5 years
- Documents that verify their competence in early care and education, including:
  - A professional resource file
  - Parent opinion questionnaires
  - The CDA Assessment Observation Instrument
  - An oral interview
  - A written assessment

Source: CDA Credentialing Program, available at the Council for Professional Recognition http://www.cdacouncil.org. Used with permission.

and educational experiences. The standards represent key concepts supported by research evidence that are now a part of best practice recommendations (Lally, 2003). These include the importance of:

- Continuity of relationships among parents, teachers, and children
- Attachment to primary caregivers
- Reading infants' cues
- The need for attention to individual children's sensitivities and temperamental characteristics in group care
- The interrelatedness of developmental domains
- The role of day-to-day encounters in shaping the child's development of self

It is important for professionals to know the standards of their profession because they represent the knowledge base for that profession. Infant and toddler professionals can be proud that there is specialized knowledge they should have in order to provide optimal care and education experiences for babies.

THE PROFESSIONAL'S EXPERIENCE

What's Different About Being an Infant and Toddler Professional?

The primary difference between infant and toddler professionals and professionals that work with older children centers on the intensity and intimacy of relationships. *First, there is the relationship with the infant or toddler.* There is a physical and emotional intensity about working with infants and toddlers (Honig, 2000; Recchia & Loizou, 2002). Keenan (1997, 1998), in her journey to become an infant and toddler professional, noted that in this work professionals provide more intimate contact and physical support with infants and toddlers than they do when working with older children.

The physical nature of the work requires an infant and toddler professional to be involved in the most intimate routines with the infant and toddler—diapering, toileting, feeding, wiping noses, and drying tears. The emotional nature of the work requires that professionals and infants and toddlers develop an attachment to each other—an emotional connection. While other professions do not recommend an emotional relationship with the client, it *is* professional for infant and toddler professionals to have an emotional connection with each child, because that is what infants and toddlers need to thrive. Infants and toddlers need that emotional bond to the professional because (as has been emphasized through this textbook) it is through relationships that babies develop their sense of self-worth, their basic ability to trust others, their concept of how adults and people in general will treat them, and how effective they can be in relationships and in mastering their environment. Infant and toddler professionals must be emotionally available each day with each child in order to ensure that babies thrive. In addition to making emotional connections, infant and toddler professionals create an environment where everyone, including the professionals, can *live* together, not just *learn* together.

Greenman, Stonehouse, and Schweikert (2008) highlight the importance of infant and toddler professionals in center or family child care and education programs creating a homelike environment. They emphasize that because children and adults live together for often many hours during the day, we need to consider that child care settings should be great places to live.

The second relationship that can be different for professionals of infants and toddlers is with families. Infant and toddler professionals, because of the emotional nature of the work, can sometimes have conflicting ideas with parents about what is best for the children. It can be challenging for families to share the care with professionals without becoming jealous or resentful, especially—which is important for the child—if the professional develops a close relationship with the infant or toddler. It can be challenging for the professional not to become competitive with the family over who knows what is best for the child. More so than professionals who work with older children, infant and toddler professionals must have *very* close relationships with families—constantly sharing information, delicately negotiating conflicts, and enthusiastically supporting the parent–child relationship.

The third relationship that is different for infant and toddler professionals is with other staff.

> Team collaboration takes on a particular significance in infant child care due to the physical and emotional demands of caring for such young children, the need for lower ratios of adults to children, and the inability of the children being cared for to speak for themselves. (Recchia & Loizou, 2002, p. 134)

Infant and toddler professionals must work as a team in center care and education programs and trust each other completely. When a baby needs to have a diaper changed in a center program, the teacher who is diapering trusts that the other teachers are automatically emotionally and physically available to the other children. So much of the communication is nonverbal. Professionals must work closely together, often in a small space, and respect each other's style of interacting with the children. Goals for the children must be made explicit. Tasks must be divided fairly. We will discuss how to develop a caring community and use effective communication and conflict resolution strategies later in the chapter.

Infant and Toddler Professionals Must Know Themselves Well

Infant and toddler professionals must have self-awareness—"personal integration and inner security" (Cartwright, 1999, p. 4). This means that professionals will not impose their personal needs onto their relationships with children, nor do they project intentions onto an infant or toddler, such as thinking that an infant is crying *just* to aggravate them or that a toddler is saying "No" *just* to annoy them. Honig (1986) emphasizes how caregivers can do some internal personal history searching to make them more responsive professionals:

> One interesting way for caregivers to feel more comfortable about floor games and creative games with babies is to do some internal personal history searching. Inside each of us are old record players. Some records play positive praises and comforting comments from our past. Some of our old personal records carry warning, shaming, prohibitions about being a silly child, a naughty child, a bad baby. A caregiver needs to leave on the nurturant positive record players that can support and encourage safe explorations and expressions of curiosity and delight. She or he may have to work hard to turn off punitive and disapproving records playing from the past. Such hard work will pay off as the caregiver becomes a person who is freer to enjoy toddlers with their "messiness" and with their delightful whimsies. (p. 209)

Infant and toddler professionals must reflect on how they handle separation and grieving. Professionals may have their heart broken because they must say good-bye to a child who has been with them since he was an infant and now is ready to transition to a preschool or kindergarten classroom. But infant and toddler professionals are willing to have their heart broken when a child transitions into a classroom for older children because they have been willing to invest in a strong, positive relationship with a child for 3 years. They know that the emotional connections developed because of *continuity of care* and *primary care* are absolutely vital for young children's optimal emotional and social development. If professionals have not done the work of reflecting on how they handle close relationships and good-byes, then the professionals may protect their own feelings rather than implement practices that they know are necessary for infants' and toddlers' well-being.

> Knowing ourselves involves exploring our strengths and vulnerabilities. We need to wonder about, and try to understand the meaning of, our reactions ("I got angry so quickly. Why is that?"), our frustrations

("I really get aggravated with judgmental staff members."), and the parts of our job that bring us joy ("I love it when families grade from the program."). This exploration can sometimes be difficult or uncomfortable. (Parlakian & Seibel, 2001, p. 6)

Parlakian and Seibel (2001) note that when we, as infant and toddler professionals, are self-reflective, we can "better manage our emotional responses, better recognize our limitations, and better leverage our skills and strengths" (p. 6). A reflective professional also develops vision, values, and a philosophy of practice.

PROFESSIONAL DEVELOPMENT: VISIONS, VALUES, AND PHILOSOPHY

> If we are going to have infant care, then why not create places where babies love to go and we love to have them go? Instead of setting our sights so low, why not create places where our children will be amazed, enlivened, and overjoyed each day? Why stop at "Do no harm?" (Lally, 2003, p. 34)

Becoming the professional you want to be requires courage, commitment, and caring. Your values and vision will guide you to make important difficult decisions regarding your practice. Part of being a reflective, theory-based professional is to reflect on your vision for children and families, professional philosophy, ethical values, and professional plan (your vision for yourself).

What if teachers in a center are being bounced around from classroom to classroom each day with no regard for the relationship that you know is critical for infants' development? Because you have knowledge of and a value for the importance of relationships, including primary and continuity of care, you problem solve with others to try to make the situation better for babies. Your values and vision are a guide to your behavior in this situation and others. How do you develop a vision?

Your Vision

> *Imagine the child care of our dreams, not just child care that's good enough. (Whitebook)*

To develop a vision, reflect and discuss with others the following questions:

- What is the primary purpose of your work?
- What do you wish for infants and toddlers?
- What do you wish for families of infants and toddlers?
- What do you wish for programs for infants and toddlers?
- What do you wish for your community, nation, and world to support infants' and toddlers' optimal development?

A vision is different from a mission statement, as noted by Carter and Curtis (1998) and others:

> A mission statement is about purpose, but it is seldom about a dream. Typically, a mission statement tries to address a problem with a statement of services. A vision, on the other hand, goes beyond how things are to describe how we would like them to be. In the words of Susan Gross (1987), a vision is "what the world or society or an environment or community would like if that purpose were realized." (p. 19)

To develop your vision, ask, "What kind of life and experiences do I want for children and families?" Carter and Curtis (1998) tell us to "think of your vision like the breath in your body. The more attention you give to it, the more it fortifies you" (p. 11). Another way for infant and toddler professionals to clarify their vision and values is to develop a philosophy statement.

A Professional Philosophy Statement

A professional's philosophy statement includes what you believe about the rights of children, goals for children, what children need, how they learn best, the definition of *quality* and why it matters for children and families. It includes what you believe about the role and responsibilities of the infant and toddler professional with children and families, your attitudes about inclusion of children with diverse needs and abilities, the critical aspects of an environment, and what type of curriculum and assessment process you think is important to provide. Developing a philosophy is a process rather than a product. It is ongoing and professionals should rewrite it often in their careers as they grow in knowledge and experience. Professionals can use their philosophy statement to reflect on their values and stay true to their principles as they progress in the profession.

Developing and Using a Code of Ethics

Ethics is how we treat children, families, colleagues, and community members—the people we work with, work for, and come to work to serve. (Israel)

NAEYC and CEC have developed codes of ethical conduct for early childhood professionals. A code of ethics states the values of the profession and the guidelines for responsible behavior. See Box 16.1 for definitions of *code of ethics, values,* and *core values.*

NAEYC's (2005) Code of Ethics is divided into sections:

Section I identifies the ethical responsibilities to children

Section II identifies the ethical responsibilities to families

Section III identifies the ethical responsibilities to colleagues

Section IV identifies the ethical responsibilities to community and society

Infant and toddler professionals are encouraged to become familiar with this Code of Ethics and apply it to their work with children, families, colleagues, and the community and society.

The Division for Early Childhood (DEC) of the Council for Exceptional Children (CEC) has developed a Code of Ethics for professionals working with children with disabilities. The Code was under revision at the time this book went to press. The Code provides principles and guidelines for practice including professional practice, professional development and preparation, responsive family practices, and ethical and evidence-based practices.

Both the NAEYC and DEC codes of ethics provide guidelines for your vision, your values, and your personal philosophy. Infant and toddler professionals work in organizations, though. How can organizations support infant and toddler professional development?

ORGANIZATIONAL STRUCTURE, PROGRAMS, AND POLICIES

Infant and toddler professionals (except for family child care home providers) usually work within an organizational structure in a program. Carter and Curtis (1998) note that "while a growing emphasis has been placed on staff qualifications and training, little attention has been given to the working conditions and resources caregivers and teachers need to do their jobs well" (p. 19). When a structure is in place, it can either support or undermine the professional's development.

Box 16.1

Ethics Terminology

code of ethics: Defines the core values of the field and gives guidance for what professionals should do in situations in which they encounter conflicting obligations or responsibilities in their work.

values: Qualities or principles that individuals believe to be desirable or worthwhile and that they prize for themselves, for others, and for the world in which they live.

core values: Commitments held by a profession that are consciously and knowingly embraced by its practitioners because they make a contribution to society. There is a difference between personal values and core values of a profession.

The Organization of a Program: Are You Treated Like a Professional?

Bittel (reported in Shoemaker, 2000) discusses how supervisors can treat their employees as professionals:

1. Realize that professional employees want to be recognized as members of a profession.
2. Ensure that credit and recognition from top management and parents is given to employees for outstanding work and unusual accomplishments.
3. Give proper dignity to the title of each position held by each employee.
4. Adopt liberal policies with respect to time off for personal reasons.
5. Encourage knowledgeable workers to take part in the activities of their professional societies. (p. 202)

Decker and Decker (2001) note that in early childhood programs "the most important role of the administrator is to enable conditions that lead to enriching professional life for staff" (p. 122). As you consider employment in a particular program, you may want to reflect on the organizational structure, policies, and procedures of the program. Ask for an organizational chart to determine where you fit in the organizational structure. Some center programs may have a board of directors who have authority over the program director, who then is responsible for office staff, maintenance staff, and head teachers in a center. Other organizations may have different structures.

As a potential employee, you will want to consider the policy and procedure manual developed by the program. This manual should contain the goals or specific purposes of the program and how the program will achieve these goals. Policies are written as comprehensive statements of decisions, principles, or courses of action to achieve the goals. Policies directly answer the question "What is to be done, and by whom?" For example, there may be a statement that one of the teacher's responsibilities is to supervise teaching assistants who work in the same classroom as the teacher. Job descriptions are critical to your understanding of the role and responsibilities of a particular position in a program.

The organizational structure, policies, and procedures will inform you of the type of program to which you are applying, including the goals, procedures for achieving those goals, and who is responsible for accomplishing the goals. You also may want to consider if the program emphasizes shared decision making.

Shared Decision Making

Shared decision making is a concept discussed by Jorde-Bloom (1995) to emphasize the importance of the participation of professionals in decisions that are made in the program where they work. Meaningful participation by all of the professionals who work together in a program enhances the trust and commitment to the organization. In a program that emphasizes shared decision making, a professional would be involved in a variety of decisions. Some examples of decisions that management might share with the infant and toddler professional are:

shared decision making
Meaningful, collaborative decision making.

1. Staff supervision and professional development
   - Establish guidelines and procedures for staff orientation.
   - Establish guidelines for supervision of teaching staff.
   - Determine the type and frequency of in-service training.
2. Instructional practices, grouping, and scheduling
   - Determine the daily schedule of classroom activities.
   - Select instructional materials and equipment.
   - Determine the content of the curriculum.

3. Enrollment and grouping
   - Determine group size and patterns (e.g., mixed-age grouping).
   - Determine the placement of children with special needs.
4. Fiscal policies and practice
   - Set priorities for classroom expenditures.
   - Determine fund-raising priorities and goals.
5. Human resources allocation
   - Determine staff hiring criteria and procedures.
   - Determine the staffing pattern and teaching assignments.
   - Determine the criteria for promotion and advancement.
6. Centerwide goals and educational objectives
   - Determine the center's philosophy.
   - Determine staff meeting agendas.
   - Establish a code of conduct (e.g., dress, confidentiality).
7. Parent relations
   - Determine who serves as the primary contact with parents.
   - Set expectations for teacher's involvement with parents.
   - Determine format and frequency of parent conferences.
8. Community relations
   - Determine the type of contacts with community agencies.
   - Establish marketing and public relations priorities.
   - Determine the content of press releases.
9. Facilities management
   - Determine how space is allocated.
   - Determine how space is arranged.
   - Determine capital improvement priorities.
10. Evaluation practices
    - Determine the type and frequency of child assessments.
    - Determine guidelines for staff performance appraisals.
    - Determine the type and frequency of programwide evaluations.*

Shared decision making may take place in some or most of the ways described. Usually there is a continuum of the professional's level of participation in these decisions. When there is shared decision making in an infant-toddler program, then there is likely to be improved employee morale, job satisfaction, and commitment to the organization (Jorde-Bloom, 1995). As you look for employment, you may want to consider whether shared decision making is emphasized in the organization to which you are applying.

As an administrator in infant and toddler organizations, you will want to emphasize:

1. Strong leadership that encourages creativity and success
2. Empowerment of teachers to make some decisions on their own

---

* From Bloom, P. J. (2000). *Circle of influence: Implementing shared decision making and participative management* (pp. 20–22). Lake Forest, IL: New Horizons. Reprinted with permission.

3. The opportunity for professional growth and career advancement

4. Membership and participation in professional organizations

5. The feeling of support and collaboration among staff

6. Real opportunities to work with peers to gather information, share ideas, and get support

All professionals deserve a quality work environment, as described by Eggbeer, Mann, and Gilkerson (2003):

> All individuals working with babies and toddlers deserve a work environment that values and supports their curiosity, their attempts to understand the meaning of behavior, their efforts to observe closely and to try new things, and their striving to be a more responsive partner to the children in their care and to the parents of these children. (p. 39)

A supportive program structure and shared decision making can support professional development. Of course, in a bioecological model (Bronfenbrenner, 2004), we know that funding, public policies, and the value our country places on infants, toddlers, and their families affect the work environment.

DEVELOPING RELATIONSHIPS AND COMMUNITY WITHIN THE PROGRAM FOR PROFESSIONAL DEVELOPMENT

Relationships with other staff in a program or in your professional organization are among the most important aspects of your work, contributing to your positive or negative feelings about the work situation and your career as an infant and toddler professional (Klinkner, Riley, & Roach, 2005) Whether your relationships with other professionals are productive or destructive will also affect the children and families with whom you work. When everyone on a staff is working together and there is a sense of community in the workplace, then positive feelings filter down to the staff's relationships with children and families. In this section we will explore a variety of ways that relationships can support professional development.

Developing a Professional Relationship-Based Community

The skills needed to create a supportive and inspiring workplace include *respect, reflect,* and *relate*—concepts that we can apply to professionals' relationships with each other as well as their relationships with children. Carter and Curtis (1998) state that professionals need to discover who they can be *together*:

> To build a group culture and a sense of community, we need to know who we are and why we are here, and to begin to discover who we can be together. (p. 85)

This process starts with respect.

Respect

Respect for your teammates includes recognizing their humanity—their need for feeling as if they are contributing and valued members of the team. It is recognizing that the need for emotional connections is just as strong for adults as it is for children. And, it is respecting that each person has strengths and can contribute in different ways.

Zoglio (1997) asks the following questions, which we think captures part of what it means to respect others on your team:

1. At meetings, do you listen well to others?

2. When you disagree with others, how often do you differ with the idea, not the person, encouraging members to share even unusual ideas or minority opinions?

3. How often do you recognize special talents of your colleagues by asking them for input on particular projects?

4. If other members miss a meeting, how often do you let them know that they were missed, perhaps expressing disappointment because you would have liked their input on something?

5. How often do you personally compliment team members when they offer ideas, facilitate decision making, or put aside personal interests for the good of the group?

Besides respecting the strengths of others, you can also reflect on your emotional and recognition needs as a team member and how you are contributing to the program.

Reflect

To become a relationship-based team member you can ask yourself: "What are my communication skills and how do I handle conflict?" When you are communicating with others, do you express yourself clearly? Do you listen with your eyes? Do you let others finish their sentences before you respond? What are your **responding habits?**

Zoglio (1997) suggests questions that can help you reflect on your responding habits. We have added the examples after each question to be relevant to the infant and toddler profession.

responding habits
Typical ways of reacting to other professionals.

1. Do you demonstrate that you are listening by reflecting the feeling of the speaker? (*"So, you are feeling upset with the parent who yelled at you."*)

2. Do you check your understanding of what others say by paraphrasing the content? (*"Your main concern is finding time to talk with Visha's parent?"*)

3. Do you try to expand your understanding of what was said by asking related questions? (*"Are you saying that Visha's mom was upset with you because she thought you didn't talk with her enough?"*)

4. Do you begin your response with agreement first and objections second? (*"I agree with you about the importance of having a special conference with each parent each month. I'm concerned about how we will find time to do that."*)

5. When disagreeing, do you state under what conditions you agree? (*"I could go along with that idea if we can do it within the work day and not have to come out again at night."*)

6. When disagreeing, do you show respect for the individual's thinking, sharing, and taking a risk? (*"That's a creative idea; let's talk to the coordinator about discussing it at the next staff meeting."*)

Despite reflecting on and using great communication skills, conflicts happen! When people work closely together in an environment where decisions with teammates often have to be made quickly and where you *live* together every day for long periods of time, then there are going to be differences of opinion, disagreements about practice, and diversity in how people relate to each other. How you and your teammates resolve conflicts will make or break your experience in the workplace. **Conflict resolution skills** are among the most important that you can learn. Zoglio (1997) identifies steps to a win–win conflict management strategy:

conflict resolution skills
Skills for deciding solutions to disagreements.

1. Prepare powerfully.
   - Identify your position/interest. Ask, "What do I want? Why do I want it?"
   - Speculate on the other party's stated position and underlying interests. Ask, "What do they want? Why do they want it?"

2. Approach positively.
   - Acknowledge that you have thought about the other party's needs: "I've thought about what's important to you. You'd like _____. Is that pretty close?"
   - State your win–win intent: "I really want to find a solution that will satisfy both of us."
   - Seek commitment to a win–win (collaborative) process.
3. Clarify both points of view.
   - Check any areas of agreement: "Let's review where we agree. We both want _____. Right?"
   - Clarify areas of disagreement: "Let's review where we differ. You would like _____, and I would like _____. Right?"
4. Create alternatives.
   - Agree not to evaluate solutions, but to generate possibilities.
   - Brainstorm alternatives together.
5. Select a solution and agree on implementation.

These strategies work if the conflict is not about the health, safety, or emotional well-being of infants and toddlers and also if the conflict is not about philosophy, beliefs, or ethics. When the conflicts are about these matters—for example, whether to pick up crying toddlers or not—then there has to be a discussion of why you think as you do, drawing upon research and what you know about the importance of a child learning to trust others and develop self-regulation, the foundation for emotional health and learning. Being an ethical professional entails supporting your point of view with scientific evidence and standing by your principles of "do no harm" and "meet the emotional and social needs of children." You may need to ask a third person to help you and the other staff member sort out the reasons for why a certain practice is critical to the health and well-being of children and families. Having an attitude of "let's find out" what information is available can lead to collaborative learning as a way to solve conflict.

Respond with Relationships in Mind

Respond to others by developing and committing to agreements. Agreements that are created in a collaborative way before disagreements occur make explicit basic values for how professionals will treat each other. Here are some areas for staff agreements, and approaches to criticism when those agreements are broken, as proposed by Carter (1992):

1. We will each have an attitude of flexibility and cooperation in our work here, thinking of the needs of others and the group as a whole, along with our own needs.
2. We will each carry a full share of the workload, which includes some extra hours outside our work schedule (i.e., parent–teacher conferences, meetings, planning and preparation of activities, recordkeeping, progress reports).
3. We will each communicate directly and honestly with each other. We will be respectful and honorable in our interactions.
4. When problems or difficulties related to our work arise, we will address them rather than ignore or avoid them.
5. We will all be informed of significant problems that affect the center. These will be communicated in person as soon as possible and in writing as necessary.
6. We understand that it is appropriate to seek help from the director on sensitive or difficult issues.
7. When necessary, we will use a criticism/self-criticism discussion process to identify attitudes and behaviors that are negatively affecting our agreements. (pp. 78–79)

Agreements are necessary for those times when the core values for how professionals treat each other are violated. However, responding to others in a caring and compassionate way that supports positive relationships can usually prevent troubles and lead to mutually satisfying solutions to problems.

The terms *respect, reflect,* and *relate* can be used to remind professionals of the important steps in developing a community of caring. By making a commitment to your own and others' sense of well-being in the workplace you are modeling your focus on the importance of healthy relationships for families and children and making it possible to do relationship-based work with them. Let's examine more closely how to ensure the professional growth of you and others in your caring community by using a **reflective practice model** of professional development that includes reflective supervision and/or **mentoring**.

reflective practice model
Thoughtful consideration of your own beliefs and performance.

mentoring
Guiding another professional.

A Reflective Practice Model

There are two major characteristics of a reflective practice model. One is that professionals engage in reflecting on their professional practice and constructing their knowledge through active engagement in the problems of practice. The second is that there are relationships with other professionals that enhance and support the professionals' self-reflection. In regard to the first characteristic, professionals are encouraged to "reflect and construct knowledge for themselves in an active and participatory manner" (Friedman, 2004, p. 65). In a reflective practice model of professional development, professionals are encouraged to experience and solve real problems with an "emphasis on *how* classroom strategies were implemented and *why* teachers engaged in certain practices" (p. 65). In regard to the second characteristic, there is a relationship that is established between a professional and another who is good at helping others grow professionally. There is a relationship established that renews each partner in the relationship.

Both reflective supervision and mentoring are relationships for learning. In these relationships for learning, there are regular meetings and strategies for supporting a person's professional development. Think about reflective supervision and mentoring both from the perspective of the one receiving supervision and mentoring *and* as one who is in the role of being a reflective supervisor or mentor. It is likely that the infant and toddler professional will be in both roles at some point in his or her career.

In both reflective supervision and the mentoring process, the golden rule is revisited:

> *Treat adults as you want them to treat children. (Carter & Curtis, 1998, p. 123)*
>
> *Do unto others as you would have others do unto others. (Pawl & St. John, 1998)*

Both rules emphasize the idea that if we want professionals to treat children and families in thoughtful ways that build on the children's and families' ability to make decisions and problem solve, then we need to treat professionals in the same way in the mentoring process.

Reflective Supervision

Carly was looking forward to her weekly meeting with her reflective supervisor. Mia actually listened to her and empowered her to think through problems. Carly couldn't wait to tell Mia about her problem with Sheila, a new toddler in her class who was biting Cal, the smallest child in her group.

Reflective supervision entails regular meetings where the two parties discuss what they are feeling and thinking with a supportive and thoughtful partner (Parlakian & Seibel, 2001).

ZERO TO THREE describes three necessary ingredients for reflective supervision to work—regularity, collaboration, and reflection. Fenichel (1992) emphasizes that each member of the relationship shares power, that there are mutual expectations for the relationship, and that there is open communication. Reflective supervision requires trust in one another, confidentiality, and trust in the ability of the supervisee to solve her own problems. The reflective supervisor provides the time and space for thoughtful reflection. The reflective supervisor engages in active listening (rephrasing the meaning of what the other says and does) and thoughtful questioning.

> *ZERO TO THREE describes supervision as an ongoing relationship, characterized by continuity and predictability, where power is shared, and where the supervisee has the opportunity to continually conceptualize what he/she is observing, feeling, and doing. In their words, supervision is a relationship for learning. (Gilkerson)*

Mentoring and Being Mentored

Mentors, as defined by Bellm, Whitebook, and Hnatiuk (1997), are guides and role models who help whoever they are mentoring—their **protégés,** or **mentees**—to develop their *own* professional goals. They are capable of developing a supportive relationship with their protégés that is based on trust and confidentiality. Whitebook and Bellm (1996) describe a mentor as someone who has training and experience in child development/early childhood education and in the teaching of adults.

protégé
The person being mentored; a mentee.

mentee
A person being mentored; a protégé.

Bellm and colleagues (1997) identify the goals of a mentoring program in a child development and education program:

1. Help experienced, skilled early childhood professionals to become mentors in order to encourage them to stay in early childhood classrooms and homes or in an early childhood career by providing recognition of their contribution and skills, and whenever possible, financial incentives.

2. Provide mentors with opportunities to develop their skills in communication, leadership, and adult education.

3. Create opportunities for new and experienced professionals to gain knowledge, reflect on their own practice, set professional goals, and improve their practices.

Responsibilities of the Mentor

What are the responsibilities of mentors? As proposed by Bellm and colleagues (1997), mentors:

- Share information
- Link their mentees to appropriate resources
- Share teaching strategies and information
- Guide and give ideas
- Assist the mentee—for example, in setting up the classroom
- Observe and discuss what was observed
- Promote self-observation and analysis
- Encourage reflection and model professionalism

Responsibilities of the Mentee

Protégés also have responsibilities as they participate in the relationship for learning. According to Bellm and colleagues (1997), protégés think about what they want to learn, are willing to examine their own practices, and engage in problem solving for change and improvement.

The mentoring relationship is built on trust, confidentiality, and commitment to each other. Mentors are not in a position to evaluate the mentee's job performance—that responsibility is for a **supervisor.** For trust to develop, the protégé and the mentor must be able to

supervisor
One who manages, directs, and evaluates another in the workplace.

discuss difficult issues and the challenges that the protégé is experiencing without fear of reprisal or judgment. The only exception, of course, is if the mentor suspects that the mentee is neglecting or abusing children. It must be made clear at the beginning of the relationship that the mentor is ethically and legally required to report suspected child abuse.

Parlakian and Seibel (2001) recommend that the following questions be used to create a more positive reflective supervision and mentoring relationship. If you are the one being supervised then you could suggest that you would like to complete the questionnaire to help your mentor get to know you.

1. How did you become interested in infant-family issues?
2. When did you start the program? What positions have you held with this program?
3. Where did you work before?
4. What is your educational background?
5. How long have you been in your current position?
6. What are the best things about your job? What are the things you like the least about your job?
7. What do you find really motivating about working here?
8. What would you change about your job if you could? The organization?
9. What are your long-term goals? What would you like to be doing 5 years from now?
10. What do you think you are learning on the job right now? What are you struggling with at the moment?
11. What skills or abilities would you like to develop? (p. 19)

BECOMING AN ADVOCATE

> Never doubt that a small group of committed citizens can change the world. Indeed, it is the only thing that ever has. (Margaret Mead)

The role of being an advocate for children, families, programs, communities, and yourself is the last characteristic of an infant and toddler professional that we will discuss.

advocate
An enthusiastic supporter and promoter of a cause.

An **advocate** is an enthusiastic supporter of a cause. We hope that you will become an advocate for the importance of the early years and relationship-based practice. As Margaret Mead stated, a small group of committed citizens can change the world. You have learned information in this book that will guide your advocacy efforts.

> Early learning begets later learning and early success breeds later success. (Heckerman)

We know that the research on brain development concludes that what happens during the first months and years matters a lot (Shonkoff & Phillips, 2000). We recognize the importance of relationships and responsive adult–child interactions for the optimal development of children's capacities in emotional, social, cognitive, language, and motor domains. We know how important it is to support families in their efforts to raise their children, and we know the effect of quality programs on children's development and sense of well-being. We know the importance of individualizing for children's unique strengths and interests, of children choosing among opportunities in an environment that the teacher intentionally provides, and of responsive planning. We know the power of the infant and toddler profession to make change in practice to become more relationship based by developing standards for professional development, developing a vision, using the code of ethics, embracing reflective professional development practices, and advocating for the profession. We know that we need to advocate at the local, state, and national level because social policies affect the quality of life for children, families, and infant and toddler professionals.

We know these things and now we must share this information with others. The authors of the book *From Neurons to Neighborhoods* (Shonkoff & Phillips, 2000) ask us to rethink the meaning of "both shared responsibility for children and strategic investment in their future" (p. 414).

In the first chapter we said our goal is that you gain an appreciation for how vitally important the prenatal period and the first 3 years of life are for children and the future adults they will become. Our hope is that you will become knowledgeable about and gain a passion for promoting the well-being, competence, and quality of life for infants and toddlers and their families.

We hope that we have accomplished our goal.

Teachers advocate for children when they value a child's work and make their learning visible.

SUMMARY

myeducationlab

Go to MyEducationLab and complete the Building Teaching Skills and Dispositions exercise in Chapter 16.

We end the book by coming full circle in our quest for quality experiences for infants and toddlers. The infant and toddler professionals are the ones who ensure that quality will be created and will continue. The following points are covered in this chapter:

- Professionals commit to a standard of performance that earns the respect of others.

- The infant and toddler profession meets the criteria determined to be necessary in order to be a profession.

- Early childhood professional standards include the values of the profession as well as a vision for the preparation of early childhood professionals.

- It is important for professionals to know the standards of their profession because they represent the knowledge base for that profession.

- The primary difference between infant and toddler professionals and professionals who work with older children centers on the intensity and intimacy of relationships.

- Part of being a reflective, theory-based professional is to reflect on your vision for children and families, professional philosophy, ethical values, and professional plan (your vision for yourself).

- The organizational structure of a program can support or undermine the professional.

- The professional will want to participate in shared decision making.

- A reflective practice model includes reflective supervision and mentoring.

- Advocacy is an important part of what it means to be a professional.

- Our goal in this book was for you to recognize the importance of relationships and responsive adult–child interactions for the optimal development of infants' and toddlers' capacities in emotional, social, cognitive, language, and motor domains.

Key Terms

advocate
conflict resolution skills
mentee
mentoring

professional
protégé
reflective practice model
responding habits

shared decision making
standards of practice
supervisor

REFLECTIONS AND RESOURCES FOR THE READER

Reflections

1. What are the key attributes of the infant and toddler profession?
2. Describe the knowledge, skills, and dispositions that an infant and toddler professional must have to work with children who have a range of abilities and disabilities.
3. What are the unique challenges of the infant and toddler professional?

Observation and Application Opportunities

1. Design a vision statement for an infant and toddler program.
2. A teammate is using practices that you think are harmful to the children (such as not comforting an infant who is crying). What are your ethical responsibilities to the children, families, colleagues, and the community and society? How would you communicate your concerns to your teammate?
3. Write a letter to a legislator on the importance of the infant and toddler years.

Supplementary Articles and Books to Read

Helm, J. H. (2007). Energize your professional development by connecting with a purpose: Building communities of practice. *Young Children, 62*(4), 12–16.

Klinkner, J. M., Riley, D., & Roach, M. A. (2005). Organizational climate as a tool for child care staff retention. *Young Children, 60*(6), 90–95.

Lutton, A. (2006). NAEYC Early Childhood Associate Degree System: Filling a gap in the U.S. teacher education system. *Young Children, 61*(5), 58–59.

NAEYC. (2006). Accreditation. Building recognition for the mark of quality. *Young Children, 61*(2), 56–58.

Parlakian, R. (2003). *Look, listen, and learn: Reflective supervision and relationship-based work.* Arlington, VA: ZERO TO THREE.

Seibel, N. (2003). *Relationship-based workplace: What it is and how to do it.* Arlington, VA: ZERO TO THREE.

Interesting Links

myeducationlab

These and other web links are included in this chapter on MyEducationLab.

http://www.naeyc.org/policy/toolbox/pdf/toolkit.pdf
NAEYC Advocacy Toolkit   Strategies for becoming a strong advocate for children, families, and programs are provided here.

http://www.naeyc.org/ece/links.asp
National Association for the Education of Young Children   This page on the NAEYC Web site provides links to national early childhood organizations.

http://www.ehsnrc.org/
Early Head Start National Resource Center   This Web site, developed by ZERO TO THREE for Early Head Start, is a storehouse of early childhood expertise. It promotes the sharing of information, including recent conferences and webinars.

http://www.ccie.com/
Child Care Information Exchange   This site promotes the exchange of ideas among leaders in early childhood programs worldwide through its magazine, books, training products and seminars, and international conference.

http://www.familiesandwork.org/
Families and Work Institute   The institute is a nonprofit center providing data on the changing workforce, family, and community. It offers some of the most comprehensive research on the U.S. workforce available.

Appendices

Appendix A   Portraits of Development   392

Appendix B   Portraits of Development (Spanish)   410

Appendix C   Developmental Trends and Responsive Interactions (Spanish)   432

Appendix D   Planning Guides   456

Appendix A

Portraits of Development

Portraits of Infants and Toddlers

	Development	Example
0–4 Months		
Emotions/ Attachment	· Infants are taking in a lot of information about the world. · Infants can get overwhelmed and begin to yawn, look away, or fuss. · Infants begin to calm themselves by sucking on their hands or listening to an adult talk quietly to them. · Infants gaze into their teacher's eyes as she feeds them. · Infants turn their heads toward a familiar voice. · Infants relax and allow themselves to be comforted by familiar people. · Infants cry when they are hungry, tired, or uncomfortable.	Carlos followed Karen with his eyes wherever she went in the room. When she came close to him, he looked at her as though he wanted her to join him. Accepting his invitation to play, she sat with him on the floor. As he began to tire and fuss, she swaddled him in a blanket, held him close, and spoke softly to him.
Learning with Peers	· Infants like to look at each other (visual regard). · Infants prefer to look at faces, especially the edges and the eyes. · Infants may cry when they hear other babies cry (contagion).	After the teacher put Tamika by Sam on a blanket on the floor, Tamika stared intently at Sam.
Cognitive	· Infants follow a moving object visually. · Infants cry to bring an adult to comfort or feed them. · Infants will look around the room with interest. · Infants begin to reach for a toy. · Infants notice that their arms or legs made something happen and will repeat the movement. · Infants recognize familiar people and objects. · Infants begin to bring objects to mouth.	Megan lifted her head, resting on her arms as she lay on the blanket. With a serious expression on her face, she watched the teachers and children around her. Willie kicked the mobile hanging over him and made it wiggle. He stopped, looked at it, and then kicked some more, watching the mobile to see if anything might happen.
Language	· Infants may startle if they hear a loud sound. · Infants hear the differences in sounds. · Infants may stop crying when they hear a familiar adult's voice. · Infants prefer to hear talk that is directed toward them. · Infants listen when an adult talks or sings to them while looking at them. · Infants cry when they are in pain, are hungry, or are distressed. · By 2 months of age babies have different cries for hunger and pain. · Infants "coo" (make soft vowel sounds). · Infants smile and laugh toward the end of this age period. · Infants will stare at interesting pictures in books.	Brenda held Jordon so they could gaze into each other's eyes. Jordon cooed softly and Brenda cooed back. Then she waited for Jordon to take another turn. Erica gave her father a big smile when he picked her up out of her crib.

Acknowledgments to Florida State University Center for Prevention & Early Intervention Policy, www.cpeip.fus.edu, for their formatting suggestions for this material.

Teacher or Parent–Child Interaction	Environment
0–4 Months	

• Keep young babies close to you, in your arms, in a snuggly, or on a blanket nearby.	• Being close to a familiar teacher is best.
• Recognize the signals that indicate a baby wants to be with you—intent gazing, reaching, a happy look—and respond with quiet, verbal and nonverbal turn taking.	• A serene, quiet space with gentle lighting limits the information an infant needs to take in.
• Recognize the signals that indicate a baby needs a break—yawning, drooling, looking away—and sit back quietly and wait while the baby regroups.	• Avoid playing background music all day.
	• Limit the number of objects, sounds, color, and movements around a young infant.
• Comfort babies whenever they cry.	• The teacher is the most interesting thing for a baby to watch, but other babies, mirrors, and toys within the baby's visual range of focus are also interesting.

• Hold two babies so they can look at each other.	• The arms of teachers provide the best environment.
• Place a few babies on a blanket on the floor so that they can look at and touch each other.	• Blankets on the floor—put two babies beside each other or so their toes are touching each other.

• Slowly move a small toy from one side to another while the infant follows it with his gaze.	• Arrange the space so that infants can see some activity but still be protected.
• Respond quickly to the baby's cries.	• Provide a few interesting things to look at—small toys on the floor during tummy time, dangling toys when infants are on their backs.
• Provide quiet time for babies to look at what is happening around them. Talk about what they see.	• Provide nonbreakable mirrors.
• React to infants' expressions with clear, even exaggerated facial expressions and language.	

• Use infant-directed speech.	• The best environment is in the arms of a caring adult who holds the baby and talks softly.
• Hold and talk to babies.	
Engage in long eye gazes while having conversational dances. Respect the baby if he needs a break and turns his head away.	• Provide toys that make pleasant sounds. Gently hold the toy and share the sounds with the baby.
• Read books with rhythmic phrases and books with one picture on a page with 2- to 4-month-olds.	• Provide interesting materials to touch while you comment on the textures.
• Interpret babies' burps, cries, yawns, stretching, and sounds as forms of communication. Say, "Oh, you're telling me you're sleepy."	• Add mirrors low along a wall. Babies will look and possibly make sounds.
• Be an empathic language partner—comment on the baby's feelings.	
• Use words and sounds to comfort babies.	

Development		Example

0–4 Months

| Motor | · Infants lift head when held at shoulder—hold head steady and erect.
 · On tummy, Infants lift their head and shoulders off the ground and can hold a toy in hand.
 · Infants turn head toward a familiar voice.
 · Infants hold body still to pay attention; wiggle and move to encourage continued interaction.
 · On back, infants thrust arms and legs in play.
 · Infants turn from side to back.
 · Infants hold finger, light toy with reflexive grasp.
 · Infants suck on own fingers and hands, objects.
 · Infants move arms and legs. | Rosie held her head up and looked around at the other children as Sharon held her against her shoulder.

 Robert, on his tummy on a blanket, lifted his head to see himself in the mirror mounted at floor level on the wall.

 Jen held a rattle placed in her hand, but seemed unaware it was there.

 Filipe brought his fingers to his mouth and sucked on them, while looking intently at the toddlers. |

4–8 Months

Emotions/ Attachment	· Infants like to look at their hands and feet. · Infants wave their arms and kick in excitement when they see a familiar person. · Infants will smile at a teacher expecting her to smile back. · Infants use their faces and bodies to express many feelings: everything from frowning and crying to laughing out loud. · Infants express their feelings more clearly to familiar people and are more reserved with strangers.	Deborah loves being carried in her teacher's arms as they move around the room "talking" about the things they see. Her eyes are wide and bright, she smiles, and she makes cooing sounds as though taking her turn in the conversation. When a visitor enters the room, Deborah gets very quiet and serious, and holds tightly to her teacher's shoulder as she looks at the visitor.
Learning with Peers	· Infants touch a peer, vocalize to each other, get excited, approach other babies, smile and laugh at each other. · Babies may treat other babies like objects—crawling over them, licking or sucking on them, or sitting on them. They are just learning the difference between people and objects. Infants may poke, push, or pat another baby to see what that other infant will do. They often look very surprised at the reaction they get.	Anna crawled over to Nadia who was lying on the floor. Touching Nadia's hair, Anna laughed out loud.
Cognitive	· Infants like to examine toys. · Infants like to make toys do something—make a sound, put one inside another. · Infants imitate adult expressions and gestures. · Infants turn toward a sound to see where it came from. · Infants look for toys they dropped.	Angela is interested in everything. She watches her friends and then looks at the teacher and smiles. Roger reaches out to touch a dangling toy. When it swings, making a sound, he reaches out to do it again.

Teacher or Parent–Child Interaction	Environment

0–4 Months

- Change the baby's position: sometimes on his back, sometimes on his tummy. Even when holding the baby, sometimes cradle him in your arms, sometimes hold him upright against your shoulder.
- When baby is on the floor, lie down face-to-face with him.
- When baby is on her back, reaching for a toy a little beyond her head, support her trunk as she rolls over.

- A stiff blanket (to prevent the danger of suffocation) on the floor provides space for early movements.
- Small, interesting toys, pictures, and books to look at will encourage babies to lift their heads. A mirror bolted to the wall at floor level always provides something interesting to look at.
- As babies begin to reach, they enjoy stable bars that dangle toys for them to bat at or reach and grasp.

4–8 Months

- Provide opportunities for babies to look in mirrors as they play.
- Mirror the emotional expressions of the Infant and add appropriate words: "I'm so excited to see you today!"
- Respond to babies in a way that helps them be calm and active; if babies are crying, soothe them.

- Mount unbreakable mirrors on walls.
- Provide floor time where babies play with their feet while on their backs and move around on the ground.
- Books and posters of photographs of real faces with different emotional expressions are very interesting to infants.

- Move to music with a baby in each arm.
- While holding one baby in your lap, point out and talk about what another baby is doing.
- Place two babies on their tummies facing a mirror.
- Instead of saying "Don't" or "Stop that" to exploring babies, say "Touch gently." Tell children what you want them to do—model it for them.

- Hang a safety mirror horizontally on the wall, so the bottom is touching the floor.
- Cover an inner tube with soft cloth. Sit two babies in the inner tube so that their feet are touching each other.

- Hold the infant in your arms as you walk around, looking at things and talking about them.
- Sit nearby and talk to the baby about the toys she is looking at.
- Call the baby by name from a short distance to reassure her you are nearby.

- Provide a variety of small toys to handle and examine.
- Provide toys that make sounds when a baby moves them, fit inside each other, or dangle and move when touched.
- Offer board books.

Development	Example
4–8 Months	

	Development	Example
Language	• Infants turn their head toward a noise or someone speaking their name. • Infants enjoy adults talking, singing, and laughing with them. • Babies vocalize with intention to get a response from the adult. • Babies make high-pitched squeals. • Infants practice their sounds when exploring and with favorite adults. • Infants begin to babble—at first with one consonant and then by combining two consonants. • Infants engage in turn-taking conversations with adults. • Babies will look at different pictures in a book and get excited at a favorite one or at the enthusiastic tone of an adult who is reading to them.	As Danielle, the infant teacher, was holding Donovan on her lap, she pointed to the pictures in the sturdy board book. "Look," she said, pointing to the picture, "a ball. There's your ball," as she pointed to a ball on the floor. Donovan looked at the picture, then at the ball on the floor, and back to the picture. "Tt" said Afi as he lay in his teacher's arms looking up at her. "Tada" exclaimed his teacher back to him. "Tt" repeated Afi as he took his turn in the conversation.
Motor	• Infants turn from back to side, later roll from back to front. • Infants sit—first with support but steady alone by the end of this period. • Infants reach with one arm. • Infants use raking grasp. • Infants crawl. • Infants shake, bang, hold, let go of objects. • Infants move objects from hand to hand. • Infants can hold their own bottle. • Infants can bring objects to their mouth.	Micky rolls from his back to his tummy to reach a toy, then rolls back over to play with it. Erin, sitting steadily alone, loves using both hands to pick up objects and study them. Freddy loves being held while he has his bottle, but he insists on holding it himself.
8–12 Months	
Emotions/ Attachment	• Mobile infants may be fearful with strangers. • Mobile infants will call upon familiar adults to help them when they are upset. • Mobile infants will look at a familiar adult to determine whether a situation is safe or dangerous. • Mobile infants will cling to a familiar adult when they are in a strange situation. • Mobile infants will find humor in silly games and adults making big facial expressions.	Jamie is enjoying his new ability to quickly crawl anywhere he wants to go. He loves the little climber that lets him look out the window. But when the ramp feels a little shaky, he likes to look back at his teacher. Fred—just making sure he's still safe.

Teacher or Parent–Child Interaction	Environment
4–8 Months	

Teacher or Parent–Child Interaction	Environment
· Use Infant-directed speech. · Talk with babies often. Show them new objects and people and name them. · Repeat the sounds that infants make and wait for the infant to make the sound again (turn taking). · Use sign language for several familiar items such as "milk" or "dog." · Sing songs and say finger-plays. · Use words to describe children's feelings expressed through gestures, body postures, and sounds. · Read simple books with one to two pictures on a page. Point to the pictures as you say the name of the picture. · Read the same books over and over. · Use joint attention strategies—point at a toy or picture in a book when you say the name or talk about it.	· Provide interesting toys and materials for babies to handle and explore. · Provide cardboard books with handles so that babies can crawl to them and pick them up. · Books with handles encourage babies to hang on to them. · Make a peek-a-boo picture book by gluing a piece of cloth over each picture. · Create a cozy book corner where teachers can be comfortable and read to babies. · Provide sound boxes (safely sealed) with different objects in them that make different sounds when shaken. · Add puppets to the environment. Use them at times to "talk" to the child. Put the puppet on the child's hand and wait to see what the child says or does.
· Stay near the baby who is just beginning to sit alone. · Know the progression of motor development; emotionally encourage and physically support new attempts. · Believe in the lifelong health benefits of an active lifestyle.	· Provide safe places for rolling, sitting, and crawling. Protect babies from anything that might fall on them. · Provide small, washable lightweight objects (too large for choking) for handling and tossing, and provide containers for objects.

Teacher or Parent–Child Interaction	Environment
8–12 Months	

Teacher or Parent–Child Interaction	Environment
· Encourage mobile infants to move off and explore by reassuring them that you are watching and keeping them safe. · Understand that mobile infants may become afraid of new situations that wouldn't have been frightening a few months ago. Be comforting and reassuring.	· Play peek-a-boo. · Read stories about mothers and fathers who go away and come back. · Read books with flaps to lift to find things. · Keep room arrangements and routines predictable.

Development		Example
	8–12 Months	
Learning with Peers	· Infants may show a peer an object, sit by each other, crawl after and around each other, play chase-and-retrieve games. · Babies smile and laugh at each other. · Babies make sounds to and with each other—may say first words with peers. · Peek-a-boo is a favorite game as babies explore separation: coming and going, in sight and out of sight. · Infants can learn to touch each other gently. · Because infants become more goal oriented at this age, they may push another baby's hand away from a toy or crawl over another baby to get a toy.	Shamaine peeked around the low toy shelf and saw Carla crawling toward her. Shamaine quickly turned around and crawled away with Carla close behind.
Cognitive	· Mobile infants like to take the pieces of a toy apart and put them back together. · Mobile infants like toys that do something when you touch them, pull them, bang them. · Mobile infants begin very simple pretend play, such as lifting a cup to their mouth. · Mobile infants like to find small toys hidden under a cloth or cup. · Mobile infants like to pick up and examine a tiny item like a Cheerio. · Mobile infants point to objects, knowing you can also see them.	Charlie loves to take each plastic animal out of the bucket and look at it. When the bucket is empty, he tosses it aside. Aliya likes the push button and the swinging doors on the busy box, but can't work all the mechanisms yet. Her teacher expresses surprise with Aliya when the doors pop open, and everyone once in a while shows her how to work another of the knobs.
Language	· Mobile infants are beginning to play social games such as peek-a-boo or "so big." · Infants enjoy listening to sound play (rhymes), songs, and finger-plays. · Babbling continues to develop with combined syllables such as "dada," "mama," and "tutu," but now the infant may be using these sounds specifically for mom or dad. · Infants will use sounds consistently for an object or person or animal. · If they hear another language with an adult through interactive conversational strategies, then infants can "keep the brain open to the sounds of a second language." · Infants may begin to use single words. · At the end of the age period, infants may begin to point to engage an adult. · They are using facial expressions and gestures such as shaking head or stretching arms out to be picked up to communicate to adults or peers.	One of Dana's first words was "mama," which she said over and over again when she saw her mother. One of Trishanna's first words was "mama," which she excitedly said over and over again when she saw her mother.

Teacher or Parent–Child Interaction	Environment

8–12 Months

· Name parts of infants' bodies as two infants sit close to each other: *Here is baby's eyes* *Here is baby's nose* *Touch the part that sees* *Touch the part that blows* · Place a baby with one other baby (pairs), because more frequent, complex, and intense peer interaction occurs than when a child is with many peers. · Understand that infants are not being "naughty" when they push another child's hand away. Say "Jenny was holding that toy. Let's find you a different toy."	· While feeding, place high chairs so children can see each other. · Set up cozy corners in the room where babies can "disappear" (but adults can still see them). · Hang a long wide cloth (so babies won't get tangled in it) from the ceiling. Babies love to crawl around it. · Place containers with different sizes of blocks in them between two babies. Sit beside them as they begin to explore the materials. Talk about what each one is doing.
· Help the baby focus on what is interesting to him, using your presence, your interest, and your enthusiasm to support his attention and exploration. · Use your emotional expressions and words to show the mobile infant that you delight in his discoveries. · Use words to describe the child's activity: "Look, you found a Cheerio. You're picking it up with your fingers."	· Provide toys like stacking cups, rings on a post, pop-beads, and tubs full of small, interesting objects such as toy animals. · Provide child-size replicas of dishes or household tools. · Provide toys that respond to children's actions—busy boxes, water-filled pads. · Provide sensory materials such as water and sand with a variety of tools. · Provide board books with photos.
· Play familiar games such as peek-a-boo, pat-a-cake, or "how big are you?" · Respond to infants' nonverbal communication with words. · Look at and wait for infants to initiate sounds or words. · Imitate the sounds and then expand, elaborate, and extend the baby's language. · Model the next step in language development. · Use self-talk and parallel talk. · Talk often in a responsive way using a varied vocabulary. Don't bombard the child. · Read books with enthusiasm, changing the tone of your voice with different characters. · Talk about the pictures and the story as you read it. Engage babies in the story with your voice and gestures. · Wait while looking at a picture for babies to communicate sounds, point, or use facial expressions.	· Create a cozy book corner where babies can easily reach and handle books. · Create an "All About Me" book—small photo albums for each child with pictures of themselves, their family, their favorite toys, peers, teachers, and the family pets. Make them available to the children. Change the pictures as the child grows. · Musical push toys encourage infants to handle them and make sounds.

Development		Example
	8–12 Months	
Motor	· Mobile infants pull to stand. · Mobile infants cruise. · Mobile infants stand alone. · Mobile infants walk with help and then alone. · Mobile infants sit in a chair. · Mobile infants finger-feed. · Mobile infants use spoon, tippy cup. · Mobile infants use pincer grasp.	Hershel crawls to his teacher's side, then holds her leg as he pulls up to stand. Jem sits at the lunch table, alternating between using her spoon and her fingers to enjoy her meal.
	12–18 Months	
Emotions/ Attachment	· Mobile infants will imitate the actions of familiar adults, such as using the phone or caring for a baby doll. · Mobile infants will seek adult attention by pulling on their leg or taking their hand. · Mobile infants will use a favorite blanket or stuffed animal to help calm themselves. · Mobile infants will protest loudly when their parents leave them. · Mobile infants will relax and be comforted by cuddling with a familiar adult. · Mobile infants will let their likes and dislikes be clearly known.	Amelia carries her teddy bear around all morning. Sometimes she copies her teacher Sophia's actions, patting its back or "feeding it a bottle." When she gets tired, she rubs teddy against her ear and sucks her thumb.
Learning with Peers	· Imitation (motor) and interactive turns begin. Toddlers may copy each other—if one gives a toy to another child, the other may imitate. · Mobile infants begin to talk to each other. · Infants may show concern when other babies are distressed. · Mobile infants may take a toy away from another child, say "no," push away another child, clutch toy to self and say "Mine." · Infants are little scientists at this age, experimenting to see how things work. This affects how they get along with peers. They are constantly doing things to other children to see what response they will get. · Biting may appear as infants bite others "to see what happens," to get the toy they want, to express frustration. Infants are on the cusp of communicating well; they may communicate through their mouths in the form of a bite.	Rashinda banged her spoon on the table; soon two others tried it. They seemed to be physically following each other's lead (as in a conversation). First, Carmen tried pushing Toby away from her rocking horse. When that didn't work she leaned over and took a bite out of his arm.

Teacher or Parent–Child Interaction	**Environment**

8–12 Months

· Stay alert when practicing walkers need a little help—and when to let them keep trying. · Allow time for older infants to practice feeding themselves.	· Safe places to pull up to stand. · Push and pull toys to help support practicing walkers. · Busy boxes. · Board books for turning pages, lifting flaps, and poking fingers through holes.

12–18 Months

· Demonstrate your interest in babies' activities. · Show your pride in babies' accomplishments. · Let babies use you as a secure base from which to explore the world. · Let babies know you understand their feelings and respond with respect. · These are still very young children who needs lots of cuddling and holding.	· Provide child-size copies of tools adults use: telephones, dishes, keys, etc. · Post photographs of the infants with their family on the wall. · Laminate photos of the infants with their family for carrying around. · Make photo albums of the children at your program and talk about the pictures. · Have adult chairs and quiet, comfortable spaces for holding children.

· Show mobile infants how to roll down a small hill together. · Help mobile toddlers learn each other's names by singing greeting and good-bye songs with the children's names in them: "Here is Tanya, how are you?" and "Here is Henry, how are you?" as you point to or touch each child who comes by you or is sitting in your lap. · Comment on prosocial behavior. Say "You gave him the doll. He likes that!" Babies may not understand your words, but they will be able to tell by your tone of voice that you are pleased with them. · They will enjoy looking at books together by forming an informal group (this means they move in and out of the group) around the legs, lap, and arms of a favorite parent or teacher.	· Provide a large cardboard box, open on each end. Encourage babies to crawl in and out of the box with each other. Windows on the side encourage babies to peek at each other through the windows. · Dolls, trucks, cars, and other play materials encourage interactions among peers. · They love sand and water and playing with different sizes of safe bottles and balls. When each has his own bin or tub of water or sand, play goes more smoothly. · Outside, large sandboxes or push toys encourage interactive play.

Development		Example
	12–18 Months	
Cognitive	• Mobile infants like to use their mobility to explore—crawling, walking, climbing, running. • Mobile infants enjoy playing with sand, water, and play dough with different kinds of tools. • Mobile infants are interested in spatial relationships in puzzles and pegboards. • Mobile infants use tools such as keys or telephones in their pretend play. • Mobile infants enjoy looking at books and naming objects, animals, or body parts.	Alexis and Dan are gleeful about being on two feet. They follow each other around, one daringly balancing his way up the sloping surface with the other right behind. Sometimes they both try to squeeze into the area under the slide. Meredith loves to cuddle on her teacher's lap, pointing at pictures in books while her teacher names the animals, or asks her to find a certain animal.
Language	• Mobile infants can follow simple directions such as "Come here" or "Go get your shoes" without you gesturing. • Mobile infants play a social game without you demonstrating the action. • Mobile infants will point to engage adults and peers. • Rapid word learning—a language explosion—may occur with the children learning many new words. • Mobile infants will combine words toward the end of this age period. • Mobile infants will jabber (stringing many sounds together) using adultlike intonation. • Mobile infants will use gestures and language to reject, request, comment, refuse, demand, and name objects and people. • Mobile infants use language to maintain an interaction or conversation with an adult or peer.	Janeika's teacher said, "Let's play pat-a-cake," and Janeika started clapping her hands together. Ross looked up expectantly at his teacher, jabbering many sounds together as if asking her a question.
Motor	• Mobile infants stack and line up blocks. • Mobile infants can dress and undress self, arm into sleeve, foot into shoe. • Mobile infants can walk. • Mobile infants walk while carrying objects in each hand. • Mobile infants climb stairs.	Gary stood at the table, carefully using both hands to build a tower with colored blocks. Michelle toddled across the room, with her teddy bear in one hand and her blanket in the other.
	18–24 Months	
Emotions/ Attachment	• Toddlers begin to control some impulses, saying, "no, no, no" as they begin to throw blocks. • Toddlers may stop their actions when told to by a teacher. • Toddlers may not want to stop playing when their parent comes to pick them up. • Toddlers may cry when they are unable to master what they are trying to do. • Toddlers know their own names and may use "me" and "mine."	Frankie climbs up onto the table, looking his disapproving teacher right in the eye and says "no, no, no."

Teacher or Parent–Child Interaction	Environment
12–18 Months	

· Allow mobile infants protected time and space to explore. · Stay nearby to express interest, provide words, and make the activity more elaborate and complex. · Help mobile infants express their interest in each other gently. · Express enthusiasm for the things that interest mobile infants.	· Provide simple puzzles, pegboards, shape forms, wooden beads with thick strings. · Provide small climbers, tunnels, interesting pathways. · Provide toys that respond to winding, turning on and off. · Provide simple props for pretend play.
· Stay on topic in a conversation with a mobile infant. See how many turns the child will take. · Respond to the intonation of the child's jabbering. For example, if it seems as if the child is asking a question, answer what you think the child might be asking. · Respond to mobile infants' pointing and other nonverbal communication with language. · Use words that describe and compare sizes, shapes, and sounds. · When a mobile infant uses words such as "I jump," model the next step in language development by saying "You're jumping," adding the "ing" to the word. · Read longer stories, pausing to encourage mobile infants to talk about pictures and story.	· Introduce art materials such as play dough, clay, and paint. · Add paper towel rolls for mobile infants to walk and pull objects behind them or push them. · Sturdy music boxes encourage mobile infants to push buttons to "make music." · Drums and other musical instruments can be made available. · Add a sturdy CD player with a story from a parent taped on it. · Use a tape recorder to tape mobile infants' voices and play it back to them. · Provide bubble making materials. · Provide spaces for two or three children to encourage peer conversation.
· Imitate baby's growing variety of movements. · Introduce songs with little dances and movements. · Provide time and patience while a toddler practices putting on his own jacket.	· Stable, low-to-the-ground riding toys. · Stable, low-to-the-ground rocking toys. · Skill-based manipulatives such as stacking cups, rings on a stick.
18–24 Months	
· Keep your sense of humor. Understand that sometimes toddlers can stop themselves from doing things, but sometimes they cannot. · Respect the strong feelings of toddlers. Taking turns and sharing come later—now "me" and "mine" are an important part of developing a strong sense of self.	· Provide spaces that allow children to explore without ever being out of sight. · Have enough copies of the same toy for several children to each have one without sharing or taking turns. · Let children bring comfort items like blankets or stuffed animals to your program. Provide a quiet place where they can comfort themselves.

Development		Example
	18–24 Months	

Learning with Peers	· Friendships can develop early. Friends are more likely to touch, lean on one another, and smile at each other than are children who are not friends. · Toddlers imitate each others sounds and words and talk to each other and begin to communicate with others across more space. · Toddlers give or offer a toy or food to another toddler. · Toddlers may get adult and pull adult to help another child or will help another child by getting a tissue, for example. · Toddlers can show kindness to other babies who are feeling distressed. A mobile infant or toddler, however, may assume that what will comfort him will also comfort the distressed child. · Children take turns (e.g., with a ball, or jumping up). They may have toddler kinesthetic conversations as they follow a leader in moving around the room—moving in and out of the group, taking turns as leader and follower—as if in a conversation of listening and talking, learning valuable turn-taking skills. · Pushing, shoving, grabbing, and hitting may occur as children struggle over "mine for as long as I want it" and "yours, but I want it, too." Toddlers may fight over small toys more than large, nonmovable objects.	Paulie looked as if he was waiting by the door for Jamie to appear at the beginning of the day. When Jamie and his mom came in the door, Paulie toddled over and took Jamie's hand, a big smile on his face. Tanya jumped (half fell) off a board several inches off the ground. Soon three toddlers were standing on the board and half jumping, half stepping off and on the board, enjoying the activity immensely.
Cognitive	· Young toddlers enjoy the ease of their movement and like to use their hands to carry things around. · Young toddlers understand they can cause things to happen. · Young toddlers understand and remember the details of routines. · Young toddlers use objects as substitutes for other objects in their pretend play. · Young toddlers enjoy increasingly challenging materials that suggest activities such as building, sorting, matching shapes.	Before breakfast, Chris puts out his hands for the little song of thanks. When a child arrives and joins the table late, he reaches out for everyone to sing again. Lynn and Matt build little towers of blocks and then drive play trucks into them and knock them down. Fran takes out the box of one-inch blocks and makes one pile of red blocks, one pile of blue blocks.
Language	· Toddlers can go get familiar toys from another room in the house when an adult asks them to and can follow directions such as "close the door." · Toddlers combine words to name things ("that cat"), to deny ("no bite"), and to reject ("no more"). · Toddlers are combining two to three words together with meaning. · Toddlers use language for a variety of purposes, including asking, "What that?" · Toddlers point to an increasing number of pictures in books when an adult talks about the picture.	"Hi, Kitty," "open door," and "hat on" were just a few of the two-word combinations Cheral used at 20 months of age. Tyra moved quickly over to the bookshelf, picked up a book with a bright cover, and rushed back to his teacher. After sitting comfortably in her lap, he opened the book and enthusiastically started pointing to the pictures as his teacher named them.

Teacher or Parent–Child Interaction	Environment

18–24 Months

- When inside or outside, nurture toddlers as they come and go to "refuel" emotionally with a special teacher, encouraging several toddlers to sit together beside you or in your lap. Allow toddlers to touch each other gently.
- Encourage several toddlers to make animal sounds together and imitate each other as you show them the pictures in a book.
- Ask one child to help another child by getting a tissue, turning the faucet on, opening a door, etc.
- Encourage kindness with one another. If one toddler cries, ask another what "we" could do to help.
- Encourage two peers to set a table together or sponge it off together after eating. Watch them imitate each other.
- Sing songs, encouraging toddlers to take turns with the actions.

- Inside and outside: Provide sand areas large enough for several toddlers and expect them to sit right in the middle of the area.
- Blankets on the floor or ground or over a table provide a spot for peers to play.
- Provide wagons: Pulling or pushing a friend in a wagon will result in squeals of delight.
- Provide balls and pull-toys that encourage interactive play.
- Places to jump safely encourage social exchanges.
- Provide musical toys, several of each kind, so children can make beautiful music together. Sometimes one will lead and another will follow, or vice versa.

- Maintain predictable routines, reminding children of the order with questions like, "It's time to eat. What do we do?"
- Keep materials in orderly and predictable places.
- Provide scaffolding as toddlers think about their activities, with questions such as "What will you do next?" or "What will you buy at the store?"

- Have toys and materials arranged so that toddlers can make choices, reach them, and put them away (with reminders).
- Frequently review the materials you have available to ensure that you are keeping a balance between what is familiar and what is a little challenging.

- Read books with longer stories, pausing as you go through the book to encourage toddlers to talk about the pictures and the story. Ask open-ended questions such as "How does the bear feel?"
- Wonder often with the child: "I wonder what will happen to the bear."
- Engage toddlers in conversation, trying to stay on the same topic as the child.
- Introduce new conversations about interesting objects and events.

- Set up an elaborate obstacle course and use words such as "in," "out," "over," "through," "around," "up," and "down" as the toddler goes through the course.
- Provide new books each week but keep children's favorites available.
- Provide a wider variety of art materials.
- Provide sensory materials.

Development		Example

18–24 Months

| Motor | · Toddlers point to objects to communicate.

· Toddlers make marks on paper.

· Toddlers pound, shape clay.

· Toddlers run.

· Toddlers sit on and get up from small chairs alone.

· Toddlers are developing spatial confidence—explore their body in space. | Mindy rolled the dough with her hands, then used tools to make designs.

Joseph sat down at the table to eat, then took his dirty dishes to the tub. |

24–36 Months

| Emotions/
Attachment | · Toddlers can sometimes be independent, but they like to know the teacher is close by.

· Toddlers like to study pictures of themselves, their friends, and their families.

· Toddlers listen to your words and the tone of your voice when you talk about them. They want you to be interested and proud of them.

· Toddlers need clear and consistent limits. They will forget rules, or test rules, but feel secure when you remind them and help them to follow the rules.

· Toddlers may use words to express their feelings, or they may hit or bite.

· Toddlers care about the feelings of others and will comfort someone who is sad or hurt. | Kiki carried her baby doll over to the photos of her own family on the wall. She crooned to her baby while looking at her own mother's face. |
| Learning
with Peers | · Toddler friendship is "proximity seeking," wanting to be close and to show affection, such as smiling, laughing, and hugging. Friendships continue to develop and deepen.

· They exchange information and can imitate past action of others.

· Toddlers may congregate and cluster together. When a teacher begins an interesting activity with one child, children often come running from the corners of the room.

· Some toddlers are capable of inventing a variety of ways to help others who are hurt or sad.

· Peers work together toward a common goal, with one the leader and one the follower.

· Object, personal space, and verbal struggles can occur. Toddlers also engage in playful exchanges—rough and tumble, run and chase, and verbal games.

· Some children may gain a reputation with peers for aggressive or kind behavior.

· Children become more positive and less negative in their social play between 24 and 36 months.

· Dominance of one child over another can occur. | Maria and Sally played on opposite sides of the small shelf of toys for 30 minutes, peeking over at each other every few minutes, and telling each other, "boat" "my boat," "hi," "want juice," "look at me," and saying each other's names over and over.

When a fire truck went by outside, several toddlers rushed to the window to look.

Josh and Mike pushed, pulled, rolled, and grunted as they worked hard to roll the huge pumpkin from inside to the playground where the toddlers and their teachers were going to cut it open and scoop out all of the seeds. |

Teacher or Parent–Child Interaction	Environment

18–24 Months

• Provide materials that challenge toddlers' growing use of their fingers.	• Art materials with thick paint brushes and markers, large surfaces for painting.
• Stay present with toddlers as they try new skills and support them.	• Smaller, skill-based manipulates such as connecting beads and pegboards.
• Provide opportunities for climbing, walking, running.	• Lots of space for movement—dancing, riding toys, climbing, slides.

24–36 Months

• Establish clear and consistent rules. Be prepared to remind the toddlers frequently of how to follow the rules: "We don't bite. Biting hurts."	• Provide many photographs of the children with their family: on the walls, in little books, and laminated to carry around.
• Give toddlers enough of your time and attention so that they feel understood.	• Provide protected spaces for quiet play.
• Echo the enthusiasm toddlers can bring to their play.	• Maintain predictable routines and room arrangement.
• Notice and comment on the interactions that toddlers are watching and thinking about.	• Provide books that tell simple stories of coming and going, of families, and of friendship.
	• Sing songs about feelings such as "When you're happy and you know it" and "When you're sad, angry . . ."

• Create situations where two toddlers need to work together—for example, to roll a pumpkin from one place to another or carry a bucket of "heavy" blocks from inside to outside.	• Place hats and easy-to-put-on dress-up clothes in a cozy corner with a big mirror.
• Put a band-aid on a doll's arm or leg and encourage toddlers to take care of the baby.	• Spaces on or under a short loft encourage peer interaction.
• Ask the toddlers, "How can we help Joey? He's sad; he's crying."	• Provide several types of dolls as well as safe feeding utensils, blankets, and small beds. Sit close and watch as toddlers pretend to care for their babies.
• Try to change the image of a child who is gaining a reputation for aggression. Keep the child close, show her how to touch gently, and comment on her helpful behavior. Give her an interesting toy that might interest other children to engage with her. Stay close and teach her how to play.	• Provide open-ended materials such as blocks, and activities that require cooperation such as painting with big brushes and water on outside walls or filling a big bucket with water from smaller containers.
	• Large motor equipment such as climbers or rocking boats encourage toddlers to work together toward a common goal: everyone moving to the top of the climber or rocking the boat with everyone in it.

Development	Example
24–36 Months	

Cognitive
- Older toddlers begin to understand concepts such as color, size, shape, time, and weight.
- Older toddlers are interested in the story and pictures in storybooks.
- Older toddlers create new stories in pretend play or new structures in block building, becoming more imaginative and creative.
- Assign roles to toys and other children in pretend play; use chairs, blankets, and bookcases as substitutes for items in pretend play.

Example: Erick is feeling a little sad and carries a picture of his mommy around with him, saying, "After nap."

Sara takes charge of the dramatic play corner, handing out dolls and stuffed animals. She puts on a hat and says, "Mommy going shopping."

Language
- Toddlers understand more complex directions and remember words to short songs and finger-plays.
- Toddlers use many 2- to 4-word sentences.
- Toddlers can point to and name body parts.
- Toddlers add "ing" to words.
- Toddlers begin using prepositions such as "on" and "in."
- Toddlers add an "s" to words to indicate plurals.
- Toddlers may begin to ask "Why?"
- Toddlers will begin to tell you stories about what they did or what they saw.
- Toward the end of this period, a toddler can use the pictures to tell you what is happening in a story.

Example: Mindy started to add "ing" to words she had been saying for several months. She said, "I running" and "I eating" rather than "I run" and "I eat."

"Look, he's playing," exclaimed Treat as he pointed to a picture in his favorite book.

Motor
- Toddlers thread beads, use scissors, paint with fingers or brushes, and do simple puzzles.
- Toddlers throw and kick a ball.
- Toddlers stand on one foot.
- Toddlers stand and walk on tiptoes.
- Toddlers climb stairs with one foot on each step.
- Toddlers climb, slide, and jump.
- Toddlers eat with spoon and fork.
- Toddlers can dress self.
- Toddlers can pour milk from small pitcher.

Example: Robert doesn't even have to think about his body as he runs to greet his dad at the end of the day.

Peggy and Misha make a game out of imitating each other's tiptoe steps, postures, and gestures.

Lawrence and Evelyn use the dress-up clothes for their game, struggling a little to pull on the pieces.

Teacher or Parent–Child Interaction	Environment

24–36 Months

Teacher or Parent–Child Interaction	Environment
· Ask children how they might solve problems that occur and let them figure out answers. · Support children working together with materials to share ideas. · Use language that describes time "now, later, before nap, after lunch"), weight ("heavy, light"), size ("bigger, smaller"). · Count things during the day.	· Provide play opportunities that promote comparison of sizes, weights, colors, shapes, and quantities. · Have books available in all areas of the program. Have several copies of old favorites and bring in new books. · Allow children to combine materials from different areas in creative ways. · Present new material or new combinations of materials.
· Answer their "why" questions with patience and enthusiasm. · Listen with your eyes to toddlers' "stories" that they tell. · Model saying words that are plurals, such as "dogs," "elephants," and so on. · Use descriptive words such as "mozzarella cheese" rather than just "cheese," or "bluejay" rather than just the word "bird." · Have long conversations with toddlers, following their lead. · Read books to small informal groups or to individual children.	· Provide pictures for children to match. · Puzzles of animals, people, vehicles, and food are important. · Books with many pictures and short stories can be added to the environment. · Dramatic play materials encourage conversation.
· Be aware of the balance of time between active and quiet activities. · Watch for increasing accuracy in fine motor skills, as subtle issues may begin to be apparent. · Be available with encouragement and patience as toddlers increasingly feed, dress, and toilet themselves.	· Provide a variety of materials to practice fine motor skills: simple puzzles, shape boxes, threading beads, table blocks, clay, art materials. · Space, opportunity, and structures to encourage movement—outdoor time, obstacle courses, dancing, and riding toys.

Appendix B
Portraits of Development—Spanish

Retratos de Bebés y Niños Pequenos

	Desarrollo	Ejemplo
	0 a 4 meses (bebé)	
Los sentimientos/ Las ataduras	· Los bebés absorben una gran cantidad de información acerca del mundo. · Los bebés pueden sentirse abrumados y comenzar a bostezar, mirar hacia otro lado o molestarse. · Los bebés comienzan a calmarse chupándose las manos o escuchando a un adulto que les hable suavemente. · Los bebés miran fijamente a los ojos de su maestra mientras les da de comer. · Los bebés voltean la cabeza hacia voces conocidas. · Los bebés se calman y se consuelan con personas conocidas. · Los bebés lloran cuando tienen hambre o están cansados o incómodos.	Carlos seguía a Karen con los ojos por donde quiera que fuera por el salón. Cuando ella se le acercó, la miró como si quisiera que ella se quedara con él. Karen aceptó la invitación a jugar y se sentó con él en el piso. En cuanto comenzó a cansarse y a ponerse molesto, Karen lo envolvió en una manta, lo abrazó estrechamente y le habló con voz suave.
El aprender entre los pares	· A los bebés les gusta mirarse mutuamente (mirada visual). · Los bebés prefieren mirar caras, especialmente los bordes y los ojos. · Puede que los bebés lloren cuando oyen llorar a otros bebés (contagio).	Después de que la profesora puso a Tamika y a Sam sobre una manta en el piso, Tamika se quedó mirando fijamente a Sam.
La Cognición	· Los bebés siguen visualmente un objeto en movimiento. · Los bebés lloran para atraer la atención del adulto a fin de que los consuele o les dé de comer. · Los bebés miran a su alrededor por el salón con interés. · Los bebés comienzan a intentar alcanzar juguetes. · Los bebés notan que sus brazos y piernas han causado algo y repiten el movimiento. · Los bebés reconocen personas y objetos. · Los bebés comienzan a llevarse objetos a la boca.	Megan levantó la cabeza, apoyándose en los brazos mientras estaba recostada sobre la manta. Con una expresión seria miró a la maestra y a los niños a su alrededor. Willy comenzó a patear el móvil que colgaba encima y logró que se meneara. Luego paró, lo miró y volvió a patearlo mirándolo para ver si pasaba algo.

Interacciones entre Maestro o Padre/Madre–Niño	Ambiente

0 a 4 meses (bebé)

• Mantenga a los bebés pequeños cerca, en brazos, en un saco de bebé, o sobre una manta.	• Estar cerca de una maestra conocida es lo mejor.
• Reconozca las señales de por qué el bebé quiere estar con usted—mirada fija, tenderle los brazos, mirada feliz—y respóndale hablándole suavemente, alternando la comunicación verbal y no verbal.	• Un espacio sereno y tranquilo con luces bajas, limita la información que el bebé necesita absorber.
	• Evite tener música de fondo todo el día.
• Reconozca las señales que indican que el bebé necesita un descanso—bostezar, babear, mirar hacia otro lado—y apártese en silencio esperando a que el bebé se recupere.	• Limite el número de objetos, sonidos, colores y movimientos alrededor de un bebé pequeño.
• Consuele a los bebés cuando lloren.	• La maestra es lo más interesante que el bebé tiene para mirar, pero para otros bebés, los espejos y juguetes que se encuentran en su campo visual, también son interesantes.

• Sostenga a dos bebés para que puedan mirarse mutuamente.	• Los brazos de la maestras ofrecen el mejor ambiente.
• Ponga varios bebés sobre una manta en el piso para que puedan mirarse y tocarse entre sí.	• Ponga a dos bebés sobre unas mantas en el piso—uno junto a otro, de manera que los dos se estén tocando con los dedos de los pies.

• Mueva lentamente un juguete pequeño de lado a lado mientras el bebé lo sigue con la mirada.	• Organice el espacio de manera que los bebés puedan ver actividad sin dejar de estar protegidos.
• Responda rápidamente al llanto del niño.	• Suministre unos cuantos objetos interesantes para mirar—juguetes pequeños en el piso, cuando están boca abajo; juguetes colgantes cuando los bebés están boca arriba
• Déles tiempo a los bebés para que estén tranquilos mirando lo que pasa a su alrededor. Hable acerca de lo que ven.	• Ponga espejos irrompibles a disposición de los bebés.
• Reaccione ante las expresiones de los bebés con expresiones y lenguaje claro y hasta exagerado.	

Desarrollo		Ejemplo
	0 a 4 meses (bebé)	
El Lenguaje	· Los bebés se pueden asustar si oyen un ruido fuerte.	Brenda sostenía a Jordán de manera que pudieran mirarse a los ojos. Jordán arrulló suavemente y Brenda le arrulló también. Luego, ella esperó a que Jordán lo volviera a hacer.
	· Los bebés captan las diferencias entre los sonidos.	
	· Los bebés pueden dejar de llorar cuando oyen la voz de un adulto conocido.	
	· Los bebés prefieren oír hablar cuando se les habla a ellos de forma directa.	Érica le sonrió de oreja a oreja a su padre cuando él la levantó de la cuna.
	· Los bebés escuchan cuando un adulto les habla o les canta mientras los mira.	
	· Los bebés lloran cuando sienten dolor, tienen hambre o están afligidos.	
	· A los 2 meses de edad, los bebés tienen llantos específicos de hambre y dolor.	
	· Los bebés "arrullan" (producen sonidos vocálicos suaves).	
	· Hacia el final de este período, los bebés sonríen y se ríen.	
	· Los bebés miran fijamente imágenes interesantes en libros.	
El desarrollo musculoso	· Los bebés levantan la cabeza cuando los llevan en brazos contra el hombro; sostienen la cabeza firme y erguida.	Rosie mantuvo la cabeza erguida y miró a su alrededor a los otros niños mientras Sharon la llevaba contra el hombro.
	· Boca abajo, los bebés levantan la cabeza y los hombros y pueden sostener un juguete en la mano.	Robert, boca abajo sobre una manta, levantó la cabeza para mirarse al espejo montado a nivel del suelo en la pared.
	· Los bebés giran la cabeza hacia una voz conocida.	
	· Los bebés se quedan quietos para prestar atención; se contonean y se mueven para inducir la continuación de la interacción.	Jen tenía un sonajero en la mano, pero no parecía darse cuenta de que lo tenía.
	· De espaldas, los bebés estiran los brazos y las piernas a manera de juego.	Filipe se llevó los dedos a la boca y se los chupó mientras miraba atentamente a los niños pequeños.
	· Estando de lado, los bebés se dan vuelta para quedar de espaldas.	
	· Los bebés sujetan un dedo o un juguete liviano con agarre reflejo.	
	· Los bebés se chupan los dedos, las manos y otros objetos.	
	· Los bebés mueven los brazos y las piernas.	

Interacciones entre Maestro o Padre/Madre–Niño	Ambiente

0 a 4 meses (bebé)

- Use lenguaje dirigido al bebé.
- Tenga a los bebés en brazos y hábleles suavemente. Mírelos largamente a los ojos mientras baila conversando. Respete al bebé si necesita un descanso y aparta la cabeza.
- Lea libros con frases rítmicas y con una sola imagen en una página, con 2 imágenes a los de 4 meses de edad.
- Interprete los eructos, llantos, bostezos, estiramientos y sonidos de los bebés como formas de comunicación. Diga "Ah, me estás diciendo que tienes sueño".
- Cante canciones de cuna y otras canciones.
- Sea un compañero de lenguaje que se identifique y comente los sentimientos del bebé.
- Diga palabras y produzca sonidos para consolar a los bebés.

- El mejor ambiente son los brazos de un adulto afectuoso que tenga al bebé en brazos y le hable suavemente.
- Suministre juguetes que produzcan sonidos agradables. Sostenga con cuidado el juguete e intercambie sonidos con el bebé.
- Suministre materiales interesantes para tocar mientras comenta las texturas.
- Coloque espejos bajos a lo largo de una pared. Los bebés se miran y es posible que produzcan sonidos.

- Cambie la posición del bebé; a veces de espaldas, otras boca abajo. Cuando lleve en brazos al bebé, acúnelo en sus brazos o sosténgalo erguido contra el hombro.
- Cuando el bebé está en el piso, acuéstese cara a cara junto a él.
- Cuando la bebé está de espaldas y trata de alcanzar un juguete un poco más allá de su cabeza, sosténgale el tronco mientras rueda.

- Una manta rígida (contra el riesgo de asfixia) en el suelo da espacio para los primeros movimientos.
- Los juguetes pequeños e interesantes, las imágenes, y los libros para mirar cuando quieran animan a los bebés a levantar la cabeza. Un espejo atornillado a la pared a nivel del suelo siempre ofrece algo interesante que mirar.
- A medida que comienzan a estirarse para alcanzar, a los bebés les gustan las barras estables con juguetes colgantes que puedan batear, alcanzar y agarrar.

Desarrollo		Ejemplo
	4 a 8 meses (bebé)	
Los sentimientos/ Las ataduras	• A los bebés les gusta mirarse las manos y los pies. • Los bebés agitan los brazos y patalean emocionados cuando ven a una persona conocida. • Los bebés le sonríen a la maestra esperando que ella les sonría también. • Con la cara y el cuerpo, los bebés expresan muchos sentimientos: desde fruncir el ceño y llorar hasta reírse a carcajadas. • Los bebés expresan sus sentimientos claramente ante personas conocidas, y son más reservados con los desconocidos	A Deborah le encanta que la maestra la lleve en brazos mientras va por el salón "hablándole" de lo que ven. Tiene los ojos bien abiertos y brillantes, sonríe y hace ruiditos de arrullo cuando le corresponde hablar en la conversación. Cuando un visitante entra en el salón, Deborah se queda muy callada y seria, y se sujeta firmemente al hombro de la maestra mirando al visitante.
El aprender entre los pares	• Los bebés tocan a otros bebés, se dirigen vocalizaciones, se entusiasman, se acercan a otros bebés, sonríen y se ríen unos de otros. • Los bebés pueden tratar a otros bebés como si fueran objetos - pasándoles por encima al gatear, lamiéndolos, chupándolos, sentándose encima. Están simplemente aprendiendo la diferencia entre personas y objetos. Los bebés pueden pinchar con el dedo, empujar, dar palmaditas a otros bebés, para ver lo que el otro bebé va a hacer. A menudo se sorprenden con la reacción que logran.reacción que logran.	Ana le pasó por encima gateando a Nadia que estaba acostada en el piso. Tocándole el pelo a Nadia. Ana se rió a carcajadas.
La Cognición	• A los bebés les gusta examinar los juguetes. • A los bebés les gusta hacer que los juguetes hagan algo— sonar, encajarse uno dentro de otro. • Los bebés imitan las expresiones y los gestos de los adultos. • Los bebés se vuelven hacia los sonidos para ver de dónde vienen. • Los bebés buscan juguetes que han dejado caer.	Ángela se interesa en todo. Mira a sus amigos y luego mira a la maestra y sonríe. Roger se estira para tocar un juguete colgante. Cuando se balancea y suena, Roger se estira para hacerlo de nuevo.
El Lenguaje	• Los bebés giran la cabeza hacia un ruido, o una persona que dice su nombre. • A los bebés les gusta que los adultos hablen, canten y se rían con ellos. • Los bebés vocalizan con la intención de obtener una respuesta del adulto. • Los bebés dan chillidos agudos. • Los bebés practican sus sonidos cuando exploran y cuando están con adultos conocidos. • Los bebés comienzan a balbucear; al principio una consonante y luego combinaciones de dos consonantes. • Los bebés participan en conversaciones turnándose con los adultos. • Los bebés miran distintas imágenes de un libro y se emocionan cuando ven una que les gusta o cuando les gusta el tono entusiasta del adulto que lee.	Mientras sostenía a Donovan en su regazo, Daniela, la maestra del bebé, señalaba con el dedo las imágenes del libro de tapas de cartón. "Mira," dijo señalando la imagen, "una pelota." Luego dijo "Ahí está tu pelota" y señaló hacia una pelota en el piso. Donovan miró la imagen, luego la pelota en el piso y finalmente volvió a mirar la imagen. "Tt" dijo Afi cuando estaba en brazos de su maestra mirándola. "Tada" le dijo la maestra. "Tt" repitió Afi cuando le tocó hablar en la conversación.

Interacciones entre Maestro o Padre/Madre-Niño	Ambiente

4 a 8 meses (bebé)

• Déles a los bebés oportunidades para que se miren al espejo mientras juegan. • Refleje las expresiones emocionales del bebé y agregue palabras apropiadas: "Estoy tan contenta de verte hoy." • Responda a los bebés de una manera que les ayude a calmarse y mantenerse activos. Si el bebé llora, cálmelo.	• Monte espejos irrompibles en las paredes. • Deje que los bebés pasen un rato en el piso mientras están boca arriba, jugando con sus pies y moviéndose por el piso. • Los libros y los álbumes de fotografías con caras reales mostrando diferentes expresiones emocionales son muy interesantes para los bebés.
• Muévase al ritmo de la música con un bebé en cada brazo. • Con un bebé sobre el regazo, apunte y hable sobre lo que el otro bebé está haciendo. • Ponga a dos bebés boca bajo frente a un espejo. • En vez de decirles "No" y "Deja de hacer eso" a los bebés que están explorando, dígales, "Tócalo con cuidado." Dígales a los niños lo que usted quiere que hagan...muéstreselo.	• Cuelgue un espejo seguro en la pared de manera horizontal, para que la parte de abajo esté tocando el piso. • Cubra la cámara de aire de la rueda de un auto con un paño suave. Siente a dos bebés en la cámara para que se toquen con los pies.
• Lleve en brazos al bebé, mientras camina por el salón mirando cosas y hablando acerca de ellas. • Siéntese cerca y háblele al bebé sobre los juguetes que está mirando. • Llame al bebé por su nombre a poca distancia para asegurarle que está cerca.	• Suministre una variedad de juguetes pequeños para que los manipule y los examine. • Suministre juguetes que suenan cuando se mueven, se encajan unos dentro de otros o se cuelgan y mueven cuando se tocan. • Ofrezca libros de tapas de cartón.
• Use lenguaje dirigido al bebé. • Hable a menudo con los bebés. Muéstreles objetos y personas nuevos y nómbrelos. • Repita los sonidos que los bebés producen y espere a que repitan el sonido (turnarse). • Refiérase a varios artículos conocidos, tales como "leche" o "perro," con lenguaje de señas. • Cante canciones y haga juegos de dedos. • Describa con palabras los sentimientos de los niños expresados a través de gestos, posturas corporales y sonidos. • Léale libros sencillos con una o dos imágenes por página. Señale con el dedo las imágenes mientras dice el nombre de la imagen. • Léale los mismos libros una y otra vez. • Aplique estrategias de atención conjunta—señale con el dedo un juguete o una imagen de un libro diciendo el nombre o hablando al respecto.	• Suministre juguetes y materiales interesantes para que los bebés los manipulen y examinen. • Suministre libros de cartón con asas para que pueden gatear hasta ellos y tomarlos. • Los libros con asas animan a los bebés a llevarlos. • Haga un libro de imágenes *de te veo, no te veo* pegando un pedazo de tela sobre cada imagen. • Forme un rincón de lectura acogedor donde las maestras puedan estar cómodas y leer a los bebés. • Suministre cajas de sonido (bien selladas) con distintos objetos adentro que produzcan distintos sonidos al sacudirlas. • Incorpore títeres al ambiente. Úselos a veces para "hablar" con el niño. Coloque los títeres en la mano del niño y espere a ver lo que el niño dice o hace.

Desarrollo		Ejemplo
4 a 8 meses (bebé)		
El desarrollo musculoso	• Los bebés de espaldas se ponen de lado y luego se vuelven a poner de espaldas.	Estando de espaldas, Micky rueda para quedar boca abajo y alcanzar un juguete, luego vuelve a rodar para jugar con el juguete.
	• Al final de este período, los bebés se sientan; primero con apoyo pero luego estables y solos.	A Erin, sentada sola establemente, le gusta recoger objetos con las dos manos y examinarlos.
	• Los bebés se estiran para alcanzar objetos con el brazo.	A Freddy le gusta que lo tomen en brazos mientras toma su biberón, aunque insiste en sujetarlo solo.
	• Los bebés agarran rastrillando.	
	• Los bebés gatean.	
	• Los bebés sacuden, golpean, sujetan y sueltan objetos.	
	• Los bebés se pasan objetos de una mano a otra.	
	• Los bebés pueden sostener su biberón.	
	• Los bebés se pueden llevar objetos a la boca.	
8 a 12 meses (bebé móvil)		
Los sentimientos/ Las ataduras	• Los bebés móviles pueden tenerle miedo a los desconocidos.	Jaime está disfrutando de su nueva habilidad, que es ir gateando rápidamente a donde quiera ir. Le encanta el pequeño trepador que le permite mirar por la ventana. Pero cuando siente que la rampa es un poco inestable, se vuelve a mirar a Federico, su maestro, para asegurarse de que no hay peligro.
	• Los bebés móviles pueden llamar a los adultos conocidos para que los ayuden cuando están enojados.	
	• Los bebés móviles miran al adulto conocido para determinar si una situación es peligrosa o no.	
	• Los bebés móviles se aferran al adulto cuando están en una situación desconocida.	
	• A los bebés móviles les parecen divertidos los juegos tontos y las expresiones faciales exageradas que ponen los adultos.	
El aprender entre los pares	• Los bebés pueden mostrar a otros bebés un objeto, sentarse juntos, perseguirse gateando y jugar a perseguir y recoger objetos.	Shamaine miró la estantería baja de juguetes y vio que Carla venía gateando hacia ella. Shamaine se dio la vuelta rápidamente y se alejó gateando con Carla siguiéndola de cerca.
	• Los bebés se sonríen y se ríen entre sí.	Kai pasó gateando por encima de las piernas de Bridger para alcanzar un juguete que estaba al otro lado de Bridger.
	• Los bebés se dirigen sonidos—y es posible que sus primeras palabras se las digan entre sí.	
	• Uno de los juegos preferidos de los bebés es el *te veo, no te veo* mientras exploran la separación: irse y volver, aparecer y desaparecer.	
	• Los bebés pueden aprender a tocarse uno al otro con cuidado.	
	• Como a esta edad los bebés actúan en gran medida en función de sus objetivos, pueden apartar la mano de un bebé que esté tocando un juguete, o gatearle por encima para alcanzar un juguete.	

Interacciones entre Maestro o Padre/Madre–Niño	Ambiente

4 a 8 meses (bebé)

- Quédese cerca del bebé que recién comienza a sentarse solo.
- Conozca el avance del desarrollo motor; anime emocionalmente y apoye físicamente al bebé en sus nuevos intentos.
- Crea en los beneficios a largo plazo para la salud de un estilo de vida activo.

- Deles lugares seguros para rodar, sentarse y gatear. Proteja a los bebés de cualquier cosa que pueda caerles encima.
- Deles objetos livianos pequeños y lavables (grandes para evitar que se asfixien) para que los manipulen y los lancen, y deles recipientes para los objetos.

8 a 12 meses (bebé móvil)

- Anime a los bebés móviles a moverse y explorar asegurándoles que usted los está mirando y cuidando.
- Entienda que los bebés móviles pueden asustarse ante situaciones nuevas que quizás no los habrían asustado hace unos meses. Consuélelos y tranquilícelos.

- Juegue al *te veo, no te veo*.
- Léales cuentos sobre madres y padres que se van y vuelven.
- Léales libros con solapas que se pueden levantar para encontrar cosas.
- Mantenga una previsibilidad de hábitos y rutinas del salón.

- Nombre partes del cuerpo del bebé mientras dos bebés están sentados juntos:

  Estos son los ojos del bebé Esta es la nariz del bebé Toca la parte con que ves Tócate la parte que te suenas
- Ponga un bebé con otro (en parejas) porque las interacciones más frecuentes, complejas e intensas entre niños se producen cuando un niño está con varios compañeros.
- Comprenda que los bebés no son "malos" cuando le apartan la mano al otro. Diga "Jenny tenía ese juguete. Vamos a buscarte otro."

- Mientras están comiendo, coloque las sillas altas de manera que los niños se puedan ver unos a los otros.
- Disponga de rincones agradables en el salón donde los bebés puedan "desaparecer" (pero pudiendo aún ser vistos por adultos).
- Cuelgue del techo un paño largo y ancho (para que los bebés no se enreden en él). A los bebés les encanta gatear alrededor.
- Ponga contenedores con bloques de diferentes tamaños entre dos bebés. Quédese sentada junto a ellos mientras comienzan a explorar los materiales. Hable acerca de lo que está haciendo cada uno.

	Desarrollo	Ejemplo
	8 a 12 meses (bebé móvil)	
La Cognición	· A los bebés móviles les gusta desarmar los juguetes y luego volver a armarlos. · A los bebés móviles les gustan los juguetes que hacen algo cuando se tocan, se jalan o se golpean. · Los bebés móviles comienzan juegos imaginarios muy simples, tales como llevarse un vaso a la boca. · A los bebés móviles les gusta encontrar juguetes pequeños debajo de un paño o de un vaso. · A los bebés móviles les gusta levantar y examinar objetos pequeños tales como un Cheerio. · Los bebés móviles muestran objetos con el dedo sabiendo que usted también puede verlos.	A Carlos le encanta sacar cada uno de los animales de plástico del balde y mirarlo. Cuando el balde queda vacío, lo lanza a un lado. A Aliya le gusta el botón que se aprieta y las puertas oscilantes de la caja mecánica, pero todavía no puede hacer funcionar todos los mecanismos. Su maestra expresa sorpresa a Aliya cuando las puertas se abren y, de vez en cuando, le enseña cómo funciona otra de las perillas.
El Lenguaje	· Los bebés móviles comienzan a participar en juegos sociales tales como el *te veo, no te veo* o el *"así de grande."* · A los bebés les gusta escuchar juegos de sonidos (rimas), canciones y juegos de dedos. · El balbuceo continúa desarrollándose con sílabas combinadas tales como "dada," "mama," "nana" y "tutu" y a esta altura el bebé puede usar estos sonidos específicamente para referirse a su mamá o su papá. · Los bebés repiten sonidos consistentemente para referirse a un objeto, una persona o un animal. · Si oyen otro lenguaje *con* un adulto a través de estrategias conversacionales interactivas, los bebés pueden "tener una actitud abierta hacia los sonidos de un lenguaje extranjero." · Los bebés pueden comenzar a decir palabras aisladas. · Al final de este período, los bebés pueden comenzar a señalar con el dedo para atraer la atención de un adulto. · Los bebés emplean expresiones faciales y gestos tales como agitar la cabeza o los brazos para que los tomen en brazos, y así comunicarse con los adultos o con sus compañeros.	Una de las primeras palabras de Dana fue "mamá," y la repetía una y otra vez cuando veía a su madre. Una de las primera palabras de Trishanna fue "mamá," y la repetía con entusiasmo una y otra vez cuando veía a su madre.
El desarrollo musculoso	· Los bebés móviles jalan de algo para ponerse de pie. · Los bebés móviles se pasean. · Los bebés móviles se quedan de pie solos. · Los bebés móviles caminan con ayuda al principio y después solos. · Los bebés móviles se sientan en una silla. · Los bebés móviles comen con los dedos. · Los bebés móviles pueden usar una cuchara y un vaso hermético. · Los bebés móviles agarran atenazando.	Hershel gatea hasta su maestra, luego se agarra de su pierna y jala para ponerse de pie. Jem se sienta a la mesa del almuerzo, y alterna la cuchara y los dedos para disfrutar de la comida.

Interacciones entre Maestro o Padre/Madre–Niño	Ambiente

8 a 12 meses (bebé móvil)

- Con su presencia, su interés y su entusiasmo, ayude al bebé a concentrarse en lo que le interesa para apoyarlo en su atención y exploración.
- Con sus expresiones y palabras afectivas, demuéstrele al bebé móvil que usted disfruta de sus descubrimientos.
- Con palabras, describa la actividad del niño: "Mira, encontraste un Cheerio. Lo estás recogiendo con los dedos."

- Suministre juguetes tales como vasos para apilar, anillos en poste, piezas que se interconectan y cubos llenos de objetos pequeños interesantes, tales como animales de juguete.
- Suministre réplicas tamaño infantil de platos o herramientas domésticas.
- Suministre juguetes que reaccionen—cajas mecánicas, almohadillas llenas de agua.
- Suministre materiales sensoriales, como agua y arena con una variedad de herramientas.
- Suministre libros de tapas de cartón con fotos.

- Organice juegos conocidos tales como te veo—no te veo, palmitas—palmitas o "¿cómo eres de grande?"
- Responda con palabras a la comunicación no verbal de los bebés.
- Observe y espere a que los bebés inicien sonidos o palabras.
- Imite los sonidos y luego expanda, detalle y amplíe el lenguaje del bebé.
- Modele el siguiente paso en el desarrollo del lenguaje.
- Emplee hablarse a sí mismo y hablar en paralelo.
- Hable a menudo de manera receptiva con un vocabulario variado. No bombardee al niño con palabras.
- Lea los libros con entusiasmo—cambiando el tono de su voz con los distintos personajes.
- Hable sobre las imágenes y el cuento a medida que lee. Involucre a los bebés con la voz y los gestos.
- Mientras miran una imagen, espere a que el bebé produzca sonidos, señale con el dedo o haga expresiones faciales.

- Cree un rincón de lectura acogedor en que los bebés puedan alcanzar fácilmente los libros y manipularlos.
- Haga un libro "Todo sobre mí"—álbumes pequeños de fotos para cada niño con imágenes de ellos, su familia, sus juguetes preferidos, sus compañeros, sus maestras y los animales domésticos de la familia. Déjelos al alcance de los niños. Cambie las imágenes a medida que el niño crece.
- Los juguetes musicales para empujar animan a los bebés a manipularlos y producir sonidos.

- Esté atenta para saber cuándo ayudar al bebé que comienza a caminar y cuándo dejar que lo siga intentando.
- Dé tiempo para que los bebés mayores practiquen comer solos.

- Lugares seguros para ponerse de pie apoyándose en algo.
- Juguetes para empujar y jalar para que los que comienzan a caminar puedan jalar y empujar.
- Cajas mecánicas.
- Libros de cartón para pasar las páginas, levantar las solapas y meter los dedos a través de los agujeros.

Desarrollo	Ejemplo
12 a 18 meses (bebé móvil)	

Los sentimientos/ Las ataduras
- Los bebés móviles imitan las acciones de los adultos conocidos, tales como hablar por teléfono o llevar en brazos a una muñeca bebé.
- Los bebés móviles intentan atraer la atención del adulto jalándole la pierna o tomándole la mano.
- Los bebés móviles se calman con su manta o su animal de peluche favorito.
- Los bebés móviles protestan ruidosamente cuando sus padres los dejan.
- Los bebés móviles se relajan y se consuelan acurrucándose con un adulto conocido.
- Los bebés móviles hacen saber claramente lo que les gusta y lo que no les gusta.

Amelia carga toda la mañana su osito de peluche por todos los lados. A veces copia las acciones de Sofía, su maestra, dándole al osito palmaditas en la espalda o alimentándole con biberón. Cuando se cansa, se frota el osito contra la oreja y se chupa el pulgar.

El aprender entre los pares
- Comienzan los turnos imitativos (motores) e interactivos. Los niños pequeños pueden imitarse unos a otros—si un bebé le da un juguete a otro, el otro puede imitarlo.
- Los bebés móviles comienzan a hablarse unos a otros.
- Los bebés pueden demostrar preocupación cuando otros bebés están afligidos.
- Los bebés móviles pueden quitarle el juguete a otro bebé, decirle "no," empujarlo, agarrar firmemente el juguete y decir "mío."
- A esta edad, los bebés son pequeños científicos que experimentan para ver cómo funcionan las cosas. Esto afecta la relación que tienen con sus compañeros, pues están constantemente haciéndoles cosas para ver cómo reaccionan.
- Morder puede aparecer cuando los bebés muerden a otros "para ver lo que pasa," para obtener el juguete que quieren, para expresar su frustración. Los bebés están al borde de comunicarse bien; pueden comunicarse por la boca en forma de mordedura.

Rashida golpeó la mesa con la cuchara; poco después, otros dos comenzaron a hacerlo. Parecían estar siguiendo el ejemplo físicamente (como si estuvieran conversando).

Primero, Carmen intentó alejar a Toby del caballito de balancín. Cuando eso no dio resultado, se inclinó hacia él y lo mordió en el brazo.

La Cognición
- A los bebés móviles les gusta poner en práctica su movilidad para explorar gateando, caminando, trepando, corriendo, etc.
- Los bebés móviles disfrutan jugando en la arena, el agua, con plastilina y varios tipos de herramientas.
- A los bebés móviles les interesan las relaciones espaciales de rompecabezas y tableros con agujeros.
- Los bebés móviles utilizan herramientas tales como llaves o teléfonos en sus juegos imaginarios.
- Los bebés móviles disfrutan al mirar libros y nombrar objetos, animales o partes del cuerpo.

Alexis y Dan están contentísimos de estar de pie. Se siguen mutuamente por todas partes, uno subiendo atrevidamente por un plano inclinado, con el otro inmediatamente detrás. A veces los dos intentan meterse debajo del tobogán.

A Meredith le encanta acurrucarse en el regazo de su maestra y mostrar con el dedo imágenes en libros mientras la maestra nombra los animales o le pide que encuentre uno en particular.

Interacciones entre Maestro o Padre/Madre–Niño	Ambiente

12 a 18 meses (bebé móvil)

• Muestre interés en las actividades del bebé.	• Disponga de objetos de mayores en tamaño infantil: teléfonos, platos, llaves, etc.
• Muestre su orgullo por los logros del bebé.	• Ponga fotografías de bebés con su familia en la pared.
• Deje que los bebés la utilicen como una base firme, para explorar el mundo.	• Lamine las fotos del bebé con su familia para que las lleve consigo.
• Deje que los bebés sepan que usted entiende lo que sienten y responda respetuosamente.	• Haga álbumes de fotos de los niños del programa y hable acerca de las fotos.
• Estos niños son todavía muy pequeños, y necesitan que se les acurruque y abrace mucho.	• Disponga de sillas de adulto y espacios tranquilos y cómodos para tener a los niños en brazos.

• Muéstreles a los niños pequeños móviles cómo rodar juntos por una pequeña pendiente.	• Suministre una caja de cartón grande abierta por los dos lados. Anímelos a entrar y salir de la caja gateando juntos. Ventanas a los lados de la caja estimulan a los bebés para que se miren entre ellos por la ventana.
• Ayude a los niños pequeños móviles a que aprendan los nombres de los demás, cantando canciones de saludo y despedida incluyendo los nombres de los niños: "Esta es Tania, ¿cómo estás?" y "Este es Enrique, ¿cómo estás?" y apuntando o tocando a cada niño que pasa junto a usted o al que está sentado en su regazo.	• Muñecas, camiones, autos y otros materiales de juego, promueven las interacciones entre compañeros.
• Comente el comportamiento social activo. Diga "Le diste la muñeca. Eso le gusta." Puede que los bebés no entiendan sus palabras, pero son capaces de darse cuenta por el tono de voz que usted está contenta con ellos.	• A los bebés les encanta la arena y el agua y jugar con botellas y pelotas seguras de diferentes tamaños. Cuando cada uno tiene su propio contenedor o cubo con agua o arena, el juego se desarrolla sin altibajos.
• A los bebés les gusta mirar libros juntos, creando grupos informales (esto significa que entrar y salir del grupo) alrededor de las piernas, el regazo y los brazos del padre, la madre o la maestra que más les gusta.	• Al aire libre, grandes cajas de arena o juguetes para empujar, estimulan el juego interactivo. Tendencias de Desarrollo e Interacciones Receptivas.

• Déle a los bebés móviles tiempo y espacio protegido para explorar.	• Suministre rompecabezas simples, tableros con agujeros, formas, cuentas de madera con cordones gruesos.
• Quédese cerca para expresar interés, sugerir palabras y hacer que la actividad sea más elaborada y compleja.	• Suministre trepadores pequeños, túneles y trayectos interesantes.
• Ayude a los bebés móviles a que expresen su interés en otros bebés cuidadosamente.	• Suministre juguetes que funcionen al darle cuerda, o que se enciendan y apaguen.
• Exprese entusiasmo por lo que les interesa a los bebés móviles.	• Suministre artículos simples para el juego imaginario.

Desarrollo	Ejemplo

12 a 18 meses (bebé móvil)

| El Lenguaje | • Los bebés móviles pueden seguir instrucciones sencillas tales como "Ven aquí" o "Trae tus zapatos" sin que haya que hacer gestos.
• Los bebés móviles pueden jugar socialmente sin que haya que demostrar la acción. Por ejemplo, cuando usted dice "Dile adiós" ellos mueven las manos aunque usted no les muestre cómo hacerlo.
• Los bebés móviles señalan con el dedo para llamar la atención de los adultos y de sus compañeros.
• Se puede producir un aprendizaje rápido de palabras—una explosión de lenguaje—en los niños que están aprendiendo muchas palabras nuevas.
• Hacia el final de este período, los bebés móviles combinan palabras.
• Los bebés móviles farfullan (hilando muchos sonidos) con la misma entonación que los adultos.
• Los bebés móviles hacen gestos y se valen de palabras para rechazar, pedir, comentar, negarse, exigir y nombrar objetos y personas.
• Los bebés móviles se valen del lenguaje para mantener una interacción o conversación con un adulto o uno de sus compañeros. | La maestra de Janina le dijo "Juguemos a dar palmitas, palmitas," y Janina comenzó a aplaudir.

Ross miró a su maestra con expectación, farfullando muchos sonidos juntos como si le hiciera una pregunta. |
| El desarrollo musculoso | • Los bebés móviles apilan y alinean bloques.
• Los bebés móviles pueden vestirse y desvestirse solos, meter el brazo en una manga y el pie dentro de un zapato.
• Los bebés móviles pueden caminar.
• Los bebés móviles caminan con objetos en las manos.
• Los bebés móviles suben escaleras. | Gary se paró frente a la mesa y construyó cuidadosamente con las dos manos una torre con bloques de colores.

Michelle caminó por la habitación con su osito de peluche en una mano y su manta en la otra. |

18 a 24 meses (niños pequeños)

| Los sentimientos/ Las ataduras | • Los niños pequeños comienzan a controlar ciertos impulsos diciendo "no, no, no" a medida que comienzan a lanzar bloques.
• Los niños pequeños pueden dejar lo que están haciendo cuando la maestra se lo dice.
• Los niños pequeños pueden no querer dejar de jugar cuando su padre o su madre viene a buscarlos.
• Los niños pequeños pueden llorar cuando no consiguen hacer algo que están intentando.
• Los niños pequeños saben su propio nombre y puede que usen el "mi" y "mío." | Francisco se sube a la mesa mientras mira directamente a los ojos de la maestra que desaprueba lo que él hace, y dice "no, no, no." |

Interacciones entre Maestro o Padre/Madre–Niño	Ambiente

12 a 18 meses (bebé móvil)

- Mantenga el tema en una conversación con un bebé móvil. Vea cuántas veces hablará el niño.
- Responda a la entonación del parloteo del niño. Por ejemplo, si parece que el niño hace una pregunta, responda a lo que usted cree que el niño puede estar preguntando.
- Responda con palabras a las señales hechas con los dedos y otros medios de comunicación no verbal de los bebés móviles.
- Describa y compare con palabras tamaños, formas y sonidos.
- Cuando un bebé móvil dice palabras tales como "Yo salto," modele el próximo paso en el desarrollo del lenguaje diciendo "Tú estás saltando," añadiendo "ando o iendo" a la palabra. Haga esto tanto con el contenido de las palabras como con la estructura de las palabras u oraciones.
- Léale libros con cuentos más largos, haga pausas a medida que avanza por el libro para animar a los bebés móviles a hablar sobre las imágenes y el cuento.

- Introduzca materiales de arte tales como plastilina, arcilla y pintura.
- Déle rollos de toallas de papel a los bebés móviles para que produzcan sonidos.
- Los juguetes musicales para jalar animan a los bebés móviles a caminar y jalarlos o empujarlos.
- Las cajas de música resistentes animan a los bebés móviles a apretar botones para "hacer música."
- Se pueden poner a disposición tambores y otros instrumentos musicales.
- Incorpore un reproductor de CD resistente con un cuento que haya grabado el padre o la madre.
- Grabe las voces de los bebés móviles con una grabadora y haga que las escuchen.
- Suministre materiales para hacer burbujas.
- Facilite espacios para animar a dos o tres niños a conversar con sus compañeros.

- Imite la cada vez mayor variedad de movimientos del bebé.
- Introduzca canciones con pequeños bailes y movimientos.
- Dé tiempo y tenga paciencia mientras el niño pequeño practica ponerse solo la chaqueta.

- Juguetes para montar estables y no muy altos.
- Juguetes mecedores estables y no muy altos.
- Juegos de manipulación basados en habilidades, tales como apilar vasos o ensartar aros en un palo.

18 a 24 meses (niños pequeños)

- Mantenga su sentido del humor. Entienda que los niños pequeños pueden dejar de hacer ciertas cosas a veces, pero no siempre.
- Respete los sentimientos fuertes de los niños pequeños. El turnarse y compartir viene después; ahora "mí" y "mío" son una etapa importante del desarrollo de un sólido sentido de identidad.

- Disponga espacios que permita que los niños exploren, pero siempre sin perderlos de vista.
- Tenga suficientes juguetes iguales para que varios niños puedan tener el suyo, sin tener que compartir o turnarse.
- Deje que los niños traigan al programa artículos que los calmen, tales como mantas o animales de peluche. Asígneles un lugar tranquilo donde puedan consolarse solos.

424

APPENDIX B

Desarrollo	Ejemplo

18 a 24 meses (niños pequeños)

El aprender entre los pares

- Las amistades pueden desarrollarse a muy temprana edad. Los amigos son más propensos a tocarse, apoyarse y sonreírse entre sí, que otros niños que no son amigos.
- Los niños pequeños imitan mutuamente los sonidos y las palabras que dicen y se hablan y comienzan a comunicarse con los demás a mayores distancias.
- Los niños pequeños dan u ofrecen un juguete o comida a otros niños pequeños
- Los niños pequeños pueden llamar a un adulto y jalar al adulto para que ayude a otro niño, o pueden ayudar a otro niño llevándole un pañuelito de papel, por ejemplo.
- Los niños pequeños demuestran bondad hacia otros bebés que se sienten afligidos. Sin embargo, el bebé o niño pequeño móvil puede suponer que lo que lo consuela a él, también consuela al afligido
- Los niños pueden turnarse, por ejemplo, con una pelota o para saltar. Pueden tener conversaciones cinéticas de niño pequeño mientras siguen a un líder por el salón—entrando y saliendo del grupo, turnándose para ser líder y seguidor— como si estuvieran en una conversación, en la cual escuchan y hablan, aprendiendo la importante habilidad de cómo turnarse.
- Empujar, dar empujones, agarrar y golpear pueden ocurrir a medida que los niños luchan con la idea de "mío durante todo el tiempo que yo quiera" y "tuyo, pero yo también lo quiero." Los niños pequeños puede que se peleen más por juguetes pequeños, que por objetos grandes que no se mueven.

Paulie parecía estar esperando en la puerta a que apareciera Jamie al principio de la jornada. Cuando Jaime y su mamá llegaron, Paulie se dirigió hacia ellos y le tomó la mano a Jaime con una gran sonrisa en la cara.

Tania saltó (medio se cayó) de una tabla situada a varias pulgadas del suelo. Pronto tres niños pequeños estaban parados sobre la tabla, y casi saltando, casi bajando de la tabla y disfrutando inmensamente de la actividad.

La Cognición

- Los niños pequeños de corta edad disfrutan de su facilidad de movimiento y les gusta llevar cosas en las manos.
- Los niños pequeños entienden que pueden hacer que ocurran cosas.
- Los niños pequeños entienden y recuerdan los detalles de las rutinas.
- Los niños pequeños sustituyen unos objetos por otros en su juego imaginario.
- Los niños pequeños disfrutan cada vez más de los materiales problemáticos que sugieren actividades tales como construir y hacer corresponder formas.

Antes del desayuno, Chris tiende las manos para la cancioncita de gracias. Cuando un niño llega más tarde y se sienta a la mesa, Chris tiende las manos para que todos canten nuevamente.

Lynn y Matt construyen pequeñas torres de bloques y luego las chocan con camiones de juguete para derribarlas

Fran saca de la caja bloques de una pulgada y hace una pila de bloques rojos y una pila de bloques azules.

Interacciones entre Maestro o Padre/Madre–Niño	Ambiente

18 a 24 meses (niños pequeños)

- Ya esté adentro o afuera, atienda a los niños pequeños cuando entran a "reponerse" emocionalmente con su maestra especial animando a varios niños pequeños a sentarse junto a usted o en su regazo. Permita que los niños pequeños se toquen mutuamente con cuidado.

- Anime a que varios niños pequeños hagan sonidos de animales y se imiten entre sí mientras les muestra las imágenes de un libro.

- Pídale a un niño que ayude a otro, trayendo un pañuelito de papel, abriendo la llave del agua, abriendo la puerta, etc.

- Estimule la bondad mutua. Si un niño pequeño llora, pregúntele a otro lo que "podríamos" hacer para ayudarlo.

- Anime a dos niños pequeños a que pongan la mesa o la limpien después de comer. Mire como se imitan.

- Cante canciones, animando a los niños pequeños a que se turnen con las acciones.

- Adentro y afuera: Ponga a su disposición áreas con arena que sean suficientemente grandes para varios niños pequeños, es de esperar que se sienten justo en el medio del área.

- Las mantas sobre el piso, el suelo o una mesa son un centro para que los niños pequeños jueguen.

- Suministre vagones: Empujar o jalar a un amigo en un vagón dará como resultado chillidos de deleite.

- Suministre pelotas y juguetes para jalar que estimulen el juego interactivo.

- Lugares para saltar sin peligro estimulan los intercambios sociales.

- Suministre juguetes musicales, varios de cada clase, para que los niños puedan tocar juntos una música bella. A veces uno dirigirá y el otro le seguirá, o viceversa.

- Mantenga rutinas predecibles recordándole a los niños el orden de las etapas con preguntas tales como "Es hora de comer. ¿Qué hacemos?"

- Tenga los materiales en lugares predecibles y ordenados.

- Con preguntas tales como "¿Qué vas a hacer ahora? ¿Qué vas a comprar en la tienda? Apoye a los niños pequeños cuando piensen en sus actividades.

- Tenga los juguetes y los materiales organizados de manera que los niños pequeños puedan escogerlos, alcanzarlos y guardarlos (con recordatorios).

- Revise frecuentemente los materiales a su disposición para asegurarse de que mantiene un equilibrio entre lo que es conocido y lo que es un poco difícil.

Desarrollo		Ejemplo
18 a 24 meses (niños pequeños)		
El Lenguaje	• Los niños pequeños pueden ir a buscar juguetes conocidos en otra habitación de la casa cuando un adulto se los pide, y pueden seguir instrucciones tales como "cierra la puerta." • Los niños pequeños combinan palabras para nombrar cosas ("ese gato"), para negar ("no muerde") y para rechazar ("no más"). • Los niños pequeños combinan dos o tres palabras con significado. • Los niños pequeños se valen del lenguaje para varios propósitos, tales como preguntar "¿Qué eso?" • Los niños pequeños señalan una cantidad de imágenes cada vez mayor en los libros cuando un adulto les habla sobre la imagen.	"Hola Kitty," "puerta abierta" y "sombrero puesto" fueron sólo algunas de las combinaciones de dos palabras que Cheral dijo a los 20 meses de edad. Tyra corrió rápidamente hasta el librero, tomó un libro con tapa brillante y regresó de prisa hasta su maestra. Después de sentarse cómodamente en su regazo, abrió el libro y comenzó a señalar con entusiasmo las imágenes mientras su maestra las nombraba.
El desarrollo musculoso	• Los niños pequeños señalan objetos con el dedo para comunicarse. • Los niños pequeños hacen marcas en un papel. • Los niños pequeños trabajan y dan forma a la plastilina. • Los niños pequeños corren. • Los niños pequeños se sientan y se levantan solos de sillas pequeñas. • Los niños pequeños están desarrollando su confianza espacial; explorando su cuerpo en el espacio.	Mindy estiró la plastilina con las manos y luego hizo figuras con las herramientas. Joseph se sentó a la mesa para comer, luego llevó los platos sucios al fregadero.
24 a 36 meses (niños pequeños)		
Los sentimientos/ Las ataduras	• Los niños pequeños a veces pueden ser independientes, pero les gusta saber que la maestra está cerca. • A los niños pequeños les gusta mirar fotos de sí mismos, sus amigos y su familia. • Los niños pequeños oyen sus palabras y el tono de su voz cuando usted habla acerca de ellos. Quieren que usted se interese en ellos y se enorgullezca de sus logros. • Los niños pequeños necesitan límites claros y consistentes. Olvidarán o pondrán a prueba las reglas, pero se sentirán a gusto cuando usted les recuerda las reglas y les ayuda a obedecerlas. • Los niños pequeños pueden utilizar palabras para expresar sus sentimientos, o pueden dar golpes o morder. • Los niños pequeños se ocupan de los sentimientos de los demás, y consuelan a quien esté triste o le llevan una curita a quien se haya lastimado.	Kiki llevó su bebé a ver las fotos de su propia familia en la pared, y la arrullaba mientras miraba la cara de su propia madre.

Interacciones entre Maestro o Padre/Madre–Niño	Ambiente

18 a 24 meses (niños pequeños)

- Léale libros con cuentos más largos, haga pausas a medida que avanza por el libro para animar a los niños pequeños a hablar sobre las imágenes y la historia. Haga preguntas abiertas tales como "¿Cómo se siente el oso?"
- Pregúntese a menudo con el niño: "Me pregunto qué va a pasar con el oso."
- Haga que los niños pequeños conversen intentando mantenerse en el mismo tema que el niño.
- Introduzca nuevas conversaciones sobre objetos y eventos.

- Disponga una pista de obstáculos complicada y use palabras tales como "adentro," "afuera," "por arriba," "a través," "alrededor," "arriba" y "abajo" mientras el niño pequeño recorre la pista.
- Suministre libros nuevos todas las semanas, pero mantenga cerca los libros preferidos de los niños.
- Suministre una mayor variedad de materiales de arte.
- Déle materiales que estimulen los sentidos.

- Ponga a disposición de los niños materiales pequeños que los induzcan a poner en práctica su creciente capacidad de manipulación de objetos con los dedos.
- Quédese con los niños pequeños y apóyelos mientras intentan poner en práctica capacidades recientemente desarrolladas.
- Deles oportunidades de trepar, caminar y correr.

- Materiales de arte tales como brochas gordas, marcadores y superficies grandes para pintar.
- Articulos pequeños, tales como cuentas que se interconectan y tableros para clavijas, para practicar actividades de manipulación.
- Mucho espacio para el movimiento: bailes, juguetes para montar, estructuras para trepar, toboganes.

24 a 36 meses (niños pequeños)

- Establezca reglas claras y consistentes. Esté preparada para recordar a los niños pequeños con frecuencia, la manera de obedecer las reglas: "No se muerde; morder duele."
- Dedique a los niños pequeños suficiente tiempo y atención para que se sientan comprendidos.
- Haga eco al entusiasmo que los niños pequeños pueden darle a su propio juego.
- Note y comente las interacciones que los niños pequeños están mirando y en las que están pensando.

- Tenga muchas fotografías de niños con sus familias en las paredes, en libros pequeños, y laminadas para que las lleven consigo.
- Disponga espacios protegidos para el juego tranquilo.
- Mantenga rutinas y disposiciones de salón previsibles.
- Tenga libros con cuentos simples sobre ir y venir, familias y amistad.
- Canten canciones sobre sentimientos tales como "Cuando estás contento y lo sabes" y "Cuando estás triste y enojado..."

Desarrollo	Ejemplo
24 a 36 meses (niños pequeños)	

El aprender entre los pares

- La amistad de los niños pequeños es "búsqueda de proximidad," deseo de estar cerca y mostrar cariño como sonreír, reírse y abrazarse. Los amigos se prefieren mutuamente como compañeros de interacción. Las amistades continúan desarrollándose y se profundizan.
- Los niños pequeños intercambian información y pueden imitar las acciones pasadas de los demás.
- Los niños pequeños pueden congregarse y amontonarse. Cuando una maestra comienza a hacer una actividad interesante con un niño, por lo general los otros llegan corriendo de todas partes del salón.
- Algunos niños pequeños son capaces de idear maneras diferentes de ayudar a otros cuando se han lastimado o están tristes. Algunos pueden tener un impresionante repertorio de comportamientos altruistas, y si algo no funciona, intentan hacer otra cosa.
- Los compañeros colaboran hacia metas comunes, haciendo uno de líder y otro de seguidor.
- Pueden producirse peleas por objetos, espacio personal y palabras. Los niños pequeños también se dedican a intercambios juguetones, tal como empujar y caerse bruscamente, correr y perseguirse, y realizar juegos verbales.
- Algunos niños pueden ganarse cierta reputación entre sus compañeros por comportamiento agresivo o bondadoso.
- Los niños se vuelven más positivos y menos negativos en su juego social entre los 24 y los 36 meses de edad.
- Puede haber dominación de un niño sobre otro.

María y Sally jugaron durante 30 minutos en extremos opuestos de la pequeña estantería de juguetes, mirándose mutuamente cada varios minutos y diciéndose "barco," "mi barco," "hola," "quiero jugo," "mírame" y llamándose por su nombre una y otra vez.

Cuando pasó un camión de bomberos afuera, varios niños pequeños se acercaron corriendo para mirar por la ventana.

José y Miguel empujaron, jalaron, rodaron y resoplaron haciendo rodar una gran calabaza desde dentro hasta el patio de juegos, donde los niños pequeños y sus maestras iban a abrirla y sacarle las semillas.

La Cognición

- Los niños pequeños de más edad comienzan a entender conceptos tales como el color, el tamaño, la forma, el tiempo y el peso.
- Los niños pequeños de más edad se interesan en las historias y en las imágenes de libros de cuentos.
- Los niños pequeños mayores crean nuevos cuentos en el juego imaginario o nuevas estructuras en la construcción de bloques y se vuelven más imaginativos y creativos.
- Asigne papeles a los juguetes y a otros niños en el juego imaginario; utilice sillas, mantas y estanterías como sustitutos en el juego imaginario.

Eric se siente un poco triste y lleva una foto de su mamá diciendo, "después de siesta."

Sara se encarga de la esquina de juego dramático entregando muñecas y animales de peluche. Se pone un sombrero y dice "la mamá va a comprar."

Interacciones entre Maestro o Padre/Madre–Niño	Ambiente

24 a 36 meses (niños pequeños)

- Organice situaciones en que dos niños pequeños deban trabajar juntos—como por ejemplo, hacer rodar una calabaza de un lugar a otro, o traer de afuera un balde con bloques "pesados."

- Póngale una curita a una muñeca en el brazo o en la pierna y anime a los niños pequeños a que cuiden al bebé.

- Pregunte a los niños pequeños "¿cómo podemos ayudar a José? Está triste, está llorando."

- Intente cambiar la imagen de la niña que se está ganando una reputación de agresividad. Téngala cerca, muéstrele cómo tocar con cuidado y comente su comportamiento servicial. Déle un juguete interesante que pueda inducir a otros niños a jugar con ella. Manténgase cerca y enséñele a jugar.

- Coloque sombreros y ropa que sea fácil de poner, en un rincón acogedor y con un espejo grande.

- Los niños pequeños disfrutarán de una mutua compañía cuando los amigos cambian de aspecto poniéndose un sombrero de ala ancha o unos zapatos grandes.

- Los espacios que quedan encima o debajo de un ático bajo estimulan la interacción entre los niños pequeños.

- Suministre varios tipos de muñecas, así como cubiertos de mesa no peligrosos, mantas y camas pequeñas. Siéntese cerca y mire como los niños pequeños juegan a cuidar a sus bebés.

- Suministre materiales sin propósito específico, como bloques, y actividades que requieran cooperación, tales como pintar con agua un muro exterior utilizando una brocha gorda, o llenar de agua un balde grande con envases pequeños.

- Un equipo de motor grande, como los trepadores o los barcos de balancín, animan a los niños pequeños a colaborar para alcanzar una meta común: todos se van a la parte de arriba del trepador, o balancean el barco con todos dentro.

- Pregúntele a los niños cómo podrían resolver problemas que se presentan y luego deje que los resuelvan solos.

- Apoye a los niños que trabajan juntos con materiales para que compartan ideas.

- Hable con un lenguaje que describa el tiempo ("ahora," "más tarde," "antes de la siesta," "después de almuerzo"), peso ("pesado," "ligero"), tamaño ("grande," "pequeño").

- Cuente cosas durante el día.

- Facilite oportunidades de juego que promuevan la comparación de tamaños, pesos, colores, formas y cantidades.

- Ponga por todas partes libros para los niños. Tenga varias copias de libros favoritos antiguos, y traiga libros nuevos.

- Permita que los niños combinen materiales de diferentes áreas de maneras creativas.

- Presente nuevos materiales o nuevas combinaciones de materiales.

Desarrollo		Ejemplo
24 a 36 meses (niños pequeños)		

	Desarrollo	Ejemplo
El Lenguaje	• Los niños pequeños comprenden instrucciones complejas y recuerdan palabras de canciones cortas y juegos de dedos. • Los niños pequeños se valen de muchas oraciones de dos a cuatro palabras. • Los niños pequeños pueden señalar con el dedo y nombrar muchas partes del cuerpo. • Los niños pequeños añaden "ando o iendo" a las palabras. • Los niños pequeños comienzan a usar preposiciones tales como "sobre" y "dentro." • Los niños pequeños añaden una "s" a las palabras para indicar plurales. • Los niños pequeños podrían empezar a preguntar "¿Por qué?" • Los niños pequeños comienzan a contar historias sobre lo que hicieron o lo que vieron. • Hacia el final de este período, el niño pequeño puede usar las imágenes para contar lo que ocurre en un cuento.	Mindy comenzó a añadir "ando o iendo" a las palabras que había estado diciendo durante meses. Dijo "Yo corriendo" y "Yo comiendo" en vez de "Yo corro" y "Yo como." "Mira, está jugando," exclamó Treat mientras señalaba con el dedo una imagen en su libro preferido.
El desarrollo musculoso	• Los niños pequeños ensartan cuentas, usan las tijeras, pintan con los dedos o con pinceles, arman rompecabezas sencillos. • Los niños pequeños lanzan y patean una pelota. • Los niños pequeños se paran en un solo pie. • Los niños pequeños se paran y caminan en puntillas. • Los niños pequeños suben escaleras poniendo un pie en cada escalón. • Los niños pequeños trepan, se deslizan y saltan. • Los niños pequeños comen con cuchara y tenedor. • Los niños pequeños se pueden vestir solos. • Los niños pequeños pueden verter leche de una jarra pequeña.	Robert ni siquiera tiene que pensar en su cuerpo cuando corre para saludar a su papá al final del día. Peggy y Misha inventan un juego imitándose mutuamente los pasos en puntillas, posturas y gestos. Forcejeando un poco, Lawrence y Evelyn juegan con la ropa para disfrazarse.

Interacciones entre Maestro o Padre/Madre–Niño	Ambiente

24 a 36 meses (niños pequeños)

- Responda sus preguntas de "por qué" con paciencia y entusiasmo. Así es como los niños aprenden y desarrollan interacciones sociales.
- Escuche con sus ojos las "historias" que los niños pequeños cuentan.
- Modele decir palabras plurales, tales como "perros," "elefantes," etc.
- Use palabras descriptivas tales como "queso mozarella" en vez de sólo "queso" o "urraca de América" en vez de sólo "pájaro."
- Tenga conversaciones largas con los niños pequeños, siguiendo lo que dicen.
- Lea libros a grupos informales pequeños o a niños por separado.

- Déle imágenes para que los niños las hagan corresponder.
- Los rompecabezas de animales, personas, vehículos y alimentos son importantes.
- Se pueden agregar al ambiente libros con muchas imágenes y cuentos cortos.
- Los materiales para el juego dramático estimulan la conversación.

- Esté consciente del equilibrio necesario entre el tiempo dedicado a actividades enérgicas y a actividades tranquilas.
- Esté atento al aumento de precisión de las capacidades motrices ligeras, pues pueden comenzar a manifestarse sutiles problemas.
- Esté a disposición de los niños pequeños animándolos y teniéndoles paciencia conforme comen, se visten y van al baño solos con más frecuencia.

- Ponga a su disposición una variedad de materiales para practicar capacidades motrices ligeras: rompecabezas simples, cajas de formas, cuentas para hacer collares, bloques de mesa, arcilla, materiales de arte.
- Espacio, oportunidad y estructuras para fomentar el movimiento: períodos de tiempo al aire libre, carreras de obstáculos, bailes y juguetes para montar.

Appendix C

Developmental Trends and Responsive Interactions—Spanish

Tendencias de Desarrollo e Interacciones Receptivas (Capítulo 6)

Tanto los bebés como los niños pequeños desarrollan un sólido sentido de identidad a través del aumento de la autor-regulación, el aprendizaje de la expresión emocional efectiva y el desarrollo de relaciones de cariño.

Desarrollo	Ejemplo
0 a 4 meses (bebé)	
· Los bebés absorben una gran cantidad de información acerca del mundo. · Los bebés pueden sentirse abrumados y comenzar a bostezar, mirar hacia otro lado o molestarse. · Los bebés comienzan a calmarse chupándose las manos o escuchando a un adulto que les hable suavemente. · Los bebés miran fijamente a los ojos de su maestra mientras les da de comer. · Los bebés voltean la cabeza hacia voces conocidas. · Los bebés se calman y se consuelan con personas conocidas. · Los bebés lloran cuando tienen hambre o están cansados o incómodos	Carlos seguía a Karen con los ojos por donde quiera que fuera por el salón. Cuando ella se le acercó, la miró como si quisiera que ella se quedara con él. Karen aceptó la invitación a jugar y se sentó con él en el piso. En cuanto comenzó a cansarse y a ponerse molesto, Karen lo envolvió en una manta, lo abrazó estrechamente y le habló con voz suave.
4 a 8 meses (bebé)	
· A los bebés les gusta mirarse las manos y los pies. · Los bebés agitan los brazos y patalean emocionados cuando ven a una persona conocida. · Los bebés le sonríen a la maestra esperando que ella les sonría también. · Con la cara y el cuerpo, los bebés expresan muchos sentimientos: desde fruncir el ceño y llorar hasta reírse a carcajadas. · Los bebés expresan sus sentimientos claramente ante personas conocidas, y son más reservados con los desconocidos.	A Deborah le encanta que la maestra la lleve en brazos mientras va por el salón "hablándole" de lo que ven. Tiene los ojos bien abiertos y brillantes, sonríe y hace ruiditos de arrullo cuando le corresponde hablar en la conversación. Cuando un visitante entra en el salón, Deborah se queda muy callada y seria, y se sujeta firmemente al hombro de la maestra mirando al visitante.
8 a 12 meses (bebé móvil)	
· Los bebés móviles pueden tenerle miedo a los desconocidos. · Los bebés móviles pueden llamar a los adultos conocidos para que los ayuden cuando están enojados. · Los bebés móviles miran al adulto conocido para determinar si una situación es peligrosa o no. · Los bebés móviles se aferran al adulto cuando están en una situación desconocida. · A los bebés móviles les parecen divertidos los juegos tontos y las expresiones faciales exageradas que ponen los adultos.	Jaime está disfrutando de su nueva habilidad, que es ir gateando rápidamente a donde quiera ir. Le encanta el pequeño trepador que le permite mirar por la ventana. Pero cuando siente que la rampa es un poco inestable, se vuelve a mirar a Federico, su maestro, para asegurarse de que no hay peligro.

Interacciones entre Maestro o Padre/Madre–Niño	Ambiente

0 a 4 meses (bebé)

- Mantenga a los bebés pequeños cerca, en brazos, en un saco de bebé, o sobre una manta.
- Reconozca las señales de por qué el bebé quiere estar con usted—mirada fija, tenderle los brazos, mirada feliz—y respóndale hablándole suavemente, alternando la comunicación verbal y no verbal.
- Reconozca las señales que indican que el bebé necesita un descanso—bostezar, babear, mirar hacia otro lado—y apártese en silencio esperando a que el bebé se recupere.
- Consuele a los bebés cuando lloren.

- Estar cerca de una maestra conocida es lo mejor.
- Un espacio sereno y tranquilo con luces bajas, limita la información que el bebé necesita absorber.
- Evite tener música de fondo todo el día.
- Limite el número de objetos, sonidos, colores y movimientos alrededor de un bebé pequeño.
- La maestra es lo más interesante que el bebé tiene para mirar, pero para otros bebés, los espejos y juguetes que se encuentran en su campo visual, también son interesantes.

4 a 8 meses (bebé)

- Déles a los bebés oportunidades para que se miren al espejo mientras juegan.
- Refleje las expresiones emocionales del bebé y agregue palabras apropiadas: "Estoy tan contenta de verte hoy."
- Responda a los bebés de una manera que les ayude a calmarse y mantenerse activos. Si el bebé llora, cálmelo.

- Monte espejos irrompibles en las paredes.
- Deje que los bebés pasen un rato en el piso mientras están boca arriba, jugando con sus pies y moviéndose por el piso.
- Los libros y los álbumes de fotografías con caras reales mostrando diferentes expresiones emocionales son muy interesantes para los bebés.

8 a 12 meses (bebé móvil)

- Anime a los bebés móviles a moverse y explorar asegurándoles que usted los está mirando y cuidando.
- Entienda que los bebés móviles pueden asustarse ante situaciones nuevas que quizás no los habrían asustado hace unos meses. Consuélelos y tranquilícelos.

- Juegue al te veo, no te veo.
- Léales cuentos sobre madres y padres que se van y vuelven.
- Léales libros con solapas que se pueden levantar para encontrar cosas.
- Mantenga una previsibilidad de hábitos y rutinas del salón.

Desarrollo	Ejemplo

12 a 18 meses (bebé móvil)

- Los bebés móviles imitan las acciones de los adultos conocidos, tales como hablar por teléfono o llevar en brazos a una muñeca bebé.
- Los bebés móviles intentan atraer la atención del adulto jalándole la pierna o tomándole la mano.
- Los bebés móviles se calman con su manta o su animal de peluche favorito.
- Los bebés móviles protestan ruidosamente cuando sus padres los dejan.
- Los bebés móviles se relajan y se consuelan acurrucándose con un adulto conocido.
- Los bebés móviles hacen saber claramente lo que les gusta y lo que no les gusta.

Amelia carga toda la mañana su osito de peluche por todos los lados. A veces copia las acciones de Sofía, su maestra, dándole al osito palmaditas en la espalda o alimentándole con biberón. Cuando se cansa, se frota el osito contra la oreja y se chupa el pulgar.

18 a 24 meses (niños pequeños)

- Los niños pequeños comienzan a controlar ciertos impulsos diciendo "no, no, no" a medida que comienzan a lanzar bloques.
- Los niños pequeños pueden dejar lo que están haciendo cuando la maestra se lo dice.
- Los niños pequeños pueden no querer dejar de jugar cuando su padre o su madre viene a buscarlos.
- Los niños pequeños pueden llorar cuando no consiguen hacer algo que están intentando.
- Los niños pequeños saben su propio nombre y puede que usen el "mi" y "mío."

Francisco se sube a la mesa mientras mira directamente a los ojos de la maestra que desaprueba lo que él hace, y dice "no, no, no."

24 a 36 meses (niños pequeños)

- Los niños pequeños a veces pueden ser independientes, pero les gusta saber que la maestra está cerca.
- A los niños pequeños les gusta mirar fotos de sí mismos, sus amigos y su familia.
- Los niños pequeños oyen sus palabras y el tono de su voz cuando usted habla acerca de ellos. Quieren que usted se interese en ellos y se enorgullezca de sus logros.
- Los niños pequeños necesitan límites claros y consistentes. Olvidarán o pondrán a prueba las reglas, pero se sentirán a gusto cuando usted les recuerda las reglas y les ayuda a obedecerlas.
- Los niños pequeños pueden utilizar palabras para expresar sus sentimientos, o pueden dar golpes o morder.
- Los niños pequeños se ocupan de los sentimientos de los demás, y consuelan a quien esté triste o le llevan una curita a quien se haya lastimado.

Kiki llevó su bebé a ver las fotos de su propia familia en la pared, y la arrullaba mientras miraba la cara de su propia madre.

Interacciones entre Maestro o Padre/Madre–Niño	Ambiente

12 a 18 meses (bebé móvil)

- Muestre interés en las actividades del bebé.
- Muestre su orgullo por los logros del bebé.
- Deje que los bebés la utilicen como una base firme, para explorar el mundo.
- Deje que los bebés sepan que usted entiende lo que sienten y responda respetuosamente.
- Estos niños son todavía muy pequeños, y necesitan que se les acurruque y abrace mucho.

- Disponga de objetos de mayores en tamaño infantil: teléfonos, platos, llaves, etc.
- Ponga fotografías de bebés con su familia en la pared.
- Lamine las fotos del bebé con su familia para que las lleve consigo.
- Haga álbumes de fotos de los niños del programa y hable acerca de las fotos.
- Disponga de sillas de adulto y espacios tranquilos y cómodos para tener a los niños en brazos.

18 a 24 meses (niños pequeños)

- Mantenga su sentido del humor. Entienda que los niños pequeños pueden dejar de hacer ciertas cosas a veces, pero no siempre.
- Respete los sentimientos fuertes de los niños pequeños. El turnarse y compartir viene después; ahora "mí" y "mío" son una etapa importante del desarrollo de un sólido sentido de identidad.

- Disponga espacios que permita que los niños exploren, pero siempre sin perderlos de vista.
- Tenga suficientes juguetes iguales para que varios niños puedan tener el suyo, sin tener que compartir o turnarse.
- Deje que los niños traigan al programa artículos que los calmen, tales como mantas o animales de peluche. Asígneles un lugar tranquilo donde puedan consolarse solos.

24 a 36 meses (niños pequeños)

- Establezca reglas claras y consistentes. Esté preparada para recordar a los niños pequeños con frecuencia, la manera de obedecer las reglas: "No se muerde; morder duele."
- Dedique a los niños pequeños suficiente tiempo y atención para que se sientan comprendidos.
- Haga eco al entusiasmo que los niños pequeños pueden darle a su propio juego.
- Note y comente las interacciones que los niños pequeños están mirando y en las que están pensando.

- Tenga muchas fotografías de niños con sus familias en las paredes, en libros pequeños, y laminadas para que las lleven consigo.
- Disponga espacios protegidos para el juego tranquilo.
- Mantenga rutinas y disposiciones de salón previsibles.
- Tenga libros con cuentos simples sobre ir y venir, familias y amistad.
- Canten canciones sobre sentimientos tales como "Cuando estás contento y lo sabes" y "Cuando estás triste y enojado..."

Tendencias de Desarrollo e Interacciones Receptivas (Capítulo 7)

Habilidades: Comunicarse con sus compañeros, ser socialmente activo, jugar con sus compañeros, y controlar emociones negativas y conflictos durante interacciones con los compañeros.

Desarrollo	Ejemplo
0 a 4 meses (bebé)	
• A los bebés les gusta mirarse mutuamente (mirada visual). • Los bebés prefieren mirar caras, especialmente los bordes y los ojos. • Puede que los bebés lloren cuando oyen llorar a otros bebés (contagio).	Después de que la profesora puso a Tamika y a Sam sobre una manta en el piso, Tamika se quedó mirando fijamente a Sam.
4 a 8 meses (bebé)	
• Los bebés tocan a otros bebés, se dirigen vocalizaciones, se entusiasman, se acercan a otros bebés, sonríen y se ríen unos de otros. • Los bebés pueden tratar a otros bebés como si fueran objetos—pasándoles por encima al gatear, lamiéndolos, chupándolos, sentándose encima. Están simplemente aprendiendo la diferencia entre personas y objetos. Los bebés pueden pinchar con el dedo, empujar, dar palmaditas a otros bebés, para ver lo que el otro bebé va a hacer. A menudo se sorprenden con la reacción que logran.	Amna le pasó por encima gateando a Nadia que estaba acostada en el piso. Tocándole el pelo a Nadia, Amna se rió a carcajadas.
8 a 12 meses (bebé móvil)	
• Los bebés pueden mostrar a otros bebés un objeto, sentarse juntos, perseguirse gateando y jugar a perseguir y recoger objetos. • Los bebés se sonríen y se ríen entre sí. • Los bebés se dirigen sonidos—y es posible que sus primeras palabras se las digan entre sí. • Uno de los juegos preferidos de los bebés es el *te veo, no te veo* mientras exploran la separación: irse y volver, aparecer y desaparecer. • Los bebés pueden aprender a tocarse uno al otro con cuidado. • Como a esta edad los bebés actúan en gran medida en función de sus objetivos, pueden apartar la mano de un bebé que esté tocando un juguete, o gatearle por encima para alcanzar un juguete.	Shamaine miró la estantería baja de juguetes y vio que Carla venía gateando hacia ella. Shamaine se dio la vuelta rápidamente y se alejó gateando con Carla siguiéndola de cerca. Kai pasó gateando por encima de las piernas de Bridger para alcanzar un juguete que estaba al otro lado de Bridger.

Interacción entre Maestra-Niño, o Padre/Madre–Niño	Ambiente

0 a 4 meses (bebé)

- Sostenga a dos bebés para que puedan mirarse mutuamente.
- Ponga varios bebés sobre una manta en el piso para que puedan mirarse y tocarse entre sí.

- Los brazos de la maestras ofrecen el mejor ambiente.
- Ponga a dos bebés sobre unas mantas en el piso—uno junto a otro, de manera que los dos se estén tocando con los dedos de los pies.

4 a 8 meses (bebé)

- Muévase al ritmo de la música con un bebé en cada brazo.
- Con un bebé sobre el regazo, apunte y hable sobre lo que el otro bebé está haciendo.
- Ponga a dos bebés boca bajo frente a un espejo.
- En vez de decirles "No" y "Deja de hacer eso" a los bebés que están explorando, dígales, "Tócalo con cuidado." Dígales a los niños lo que usted quiere que hagan . . . muéstreselo.

- Cuelgue un espejo seguro en la pared de manera horizontal, para que la parte de abajo esté tocando el piso.
- Cubra la cámara de aire de la rueda de un auto con un paño suave. Siente a dos bebés en la cámara para que se toquen con los pies.

8 a 12 meses (bebé móvil)

- Nombre partes del cuerpo del bebé mientras dos bebés están sentados juntos:

  Estos son los ojos del bebé

  Esta es la nariz del bebé

  Toca la parte con que ves

  Tócate la parte que te suenas

- Ponga un bebé con otro (en parejas) porque las interacciones más frecuentes, complejas e intensas entre niños se producen cuando un niño está con varios compañeros.
- Comprenda que los bebés no son "malos" cuando le apartan la mano al otro. Diga "Jenny tenía ese juguete. Vamos a buscarte otro."

- Mientras están comiendo, coloque las sillas altas de manera que los niños se puedan ver unos a los otros.
- Disponga de rincones agradables en el salón donde los bebés puedan "desaparecer" (pero pudiendo aún ser vistos por adultos).
- Cuelgue del techo un paño largo y ancho (para que los bebés no se enreden en él). A los bebés les encanta gatear alrededor.
- Ponga contenedores con bloques de diferentes tamaños entre dos bebés. Quédese sentada junto a ellos mientras comienzan a explorar los materiales. Hable acerca de lo que está haciendo cada uno.

Desarrollo	Ejemplo

12 a 18 meses (bebé móvil)

- Comienzan los turnos imitativos (motores) e interactivos. Los niños pequeños pueden imitarse unos a otros—si un bebé le da un juguete a otro, el otro puede imitarlo.
- Los bebés móviles comienzan a hablarse unos a otros.
- Los bebés pueden demostrar preocupación cuando otros bebés están afligidos.
- Los bebés móviles pueden quitarle el juguete a otro bebé, decirle "no," empujarlo, agarrar firmemente el juguete y decir "mío."
- A esta edad, los bebés son pequeños científicos que experimentan para ver cómo funcionan las cosas. Esto afecta la relación que tienen con sus compañeros, pues están constantemente haciéndoles cosas para ver cómo reaccionan.
- Morder puede aparecer cuando los bebés muerden a otros "para ver lo que pasa," para obtener el juguete que quieren, para expresar su frustración. Los bebés están al borde de comunicarse bien; pueden comunicarse por la boca en forma de mordedura.

Rashida golpeó la mesa con la cuchara; poco después, otros dos comenzaron a hacerlo. Parecían estar siguiendo el ejemplo físicamente (como si estuvieran conversando).

Primero, Carmen intentó alejar a Toby del caballito de balancín.

Cuando eso no dio resultado, se inclinó hacia él y lo mordió en el brazo.

18 a 24 mese s (niños pequeños)

- Las amistades pueden desarrollarse a muy temprana edad. Los amigos son más propensos a tocarse, apoyarse y sonreírse entre sí, que otros niños que no son amigos.
- Los niños pequeños imitan mutuamente los sonidos y las palabras que dicen y se hablan y comienzan a comunicarse con los demás a mayores distancias.
- Los niños pequeños dan u ofrecen un juguete o comida a otros niños pequeños.
- Los niños pequeños pueden llamar a un adulto y jalar al adulto para que ayude a otro niño, o pueden ayudar a otro niño llevándole un pañuelito de papel, por ejemplo.
- Los niños pequeños demuestran bondad hacia otros bebés que se sienten afligidos. Sin embargo, el bebé o niño pequeño móvil puede suponer que lo que lo consuela a él, también consuela al afligido.
- Los niños pueden turnarse, por ejemplo, con una pelota o para saltar. Pueden tener conversaciones cinéticas de niño pequeño mientras siguen a un líder por el salón—entrando y saliendo del grupo, turnándose para ser líder y seguidor—como si estuvieran en una conversación, en la cual escuchan y hablan, aprendiendo la importante habilidad de cómo turnarse.
- Empujar, dar empujones, agarrar y golpear pueden ocurrir a medida que los niños luchan con la idea de "mío durante todo el tiempo que yo quiera" y "tuyo, pero yo también lo quiero." Los niños pequeños puede que se peleen más por juguetes pequeños, que por objetos grandes que no se mueven.

Paulie parecía estar esperando en la puerta a que apareciera Jamie al principio de la jornada. Cuando Jaime y su mamá llegaron, Paulie se dirigió hacia ellos y le tomó la mano a Jaime con una gran sonrisa en la cara.

Tania saltó (medio se cayó) de una tabla situada a varias pulgadas del suelo. Pronto tres niños pequeños estaban parados sobre la tabla, y casi saltando, casi bajando de la tabla y disfrutando inmensamente de la actividad.

Interacción entre Maestra-Niño, o Padre/Madre–Niño	Ambiente

12 a 18 meses (bebé móvil)

- Muéstreles a los niños pequeños móviles cómo rodar juntos por una pequeña pendiente.
- Ayude a los niños pequeños móviles a que aprendan los nombres de los demás, cantando canciones de saludo y despedida incluyendo los nombres de los niños: "Esta es Tania, ¿cómo estás?" y "Este es Enrique, ¿cómo estás?" y apuntando o tocando a cada niño que pasa junto a usted o al que está sentado en su regazo.
- Comente el comportamiento social activo. Diga "Le diste la muñeca. Eso le gusta." Puede que los bebés no entiendan sus palabras, pero son capaces de darse cuenta por el tono de voz que usted está contenta con ellos.
- A los bebés les gusta mirar libros juntos, creando grupos informales (esto significa que entrar y salir del grupo) alrededor de las piernas, el regazo y los brazos del padre, la madre o la maestra que más les gusta.

- Suministre una caja de cartón grande abierta por los dos lados. Anímelos a entrar y salir de la caja gateando juntos. Ventanas a los lados de la caja estimulan a los bebés para que se miren entre ellos por la ventana.
- Muñecas, camiones, autos y otros materiales de juego, promueven las interacciones entre compañeros.
- A los bebés les encanta la arena y el agua y jugar con botellas y pelotas seguras de diferentes tamaños. Cuando cada uno tiene su propio contenedor o cubo con agua o arena, el juego se desarrolla sin altibajos.
- Al aire libre, grandes cajas de arena o juguetes para empujar, estimulan el juego interactivo.

18 a 24 meses (niños pequeños)

- Ya esté adentro o afuera, atienda a los niños pequeños cuando entran a "reponerse" emocionalmente con su maestra especial animando a varios niños pequeños a sentarse junto a usted o en su regazo. Permita que los niños pequeños se toquen mutuamente con cuidado.
- Anime a que varios niños pequeños hagan sonidos de animales y se imiten entre sí mientras les muestra las imágenes de un libro.
- Pídale a un niño que ayude a otro, trayendo un pañuelito de papel, abriendo la llave del agua, abriendo la puerta, etc.
- Estimule la bondad mutua. Si un niño pequeño llora, pregúntele a otro lo que "podríamos" hacer para ayudarlo.
- Anime a dos niños pequeños a que pongan la mesa o la limpien después de comer. Mire como se imitan.
- Cante canciones, animando a los niños pequeños a que se turnen con las acciones.

- Adentro y afuera: Ponga a su disposición áreas con arena que sean suficientemente grandes para varios niños pequeños, es de esperar que se sienten justo en el medio del área.
- Las mantas sobre el piso, el suelo o una mesa son un centro para que los niños pequeños jueguen.
- Suministre vagones: Empujar o jalar a un amigo en un vagón dará como resultado chillidos de deleite.
- Suministre pelotas y juguetes para jalar que estimulen el juego interactivo.
- Lugares para saltar sin peligro estimulan los intercambios sociales.
- Suministre juguetes musicales, varios de cada clase, para que los niños puedan tocar juntos una música bella. A veces uno dirigirá y el otro le seguirá, o viceversa.

Desarrollo	Ejemplo

24 a 36 meses (niños pequeños)

- La amistad de los niños pequeños es "búsqueda de proximidad," deseo de estar cerca y mostrar cariño como sonreír, reírse y abrazarse. Los amigos se prefieren mutuamente como compañeros de interacción. Las amistades continúan desarrollándose y se profundizan.
- Los niños pequeños intercambian información y pueden imitar las acciones pasadas de los demás.
- Los niños pequeños pueden congregarse y amontonarse. Cuando una maestra comienza a hacer una actividad interesante con un niño, por lo general los otros llegan corriendo de todas partes del salón.
- Algunos niños pequeños son capaces de idear maneras diferentes de ayudar a otros cuando se han lastimado o están tristes. Algunos pueden tener un impresionante repertorio de comportamientos altruistas, y si algo no funciona, intentan hacer otra cosa.
- Los compañeros colaboran hacia metas comunes, haciendo uno de líder y otro de seguidor.
- Pueden producirse peleas por objetos, espacio personal y palabras. Los niños pequeños también se dedican a intercambios juguetones, tal como empujar y caerse bruscamente, correr y perseguirse, y realizar juegos verbales.
- Algunos niños pueden ganarse cierta reputación entre sus compañeros por comportamiento agresivo o bondadoso.
- Los niños se vuelven más positivos y menos negativos en su juego social entre los 24 y los 36 meses de edad.
- Puede haber dominación de un niño sobre otro.

María y Sally jugaron durante 30 minutos en extremos opuestos de la pequeña estantería de juguetes, mirándose mutuamente cada varios minutos y diciéndose "barco," "mi barco," "hola," "quiero jugo," "mírame" y llamándose por su nombre una y otra vez.

Cuando pasó un camión de bomberos afuera, varios niños pequeños se acercaron corriendo para mirar por la ventana.

José y Miguel empujaron, jalaron, rodaron y resoplaron haciendo rodar una gran calabaza desde dentro hasta el patio de juegos, donde los niños pequeños y sus maestras iban a abrirla y sacarle las semillas.

Interacción entre Maestra-Niño, o Padre/Madre–Niño	Ambiente

24 a 36 meses (niños pequeños)

- Organice situaciones en que dos niños pequeños deban trabajar juntos—como por ejemplo, hacer rodar una calabaza de un lugar a otro, o traer de afuera un balde con bloques "pesados."

- Póngale una curita a una muñeca en el brazo o en la pierna y anime a los niños pequeños a que cuiden al bebé.

- Pregunte a los niños pequeños "¿cómo podemos ayudar a José? Está triste, está llorando."

- Intente cambiar la imagen de la niña que se está ganando una reputación de agresividad. Téngala cerca, muéstrele cómo tocar con cuidado y comente su comportamiento servicial. Déle un juguete interesante que pueda inducir a otros niños a jugar con ella. Manténgase cerca y enséñele a jugar.

- Coloque sombreros y ropa que sea fácil de poner, en un rincón acogedor y con un espejo grande.

- Los niños pequeños disfrutarán de una mutua compañía cuando los amigos cambian de aspecto poniéndose un sombrero de ala ancha o unos zapatos grandes.

- Los espacios que quedan encima o debajo de un ático bajo estimulan la interacción entre los niños pequeños.

- Suministre varios tipos de muñecas, así como cubiertos de mesa no peligrosos, mantas y camas pequeñas. Siéntese cerca y mire como los niños pequeños juegan a cuidar a sus bebés.

- Suministre materiales sin propósito específico, como bloques, y actividades que requieran cooperación, tales como pintar con agua un muro exterior utilizando una brocha gorda, o llenar de agua un balde grande con envases pequeños.

- Un equipo de motor grande, como los trepadores o los barcos de balancín, animan a los niños pequeños a colaborar para alcanzar una meta común: todos se van a la parte de arriba del trepador, o balancean el barco con todos dentro.

Tendencias de Desarrollo e Interacciones Receptivas (Capítulo 8)

Los bebés y los niños pequeños se conocen a sí mismos, a los demás y al mundo, a través de sus propias capacidades y atributos, utilizando instrumentos cognitivos de aprendizaje y conceptos básicos.

Desarrollo	Ejemplo
0 a 4 meses (bebé)	
• Los bebés siguen visualmente un objeto en movimiento. • Los bebés lloran para atraer la atención del adulto a fin de que los consuele o les dé de comer. • Los bebés miran a su alrededor por el salón con interés. • Los bebés comienzan a intentar alcanzar juguetes. • Los bebés notan que sus brazos y piernas han causado algo y repiten el movimiento. • Los bebés reconocen personas y objetos. • Los bebés comienzan a llevarse objetos a la boca.	Megan levantó la cabeza, apoyándose en los brazos mientras estaba recostada sobre la manta. Con una expresión seria miró a la maestra y a los niños a su alrededor. Willy comenzó a patear el móvil que colgaba encima y logró que se meneara. Luego paró, lo miró y volvió a patearlo mirándolo para ver si pasaba algo.
4 a 8 meses (bebé)	
• A los bebés les gusta examinar los juguetes. • A los bebés les gusta hacer que los juguetes hagan algo—sonar, encajarse uno dentro de otro. • Los bebés imitan las expresiones y los gestos de los adultos. • Los bebés se vuelven hacia los sonidos para ver de dónde vienen. • Los bebés buscan juguetes que han dejado caer.	Ángela se interesa en todo. Mira a sus amigos y luego mira a la maestra y sonríe. Roger se estira para tocar un juguete colgante. Cuando se balancea y suena, Roger se estira para hacerlo de nuevo.
8 a 12 meses (bebé móvil)	
• A los bebés móviles les gusta desarmar los juguetes y luego volver a armarlos. • A los bebés móviles les gustan los juguetes que hacen algo cuando se tocan, se jalan o se golpean. • Los bebés móviles comienzan juegos imaginarios muy simples, tales como llevarse un vaso a la boca. • A los bebés móviles les gusta encontrar juguetes pequeños debajo de un paño o de un vaso. • A los bebés móviles les gusta levantar y examinar objetos pequeños tales como un Cheerio. • Los bebés móviles muestran objetos con el dedo sabiendo que usted también puede verlos.	A Carlos le encanta sacar cada uno de los animales de plástico del balde y mirarlo. Cuando el balde queda vacío, lo lanza a un lado. A Aliya le gusta el botón que se aprieta y las puertas oscilantes de la caja mecánica, pero todavía no puede hacer funcionar todos los mecanismos. Su maestra expresa sorpresa a Aliya cuando las puertas se abren y, de vez en cuando, le enseña cómo funciona otra de las perillas.

Interacción entre Maestra-Niño, o Padre/Madre–Niño	Ambiente

0 a 4 meses (bebé)

- Mueva lentamente un juguete pequeño de lado a lado mientras el bebé lo sigue con la mirada.
- Responda rápidamente al llanto del niño.
- Déles tiempo a los bebés para que estén tranquilos mirando lo que pasa a su alrededor. Hable acerca de lo que ven.
- Reaccione ante las expresiones de los bebés con expresiones y lenguaje claro y hasta exagerado.

- Organice el espacio de manera que los bebés puedan ver actividad sin dejar de estar protegidos.
- Suministre unos cuantos objetos interesantes para mirar—juguetes pequeños en el piso, cuando están boca abajo; juguetes colgantes cuando los bebés están boca arriba.
- Ponga espejos irrompibles a disposición de los bebés.

4 a 8 meses (bebé)

- Lleve en brazos al bebé, mientras camina por el salón mirando cosas y hablando acerca de ellas.
- Siéntese cerca y háblele al bebé sobre los juguetes que está mirando.
- Llame al bebé por su nombre a poca distancia para asegurarle que está cerca.

- Suministre una variedad de juguetes pequeños para que los manipule y los examine.
- Suministre juguetes que suenan cuando se mueven, se encajan unos dentro de otros o se cuelgan y mueven cuando se tocan.
- Ofrezca libros de tapas de cartón.

8 a 12 meses (bebé móvil)

- Con su presencia, su interés y su entusiasmo, ayude al bebé a concentrarse en lo que le interesa para apoyarlo en su atención y exploración.
- Con sus expresiones y palabras afectivas, demuéstrele al bebé móvil que usted disfruta de sus descubrimientos.
- Con palabras, describa la actividad del niño: "Mira, encontraste un Cheerio. Lo estás recogiendo con los dedos."

- Suministre juguetes tales como vasos para apilar, anillos en poste, piezas que se interconectan y cubos llenos de objetos pequeños interesantes, tales como animales de juguete.
- Suministre réplicas tamaño infantil de platos o herramientas domésticas.
- Suministre juguetes que reaccionen—cajas mecánicas, almohadillas llenas de agua.
- Suministre materiales sensoriales, como agua y arena con una variedad de herramientas.
- Suministre libros de tapas de cartón con fotos.

Desarrollo	Ejemplo

12 a 18 meses (bebé móvil)

- A los bebés móviles les gusta poner en práctica su movilidad para explorar gateando, caminando, trepando, corriendo, etc.
- Los bebés móviles disfrutan jugando en la arena, el agua, con plastilina y varios tipos de herramientas.
- A los bebés móviles les interesan las relaciones espaciales de rompecabezas y tableros con agujeros.
- Los bebés móviles utilizan herramientas tales como llaves o teléfonos en sus juegos imaginarios.
- Los bebés móviles disfrutan al mirar libros y nombrar objetos, animales o partes del cuerpo.

Alexis y Dan están contentísimos de estar de pie. Se siguen mutuamente por todas partes, uno subiendo atrevidamente por un plano inclinado, con el otro inmediatamente detrás. A veces los dos intentan meterse debajo del tobogán.

A Meredith le encanta acurrucarse en el regazo de su maestra y mostrar con el dedo imágenes en libros mientras la maestra nombra los animales o le pide que encuentre uno en particular.

18 a 24 meses (niños pequeños)

- Los niños pequeños de corta edad disfrutan de su facilidad de movimiento y les gusta llevar cosas en las manos.
- Los niños pequeños entienden que pueden hacer que ocurran cosas.
- Los niños pequeños entienden y recuerdan los detalles de las rutinas.
- Los niños pequeños sustituyen unos objetos por otros en su juego imaginario.
- Los niños pequeños disfrutan cada vez más de los materiales problemáticos que sugieren actividades tales como construir y hacer corresponder formas.

Antes del desayuno, Chris tiende las manos para la cancioncita de gracias. Cuando un niño llega más tarde y se sienta a la mesa, Chris tiende las manos para que todos canten nuevamente.

Lynn y Matt construyen pequeñas torres de bloques y luego las chocan con camiones de juguete para derribarlas.

Fran saca de la caja bloques de una pulgada y hace una pila de bloques rojos y una pila de bloques azules.

24 a 36 meses (niños pequeños)

- Los niños pequeños de más edad comienzan a entender conceptos tales como el color, el tamaño, la forma, el tiempo y el peso.
- Los niños pequeños de más edad se interesan en las historias y en las imágenes de libros de cuentos.
- Los niños pequeños mayores crean nuevos cuentos en el juego imaginario o nuevas estructuras en la construcción de bloques y se vuelven más imaginativos y creativos.
- Asigne papeles a los juguetes y a otros niños en el juego imaginario; utilice sillas, mantas y estanterías como sustitutos en el juego imaginario.

Eric se siente un poco triste y lleva una foto de su mamá diciendo, "después de siesta."

Sara se encarga de la esquina de juego dramático entregando muñecas y animales de peluche. Se pone un sombrero y dice "la mamá va a comprar."

Interacción entre Maestra-Niño, o Padre/Madre–Niño	Ambiente

12 a 18 meses (bebé móvil)

- Déle a los bebés móviles tiempo y espacio protegido para explorar.
- Quédese cerca para expresar interés, sugerir palabras y hacer que la actividad sea más elaborada y compleja.
- Ayude a los bebés móviles a que expresen su interés en otros bebés cuidadosamente.
- Exprese entusiasmo por lo que les interesa a los bebés móviles.

- Suministre rompecabezas simples, tableros con agujeros, formas, cuentas de madera con cordones gruesos.
- Suministre trepadores pequeños, túneles y trayectos interesantes.
- Suministre juguetes que funcionen al darle cuerda, o que se enciendan y apaguen.
- Suministre artículos simples para el juego imaginario.

18 a 24 meses (niños pequeños)

- Mantenga rutinas predecibles recordándole a los niños el orden de las etapas con preguntas tales como "Es hora de comer. ¿Qué hacemos?"
- Tenga los materiales en lugares predecibles y ordenados.
- Con preguntas tales como "¿Qué vas a hacer ahora? ¿Qué vas a comprar en la tienda? apoye a los niños pequeños cuando piensen en sus actividades.

- Tenga los juguetes y los materiales organizados de manera que los niños pequeños puedan escogerlos, alcanzarlos y guardarlos (con recordatorios).
- Revise frecuentemente los materiales a su disposición para asegurarse de que mantiene un equilibrio entre lo que es conocido y lo que es un poco difícil.

24 a 36 meses (niños pequeños)

- Pregúntele a los niños cómo podrían resolver problemas que se presentan y luego deje que los resuelvan solos.
- Apoye a los niños que trabajan juntos con materiales para que compartan ideas.
- Hable con un lenguaje que describa el tiempo ("ahora," "más tarde," "antes de la siesta," "después de almuerzo"), peso ("pesado," "ligero"), tamaño ("grande," "pequeño").
- Cuente cosas durante el día.

- Facilite oportunidades de juego que promuevan la comparación de tamaños, pesos, colores, formas y cantidades.
- Ponga por todas partes libros para los niños. Tenga varias copias de libros favoritos antiguos, y traiga libros nuevos.
- Permita que los niños combinen materiales de diferentes áreas de maneras creativas.
- Presente nuevos materiales o nuevas combinaciones de materiales.

Tendencias de Desarrollo e Interacciones Receptivas (Capítulo 9)

Los bebés y los niños pequeños desarrollan la capacidad de entender, expresar y decir palabras.

Desarrollo	Ejemplo
0 a 4 meses (bebé)	

Desarrollo	Ejemplo
• Los bebés se pueden asustar si oyen un ruido fuerte. • Los bebés captan las diferencias entre los sonidos. • Los bebés pueden dejar de llorar cuando oyen la voz de un adulto conocido. • Los bebés prefieren oír hablar cuando se les habla a ellos de forma directa. • Los bebés escuchan cuando un adulto les habla o les canta mientras los mira. • Los bebés lloran cuando sienten dolor, tienen hambre o están afligidos. • A los 2 meses de edad, los bebés tienen llantos específicos de hambre y dolor. • Los bebés "arrullan" (producen sonidos vocálicos suaves). • Hacia el final de este período, los bebés sonríen y se ríen. • Los bebés miran fijamente imágenes interesantes en libros.	Brenda sostenía a Jordán de manera que pudieran mirarse a los ojos. Jordán arrulló suavemente y Brenda le arrulló también. Luego, ella esperó a que Jordán lo volviera a hacer. Érica le sonrió de oreja a oreja a su padre cuando él la levantó de la cuna.

| **4 a 8 meses (bebé)** | |

Desarrollo	Ejemplo
• Los bebés giran la cabeza hacia un ruido, o una persona que dice su nombre. • A los bebés les gusta que los adultos hablen, canten y se rían con ellos. • Los bebés vocalizan con la intención de obtener una respuesta del adulto. • Los bebés dan chillidos agudos. • Los bebés practican sus sonidos cuando exploran y cuando están con adultos conocidos. • Los bebés comienzan a balbucear; al principio una consonante y luego combinaciones de dos consonantes. • Los bebés participan en conversaciones turnándose con los adultos. • Los bebés miran distintas imágenes de un libro y se emocionan cuando ven una que les gusta o cuando les gusta el tono entusiasta del adulto que lee.	Mientras sostenía a Donovan en su regazo, Daniela, la maestra del bebé, señalaba con el dedo las imágenes del libro de tapas de cartón. "Mira," dijo señalando la imagen, "una pelota." Luego dijo "Ahí está tu pelota" y señaló hacia una pelota en el piso. Donovan miró la imagen, luego la pelota en el piso y finalmente volvió a mirar la imagen. "Tt" dijo Afi cuando estaba en brazos de su maestra mirándola. "Tada" le dijo la maestra. "Tt" repitió Afi cuando le tocó hablar en la conversación.

Interacción entre Maestra-Niño, o Padre/Madre–Niño	Ambiente

0 a 4 meses (bebé)

- Use lenguaje dirigido al bebé.
- Tenga a los bebés en brazos y hábleles suavemente. Mírelos largamente a los ojos mientras baila conversando. Respete al bebé si necesita un descanso y aparta la cabeza.
- Lea libros con frases rítmicas y con una sola imagen en una página, con 2 imágenes a los de 4 meses de edad.
- Interprete los eructos, llantos, bostezos, estiramientos y sonidos de los bebés como formas de comunicación. Diga "Ah, me estás diciendo que tienes sueño."
- Cante canciones de cuna y otras canciones.
- Sea un compañero de lenguaje que se identifique y comente los sentimientos del bebé.
- Diga palabras y produzca sonidos para consolar a los bebés.

- El mejor ambiente son los brazos de un adulto afectuoso que tenga al bebé en brazos y le hable suavemente.
- Suministre juguetes que produzcan sonidos agradables. Sostenga con cuidado el juguete e intercambie sonidos con el bebé.
- Suministre materiales interesantes para tocar mientras comenta las texturas.
- Coloque espejos bajos a lo largo de una pared. Los bebés se miran y es posible que produzcan sonidos.

4 a 8 meses (bebé)

- Use lenguaje dirigido al bebé.
- Hable a menudo con los bebés. Muéstreles objetos y personas nuevos y nómbrelos.
- Repita los sonidos que los bebés producen y espere a que repitan el sonido (turnarse).
- Refiérase a varios artículos conocidos, tales como "leche" o "perro," con lenguaje de señas.
- Cante canciones y haga juegos de dedos.
- Describa con palabras los sentimientos de los niños expresados a través de gestos, posturas corporales y sonidos.
- Léale libros sencillos con una o dos imágenes por página. Señale con el dedo las imágenes mientras dice el nombre de la imagen.
- Léale los mismos libros una y otra vez.
- Aplique estrategias de atención conjunta—señale con el dedo un juguete o una imagen de un libro diciendo el nombre o hablando al respecto.

- Suministre juguetes y materiales interesantes para que los bebés los manipulen y examinen.
- Suministre libros de cartón con asas para que pueden gatear hasta ellos y tomarlos.
- Los libros con asas animan a los bebés a llevarlos.
- Haga un libro de imágenes de te veo, no te veo pegando un pedazo de tela sobre cada imagen.
- Forme un rincón de lectura acogedor donde las maestras puedan estar cómodas y leer a los bebés.
- Suministre cajas de sonido (bien selladas) con distintos objetos adentro que produzcan distintos sonidos al sacudirlas.
- Incorpore títeres al ambiente. Úselos a veces para "hablar" con el niño. Coloque los títeres en la mano del niño y espere a ver lo que el niño dice o hace.

Desarrollo	Ejemplo

8 a 12 meses (bebé móvil)

Desarrollo	Ejemplo
• Los bebés móviles comienzan a participar en juegos sociales tales como el *te veo, no te veo* o el "*así de grande.*"	Una de las primeras palabras de Dana fue "mamá," y la repetía una y otra vez cuando veía a su madre.
• A los bebés les gusta escuchar juegos de sonidos (rimas), canciones y juegos de dedos.	Una de las primera palabras de Trishanna fue "mamá," y la repetía con entusiasmo una y otra vez cuando veía a su madre.
• El balbuceo continúa desarrollándose con sílabas combinadas tales como "dada," "mama," "nana" y "tutu" y a esta altura el bebé puede usar estos sonidos específicamente para referirse a su mamá o su papá.	
• Los bebés repiten sonidos consistentemente para referirse a un objeto, una persona o un animal.	
• Si oyen otro lenguaje *con* un adulto a través de estrategias conversacionales interactivas, los bebés pueden "tener una actitud abierta hacia los sonidos de un lenguaje extranjero."	
• Los bebés pueden comenzar a decir palabras aisladas.	
• Al final de este período, los bebés pueden comenzar a señalar con el dedo para atraer la atención de un adulto.	
• Los bebés emplean expresiones faciales y gestos tales como agitar la cabeza o los brazos para que los tomen en brazos, y así comunicarse con los adultos o con sus compañeros.	

12 a 18 meses (bebé móvil)

Desarrollo	Ejemplo
• Los bebés móviles pueden seguir instrucciones sencillas tales como "Ven aquí" o "Trae tus zapatos" sin que haya que hacer gestos.	La maestra de Janina le dijo "Juguemos a dar palmitas, palmitas," y Janina comenzó a aplaudir.
• Los bebés móviles pueden jugar socialmente sin que haya que demostrar la acción. Por ejemplo, cuando usted dice "Dile adiós" ellos mueven las manos aunque usted no les muestre cómo hacerlo.	Ross miró a su maestra con expectación, farfullando muchos sonidos juntos como si le hiciera una pregunta.
• Los bebés móviles señalan con el dedo para llamar la atención de los adultos y de sus compañeros.	
• Se puede producir un aprendizaje rápido de palabras—una explosión de lenguaje—en los niños que están aprendiendo muchas palabras nuevas.	
• Hacia el final de este período, los bebés móviles combinan palabras.	
• Los bebés móviles farfullan (hilando muchos sonidos) con la misma entonación que los adultos.	
• Los bebés móviles hacen gestos y se valen de palabras para rechazar, pedir, comentar, negarse, exigir y nombrar objetos y personas.	
• Los bebés móviles se valen del lenguaje para mantener una interacción o conversación con un adulto o uno de sus compañeros.	

Interacción entre Maestra-Niño, o Padre/Madre–Niño	Ambiente

8 a 12 meses (bebé móvil)

- Organice juegos conocidos tales como te veo—no te veo, palmitas—palmitas o "*¿cómo eres de grande?*"
- Responda con palabras a la comunicación no verbal de los bebés.
- Observe y espere a que los bebés inicien sonidos o palabras.
- Imite los sonidos y luego expanda, detalle y amplíe el lenguaje del bebé.
- Modele el siguiente paso en el desarrollo del lenguaje.
- Emplee hablarse a sí mismo y hablar en paralelo.
- Hable a menudo de manera receptiva con un vocabulario variado. No bombardee al niño con palabras.
- Lea los libros con entusiasmo—cambiando el tono de su voz con los distintos personajes.
- Hable sobre las imágenes y el cuento a medida que lee. Involucre a los bebés con la voz y los gestos.
- Mientras miran una imagen, espere a que el bebé produzca sonidos, señale con el dedo o haga expresiones faciales.

- Cree un rincón de lectura acogedor en que los bebés puedan alcanzar fácilmente los libros y manipularlos.
- Haga un libro "Todo sobre mí"—álbumes pequeños de fotos para cada niño con imágenes de ellos, su familia, sus juguetes preferidos, sus compañeros, sus maestras y los animales domésticos de la familia. Déjelos al alcance de los niños. Cambie las imágenes a medida que el niño crece.
- Los juguetes musicales para empujar animan a los bebés a manipularlos y producir sonidos.

12 a 18 meses (bebé móvil)

- Mantenga el tema en una conversación con un bebé móvil. Vea cuántas veces hablará el niño.
- Responda a la entonación del parloteo del niño. Por ejemplo, si parece que el niño hace una pregunta, responda a lo que usted cree que el niño puede estar preguntando.
- Responda con palabras a las señales hechas con los dedos y otros medios de comunicación no verbal de los bebés móviles.
- Describa y compare con palabras tamaños, formas y sonidos.
- Cuando un bebé móvil dice palabras tales como "Yo salto," modele el próximo paso en el desarrollo del lenguaje diciendo "Tú estás saltando," añadiendo "ando o iendo" a la palabra. Haga esto tanto con el contenido de las palabras como con la estructura de las palabras u oraciones.
- Léale libros con cuentos más largos, haga pausas a medida que avanza por el libro para animar a los bebés móviles a hablar sobre las imágenes y el cuento.

- Introduzca materiales de arte tales como plastilina, arcilla y pintura.
- Déle rollos de toallas de papel a los bebés móviles para que produzcan sonidos.
- Los juguetes musicales para jalar animan a los bebés móviles a caminar y jalarlos o empujarlos.
- Las cajas de música resistentes animan a los bebés móviles a apretar botones para "hacer música."
- Se pueden poner a disposición tambores y otros instrumentos musicales.
- Incorpore un reproductor de CD resistente con un cuento que haya grabado el padre o la madre.
- Grabe las voces de los bebés móviles con una grabadora y haga que las escuchen.
- Suministre materiales para hacer burbujas.
- Facilite espacios para animar a dos o tres niños a conversar con sus compañeros.

Desarrollo	Ejemplo

18 a 24 meses (niño pequeño)

· Los niños pequeños pueden ir a buscar juguetes conocidos en otra habitación de la casa cuando un adulto se los pide, y pueden seguir instrucciones tales como "cierra la puerta." · Los niños pequeños combinan palabras para nombrar cosas ("ese gato"), para negar ("no muerde") y para rechazar ("no más"). · Los niños pequeños combinan dos o tres palabras con significado. · Los niños pequeños se valen del lenguaje para varios propósitos, tales como preguntar "¿Qué eso?" · Los niños pequeños señalan una cantidad de imágenes cada vez mayor en los libros cuando un adulto les habla sobre la imagen.	"Hola Kitty," "puerta abierta" y "sombrero puesto" fueron sólo algunas de las combinaciones de dos palabras que Cheral dijo a los 20 meses de edad. Tyra corrió rápidamente hasta el librero, tomó un libro con tapa brillante y regresó de prisa hasta su maestra. Después de sentarse cómodamente en su regazo, abrió el libro y comenzó a señalar con entusiasmo las imágenes mientras su maestra las nombraba.

24 a 36 meses (niño pequeño)

· Los niños pequeños comprenden instrucciones complejas y recuerdan palabras de canciones cortas y juegos de dedos. · Los niños pequeños se valen de muchas oraciones de dos a cuatro palabras. · Los niños pequeños pueden señalar con el dedo y nombrar muchas partes del cuerpo. · Los niños pequeños añaden "ando o iendo" a las palabras. · Los niños pequeños comienzan a usar preposiciones tales como "sobre" y "dentro." · Los niños pequeños añaden una "s" a las palabras para indicar plurales. · Los niños pequeños podrían empezar a preguntar "¿Por qué?" · Los niños pequeños comienzan a contar historias sobre lo que hicieron o lo que vieron. · Hacia el final de este período, el niño pequeño puede usar las imágenes para contar lo que ocurre en un cuento.	Mindy comenzó a añadir "ando o iendo" a las palabras que había estado diciendo durante meses. Dijo "Yo corriendo" y "Yo comiendo" en vez de "Yo corro" y "Yo como." "Mira, está jugando," exclamó Treat mientras señalaba con el dedo una imagen en su libro preferido.

Interacción entre Maestra-Niño, o Padre/Madre–Niño	Ambiente

18 a 24 meses (niño pequeño)

- Léale libros con cuentos más largos, haga pausas a medida que avanza por el libro para animar a los niños pequeños a hablar sobre las imágenes y la historia. Haga preguntas abiertas tales como "¿Cómo se siente el oso?"
- Pregúntese a menudo con el niño: "Me pregunto qué va a pasar con el oso."
- Haga que los niños pequeños conversen intentando mantenerse en el mismo tema que el niño.
- Introduzca nuevas conversaciones sobre objetos y acontecimientos interesantes.

- Disponga una pista de obstáculos complicada y use palabras tales como "adentro," "afuera," "por arriba," "a través," "alrededor," "arriba" y "abajo" mientras el niño pequeño recorre la pista.
- Suministre libros nuevos todas las semanas, pero mantenga cerca los libros preferidos de los niños.
- Suministre una mayor variedad de materiales de arte.
- Déle materiales que estimulen los sentidos.

24 a 36 meses (niño pequeño)

- Responda sus preguntas de "por qué" con paciencia y entusiasmo. Así es como los niños aprenden y desarrollan interacciones sociales.
- Escuche con sus ojos las "historias" que los niños pequeños cuentan.
- Modele decir palabras plurales, tales como "perros," "elefantes," etc.
- Use palabras descriptivas tales como "queso mozarella" en vez de sólo "queso" o "urraca de América" en vez de sólo "pájaro."
- Tenga conversaciones largas con los niños pequeños, siguiendo lo que dicen.
- Lea libros a grupos informales pequeños o a niños por separado.

- Déle imágenes para que los niños las hagan corresponder.
- Los rompecabezas de animales, personas, vehículos y alimentos son importantes.
- Se pueden agregar al ambiente libros con muchas imágenes y cuentos cortos.
- Los materiales para el juego dramático estimulan la conversación.

Tendencias de desarrollo e interacciones receptivas (Capítulo 10)

Los bebés y los niños pequeños desarrollan capacidades motrices para la locomoción, el uso de herramientas y la coordinación de información perceptiva con acciones motrices.

Desarrollo	Ejemplo
0 a 4 meses (bebé)	
· Los bebés levantan la cabeza cuando los llevan en brazos contra el hombro; sostienen la cabeza firme y erguida.	Rosie mantuvo la cabeza erguida y miró a su alrededor a los otros niños mientras Sharon la llevaba contra el hombro.
· Boca abajo, los bebés levantan la cabeza y los hombros y pueden sostener un juguete en la mano.	Robert, boca abajo sobre una manta, levantó la cabeza para mirarse al espejo montado a nivel del suelo en la pared.
· Los bebés giran la cabeza hacia una voz conocida.	Jen tenía un sonajero en la mano, pero no parecía darse cuenta de que lo tenía.
· Los bebés se quedan quietos para prestar atención; se contonean y se mueven para inducir la continuación de la interacción.	Filipe se llevó los dedos a la boca y se los chupó mientras miraba atentamente a los niños pequeños.
· De espaldas, los bebés estiran los brazos y las piernas a manera de juego.	
· Estando de lado, los bebés se dan vuelta para quedar de espaldas.	
· Los bebés sujetan un dedo o un juguete liviano con agarre reflejo.	
· Los bebés se chupan los dedos, las manos y otros objetos.	
· Los bebés mueven los brazos y las piernas.	
4 a 8 meses (bebé)	
· Los bebés de espaldas se ponen de lado y luego se vuelven a poner de espaldas.	Estando de espaldas, Micky rueda para quedar boca abajo y alcanzar un juguete, luego vuelve a rodar para jugar con el juguete.
· Al final de este período, los bebés se sientan; primero con apoyo pero luego estables y solos.	A Erin, sentada sola establemente, le gusta recoger objetos con las dos manos y examinarlos.
· Los bebés se estiran para alcanzar objetos con el brazo.	A Freddy le gusta que lo tomen en brazos mientras toma su biberón, aunque insiste en sujetarlo solo.
· Los bebés agarran rastrillando.	
· Los bebés gatean.	
· Los bebés sacuden, golpean, sujetan y sueltan objetos.	
· Los bebés se pasan objetos de una mano a otra.	
· Los bebés pueden sostener su biberón.	
· Los bebés se pueden llevar objetos a la boca.	
8 a 12 meses (bebé móvil)	
· Los bebés móviles jalan de algo para ponerse de pie.	Hershel gatea hasta su maestra, luego se agarra de su pierna y jala para ponerse de pie.
· Los bebés móviles se pasean.	Jem se sienta a la mesa del almuerzo, y alterna la cuchara y los dedos para disfrutar de la comida.
· Los bebés móviles se quedan de pie solos.	
· Los bebés móviles caminan con ayuda al principio y después solos.	
· Los bebés móviles se sientan en una silla.	
· Los bebés móviles comen con los dedos.	
· Los bebés móviles pueden usar una cuchara y un vaso hermético.	
· Los bebés móviles agarran atenazando.	

Interacciones entre el niño y la maestra, el padre o la madre	Ambiente

0 a 4 meses (bebé)

- Cambie la posición del bebé; a veces de espaldas, otras boca abajo. Cuando lleve en brazos al bebé, acúnelo en sus brazos o sosténgalo erguido contra el hombro.
- Cuando el bebé está en el piso, acuéstese cara a cara junto a él.
- Cuando la bebé está de espaldas y trata de alcanzar un juguete un poco más allá de su cabeza, sosténgale el tronco mientras rueda.

- Una manta rígida (contra el riesgo de asfixia) en el suelo da espacio para los primeros movimientos.
- Los juguetes pequeños e interesantes, las imágenes, y los libros para mirar cuando quieran animan a los bebés a levantar la cabeza. Un espejo atornillado a la pared a nivel del suelo siempre ofrece algo interesante que mirar.
- A medida que comienzan a estirarse para alcanzar, a los bebés les gustan las barras estables con juguetes colgantes que puedan batear, alcanzar y agarrar.

4 a 8 meses (bebé)

- Quédese cerca del bebé que recién comienza a sentarse solo.
- Conozca el avance del desarrollo motor; anime emocionalmente y apoye físicamente al bebé en sus nuevos intentos.
- Crea en los beneficios a largo plazo para la salud de un estilo de vida activo.

- Deles lugares seguros para rodar, sentarse y gatear. Proteja a los bebés de cualquier cosa que pueda caerles encima.
- Deles objetos livianos pequeños y lavables (grandes para evitar que se asfixien) para que los manipulen y los lancen, y deles recipientes para los objetos.

8 a 12 meses (bebé móvil)

- Esté atenta para saber cuándo ayudar al bebé que comienza a caminar y cuándo dejar que lo siga intentando.
- Dé tiempo para que los bebés mayores practiquen comer solos.

- Lugares seguros para ponerse de pie apoyándose en algo.
- Juguetes para empujar y jalar para que los que comienzan a caminar puedan jalar y empujar.
- Cajas mecánicas.
- Libros de cartón para pasar las páginas, levantar las solapas y meter los dedos a través de los agujeros.

Desarrollo	Ejemplo
12 a 18 meses (bebé móvil)	

- Los bebés móviles apilan y alinean bloques.
- Los bebés móviles pueden vestirse y desvestirse solos, meter el brazo en una manga y el pie dentro de un zapato.
- Los bebés móviles pueden caminar.
- Los bebés móviles caminan con objetos en las manos.
- Los bebés móviles suben escaleras.

Gary se paró frente a la mesa y construyó cuidadosamente con las dos manos una torre con bloques de colores.

Michelle caminó por la habitación con su osito de peluche en una mano y su manta en la otra.

18 a 24 meses (niño pequeño)

- Los niños pequeños señalan objetos con el dedo para comunicarse.
- Los niños pequeños hacen marcas en un papel.
- Los niños pequeños trabajan y dan forma a la plastilina.
- Los niños pequeños corren.
- Los niños pequeños se sientan y se levantan solos de sillas pequeñas.
- Los niños pequeños están desarrollando su confianza espacial; explorando su cuerpo en el espacio.

Mindy estiró la plastilina con las manos y luego hizo figuras con las herramientas.

Joseph se sentó a la mesa para comer, luego llevó los platos sucios al fregadero.

24 a 36 meses (niño pequeño)

- Los niños pequeños ensartan cuentas, usan las tijeras, pintan con los dedos o con pinceles, arman rompecabezas sencillos.
- Los niños pequeños lanzan y patean una pelota.
- Los niños pequeños se paran en un solo pie.
- Los niños pequeños se paran y caminan en puntillas.
- Los niños pequeños suben escaleras poniendo un pie en cada escalón.
- Los niños pequeños trepan, se deslizan y saltan.
- Los niños pequeños comen con cuchara y tenedor.
- Los niños pequeños se pueden vestir solos.
- Los niños pequeños pueden verter leche de una jarra pequeña.

Robert ni siquiera tiene que pensar en su cuerpo cuando corre para saludar a su papá al final del día.

Peggy y Misha inventan un juego imitándose mutuamente los pasos en puntillas, posturas y gestos.

Forcejeando un poco, Lawrence y Evelyn juegan con la ropa para disfrazarse.

Interacciones entre el niño y la maestra, el padre o la madre	Ambiente

12 a 18 meses (bebé móvil)

- Imite la cada vez mayor variedad de movimientos del bebé.
- Introduzca canciones con pequeños bailes y movimientos.
- Dé tiempo y tenga paciencia mientras el niño pequeño practica ponerse solo la chaqueta.

- Juguetes para montar estables y no muy altos.
- Juguetes mecedores estables y no muy altos.
- Juegos de manipulación basados en habilidades, tales como apilar vasos o ensartar aros en un palo.

18 a 24 meses (niño pequeño)

- Ponga a disposición de los niños materiales pequeños que los induzcan a poner en práctica su creciente capacidad de manipulación de objetos con los dedos.
- Quédese con los niños pequeños y apóyelos mientras intentan poner en práctica capacidades recientemente desarrolladas.
- Deles oportunidades de trepar, caminar y correr.

- Materi.ales de arte tales como brochas gordas, marcadores y superficies grandes para pintar.
- Articulos pequeños, tales como cuentas que se interconectan y tableros para clavijas, para practicar actividades de manipulación.
- Mucho espacio para el movimiento: bailes, juguetes para montar, estructuras para trepar, toboganes.

24 a 36 meses (niño pequeño)

- Esté consciente del equilibrio necesario entre el tiempo dedicado a actividades enérgicas y a actividades tranquilas.
- Esté atento al aumento de precisión de las capacidades motrices ligeras, pues pueden comenzar a manifestarse sutiles problemas.
- Esté a disposición de los niños pequeños animándolos y teniéndoles paciencia conforme comen, se visten y van al baño solos con más frecuencia.

- Ponga a su disposición una variedad de materiales para practicar capacidades motrices ligeras: rompecabezas simples, cajas de formas, cuentas para hacer collares, bloques de mesa, arcilla, materiales de arte.
- Espacio, oportunidad y estructuras para fomentar el movimiento: períodos de tiempo al aire libre, carreras de obstáculos, bailes y juguetes para montar.

Appendix D
Planning Guides

DIRECTIONS FOR USING THE PLANNING GUIDES

Individual Child Planning Guides

1. **Choose which Individual Child Planning Guide you would like to use.** Version 1 divides the *Reflect* section into developmental domains, while Version 2 provides a space under the *Reflect* section for you to write a sentence or two about the child's development that integrates the domains.

2. **Choose the child or children to observe during the week.** In a center program, teachers decide which children each teacher will observe during the week. In a center using a primary caregiving system, each teacher will complete a guide on her primary group children. In a family child care home, the teacher can choose several children to observe during a particular week. For a home visiting program, the home visitor completes the guide with the family.

3. **Complete the *Respect* section.** For both versions, each teacher writes an anecdotal record; uses a photograph (or series of photographs) of the child involved with the teacher, peers, equipment, toys, materials, and experiences; or uses other documentation (for example, an example of the child's scribbling). You can attach these to the page.

4. **Complete the *Reflect* section.** This section is completed by you, with other teachers, and/or with family members. When completing the section *What am I doing?,* objectively describe the behavior represented under the *Respect* section. You could use the Chart of Concepts and the Developmental Trends and Responsive Interaction Charts found in chapters 6 through 10 to help you complete *What am I learning?.* For Version 1, describe what concepts the child is exploring and/or describe development. For Version 2, describe what concepts the child is exploring and what the child may be thinking.

5. **Complete the *Relate* section.** This section is completed by you, with other teachers, and/or with family members. In both versions, decide what interactions and changes in the environment are responsive to the concepts the child is exploring and the development observed.

6. **Create a portfolio for each child and include the Individual Child Planning Guides.** Use them to reflect on changes in the child's interests and the child's developmental progress over time. Give the portfolios to the family of the child when the child changes rooms or when the child leaves the program.

Group Planning Guides

1. **Complete the Individually Responsive Group Planning Guide with other teachers and/or with family members.** Each teacher in a center-based program brings her completed Individual Child Planning Guides to a team meeting. The team discusses the information from the individual guides, and then completes the group guide by summarizing the concepts and developmental efforts of the individual children observed that week. You could use resource books that provide ideas about interactions, equipment, and experiences, and then choose *opportunities* that are responsive to the individual children and the group. Provide the opportunities during the following week.

2. **Complete the Group Planning for Routines Guide each month.**

Individual Child Planning Guide: Version 1

Child's Name: _____ Plans for Week of (Date): _____

Person Completing the Guide: _____

Respect: Child's Emotions, Effort, Goals, Learning, and Relationships

Write an observation or use a picture or other documentation here—date all notes:

Respect and Reflect	**Relate**
	What will you do to support my development and learning?
What am I doing?	**Responsive Interactions**
How am I feeling?	
What am I learning?	
• *Emotional*	**Environment, Toys, Materials, and Experiences**
• *Social*	
• *Cognitive*	
• *Language*	
• *Motor*	

Individual Child Planning Guide: Version 2

Child's Name: _____ Plans for Week of (Date): _____

Person(s) Completing the Guide: _____

_____

_____

Respect: Child's Emotions, Effort, Goals, Learning, and Relationships
Write an observation or use a picture or other documentation here—date all notes:

Reflect

What am I doing?

How am I feeling?

What am I learning?

Relate

What will you do to support my development and learning?

Responsive Interactions

Environment, Toys, Materials, and Experiences

Individually Responsive Group Planning Guide

Name of Group: _____

Week of: _____

Person(s) Completing This Guide: _____

Respect and Reflect

(Use information from the individual planning guides.)

Relate: Plans for the Week to Meet Children's Interests and Needs

Songs/Finger-Plays

Stories/Books

Responsive Interactions

Environment, Toys, Materials, and Opportunities

Experiences with Families

Special Experiences

Group Planning for Routines

Name of Group: _____

Week of: _____

Person(s) Completing This Form: _____

Developing a caring community: Think about what is happening and what could happen to develop a relationship-based program for children, families, and teachers.

Routine	What is going well for the children and teachers?	What could we do to improve the experience for children, families, and the teachers?
Greeting time or good-bye time		
Feeding infants and toddler eating times		
Infant sleep and toddler nap time		
Diapering		
Toileting		
Play times		
Outdoor times		
Transitions		

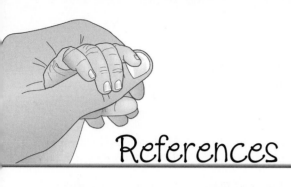

References

AAP (American Academy of Pediatrics). (1997). Breastfeeding and the use of human milk. *Pediatrics, 100*(6), 1035–1039.

AAP (American Academy of Pediatrics). (1999). Newborn and infant hearing loss: Detection and intervention. *Pediatrics, 103*(2), 527–530.

AAP (American Academy of Pediatrics). (2000a). Fetal alcohol syndrome and alcohol-related neurodevelopmental disorders. *Pediatrics, 106*(2), 358–361.

AAP (American Academy of Pediatrics). (2000b). Task force on infant sleep position and sudden infant death syndrome. Changing concepts of sudden infant death syndrome: implications for infant sleeping environment and sleep position. *Pediatrics, 105*(26), 650–656.

AAP (American Academy of Pediatrics). (2004). U.S. government should ban baby walkers. Retrieved September 21, 2008, from http://www.aap.org

AAP (American Academy of Pediatrics). (2005a). AAP recommendations on SIDS 2005. Retrieved September 10, 2008, from http://www.aap.org

AAP (American Academy of Pediatrics). (2005b). The changing concept of sudden infant death syndrome: Diagnostic coding shifts, controversies regarding the sleeping environment, and new variables to consider in reducing risk. *Pediatrics, 116*(5), 1245–1255.

Abramson, S., & Huggins, S. (2001). A review of *Bambini: The Italian approach to infant/toddler care. Focus on Infants and Toddlers, 15*(1), 3, 6–7.

Acredolo, L., Brown, C., & Goodwyn, S. (2000). Impact of symbolic gesturing on early language development. *Journal of Nonverbal Behavior, 24*(2), 81–103.

Acredolo, L., & Goodwyn, S. (1985). Symbolic gesturing in language development: A case study. *Human Development, 28*, 40–49.

Acredolo, L., & Goodwyn, S. (2002). *Baby signs: How to talk with your baby before your baby can talk.* New York: McGraw-Hill.

Adamson, L. B., Bakeman, R., & Deckner, D. J. (2004). The development of symbol-infused joint engagement. *Child Development, 75*(4), 1171–1189.

Adolph, K. E. (2008). Learning to move. *Current Directions in Psychological Science, 17*, 213–218.

Adolph, K. E., & Eppler, M. A. (2002). Flexibility and specificity in infant motor skill acquisition. In J. Fagan (Ed.), *Progress in infancy research* (Vol. 2, pp. 121–167). Mahwah, NJ: Erlbaum.

Adolph, K. E., & Vereijken, B. (2003). What changes in infant walking and why. *Child Development, 74*(2), 475–497.

Adolph, K. E., Vereijken, B., & Denney, M. (1998). Learning to crawl. *Child Development, 69*(5), 1299–1312.

Ainsworth, M. D. S., Bell, S. M., & Stayton, D. J. (1971). Individual differences in the strange situation behavior of one-year-olds. In H. R. Schaffer (Ed.), *The origins of human social relations* (pp. 17–58). San Diego, CA: Academic Press.

Ainsworth, M. D. S., Blehar, M. C., Waters, E., & Wall, S. (1978). *Patterns of attachment: A psychological study of the strange situation.* Hillsdale, NJ: Erlbaum.

Als, H., Lester, B., Tronick, E. Z., & Brazelton, T. B. (1982). Towards a research instrument for the assessment of preterm infants' behavior (A.P.I.B.). In H. E. Fitzgerald, B. M. Lester, & M. W. Yogman (Eds.), *Theory and research in behavioral pediatrics* (Vol. 1, pp. 85–132). New York: Plenum.

Amato, P. R., & Rivera, F. (1999). Paternal involvement and children's behavior problems. *Journal of Marriage and the Family, 61*(22), 375–384.

American Speech–Language–Hearing Association. (1997–2009). Typical speech and language development. Retrieved March 10, 2009, from http://www.asha.org/public/speech/development/01.htm

The Annie E. Casey Foundation. (2008). *KIDS COUNT data book.* Retrieved February 11, 2009, from http://www.kidscount.org/datacenter/compare_results.jsp?i=689

APHA (American Public Health Association) & AAP (American Academy of Pediatrics). (2002). *Caring for our children: National health and safety performance standards: Guidelines for out-of-home child care programs.* Washington, DC: Authors.

Appleton, T. R., Clifton, R. K., & Goldberg, S. (1975). The development of behavioral competence in infancy. *Review of Child Development Research, 4*, 101–185.

Arnett, J. (1989). Caregivers in child care centers. Does training matter? *Journal of Applied Developmental Psychology, 10*, 541–552.

ASCAA (American Sickle Cell Anemia Assocation). (2007). Available from http://www.ascaa.org/

Aslin, R. N., Saffran, J. R., & Newport, E. L. (1998). Computation of conditional probability statistics by 8-month-old infants. *Psychological Science, 9*, 321–324.

Astington, J. W., & Barriault, T. (2001). Children's theory of mind: How young children come to understand that people have thoughts and feelings. *Infants and Young Children, 13*(3), 1–12.

BabyCenter. (2008). *Motor development: Ten red flags.* Retrieved February 9, 2009, from the BabyCenter Web site: http://www.babycenter.com/0-motor-development-ten-red-flags_11640.bc

Badaly, D., & Adolph, K. E. (2008). Beyond the average: Walking infants take steps longer than their leg length. *Infant Behavior and Development, 31,* 554–558.

Bahrick, L. E. (1995). Intermodal origins of self-perception. In P. Rochat (Ed.), *The self in infancy: Theory and research advances in psychology* (pp. 349–373). Amsterdam: North Holland/Elsevier.

Bailey, T. M., & Plunkett, K. (2002). Phonological specificity in early words. *Cognitive Development, 17*(2), 1265–1282.

Baillargeon, R. (1993). The object concept revisited: New directions in the investigation of infant's physical knowledge. In C. Granrud (Ed.), *Visual perception and cognition in infancy* (pp. 265–315). Hillsdale, NJ: Erlbaum.

Baldwin, E., Friedman, K., & Harvey, S. (1997, Fall). In the best interests of breastfed children. Retrieved March 26, 2009, from http://www.llli.org/Law/LawInterest.html

Bancroft, J. (1989). *Human sexuality and its problems.* Edinburgh: Churchill Livingstone.

Bandura, A. (1965). Influence of models' reinforcement contingencies on the acquisition of imitative responses. *Journal of Personality and Social Psychology, 1,* 587–595.

Bandura, A. (1977). *Social learning theory.* Upper Saddle River, NJ: Prentice Hall.

Bandura, A. (1989). Social cognitive theory. In R. Vasta (Ed.), *Annals of child development* (Vol. 6). Greenwich, CT: JAI.

Bandura, A. (1997). *Self-efficacy: The exercise of control.* New York: Freeman.

Bandura, A. (2001). Social cognitive theory: An agentive perspective. *Review of Psychology, 52,* 1–26.

Barrera, I., & Corso, R. (2003). *Skilled dialogue: Strategies for responding to cultural diversity in early childhood.* Baltimore: Brookes.

Barrera, I., & Kramer, L. (1997). From monologues to skilled dialogues: Teaching the process of crafting culturally competent early childhood environments. In P. Winton, J. McCollum, & C. Catlett (Eds.), *Reforming personnel preparation in early intervention: Issues, models, and practical strategies* (pp. 217–252). Baltimore: Brookes.

Baumrind, D. (1991). The influence of parenting style on adolescent competence and substance use. *Journal of Early Adolescence, 11*(1), 56–95.

Beard, J. L., Connor, J. D., & Jones, B. C. (1997). Brain iron: Location and function. *Progress in Food and Nutrition Science, 17,* 183–221.

Beckerman, S., & Valentine, P. (2002). *Cultures of multiple fathers: The theory and practice of partible paternity in South America.* Gainesville: University of Florida Press.

Bellagamba, F., Camaioni, L., & Colonnesi, C. (2006). Change in children's understanding of others' intentional actions. *Developmental Science, 9*(2), 182–188.

Bellm, D., Whitebook, M., & Hnatiuk, P. (1997). *The early childhood mentoring curriculum: A handbook for mentors.* Washington, DC: National Center for the Early Childhood Work Force.

Belsky, J., & Fearon, R. M. P. (2002). Early attachment security, subsequent maternal sensitivity, and later child development: Does continuity in development depend upon continuity of caregiving? *Attachment and Human Development, 4,* 361–387.

Berger, S. E., & Adolph, K. E. (2003). Infants use handrails as tools in a locomotor task. *Developmental Psychology, 39*(3), 594–605.

Bernadette-Shapiro, S., Ehrensaft, D., & Shapiro, J. L. (1996). Father participation in child care and the development of empathy in sons: An empirical study. *Family Therapy, 23*(2), 77–93.

Besag, F. M. (2002). Childhood epilepsy in relation to mental handicap and behavioural disorders. *Journal of Child Psychology and Psychiatry, 43,* 103–131.

Bettelheim, B. (1987, March). The importance of play. *Atlantic,* 35–46.

Biller, H., & Meredith, D. (1974). *Father power.* New York: McKay.

Bing, E. (1982). The effect of child-rearing practices on the development of differential cognitive abilities. *Child Development, 34,* 631–639.

Blasco, P. M. (2001). *Early intervention services for infants, toddlers, and their families.* Boston: Allyn & Bacon.

Bloom, P. J. (2000). *Circle of influence: Implementing shared decision making and participative management.* Lake Forest, IL: New Horizons.

Bobath, K. (1980). *A neurophysiological basis for the treatment of cerebral palsy.* Philadelphia: Lippencott.

Borke, J., Lamm, B., Eickhorst, A., & Keller, H. (2007). Father-infant interaction, paternal ideas about early child care, and their consequences for the development of children's self-recognition. *Journal of Genetic Psychology, 168*(4), 365–379.

Bower, T. G. R. (1977). *A primer of infant development.* San Francisco: Freeman.

Bowlby, J. (1969). *Attachment and Loss: Vol. 1. Attachment.* New York: Basic Books.

Bowlby, J. (1982). *Attachment.* New York: Basic Books.

Bowlby, J. (1988). *A Secure Base: Parent–Child Attachment and Healthy Human Development.* New York: Basic Books.

Brannon, E. M. (2002). The development of ordinal numerical knowledge in infancy. *Cognition, 83,* 223–240.

Braungart-Rieker, J. M., Garwood, M. M., Powers, B. P., & Wang, X. (2001). Parental sensitivity, infant affect, and affect regulation: Predictors of later attachment. *Child Development, 72*(1), 252–270.

Brazelton, T. B. (1972). Implications of infant development among the Mayan Indians of Mexico. *Human Development, 15*(2), 90–111.

Brazelton, T. B. (1992). *Touchpoints: Your child's emotional and behavioral development.* Reading, MA: Perseus.

Brazelton, T. B., & Greenspan, S. I. (2000). *The irreducible needs of children: What every child must have to grow, learn, and flourish.* New York: Perseus.

Brazelton, T. B., & Sparrow, J. D. (2004). *Toilet training: The Brazelton way.* Cambridge, MA: Da Capo.

Brems, S., & Berg, A. (1988). *"Eating down" during pregnancy: Nutrition, obstetrics, and culture considerations in the third world.* Washington, DC: UN Advisory Group on Nutrition.

Breslin, D. (2005). Children's capacity to develop resiliency: How to nurture it. *Young Children, 60*(1), 47–57.

Bretherton, I. (1985). Attachment theory: Retrospect and prospect. *Monographs of the Society for Research in Child Development, 50*(1/2), 3–35.

Bricker, D., & Squires, J. (2009). *Ages and Stages Questionnaires, Third Edition (ASQ-3). A parent-completed monitoring system.* Baltimore: Brookes.

Bromwich, R. (1997). *Working with families and their infants at risk.* Austin, TX: Pro-Ed.

Bronfenbrenner, U. (1979). *The ecology of human development.* Cambridge, MA: Harvard University Press.

Bronfenbrenner, U. (1986). Ecology of the family as a context for human development: Research perspectives. *Developmental Psychology, 22*(6), 723–741.

Bronfenbrenner, U. (1994). Who cares for the children. In H. Nuba, M. Searson, & D. L. Sheiman (Eds.), *Resources for early childhood: A handbook.* New York: Garland.

Bronfenbrenner, U. (Ed.). (2004). *Making human beings human: Bioecological perspectives on human development.* Thousand Oaks, CA: Sage.

Bronson, M. B. (2000a). Recognizing and supporting the development of self-regulation in young children. *Young Children, 55*(2), 32–37.

Bronson, M. B. (2000b). *Self-regulation in early childhood: Nature and nurture.* New York: Guilford Press.

Bronte-Tinkew, J., Carrano, J., & Guzman, L. (2006). Resident fathers' perceptions of their roles and links to involvement with infants. *Fathering: A Journal of Theory, Research, & Practice About Men as Fathers, 4*(3), 254–285.

Brook, J. S., Zheng, L., Whiteman, M., & Brook, D. (2001). Aggression in toddlers: Associations with parenting and marital relations. *Journal of Genetic Psychology, 162*(2), 228–241.

Brooks, R., & Meltzoff, A. N. (2005). The development of gaze following and its relation to language. *Developmental Science, 8*(6), 535–543.

Brown, R. (1973). *A first language: The early stages.* London: Allen & Unwin.

Brown University (2006, May 2). Fussy babies and postpartum depression linked, study finds. *ScienceDaily.* Retrieved January 22, 2009, from http://www.sciencedaily.com/releases/2006/05/060502090732.htm

Brownell, C. A., & Carriger, M. (1990). Changes in cooperation and self-determination during the second year. *Child Development, 61,* 1164–1174.

Brownell, C. A., & Kopp, C. B. (2007). *Socioemotional development in the toddler years. Transitions and transformations.* New York: Guilford Press.

Brownell, C. A., Ramani, G. B., & Zerwas, S. (2006). Becoming a social partner with peers: Cooperation and social understanding in one- and two-year-olds. *Child Development, 77*(4), 803–821.

Brownlee, J., & Bakeman, R. (1981). Hitting in toddler-peer interactions. *Child Development, 52*(3), 1076–1080.

Bruder, M. B., & Brand, M. (1995). A comparison of two types of early intervention environments serving toddler-age children with disabilities. *Infant-Toddler Intervention: The Transdisciplinary Journal, 5,* 207–217.

Bruner, J. (1966). *Toward a theory of instruction.* Cambridge, MA: Harvard University Press.

Bruner, J. (1983). *Child's talk.* New York: Norton.

Bruner, J. (1996a). *The culture of education.* Cambridge, MA: Harvard University Press.

Bruner, J. (1996b). What we have learned about early learning. *European Early Childhood Education Research Journal, 4*(1), 5–16.

Buell, M. J., Gamel-McCormick, M., & Hallam, R. A. (1999, December). Inclusion in a child development and education context: Experiences and attitudes of family child development and education providers. *Topics in Early Childhood Special Education, 19,* 217–224.

Burchinal, M. R., Howes, C., & Kontos, S. (2002). Structural predictors of child care quality in child care homes. *Early Childhood Research Quarterly, 17,* 87–105.

Burchinal, M. R., Roberts, J. E., Nabors, L. A., & Bryant, D. M. (1996). Quality of center child care and infant cognitive and language development. *Child Development, 67,* 606–620.

Bureau of Labor Statistics. (June, 2008). *Labor force participation of mothers with infants in 2007.* Retrieved September 1, 2008, from http://www.bls.gov/opub/ted/2008/jun/wk1/art03.htm

Butterfield, P. (2002). Child care is rich in routines. *Zero to Three, 22*(4), 29–32.

Cahill, L. (2005). His brain, her brain. *Scientific American, 292*(5), 40–47.

Campbell, D. W., & Eaton, W. O. (1999). Sex differences in the activity levels of infants. *Infant and Child Development, 8,* 1–17.

Campbell, S. B. (1995). Depression in first-time mothers: Mother–infant interaction and depression chronicity. *Developmental Psychology, 31*(3), 349–357.

Camras, L. A. (1992). Expressive development and basic emotions. *Cognition and Emotion, 6*(3), 269–283.

Camras, L. A., Oster, H., Campos, J., Campos, R., Ujiie, T., & Miyake, K. (1998). Production of emotional facial expressions in European American, Japanese, and Chinese infants. *Developmental Psychology, 34*(4), 616–628.

Canterino, J. C., VanHorn, L. G., Harrigan, J., Ananth, C., & Vintzileos, A. (1999). Domestic abuse in pregnancy: A comparison of a self-completed domestic abuse questionnaire with a directed interview. *American Journal of Obstetrics and Gynecology, 181*(5), 1049–1051.

Capatides, J., Collins, C. C., & Bennett, L. (1996). *Peer interaction in toddlers: Parallel play revisited.* Paper presented at the conference "Ask the Child: Why, When, and How?" Teachers College Press, New York.

Capizzano. J., & Adams, G. (2000). The hours that children under 5 spend in child care. *New federalism: National survey of America's families,* Series B (No. B-8). Washington, DC: Urban Institute.

Carey, S. (1978). The child as word learner. In M. Halle, J. Bresnan, & G. A. Miller (Eds.), *Linguistic theory and psychological reality* (pp. 264–293). Cambridge, MA: MIT Press.

Carlson, M., & McLanahan, S. (2002). *Characteristics and antecedents of involvement by young, unmarried fathers.* (Working Paper #02–09–FF). Princeton University: Center for Research on Child Wellbeing.

Carson, D. K., Klee, T., Perry, C. K. Muskina, G., & Donaghy, T. (1998). Comparisons of children with delayed and normal language at 24 months of age on measures of behavioral difficulties, social and cognitive development. *Infant Mental Health Journal, 19,* 59–75.

Carson, J., & Parke, R. D. (1996). Reciprocal negative affect in parent–child interactions and children's peer competency. *Child Development, 67,* 2217–2226.

Carter, M. (1992). Honoring diversity: Problems and possibilities for staff and organization. In B. Neugebauer (Ed.), *Alike and different: Exploring our humanity with young children* (Rev. ed.). Washington, DC: NAEYC.

Carter, M., & Curtis, D. (1998). *The visionary director: A handbook for dreaming, organizing, and improvising in your center.* St. Paul, MN: Redleaf.

Cartwright, S. (1999). What makes good preschool teachers? *Young Children, 54*(4), 4–7.

Caruso, D. A. (1988). Play and learning in infancy: Research and implications. *Young Children, 43*(6), 63–70.

Cassels, C. (2008, August 22). *Widespread, Newborn Screening for Fragile X Under Way.* Retrieved February 6, 2009, from http://www.medscapre.com/viewarticle/579468

Cathcart, M., & Robles, R. (1996). *Parenting our children: In the best interest of the nation.* Washington, DC: U.S. Commission on Child and Family Welfare.

Cawlfield, M. E. (1992). Velcro time: The language connection. *Young Children, 47*(4), 26–30.

CCW (Center for the Childcare Workforce). (2004). *Current data on the salaries and benefits of the U.S. early childhood education workforce.* Washington, DC: Author.

CDC (Centers for Disease Control and Prevention). (2004). Smoking during pregnancy—U.S., 1990–2002. *Morbidity and Mortality Weekly Report, 53*(39), 911–915.

CDC (Centers for Disease Control and Prevention). (2006) *Violence and reproductive health: Home.* Retrieved February 11, 2009, from http://www.cdc.gov/reproductivehealth/violence/

CFF (Cystic Fibrosis Foundation). (2009). *What is Cystic Fibrosis?* Retrieved February 9, 2009, from http://www.cff.org/AboutCF/

Chang, A., & Aronson, S. (2002). Introduction. In American Public Health Association & American Academy of Pediatrics,

Caring for our children: National health and safety performance standards: Guidelines for out-of-home child care programs. Washington, DC: APHA & AAP.

Chao, R. K. (1994). Beyond parental control and authoritarian parenting style: Understanding Chinese parenting through the cultural notion of training. *Child Development, 65*(4), 1111–1119.

Chen, D., & Haney, M. (1999). *Promoting learning through active interaction. Project PLAI. Final report.* Northridge: California State University. (ERIC Document Reproduction Service No. ED432118)

Chen, X., Hastings, P. D., Rubin, K. H., Chen, H., Cen, G., & Stewart, S. L. (1998). Child-rearing attitudes and behavioral inhibition in Chinese and Canadian toddlers: A cross-cultural study. *Developmental Psychology, 34*(4), 677–686.

Cherlin, A. J., Furstenberg, F. F., Chase-Lansdale, P. L., Kiernan, K., Robins, P., Morrison, D., et al. (1991). Longitudinal studies of effects of divorce on children in Great Britain and the United States. *Science, 252,* 1386–1389.

Child Care Services Association. (2000). *T.E.A.C.H. Early Childhood: Celebrating ten years.* Chapel Hill, NC: Author.

Child poverty fact sheet. (2001). Information is available from the National Center for Children in Poverty Web site: http://www.nccp.org/

Children's Defense Fund. (2006). *Annual report 2006.* Retrieved August 25, 2008, from http://www.childrensdefense.org/site/DocServer/2006_annual_report.pdf?docID=5141

Child Trends. (2002). *Databank.* Retrieved April 15, 2008, from http://www.childtrendsdatabank.org

Child Welfare Information Gateway. (2008). *Parent education. Issue brief.* Retrieved August 23, 2008, from http://www.childwelfare.gov/pubs/issue_briefs/parented/

Chiriboga, C. A. (1991). Abuse of children: Fetal and pediatric AIDS, fetal alcohol syndrome, fetal cocaine effects, and the battered child syndrome. In L. P. Rowland (Ed.), *Merritt's textbook of neurology* (pp. 995–1000). Baltimore: Williams & Wilkins.

Chomsky, N. (1975). *Reflections on language.* New York: Pantheon Books.

Chrisman, K., & Couchenour, D. (2003). Developing concepts of gender roles. In C. Copple (Ed.), *A world of difference* (pp. 116–117). Washington, DC: NAEYC.

Christie-Mizell, C., Peralta, R. L., & Laske, M. T. (2008). *Maternal depression and race: The consequences of neighborhood perceptions and neighborhood location.* Paper presented at the annual meeting of the American Sociological Association Annual Meeting, Boston, MA. Retrieved January 15, 2009, from http://www.allacademic.com/meta/p241248_index.html

Chugani, H. T. (1997). Neuroimaging of developmental non-linearity and developmental pathologies. In R. W. Thatcher, G. R. Lyon, J. Rumsey, & N. Krasnegor (Eds.), *Developmental neuroimaging: Mapping the development of brain and behavior* (pp. 187–195). San Diego, CA: Academic Press.

Chugani, H. T. (1998). A critical period of brain development: Studies of cerebral glucose utilization with PET. *Preventive Medicine, 27,* 487–497.

Clark, R., & Fenichel, E. (2001, August–September). Mothers, babies, and depression: Questions and answers. *Zero to Three, 22*(1), 48–50.

Clarke-Stewart, K. A., Vandell, D. L., Burchinal, M., O'Brien, M., & McCartney, K. (2002). Do regulable features of child-care homes affect children's development? *Early Child Research Quarterly, 17,* 52–86.

Clifton, R. K., Rochat, P., Robin, D., & Berthier, N. E. (1994). Multimodal perception in the control of infant reaching. *Journal of Experimental Psychology: Human Perception and Performance, 20*(4), 876–886.

Coleman, J. G. (1999). *The early intervention dictionary: A multidisciplinary guide to terminology.* Bethesda, MD: Woodbine.

Coley, R. L., & Chase-Lansdale, P. L. (1999). Stability and change in paternal involvement among urban African-American fathers. *Journal of Family Psychology, 13*(3), 416–435.

Coll, C. G., & Magnuson, K. (2000). Cultural differences as sources of developmental vulnerabilities and resources. In J. P. Shonkoff & S. J. Meisels (Eds.), *Handbook of early childhood intervention* (2nd ed., pp. 94–114). New York: Cambridge University Press.

Collier, A. M., & Henderson, F. W. (2000). Respiratory disease in infants and toddlers. In D. Cryer & T. Harms (Eds.), *Infants and toddlers in out-of-home care* (pp. 163–178). Baltimore: Brookes.

Collins, W. A., Maccoby, E. E., Steinberg, L., Hetherington, E. M., & Bornstein, M. H. (2000). Contemporary research on parenting: The case for nature and nurture. *American Psychologist, 55,* 218–232.

Connellan, J., Baron-Cohen, S., Wheelwright, S., Ba'tki, A., & Ahluwalin, J. (2001). Sex differences in human neonatal social perception. *Infant Behavior and Development, 23,* 113–118.

Cooper, P. J., & Murray, L. (1998). Postnatal depression. *British Medical Journal, 316,* 1884–1886.

Cooper, R. P., & Aslin, R. N. (1990). Preference for infant-directed speech in the first month after birth. *Child Development, 61*(5), 1584–1595.

Coplan, R., Rubin, K. H., Fox, N. A., Calkins, S., & Stewart, S. (1994). Being alone, playing alone, and acting alone: Distinguishing among reticence and passive and active solitude in young children. *Child Development, 65*(1), 129–137.

Copple, C. (Ed.). (2003). *A world of difference: Readings on teaching young children in a diverse society.* Washington, DC: NAEYC.

Copple, C., & Bredecamp, S. (Eds.). (2009). *Developmentally appropriate practice in early childhood programs* (3rd ed.) Washington, DC: NAEYC.

Cote, S. M., Vaillancourt, T., LeBlanc, J. C., Nagin, D. S., & Tremblay, R. E. (2006). The development of physical aggression from toddlerhood to pre-adolescence: A nation wide longitudinal study of Canadian children (Clinical report). *Journal of Abnormal Child Psychology, 34*(1), 71–86.

Council for Exceptional Children (2009). *What every special educator must know—ethics, standards, and guidelines for special educators* (6th ed.). Arlington, VA: Author.

Cowan, C. P., & Cowan, P. A. (1992). *When partners become parents.* New York: Erlbaum.

Cox, M. J., Owen, M. T., Henderson, V. K., & Margand, N. A. (1992). Prediction of infant–father and infant–mother attachment. *Developmental Psychology, 28,* 474–483.

CQO Study Team. (1995). *Cost, quality, and child outcomes in child care centers.* Public report, Denver: University of Colorado Denver.

Crittenden, P. (1995). Attachment and psychopathology. In S. Goldbert, R. Muir, & J. Kerr (Eds.), *Attachment theory: Social, developmental, and clinical perspectives* (pp. 367–406). Hillsdale, NJ: Analytic Press.

Crockenberg, S., Leerkes, E., & Lekka, S.K. (2007). Pathways from marital aggression to infant emotion regulation: The development of withdrawal in infancy. *Infant Behavior and Development, 30*(1), 97–113.

Cross, A. F., Traub, E. K., Hutter-Pishagi, L., & Shelton, G. (2004). Elements of successful inclusion for children with significant disabilities. *Topics in Early Childhood Special Education, 24*(3), 169–184.

Cryer, D., Harms, T., & Bourland, B. (1988). *Active learning for threes.* Menlo Park, CA: Addison-Wesley.

CWIG (Child Welfare Information Gateway). (2001). Understanding the effects of maltreatment on early brain development. Retrieved February 22, 2009, from http://www.childwelfare.gov/pubs/focus/earlybrain/earlybraina.cfm

Damasio, A. (2003). *Looking for Spinoza: Joy, sorrow, and the feeling brain.* Orlando, FL: Harcourt.

Damasio, A., & Damasio, H. (1999). Brain and language. In *The Scientific American book of the brain,* by the editors of *Scientific American Magazine.* Guilford, CT: Lyons.

Darling, N. (1999, March). Parenting style and its correlates. *ERIC Digest* (ED427896). Champaign, IL: ERIC Clearinghouse on Elementary and Early Childhood Education.

DaRos, D., & Kovach, B. (1998). Assisting toddlers and caregivers during conflict resolutions: Interactions that promote socialization. *Childhood Education, 75*(1), 25.

Darwin, C. (1859). *On the origin of species by means of natural selection.* London: John Murray.

de Boer, B., & Kuhl, P. K. (2003). Investigating the role of infant-directed speech with a computer model. *Acoustics Research Letters Online (ARLO), 4*(4), 129–134. Available from the ARLO Web site: http://scitation.aip.org/ARLO/top.jsp

DEC (Division for Early Childhood). (2008). Code of ethics. Retrieved January 15, 2009, from http://www.dec-sped.org/uploads/docs/about_dec/position_concept_papers/Code%20of%20Ethics_Field%20Review%2011_08.pdf

DeCasper, A., & Fifer, W. (1980). Of human bonding: Newborns prefer their mothers' voices. *Science, 208,* 1174–1176.

DeCasper, A., & Spence, M. J. (1986). Prenatal maternal speech influences newborns' perception of speech sounds. *Infant Behavior and Development, 9,* 133–150.

Decker, C. A., & Decker, J. R. (2001). *Planning and administering early childhood programs* (7th ed.). Upper Saddle River, NJ: Merrill/Prentice Hall.

de Hann, D., & Singer, E. (2003). Use your words: A sociocultural approach to the teacher's role in the transition from physical to verbal strategies of resolving peer conflicts among toddlers. *Journal of Early Childhood Research, 1*(1), 95–109.

DeHouwer, A. (1999, July). Two or more languages in early childhood: Some general points and practical recommendations. *ERIC Digest* (ED433697). District of Columbia: ERIC Clearinghouse on Languages and Linguistics.

Delamonica, E., & Minujin, A. (2007). Incidence, depth and severity of children in poverty. *Social Indicators Research, 82,* 361–374.

Delaney, C. (2000). Making babies in a Turkish village. In J. DeLoache & A. Gottlieb (Eds.), *A world of babies: Imagined child care guides for seven societies* (pp. 117–144). Cambridge, England: Cambridge University Press.

DeLoache, J. (2000). Cognitive development in infants. In D. Cryer & T. Harmes (Eds.), *Infants and toddlers in out of home care* (pp. 7–48). Baltimore: Brookes.

DeLoache, J. S., Pierroutsakos, S. L., Troseth, G. L., Uttah, D. H., Rosengren, K. S., & Gottlieb, A. (1998). Grasping the nature of pictures. *Psychological Science, 9,* 205–210.

DeLoache, J. S., Pierroutsakos, S. L. T., & Troseth, G. L. (1997). The three Rs of pictorial competence. *Annals of Child Development, 12,* 1–48.

DeLoache, J. S., Strauss, M. S., & Maynard, J. (1979). Picture perception in infancy. *Infant Behavior and Development, 2,* 77–89.

Denckla, M. B. (1989). Executive function: The overlap zone between attention deficit hyperactivity disorder and learning disabilities. *International Pediatrics, 4,* 155–160.

Derman-Sparks, L., & The A.B.C. Task Force. (2003). Expanding awareness of gender roles. In C. Copple (Ed.), *A world of difference* (pp. 118–119). Washington, DC: NAEYC.

DeStefano, C. T., & Mueller, E. (1982). Environmental determinants of peer social activity in 18-month-old males. *Infant Behavior and Development, 5,* 175–183.

DeVries, R., & Zan, B. (1996). A constructivist perspective on the role of the sociomoral atmosphere in promoting children's development. In C. T. Fosnet (Ed.), *Constructivism: Theory, perspectives, and practice* (pp. 103–119). New York: Teachers College Press.

de Wolff, M. S. & van IJzendourn, M. H. (1997). Sensitivity and attachment: A meta-analysis on parental antecedents of infant attachment. *Child Development, 68,* 571–591.

Diamond, K. E. (2001). Relationships among young children's ideas, emotional understanding, and social contact with classmates with disabilities. *Topics in Early Childhood Special Education, 21,* 104–113.

Dicker, S., Gordon, E., & Knitzer, J. (2001). *Improving the odds for the healthy development of young children in foster care.* New York: National Center for Children in Poverty.

Diener, P. (1992). Family day care and children with disabilities. In D. Peters & A. Pence (Eds.), *Family day care: Current research for informed public policy* (pp. 129–146). New York: Teachers College Press.

Dietrich, S. L. (2005). A look at friendships between preschool children with and without disabilities in two inclusive classrooms. *Journal of Early Childhood Research, 3*(2), 193–215.

Dodge, D. T., Rudick, S., Berke, K., & Dumbro, A. (2006). *The creative curriculum for infants, toddlers & twos* (2nd ed.). Washington, DC: Teaching Strategies.

Doescher, S., Hare, J., & Morrow, A. M. (1996). *Parenting after divorce.* Corvallis: Oregon State University Extension Service.

Dombro, A., Colker, L., & Dodge, D. T. (1998). *A journal for using "The Creative Curriculum for Infants and Toddlers."* St. Paul, MN: Redleaf.

Donahoo, S. (2003, Spring). Single parenting and children's academic achievement. *NPIN Parent News.*

Dunham, P., & Dunham, F. (1996). The semantically reciprocating robot: Adult influences on children's early conversational skills. *Social Development, 5,* 261–274.

EHSRE (Early Head Start Research and Evaluation Project). (1996–Current). Retrieved September 4, 2008, from http://www.acf.hhs.gov/programs/opre/ehs/ehs_resrch/index.html

Eaton, W. O. (2009). Motor activity level. Retrieved February 1, 2009, from http://home.cc.umanitoba.ca/~eaton/child-development-motor-activity-level.htm

Eckerman, C. O., & Didow, S. M. (2001). *Peer and infant social communicative development.* London: Blackwell.

Eckerman, C. O., Whatley, J. L., & Kutz, S. L. (1975). Growth of social play with peers during the second year of life. *Developmental Psychology, 11*(1), 42–49.

Edin, K. (2000). What do low-income single mothers say about marriage? *Social Problems, 47,* 112–133.

Edwards, C., Gandini, L., & Forman, G. (Eds.). (1998). *The hundred languages of children: The Reggio Emilia approach—Advanced reflections.* Greenwich, CT: Ablex.

Edwards, C., & Raikes, H. (2002). Extending the dance: Relationship-based approaches to infant/toddler care and education. *Young Children, 57*(4), 10–17.

Egeland, B., Weinfield, N., Bosquet, M., & Cheng, V. K. (2000). Remembering, repeating, and working through: Lessons from attachment-based interventions. In J. D. Osofsky & H. E. Fitzgerald, *WAIMH handbook of infant mental health: Vol. 4. Infant mental health in groups at high risk* (pp. 35–90). New York: Wiley.

Eggbeer, L., Mann, T., & Gilkerson, L. (2003). Preparing infant–family practitioners: A work in progress. *Zero to Three, 24*(1), 35–40.

EHSREP (Early Head Start Research and Evaluation Project). (2006). Research to practice: Depression in the lives of Early Head Start families. Retrieved February 9, 2009, from http://www.acf.hhs.gov/programs/opre/ehs/ehs_resrch/reports/dissemination/research_briefs/4pg_depression.html

Eimas, P. D., & Quinn, P. C. (1994). Studies on the formation of perceptually based basic-level catagories in young infants. *Child Development, 65,* 903–917.

Eisenberg, A., Murkoff, H. E., & Hathaway, S. (1991). *What to expect when you're expecting.* New York: Workman.

Eisenberg, N., Cumberland, A., & Spinrad, T. L. (1998). Parental socialization of emotion. *Psychological Inquiry, 9*(4), 241–273.

Elicker, J., Fortner-Wood, C., & Noppe, I. C. (1999). The context of infant attachment in family child care. *Journal of Applied Developmental Psychology, 20*(2), 319–336.

Ellis, S., & Siegler, R. S. (1997). Planning as a strategy choice, or why don't children plan when they should? In S. L. Friedman & E. K. Scholnick (Eds.), *The developmental psychology of planning: Why, how, and when do we plan?* (pp. 183–208). Mahwah, NJ: Erlbaum.

Ellison, P. T. (2001). *On fertile ground.* Cambridge, MA: Harvard University Press.

Emde, R. N. (1988). The effect of relationships on relationships: A developmental approach to clinical intervention. In R. A. Hinde & J. Stevenson-Hinde (Eds.), *Relationships within families* (pp. 334–364). Oxford: Clarendon.

Emde, R. N. (1994). Individuality, context, and the search for meaning. *Child Development, 65,* 719–737.

Emde, R. N. (1998). Early emotional development: New modes of thinking for research and intervention. *Pediatrics, 102,* 1236–1243.

Emde, R. N. (2001). In L. Gandini & C. Edwards (Eds.), *Bambini: The Italian approach to infant/toddler care* (pp. vii–xiv). New York: Teachers College Press.

Emde, R. N., Biringen, Z., Clyman, R. B., & Oppenheim, D. (1991). The moral self of infancy: Affective core and procedural knowledge. *Developmental Review, 11,* 251–270.

Emde, R. N., & Robinson, J. L. (2000). Guiding principles for a theory of early intervention: A developmental-psychoanalytic perspective. In J. P. Shonkoff & S. J. Meisels (Eds.), *Handbook of early intervention* (pp. 160–178). New York: Cambridge University Press.

Erikson, E. (1950). *Childhood and society.* New York: Norton.

Erikson, E. (1959, 1980, Reissued 1994). *Identity and the life cycle.* New York: W.W. Norton & Company.

Erikson, E. (1963). *Childhood and society* (2nd ed.). New York: Norton.

Erickson, M. F., & Kurz-Riemer, K. (1999). *Infants, toddlers and families: A framework for support and intervention.* New York: Guilford Press.

Eslinger, P. J. (1996). Conceptualizing, describing, and measuring components of executive function: A summary. In G. R. Lyon & N. Krasnegor (Eds.), *Attention, memory, and executive function* (pp. 367–395). Baltimore: Brookes.

Fabes, R. A., Eisenberg, N., Jones, S., Smith, M., Guthrie, I., Powlin, R., et al. (1999). Regulation, emotionality, and preschoolers' socially competent peer interactions. *Child Development, 70*(2), 432–442.

Fabes, R. A., Hanish, L. D., & Martin, C. L. (2003). Children at play: The role of peers in understanding the effects of child care. *Child Development, 74*(4), 1039–1044.

Fabes, R. A., Martin, C. L., & Hanish, L. D. (2004). The next 50 years: Considering gender as a context for understanding young children's peer relationships. *Merrill-Palmer Quarterly, 50*(3), 260–274.

Fattal-Valevski, A., Leitner, Y., Kutai, M., Tal-Posener, E., Tomer, A., & Lieberman, D. (1999). Neurodevelopmental outcome in children with intrauterine growth retardation: A 3-year follow-up. *Journal of Child Neurology, 14,* 724–727.

Feigenson, L., Carey, S., & Spelke, E. (2002, February). Infants' discrimination of number vs. continuous extent. *Cognitive Psychology, 44,* 33–66.

Feldman, R., Greenbaum, C. W., Yirmiya, N. (1999). Mother–infant affect synchrony as an antecedent of the emergence of self-control. *Developmental Psychology, 35*(1), 223–231.

Feldman, R., Eidelman, A., Sirota, L., & Weller, A. (2002). Comparison of skin-to-skin (kangaroo) and traditional care. *Pediatrics, 110*(1), 16–27.

Fenichel, E. (Ed.). (1992). *Learning through supervision and mentorship: A sourcebook.* Arlington, VA: ZERO TO THREE.

Fenichel, E. (2002). Relationships at risk: The policy environment as a context for infant development. *Infants and Young Children, 15*(2), 49–56.

Fernald, A. (1985). Four-month-old infants prefer to listen to motherese. *Infant Behaviour and Development, 8,* 181–195.

Fetal development. (2004, May 8). Retrieved January 19, 2005, from the *MedlinePlus Medical Encyclopedia,* an online service of the National Library of Medicine and the National Institutes of Health, http://www.nlm.nih.gov/medlineplus/ency/article/002398.htm

Field, T. (1998). Maternal depression effects on infants and early interventions. *Preventive Medicine, 27,* 200–203.

Field, T., & Brazelton, T. B. (1990). *Advances in touch.* Skillman, NJ: Johnson & Johnson.

Fitchen, J. M. (1995). The single-parent family, child poverty, and welfare reform. *Human Organization, 54,* 355–362.

Flavell, J. H. (1977). *Cognitive development.* Upper Saddle River, NJ: Prentice Hall.

Flavell, J. H. (1996). Piaget's legacy. *Psychological Science, 7,* 200–203.

Forman, D. R., O'Hara, M. W., Larsen, K., Coy, K. C., Gorman, L. L., & Stuart, S. (2003). Infant emotionality: Observational methods and the validity of maternal reports. *Infancy, 4*(4), 541–565.

Foumbi, J., & Lovich, R. (1997). *Global 1997: Role of men in the lives of children: A study on how improving knowledge about men* in families helps strengthen programming for children and women. New York: UNICEF.

Fox, N. A., & Calkins, S. (1993). Pathways to aggression and social withdrawl: Interactions among temperament, attachment, and regulation. In K. H. Rubin & J. Asendorpf (Eds.), *Social withdrawal, inhibition, and shyness in childhood* (pp. 81–100). Hillsdale, NJ: Erlbaum.

Fox, N. A., Henderson, H. A., Rubin, K. H., Calkins, S., & Schmidt, L. A. (2001). Continuity and discontinuity of behavioral inhibition and exuberance: Psychophysiological and behavioral influences across the first four years of life. *Child Development, 72*(1), 1–21.

Fox, N. A., Rubin, K.H., Calkins, S., Marshall, T., Coplan, R., Porges, W., et al. (1995). Frontal activation asymmetry and social competence at four years of age. *Child Development, 66,* 1770–1784.

Fraiberg, S. (1996). *The magic years: Understanding and handling the problems of childhood* (Reissue ed.). New York: Fireside.

Frank, D. A., Jacobs, R. R., Beeghly, M., Augustyn, M., Bellinger, D., Cabral, H., et al. (2002). Level of prenatal cocaine exposure and scores on the Bayley Scales of Infant Development: Modifying effects of caregiver, early intervention, and birth weight. *Pediatrics, 110*(6), 1143–1152.

Frank, E., & Rowe, D. (1990, June). Adoptive parents and their babies: Minimizing the risks to emotional development in the first three years. *Zero to Three, 10*(5), 19–25.

Frascarolo, F. (2004). Paternal involvement in child care and infant sociability. *Infant Mental Health Journal, 25*(6), 509–521.

Freedland, R. L., & Bertenthal, B. I. (1994). Developmental changes in interlimb coordination: Transition to hands and knees crawling. *Psychological Science, 5*(1), 26–33.

Friedman, D. L. (2004). When teachers participate, reflect, and choose change. *Young Children, 59*(6), 64–70.

Gable, S., Belsky, J., & Crnic, K. (1992). Marriage, parenting, and child development: Progress and prospects. *Journal of Family Psychology, 5*(3–4), 276–294.

Gable, S., & Cole, K. (2000, October). Parents' child care arrangements and their ecological correlates. *Early Education and Development, 11*(5), 549–572.

Gaensbauer, T. (2004). Telling their stories: Representation and reenactment of traumatic experiences occurring in the first year of life. *Zero to Three, 24*(5), 25–31.

Galinsky, E., Howes, C., & Kontos, S. (1995). *The family child care training study: Highlights of findings.* New York: Families and Work Institute.

Galluzzo, D., Matheson, C., Moore, J., & Howes, C. (1990). Social orientation to adults and peers in infant day care. In N. A. Fox & F. Fien (Eds.), *Infant day care: The current debate* (pp. 183–192). New York: Ablex.

Gandini, L., & Edwards, C. (Eds.). (2001). *Bambini: The Italian approach to infant/toddler care.* New York: Teachers College Press.

Gandini, L., & Goldhaber, J. (2001). Two reflections about documentation. In L. Gandini & C. Edwards (Eds.), *Bambini:*

The Italian approach to infant/toddler care (pp. 124–145). New York: Teachers College Press.

Garbarino, J., & Ganzel, B. (2000). The human ecology of early risk. In J. P. Shonkoff & S. J. Meisels (Eds.), *Handbook of early childhood intervention* (2nd ed., pp. 76–93). New York: Cambridge University Press.

Garcia, E. (1992). Effective instruction for language minority students: The teacher. *Journal of Education, 173*(2), 130–141.

Geist, E. (2003). Infants and toddlers exploring mathematics. *Young Children, 58*(1), 10–12.

Genesee, F., Nicoladis, E., & Paradis, J. (1996). Language differentiation in early bilingual development. *Journal of Developmental and Behavioral Pediatrics, 22,* 611–631.

George, C., & Soloman, J. (2003). *Babies' attachment to parents affected by overnights.* Retrieved February 9, 2009, from http://www.newswise.com/articles/view/?id=DIVORCE.MLS

Gergely, G., Bekkering, H., & Király, I. (2002). Rational imitation in preverbal infants. *Nature, 415,* 755

Gergely, G., & Csibra, G. (2006). Sylvia's recipe: The role of imitation and pedagogy in the transmission of cultural knowledge. In N. J. Enfield & S. C. Levenson (Eds.), *Roots of human sociality: Culture, cognition, and human interaction* (pp. 229–255). Oxford: Berg. Retrieved February 9, 2009, from http://www.cbcd.bbk.ac.uk/people/scientificstaff/gergo/pub/index.html/pub/sylvia.pdf

Gesell, A. (1946). The ontogenesis of infant behavior. In L. Carmichael (Ed.), *Manual of child psychology* (pp. 295–331). New York: Wiley.

Gibson, E. J., & Pick, A. D. (2003). *An ecological approach to perceptual learning and development.* London: Oxford University Press.

Girolametto, L. (2000). Directiveness in teachers' language input to toddlers and preschoolers in daycare. *Journal of Speech, Languages, and Hearing Research, 43*(5), 1101.

Goffman, E. (1976). Replies and responses. *Language and Society, 5*(3), 257–313.

Goldfield, E. C. (1989). Transition from rocking to crawling: Postural constraints on infant movement. *Developmental Psychology, 25*(6), 913–919.

Golombok, S. (2000). *Parenting: What really counts?* London: Routledge.

Golombok, S., Tasker, F., & Murray, C. (1997). Children raised in fatherless families from infancy: Family relationships and the socioemotional development of children of lesbian and single heterosexual mothers. *Journal of Child Psychology and Psychiatry, 38,* 783–791.

Golub, M. S., Keen, C. L., Gershwin, M. E., & Hendrickx, A. G. (1995). Developmental zinc deficiency and behavior. *Journal of Nutrition, 125,* 2263S–2271S.

Gonzalez-Mena, J. (2001). *Multicultural issues in child care* (3rd ed.). Mountain View, CA: Mayfield Publishing Co.

Gonzalez-Mena, J. (2006). *50 early childhood strategies for working and communicating with diverse families.* Upper Saddle River, NJ: Merrill/Prentice Hall.

Gonzalez-Mena, J. (2008). *Diversity in early care and education: Honoring differences* (5th ed.). Washington, DC: NAEYC.

Gonzalez-Mena, J., & Eyer, D. W. (2001). *Infants, toddlers, and caregivers* (5th ed.). Mountain View, CA: Mayfield.

Gonzalez-Mena, J., & Eyer, D. W. (2009). *Infants, toddlers, and caregivers: A curriculum of respectful, responsive care and education* (8th ed.). Boston: McGraw-Hill College.

Goodnow, J. J., Cashmore, J., Cotton, S., & Knight, R. (1984). Mothers' developmental timetables in two cultural groups. *International Journal of Psychology, 19,* 193–205.

Goodwyn, S., Acredolo, L., & Brown, C. (2000). Impact of symbolic gesturing on early language development. *Journal of Nonverbal Behavior, 24*(2), 81–103.

Gopnik, A., Meltzoff, A. N., & Kuhl, P. K. (1999). *The scientist in the crib: Minds, brains, and how children learn.* New York: Morrow.

Gottlieb, A. (2000). Luring your child into this life: A Beng path for infant care. In J. DeLoache & A. Gottlieb (Eds.), *A world of babies: Imagined child care guides for seven societies* (pp. 55–90). Cambridge, England: Cambridge University Press.

Gottlieb, G. (1992). *Individual development and evolution: The genesis of novel behavior.* New York: Oxford University Press.

Gottman, J. M., Katz, L. F., & Hooven, C. (1997). *Meta-emotion: How families communicate emotionally.* Mahwah, NJ: Erlbaum.

Gowen, J. W. (1995). The early development of symbolic play. *Young Children, 50*(3), 75–84.

Grabmeier, J. (1999). *Infants use sign language to communicate at Ohio State school.* Retrieved February 9, 2009, from http://www.scienceblog.com/community/older/1999/C/1999-02749.html

Greenman, J. (1988). *Caring spaces, learning places: Children's environments that work.* Redmond, WA: Exchange.

Greenman, J., & Stonehouse, A. (1996). *Prime times: A handbook for excellence in infant and toddler programs.* St. Paul, MN: Redleaf.

Greenspan, S. I. (1997). The growth of the mind and the endangered origins of intelligence. Reading, MA: Perseus Books.

Greenspan, S. I., & Greenspan, N. T. (1994). *First feelings: Milestones in the emotional development of your baby and child.* New York: Penguin. (Original work published 1985)

Griffin, A. (1998). Infant/toddler sleep in the child care context: Patterns, problems, and relationships. *Zero to Three, 19*(2) 24–29.

Gross, S. (1987). The power of purpose. *Child Care Information Exchange, 56.*

Grossman, K., Grossman, K. E., Spangler, G., Suess, G., & Unzer, L. (1985). Maternal sensitivity and the newborn's orientation responses as related to quality of attachment in northern Germany. In I. Bretherton & E. Waters (Eds.), *Growing points of attachment theory and research. Monographs of the Society for Research in Child Development* (233–256). Chicago: University of Chicago Press.

Gunnar, M., & Cheatham, C. L. (2003). Brain and behavior interface: Stress and the developing brain. *Infant Mental Health Journal, 24*(3), 195–211.

Gunnar, M. R., & Quevedo, K. (2007). The neurobiology of stress and development. *Annual Review of Psychology, 58*(1), 145.

Gunnar, M. R., Tout, K., de Haan, M., Pierce, S., & Stansbury, K. (1997). Temperament, social competence, and adrenocortical activity in preschoolers. *Developmental Psychobiology, 31*(1), 65–85.

Guralnik, M. J. (2000). The early intervention system and out-of-home child care. In D. Cryer & T. Harms (Eds.), *Infants and toddlers in out-of-home care* (pp. 207–234). Baltimore: Brookes.

Haith, M. M. (1980). *Rules that babies look by: The organization of newborn visual activity.* Hillsdale, NJ: Erlbaurn.

Hanna, E., & Meltzoff, A. N. (1993). Peer imitation by toddlers in a laboratory, home, and day-care contexts: Implications for social learning and memory. *Developmental Psychology, 4,* 701–710.

Harel, J., Scher, A. (2003). Insufficient responsiveness in ambivalent mother–infant relationships: Contextual and affective aspects. *Infant Behavior and Development, 26*(3), 371–383.

Harmes, T., Cryer, D., & Clifford, R. M. (2006). *Infant/toddler environment rating scale.* New York: Teachers College Press.

Hart, B., & Risley, T. R. (1992). American parenting of language-learning children: Persisting differences in family–child interactions observed in natural home environments. *Developmental Psychology, 28,* 1096–1105.

Hart, B., & Risley, T. R. (1995). *Meaningful differences in the everyday experience of young American children.* Baltimore: Brookes.

Hart, B., & Risley, T. R. (1999). *The social world of children learning to talk.* Baltimore: Brookes.

Hast, F., & Hollyfield, A. (1999). *Infant and toddler experiences.* St. Paul, MN: Redleaf Press.

Hauser-Cram, P. (1996). Mastery motivation in toddlers with developmental disabilities. *Child Development, 67,* 236–248.

Hawley, P., & Little, T. (1999). On winning some and losing some: A social relations approach to social dominance in toddlers. *Merrill-Palmer Quarterly, 45*(2), 185–214.

Hay, D. F., Payne, A., & Chadwick, A. (2004). Peer relations in childhood. *Journal of Child Psychology and Psychiatry, 45,* 84–108.

Helburn, S. W. (Ed.). (1995). *Cost, quality, and child outcomes in child care centers* [Technical report]. Denver: Department of Economics, Center for Research in Economic and Social Policy, University of Colorado Denver.

Henderson, H. A., Marshall, P., Fox, N. A., & Rubin, K. H. (2004). Converging psychophysiological and behavioral evidence for subtypes of social withdrawal in preschoolers. *Child Development, 75,* 251–263.

HGP (Human Genome Project). (2008). *Human Genome Project Information.* Retrieved February 9, 2009, from, http://www.ornl.gov/sci/techresources/Human_Genome/home.shtml

High/Scope. (2008). *Assessment.* Retrieved September 5, 2008, from http://www.highscope.org/Content.asp?ContentId=372

Hinde, R. (1988). Introduction. In R. Hinde & J. Stevenson-Hinde (Eds.), *Relationships within families: Mutual influences* (pp. 1–4). Oxford, England: Clarendon.

Hinde, R. (1992a). Developmental psychology in the context of older behavioral sciences. *Developmental Psychology, 28,* 1018–1029.

Hinde, R. (1992b). Ethological and relationship approaches. In R. Vasta (Ed.), *Six theories of child development: Revised formulations and current issues* (pp. 251–285). London: JKP Press.

Hinde, R., & Stevenson-Hinde, J. (1987). Interpersonal relationships and child development. *Developmental Review, 7,* 1–21.

Hirsch, E. S. (1996). *The block book* (3rd ed.). Washington, DC: NAEYC.

Hodgkinson, H. (2003). *Leaving too many children behind: A demographer's view on the neglect of America's youngest children.* Available from the Institute for Educational Leadership Web site: http://www.iel.org

Holdgrafer, G. (1991). Quantity of communicative behavior in children from birth to 30 months. *Perceptual and Motor Skills, 72,* 803–806.

Holdgrafer, G., & Dunst, C. J. (1990). Use of low-structured observation for assessing communicative intents in young children. *First Language, 10*(3), 243–253.

Honig, A. (1986). Tuning in to toddlers: A communication challenge. *Early Child Development and Care, 25,* 207–219.

Honig, A. (1993). Mental health for babies: What do theory and research tell us? *Young Children, 48*(3), 69–76.

Honig, A. (1994). Helping toddlers with group entry skills. *Zero to Three, 14*(5), 15–19.

Honig, A. (1995). Singing with infants and toddlers. *Young Children, 50*(5), 72–78.

Honig, A. (2000). Raising happy achieving children in the new millennium. *Early Child Development and Care, 163,* 79–106.

Honig, A. (2001). How infants and toddlers move through space. *Scholastic Early Childhood Today, 15*(7), 26–27.

Honig, A. (2002a). Choosing childcare for young children. In M. Bornstein (Ed.), *Handbook of parenting* (Vol. 4, pp. 411–435). Hillsdale, NJ: Erlbaum.

Honig, A. (2002b). Playing it out: The aftermath of September 11th in early care and education. *Zero to Three, 22*(3), 52.

Honig, A. (2002c). *Secure relationships: Nurturing infant toddler attachment in early care settings.* Washington, DC: NAEYC.

Honig, A. (2003a). Beauty for babies. *Scholastic Early Childhood Today, 17*(7), 22–25.

Honig, A. (2003b, September). Helping babies feel secure. *Scholastic Early Childhood Today, 18*(1), 27–29.

Honig, A. (2007). Choosing great books for babies: Helping children develop a love of reading. *Early Childhood Today (3), 21*(4), 24–26.

Honig, H. S., & Brophy, H. E. (1996). *Talking with your baby: Family as a first school.* Syracuse, NY: Syracuse University Press.

Howes, C. (1980). Peer play scale as an index of complexity of peer interaction. *Developmental Psychology, 16,* 371–372.

Howes, C. (1988). Peer interaction in young children. *Monographs of the Society for Research in Child Development, 53*(1), (Serial No. 217).

Howes, C. (1996). The earliest friendships. In W. M. Bukowksi, A. F. Newcomb, & W. W. Harup (Eds.), *The company they keep: Friendship in childhood and adolescence.* Boston: Cambridge University Press.

Howes, C. (2000). Social development, family, and attachment relationships. In D. Cryer & T. Harms (Eds.), *Infants and toddlers in out-of-home care.* Baltimore: Brookes.

Howes, D. (2006). Disabled children, parent–child interaction and attachment. *Child and Family Social Work, 11,* 95–106.

Howes, C., & Farver, J. (1987). Toddlers' responses to the distress of their peers. *Journal of Applied Developmental Psychology, 8,* 441–452.

Howes, C., & Hamilton, C. E. (1992). Children's relationships with caregivers: Mothers and childcare teachers. *Child Development, 63,* 859–866.

Howes, C., & Hamilton, C. E. (1993). The changing experience of childcare: Changes in teacher and in teacher–child relationships and children's social competence with peers. *Early Childhood Research Quarterly, 8,* 15–30.

Howes, C., Hamilton, C. E., & Matheson, C. (1994). Children's relationship with peers: Differential associations with aspects of the teacher–child relationship. *Child Development, 65,* 253–263.

Howes, C., Matheson, C., & Hamilton, C. E. (1992). Sequences in the development of competent play with peers: Social and social-pretend play. *Developmental Psychology, 28,* 961–974.

Howes, C., Phillips, D., & Whitebook, M. (1992). Thresholds of quality: Implications for the social development of children in center-based child care. *Child Development, 63,* 449–460.

Howes, C., & Phillipsen, L. (1998). Continuity in children's relations with peers. *Social Development, 7*(3), 340–349.

Howes, C., & Smith, E. (1995). Relations among child care quality, teacher behavior, children's play activities, emotional security, and cognitive activity in child care. *Early Childhood Research Quarterly, 10,* 381–404.

Howes, C., Unger, O., & Seidner, L. (1989). Social pretend play in toddlers: Parallels with social play and with solitary pretend. *Child Development, 60,* 77–84.

Head Start. (2008). FY 2008 Office of Head Start Monitoring Protocol. Available from http://eclkc.ohs.hhs.gov/

Huda, S. N., Grantham-McGregor, S. M., & Tomkins, A. (1999). Biochemical hypothyroidism secondary to iodine deficiency is associated with poor school achievement and cognition in Bangladeshi children. *Journal of Nutrition, 129,* 980–987.

Hussey-Gardner, B. (2003). *Parenting to make a difference.* Palo Alto, CA: Vort.

Huttenlocher, J., Haight, W., Bryk, A., Seltzer, M., & Lyons, T. (1991). Early vocabulary growth: Relation to language input and gender. *Developmental Psychology, 27*(2), 236–248.

Huttenlocher, P. R. (1984). Synapse elimination and plasticity in developing human cerebral cortex. *American Journal of Mental Defiency, 88,* 488–496.

Hyson, M. (2003). Preparing early childhood professionals: NAEYC's standards for programs. Washington, DC: NAEYC.

IRSF (International Rett Syndrome Research Foundation). (2008). Retrieved March 4, 2009, from http://www.rettsyndrome.org/

Ilari, B., & Johnson-Green, E. (2002, September). Musical resources for children. *Zero to Three, 23*(1), 49–52.

Irwin, J., Carter, A. S., & Briggs-Gowan, M. I. (2002). The social-emotional development of "late-talking" toddlers. *Journal of the American Academy of Child and Adolescent Psychiatry, 41*(11), 1324–1332.

Irvine, J. T. (1978). Wolof "magical thinking": Culture and conservation revisited. *Journal of Cross-Cultural Psychology, 9,* 300–310.

Isbell, R., & Isbell, C. (2003). *The complete learning spaces book for infants and toddlers.* Beltsville, MD: Gryphon House.

Ispa, J. M., Fine, M. A., Halgunseth, L. C., Harper, S., Robinson, J., Boyce, L., et al. (2004). Maternal intrusiveness, maternal warmth, and mother–toddler relationship outcomes: Variations across low-income ethnic and acculturation groups. *Child Development, 75*(6), 1613–1631.

Israel, M. S. (2004). Ethical dilemmas for early childhood educators: The ethics of being accountable. *Young Children, 59*(6), 24–32.

Izard, C. E., & Malatesta, C. Z. (1987). Perspectives on emotional development: Differential emotions theory of early emotional development. In J. D. Osofsky (Ed.), *Handbook of infant development* (pp. 494–554). New York: Wiley.

Jablon, J. R., Dombro, A., & Dichtelmiller, M. L. (1999). *The power of observation.* Washington, DC: Teaching Strategies.

Jacobson, J., & Jacobson, S. W. (2002). Effects of prenatal alcohol exposure on child development. *Alcohol Research and Health, 26*(4), 282–286.

Jacobvitz, D., & Hazen, H. (1999). Developmental pathways from infant disorganization to childhood peer relationships. In J. Solomon & C. George (Eds.), *Attachment disorganization* (pp. 127–159). New York: Guilford Press.

Jeffer, F., Bakermans-Kranenburg, M.J., & van IJzendoorn, M.H. (2005). The importance of parenting in the development of disorganized attachment: Evidence from a preventive intervention study in adoptive families. *Journal of Child Psychology and Psychiatry, 46*(3), 263–274.

Jennings, K. D., Connors, R. E., & Stegman, C. E. (1988). Does a physical handicap alter the development of mastery motivation during the preschool years? *Journal of the American Academy of Child and Adolescent Psychiatry, 27,* 312–317.

Johnson, J. E., Christie, J. F., & Yawkey, T. D. (1999). *Play and early childhood development* (2nd ed.). Boston, MA: Allyn and Bacon/Merrill Education.

Johnson, M. (2005). *Developmental cognitive neuroscience* (2nd ed.). Oxford: Blackwell.

Johnston, K. (1990). Mental health consultation to day care providers: The San Francisco daycare consultants program. *Zero to Three, 10*(3), 7–9.

Jordan, K. E., & Brannon, E. M. (2006). The multisensory representation of number in infancy. *Proceedings of the National Academy of Sciences, 103,* 3486–3489.

Jorde-Bloom, P. (1995). Shared decision making: The centerpiece of participatory management. *Young Children, 50*(4), 55–60.

Kagan, J. (1997). Temperament and the reactions to the unfamiliarity. *Child Development, 68,* 139–143.

Kantor, D. (2006). *Rett syndrome–Overview.* Retrieved March 4, 2009, from http://www.umn.edu/ency/article/001536.htm

Kaplan Early Learning Company Catalog. (2008). Retrieved September 21, 2008, from http://www.kaplanco.com

Kaplan, H., & Dove, H. (1987). Infant development among the Ache of eastern Paraguay. *Developmental Psychology, 23*(2), 190–198.

Kaplan, L. (1978). *Oneness and separateness.* New York: Simon & Schuster.

Katz, J. (2004). Building peer relationships in talk: Toddlers' peer conversations in child care. *Discourse Studies, 6*(3), 329–347.

Katz, J., & Snow, C. (2000). Language development in early childhood: The role of social interaction. In D. H. Cryer (Ed.), *Infants and toddlers in out-of-home care* (pp. 49–86). Baltimore: Brookes.

Katz, L. G. (1987). The nature of professions: Where is early childhood education? In L. G. Katz (Ed.), *Current topics in early childhood education* (Vol. 7). Norwood, NJ: Ablex.

Kearney, P., & Griffin, T. (2001). Between joy and sorrow: Being a parent of a child with developmental disability. *Journal of Advanced Nursing, 34*(5), 582–593.

Keenan, M. (1997). Shifting gears for infants and toddlers. *Child Care Information Exchange, 113,* 92–98.

Keenan, M. (1998). Making the transition from preschool to infant/toddler teacher. *Young Children, 53*(2), 5–11.

Keller, H. (2002). *Culture and development: Developmental pathways to individualism and interrelatedness.* Online readings in psychology and culture, available from the Center for Cross-Cultural Research Web site: http://www.ac.wwu.edu/~culture/contents_complete.htm

Keller, H., Lamm, B., Abels, M., Yovsi, R. D., Borke, J., Jensen, H., et al. (2006). Cultural models, socialization goals, and parenting ethnotheories: A multi-cultural analysis. *Journal of Cross-Cultural Psychology, 37,* 155–172.

Kelley, S. A., Brownell, C. A., & Campbell, S. B. (2000). Mastery motivation and self-evaluative affect in toddlers: Longitudinal relations with maternal behavior. *Child Development, 71*(4), 1061–1071.

Kerig, P. K., Cowan, P. A., & Cowan, C. P. (1993). Marital quality and gender differences in parent–child interaction. *Developmental Psychology, 29*(6), 931–939.

Kesner, J. E., & McKenry, P. C. (2001). Single parenthood and social competence in children of color. *Families in Society: The Journal of Contemporary Human Services, 82,* 135–143.

KIDS COUNT census data online. (2006). *2000 Census data—income and poverty profile for United States.* Retrieved August 24, 2008, from http://www.kidscount.org/cgi-bin/aeccensus.cgi?action=profileresults&area=00N&areaparent=00N&printerfriendly=0&section=5

KidsHealth. (2008). *Abusive head trauma (shaken baby syndrome).* Retrieved September 4, 2008, from http://www.kidshealth.org/parent/medical/brain/shaken.html

KidsHealth. (2009). *A primer on preemies.* Retrieved January 20, 2009, from http://health.msn.com/kids-health/articlepage.aspx?cp-documentid=100151172

Kim, Y. M., Sugai, G., & Kim, G. (1999). Early intervention needs of children at risk due to prenatal drug exposure: A survey of early childhood educators. *Journal of Research in Childhood Education, 13*(2), 207–214.

Kinch, A. F., & Schweinhart, L. J. (2004). Achieving high-quality child care: How ten programs deliver excellence parents can afford. Available from http://www.naeyc.org/ece/

Kitayama, S., & Marcus, H. R. (2000). The pursuit of happiness and the realization of sympathy: Cultural patterns of self, social relations, and well-being. In E. Diener & E. M. Suh (Eds.), *Culture and subjective well-being* (pp. 113–161). Cambridge, MA: MIT Press.

Klinkner, J. M., Riley, D., & Roach, M. A. (2005). Organizational climate as a tool for child care staff retention. *Young Children, 60*(6), 90–95.

Klinnert, M., Emde, R. N., Butterfield, P., & Campos, J. J. (1986). Social referencing: The infant's use of emotional signals from a friendly adult with mother present. *Developmental Psychology, 22*(4), 427–432.

Konner, M. (1977). Infancy among the Kalihari Desert San. In P. H. Liederman, S. R. Tulin, & A. Rosenfeld (Eds.), *Culture and infancy: Variations in the human experience* (pp. 287–327). New York: Academic Press.

Kontos, S. (1988). Family day care as an integrated early intervention setting. *Topics in Early Childhood Special Education, 8*(2), 1–4.

Kontos, S., Howes, C., Shinn, M., & Galinsky, E. (1995). *Quality in family child care and relative care.* New York: Teachers College Press.

Kopp, C. B. (2000). Self-regulation in children. In J. J. Smelser & P. B. Baltes (Eds.), *International encyclopedia of the social and behavioral sciences.* Oxford, England: Elsevier.

Kranowitz, C. S., & Silver, L. B. (1998). *The out-of-sync child: Recognizing and coping with sensory integration dysfunction.* New York: Perigee.

Krøjgaard, P. (2005). Infants' search for hidden persons. *International Journal of Behavioral Development, 29*(1), 70–79.

Kubicek, L. F. (2003). Fresh perspectives on young children and family routines. *Zero to Three, 22*(4), 4–9.

Kuhl, P. K. (2000). A new view of language acquisition. *PNAS, 97*(22), 11850–11857.

Kuhl, P. K. (2007). Is speech learning 'gated' by the social brain? *Developmental Science, 10*(1), 110–120.

Kuhl, P. K., Williams, K. A., Lacerda, F., Stevens, K. N., & Lindblom, B. (1992). Linguistic experience alters phonetic perception in infants by 6 months of age. *Science, 255,* 606–608.

Kumin, L. (1998). *Comprehensive speech and language treatment for infants, toddlers, and children with Down syndrome.* Retrieved September 3, 2008, from Down Syndrome: Health Issues Web site: http://www.ds-health.com/speech.htm

Kupetz, B., & Green, E. (1997). Sharing books with infants and toddlers: Facing the challenges. *Young Children, 52*(2), 22–27.

Kutner, L. (1993). *Pregnancy and the first year.* New York: Morrow.

LaFrenierse, P. J., & Sroufe, L. A. (1985). Profiles of peer competence in the preschool: Interrelations between measures, influence of social ecology, and relations to attachment history. *Developmental Psychology, 21,* 56–69.

Laible, D. J., & Thompson, R. A. (2002). Mother–child conflict in the toddler years: Lessons in emotion, morality, and relationships. *Child Development, 73*(4), 1187–1203.

Lally, J. R. (1995). The impact of child care policies and practices on infant/toddler identity formation. *Young Children, 51*(1), 58–67.

Lally, J. R. (2003). Infant-toddler child care in the United States: Where has it been? Where is it now? Where is it going? *Zero to Three, 24*(1), 29–34.

Lally, J. R., Griffin, A., Fenichel, E., Segal, M., Szanton, E., & Weissbourd, B. (1995). *Caring for infants and toddlers in groups: Developmentally appropriate practice.* Washington, DC: ZERO TO THREE.

Lally, J. R., & Keith, H. (1997). Early Head Start: The first two years. *Zero to Three, 17*(3), 3–8.

Lally, J. R., Torres, Y., & Phelps, P. (1994). Caring for infants and toddlers in groups: Necessary considerations for emotional, social, and cognitive development. *Zero to Three, 14*(5), 1–8.

Lamb, M. (1998). Nonparental child care: Context, quality, correlates. In W. Damon, I. E. Sigel, & K. A. Renninger (Eds.), *Handbook of child psychology: Vol. 4. Child psychology in practice.* New York: Wiley.

Lamb, M. E. (2004). *The role of the father in child development,* 4th Ed. New York: John Wiley & Sons.

Lamb, M. E., Bornstein, M. H., & Teti, D. (2002). *Development in infancy* (4th ed.). Hillsdale, NJ: Erlbaum.

Lawrence, R. A. (1997). A review of the medical benefits and contraindications to breastfeeding in the United States. *Maternal and child health: Technical information bulletin.* Washington, DC: National Center for Maternal and Child Health.

Layzer, J., Goodson, B., Bernstein, L. & Price, C. (2001). *National evaluation of family support programs.* Cambridge, MA: Abt Associates.

Lazarov, M., & Evans, A. (2000). Breastfeeding: Encouraging the best for low-income women. *Zero to Three, 21*(1), 15–23.

Legerstee, M., & Barillas, Y. (2003). Sharing attention and pointing to objects at 12 months: Is the intentional stance implied? *Cognitive Development, 18*(1), 91–110.

Lerner, C., & Dombro, A. (2000). *Learning and growing together: Understanding and supporting your child's development.* Washington, DC: ZERO TO THREE.

Lew, A. R., & Butterworth, G. (1997). The development of hand-mouth coordination in 2- to 5-month-old infants: Similarities with reaching and grasping. *Infant Behavior and Development, 20*(1), 59–69.

Lewis, M. L. (1993). Self-conscious emotions: Embarrassment, pride, shame, and guilt. In M. Lewis & J. M. Haviland-Jones (Eds.), *Handbook of emotions* (pp. 563–573). New York: Guilford Press.

Lewis, R. (2007). *Postural Drainage.* Retrieved September 4, 2008, from Medline Plus Web site: http://www.nim.nih.gov/medlineplus/ency/imagepages/18084.htm

Lewkowicz, D. J., & Lickliter, R. (Eds.). (1994). *The development of intersensory perception: Comparative perspectives.* Hillsdale, NJ: Erlbaum.

Lieberman, A. (1993). *The emotional life of a toddler.* New York: Free Press.

Lieberman, A., Silverman, R., & Pawl, J. (2000). Infant–parent psychotherapy: Core concepts and current approaches. In C. H. Zeanah (Ed.), *Handbook of infant mental health* (pp. 472–484). New York: Guilford Press.

Lorenz, K. (1966). *On aggression.* New York: Harcourt, Brace & World.

Love, J. M., Kisker, E. E., Ross, C., Raikes, H., Constantine, J., Boller, K., et al. (2005). The effectiveness of Early Head Start for 3-year-old children and their parents: Lessons for policy and programs. *Developmental Psychology, 41*(6), 885–901.

Lowenthal, B. (1995). Strategies that promote social skills in toddlers with special needs in the inclusive setting. *Infant-Toddler Intervention: The Trandisciplinary Journal, 5*(1), 15–22.

Lozoff, B., Klein, N. K., Nelson, E. C., McClish, D. K., Manuel, M., & Chacon, M. E. (1998). Behavior of infants with iron-deficiency anemia. *Child Development, 69,* 24–36.

Lu, M. (1998). Language learning in social and cultural contexts. *ERIC Digest* (ED423531). Bloomington, IN: ERIC Clearinghouse on Reading, English, and Communication.

Lu, M. (2000). Language development in the early years. *ERIC Digest* (ED446336). Bloomington, IN: ERIC Clearinghouse on Reading, English, and Communication.

Lussier, B. J. (1994). Effect of three adult interaction styles on infant engagement. *Journal of Early Intervention, 18*(1), 12–24.

Lutchmaya, S., & Baron-Cohen, S. (2002). Human sex differences in social and nonsocial looking preferences at 12 months of age. *Infant Behavior and Development, 25*(3), 319–326.

Lynch, E. W., & Hanson, M. J. (1998). Steps in the right direction. In E. W. Lynch & M. J. Hanson (Eds.), *Developing cross-cultural competence: A guide for working with parents and families* (pp. 491–512). Baltimore: Brookes.

Maccoby, E. E. (1998). *The two sexes: Growing up apart, coming together.* Cambridge, MA: Belknap.

Maccoby, E. E., & Martin, J. A. (1983). Socialization in the context of the family: Parent–child interaction. In P. H. Mussen & E. M. Hetherington (Eds.), *Handbook of child psychology* (Vol. 4, pp. 1–102). New York: Wiley.

Magill-Evans, J., Harrison, M. Benzies, K., Gierl, M., & Kimak, C. (2007). Effects of parenting education on first-time fathers' skills in interactions with their infants. *Fathering: A journal of theory, research, & practice about men as fathers, 5*(1), 42–57.

Mahler, M. S. (1975). *The psychological birth of the human infant.* New York: Basic Books.

Mahoney, G., Fors, S., & Wood, S. (1990). Material directed behavior revisited. *American Journal on Mental Retardation, 94,* 398–406.

Main, M. (2000). The organized categories of infant, child, and adult attachment: Flexible vs. inflexible attention under attachment-related stress. *Journal of the American Psychoanalytic Association, 48,* 1055–1096.

Main, M., & Cassidy, J. (1988). Categories of response with the parent at age 6: Predicted from infant attachment classifications and stable over a one-month period. *Developmental Psychology, 24,* 415–426.

Main, M., & Goldwyn, R. (1994). Adult attachment rating and classification systems. In M. Main (Ed.), *A typology of human attachment organization assessed in discourse, drawings, and interviews.* New York: Cambridge University Press.

Main, M., Kaplan, N., & Cassidy, J. (1985). Security in infancy, childhood, and adulthood: A move to the level of representation. In I. Bretherton & E. Waters (Eds.), *Growing points of attachment theory and research, Monographs of the Society for Research in Child Development, 50*(Serial No. 209), 66–104.

Malaguzzi, L., & Gandini, L. (1993). For an education based on relationships. *Young Children, 49*(1), 9–12.

Malatesta, C. Z., Culver, C., Tesman, J. R., & Shepard, B. (1989). The development of emotional expression during the first two years of life. *Monographs of the Society for Research in Child Development, 54*(Serial No. 219), 1–104.

Malina, R. M. (2004). Motor development during infancy and early childhood: Overview and suggested directions for research. *International Journal of Sport and Health Medicine, 2,* 50–66.

Mandler, J. M., & McDonough, L. (1996). Concept formation in infancy. *Cognitive Development, 8,* 291–318.

Mangione, P. L., Lally, R. J., & Signer, S. (1990). The ages of infancy: Caring for young, mobile, and older infants [Video magazine]. Sacramento, CA: CDE Press.

Marcus, H. R., & Kitayama, S. (1991). Culture and the self: Implications for cognition, emotion, and motivation. *Psychological Review, 98,* 222–253.

Marsden, D. B., Dombro, A. L., Dichtelmiller, M. L. (2003). *The Ounce Scale user's guide.* New York: Pearson Early Learning.

Maslow, A. H. (1968). *Toward a psychology of being.* New York: Van Nostrand Reinhold.

Matthey, S., Barnett, B., Ungerer, J., & Waters, B. (2000). Paternal and maternal depressed mood during the transition to parenthood. *Journal of Affective Disorders, 60*(2), 75–85.

Maxted, A. E., Dickstein, S., Miller-Loncar, C., High, P., Spritz, B., Liu, J., Lester, B. M. (2005). Infant colic and maternal depression. *Infant Mental Health Journal, 26*(1), 56–68.

Mayberry, R. I., Lock, E., & Kazmi, H. (2002). Linguistic ability and early language exposure. *Nature, 417*(6884), 38.

McCartney, K. (1984). Effect of quality of day-care environment on children's language development. *Developmental Psychology, 20,* 244–260.

McCullough, A. L., Kirksey, A., Wachs, T. D., McGabe, G. P., Bassily, N. S., Bishry, Z., et al. (1990, June). Vitamin B-6 status of Egyptian mothers: Relation to infant behavior and maternal–infant interactions. *American Journal of Clinical Nutrition, 51*(6), 1067–1074.

McDevitt, T. M., & Ormrod, J. E. (2002). *Child development and education.* Upper Saddle River, NJ: Merrill/Prentice Hall.

McElwain, N. L., Cox, M. J., Burchinal, M. R., & Macfie, J. (2003). Differentiating among insecure mother–infant attachment classifications: A focus on child–friend interaction and exploration during solitary play at 36 months. *Attachment & Human Development, 5*(2), 136–164.

McElwain, N. L., & Booth-LaForce, C. (2006). Maternal sensitivity to infant distress and non-distress as predictors of infant–mother attachment security. *Journal of Family Psychology, 20*(2), 247–255.

McFarlane, J. (1975). Olfaction in the development of social preferences in the human neonate. In M. Hofer (Ed.), *Parent–infant interaction.* Amsterdam: Elsevier.

McKenna, J. (nd). *Rethinking "healthy" infant sleep.* Retrieved September 2, 2008, from The Natural Child Project: http://www.naturalchild.org/james_mckenna/rethinking.html

McLane, J. B., & McNamee, G. D. (1991). The beginnings of literacy. *Zero to Three, 12*(1), 1–8.

Mehler, J., Jusczyk, P., Lambertz, G., Halsted, N., Bertoncini, J., & Ameil-Tison, C. (1988). A precurser of language acquisition in young infants. *Cognition, 29,* 143–178.

Meisels, S. J., Dombro, A., Marsden, D. B., Weston, D. R., & Jewkes, A. M. (2003). *The Ounce Scale.* New York: Pearson Early Learning.

Meltzoff, A. N. (1995). Understanding the intentions of others: Reenactment of intended acts of others by 10-month-old children. *Developmental Psychology, 31,* 838–850.

Meltzoff, A. N. (2005). Imitation and other minds: The "Like Me" hypothesis. In S. Hurley & N. Chater (Eds.), *Perspectives on imitation: From cognitive neuroscience to social science* (pp. 55–77). Cambridge: MIT Press.

Meltzoff, A. N., & Moore, M. K. (1977). Imitation of facial and manual gestures by human neonates. *Science, 198,* 75–78.

Mennella, J. A., & Beauchamp, G. K. (2002). Flavor experiences during formula feeding are related to preferences during childhood. *Early Human Development, 68,* 71–82.

Meyers, A., & Chawla, N. (2000). Nutrition and the social, emotional, and cognitive development of infants and young children. *Zero to Three, 21*(1), 5–11.

Michigan State University (nd). American Sign Language browser. Retrieved March 4, 2009, from http://aslbrowser.commtechlab.msu.edu/

Miller, K. (1999). *Simple steps: Developmental activities for infants, toddlers, and two-year-olds.* Beltsville, MD: Gryphon House.

Milne, A. A. (1926). *Winnie-the-Pooh.* London, England: Methuen & Co. Ltd.

Milne, A. A. (1991). *Winnie-the-Pooh.* New York: Dutton. (Original work published 1926)

Minkler, M. (2002). *Grandparents and other relatives raising children: Characteristics, needs, best practices, & implications for*

the aging network. Washington, DC: Administration on Aging, Department of Health and Human Services.

Mischel, W. (1961). Father absence and the delay of gratification. *Journal of Abnormal and Social Psychology, 62,* 116–124.

Miyake, K., Chen, S. J., & Campos, J. J. (1985). Infant temperament, mother's mode of interaction, and attachment in Japan: An interim report. In I. Bretherton & E. Waters (Eds.), *Growing points of attachment theory and research, Monographs of the Society for Research in Child Development, 50*(Serial No. 209), 276–297.

MOD (March of Dimes). (2009a). *Cerebral palsy. Quick reference: fact sheets.* Retrieved February 10, 2008, http://www.marchofdimes.com

MOD (March of Dimes). (2009b). *Genital herpes and pregnancy. Quick reference: fact sheets.* Retrieved July 1, 2005, from http://www.modimes.com

MOD (March of Dimes). (2009c). *Multiples: twins, triplets, and beyond.* Retrieved January 20, 2009, from http://search.marchofdimes.com/cgi-bin/MsmGo.exe?grab_id=6&page_id=10092800&query=twins&hiword=TWIN+TWINING+TWINLESS+twins+

MOD (March of Dimes). (2009d). *Preterm births rise 36 percent since early 1980s.* Retrieved January 20, 2009, from http://www.marchofdimes.com/peristats/whatsnew.aspx?id=35&dv=wn

MOD (March of Dimes). (2009e). *Sexually transmitted infections in pregnancy.* Retrieved January 21, 2009, from http://www.marchofdimes.com/professionals/14332_1226.asp

Moller, L., & Serbin, L. (1996). Antecedents of toddler gender segregation: Cognitive consonance, gender-typed toy preferences, and behavioral compatibility. *Sex Roles: A Journal of Research, 34*(7–8), 445–461.

Mondschein, E. R., Adolph, K. E., & Tamis-LeMonda, C. S. (2000). Gender bias in mothers' expectations about infant crawling. *Journal of Experimental Child Psychology, 77*(4), 304–316.

Moon, C., Cooper, R. P., & Fifer, W. P. (1993). Two-day-olds prefer their native language. *Infant Behavior and Development, 16*(4), 495–500.

Morgan, G. A., Harmon, R. J., & Maslin-Cole, C. A. (1999). Imitation of facial and manual gestures by human neonates. *Science, 198,* 75–78.

Morgan Stanley Children's Hospital of New York—Pres by terian. (nd). Age Appropriate Vision Milestones, http://childrensnyp.org/

Mosley, J., & Thompson, E. (1995). Fathering behavior and child outcomes: The role of race and poverty. In W. Marsiglio (Ed.), *Fatherhood: Contemporary theory, research, and social policy.* Thousand Oaks, CA: Sage.

Mother's day: More than candy and flowers, working parent's need paid time-off. (2002). Retrieved February 10, 2009, from http://www.childpolicyintl.org/issuebrief/issuebrief5.htm

Müller, E. (2007). Collaborative partnerships between SEAs and Parent Training and Information Centers (PTIs). Retrieved February 11, 2009, from http://www.nichcy.org/products/pages/default.aspx?productid=7437

Muir, E., Lojkasek, M., & Cohen, N. (1999). *Watch, wait, and wonder: A manual describing a dyadic infant-led approach to problems in infancy and early childhood.* Toronto, Ontario, Canada: Hincks-Dellcrest.

Mulligan, S. (1997). Group activities: One child at a time. *Child Care Plus, 8*(1), 1.

Murphy, L. B. (1936). Sympathetic behavior in young children. *Journal of Experimental Education, 5,* 79–90.

Murphy, L. B. (1994). Hopping, jumping, leaping, skipping, and loping: Savoring the possibilities of locomotion. *Zero to Three, 15*(1), 27.

Murray, A. D., & Yingling, J. L. (2000). Competence in language at 24 months: Relations with attachment security and home stimulation. *Journal of Genetic Psychology, 161*(2), 133–140.

Murray, L., & Cooper, P. J. (1999, August). Effects of postnatal depression on infant development. *Archives of Disease in Childhood, 77,* 99–101.

NAEYC (National Association for the Education of Young Children). (2005). *Code of ethical conduct and statement of commitment.* Retrieved from http://www.naeyc.org/about/positions/PSethO5.asp

NAEYC (National Association for the Education of Young Children). (2006a). NAEYC accreditation. Assessment in the new NAEYC accreditation system. *Young Children, 61*(3), 60–62.

NAEYC (National Association for the Education of Young Children). (2006b). *NAEYC early childhood program standards and accreditation criteria.* Retrieved October 20, 2007, from http://www.naeyc.org/academy/standards/

NAEYC (National Association for the Education of Young Children). (2008). *Standards for professional preparation.* Retrieved February 6, 2009, from http://www.naeyc.org/faculty/college.asp

NAFCC (National Association for Family Child Care). (2009). *NAFCC's restructured accreditation process.* Retrieved February 9, 2009, from http://www.nafcc.org/restructuredprocess/overview.htm

Nag, M. (1994). Beliefs and practices about food during pregnancy. *Economic and Political Weekly,* 2427–2438.

Namy, L. (2001). What's in a name when it isn't a word? 17-month-olds' mapping of nonverbal symbols to object categories. *Infancy, 2*(1), 73–86.

Namy, L., & Waxman, S. R. (1998). Words and gestures: Infants' interpretations of different forms of symbolic reference. *Child Development, 69*(2), 295–308.

National SIDS/Infant Death Resource Center. (2007, May). *Helping Baby "Back to Sleep."* Retrieved September 17, 2008, from http://www.sidcenter.org/documents/sidrc/BackToSleep.pdf

NCCIC (National Child Care Information and Technical Assistance Center). (2004). Overview of tiered strategies: Quality rating, reimbursement, licensing. Retrieved March 1, 2009, from http://www.ncic.acf.hhs.gov/

NCCIC (National Child Care Information and Technical Assistance Center). (2007). *Brain devlopment.* Retrieved February 11, 2009, from http://nccic-acf.hhs.gov/poptopics/brain.html

NCCIC (National Child Care Information and Technical Assistance Center). (2009). *Child care technical assistance network.* Retrieved January 23, 2009, from http://nccic.acf.hhs.gov/cctan/index.html

NCSBS (National Center on Shaken Baby Syndrome). (2009). *Physical consequences of shaking.* Retrieved February 11, 2009, from http://www.dontshake.org/

NCTM (National Council of Teachers of Mathematics). (2000). *Principles and standards for school mathematics.* Washington, DC: Author.

NDSS (National Down Syndrome Society). (2005). Available at the NDSS Web site, http://www.ndss.org

NECTAC (National Early Childhood Technical Assistance Center). (2005). *Minimum components under IDEA for a statewide, comprehensive system of early intervention services to infants and toddlers with special needs (Including American Indian and homeless infants and toddlers).* Retrieved February 6, 2009, from http://www.nectac.org/partc/componen.asp.

Newman, R. S., & Hussain, I. (2006). Changes in preference for infant-directed speech in low and moderate noise by 4.5- to 13-month-olds. *Infancy, 10*(1), 61–76.

NFXF (National Fragile X Foundation). (2008). *What is fragile X?* Available at the NFXF Web site, http://www.fragilex.org/html/what.htm

NICHCY. (2003). *Pervasive developmental disorders. Fact sheet 20.* Retrieved February 6, 2009, from http://old.nichcy.org/pubs/factshe/fs20txt.htm

NICHD Early Child Care Research Network. (1996). Characteristics of infant child care: Factors contributing to positive caregiving. *Early Childhood Research Quarterly, 11,* 269–306.

NICHD Early Child Care Research Network. (1997). The effects of infant child care on infant–mother attachment security: Results of the NICHD study of early child care. *Child Development, 68,* 860–879.

NICHD Early Child Care Research Network. (1998). Relations between family predictors and child outcomes: Are they weaker for children in child care? *Developmental Psychology, 34,* 1119–1128.

NICHD Early Child Care Research Network. (2000a). Characteristics and quality of child care for toddlers and preschoolers. *Applied Developmental Science, 4*(3), 116–135.

NICHD Early Child Care Research Network. (2000b). The relation of child care to cognitive and language development. *Child Development, 71*(4), 960–980.

NICHD Early Child Care Research Network. (2001a). Child care and children's peer interaction at 24 and 36 months. *Child Development, 72*(5), 1478–1501.

NICHD Early Child Care Research Network. (2001b). Nonmaternal care and family factors in early development: An overview of the NICHD study of early child care. *Journal of Applied Developmental Psychology, 22,* 457–492.

NICHD Early Child Care Research Network. (2002a). Child care structure, process, outcome: Direct and indirect effects of child care quality on young children's development. *Psychological Science, 13,* 199–206.

NICHD Early Childhood Research Network. (2002b). The interaction of childcare and family in relation to child development at 24 and 36 months. *Applied Developmental Science, 6*(3), 144–157.

NICHD Early Child Care Research Network. (2003). Child care and mother–child interaction from 36 months through first grade. *Infant Behavior and Development, 26,* 345–370.

NICHD Early Child Care Research Network. (2004). Father's and mother's parenting behavior and beliefs as predictors of child social adjustment in the transition to school. *Journal of Family Psychology, 18*(4), 628–638.

Nicoladis, E., & Genesee, F. (1996). A longitudinal study of pragmatic differentiation in young bilingual children. *Language Learning, 46*(3), 439–464.

NIH (National Institutes of Health). (2000). *National Institutes of Health consensus development statement. Phenylketonuria: Screening and management.* Washington, DC: Author.

NTSADA (National Tay-Sachs & Allied Diseases Association, Inc.). (2009). What is Tay-Sachs disease? Retrieved February 11, 2009, from http://www.ntsad.org/

NWHIC (National Women's Health Information Center). (2009). *Pregnancy and a healthy diet.* Retrieved February 11, 2009, from http://www.4woman.gov/

O'Brien, M. (1997). *Inclusive child care for infants and toddlers: Meeting individual and special needs.* Baltimore: Brookes.

Ødegaard, E. E. (2006). What's worth talking about? Meaning-making in toddler-initiated conarratives in preschool. *Early Years, 26*(1), 79–92.

Odom, S., & Diamond, K. (1998). Inclusion of young children with special needs in early childhood education: The research base. *Early Childhood Research Quarterly, 13*(1), 3–25.

Olson, J. M., Vernon, P. S., Harris, J. A., & Jang, K. L. (2001). The heritability of attitudes: A study of twins. *Journal of Personality and Social Psychology, 80,* 845–860.

Olson, M. R., & Haynes, J. A. (1993). Successful single parents. *Families in Society: The Journal of Contemporary Human Services, 74,* 259–267.

Oser, C., & Cohen, J. (2003). *America's babies: The Zero to Three policy center data book.* Washington, DC: ZERO TO THREE.

OTIS. (2005). *DEET (N, N-ethyl-m-toluamide) and pregnancy.* Retrieved February 11, 2009, from http://www.otispregnancy.org/pdf/DEET.pdf

Ozonoff, S., Macari, S., Young, G. S., Goldring, S., Thompson, M., & Rogers, S. J. (2008). Atypical object exploration at 12 months of age is associated with autism in a prospective sample. *Autism: the International Journal of Research and Practice, 12*(5), 457–472.

Pan, B. A., Imbens-Bailey, A., Winner, K., & Snow, C. (1996). Communicative intents expressed by parents in interaction with young children. *Merrill-Palmer Quarterly, 42,* 248–266.

Park, K. A., & Waters, E. (1989). Security of attachment and preschool friendships. *Child Development, 60*(5), 1076–1081.

Parke, R. D. (1996). *Fatherhood.* Cambridge, MA: Harvard University Press.

Parke, R. D. (2000). Father involvement: A developmental psychological perspective. *Marriage and Family Review, 29*(2/3), 43–58.

Parke, R. D. (2002). Fathers and familes. In M. H. Bornstein (Ed.), *Handbook of parenting:* Vol. 3: Being and becoming a parent (2nd ed., pp. 27–63). Mahwah, NJ: Lawrence Erlbaum.

Parke, R. D. (2004). Fathers, families, and the future. A plethora of plausible predictions. *Merrill-Palmer Quarterly, 50*(4), 456–470.

Parke, R., & Swain, D. (1976). The father's role in infancy. *Family Coordinator, 25,* 365–372.

Parkinson, G. M. (2002). High incidence of language disorder in children with focal epilepsies. *Developmental Medicine and Child Neurology, 44,* 533–537.

Parlakian, R. (2003). *Before the ABCs: Promoting school readiness in infants and toddlers.* Washington, DC: ZERO TO THREE.

Parlakian, R., & Seibel, N. (2001). *Being in charge: Reflective leadership in infant/family programs.* Washington, DC: ZERO TO THREE.

Parten, M. B. (1932). Social participation among preschool children. *Journal of Abnormal and Social Psychology, 27,* 243–269.

Parten, M. B. (1933). Social play among preschool children. *Journal of Abnormal and Social Psychology, 28,* 136–147.

Patterson, C. (1992). Children of lesbian and gay parents. *Child Development, 63,* 1025–1042.

Patterson, C. (2006). Children of lesbian and gay parents. *Current Directions in Psychological Science, 15*(5), 241–244.

Pawl, J. H. (1995). The therapeutic relationship as human connectedness: Being held in another's mind. *Zero to Three, 15*(4), 1–5.

Pawl, J. H., & St. John, M. (1998). How you are is as important as what you do . . . in making a positive difference for infants, toddlers, and their families. Washington, DC: ZERO TO THREE.

Pearson, B. Z., Fernandez, S. C., Lewedeg, V., & Oller, D. K. (1997). The relation of input factors to lexical learning by bilingual infants. *Applied Psycholinguistics, 18*(1), 41–58.

Pearson, B. Z., Fernandez, S. C., & Oller, D. K. (1993). Lexical development in bilingual infants and toddlers: Comparison to monolingual norms. *Language Learning, 43*(1), 93–120.

Penn, H. (2005). *Unequal childhoods: Young children's lives in poor countries.* London: Routledge.

Perera, F. P., Illman, S. M., Kinney, P. L., Whyatt, R. M., Kelvin, E. A., Shepard, P., et al. (2002). The challenge of preventing environmentally related disease in young children: Community-based research in New York City. *Environmental Health Perspectives, 110*(2), 197–204.

Perrin, E. C. (2002). Technical report: Coparent or second-parent adoption by same-sex parents. *Pediatrics, 109*(2), 341–344.

Perry, B. (1996). *Maltreated children: Experience, brain development, and the next generation.* New York: Norton.

Perry, B. (1999, July–August). Time is precious in early childhood development. *Good Health Magazine,* 1.

Perry, B. (2001, April). The importance of pleasure in play. *Scholastic Early Childhood Today,* 24–25.

Perry, B., & Pollard, R. (1997). Altered brain development following global neglect in early childhood. *Neuroscience.* Proceedings from the annual meeting, New Orleans.

Petersen, S., Jones, L., McGinley, K. A. (2008). *Early learning guidelines for infants and toddlers: Recommendations to states.*

Washington, DC: ZERO TO THREE. Also retrieved January 23, 2009, from http://www.zerotothree.org/site/DocServer/ Early_Learning_Guidelines_for_Infants_and_Toddlers.pdf? docID=4961

Petersen, S. H., & Wittmer, D. S. (2008). *Endless opportunities for infants and toddlers: A relationship-based approach.* Upper Saddle River, NJ: Merrill/Prentice Hall.

Petitto, L. A., Katerelos, M., Levy, B. Gauna, K. Tetreault, K., & Ferraro, V. (2001). Bilingual signed and spoken language acquisition from birth: Implications for the mechanisms underlying early bilingual language acquisition. *Journal of Child Language, 28*(2), 453–496.

Pham, L. (1994). Infant dual language acquisition revisited. *Journal of Educational Issues of Language Minority Students, 14,* 185–210.

Phillips, D., & Adams, G. (2001). Child care and our youngest children. *The Future of Children Journal: Caring for Infants and Toddlers, 11*(1), 35–52.

Piaget, J. (1952). *The origins of intelligence in children.* New York: Norton.

Piaget, J. (1954). *The construction of reality in the child.* New York: Basic Books.

Piaget, J. (1962). *Play, dreams and imitation in childhood.* New York: Norton.

Piaget, J. (1997). *The moral judgment of the child.* New York: Free Press Paperbacks. (Original work published 1965)

Piaget, J. (2002). *The language and thought of the child.* Routledge Classics, New York: Routledge. (Original work published 1926)

Piaget, J., & Inhelder, B. (2000). *The psychology of the child.* New York: Basic Books. (Original work published 1969)

Piek, J. P., & Gasson, N. (2002). Limb and gender differences in the development of coordination in early infancy. *Human Movement Science, 21*(5–6), 621–639.

Pierroutsakos, S. L. (2000). Infants of the dreaming: A Warlpiri guide to child care. In J. DeLoache & A. Gottlieb (Eds.), *A world of babies: Imagined child care guides for seven societies.* Cambridge, England: Cambridge University Press.

Pines, M. (1979). Good samaritans at age two? *Psychology Today,* 66–73.

Pines, M. (1984). Children's winning ways. *Psychology Today,* 59–65.

PITC (Program for Infant/Toddler Care). (2008). Retrieved September 29, 2008, from http://www.pitc.org/

Plusquellec, P., Francois, N., Boivin, M., Perusse, D., & Tremblay, R. E. (2007). Dominance among unfamiliar peers starts in infancy. *Infant Mental Health Journal, 28*(3), 324–343.

Pollak, S. D., & Kistler, D. J. (2002). Early experience is associated with the development of categorical representations for facial expressions of emotion. *Proceedings of the National Academy of Science, 99*(13), 9072–9076.

Popenoe, D. (1999). Challenging the culture of fatherlessness. In W. F. Horn, D. E. Eberly, D. Blankenhorn, & M. B. Pearlstein (Eds.), *The fatherhood movement: A call to action* (pp. 17–24). Lanham, MD: Lexington.

Post, J., & Hohmann, M. (2000). *Tender care and early learning: Supporting infants and toddlers in child care settings.* Ypsilanti, MI: High/Scope.

Poulsen, M. (1993). Strategies for building resilience in infants and young children at risk. *Infants and Young Children, 6*(2), 29–40.

Pratt, M. (1999). The importance of infant/toddler interactions. *Young Children, 54*(4), 26–29.

Press, B., & Greenspan, S. I. (1985). The toddler group: A setting for adaptive social/emotional development of disadvantaged one- and two-year-olds in a peer group. *Zero to Three, 5*(4), 6–11.

Pretti-Frontczak, K., & Bricker, D. (2004). An activity-based approach to early intervention. Baltimore: Brookes.

Prizant, B., Wetherby, A., & Roberts, J. (1993). Communication disorders in infants and toddlers. In J. Charles & H. Zeanah (Eds.), *Handbook of infant mental health.* New York: Guilford Press.

Pruden, S. M., Hirsh-Pasek, K., Golinkoff, R. M., & Hennon, E. A. (2006). The birth of words: Ten-month-olds learn words through perceptual salience. *Child Development, 77*(2), 266–280.

Pruett, K. D. (1999). Me, myself, and I: How children build their sense of self. Lanham, MD: Goddard Press.

Pruett, K. D. (2000). *Fatherneed.* New York: Free Press.

Radin, N. (1982). *Paternal involvement in child care index.* Ann Arbor: University of Michigan School of Social work.

Raikes, H. (1993). Relationship duration in infant care: Time with a high-ability teacher and infant–teacher attachment. *Early Childhood Research Quarterly, 8,* 309–325.

Rakic, P., Bourgeois, J. P., & Goldman-Rakic, P. S. (1994). Synaptic development of the cerebral cortex: Implications for learning, memory, and mental illness. In J. van Pelt, M. A. Corona, H. B. M. Uylings, & P. H. Lopes da Silva (Eds.), *The self-organizing brain: From growth cones to functional networks* (pp. 227–243). Amsterdam: Elsevier Science.

Recchia, S. L., & Loizou, E. (2002). Becoming an infant caregiver: Three profiles of personal and professional growth. *Journal of Research in Childhood Education, 16*(2), 133–147.

Redding, R. E., Morgan, G. A., & Harmon, R. J. (1988). Mastery motivation in infants and toddlers: Is it greatest when tasks are moderately challenging? *Infant Behavior and Development, 11,* 419–430.

Reese, E., & Fivush, R. (1993). Parental styles of talking about the past. *Developmental Psychology, 29*(3), 596–606.

Reindle, N. (2004). *The zone of proximal development in block play.* Paper and documentation panel presented in a University of Colorado–Denver course titled Advanced Developmentally Appropriate Practice.

Repacholi, B. M. (1998). Infants' use of attentional cues to identify the referent of another person's emotional expression. *Developmental Psychology, 33*(5), 1017–1025.

Restak, R. (2001). *The secret life of the brain.* Washington, DC: Joseph Henry Press.

Richardson, H. (1997). Kangaroo care: Why does it work? *Midwifery Today, 44,* 50–51.

Rinaldi, C. (2001). Reggio Emilia: The image of the child and the child's environment as a fundamental principle. In L. Gandini

& C. Edwards (Eds.), *Bambini: The Italian approach to infant care* (pp. 49–55). New York: Teachers College Press.

Roberts, S. B., & Heyman, M. B. (2000). How to feed babies and toddlers in the 21st century. *Zero to Three, 21*(1), 24–28.

Robertson, A. S. (1998). The parenting education spectrum: A look at the scope of parenting programs that should be available within a community. *Parent News: National Parent Information Network.*

Robin, D. J., Berthier, N. E., & Clifton, R. K. (1996). Infants' predictive reaching for moving objects in the dark. *Developmental Psychology, 32,* 824–835.

Robinson, J. L., & Acevedo, M. C. (2001). Infant reactivity and reliance on mother during emotion challenges: Prediction of cognition and language skills in a low-income sample. *Child Development, 72*(2), 402–416.

Rochat, P. (2001). *The infant's world.* Cambridge, MA: Harvard University Press.

Rogoff, B. (2003). *The cultural nature of human development.* New York: Oxford University Press.

Roopnarine, J. L., & Field, T. M. (1983). Peer-directed behaviors of infants and toddlers during nursery school play. *Infant Behavior and Development, 6*(1), 133.

Rosenkoetter, S., & Barton, L. (2002). Bridges to literacy: Early routines that promote later school success. *Zero to Three, 22*(4) 33–38.

Ross, H. S., & Lollis, S. P. (1989). A social relations analysis of toddler peer relationships. *Child Development, 60*(5), 1082–1092.

Rothbart, M. K. (1989). *Temperament and development.* Chichester, England: Wiley.

Rothbart, M. K., & Bates, J. E. (1998). Temperament. In W. Damon (Ed.), *Handbook of child psychology: Volume 3. Social, emotional, and personality development* (5th ed.). New York: Wiley.

Rothbart, M. K., & Derryberry, D. (1981). Development of individual differences in temperament. In M. E. Lamb & A. L. Brown (Eds.), *Advances in developmental psychology* (Vol. 1, pp. 37–86). Hillsdale, NJ: Erlbaum.

Rouse, K. (1998). Infant and toddler resilience. *Early Childhood Education Journal, 26*(1), 47–52.

Rovee-Collier, C. K., Sullivan, M. W., Enright, M., Lucas, D., & Fagan, J. W. (1980). Reactivism of infant memory. *Science, 208,* 1159–1161.

RSRF (Rett Syndrome Research Foundation). (2009). Available from the RSRF Web site: http://www.rsrf.org/

Rubin, K. H. (1998). Social and emotional development from a cultural perspective. *Developmental Psychology, 34*(4), 611–615.

Rubin, K. H., Bukowski, W., & Laurensen, B. (Eds.). (2008). *Handbook of peer interactions, relationships, and groups.* New York: Guilford.

Rubin, K. H., Bukowski, W., & Parker, J. G. (1998). Peer interactions, relationships, and groups. In W. Damon (Ed.), *Handbook of child psychology: Vol. 3. Social, emotional, and personality development* (5th ed.). New York: Wiley.

Rubin, K. H., Burgess, K. B., Dwyer, K. M., & Hastings, P. D. (2003). Predicting preschoolers' externalizing behaviors from toddler temperament, conflict, and maternal negativity. *Developmental Psychology, 39*(1), 164–177.

Rubin, K. H., Burgess, K., & Hastings, P. (2002). Stability and social-behavioral consequences of toddlers' inhibited temperament and parenting behaviors. *Child Development, 73*(2), 483–496.

Rubin, K. H., & Coplan, R. J. (2004). Paying attention to and not neglecting social withdrawal and social isolation. *Merrill-Palmer Quarterly, 50*(4), 506–535.

Runyan, D. K., Hunter, W. M., Socolar, R. R. S., Amaya-Jackson, L., English, D., Landsverk, J., et al. (1996). Children who prosper in unfavorable environments: The relationship to social capital. *Pediatrics, 101*(1), 12–18.

Ruopp, R. R., Travers, J., Glantz, R., & Coelen, C. (1979). *Children at the center: Final report of the National Day Care Study* (Vol. 1). Cambridge, MA: Abt Associates.

Rutherford, E., & Mussen, P. (1968). Generosity in nursery school boys. *Child Development, 39,* 755–764.

Saffran, J. R. (2002). Constraints on statistical language learning. *Journal of Memory and Language, 47,* 172–196.

Saffran, J. R., Loman, M. M., & Robertson, R. W. (2000). Infant memory for musical experiences. *Cognition, 77*(1), B15–B23.

Sameroff, A. J. (1998). Management of clinical problems and emotional care: Environmental risk factors in infancy. *Pediatrics, 102*(5), 1287–1292.

Sameroff, A. J., & Chandler, M. (1975). Reproductive risk and the continuum of caretaking casualty. In F. Horowitz, M. Hetherington, & S. Scar-Salaperk (Eds.), *Review of child development research* (Vol. 4, pp. 187–244). Chicago: University of Chicago Press.

Sameroff, A. J., & Feise, B. H. (2000). Transactional regulation: The development ecology of early intervention. In J. P. Shonkoff & S. J. Meisels (Eds.), *Handbook of early childhood intervention* (2nd ed., pp. 135–159). New York: Cambridge University Press.

Sameroff, A. J., & MacKenzie, M. J. (2003). A quarter-century of the transactional model: How have things changed? *Zero to Three, 24*(1), 14–22.

Sánchez, S. Y., & Thorp, E. K. (1998a). Discovering meanings of continuity: Implications for the infant/family field. In Emily Fenichel (Ed.), *Bulletin of Zero to Three: National Center for Infants, Toddlers, and Families, 18*(6), 1–5.

Sánchez, S. Y., & Thorp, E. K. (1998b). Policies on linguistic continuity: A family's right, a practitioner's choice, or an opportunity to create shared meaning and a more equitable relationship? In Emily Fenichel (Ed.), *Bulletin of Zero to Three: National Center for Infants, Toddlers, and Families, 18*(6), 12–20.

Sánchez, S. Y., & Thorp, E. K. (1998c). The use of discontinuity in preparing early educators of culturally, linguistically, and ability-diverse young children and their families. In Emily Fenichel (Ed.), *Bulletin of Zero to Three: National Center for Infants, Toddlers, and Families, 18*(6), 27–32.

Sandall, S., Hemmeter, M. L., Smith, B., & McLean, M. (2004). *DEC recommended practices: A comprehensive guide.* Longmont, CO: Sopris West.

Santelli, B. (2003). *Parent to parent support*. Retrieved February 11, 2009, from http://www.nichcy.org/pubs/basicpar/bp2txt.htm

Sawyers, J. K., & Rogers, C. S. (2003). Helping babies play. [NAEYC resources in focus; selected excerpts.] *Young Children, 58*(3), 52–53.

SBAA (Spina Bifida Association of America). (2005). Available from the SBAA Web site: http://www.spinabifidaassociation.org

Scarborough, H. S., & Dobrich, W. (1990). Development of children with early language delay. *Journal of Speech and Hearing Research, 33*, 70–83.

Schickedanz, J. A. (2003). NAEYC resources in focus: Creating a book nook for babies and toddlers. *Young Children, 58*(2), 61.

Schmuckler, M. A., Collimore, L. M., & Dannemiller, J. L. (2007). Infants' reactions to object collision on hit and miss trajectories. *Infancy, 12*(1), 105–118.

Schorr, L. B. (1997). *Common purpose: Strengthening families and neighborhoods to rebuild America*. New York: Doubleday.

Schreiber, M. E. (1999). Time-outs for toddlers: Is our goal punishment or education? *Young Children, 54*(4), 22–25.

Schweinhart, L. (1994). *Lasting benefits of preschool programs. ERIC Digest*. Urbana, IL: ERIC Clearinghouse on Elementary and Early Childhood Education.

Scott-Little, C., Kagan, S. L., Frelow, V. S., & Reid, J. (2008). Inside the content of infant-toddler early learning guidelines. Results from analyses, issues to consider, and recommendations. Retrieved January 28, 2009, from http://ccf.tc.columbia.edu/pdf/Inside%20the%20Content%20of%20Infant-Toddler%20ELGs-Brief.pdf

Sears, W., & Sears, M. (2001). *Attachment parenting: A common-sense guide to understanding and nurturing your baby*. New York: Little, Brown.

Segatti, L., Brown-DuPaul, J., & Keyes, T. (2003). Using everyday materials to promote problem solving in toddlers. *Young Children, 58*(5), 12–18.

Seifer, R., Sameroff, A. J., Baldwin, C. P., & Baldwin, A. (1992). Child and family factors that ameliorate risk between 4 and 13 years of age. *Journal of the American Academy of Child and Adolescent Psychiatry, 31*, 893–903.

Seifer, R., Sameroff, A. J., Barrett, L. C., & Krafchuk, E. (1994). Infant temperament measured by multiple observations and mother report. *Child Development, 65*, 1478–1490.

Seligman, M. (1992). *Helplessness*. New York: Freeman.

Serbin, L., Moller, L., Gulko, J., Powlishta, K., & Colbourne, K. (1994). The emergence of gender segregation in toddler playgroups. In C. Leaper (Ed.), *Childhood gender segregation: Causes and consequences* (*New Directions for Child Development,* No. 65, pp. 7–18). San Francisco: Jossey-Bass.

Shalala calls for a new era of support to families with infants and toddlers. (1995). *Children Today, 23*(3), 4–5.

Shatz, M. (2007). Revisiting *A Toddler's Life for the Toddler Years*: conversational participation as a tool for learning across knowledge domains. In C. Brownell & C. Kopp (Eds.), *Socioemotional development in the toddler years: Transitions and transformation* (pp. 241–260). New York/London: Guilford Press.

Shaw, M. A. (1991). *Helping your child survive divorce*. New York: Birch Lane.

Shirah, S., Hewitt, T., & McNair, R. (1993). Preservice training fosters retention: The case for vocational training. *Young Children, 48*(4), 27–31.

Shoemaker, C. C. (2000). *Leadership and management of programs for young children* (2nd ed.). Upper Saddle River, NJ: Merrill/Prentice Hall.

Shonkoff, J. P., & Meisels, S. J. (2000). *Handbook of early childhood intervention* (2nd ed.). Cambridge, England: Cambridge University Press.

Shonkoff, J. P., & Phillips, D. A. (Eds.). (2000). *From neurons to neighborhoods: The science of early development*. Washington, DC: National Academy Press.

Shore, R. (1997). *Rethinking the brain: New insights into early development*. New York: Families and Work Institute.

Siegel, A. C., & Burton, R. V. (1999). Effects of baby walkers on motor and mental development in human infants. *Journal of Developmental and Behavioral Pediatrics, 20*, 355–361.

Skeels, H. M., & Dye, H. B. (1939). *A study of the effects of differential stimulation on mentally retarded children*. Proceedings and addresses of the American Association on Mental Deficiency.

Skinner, B. F. (1957). *Verbal behavior*. New York: Appleton-Century Crofts.

Small, M. F. (1998). *Our babies, ourselves: How biology and culture shape the way we parent*. New York: Anchor.

Smilansky, S., & Shefatya, L. (1990). *Facilitating play: A medium for promoting cognitive, socioemotional, and academic development in young children*. Gaithersburg, MD: Psychosocial and Educational Publications.

Smith, A. B., Dannison, L. L., & Vach-Hasse, T. (1998). When "Grandma" is "Mom": What today's teachers need to know. *Childhood Education, 75*(1), 12–16.

Smith, P. M. (2003). *You are not alone: For parents when they learn that their child has a disability*. Available from Kidsource Online: http://www.kidsource.com/NICHCY/parenting.disab.all.4.2.html

Snow, C., Burns, M. S., & Griffin, P. (1998). *Preventing reading difficulties in young children*. Washington, DC: International Reading Association.

Snow, C., & Tabors, P. (1996). Intergenerational transfer of literacy. In L. A. Benjamin & J. Ford (Eds.), *Family literacy: Directions in research and implications for practice* (pp. 73–79). Washington, DC: U.S. Department of Education.

Solchany, J. E. (2001). *Promoting maternal mental health during pregnancy*. Seattle, WA: NCAST.

Soodak, L. C., & Erwin, E. J. (2000). Valued member or tolerated participant: Parents' experiences in inclusive early childhood settings. *Journal of the Association for Persons with Severe Handicaps, 25*, 29–44.

Spectrum Health. (2009). Hearing milestones. Retrieved March 10, 2009, from https://www.spectrumhealth.org/

Spelke, E. S. (2002). Developmental neuroimaging: A developmental psychologist looks ahead. *Developmental Science, 5*(3), 392–396.

Spelke, E. S., Breinlinger, K., Jacobson, K., & Phillips, A. (1993). Gestalt relations and object perception: A developmental study. *Perception, 22,* 1483–1501.

Spelke, E. S., & Kinzler, K. D. (2007). Core knowledge. *Developmental Science, 10*(1), 89–96.

Spelke, E. S., & Owlsley, C. (1979). Infants intermodal perception of events. *Infant Behavior and Development, 2,* 13–17.

Spitz, R. A. (1945). Hospitalism: An inquiry into the genesis of psychiatric conditions of early childhood. *Psychoanalytic Study of the Child, 1,* 53–74.

Sroufe, E. A. (1990). The fate of early experience following developmental change: Longitudinal approaches to individual adaptation in childhood. *Child Development, 61,* 1363–1373.

Stanford University Medical Center. (2007, July 30). Severe trauma affects kids' brain function, say researchers. *ScienceDaily.* Retrieved August 22, 2008, from http://www.sciencedaily.com/releases/2007/07/070726184910.htm

Steckel, A. (1987). Psychosocial development of children of lesbian mothers. In F. W. Bozett (Ed.), *Gay and lesbian parents* (pp. 75–85). New York: Praeger.

Stein, M. T., Colaruso, C., Mckenna, J. J., and Powers, N. G. (2001). Cosleeping (bedsharing) among infants and toddlers. *Pediatrics, 107,* 873–877.

Stephens, K. (1999). Toilet training: Children step up to independence. *Child Care Information Exchange,* 76–80.

Stern, D. (1995). *The motherhood constellation.* New York: Basic Books.

Stern, D. (2000). *The interpersonal world of the infant.* New York: Basic Books.

Stern, F. M., & Gorga, D. (1988). Neurodevelopmental treatment (NDT): Therapeutic intervention and its efficacy. *Infants and Young Children, 1,* 22–32.

Stern, N. B. (1999). Motherhood: The emotional awakening. *Journal of Pediatric Health Care, 13,* 8–12.

Stockmeyer, S. A. (1972). A sensorimotor approach to treatment. In P. H. Pearson & C. E. Williams (Eds.), *Physical therapy services in the developmental disabilities* (pp. 186–222). Springfield, IL: Thomas.

Stroud, J. E. (1995). Block play: A foundation for literacy. *Early Childhood Education Journal, 23*(1), 9–13.

Super, C. M., & Harkness, S. (1997). The cultural structuring of child development. In J. W. Berry, P. R. Dasen, & T. S. Saraswathi (Eds.), *Handbook of cross-cultural psychology: Vol. 2. Basic processes and human development* (pp. 1–39). Boston: Allyn & Bacon.

Susman-Stillman, A., Appleyard, K., & Siebenbruner, J. (2003). For better or worse: An ecological perspective on parents' relationships and parent–infant interaction. *Zero to Three, 23*(3), 4–12.

Sutherland, P. (1992). *Cognitive development today: Piaget and his critics.* London: Chapman.

Swain, I., Zelazo, P., & Clifton, R. (1993). Newborn infants' memory for speech sounds retained over 24 hours. *Developmental Psychology, 29,* 312–323.

Sylvester, K. (2001). Caring for our youngest: Public attitudes in the United States. *The Future of Children Journal: Caring for Infants and Toddlers, 11*(1), 53–61.

Szanton, E. S. (2001). For America's infants and toddlers, are important values threatened by our zeal to "teach"? *Young Children, 56*(1), 15–21.

Tamis-LeMonda, C. S., Adolph, K. E., Lobo, S. A., Karasik, L. B., Dimitroupoulou, K. D., & Ishak, S. (2008). When infants take mothers' advice: 18-month-olds integrate perceptual and social information for guiding motor action. *Developmental Psychology, 44,* 734–746.

Tamis-LeMonda, C. S., & Cabrera, N. J. (2002). *Handbook of father involvement: Multidisciplinary perspectives.* Erlbaum.

Taylor, F., Ko, R., & Pan, M. (1999). Prenatal and reproductive health care. In E. Kramer, S. Ivey, & Y.W. Ying (Eds.), *Immigrant women's health: Problems and solutions* (pp. 121–135). San Francisco: Jossey-Bass.

Taylor, N., Donovan, W., & Leavitt, L. (2008). Consistency in infant sleeping arrangements and mother-infant interaction. *Infant Mental Health Journal, 29*(2), 77–94.

Teaching Strategies. (2008). *The Creative Curriculum system for infants, toddlers, and twos: Assessment.* Retrieved September 4, 2008, from http://www.teachingstrategies.com/page/IT2_Assessment.cfm

Thelen, E. (2000). Grounded in the world: Developmental origins of the embodied mind. *Infancy, 1,* 3–30.

Thelen, E., & Smith, L. B. (1996). A dynamic systems approach to the development of cognition and action. Cambridge, MA: MIT Press.

Thiessen, E. D., Hill, E. A., & Saffran, J. R. (2005). Infant-directed speech facilitates word segmentation. *Infancy, 7*(1), 53–71.

Thomas, A., & Chess, S. (1977). *Temperament and development.* New York: Brunner/Mazel.

Thomas, A., Chess, S., Birch, H. G., Hertzig, M. E., & Korn, S. (1963). *Behavioral individuality in early childhood.* New York: New York University Press.

Thomas, M. S. C., & Johnson, M. H. (2008). New advances in understanding sensitive periods in brain development. *Current Directions in Psychological Science, 17*(1), 1–5.

Thomas, R., & Footrakoon, O. (1998). *What curricular perspectives can tell us about parent education curricula.* Retrieved February 11, 2009, from the Parenthood in America Web site: http:parenthood.library.wise.edu/Thomas/Thomas.html

Thompson-Rangel, T. (1994). The Hispanic child and family: Developmental disabilities and occupational therapy intervention. *Developmental Disabilities Special Interest Newsletter, 16*(1), 2.

Tinbergen, N. (1951). *The study of instinct.* Oxford, England: Clarendon.

Todd, C. (2001). *The NICHD child care study results: What do they mean for parents, child care professionals, employers, and decision-makers?* Ames, IA: National Network for Child Care.

Tomasello, M. (1992). The social bases of language acquisition. *Social Development, 1,* 68–87.

Torelli, L., & Durrett, C. (2007). Landscape for learning: The impact of classroom design on infants and toddlers. Retrieved February 11, 2009, from http://www.spacesforchildren.com/impact.html

Tortora, S. (2004). Our moving bodies tell us stories, which speak of our experiences. *Zero to Three, 24*(5), 4–12.

Troy, M., & Sroufe, A. (1987). Victimization among preschoolers: Role of attachment relationships. *Journal of the American Academy of Child and Adolescent Psychiatry, 1987 26*(2): 166–172.

True, M. M., Pisani, L., & Oumar, F. (2001). Infant–mother attachment among the Dogon of Mali. *Child Development, 72,* 1451–1466.

UCP (United Cerebral Palsy). (2009). *Cerebral Palsy—Facts & Figures.* Retrieved February 11, 2009, from http://www.ucp.org/ucp_generaldoc.cfm/1/9/37/37-37/447

Ulione, M. S. (1997). Health promotion and injury prevention in a child development center. *Journal of Pediatric Nursing, 12*(3), 148–154.

UNICEF. (2008). *The state of the world's children 2008.* Retrieved August 24, 2008, from http://www.unicef.org/publications/files/SOWC_2008_Exec_Summary_EN_042908.pdf

UNICEF. (2009). Convention on the Rights of the Child. Retrieved February 3, 2009, from http://www.unicef.org/crc/

U.S. Census Bureau (2008). Retrieved August 25, 2008, from http://quickfacts.census.gov

U.S. Census Bureau (2004). *Living arrangements of children: 2004.* Retrieved February 20, 2009, from http://www.census.gov/prod/2008 pubs/p70–114.pdf

U.S. Census Bureau, American FactFinder. (2006). *Selected economic characteristics.* Retrieved February 9, 2009, from http://factfinder.census.gov/

U.S. Census Bureau, American FactFinder. (2007). *General demographic characteristics. 2007 population estimates.* Retrieved August 25, 2008, from http://factfinder.census.gov/

U.S. Consumer Product Safety Commission. (2001). *Consumer product safety alert.* Retrieved February 11, 2009, from http://www.cpsc.gov/CPSCPUB/PUBS/babywalk.pdf

U.S. Department of Health and Human Services. (2001). *Early Head Start shows significant results for low income children and parents.* Retrieved January 7, 2009, from http://www.hhs.gov/news/pres/20010112.html

U.S. Department of Health and Human Services. (2008a). Smoking and women fact sheet. Retrieved February 11, 2009, from http://www.lungusa.org/site/c.dvLUK9O0E/b.33572/

U.S. Department of Health & Human Services. (2008b). *The 2008 HHS poverty guidelines.* Retrieved August 25, 2008, from http://aspe.hhs.gov/poverty/08poverty.shtml

U.S. Department of Justice. (1997). *Commonly asked questions about child care centers and the Americans with Disabilities Act.* Retrieved February 11, 2009, from http://www.ada.gov/childq%26a.htm

U.S. Department of State. (2008). *2008 poverty guidelines.* Retrieved August 23, 2008, from http://travel.state.gov/visa/immigrants/info/info_1327.html

Uzgiris, I. C., & Hunt, J. M. (1975). *Assessment in infancy: Ordinal scales of psychological development.* Urbana: University of Illinois Press.

Vandell, D., & Wolfe, B. (2001). *Child care quality: Does it matter and does it need to be improved?* Washington, DC: U.S. Department of Health and Human Services.

Van De Zande, I., & the Santa Cruz Toddler Care Center Staff. (1995). *1, 2, 3 . . . The toddler years: A practical guide for parents and caregivers.* Santa Cruz, CA: Santa Cruz Toddler Care Center.

Van Hulle, C. A., Goldsmith, H. H., & Lemery, K. S. (2004). Genetic, environmental, and gender effects on individual differences in toddler expressive language. *Journal of Speech, Language, and Hearing Research, 47*(4), 904–1003.

Vernon, F. (2003, Spring). Sink play. *Focus on Infants and Toddlers, 15*(1), 5.

Volling, B., & Feagans, L. (1995). Infant day care and children's social competence. *Infant Behavior and Development, 18,* 177–188.

Volling, B., Notaro, P. C., & Larsen, J. J. (1998). Adult attachment styles: Relations with emotional well-being, marriage, and parenting. *Family Relations, 47*(4), 355–367.

Vygotsky, L. S. (1962). *Thought and language.* Cambridge, MA: MIT Press.

Vygotsky, L. S. (1978). *Mind in society: The development of higher psychological processes.* Cambridge, MA: Harvard University Press.

Vygotsky, L. S. (1987). Thinking and speech. In N. Minick (Trans.), *The collected works of L. S. Vygotsky: Vol. 1. Problems in general psychology.* New York: Plenum.

Wallerstein, J. S. (1985). Children of divorce: Preliminary report of a ten-year follow-up of older children and adolescents. *Journal of the American Academy of Child Psychiatry, 24*(5), 545–553.

Watamura, S., Donzella, B., Alwin, J., & Gunnar, M. (2003). Morning-to-afternoon increases in cortisol concentrations for infants and toddlers at child care: Age differences and behavioral correlates. *Child Development, 74*(4), 1006–1021.

Watemberg, N., Silver, S., Harel, S., & Lerman-Sagie, T. (2002). Significance of microcephaly among children with developmental disabilities. *Journal of Child Neurology, 17,* 117–122.

Watson, J. (1972). Smiling, cooing, and the game. *Merrill-Palmer Quarterly, 18,* 323–340.

Watson, M., & White, J. (2001). Accident prevention activities: A national survey of health authorities. *Health Education Journal, 60*(3), 275–283.

Waxman, S. R., & Markow, D. B. (1995). Words as invitations to form categories: Evidence from 12- to 13-month-old infants. *Cognitive Psychology, 29,* 257–302.

Weatherston, D. (2001). Infant mental health: A review of relevant literature. *Psychoanalytic Social Work, 8*(1), 39–69.

Weil, J. L. (1993). *Early deprivation of empathic care.* Madison, CT: International Universities Press.

Weinfield, N. S., Sroufe, A. L., Egeland, B., & Carlson, E. A. (2002). In J. Cassidy, & P. R. Shaver (Eds.), *Handbook of attachment: Theory, research, and clinical applications* (pp. 68–88). New York: Guilford Press.

Weitoft, G. R., Hjern, A., Haglund, B., & Rosén, M. (2003). Mortality, severe morbidity, and injury in children living with single parents in Sweden: A population-based study. *Lancet, 361*(9354), 289–294.

Werner, E. E. (1993). Risk, resilience, and recovery: Perspectives from the Kauai longitudinal study. *Development and Psychopathology, 9*(4), 503–515.

Werner, E. E. (2000). The power of protective factors in the early years. *Zero to Three, 20*(3), 3–5.

Werker, J. F., Pons, F., Dietrich, C., Kajikawa, S., Fais, L., & Amano, S. (2007). Infant-directed speech supports phonetic category learning in English and Japanese. *Cognition, 103,* 147–162.

Westby, C. (1980). Assessment of cognitive and language abilities through play. *Language, Speech, and Hearing Sciences in Schools, 11,* 154–168.

Whaley, K., & Rubenstein, T. (1994). How toddlers "do" friendship: A descriptive analysis of naturally occurring friendships in a group child care setting. *Journal of Social and Personal Relationships, 11,* 383–400.

Whitebook, M., & Bellm, D. (1996). Mentoring for early childhood teachers and providers: Building upon and extending tradition. *Young Children, 52*(1), 59–64.

Whitebook, M., Howes, C., & Phillips, D. (1998). *Worthy work, unlivable wages: The national child care staffing study, 1988–1997.* Washington, DC: Center for the Child Care Workforce.

Whitehurst, G. J., Zenvenberger, A. A., Crone, D. A., Schultz, M. D., Velting, O. N., & Fischel, J. E. (1999). Outcomes of an emergent literacy intervention from Head Start through second grade. *Journal of Educational Psychology, 91,* 261–272.

Wittmer, D. (1991). *Toddlers with special needs as initiators and recipients of prosocial behaviors.* Denver: University of Colorado Junior Faculty Award Report.

Wittmer, D. S. (2008). *A focus on peers in the early years: The importance of relationships.* Washington, DC: ZERO TO THREE.

Wittmer, D., & Petersen, S. (1992). Social development and interaction: Facilitating the prosocial development of typical and exceptional infants and toddlers in group settings. *Zero to Three, 12*(4), 52–60.

Wittmer, D. S., & Petersen, S. H. (2009). Issues in infant/toddler programs. In S. Feeney, A. Galper, & C. Seefeldt (Eds.), *Continuing issues in early childhood education* (3rd ed., pp. 58–82). Upper Saddle River, NJ: Merrill/Pearson.

Wober, M. (1972). Culture and the concept of intelligence: A case in Uganda. *Journal of Cross-Cultural Psychology, 3,* 327–328.

Woodward, A. L., Markman, E. M., & Fitzsimmons, C. M. (1994). Rapid word learning in 13- and 18-month-olds. *Developmental Psychology, 30,* 553–566.

WSDOH (Washington State Department of Health). (2006). *The infant and young child with sickle cell anemia.* Retrieved September 4, 2008, from http://www.doh.wa.gov/EHSPHL/PHL/Newborn/chwsick.htm

Wynn, K. (1992). Addition and subtraction by human infants. *Nature, 358,* 749–750.

Xu, F., & Carey, S. (1996). Infants' metaphysics: The case of numerical identity. *Cognitive Psychology, 30*(2), 111–153.

Yarrow, L. J. (1981). Beyond cognition: The development of mastery motivation. *Zero to Three, 1*(3), 1–5.

Yeung, W. J., Sandberg, J. F., Davis-Kean, P., & Hofferth, S. L. (2001). Children's time with fathers in intact families. *Journal of Marriage and Family, 63*(1), 136–154.

Yogman, M. W. (1982). Development of the father–infant relationship. In H. E. Fitzpatrick, B. M. Lester, & M. W. Yogman (Eds.), *Theory and research in behavioral pediatrics* (pp. 221–279). New York: Plenum.

Yogman, M. W., Kindlon, D., and Earls, F. (1995). Father involvement and cognitive/behavioral outcomes of premature infants. *Journal of the American Academy of Child and Adolescent Psychiatry, 5*(34), 58–66.

Yoshinaga-Itano, C., Sedey, A. L., Coulter, D. K., & Mehl, A. L. (1998). Language of early- and later-identified children with hearing loss. *Pediatrics, 102*(5), 1161–1172.

Zahn-Waxler, C., & Radke-Yarrow, R. (1990). The origins of empathic concern. *Motivation and Emotion, 14,* 107–130.

Zahn-Waxler, C., Radke-Yarrow, R., & King, R. A. (1979). Child rearing and children's prosocial initiations toward victims of distress. *Child Development, 50*(2), 319–330.

Zanolli, K. M., Saudargas, R. A., & Twardosz, S. (1997). The development of toddlers' responses to affectionate teacher behavior. *Early Childhood Research Quarterly, 12*(1), 99–116.

Zeanah, C. H., Boris, N. W., & Larrieu, J. A. (1997). Infant development and developmental risk: A review of the past 10 years. *Journal of the American Academy of Child and Adolescent Psychiatry, 36*(2), 165–178.

ZERO TO THREE. (1992). *Heart Start: The emotional foundations of school readiness.* Washington, DC: National Center for Clinical Infant Programs.

ZERO TO THREE. (2008). *Caring for Infants and Toddlers in Groups: Developmentally Appropriate Practice* (2nd ed.). Washington, DC: ZERO TO THREE.

ZERO TO THREE. (2009). *Brain development.* Retrieved January 20, 2009, from http://www.zerotothree.org/site/PageServer?pagename=ter_key_brainFPQ

Zinner, S. H., McGarvey, S. T., Lipsitt, L. T., & Rosner, B. (2002, September). Neonatal blood pressure and salt taste responsiveness. *Hypertension, 40,* 280–285.

Ziv, Y., Oppenheim, D., & Sagi-Schwartz, A. (2004). Social information processing in middle childhood: Relations to infant–mother attachment. *Attachment and Human Development, 6*(3), 327–349.

Zoglio, S. (1997). *Training program for teams at work.* Doylestown, PA: Tower Hill.

Zuckerman, B., Frank, D. A., Hingson, R., Amaro, H., Levenson, S. M., Kayne, H., et al. (1989). Effects of maternal marijuana and cocaine on fetal growth. *New England Journal of Medicine, 320,* 762–768.

Name Index

Abels, M., 27
Acevedo, M. C., 114, 115
Acredolo, L., 198, 199, 203
Adams, G., 136, 243, 245
Adamson, L. B., 207
Adolph, K. E., 64, 65, 221, 223, 226, 228, 229
Ahluwalia, J., 171
Ainsworth, M. D. S., 48, 56, 57, 120, 121, 246
Als, H., 112
Alwin, J., 138
Amano, S., 203
Amaro, H., 102
Amaya-Jackson, L., 4
Ameil-Tison, C., 169
Ananth, C., 104
Appleton, T. R., 225
Appleyard, K., 29
Arnett, J., 248, 261
Aronson, S., 250
Aslin, R. N., 200, 202
Astington, J. W., 177
Augustyn, M., 101

Badaly, D., 229
Bahrick, L. E., 171
Bailey, T. M., 204
Baillargeon, R., 169
Bakeman, R., 75, 207
Bakermans-Kranenburg, M. J., 5
Baldwin, A., 35
Baldwin, C. P., 35
Baldwin, E., 36
Baldwin, James, 116
Bancroft, J., 224
Bandura, A., 62, 70, 71, 139
Barillas, Y., 203
Baron-Cohen, S., 171
Barrera, I., 3, 16, 47, 193, 284, 287
Barriault, T., 177
Barton, L., 318
Bassily, N. S., 257

Ba'tki, A., 171
Baumrind, D., 34
Beard, J. L., 257
Beauchamp, G. K., 170
Beckerman, S., 32
Beeghly, M., 101
Bekkering, H., 62
Bell, S. M., 48
Bellagamba, F., 62
Bellinger, D., 101
Bellm, D., 387
Belsky, J., 30, 153
Bennett, L., 151
Benzies, K., 33
Berg, A., 101
Berger, S. E., 229
Berke, K., 266, 325
Bernstein, L., 40
Bertenthal, B. I., 228
Berthier, N. E., 232
Bertoncini, J., 169
Besag, F. M., 358
Bettelheim, B., 273
Birch, H. G., 114, 115
Biringen, Z., 246
Bishry, Z., et. al., 257
Blehar, M. C., 56, 120, 121, 246
Bloom, P. J., 382
Bodrova, E., 136
Boivin, M., 150
Boller, K., 20
Booth-LaForce, C., 5
Boris, N. W., 12, 15
Borke, J., 27
Bornstein, M. H., 11, 168
Bosquet, M., 124
Bourgeois, J. P., 92
Bourland, B., 312
Bower, T. G. R., 168
Bowlby, J., 48, 56, 119–20, 121, 165
Boyce, L., 5
Brand, M., 357
Brannon, E. M., 62, 180

Braungart-Rieker, J. M., 114
Brazelton, T. B., 21, 112, 170, 224, 333, 347
Bredecamp, S., 265
Breinlinger, K., 169
Brems, S., 101
Breslin, D., 13
Bretherton, I., 121, 122
Bricker, D., 183
Briggs-Gowan, M. I., 331
Bromwich, R., 334–35
Bronfenbrenner, U., 3, 47, 51, 52, 190, 268, 383
Bronson, M. B., 11
Bronte-Tinkew, J., 32
Brook, D., 152, 333
Brook, J. S., 152, 333
Brooks, R., 62, 202
Brophy, H. E., 207
Brown, C., 199
Brown, R., 205
Brown University, 123
Brown-DuPaul, J., 323
Brownell, C. A., 136, 144, 150, 166
Brownlee, J., 75
Bruder, M. B., 357
Bruner, J., 60–61, 64, 141, 163, 268
Bryant, D. M., 212
Bryk, A., 192, 211
Buell, M. J., 356, 366
Bukowski, W., 136, 152
Burchinal, M. R., 5, 152, 212, 245, 247, 248
Burgess, K. B., 137, 138, 139
Butterfield, P., 118, 299
Butterworth, G., 230

Cabral, H., 101
Cabrera, N. J., 32
Cahill, L., 172
Calkins, S., 138
Camaioni, L., 62
Campbell, D. W., 224

Campbell, S. B., 124, 166
Campos, J. J., 117, 118
Campos, R., 117
Camras, L. A., 117
Canterino, J. C., 104
Capatides, J., 151
Capizzano, J., 136
Carey, S., 180, 204
Carlson, E. A., 122
Carlson, M., 30
Carrano, J., 32
Carriger, M., 150
Carson, D. K., 331
Carter, A. S., 331
Carter, M., 276, 300, 373, 379, 380, 383, 385
Cartwright, S., 378
Cashmore, J., 26
Cassels, C., 358
Cassidy, J., 121, 122
Cathcart, M. B., 36
Cawlfield, M. E., 272
Cen, G., 119
Chacon, M. E., 257
Chadwick, A., 136, 138
Chandler, M., 13, 47, 49
Chang, A., 250
Chao, R. K., 35
Chase-Lansdale, P. L., 30
Chawla, N., 256, 257
Cheatham, C. L., 5
Chen, D., 5
Chen, H., 119
Chen, S. J., 117
Chen, X., 119
Cheng, V. K., 124
Chess, S., 114, 115, 224
Chiriboga, C. A., 102
Chomsky, N., 63, 64
Chrisman, K., 140
Christie-Mizell, C., 124
Chugani, H. T., 92
Clark, Frank A., 111
Clark, R., 123
Clarke-Stewart, K. A., 248
Clifford, R. M., 260
Clifton, R. K., 173, 225, 232
Clyman, R. B., 246
Cohen, J., 18, 21
Cohen, N., 127
Colaruso, C., 27, 28
Cole, K., 19
Coleman, J. G., 359, 360, 361
Coley, R. L., 30

Coll, C. G., 11
Collier, A. M., 250
Collimore, L. M., 62
Collins, C. C., 151
Collins, W. A., 11
Colonnesi, C., 62
Connellan, J., 171
Connor, J. D., 257
Connors, R. E., 180
Constantine, J., 20
Cooper, P. J., 124
Cooper, R. P., 169, 200
Coplan, R. J., 138
Copple, C., 265, 284
Corso, R., 3, 16, 47, 284, 287
Cotton, S., 26
Couchenour, D., 140
Coulter, D. K., 211
Cowan, C. P., 30, 33
Cowan, P. A., 30, 33
Cox, M. J., 5, 32, 152
Coy, K. C., 151
CQO Study Team, 243
Crittenden, P., 352
Crnic, K., 30
Crockenberg, S., 3, 119, 348–49
Crone, D. A., 320
Cross, A. F., 366, 367
Cryer, D., 260, 312
Csibra, G., 62
Culver, C., 119
Cumberland, A., 119
Curtis, D., 276, 300, 373, 379, 380, 383

Damasio, A., 124, 190, 192
Damasio, H., 190, 192
Dannemiller, J. L., 62
Dannison, L. I., 38
Darling, N., 35
DaRos, D., 151–52
Darwin, C., 56
Davis-Kean, P., 30
de Boer, B., 200, 201, 203
DeCasper, A., 169, 199, 200
Decker, C. A., 381
Decker, J. R., 381
Deckner, D. J., 207
de Haan, M., 138
de Hann, D., 336
DeHouwer, A., 197, 198, 199
Delaney, C., 101
DeLoache, J. S., 93, 175
Denckla, M. B., 163
Denney, M., 228

Derman-Sparks, L., 140
Derryberry, D., 111
de Wolff, M. S., 5
Diamond, K. E., 357, 366
Dichtelmiller, M. L., 73, 84
Dicker, S., 39
Dickstein, S., 124
Didow, S. M., 150
Diener, P., 357
Dietrich, C., 203
Dietrich, S. L., 154
Dimitroupoulou, K. D., 65
Dobrich, W., 211
Dodge, D. T., 266, 325
Doescher, S., 36
Dombro, A. L., 73, 84, 272–73, 277, 288
Donaghy, T., 331
Donahoo, S., 35
Donovan, W., 27
Donzella, B., 138
Douglass, Frederick, 122
Dove, H., 225
Dunham, F., 208
Dunham, P., 208
Dunst, C. J., 204
Durret, C., 300
Dwyer, K. M., 137
Dye, H. B., 94

Earls, F., 32
Eaton, W. O., 224
Eckerman, C. O., 145, 150
Edin, K., 30
Edwards, C., 66, 82, 141, 266, 269, 325, 326
Egeland, B., 122, 124
Eggbeer, L., 383
Eidelman, A., 169, 170
Eimas, P. D., 174
Eisenberg, N., 119, 137
Ellis, S., 172
Ellison, P. T., 26
Emde, R. N., 47, 49, 117, 118, 136, 246, 288
English, D., 4
Enright, M., 173
Eppler, M. A., 226
Erickson, M. F., 1
Erikson, E., 53, 54, 66, 70
Erwin, E. J., 366
Eslinger, P. J., 163
Evans, A., 256
Eyer, D. W., 266, 268

Fabes, R. A., 137, 139, 140
Fagan, J. W., 173
Fais, I., 203
Farver, J., 145
Fattal-Valevski, A., 357
Feason, R. M. P., 153
Feigenson, L., 180
Feise, B. H., 4, 50
Feldman, R., 5, 169, 170
Fenichel, E., 66, 123, 244, 387
Fernald, Anne, 208
Fernandez, S. C., 197
Ferraro, V., 195, 196
Field, T. M., 124, 145, 170
Fifer, W. P., 169, 199
Fine, M. A., 5
Fischel, J., 320
Fitchen, J. M., 30
Fitzsimmons, C. M., 203, 204
Fivush, R., 195
Flavell, J. H., 59, 178
Footrakoon, O., 40
Forman, D. R., 151, 282
Forman, G., 82
Fors, S., 180
Foumbi, J., 32
Fox, N. A., 138
Fraiberg, S., 125, 126
Francois, N., 150
Frank, D. A., 101, 102
Frank, E., 39
Freedland, R. L., 228
Frelow, V. S., 178
Friedman, D. L., 386
Friedman, K., 36

Gable, S., 19, 30
Gaensbauer, T., 350–51
Galinsky, E., 244, 248
Galluzzo, D., 148
Gamel-McCormick, M., 356, 366
Gandini, L., 81–82, 141, 165, 266, 269, 325, 326
Ganzel, B., 13
Garbarino, J., 13
Garcia, E., 198
Garwood, M. M., 114
Gasson, N., 224
Gauna, K., 195, 196
Geist, E., 320
Genesee, F., 196, 197
George, C., 36
Gerber, Magda, 279
Gergely, G., 62

Gesell, A., 64
Gibson, E. J., 232
Gibson, Eleanor, 232
Gibson, James, 232
Gierl, M., 33
Gilkerson, L., 383
Girolametto, L., 206
Goffman, E., 194
Goldberg, S., 225
Goldfield, E. C., 228
Goldhaber, J., 81–82, 326
Goldman-Rakic, P. S., 92
Goldring, S., 362
Goldsmith, H. H., 192, 193
Goldwyn, R., 122
Golinkoff, R. M., 202
Golombok, S., 30, 37
Gonzalez-Mena, J., 3, 11, 266, 268, 284, 330
Goodnow, J. J., 26
Goodson, B., 40
Goodwyn, S., 198, 199, 203
Gopnik, A., 26, 92, 124, 176
Gordon, E., 39
Gorman, L. L., 151
Gottlieb, A., 101, 175
Gottlieb, G., 11
Gottman, J. M., 118
Gowen, J. W., 175, 176
Grabmeier, J., 199
Grantham-McGregor, S. M., 257
Green, E., 320
Greenbaum, C. W., 5
Greenman, J., 276, 300, 307, 373, 377
Greenspan, N. T., 111–12, 117–18
Greenspan, S. I., 21, 111–12, 117–18, 175
Griffin, A., 66, 244, 298, 299
Griffin, T., 41
Grossman, K. E., 117
Gunnar, M. R., 5, 138
Guralnik, M. J., 180
Guthrie, I., 137
Guzman, L., 32

Haglund, B., 36
Haight, W., 192, 211
Haith, M. M., 168
Halgunseth, L. C., 5
Hallam, R. A., 356, 366
Halsted, N., 169
Hamilton, C. E., 5, 6, 143, 155, 160, 246
Haney, M., 5

Hanish, L. D., 139, 140
Hanson, M. J., 16
Hare, J., 36
Harel, J., 5
Harel, S., 358
Harkness, S., 172
Harmon, R. J., 165, 166
Harms, T., 260, 312
Harper, S., 5
Harrigan, J., 104
Harris, J. A., 11
Harrison, M., 33
Hart, B., 106, 193, 207, 210
Harvey, S., 36
Harwood, R. L., 193
Hast, F., 308
Hastings, P. D., 119, 137, 138, 139
Hauser-Cram, P., 180
Hawley, P., 150
Hay, D. F., 136, 138
Haynes, J. A., 30
Hazen, H., 152
Helburn, S. W., 19
Hemmeter, M. L., 265
Henderson, F. W., 250
Henderson, H. A., 138
Henderson, V. K., 32
Hennon, E. A., 202
Hertzig, M. E., 114, 115
Hetherington, E. M., 11
Hewitt, T., 248
Heyman, M. B., 258
High, P., 124
Hill, E. A., 64, 208
Hinde, R., 3, 12, 47, 48, 49, 70, 72, 136, 164, 166
Hingson, R., 102
Hirsch, E. S., 315
Hirsh-Pasek, K., 202
Hjern, A., 36
Hnatiuk, P., 387
Hofferth, S. L., 30
Hohmann, M., 266
Holdgrafter, G., 192, 204
Hollyfield, A., 308
Honig, A., 139, 268, 271, 272, 276, 279, 281, 314, 318, 319, 322, 336, 377, 378
Honig, H. S., 207
Hooven, C., 118
Howe, David, 124
Howes, C., 5, 6, 136, 143, 144, 145, 146, 148, 155, 160, 175, 176, 244, 245, 246, 248, 269, 273

Howes, S. C., 245, 247
Huda, S. N., 257
Hunt, J. M., 178
Hunter, W. M., 4
Hussain, I., 209
Hussey-Gardner, B., 224
Huttenlocher, J., 192, 211
Huttenlocher, P. R., 92
Hutter-Pishagi, L., 366, 367

Ilari, B., 318
Imbens-Bailey, A., 194
Inhelder, B., 58
Irizarry, N. L., 193
Irvine, J. T., 172
Irwin, J., 331
Ishak, S., 65
Ispa, J. M., 5
Izard, C. E., 117

Jablon, J. R., 73
Jacobs, R. R., 101
Jacobson, J., 101, 169
Jacobson, S. W., 101
Jacobvitz, D., 152
Jang, K. L., 11
Jeffer, F., 5
Jennings, K. D., 180
Jensen, H., 27
Jewkes, A. M., 84, 288
Johnson, James E., 143
Johnson, M. H., 9, 64
Johnson-Green, E., 318
Jones, B. C., 257
Jones, L., 178
Jones, S., 137
Jorde-Bloom, P., 381
Jordon, K. F., 62
Jusczyk, P., 169

Kagan, J., 138
Kagan, S. L., 178
Kajikawa, S., 203
Kantor, D., 359
Kaplan, H., 225
Kaplan, N., 122
Karasik, L. B., 65
Katerelos, M., 195, 196
Katz, J., 141, 142–43, 193,
    195, 201, 210
Katz, L. F., 118
Katz, L. G., 373
Kayne, H., 102
Kazmi, H., 212

Kearney, P., 41
Keenan, M., 377
Keith, H., 66, 268, 287
Keller, H., 27
Kelley, S. A., 166
Kerig, P. K., 30
Kesner, J. E., 30
Keyes, T., 323
Kim, G., 102
Kim, Y. M., 102
Kimak, C., 33
Kinch, A. F., 297n
Kindlon, D., 32
King, R. A., 145
Kinzler, K. D., 62, 163
Kiraly, I., 62
Kirksey, A., 257
Kisker, E. E., 20
Kistler, D. J., 119
Kitayama, S., 35
Klee, T., 331
Klein, N. K., 257
Klinkner, J. M., 383
Klinnert, M., 118
Knight, R., 26
Knitzer, J., 39
Ko, R., 101
Konner, M., 225
Kontos, S., 244, 245, 247, 248
Kopp, C. B., 11, 136
Korn, S., 114, 115
Kovach, B., 151–52
Kramer, L., 193
Krøjgaard, P., 178
Kubicek, L. F., 299
Kuhl, P. K., 26, 63–64, 92, 124,
    176, 199, 200, 201, 203
Kumin, L., 358
Kupetz, B., 320
Kurz-Riemer, K., 1
Kutai, M., 357
Kutner, L., 226
Kutz, S. L., 145

Lacerda, F., 203
LaFreniere, P. J., 152
Laibe, D. J., 337
Lally, J. R., 66, 244, 248, 268,
    270, 279, 287, 377, 379
Lally, R. J., 271, 279
Lally, Ron, 111
Lamb, M. E., 32, 168
Lambertz, Z., 169
Lamm, B., 27

Landsverk, J., 4
Larrieu, J. A., 12, 15
Larsen, J. J., 27, 30
Larsen, K., 151
Laske, M. T., 124
Lawrence, R. A., 256
Layzer, J., 40
Lazarov, M., 256
Leavitt, L., 27
Leerkes, E., 3, 119, 348–49
Legerstee, M., 203
Leitner, Y., 357
Lekka, S. K., 3, 119, 348–49
Lemery, K. S., 192, 193
Leong, D. J., 136
Lerman-Sagie, T., 358
Lerner, C., 272–73, 277
Lester, B. M., 112, 124
Levenson, S. M., 102
Levy, B., 195, 196
Lew, A. R., 230
Lewedeg, V., 197
Lewis, M. L., 117
Lewis, R., 359
Lewkowicz, D. J., 171
Lickliter, R., 171
Lieberman, A., 127, 340, 341, 348, 351
Lieberman, D., 357
Lindblom, B., 203
Lipsitt, L. T., 171
Little, T., 150
Liu, J., 124
Lobo, S. A., 65
Lock, E., 212
Loizou, E., 377, 378
Lojkasek, M., 127
Lollis, S. P., 148–49
Loman, M. M., 201
Lombardi, J., 248
Lorenz, K., 56
Love, J. M., 20
Lovich, R., 32
Lowenthal, B., 369
Lozoff, B., 257
Lu, Mei-Yu, 190, 201
Lucas, D., 173
Lutchmaya, S., 171
Lynch, E. W., 16
Lyons, T., 192, 211

Macari, S., 362
Maccoby, E. E., 11, 34, 140
Macfie, J., 5, 152
MacKenzie, M. J., 50

Magill-Evans, J., 33
Magnuson, K., 11
Mahler, Margaret, 54, 56, 116
Mahoney, G., 180
Main, M., 121, 122, 123
Malaguzzi, L., 165
Malatesta, C. Z., 117, 119
Malina, R. M., 221
Mandler, J. M., 174
Mangione, P. L., 271, 279
Mann, T., 383
Manuel, M., 257
Marcus, H. R., 35
Margand, N., 32
Markman, E. M., 203, 204
Markow, D. B., 203
Marsden, D. B., 84, 288
Martin, C. L., 139, 140
Martin, J. A., 34
Maslin-Cole, C. A., 165
Maslow, A. H., 54
Matheson, C., 143, 148, 155, 160
Maxted, A. E., 124
Mayberry, R. I., 212
Maynard, J., 175
McCantney, K., 248
McClish, D. K., 257
McCullough, A. L., 257
McDevitt, T. M., 200, 207, 208
McDonough, L., 174
McElwain, N. L., 5, 152
McFarlane, J., 170
McGabe, G. P., 257
McGarvey, S. T., 171
McGinley, K. A., 178
McKenna, J. J., 27, 28
McKenry, P. C., 30
McLanahan, S., 30
McLane, J. B., 318
McLean, M., 265
McNair, R., 248
McNamee, G. D., 318
Mehl, A. I., 211
Mehler, J., 169
Meisels, S. J., 15, 84, 288
Meltzoff, A. N., 26, 62, 92, 124, 171,
        174, 176, 202
Mennella, J. A., 170
Meyers, A., 256, 257
Miller, J. G., 193
Miller, K., 310, 322
Miller-Loncar, C., 124
Minkler, M., 38
Miyake, K., 117

Moller, L., 139, 140
Mondschein, E. R., 223
Montagner, Hubert, 142
Moon, C., 169
Moore, J., 148
Moore, M. K., 171, 176
Morgan, G. A., 165, 166
Morrow, A. M., 36
Muir, E., 127
Mulligan, S., 181
Murphy, L. B., 145, 229
Murray, C., 37
Murray, L., 124
Muskina, G., 331

Nabors, L. A., 212
Namy, L., 175, 205
Nelson, E. C., 257
Newman, R. S., 209
Newport, E. L., 202
Nicoladis, E., 196, 197
Notaro, P. C., 30

O'Brien, M., 248, 363, 364, 368
Ødegaard, E. E., 142–43
Odom, S., 357
O'Hara, M. W., 151
Oller, D. K., 197
Olson, J. M., 11
Olson, M. R., 30
Oppenheim, D., 152, 246
Ormrod, J. E., 200, 207, 208
Oser, C., 18, 21
Oster, H., 117
Oumar, F., 117
Owen, M. T., 32
Owlsley, C., 171
Ozonoff, S., 362

Pan, B. A., 194
Pan, M., 101
Paradis, J., 196
Park, K. A., 152
Parke, R. D., 32
Parker, J. G., 152
Parkinson, G. M., 358
Parlakian, R., 271, 379, 386, 388
Parten, M. B., 143
Patterson, C., 37
Pawl, J. H., 47, 126, 127, 298
Payne, A., 136, 138
Pearson, B. Z., 197
Peralta, R. L., 124
Perrin, E. C., 35

Perry, B., 94, 95, 169, 273
Perry, C. K., 331
Perussa, D., 150
Petersen, S., 18, 154
Petersen, S. H., 178
Petitto, L. A., 195, 196
Pham, L., 194
Phelps, P., 268, 279
Phillips, A., 169
Phillips, D. A., 5, 8, 9, 10, 106, 138,
        139, 144, 148, 155, 180, 181,
        194, 207, 243, 245, 248, 268,
        269, 388–89
Phillipsen, L., 136, 273
Piaget, J., 58, 59–60, 66, 70–71, 136,
        163, 166, 172, 177–78
Pick, A. D., 232
Piek, J. P., 224
Pierce, S., 138
Pierroutsakos, S. L., 175
Pines, Maya, 142
Pisani, L., 117
Plunkett, K., 204
Plusguellec, P., 150
Pollak, S. D., 119
Pollard, R., 95
Pons, F., 203
Popenoe, D., 32
Post, J., 266
Poulsen, M., 13
Powers, B. P., 114
Powers, N. G., 27, 28
Powlin, R., 137
Pratt, M., 273
Pretti Frontczak, K., 183
Price, C., 40
Pruden, S. M., 202
Pruett, K. D., 37, 165

Quevedo, K., 5
Quinn, P. C., 174

Radke-Yarrow, R., 145, 246
Raikes, H., 6, 20, 66, 246
Rakic, P., 92
Ramani, G. B., 144
Rebhorn, T., 42
Recchia, S. L., 377, 378
Redding, R. E., 166
Reese, E., 195
Reid, J., 178
Reindle, N., 315
Repacholi, B. M., 118
Restak, R., 91

Richardson, H., 169
Riley, D., 383
Rinaldi, C., 181, 326
Risley, T. R., 106, 193, 207, 210
Roach, M. A., 383
Roberts, J. E., 212
Roberts, S. B., 258
Robertson, A. S., 40
Robertson, R. W., 201
Robin, D. J., 232
Robinson, J. B., 5
Robinson, J. L., 47, 49, 114, 115
Robles, R., 36
Rochat, P., 171, 232
Rogers, C. S., 305
Rogers, S. J., 362
Rogoff, B., 172
Roopnarine, J. L., 145
Rosén, M., 36
Rosengren, K. S., 175
Rosenkoetter, S., 318
Rosner, B., 171
Ross, C., 20
Ross, H. S., 148–49
Rothbart, M. K., 111, 115
Rouse, K., 13
Rovee-Collier, C. K., 173
Rowe, D., 39
Rubenstein, T., 148
Rubin, K., 138
Rubin, K. H., 119, 136, 137, 138,
    139, 141, 152
Rudick, S., 266, 325
Runyan, D. K., 4

Saffran, J. R., 64, 201, 202, 208
Sagi-Schwartz, A., 5, 152
St. John, M., 298
Sameroff, A. J., 4, 13, 35, 47, 49, 50
Sanchez, S. Y., 198
Sandall, S., 265
Sandberg, J. F., 30
Santelli, B., 42
Saudargas, R. A., 279
Sawyers, J. K., 305
Scarborough, H. S., 211
Scher, A., 5
Schickedanz, J. A., 319
Schmidt, L. A., 138
Schmuckler, M. A., 62
Schorr, L. B., 40
Schreiber, M. E., 338
Schultz, M. D., 320
Schweikert, L., 276, 377

Schweinhart, L. J., 297n
Scott-Little, C., 178
Sears, M., 280
Sears, W., 280
Sedey, A. L., 211
Segal, M., 66, 244
Segatti, L., 323
Seibel, N., 379, 386, 388
Seidner, L., 175, 176
Seifer, R., 35
Seligman, M., 166
Seltzer, M., 192, 211
Serbin, L., 139, 140
Shalala, Donna, 20
Shatz, M., 143
Shefatya, L., 273
Shelton, G., 366, 367
Shepard, B., 119
Shinn, M., 244
Shirah, S., 248
Shoemaker, C. C., 381
Shonkoff, J. P., 8, 9, 10, 15, 106, 138,
    139, 148, 180, 181, 194, 207,
    268, 269, 388–89
Shore, R., 9, 91, 92
Siebenbruner, J., 29
Siegler, R. S., 172
Signer, S., 271, 279
Silver, S., 358
Silverman, R., 127
Singer, E., 336
Sirota, L., 169, 170
Skeels, H. M., 94
Skinner, B. F., 63
Small, M. F., 11, 26, 27
Smilansky, S., 273
Smith, A. B., 38
Smith, B., 265
Smith, E., 5, 245
Smith, L. B., 227
Smith, M., 137
Snow, C., 193, 194, 195, 201, 210
Socolar, R. R. S., 4
Solchany, J. E., 97
Soloman, J., 36
Soodak, L. C., 366
Spangler, G., 117
Sparrow, J. D., 347
Spelke, E. S., 9, 62, 163, 169,
    171, 180
Spence, M. J., 169, 200
Spinrad, T. L., 119
Spitz, R. A., 169
Spritz, B., 124

Sroufe, A., 122
Sroufe, A. L., 122
Sroufe, E. A., 121
Sroufe, L. A., 152
Stansbury, K., 138
Stayton, D. J., 48
Stegman, C. E., 180
Stein, M. T., 27, 28
Steinberg, L., 11
Stern, D., 31, 33, 57–58, 116,
    118, 176
Stern, N. B., 34
Stevens, K. N., 203
Stevenson-Hinde, J., 3, 12
Stewart, S. L., 119, 138
Stonehouse, A., 276, 373, 377
Strauss, M. S., 175
Stroud, J. E., 316
Stuart, S., 151
Suess, G., 117
Sugai, G., 102
Sullivan, M. W., 173
Super, C. M., 172
Susman-Stillman, A., 29
Sutherland, P., 60
Swain, I., 173
Sylvester, K., 244
Szanton, E. S., 66, 244, 266, 269

Tal-Posener, E., 357
Tamis-LeMonda, C. S., 32,
    65, 223
Tasker, F., 37
Taylor, F., 101
Taylor, N., 27
Tesman, J. R., 119
Teti, D., 168
Tetreault, K., 195, 196
Thelen, E., 226–27
Thiessen, E. D., 64, 208
Thomas, A., 114, 115, 224
Thomas, M. S. C., 9
Thomas, R., 40
Thompson, M., 362
Thompson, R. A., 337
Thompson-Rangel, T., 225
Thorp, E. K., 198
Tinbergen, N., 56
Tomasello, M., 190
Tomer, A., 357
Tomkins, A., 257
Torrelli, L., 300
Torres, Y., 268, 279
Tortora, S., 237

Tout, K., 138
Traub, E. K., 366, 367
Tremblay, R. E., 150
Trends, Child, 36
Tronick, E. Z., 112
Troseth, G. L., 175
Troy, M., 122
True, M. M., 117
Twardosz, S., 279

Ujiie, T., 117
Ulione, M. S., 248
Unger, O., 175, 176
Unzer, L., 117
Uttah, D. H., 175
Uzgiris, I. C., 178

Vach-Hasse, T., 38
Valentine, P., 32
Vandell, D. L., 248
Van De Zande, I., 332
VanHorn, L. G., 104
Van Hulle, C. A., 192, 193
van IJzendoom, M. H., 5
Velting, O. N., 320
Vereijken, B., 228, 229
Vernon, F., 313
Vernon, P. S., 11
Vintzileos, A., 104
Volling, B., 30

Vygotsky, L. S., 61, 64, 66, 70, 71, 136,
    139, 140, 144, 163, 164, 172,
    176–77, 190

Wachs, T. D., 257
Wall, S., 56, 120, 121, 246
Wang, X., 114
Watamura, S., 138
Watemberg, N., 358
Waters, E., 56, 120, 121, 152, 246
Watson, J., 117, 164, 166
Watson, M., 254
Waxman, S. R., 203, 205
Weatherston, D., 126
Weil, J. L., 266
Weinfield, N. S., 122, 124
Weissbourd, B., 66, 244
Weitoft, G. R., 36
Weller, A., 169, 170
Werke, J. F., 203
Werner, E. E., 13–15
Westby, C., 175, 176
Weston, D. R., 84, 288
Whaley, K., 148
Whatley, J. L., 145
Wheelwright, S., 171
White, J., 254
Whitebook, M., 5, 144, 155, 269, 387
Whitebrook, M., 248
Whitehurst, G. J., 320

Whiteman, M., 152, 333
Williams, K. A., 203
Winner, K., 194
Wittmer, D. S., 18, 66, 136, 137, 154
Wolfe, B., 248
Wood, S., 180
Woodward, A. L., 203, 204
Wynn, K., 62, 180

Xu, F., 180

Yarrow, L. J., 166
Yeung, W. J., 30
Yirmiya, N., 5
Yogman, M. W., 32
Yoshinaga-Itano, C., 211
Young, G. S., 362
Yovsi, R. D., 27

Zahn-Waxler, C., 145, 246
Zanolli, K. M., 279
Zeanah, C. H., 12, 15
Zelazo, P., 173
Zenvenberger, A. A., 320
Zerwas, S., 144
Zheng, L., 152, 333
Zinner, S. H., 171
Ziv, Y., 5, 152
Zoglio, S., 383, 384–85
Zuckerman, B., 102

Subject Index

A.B.C. Task Force, 140
Accident prevention, 253–54
Accommodation, 59
Accreditation, 263
Ache mothers, 224–25
Active play, opportunities for, 322–23
Activities
    adapting, 368–69
    intervention based on, 183
Adoptive parents, 38–39
Adult-child relationships
    effect on peer relationships, 152–53
    in relationship-based program,
        276–83
Adult child responsive interaction
        strategies, focusing on, 335–38
Advocate
    becoming an, 388–89
    defined, 388
Ages and Stages Questionnaires (ASQ), 85
Aggressive behavior, 350
Albinism, 97
Alcohol, use of, during pregnancy, 101
Allergic reactions, 257, 260, 361
American Academy of Pediatrics (AAP),
        28, 211, 236, 250, 251, 252,
        256, 257, 258–59
    "Back to Sleep" campaign, 28, 254
    Task Force on Infant Positioning and
        sudden infant death syndrome
        (SIDS), 254
American College of Obstetricians
        and Gynecologists, 100
American Public Health Association
        (APHA), 250, 251, 252,
        257, 258–59
American Sickle Cell Anemia Association
        (ASCAA), 359
Americans with Disabilities Act (1990)
        (ADA), child care and, 366
Amodal learning, cognitive development
        and, 171
Anecdotal records, 76–77

Anemia, sickle cell, 359
Anencephaly, preventing, 101
Anger, 349
Anxiety, 348–49
    biting and, 345
    during pregnancy, 103–4
Anxious-ambivalent attachment, 120, 121
Anxious-avoidant attachment, 120, 121
APGAR ratings, 104
Apnea, risk for, in premature infants, 107
Arsenic, exposure to, during
        pregnancy, 102
Asian cultures, nutrition during
        pregnancy in, 101
Asking, 334–35
Asperger's disorder, 361
Assessment, observation as part of,
        83–85
Assimilation, 59
Assumptions about nature of infants
        and toddlers, 267–68
Asthma, 361
Ataxic cerebral palsy, 234
Athetoid cerebral palsy, 234
Attachment
    anxious-ambivalent, 120, 121
    anxious-avoidant, 120, 121
    disorganized, 121
    secure, 120, 121
Attachment groups, 276
Attachment relationships, 110–32
    Ainsworth's work on, 120–21
    Bowlby's theory on, 119–20
    defined, 119
    development and learning
        through, 116–24
    child care experiences and
        emotional development, 127–32
    developmental trends and
        responsive interactions, 128–30
    infant mental health, 125–27
    importance of theory, 123
    research in late 20th century, 121–22

uniqueness of children, 110–15
    working models of, 122–23
Attachment theory, 56–57
Attention
    biting and, 345
    cognitive development and, 163–64
Attentional disorders, 360
Attention-deficit disorder, 360
Attributes
    cognitive development and, 171–72
    emotional relationships and, 114–15
    language development and, 192–93
    motor development and, 223–24
    social development and, 137–40
Attunement, 176, 279
Authoritarian parents, 34
Authoritative parents, 34
Autism, 124, 361, 362
Autonomy, biting and, 344

Babbling, 200, 201, 203
Baby. *See also* Infants
    imagined, 34
    real, 34
Baby talk, 208
Baby walkers, 236
Bayley Mental Development Index,
        245
Bedding, sanitizing, 252
Behavioral organization, hierarchy of, 112
Behavior compatibility theory, same-sex
        play and, 139
Behaviors
    aggressive, 350
    guiding children in controlling, 336
    meeting challenging, 347–53
    prosocial, 137
    recognizing, as communication, 336
Beliefs, about nature of infants and
        toddlers, 267–68
Bias, 87
Bidialectical children, 195
    language development and, 195–99

Bilingual children, language development and, 195–99
Bioecological systems theory, 51–52
    defined, 3
Biological effects on family, 26–29
Biology, effect on parenting, 26
Bipolar disorder, 124
Birth defects, structural/metabolic, 102
Blocks, opportunities with, 315–17
Books, learning to love, 319–20
Bowlby, John, theory on, 119–20
Brain, structure of, 90–93
Brain development
    effects of stress and violence on, 94–95
    importance of early experiences for, 93–94
    interaction between language and, 192
    prenatal, 105–6
    research on, 8–9
Breast-feeding
    benefits of, 256–58
    incidence of disease in, 256–57
Bushmen of the Kalahari Desert, 225

Calcium, need for, during pregnancy, 101
Capacities
    cognitive development and, 163–66
    motor development and, 221–22
    social development and, 136–37
Capacities of children, emotional relationships and, 111–14
Care and education programs that support families, 40–42
Caregiver, 7
Caregiving
    gifts of, 249
    primary, 246
Care teacher, 7
Caring for Our Children: National Health and Safety Performance Standards: Guidelines for Out-of-Home Child Care Programs, 250
Casey, Annie E., Foundation, 15
Categorizing, 174
Cause and effect
    biting and, 345
    for infants and toddlers, 178–79
Cell, genetic information in, 95
Cell membrane, 96
Census Bureau, U.S., American Fact Finder 2006, 17
Center child care, types of, 18
Center for the Childcare Workforce (CCW), 248

Central nervous system disorders, 360–61
Cephalocaudal development, 225
Cerebral palsy, 234, 360
    ataxic, 234
    athetoid, 234
    spastic, 234
Challenging behaviors, meeting, 347–53
Changing table, sanitizing, 252
Charts, 80–81
Chemical solvents, exposure to, during pregnancy, 102
Child abuse and neglect
    defined, 255
    reporting suspected cases of, 255, 256
Child abusers, characteristics of, 255–56
Child and Adult Care Food Program (CACFP), 259, 260
Child care
    Americans with Disabilities Act and, 366
    cognitive development and, 181
    emotional development and, 127–32
    language development and, 212
Child care centers, 259
Child Care Development Fund (CCDF), 261–62
Child care programs, 18–20
    evaluating quality in, 260–61
    transition of entering new, 298
Child care teacher, administering medication by, 253
Child-centered talk, 194
Child development and education as natural environment, 366
Child development and education programs
    including infants and toddlers with disabilities in, 356–70
    motor development and, 235–36
    supporting, 258–60
    teacher attitudes and strategies in, 366–70
Child Development Associate (CDA), 374–77
    credentials for, 376
Child development programs, 66
Child directed speech, 64
Childhood disintegrative disorder, 361
Child Observation Record (COR), 325
Children
    accentuating strengths of, 341
    in attachment and emotional relationships, 110–15

being attuned to cues of, 279
bidialectical, 195–99
bilingual, 195–99
in cognitive development, 162–72
as conversational partners in different cultures, 194–95
developing strong positive relationship with, 278–79
development and learning by, 271–75
development of, as both continuous and discontinuous, 12
documenting competence of, 368
effect of active exploration by, on development, 11
effect of attributes and capacities on relationships, 4
effect of nature and nurture on, 11
empathizing with goals, struggles and feelings, 335–36
encouraging developing skills in, 281–82
excluding ill, 252
following of needs by teachers, 277
giving choices you can live with, 338
guiding, in controlling impulses and behavior, 336
helping, in problem-solving and conflict management, 337
initiating of, by teachers, 282
language development and, 189–93
learning through play, 273–75
promoting capacities of, 335–38
providing limits for safety, 337
respect for emotional needs of, 329–30
respect for individual differences in, 330
responding to distress in, 281
responsiveness of teachers to emotional needs of, 277–82
in social development, 136–40
supporting relationships with important people in lives, 333–35
teaching to make clear, positive statements, 337
who bite, 342–46
Children's Bureau, 39
Children's Defense Fund, 18
Children with disabilities, early intervention for, 21
Children with special needs, 124–25
    cognitive development and, 180–81
    language development in, 211–12
    programs for parents of, 41–42
    social development and, 154–55
Child-to-teacher ratio, 155

Child Welfare Information Gateway, 08, 4
Choice questions, 209
Chromosomal abnormalities, 358–59
Chromosome, DNA of, 96–97
Chronic illness, 361
    Chronic lung disease
        (bronchopulmanory
        displasia), risk for, in
        premature infants, 107
Chronosystem, 52
Classification, opportunities for learning
        about, 321
Cleaning products, exposure to, during
        pregnancy, 102
Cleft palate, 102
Closed questions, 209
Cocaine use during pregnancy, 101–2
Cognitive consonance theory, same-sex
        play and, 139
Cognitive development and learning,
        162–86
    children with special needs, 180–81
    curiosity and, 164–66
    motivation and, 164–66
    programs that enhance, 181–86
        child care, 181
        developmental trends and
            responsive interactions, 184–86
        early intervention, 183
        for infants and toddlers at risk, 183
    theories of, 58–63
        constructivist theory of
            learning, 58–61
        core knowledge, 62
        social learning/cognitive, 62
        sociocultural, 61
    through relationships, 172–80
    uniqueness of each child, 162–72
Cognitive opportunities, 312
Cognitive process, 165
Collectivist cultures, 27
Communication
    defined, 190
    with peers, 141–42
    recognizing behavior as, 336
Communicative-linguistic
        parameters, 193
Communicators, capacity to be, 190–91
Compassion, capacity of children for, 145
Competence, 1–2
Concrete assistance, 126
Conflict, social competence and, 150
Conflict management, helping
        children in, 337

Conflict resolution skills, 384–85
Congenital infections, 361
Constraints
    ritual, 194
    system, 194
Constructivist theory of learning, 58–61
Consumer Product Safety
        Commission, 236
Continuity of care, 6, 246–47, 378
Continuity of peer groups, 155
Controlling, guiding children in,
        impulses and behavior, 336
Conversational dance, 206
Conversation-eliciting style, 209
Conversations between and among
        peers, 142–43
Cooperation, 144
COPE, 124
Core knowledge theory, 62
Core values, 380
Corporal punishment, 256
Co-sleeping, 27–28
Council for Exceptional Children (CEC),
        374, 380
    Division for Early Childhood (DEC), 72
        Code of Ethics for, 72, 380
        Recommended Practice, 265
Council for Professional Recognition,
        374–75
Counseling, genetic, 97
Counting, opportunities for learning
        about, 321
Cozy spaces, 304–7
Crawling, 228
Creative Curriculum Developmental
        Continuum for Infants, Toddlers,
        and Twos, 85
Creative Curriculum for Infants, Toddlers
        and Twos, 266, 325
Creative opportunities, 313–14
Creeping, 228
Cruising, 228–29
Cultural and linguistic continuity, 249
Cultural competence, 16
Cultural differences, emotional
        development and, 116–17
Cultural effects on family, 26–29
Culturally responsive care, 286
Cultural questions in infant and toddler
        child care, 28–29
Cultural values, differing, 27–28
Culture, peer relationships and, 140–41
Culture and language, development and
        learning and, 193–95

Cultures
    collectivist, 27
    individualist, 27
    influence on development and child-
        rearing beliefs and practices, 11
    influence on families, 3–4
    language content and, 195
    motor development and, 224–25
    relationships and, 172
    strategies for developing relationships
        with families from diverse, 284
Curiosity, 165
    cognitive development and, 164–66
Curriculum, components of, 267
Cystic fibrosis, 97, 359
Cystic Fibrosis Foundation (CFF), 359
Cytomegalovirus, 102
Cytomegela virus, 361
Cytoplasm, 96

Dance the developmental ladder, 272
Decentered symbolic play, 175
Decision making, shared, 381–83
DEET, exposure to, during pregnancy, 102
Defiance, 349
Delighting-the-senses experiences, 312–13
Demographics, effects of changes in,
        on infants, toddlers, and families,
        15–17
Dendrites, 92
Deoxyribonucleic acid (DNA), genetics
        and, 96–97
Depression
    impact of maternal, 123–24
    during pregnancy, 104
Development
    children's effect of active exploration
        by, on, 11
    conditions of risk for poor, 361–62
    during emotional relationships,
        116–24
    respect for power of, 330–31
    self-regulation as indicator, 11
    womb as environment for, 99–103
Developmental delay, 331
Developmental differences, appreciating,
        282
Developmental guidance, 126
Developmentally Appropriate Practice,
        265
Developmental milestones of newborn,
        106
Developmental outcomes, 2
Developmental profiles, 83

Developmental trends and responsive interactions, 432–55

Development and child-rearing beliefs and practices, culture influence on, 11

Diagrams, 80–81

Diapering, 251–52

Diluted bleach sanitizer, 252

Directive style, 209

Disappointment, toddlers' building ability to handle, 338

Discipline
defined, 329
differences between guidance and, 329

Discussing, 335

Disease, sanitizing and preventing spread of, 250–53

Disequilibrium, 59, 312

Disorganized attachment, 121

Dissociation, 114

Divorce, 36

Documentation, 81–83, 86

Documentations, portfolios of, 86

Domains, defined, 4

Domestic violence during pregnancy, 104

Dominance, 150

Dopamine, 92

Down syndrome, 236, 357, 358

Dynamic systems approach, 226

Early Child Care Research Network of the National Institute of Child Health and Human Development, 19

Early Childhood Education, Master's Degree Programs in, 374

Early development and education programs, 18–21
child care, 18–20
defined, 18
early intervention for children with disabilities, 21
early intervention programs for children at risk, 20–21

Early experiences, importance of timing of, 15

Early Head Start (EHS), 39, 40, 89–90, 183
home visitors for, 104
national research, 123
programs of, 66
on ratios and group size requirements in Program Performance standards, 245

Early Head Start Research and Evaluation Project, 21, 123

Early intervention
for children at risk, 20–21
for children with disabilities, 21
in cognitive development, 183
differences made by, 15
IDEA Part C, 362–66
early intervention services, 364–65
eligibility, 363
Individual Family Service Plan (IFSP), 363
making referrals, 365
language development and, 212–13

Early Learning Guidelines for Infants and Toddlers (ELG/ITs), 178

Ecology, effect on relationships, 3–4

Economic opportunity, impact of, 30

Economics as factor affecting parent-child interactions, 30

Ectoderm, 90

Edges, seeing, 168

Education, parent, 40–41

Elaborate play schemes, 139

Elaboration, semantic, 208

Emotional abuse, indicators of, 255

Emotional development
cultural differences and, 116–17
infant mental health and, 125–27
programs that enhance, 125–27
theories of, 53–58
attachment, 56–57
hierarchy of, 54
interpersonal, 57–58
of psychosocial development, 53–54
separation and individuation, 54, 56

Emotional display rules, 118–19

Emotional expression and understanding
in infancy, 117–19
in toddlers, 119

Emotional needs, respect for, in children, 329–30

Emotional reactivity, 115

Emotional regulation in infants, 111–12

Emotional relationships, 110–32
development and learning through, 116–24
programs that enhance emotional development and learning, 125–27
child care experiences and emotional development, 127–32

developmental trends and responsive interactions, 128–30
infant mental health, 125–27
uniqueness of children, 110–15

Emotional support, 126

Emotional vocabulary, building, 336

Emotions, self-regulation of, 137

Empathic language, 206

Endoderm, 90

Endorphins, 92

Environment
arranging, 369
creating and changing, 339, 342

Ethics, 380
developing and using codes of, 380
of observing, 72–73

Events, traumatic, 329

Event sampling, 78–80

Executive functioning, 163

Exosystem, 52

Experimenting, 335

Exploration, biting and, 344

Expressive language, 191, 200

Extroversion, 138

Exuberance, 138

Eyes, listening with your, 210–11

Familiarity, 148

Families
bilingual and bidialectical, 195–99
biological and cultural effects on, 26–29
culture influence on, 3–4
defined, 35
effects of changes in demographics on, 15–16
strategies for developing relationships with, 283–84
from diverse cultures, 284
structure of, 35–39
supporting child's relationship with his or her, 333–34

Family Album, 84

Family-centered program, characteristics of, 285

Family Child Care Association, 52

Family child care homes, types of, 18

Family day care homes, 259

Family support programs, 41–42

Fast mapping, 204

Father, becoming, 32–33

Fearfulness, 348–49

Feeding, social environment of, 258–59

Fetus, 97
  first trimester, 97
  language learning and, 199–200
  second trimester, 98
  third trimester, 98
Finger-plays, 211
First trimester, 97
Fluid intake, need for, during pregnancy, 101
Folic acid, need for, during pregnancy, 101
Food, safe handling, 259
Food services, policies supporting safe and healthy, 260
Foster parents, 39
Four E approach, 208
Fragile X syndrome, 358–59
Friendships, development of, 148–49
Frustration, biting and, 345
Furniture, sanitizing, 252

Games, social, 211
Gender
  motor development and, 223–24
  social development and, 139–40
Gender-segregation, 139, 140
Gender-type-toy preference theory, same-sex play and, 139
Genetic counseling, 97
Genetics
  deoxyribonucleic acid (DNA) and, 96–97
  prenatal development and, 95–97
Genetic syndromes, 358–59
Gestation
  brain development during, 90–93
  defined, 90
Gestural language, 142
Goodness, temperament and, 115–16
Grandparents, 38
Grasp, 230
  palmar, 230
  raking, 230
Group affection activities, 369
Group continuity of care, 148
Guidance
  defined, 329
  differences between discipline and, 329
  3 R approach to, 328–53
    challenging behavior and mental health issues, 347–53
    difference between discipline and, 329
    relationship-based approach to guidance reflecting, 331–32

    relating, 332–39
    respect, 329–31
  relationship realignments
    children who bite, 342–46
    separation anxiety, 339–40
    tantrums, 341–42
    toddler resistance, 340
    toilet learning, 346–47

Habituation, 164
Handwashing, 251
Head lifting, 227–28
Head Start Child Development Institute, 111
Head Start Program Performance Standards (HSPPS), 20, 183, 253
Health
  adopting policies that promote and protect, 254–56
  safety and, 249–56
Healthy development, effects of relationships on, 12
Hearing, cognitive development and, 169
Hearing impairment, 211–12, 359
Heart Start: The Emotional Foundations of Learning, 164
Helplessness, 348
Hemophilia, 97, 361
Hepatitis B, 361
Herpes simplex, 102, 361
Hexosaminidase A (Hex-A), 360
High muscle tone, 236
High/Scope approach, 266, 325
High/Scope COR for Infants and Toddlers, 84–85
Holding on, biting and, 344
Holds and enfolds, 278
Homebases, 276
Home language, 198
Home visiting programs, 89–90
Human genome project, 97
Human immunodeficiency virus (HIV), 361
Human needs, hierarchy of, 54
Human organization, hierarchy of, 112–13
Hyperbilirubinemia, risk for, in premature infants, 107
Hyper-reactivity, 360
Hypersensitivity, 359, 360
Hyposensitivity, 360
Hypothyroidism, 257

Illinois Department of Child and Family Services (IDCFS), 39
Imitation, 176
  biting and, 345
Individual differences
  broad range of, 12
  respect for, in children, 330
Individualist cultures, 27
Individualized Family Service Plan (IFSP), 363
Individuals with Disabilities Education Act (IDEA) (2004), 21, 42, 183, 362
Indulgent parents, 34
Infancy
  importance of, 6–10
  learning in, 272
Infant and toddler profession, 372–77
  defined, 7
  specific standards for, 374–77
Infant child care, cultural questions in, 28–29
Infant-directed speech, 194, 208–9
Infants
  beliefs and assumptions about nature, 267–68
  concepts learned by, 177–80
  creating routines to provide security for, 338
  defined, 6
  disabilities seen in, 357–62
  effects of changes in demographics on, 15–16
  emotional expression and understanding in, 117–19
  importance of learning to, 269–71
  irreducible needs of, 21–22
  language learning in, 200–203
  learning through play, 273–75
  needs of, 268–69
  nutritional needs of, 256–58
  prosocial development in, 144–52
  recent understanding of importance of, 7–8
  vulnerability and resiliency of, 12–15
  vulnerability to infection in, 250–51
Infants with disabilities, including, in child development and education programs, 356–70
Infant-Toddler Environmental Rating Scale (ITERS), 19, 248, 260
Infant-toddler professionals, role of, in creating relationship-based program, 275–83

Infant-toddler teacher, 65
  relationship with, 155
  responsibilities of, 276
Inferences, 76
Information
  invisible, 174
  sharing, 367
Inhibition, 138
Insight-based psychotherapy, 126–27
Interactive language, 206
Interactive stimulus, 165
Interpersonal development theory, 57–58
Interpsychological thinking, 140
Intersubjectivity, 118
Intrapsychological thinking, 140
Intraventricular hemorrage (IVH), risk
    for, in premature infants, 107
Invisible information, 174
Iodine deficiency, 257
Irreducible needs of infants and
    toddlers, 21–22

Jargoning, 204
Jaundice, risk for, in premature infants,
    107
Joint attention strategies, using, 207
Justification, 337

Kalahari Desert, Bushmen of the, 225
KIDS COUNT Census Data Online, 17
KidsHealth, 107, 361
Kuhl's perceptual mapping model, 63–64
!Kung San, 225

Labor Statistics, Bureau of, 18
Lactose intolerance, 97
Language
  brain development and, 192
  capacities of, 190–92
  defined, 190
  differences in when and how
      of use, 193
  empathic, 206
  expressive, 191, 200
  gestural, 142
  home, 198
  for infants and toddlers, 179
  interactive, 206
  in newborn, 106
  receptive, 191
  responsive, 206
  sign, 196, 199, 336
  terms and definitions, 191
Language acquisition device (LAD), 63

Language acquisition support system
    (LASS), 64
Language content, culture and, 195
Language delay, 211
Language development, theories of, 63–64
  Kuhl's perceptual mapping model,
      63–64
Language development and learning,
      189–217
  attributes in, 192–93
  bilingual and bidialectical children
      and families in, 195–99
  capacities in, 190–92
  children with special needs, 211–12
  culture and language and, 193–95
  development in relationships,
      199–206
  programs that enhance, 212
    child care, 212
      developmental trends and
          responsive interactions, 214–17
      early intervention, 212–13
    strategies to encourage language
        learning, 206–11
    strategies to support, 213
      developmental trends and
          responsive interactions, 214–17
    uniqueness of each child, 189–93
Language opportunities, 310
Lead, exposure to, during pregnancy, 102
Learned helplessness, 166
Learning
  constructivist theory of, 58–61
  as developmental, 271–75
  during emotional relationships, 116–24
  importance of, for infants and
      toddlers, 269–71
  as integrated, 271
  scaffolding of, 282
  through cognitive relationships,
      176–77
  through play, 273–75
  tools of, 173–76
Learning spaces, 304
Letting go, biting and, 344
Lexicon, 191
Licensing, 262
Lines, seeing, 168
Listening, 334
Literacy for infants and toddlers, 179
Literacy opportunities, 318–20
Low muscle tone, 236
Lyme's disease, exposure to, during
    pregnancy, 102

Macrosystem, 52
March of Dimes, 107, 234, 361
Mastery motivation, 166
Materials, adapting, 368–69
Maternal depression, impact of, 123–24
Maternal infections, 102
Mathematics, space, and shape
    opportunities, 320–22
Medication, administering, 253
Memory, 173
Mental health
  defined, 2
  infant, 125–27
  issues in, 347–53
Mental model, 60
Mentees, 387
  responsibilities of, 387–88
Mentoring, 386
  defined, 387–88
Mentors, 387
  responsibilities of, 387
Mercury, exposure to, during pregnancy,
    102
Mesoderm, 90
Mesosystem, 52
Metabolic disorders, 359–60
Microsystem, 52
Mirroring, 176
Mitigation, 337
Mobility, 237
Modeling, 176
Moment-to-moment social behavior, 151
Monolingual children, 195
Mood, temperament and, 137–38
Moro reflex, 221
Morphemes, 191
Mother, becoming, 31–32
Mother-infant bond, importance of, 27
Mother's experience as environment,
    103–4
Mother's influence, on paternal
    involvement, 30
Motivation, cognitive development and,
    164–66
Motor development, 220–40
  attributes and, 223–24
  capacities and, 221–22
  child development and education
      programs and, 235–36
  children with special needs and,
      233–35
  culture and, 224–25
  gender and, 223–24
  movement and, 226–29

movement psychotherapy and, 237
opportunities for, 322–23
perceptual-motor coordination and, 232–33
physical and occupational therapy and, 236–37
principles and progression of, 225
programs that enhance
    child development and education programs, 235–36
    developmental trends and responsive interactions, 238–40
strategies to support, 233
theories of, 64–65
tool use and, 229–31
uniqueness of each child, 220–24
Motor disorders, effects of, 234–35
Motor system, 112
Movement, motor development and, 226–29
Movement psychotherapy, motor development and, 237
Movement therapy, 237
Moving objects, seeing, 169
Muscle tone
    high, 236
    low, 236
Muscular dystrophy, 97
Music, song, and creative movement opportunities, 317–18

NAIC, 38
National Association for Children's Hospitals and Related Institutions, 236
National Association for Family Child Care (NAFCC), 262, 263
National Association for the Education of Young Children (NAEYC), 52, 72, 263, 374, 380
    Code of Ethics of, 72–73, 380
National Association for the Education of Young Children (NAEYC) standards, 375
National Center for Chronic Disease Prevention and Health Promotion (NCCDPHP), 104
National Center for Family Literacy (NCFL), 320
National Center for Infants, Toddlers, and Families, on quality, 244
National Center on Shaken Baby Sundrome (NCSBS), 361

National Child Care Information and Technical Assistance Center (NCCIC), 262
National Clearinghouse on Child Abuse and Neglect Information (NCCANI), 95, 255
National Council of Teachers of Mathematics (NCTM), 179–80
National Down Syndrome Society (NDSS), 358
National Early Childhood Technical Assistance Center (NECTAC), 362, 363
National Fragile X Foundation, 358
National Health and Safety Performance Standards, 251, 252, 253, 258, 259
National Institute of Child Health and Human Development (NICHD), 137, 269
    Early Child Care Research Network, 5–6, 19, 119, 146, 152, 155, 212, 244
    Early Childhood Research Network, 245
    study in child care, 181
    study on effects of child care on child development, 127–32
National Institute of Health (NIH), 360
National SIDS/Infant Death Resource Center, 28
National Tay-Sachs & Allied Diseases Association (NTSADA), 360
Nature, defined, 11
Negativism, 341
Neonatal intensive care units (NICU), 107
Neural tube defects, preventing, 101
Neuromuscular system, 236
Neurons, creating connections between, 91–93
Neurotransmitter chemical, 92
Newborn
    developmental milestones of, 106
    language in, 106
    postnatal brain development in, 105–6
    touch in, 105–6
NICHCY, 362
NITCCU, 178
Nonverbal communication, responding to, 206–7
Numbers for infants and toddlers, 179–80
Nurture, effect of, on children's development, 11

Nurturing opportunities, 309
Nutrition
    importance of good, 256–60
    for infants, 256–58
    in pregnancy, 100–101
    for toddlers, 256–58

Object permanence for infants and toddlers, 178
Object representation, 62
Objects, handling, 230–31
Observational Record of Caregiving Environment (ORCE), 261
Observations, 334
    defined, 73
    determining method to use, 85–86
    effect of, on children are understood, 70–72
    ethics of, 72–73
    methods of, 75–80
    observer in, 86–87
    as part of assessment, 83–85
    portfolios of, 86
    reasons for importance of, 70
    "what is" in, 73–75
Occupational therapy, motor development and, 236–37
One-to-one correspondence, opportunities for learning about, 321
Open-ended questions, 209
Opportunities
    for active play and motor development, 322–23
    with blocks, 315–17
Other-oriented guidance, 337
Ounce Scale, 84
Outdoor opportunities, 323
Outdoor play, supervision of, 254
Outdoor time, security and safety issues for, 324
Overgeneralization, 205

Palmar grasp reflex, 221, 230
Parallel talk, 207, 310
Parent-Completed, Child-Monitoring System, 85
Parent education, 40–41
Parenthood, transition from partners to, 33–34
Parenting
    biology effect on, 26
    cultural effects on, 26–29
    variations in, 29–35

Parenting styles, 34–35
  defined, 34
Parents
  adoptive, 38–39
  foster, 39
  same-sex, 37–38
  single, 36–37
Parents as Teachers, 40
Parents' relationship, impact of, 30
Parent-to-Parent support programs, 42
Parent training and information center
    (PTIC), 42
Paternal involvement, mother's influence
    on, 30
Peer development, richness of, 151–52
Peer groups, continuity of, 155
Peer interaction, biting and, 344
Peer relationships, challenges and
    conflicts in, 149–50
Peers
  communication with, 141–42
  conversations between and among,
    142–43
  play with, 143–44
  significance of quality experiences, 136
  social development with, 141–44
Perceptual mapping, 63
Perceptual-motor coordination, motor
    development and, 232–33
Permissive parents, 34
Pervasive development disorders (PDD),
    361–62
Phenylketonuria (PKU), 102, 359–60
Phonemes, 191
Physical abuse, indicators of, 255
Physical and emotional neglect,
    indicators of, 255
Physical therapy, motor development
    and, 236–37
Pincer grasp, 230
Placenta, 99
Planning guides, 456–60
Planning opportunities, 307–8
Play
  children learning through, 273–75
  decentered symbolic, 175
  elaborate schemes, 139
  encouraging, 275
  with peers, 143–44
  same-gender, 139
  same-sex, 139–40
  symbolic, 174–76
Population, changing, in United States,
    15–16

Portfolios of observations/
    documentations, 86
Portraits of development
  English, 392–409
  Spanish, 410–31
Positive comments, 335
Positive relationships, 3
Positive social relationships, 136
Positive turnarounds, 13
Postnatal brain development in
    newborn, 105–6
Post-traumatic stress disorder (PTSD),
    350–51
Postural reflexes, 221–22
Poverty, effects of relationships, 17
Pragmatics, 191
Pregnancy
  nutrition in, 100–101
  smoking in, 102
Premature, defined, 107
Premature birth, cause of, 107
Prenatal development
  defined, 6
  genetics and, 95–97
Prenatal testing, 102–3
Primary care, 378
Primary caregiving, 246
Primary teacher, continuity of care
    and, 246–47
Problem-solving, 174
  helping children in, 337
Process variables of quality, 248–49
Profession, infant and toddler, 372–77
Professional, defined, 372
Professional development, 379–83
Professional identity, 373
Professional organizations, standards set
    by, 374
Professional philosophy statement,
    380
Professional's experience, 377–79
Professional standards, 373, 374–77
  Program for Infant/Toddler Care
    (PITC), 266, 325
  Program for Infant/Toddler Caregivers
    (PITC), 183, 266
Program Review Instrument for Systems
    Monitoring (PRISM), 261
Proprioceptive system, 232
Prosocial behaviors, 137
Prosocial development
  in infants, 144–52
  in toddlers, 144–52
Prosody, 191

Protective factors, 35
  defined, 14
Protégés, 387
Proximal development, zone of, 61
Proximal-distal development, 225
Pruning, 92
Psychosocial development, theory of,
    53–54
Psychotherapy, insight-based, 126–27
Punishment, corporal, 256

Quality
  defined, 244
  evaluating, in child care programs,
    260–61
  process variables of, 248–49
  structural variables of, 245–48
Quality child development and
    education programs, social
    development and, 155
Quality of life, 2
Quality programs, policies, laws, and
    systems that support, 261–63
Quality rating systems, 262
Questions
  choice, 209
  closed, 209
  open-ended, 209
  true, 209
Quiet and calm opportunities, 308–9

Raking grasp, 230
Reaching, 232
Reaction, intensity of, 115
Receptive language, 191
Reciprocal interaction, 280
Records
  anecdotal, 76–77
  running, 77–78
Reflecting, 331–32, 384–85
Reflective practice model, 386–87
Reflective supervision, 386–87
Reflexes, 221
  Moro, 221
  palmar grasp, 221
  postural, 221–22
  rooting and sucking, 221
  step, 221
  tonic neck, 221
Reggio Emilia, 181, 325–26
Regulation
  defined, 111
  emotional, 111–12
  relationships and, 114

Relating, 332–39
Relationship-based community
    creating, 276
    developing professional, 383–88
Relationship-based curriculum, 265–93
    approaches, 323–26
Relationship-based environments,
        creating responsive, 300–307
Relationship-based model, 2–6
    defined, 2
    temperament in, 115
Relationship-based planning, responsive,
        287–93
Relationship-based programs, 66
    adult-child interactions and
        relationships in, 276–83
    infant-toddler professional's role of, in
        creating, 275–83
Relationship-based theory, 47–49, 72
    social development and, 136
Relationship-building skills, 3
Relationships, 385–86
    attachment, 119–23
    children's effect of attributes and
        capacities on, 4
    culture and, 172
    development and learning through,
        116–24
    ecology effect on, 3–4
    importance of, for children, families, and
        infant-toddler professionals, 5–6
    regulation and, 114
Releasing, 230
Resilience
    of infants and toddlers, 12–15
    vulnerability and resiliency of, 12–15
Resolution, 337
Respect, 329–31, 383–84
Respect, reflect, and relate (3 R)
        planning process, 296
Respiratory distress syndrome (RDS), risk
        for, in premature infants, 107
Responding habits, 384
Responsive interactions, using, 341–42
Responsive language, 206
Responsiveness, 5
Responsive opportunities, 307–23
    for active play and motor
        development, 322–23
    with blocks, 315–17
    cognitive, 312
    creative, 313–14
    delighting-the-senses experiences,
        312–13

language, 310
literacy, 318–20
mathematics, space, and shape,
    320–22
music, song, and creative movement,
    317–18
nurturing, 309
planning, 307–8
quiet and calm, 308–9
social, 310
writing and drawing, 315
Responsive programs, 243–63
    health and safety, 249–56
        nutrition, 256–60
    quality, 244–49, 260–63
Responsive routines, 299–300
Retinopathy of prematurity (ROP), risk
        for, in premature infants, 107
Rett's syndrome, 359, 361
Rett Syndrome Research Foundation,
        359
Risk factors, 8
    defined, 8
Ritual constraints, 194
Rocking, 228
Rolling, 227–28
Rooting reflex, 221
Routines
    defined, 297
    responsive, 299–300
Rubella, 102, 361
Running records, 77–78

Safety
    health and, 249–56
    promoting, 253–54
Same-gender play, 139
Same-sex parents, 37–38
Same-sex play, 139–40
Scaffolding, 176–77, 282–83
Schemas, 58
Screening tools, 85
Second language
    questions on, 196–97
    strategies for learning, 197
Second trimester, 98
Secure attachment, 120, 121
Security and safety issues for outdoor
        time, 324
Seeing, cognitive development and,
        167–69
Segregation, gender, 139
Self, respect for, 331
Self-fusion, 116

Self-regulation
    cognitive development and, 163
    defined, 11
    of emotions, 137
    as indicator of development, 11
    temperament and, 138
Self-talk, 207
Semantically responsive talk, 208
Semantic elaboration, 208
Semantics, 191
Sensitive periods, 9
Sensory challenges, 330
Sensory impairments, 359
Sensory integration, 232–33
Sensory perceptions, cognitive
        development and, 166–71
Separation and individuation, 54, 56
Separation anxiety, 339–40
Serotonin, 92
Sexual abuse, indicators of, 255
Sexually transmitted diseases, 102
Shaken baby syndrome, 361
Shared decision making, 381–83
Sickle cell anemia, 97, 359
Sign language, 196, 199, 336
Simultaneous bilinguals, 195
Single parents, 36–37
    influence of other adult
        relationships of, 30
Sink play, 313
Sitting, 228
Small motor and manipulative
        opportunities, 323
Smelling, cognitive development and,
        170–71
Smoking in pregnancy, 102
Social behavior, moment-to-moment, 151
Social competence
    conflict may be related to, 150
    defined, 136
    peers and, 136
Social development
    learning with peers and, 135–60
        children with special needs and,
            154–55
        culture and peer relationships,
            140–41
        learning through relationships,
            152–53
        programs that enhance social
            development and learning,
            155–60
        prosocial, in infants and toddlers,
            144–52

Social development (*Continued*)
    social development with peers,
      141–44
    uniqueness of each child, 136–40
    with peers, 141–44
Social environment of feeding,
    258–59
Social games, 211
Social interactions, 136
Social interaction theory, 64
Socialization, 329
    strategies of teacher, 160
Social learning/cognitive theory,
    62, 71
Socially competent children,
    temperament and, 137
Social opportunities, 310
Social referencing, 118
Social relationships, positive, 136
Sociocultural theory, 61, 71
Space, use for infants and toddlers,
    179
Spastic cerebral palsy, 234
Speech, infant-directed, 194, 208–9
Spina bifida, 360
    preventing, 101
Spina Bifida Association of America,
    360
Stability, 237
Standing, 228–29
Stanford University Medical Center, 9
State of alertness system, 112
Step reflex, 221
STORCH, 361
Stress, effects of, on brain development,
    94–95
Stress-response, 94
Structural/metabolic birth defects, 102
Structural variables of quality, 245–48
Subordination, 150
Sucking reflexes, 221
Sudden infant death syndrome (SIDS)
    deaths, 254–55
    drop in, 28
Supervision, reflective, 386–87
Supervisor, 388
Surfactant, defined, 107
Symbolic play, 174–76
    decentered, 175
Symbolic representation, 60
Synapse, 92, 192
Syntax, 191
Syphilis, 361
System constraints, 194

Tactile defensiveness, 359
Talk
    baby, 208
    child-centered, 194
    parallel, 207, 310
    self-, 207
    semantically responsive, 208
Tantrums, 341–42
Tasting, cognitive development and,
    170–71
Tay-Sachs disease, 97, 102, 359, 360
Teacher Interaction Scale, 261
Teachers
    attitudes and strategies of, in child
      development and education
      program, 366–70
    following of children's leads, 277
    initiating of children by, 282
    quality and characteristics of, 247–48
    responsiveness to children's emotional
      needs, 277–82
    socialization strategies of, 160
Teaching, responsive, 248–49
Teething, biting and, 344
Temperament
    emotional relationships and, 114–15
    motor development and, 224
    social development and, 137–39
    types of, 114–15
Teratogens, 101–2
Theories
    applying, in programs, 65–66
    bioecological systems, 51–52
    of cognitive development, 58–63
      constructivist theory of learning,
        58–61
      core knowledge, 62
      social learning/cognitive, 62
      sociocultural, 61
    defined, 45
    of emotional development, 53–58
      attachment, 56–57
      hierarchy of, 54
      interpersonal, 57–58
      psychosocial, 53–54
      of psychosocial development, 53–54
      separation and individuation, 54, 56
    of language development, 63–64
      Kuhl's perceptual mapping model,
        63–64
    relationship-based, 47–49
    transactional, 49–50
Theory of mind, 177
Therapeutic goals, meeting, 370

Third trimester, 98
3 R approach to guidance, 328–53
    challenging behavior and mental
      health issues, 347–53
    difference between discipline and, 329
    relationship-based approach to
      guidance
        reflecting, 331–32
        relating, 332–39
        respect, 329–31
    relationship realignments
      children who bite, 342–46
      separation anxiety, 339–40
      tantrums, 341–42
      toddler resistance, 340
      toilet learning, 346–47
Tiered quality systems, 262
Time-in, 338
Time-out, 338
Time sampling, 80–81
Toddlers
    beliefs and assumptions about nature,
      267–68
    building ability to handle
      disappointment, 338
    concepts learned by, 177–80
    creating routines to provide security
      for, 338
    cultural questions in child care for,
      28–29
    defined, 6
    disabilities seen in, 357–62
    effects of changes in demographics
      on, 15–16
    emotional expression and
      understanding in, 119
    importance of learning to, 269–71
    irreducible needs of, 21–22
    language learning in, 203–6
    learning in, 272–73
    learning through play, 273–75
    needs of, 268–69
    nutritional needs of, 256–58
    prosocial development in, 144–52
    recent understanding of importance
      of, 7–8
    resistance of, 340
    vulnerability to infection in, 250–51
Toddlers with disabilities, including, in
      child development and education
      programs, 356–70
Toddling, 229
Toilet learning, 346–47
    readiness for, 346

Tone, maintaining pleasant emotional, 281
Tonicity, 236
Tonic neck reflex, 221
Tools
  motor development and, 229–31
  use for infants and toddlers, 179
TORCH-S, 361
TORCH syndrome, 102
Touch, cognitive development and, 169–70
Toxic substances, disorders secondary to exposure to, 361
Toxins, 101–2
Toxoplasmosis, 361
Toys, sanitizing, 252
Transactional theory, 49–50
Transitions
  during day, 298–99
  defined, 297
  of entering new child care and education program, 298
Traumatic events, 329

Trilingual children, 195
True questions, 209

Undergeneralization, 205
Uninvolved parents, 34
United Cerebral Palsy, 360
United Nations (UN), Convention on the Rights of the Child, 268
United Nations Children's Fund (UNICEF), 17
Utensils, safe handling, 259

Values, 380
Velcro time, 272
Vestibular system, 232
Vigilance, 348–49
Violence, effects of, on brain development, 94–95
Visual cliff paradigm, 118
Visual impairment, 359
Vocabulary, using rich and varied, 207
Vulnerability of infants and toddlers, 12–15

Walking, 229
Washington State Department of Health, 359
"Watch, Wait, and Wonder" (Canadian program), 127
Well-being, 1
West Nile virus, exposure to, during pregnancy, 102
Windows of opportunity, 9
Womb as environment for development, 99–103
Working models of attachment, 122–23
Working sense of self, 270
Writing and drawing opportunities, 315

X chromosome, 96
X-linked disorder, 361

Y chromosome, 96

ZERO TO THREE, 164, 266, 320, 387
Zinc deficiency, 257
Zinecanteco Indians, 224

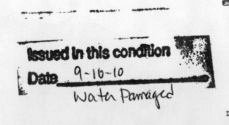